Lecture Notes in Computer Science   14256

Founding Editors

Gerhard Goos
Juris Hartmanis

The series Lecture Notes in Computer Science (LNCS), including its subseries Lecture Notes in Artificial Intelligence (LNAI) and Lecture Notes in Bioinformatics (LNBI), has established itself as a medium for the publication of new developments in computer science and information technology research, teaching, and education.

LNCS enjoys close cooperation with the computer science R & D community, the series counts many renowned academics among its volume editors and paper authors, and collaborates with prestigious societies. Its mission is to serve this international community by providing an invaluable service, mainly focused on the publication of conference and workshop proceedings and postproceedings. LNCS commenced publication in 1973.

Lazaros Iliadis · Antonios Papaleonidas ·
Plamen Angelov · Chrisina Jayne
Editors

Artificial Neural Networks and Machine Learning – ICANN 2023

32nd International Conference on Artificial Neural Networks
Heraklion, Crete, Greece, September 26–29, 2023
Proceedings, Part III

Springer

Editors
Lazaros Iliadis ⓘD
Democritus University of Thrace
Xanthi, Greece

Antonios Papaleonidas ⓘD
Democritus University of Thrace
Xanthi, Greece

Plamen Angelov ⓘD
Lancaster University
Lancaster, UK

Chrisina Jayne ⓘD
Teesside University
Middlesbrough, UK

ISSN 0302-9743   ISSN 1611-3349 (electronic)
Lecture Notes in Computer Science
ISBN 978-3-031-44212-4   ISBN 978-3-031-44213-1 (eBook)
https://doi.org/10.1007/978-3-031-44213-1

This Springer imprint is published by the registered company Springer Nature Switzerland AG
The registered company address is: Gewerbestrasse 11, 6330 Cham, Switzerland

Paper in this product is recyclable.

Preface

The European Neural Network Society (ENNS) is an association of scientists, engineers and students, conducting research on the modelling of behavioral and brain processes, and on the development of neural algorithms. The core of these efforts is the application of neural modelling to several diverse domains. According to its mission statement ENNS is the European non-profit federation of professionals that aims at achieving a worldwide professional and socially responsible development and application of artificial neural technologies.

The flagship event of ENNS is ICANN (the International Conference on Artificial Neural Networks) at which contributed research papers are presented after passing through a rigorous review process. ICANN is a dual-track conference, featuring tracks in brain-inspired computing on the one hand, and machine learning on the other, with strong crossdisciplinary interactions and applications.

The response of the international scientific community to the ICANN 2023 call for papers was more than satisfactory. In total, 947 research papers on the aforementioned research areas were submitted and 426 (45%) of them were finally accepted as full papers after a peer review process. Additionally, 19 extended abstracts were submitted and 9 of them were selected to be included in the front matter of ICANN 2023 proceedings. Due to their high academic and scientific importance, 22 short papers were also accepted.

All papers were peer reviewed by at least two independent academic referees. Where needed, a third or a fourth referee was consulted to resolve any potential conflicts. Three workshops focusing on specific research areas, namely Advances in Spiking Neural Networks (ASNN), Neurorobotics (NRR), and the challenge of Errors, Stability, Robustness, and Accuracy in Deep Neural Networks (ESRA in DNN), were organized.

The 10-volume set of LNCS 14254, 14255, 14256, 14257, 14258, 14259, 14260, 14261, 14262 and 14263 constitutes the proceedings of the 32nd International Conference on Artificial Neural Networks, ICANN 2023, held in Heraklion city, Crete, Greece, on September 26–29, 2023.

The accepted papers are related to the following topics:

Machine Learning: Deep Learning; Neural Network Theory; Neural Network Models; Graphical Models; Bayesian Networks; Kernel Methods; Generative Models; Information Theoretic Learning; Reinforcement Learning; Relational Learning; Dynamical Models; Recurrent Networks; and Ethics of AI.

Brain-Inspired Computing: Cognitive Models; Computational Neuroscience; Self-Organization; Neural Control and Planning; Hybrid Neural-Symbolic Architectures; Neural Dynamics; Cognitive Neuroscience; Brain Informatics; Perception and Action; and Spiking Neural Networks.

Neural applications in Bioinformatics; Biomedicine; Intelligent Robotics; Neuro-robotics; Language Processing; Speech Processing; Image Processing; Sensor Fusion; Pattern Recognition; Data Mining; Neural Agents; Brain-Computer Interaction; Neuromorphic Computing and Edge AI; and Evolutionary Neural Networks.

September 2023

Lazaros Iliadis
Antonios Papaleonidas
Plamen Angelov
Chrisina Jayne

Organization

General Chairs

Iliadis Lazaros   Democritus University of Thrace, Greece
Plamen Angelov   Lancaster University, UK

Program Chairs

Antonios Papaleonidas   Democritus University of Thrace, Greece
Elias Pimenidis   UWE Bristol, UK
Chrisina Jayne   Teesside University, UK

Honorary Chairs

Stefan Wermter   University of Hamburg, Germany
Vera Kurkova   Czech Academy of Sciences, Czech Republic
Nikola Kasabov   Auckland University of Technology, New Zealand

Organizing Chairs

Antonios Papaleonidas   Democritus University of Thrace, Greece
Anastasios Panagiotis Psathas   Democritus University of Thrace, Greece
George Magoulas   University of London, Birkbeck College, UK
Haralambos Mouratidis   University of Essex, UK

Award Chairs

Stefan Wermter   University of Hamburg, Germany
Chukiong Loo   University of Malaysia, Malaysia

Communication Chairs

Sebastian Otte	University of Tübingen, Germany
Anastasios Panagiotis Psathas	Democritus University of Thrace, Greece

Steering Committee

Stefan Wermter	University of Hamburg, Germany
Angelo Cangelosi	University of Manchester, UK
Igor Farkaš	Comenius University in Bratislava, Slovakia
Chrisina Jayne	Teesside University, UK
Matthias Kerzel	University of Hamburg, Germany
Alessandra Lintas	University of Lausanne, Switzerland
Kristína Malinovská (Rebrová)	Comenius University in Bratislava, Slovakia
Alessio Micheli	University of Pisa, Italy
Jaakko Peltonen	Tampere University, Finland
Brigitte Quenet	ESPCI Paris, France
Ausra Saudargiene	Lithuanian University of Health Sciences, Lithuania
Roseli Wedemann	Rio de Janeiro State University, Brazil

Local Organizing/Hybrid Facilitation Committee

Aggeliki Tsouka	Democritus University of Thrace, Greece
Anastasios Panagiotis Psathas	Democritus University of Thrace, Greece
Anna Karagianni	Democritus University of Thrace, Greece
Christina Gkizioti	Democritus University of Thrace, Greece
Ioanna-Maria Erentzi	Democritus University of Thrace, Greece
Ioannis Skopelitis	Democritus University of Thrace, Greece
Lambros Kazelis	Democritus University of Thrace, Greece
Leandros Tsatsaronis	Democritus University of Thrace, Greece
Nikiforos Mpotzoris	Democritus University of Thrace, Greece
Nikos Zervis	Democritus University of Thrace, Greece
Panagiotis Restos	Democritus University of Thrace, Greece
Tassos Giannakopoulos	Democritus University of Thrace, Greece

Program Committee

Abraham Yosipof	CLB, Israel
Adane Tarekegn	NTNU, Norway
Aditya Gilra	Centrum Wiskunde & Informatica, Netherlands
Adrien Durand-Petiteville	Federal University of Pernambuco, Brazil
Adrien Fois	LORIA, France
Alaa Marouf	Hosei University, Japan
Alessandra Sciutti	Istituto Italiano di Tecnologia, Italy
Alessandro Sperduti	University of Padua, Italy
Alessio Micheli	University of Pisa, Italy
Alex Shenfield	Sheffield Hallam University, UK
Alexander Kovalenko	Czech Technical University in Prague, Czech Republic
Alexander Krawczyk	Fulda University of Applied Sciences, Germany
Ali Minai	University of Cincinnati, USA
Aluizio Araujo	Universidade Federal de Pernambuco, Brazil
Amarda Shehu	George Mason University, USA
Amit Kumar Kundu	University of Maryland, USA
Anand Rangarajan	University of Florida, USA
Anastasios Panagiotis Psathas	Democritus University of Thrace, Greece
Andre de Carvalho	Universidade de São Paulo, Brazil
Andrej Lucny	Comenius University, Slovakia
Angel Villar-Corrales	University of Bonn, Germany
Angelo Cangelosi	University of Manchester, UK
Anna Jenul	Norwegian University of Life Sciences, Norway
Antonios Papaleonidas	Democritus University of Thrace, Greece
Arnaud Lewandowski	LISIC, ULCO, France
Arul Selvam Periyasamy	Universität Bonn, Germany
Asma Mekki	University of Sfax, Tunisia
Banafsheh Rekabdar	Portland State University, USA
Barbara Hammer	Universität Bielefeld, Germany
Baris Serhan	University of Manchester, UK
Benedikt Bagus	University of Applied Sciences Fulda, Germany
Benjamin Paaßen	Bielefeld University, Germany
Bernhard Pfahringer	University of Waikato, New Zealand
Bharath Sudharsan	NUI Galway, Ireland
Binyi Wu	Dresden University of Technology, Germany
Binyu Zhao	Harbin Institute of Technology, China
Björn Plüster	University of Hamburg, Germany
Bo Mei	Texas Christian University, USA

DongNyeong Heo	Handong Global University, South Korea
Dongyang Zhang	University of Electronic Science and Technology of China, China
Doreen Jirak	Istituto Italiano di Tecnologia, Italy
Douglas McLelland	BrainChip, France
Douglas Nyabuga	Mount Kenya University, Rwanda
Dulani Meedeniya	University of Moratuwa, Sri Lanka
Dumitru-Clementin Cercel	University Politehnica of Bucharest, Romania
Dylan Muir	SynSense, Switzerland
Efe Bozkir	Uni Tübingen, Germany
Eleftherios Kouloumpris	Aristotle University of Thessaloniki, Greece
Elias Pimenidis	University of the West of England, UK
Eliska Kloberdanz	Iowa State University, USA
Emre Neftci	Foschungszentrum Juelich, Germany
Enzo Tartaglione	Telecom Paris, France
Erwin Lopez	University of Manchester, UK
Evgeny Mirkes	University of Leicester, UK
F. Boray Tek	Istanbul Technical University, Turkey
Federico Corradi	Eindhoven University of Technology, Netherlands
Federico Errica	NEC Labs Europe, Germany
Federico Manzi	Università Cattolica del Sacro Cuore, Italy
Federico Vozzi	CNR, Italy
Fedor Scholz	University of Tuebingen, Germany
Feifei Dai	Chinese Academy of Sciences, China
Feifei Xu	Shanghai University of Electric Power, China
Feixiang Zhou	University of Leicester, UK
Felipe Moreno	FGV, Peru
Feng Wei	York University, Canada
Fengying Li	Guilin University of Electronic Technology, China
Flora Ferreira	University of Minho, Portugal
Florian Mirus	Intel Labs, Germany
Francesco Semeraro	University of Manchester, UK
Franco Scarselli	University of Siena, Italy
François Blayo	IPSEITE, Switzerland
Frank Röder	Hamburg University of Technology, Germany
Frederic Alexandre	Inria, France
Fuchang Han	Central South University, China
Fuli Wang	University of Essex, UK
Gabriela Sejnova	Czech Technical University in Prague, Czech Republic
Gaetano Di Caterina	University of Strathclyde, UK
George Bebis	University of Nevada, USA

Gerrit Ecke	Mercedes-Benz, Germany
Giannis Nikolentzos	Ecole Polytechnique, France
Gilles Marcou	University of Strasbourg, France
Giorgio Gnecco	IMT School for Advanced Studies, Italy
Glauco Amigo	Baylor University, USA
Greg Lee	Acadia University, Canada
Grégory Bourguin	LISIC/ULCO, France
Guillermo Martín-Sánchez	Champalimaud Foundation, Portugal
Gulustan Dogan	UNCW, USA
Habib Khan	Islamia College University Peshawar, Pakistan
Haizhou Du	Shanghai University of Electric Power, China
Hanli Wang	Tongji University, China
Hanno Gottschalk	TU Berlin, Germany
Hao Tong	University of Birmingham, UK
Haobo Jiang	NJUST, China
Haopeng Chen	Shanghai Jiao Tong University, China
Hazrat Ali	Hamad Bin Khalifa University, Qatar
Hina Afridi	NTNU, Gjøvik, Norway
Hiroaki Aizawa	Hiroshima University, Japan
Hiromichi Suetani	Oita University, Japan
Hiroshi Kawaguchi	Kobe University, Japan
Hiroyasu Ando	Tohoku University, Japan
Hiroyoshi Ito	University of Tsukuba, Japan
Honggang Zhang	University of Massachusetts, Boston, USA
Hongqing Yu	Open University, UK
Hongye Cao	Northwestern Polytechnical University, China
Hugo Carneiro	University of Hamburg, Germany
Hugo Eduardo Camacho Cruz	Universidad Autónoma de Tamaulipas, Mexico
Huifang Ma	Northwest Normal University, China
Hyeyoung Park	Kyungpook National University, South Korea
Ian Nabney	University of Bristol, UK
Igor Farkas	Comenius University Bratislava, Slovakia
Ikuko Nishikawa	Ritsumeikan University, Japan
Ioannis Pierros	Aristotle University of Thessaloniki, Greece
Iraklis Varlamis	Harokopio University of Athens, Greece
Ivan Tyukin	King's College London, UK
Iveta Bečková	Comenius University in Bratislava, Slovakia
Jae Hee Lee	University of Hamburg, Germany
James Yu	Southern University of Science and Technology, China
Jan Faigl	Czech Technical University in Prague, Czech Republic

Jan Feber	Czech Technical University in Prague, Czech Republic
Jan-Gerrit Habekost	University of Hamburg, Germany
Jannik Thuemmel	University of Tübingen, Germany
Jeremie Cabessa	University Paris 2, France
Jérémie Sublime	ISEP, France
Jia Cai	Guangdong University of Finance & Economics, China
Jiaan Wang	Soochow University, China
Jialiang Tang	Nanjing University of Science and Technology, China
Jian Hu	YiduCloud, Cyprus
Jianhua Xu	Nanjing Normal University, China
Jianyong Chen	Shenzhen University, China
Jichao Bi	Zhejiang Institute of Industry and Information Technology, China
Jie Shao	University of Electronic Science and Technology of China, China
Jim Smith	University of the West of England, UK
Jing Yang	Hefei University of Technology, China
Jingyi Yuan	Arizona State University, USA
Jingyun Jia	Baidu, USA
Jinling Wang	Ulster University, UK
Jiri Sima	Czech Academy of Sciences, Czech Republic
Jitesh Dundas	Independent Researcher, USA
Joost Vennekens	KU Leuven, Belgium
Jordi Cosp	Universitat Politècnica de Catalunya, Spain
Josua Spisak	University of Hamburg, Germany
Jozef Kubík	Comenius University, Slovakia
Junpei Zhong	Hong Kong Polytechnic University, China
Jurgita Kapočiūtė-Dzikienė	Vytautas Magnus University, Lithuania
K. L. Eddie Law	Macao Polytechnic University, China
Kai Tang	Independent Researcher, China
Kamil Dedecius	Czech Academy of Sciences, Czech Republic
Kang Zhang	Kyushu University, Japan
Kantaro Fujiwara	University of Tokyo, Japan
Karlis Freivalds	Institute of Electronics and Computer Science, Latvia
Khoa Phung	University of the West of England, UK
Kiran Lekkala	University of Southern California, USA
Kleanthis Malialis	University of Cyprus, Cyprus
Kohulan Rajan	Friedrich Schiller University, Germany

Koichiro Yamauchi	Chubu University, Japan
Koloud Alkhamaiseh	Western Michigan University, USA
Konstantinos Demertzis	Democritus University of Thrace, Greece
Kostadin Cvejoski	Fraunhofer IAIS, Germany
Kristína Malinovská	Comenius University in Bratislava, Slovakia
Kun Zhang	Inria and École Polytechnique, France
Laurent Mertens	KU Leuven, Belgium
Laurent Perrinet	AMU CNRS, France
Lazaros Iliadis	Democritus University of Thrace, Greece
Leandro dos Santos Coelho	Pontifical Catholic University of Parana, Brazil
Leiping Jie	Hong Kong Baptist University, China
Lenka Tětková	Technical University of Denmark, Denmark
Lia Morra	Politecnico di Torino, Italy
Liang Ge	Chongqing University, China
Liang Zhao	Dalian University of Technology, China
Limengzi Yuan	Shihezi University, China
Ling Guo	Northwest University, China
Linlin Shen	Shenzhen University, China
Lixin Zou	Wuhan University, China
Lorenzo Vorabbi	University of Bologna, Italy
Lu Wang	Macao Polytechnic University, China
Luca Pasa	University of Padova, Italy
Ľudovít Malinovský	Independent Researcher, Slovakia
Luis Alexandre	Universidade da Beira Interior, Portugal
Luis Lago	Universidad Autonoma de Madrid, Spain
Lukáš Gajdošech Gajdošech	Comenius University Bratislava, Slovakia
Lyra Puspa	Vanaya NeuroLab, Indonesia
Madalina Erascu	West University of Timisoara, Romania
Magda Friedjungová	Czech Technical University in Prague, Czech Republic
Manuel Traub	University of Tübingen, Germany
Marcello Trovati	Edge Hill University, UK
Marcin Pietron	AGH-UST, Poland
Marco Bertolini	Pfizer, Germany
Marco Podda	University of Pisa, Italy
Markus Bayer	Technical University of Darmstadt, Germany
Markus Eisenbach	Ilmenau University of Technology, Germany
Martin Ferianc	University College London, Slovakia
Martin Holena	Czech Technical University, Czech Republic
Masanari Kimura	ZOZO Research, Japan
Masato Uchida	Waseda University, Japan
Masoud Daneshtalab	Mälardalen University, Sweden

Mats Leon Richter	University of Montreal, Germany
Matthew Evanusa	University of Maryland, USA
Matthias Karlbauer	University of Tübingen, Germany
Matthias Kerzel	University of Hamburg, Germany
Matthias Möller	Örebro University, Sweden
Matthias Müller-Brockhausen	Leiden University, Netherlands
Matus Tomko	Comenius University in Bratislava, Slovakia
Mayukh Maitra	Walmart, India
Md. Delwar Hossain	Nara Institute of Science and Technology, Japan
Mehmet Aydin	University of the West of England, UK
Michail Chatzianastasis	École Polytechnique, Greece
Michail-Antisthenis Tsompanas	University of the West of England, UK
Michel Salomon	Université de Franche-Comté, France
Miguel Matey-Sanz	Universitat Jaume I, Spain
Mikołaj Morzy	Poznan University of Technology, Poland
Minal Suresh Patil	Umea universitet, Sweden
Minh Tri Lê	Inria, France
Mircea Nicolescu	University of Nevada, Reno, USA
Mohamed Elleuch	ENSI, Tunisia
Mohammed Elmahdi Khennour	Kasdi Merbah University Ouargla, Algeria
Mohib Ullah	NTNU, Norway
Monika Schak	Fulda University of Applied Sciences, Germany
Moritz Wolter	University of Bonn, Germany
Mostafa Kotb	Hamburg University, Germany
Muhammad Burhan Hafez	University of Hamburg, Germany
Nabeel Khalid	German Research Centre for Artificial Intelligence, Germany
Nabil El Malki	IRIT, France
Narendhar Gugulothu	TCS Research, India
Naresh Balaji Ravichandran	KTH Stockholm, Sweden
Natalie Kiesler	DIPF Leibniz Institute for Research and Information in Education, Germany
Nathan Duran	UWE, UK
Nermeen Abou Baker	Ruhr West University of Applied Sciences, Germany
Nick Jhones	Dundee University, UK
Nicolangelo Iannella	University of Oslo, Norway
Nicolas Couellan	ENAC, France
Nicolas Rougier	University of Bordeaux, France
Nikolaos Ioannis Bountos	National Observatory of Athens, Greece
Nikolaos Polatidis	University of Brighton, UK
Norimichi Ukita	TTI-J, Japan

Oleg Bakhteev	EPFL, Switzerland
Olga Grebenkova	Moscow Institute of Physics and Technology, Russia
Oliver Sutton	King's College London, UK
Olivier Teste	Université de Toulouse, France
Or Elroy	CLB, Israel
Oscar Fontenla-Romero	University of A Coruña, Spain
Ozan Özdenizci	Graz University of Technology, Austria
Pablo Lanillos	Spanish National Research Council, Spain
Pascal Rost	Universität Hamburg, Germany
Paul Kainen	Georgetown, USA
Paulo Cortez	University of Minho, Portugal
Pavel Petrovic	Comenius University, Slovakia
Peipei Liu	School of Cyber Security, University of Chinese Academy of Sciences, China
Peng Qiao	NUDT, China
Peter Andras	Edinburgh Napier University, UK
Peter Steiner	Technische Universität Dresden, Germany
Peter Sutor	University of Maryland, USA
Petia Georgieva	University of Aveiro/IEETA, Portugal
Petia Koprinkova-Hristova	Bulgarian Academy of Sciences, Bulgaria
Petra Vidnerová	Czech Academy of Sciences, Czech Republic
Philipp Allgeuer	University of Hamburg, Germany
Pragathi Priyadharsini Balasubramani	Indian Institute of Technology Kanpur, India
Qian Wang	Durham University, UK
Qinghua Zhou	King's College London, UK
Qingquan Zhang	Southern University of Science and Technology, China
Quentin Jodelet	Tokyo Institute of Technology, Japan
Radoslav Škoviera	Czech Technical University in Prague, Czech Republic
Raoul Heese	Fraunhofer ITWM, Germany
Ricardo Marcacini	University of São Paulo, Brazil
Riccardo Renzulli	University of Turin, Italy
Richard Duro	Universidade da Coruña, Spain
Robert Legenstein	Graz University of Technology, Austria
Rodrigo Clemente Thom de Souza	Federal University of Parana, Brazil
Rohit Dwivedula	Independent Researcher, India
Romain Ferrand	IGI TU Graz, Austria
Roman Mouček	University of West Bohemia, Czech Republic
Roseli Wedemann	Universidade do Estado do Rio de Janeiro, Brazil

Rufin VanRullen	CNRS, France
Ruijun Feng	China Telecom Beijing Research Institute, China
Ruxandra Stoean	University of Craiova, Romania
Sanchit Hira	JHU, USA
Sander Bohte	CWI, Netherlands
Sandrine Mouysset	University of Toulouse/IRIT, France
Sanka Rasnayaka	National University of Singapore, Singapore
Sašo Karakatič	University of Maribor, Slovenia
Sebastian Nowak	University Bonn, Germany
Seiya Satoh	Tokyo Denki University, Japan
Senwei Liang	LBNL, USA
Shaolin Zhu	Tianjin University, China
Shayan Gharib	University of Helsinki, Finland
Sherif Eissa	Eindhoven University of Technology, Afghanistan
Shiyong Lan	Independent Researcher, China
Shoumeng Qiu	Fudan, China
Shu Eguchi	Aomori University, Japan
Shubai Chen	Southwest University, China
Shweta Singh	International Institute of Information Technology, Hyderabad, India
Simon Hakenes	Ruhr University Bochum, Germany
Simona Doboli	Hofstra University, USA
Song Guo	Xi'an University of Architecture and Technology, China
Stanislav Frolov	Deutsches Forschungszentrum für künstliche Intelligenz (DFKI), Germany
Štefan Pócoš	Comenius University in Bratislava, Slovakia
Steven (Zvi) Lapp	Bar Ilan University, Israel
Sujala Shetty	BITS Pilani Dubai Campus, United Arab Emirates
Sumio Watanabe	Tokyo Institute of Technology, Japan
Surabhi Sinha	Adobe, USA
Takafumi Amaba	Fukuoka University, Japan
Takaharu Yaguchi	Kobe University, Japan
Takeshi Abe	Yamaguchi University, Japan
Takuya Kitamura	National Institute of Technology, Toyama College, Japan
Tatiana Tyukina	University of Leicester, UK
Teng-Sheng Moh	San Jose State University, USA
Tetsuya Hoya	Independent Researcher, Japan
Thierry Viéville	Domicile, France
Thomas Nowotny	University of Sussex, UK
Tianlin Zhang	University of Manchester, UK

Tianyi Wang	University of Hong Kong, China
Tieke He	Nanjing University, China
Tiyu Fang	Shandong University, China
Tobias Uelwer	Technical University Dortmund, Germany
Tomasz Kapuscinski	Rzeszow University of Technology, Poland
Tomasz Szandala	Wroclaw University of Technology, Poland
Toshiharu Sugawara	Waseda University, Japan
Trond Arild Tjostheim	Lund University, Sweden
Umer Mushtaq	Université Paris-Panthéon-Assas, France
Uwe Handmann	Ruhr West University, Germany
V. Ramasubramanian	International Institute of Information Technology, Bangalore, India
Valeri Mladenov	Technical University of Sofia, Bulgaria
Valerie Vaquet	Bielefeld University, Germany
Vandana Ladwani	International Institute of Information Technology, Bangalore, India
Vangelis Metsis	Texas State University, USA
Vera Kurkova	Czech Academy of Sciences, Czech Republic
Verner Ferreira	Universidade do Estado da Bahia, Brazil
Viktor Kocur	Comenius University, Slovakia
Ville Tanskanen	University of Helsinki, Finland
Viviana Cocco Mariani	PUCPR, Brazil
Vladimír Boža	Comenius University, Slovakia
Vojtech Mrazek	Brno University of Technology, Czech Republic
Weifeng Liu	China University of Petroleum (East China), China
Wenxin Yu	Southwest University of Science and Technology, China
Wenxuan Liu	Wuhan University of Technology, China
Wu Ancheng	Pingan, China
Wuliang Huang	ICT, China
Xi Cheng	NUPT, Hong Kong, China
Xia Feng	Civil Aviation University of China, China
Xian Zhong	Wuhan University of Technology, China
Xiang Zhang	National University of Defense Technology, China
Xiaochen Yuan	Macao Polytechnic University, China
Xiaodong Gu	Fudan University, China
Xiaoqing Liu	Kyushu University, Japan
Xiaowei Zhou	Macquarie University, Australia
Xiaozhuang Song	Chinese University of Hong Kong, Shenzhen, China

Xingpeng Zhang	Southwest Petroleum University, China
Xuemei Jia	Wuhan University, China
Xuewen Wang	China University of Geosciences, China
Yahong Lian	Nankai University, China
Yan Zheng	China University of Political Science and Law, China
Yang Liu	Fudan University, China
Yang Shao	Hitachi, Japan
Yangguang Cui	East China Normal University, China
Yansong Chua	China Nanhu Academy of Electronics and Information Technology, Singapore
Yapeng Gao	Taiyuan University of Technology, China
Yasufumi Sakai	Fujitsu, Japan
Ye Wang	National University of Defense Technology, China
Yeh-Ching Chung	Chinese University of Hong Kong, Shenzhen, China
Yihao Luo	Yichang Testing Technique R&D Institute, China
Yikemaiti Sataer	Southeast University, China
Yipeng Yu	Tencent, China
Yongchao Ye	Southern University of Science and Technology, China
Yoshihiko Horio	Tohoku University, Japan
Youcef Djenouri	NORCE, Norway
Yuan Li	Military Academy of Sciences, China
Yuan Panli	Shihezi University, China
Yuan Yao	Tsinghua University, China
Yuanlun Xie	University of Electronic Science and Technology of China, China
Yuanshao Zhu	Southern University of Science and Technology, China
Yucan Zhou	Institute of Information Engineering, Chinese Academy of Sciences, China
Yuchen Zheng	Shihezi University, China
Yuchun Fang	Shanghai University, China
Yue Zhao	Minzu University of China, China
Yuesong Nan	National University of Singapore, Singapore
Zaneta Swiderska-Chadaj	Warsaw University of Technology, Poland
Zdenek Straka	Czech Technical University in Prague, Czech Republic
Zhao Yang	Leiden University, Netherlands
Zhaoyun Ding	NUDT, China
Zhengwei Yang	Wuhan University, China

Invited Talks

Developmental Robotics for Language Learning, Trust and Theory of Mind

Angelo Cangelosi

University of Manchester and Alan Turing Institute, UK

Growing theoretical and experimental research on action and language processing and on number learning and gestures clearly demonstrates the role of embodiment in cognition and language processing. In psychology and neuroscience, this evidence constitutes the basis of embodied cognition, also known as grounded cognition (Pezzulo et al. 2012). In robotics and AI, these studies have important implications for the design of linguistic capabilities in cognitive agents and robots for human-robot collaboration, and have led to the new interdisciplinary approach of Developmental Robotics, as part of the wider Cognitive Robotics field (Cangelosi and Schlesinger 2015; Cangelosi and Asada 2022). During the talk we presented examples of developmental robotics models and experimental results from iCub experiments on the embodiment biases in early word acquisition and grammar learning (Morse et al. 2015; Morse and Cangelosi 2017) and experiments on pointing gestures and finger counting for number learning (De La Cruz et al. 2014). We then presented a novel developmental robotics model, and experiments, on Theory of Mind and its use for autonomous trust behavior in robots (Vinanzi et al. 2019, 2021). The implications for the use of such embodied approaches for embodied cognition in AI and cognitive sciences, and for robot companion applications, was also discussed.

Challenges of Incremental Learning

Barbara Hammer

CITEC Centre of Excellence, Bielefeld University, Germany

Smart products and AI components are increasingly available in industrial applications and everyday life. This offers great opportunities for cognitive automation and intelligent human-machine cooperation; yet it also poses significant challenges since a fundamental assumption of classical machine learning, an underlying stationary data distribution, might be easily violated. Unexpected events or outliers, sensor drift, or individual user behavior might cause changes of an underlying data distribution, typically referred to as concept drift or covariate shift. Concept drift requires a continuous adaptation of the underlying model and efficient incremental learning strategies. Within the presentation, I looked at recent developments in the context of incremental learning schemes for streaming data, putting a particular focus on the challenge of learning with drift and detecting and disentangling drift in possibly unsupervised setups and for unknown type and strength of drift. More precisely, I dealt with the following aspects: learning schemes for incremental model adaptation from streaming data in the presence of concept drift; various mathematical formalizations of concept drift and detection/quantification of drift based thereon; and decomposition and explanation of drift. I presented a couple of experimental results using benchmarks from the literature, and I offered a glimpse into mathematical guarantees which can be provided for some of the algorithms.

Reliable AI: From Mathematical Foundations to Quantum Computing

Gitta Kutyniok[1,2]

[1]Bavarian AI Chair for Mathematical Foundations of Artificial Intelligence, LMU Munich, Germany
[2]Adjunct Professor for Machine Learning, University of Tromsø, Norway

Artificial intelligence is currently leading to one breakthrough after the other, both in public life with, for instance, autonomous driving and speech recognition, and in the sciences in areas such as medical diagnostics or molecular dynamics. However, one current major drawback is the lack of reliability of such methodologies.

In this lecture we took a mathematical viewpoint towards this problem, showing the power of such approaches to reliability. We first provided an introduction into this vibrant research area, focussing specifically on deep neural networks. We then surveyed recent advances, in particular concerning generalization guarantees and explainability methods. Finally, we discussed fundamental limitations of deep neural networks and related approaches in terms of computability, which seriously affects their reliability, and we revealed a connection with quantum computing.

Intelligent Pervasive Applications for Holistic Health Management

Ilias Maglogiannis

University of Piraeus, Greece

The advancements in telemonitoring platforms, biosensors, and medical devices have paved the way for pervasive health management, allowing patients to be monitored remotely in real-time. The visual domain has become increasingly important for patient monitoring, with activity recognition and fall detection being key components. Computer vision techniques, such as deep learning, have been used to develop robust activity recognition and fall detection algorithms. These algorithms can analyze video streams from cameras, detecting and classifying various activities, and detecting falls in real time. Furthermore, wearable devices, such as smartwatches and fitness trackers, can also monitor a patient's daily activities, providing insights into their overall health and wellness, allowing for a comprehensive analysis of a patient's health. In this talk we discussed the state of the art in pervasive health management and biomedical data analytics and we presented the work done in the Computational Biomedicine Laboratory of the University of Piraeus in this domain. The talk also included Future Trends and Challenges.

Contents – Parts III

Anomaly Detection in Directed Dynamic Graphs via RDGCN and LSTAN

Mark Junjie Li[1], Zukang Gao[1(✉)], Jun Li[2], Xianyu Bao[2], Meiting Li[1], and Gen Zhao[1]

[1] College of Computer Science and Software Engineering,
Shenzhen University, Shenzhen, China
jj.li@szu.edu.cn, {2070276158,limeiting2021,2210273039}@email.szu.edu.cn
[2] Shenzhen Academy of Inspection and Quarantine, Shenzhen, China

Abstract. Anomaly detection in dynamic graphs has gained significant attention in practical applications such as cybersecurity and e-commerce. However, existing deep learning-based methods often overlook the asymmetric structural characteristics of directed dynamic graphs, limiting their applicability to such graph types. Furthermore, these methods inadequately consider the long-term and short-term temporal features of dynamic graphs, which hampers their ability to capture the evolving patterns within the graphs. This paper proposes **DyGRL**, an anomaly detection algorithm designed specifically for directed dynamic graphs. **DyGRL** utilizes a Roled-based Directed Graph Convolutional Network (RDGCN) to extract structural features from directed dynamic graphs. The RDGCN defines and aggregates node neighbor information based on their roles, effectively addressing the asymmetric nature of the graph structure. Additionally, **DyGRL** incorporates a Long Short-term Temporal Attention Network (LSTAN) to capture the evolution patterns of dynamic graphs. The LSTAN leverages a recurrent attention mechanism to efficiently extract and fuse both long-term and short-term temporal features, enabling a comprehensive understanding of graph evolution. We demonstrate the effectiveness and superiority of **DyGRL** over existing methods in detecting anomalies in directed dynamic graphs through extensive experiments on real-world datasets.

Keywords: Anomaly detection · Directed Dynamic graphs · Attention network

1 Introduction

A dynamic graphs is a sequence of static graphs that represents the relationships between nodes and edges over time, and is widely used in various fields such as social networks [18] and cybersecurity [2]. Anomaly detection in dynamic graphs aims to identify objects, points, or edges that deviate significantly from the network's underlying majority [17], which is an important task. This paper

L. Iliadis et al. (Eds.): ICANN 2023, LNCS 14256, pp. 1–12, 2023.
https://doi.org/10.1007/978-3-031-44213-1_1

focuses on detecting irregular edges in dynamic graphs, which can help diagnose errors in various systems, such as fraudulent and risky transactions in trading platforms [8,9].

It is essential to capture both the structural and temporal features of the dynamic graphs to detect anomalies in dynamic graphs. The structural features primarily comprise the dynamic graphs' node attribute and topology information. On the other hand, temporal features encompass the historical state information, including node attributes, graph structure, and edge weights in the previous timestamps. These temporal features can be divided into short-term and long-term temporal features [20]. The short-term temporal features focus on the recent evolution pattern, while the long-term temporal features focus on the global evolution patterns.

Recently, deep learning-based models have shown great strides due to their high performance in detecting the anomalies in dynamic graphs [13]. However, existing methods extract structural features of dynamic graphs by treating them as undirected, ignoring the asymmetric structural features of directed dynamic graphs. It prevents the methods from capturing unique anomalous patterns shown in Fig. 1 specific to directed dynamic graphs. Figure 1a shows node A has more out-degree relationships, whereas node B has more in-degree relationships. Intuitively, the edge $A \to B$ tends to be normal, while the edge $B \to A$ tends to be irregular. In Fig. 1b, node A and node B share many connected neighbors with similar connection patterns. Hence, the connection pattern of node B can be inferred that the edge $A \to C$, which is a normal edge, while the edge $C \to A$ is likely to be an irregular edge. Figure 1c shows a path $A \to B \to C$ in the directed graph. Based on the concept of asymmetric transitivity [15], $A \to C$ can be inferred as a normal edge, while edge $C \to A$ is likely to be an irregular edge. Additionally, when extracting the temporal features of dynamic graphs, these methods only consider short-term temporal features, neglecting the importance of long-term temporal features or not consistently extracting such features. Consequently, the model fails to capture the complete evolution pattern of the dynamic graphs.

In this paper, we propose **DyGRL**, an Anomaly Detection Algorithm in Directed Dynamic Graphs via Roled-based Directed Graph Convolutional Network(RDGCN) and Long Short-term Temporal Attention Network(LSTAN). DyGRL applies RDGCN and LSTAN to extract dynamic graphs' structure and temporal features. It also proposes a directed negative sampling training strategy to enhance model performance on directed dynamic graphs. RDGCN can extract structural features by defining and aggregating the neighbor information of each node's two roles. While LSTAN divides the snapshots into multiple ST-blocks(short-term blocks) to extract short-term temporal features and combine them with long-term temporal features from previous blocks. It also uses adaptive attention mechanisms to focus on relevant information and discard irrelevant information.

2   Related Work

Anomaly Detection in Dynamic Graphs has attracted considerable interest for decades. CM-Sketch [16] as well as Midas [2] use Count-Min Sketch to preserve the current and global number of edges and use statistical methods to measure whether the edge is anomalous or not. Some recent works use graph deep embedding methods to embed points or edges of graphs into vector spaces, where certain structural and temporal features of the graph are extracted and preserved. It can be mainly divided into two types, random walk-based and GNN-RNN based. For random walk-based methods, Netwalk [19] proposes clique embedding with random walk sampling to capture the structural features of the dynamic graphs, and temporal features are obtained by using reservoir sampling. Finally, a dynamic clustering-based anomaly detector(such as k-means) is used to score each edge. DSEDN [1] applies sparse autoencoder to generate network embeddings minimizing the pair-wise and neighborhood distance between vertex representations of every subgraph derived from random walks. For GNN-RNN based method, AddGrpah [20] combine GCN and GRU model to extract the structural-temporal features of dynamic graphs. StrGNN [3] uses enclosing subgraph generation to obtain topology information for each target edge, and then applies GCN to obtain the structural features, then applies GRU with fixed-size window to get the temporal features of the target edge.

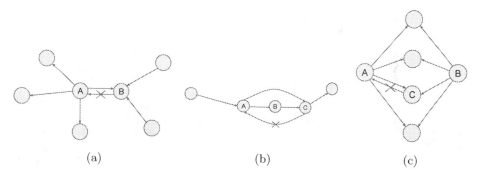

$$(a) \qquad\qquad (b) \qquad\qquad (c)$$

Fig. 1. Examples of anomalous patterns in directed dynamic graphs, (a) asymmetric anomalous patterns, and (b) anomalous patterns associated with asymmetric transitivity

3   Methodology

In this section, we will introduce the framework of DyGRL, shown in Fig. 2. DyGRL consists of three key modules, they are (1) RDGCN (Role-based Digraph Convolution Network), (2) LSTAN (Long Short-term Temporal Attention Network), (3) Anomaly detection module. Roughly, DyGRL employs RDGCN to extract the structural features of dynamic graphs. Then, DyGRL employ LSTAN

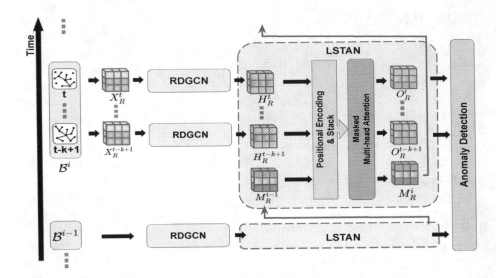

Fig. 2. The overall framework of DyGRL

to extract long-term and short-term temporal features into node embeddings adaptively. In the Anomaly detection module, DyGRL uses directed Negative Sampling to generate pseudo-negative edges in dynamic digraphs to enhance model performance on directed dynamic graphs.

3.1   Role-Based Graph Convolution Neural Network

Each node in the directed graph has two roles: source node and target node. To better distinguish the effect of two roles, We can learn source embeddings ϕ_S and target embeddings ϕ_T for each node, respectively. We define source and target neighbors for each node, and RDGCN can aggregate different neighbor information to obtain node embeddings. The neighbors of a node are considered to be highly correlated with the node, and this correlation is reflected in their connection relationship or common target and source nodes, which is referred to as asymmetric proximity. Next, we will define the neighbors of nodes and how neighbor information is aggregated.

Definition 1. *(k-hop Source/Target Neighbors). Given a digraph $\mathcal{G} = \{\mathcal{V}, \mathcal{E}\}$. For node $v_i \in \mathcal{V}$, its k-hop source neighbors are defined as $SourceNei(v_i, k) = \{v_j | \exists v_t \in \mathcal{V}, d(i,t) = k \wedge d(j,t) = k\}$, which represents the local structure when it acts as a source node, where $d(i,t)$ is the shortest path distance from v_i to v_t. For instance, if a shortest path from v_i to v_j is in this form: $v_i \underbrace{\rightarrow ... \rightarrow}_{k \ edges} v_j$, then $d(i,j) = k$. Similarly, the k-hop target neighbors of node v_i can be obtained by $TargetNei(v_i, k) = \{v_j | \exists v_t \in \mathcal{V}^t, d(t,i) = k \wedge d(t,j) = k\}$. Note that, The 0-hop neighbors of a node are itself.*

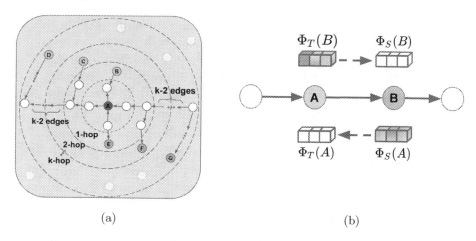

(a)   (b)

Fig. 3. (a) illustrate the k-hop source/target neighbors. (b)illustrate the information propagation of directed neighbors.

Figure 3a illustrate the k-hop source/target neighbors. To better describe the relationship between k-hop neighbors, we define the k-hop source/target adjacency matrix $A_S^{(k)}$ and $A_T^{(k)}$ of graph $\mathcal{G}$.

Definition 2. (k-hop Source/Target Adjacency Matrix). *The k-hop Adjacency Matrix $A_S^{(k)}$ and $A_T^{(k)}$ of graph $\mathcal{G}$ can be computed as follow:*

$$
\begin{cases}
A_S^{(0)} = A_T^{(0)} = I & k = 0 \\
A_S^{(k)} = A^k(A^\top)^k - Diag(A^k(A^\top)^k), & k \geqslant 1 \\
A_T^{(k)} = (A^\top)^k A^k - Diag((A^\top)^k A^k), & k \geqslant 1
\end{cases}
\tag{1}
$$

where $A_{S,ij}^{(k)} \in \{0,1\}$ and $A_{T,ij}^{(k)} \in \{0,1\}$ indicate that, whether v_i is k-hop source neighbor and destination neighbor of v_j respectively, $Diag(A)$ is a matrix composed of elements on the diagonal of matrix A. In addition, $A_T^{(k)}$ and $A_T^{(k)}$ is symmetrical, which means, if v_i is k-hop source neighbor of v_j, then v_j is also k-hop source neighbor of v_i.

Next, we designed a multi-scale convolutional network to aggregate neighbor information of different hops and use the aggregated information to learn the hidden state vector of the node. The calculation formula is as follows:

$$
Z_{S,hop}^{(k)} = \sigma(D(k,S)^{-\frac{1}{2}} \tilde{A}_S^{(k)} D(k,S)^{-\frac{1}{2}} X_S W^{(k)})
\tag{2}
$$

$$
Z_{T,hop}^{(k)} = \sigma(D(k,T)^{-\frac{1}{2}} \tilde{A}_T^{(k)} D(k,T)^{-\frac{1}{2}} X_T W^{(k)})
\tag{3}
$$

where $k \geqslant 1$ is the hop count of the current neighbors, $X_S \in \mathbb{R}^{n \times d_f}$ and $X_T \in \mathbb{R}^{n \times d_f}$ are the initial node source feature matrix and target feature matrix with d_f dimension, $\sigma(\cdot)$ denotes activation function, such as $ReLU(\cdot)$,

$Z_{S,hop}^{(k)} \in \mathbb{R}^{n \times d_h}$ and $Z_{T,hop}^{(k)} \in \mathbb{R}^{n \times d_h}$ are the hidden state matrices obtained after convolutional network aggregating the information of k hop source neighbors and target neighbors respectively, d_h is the output dimension, $\tilde{A}_R^{(k)} = A_R^{(k)} + I_N$, where $I_N \in \mathbb{R}^{n \times n}$ is the identity matrix, $D(k, R)$ denotes the degree matrix of $\tilde{A}_R^{(K)}$, such as $D(k, S)_{ii} = \sum_j \tilde{A}_{S,ij}^{(k)}$ indicates the degree of the ith node in $\tilde{A}_S^{(k)}$, $W^{(k)} \in \mathbb{R}^{d_f \times d_h}$ is a learnable parameter in the network.

Each convolution result from $Z_{R,hop}^{(k)}$ extracts structural features of different scales in the digraph. Next, RDGCN fuses multi-scale features to obtain a hidden state matrix that aggregates all k-hop neighbor information. Its calculation formula is as follows:

$$Z_{R,hop} = \sigma(\Gamma(Z_{R,hop}^{(1)}, Z_{R,hop}^{(2)}, ..., Z_{R,hop}^{(k)}))) \tag{4}$$

$$\Gamma(Z_{R,hop}^{(1)}, Z_{R,hop}^{(2)}, ..., Z_{R,hop}^{(k)}) = Concat(Z_{R,hop}^{(1)}, Z_{R,hop}^{(2)}, ..., Z_{R,hop}^{(k)})W_{\Gamma,R} \tag{5}$$

where $R \in \{S, T\}$ represents the role of the source node and target node respectively, $W_{\Gamma,R} \in \mathbb{R}^{kd_h \times d_h}$ is a learnable parameter, $Z_{R,hop} \in \mathbb{R}^{n \times d_h}$ is the hidden state matrix that combines multi-scale structural feature information.

Only aggregating structural information from k-hop neighbors does not consider preserving the asymmetric transitivity of dynamic digraphs. Therefore, RDGCN also aggregates information from directly connected nodes known as direct neighbors. Figure 3b illustrates the information propagation of directed neighbors. For an edge $A \rightarrow B$, RDGCN ensures that the source embedding of node A is similar to the source embedding of node B, while the target embedding of node B is similar to the target embedding of node A. The calculation formula for aggregated asymmetric transitivity information is as follows:

$$Z_{S,dir} = \sigma(D^{-\frac{1}{2}} \tilde{A} \tilde{D}^{-\frac{1}{2}} X_S W_{Sd}) \tag{6}$$

$$Z_{T,dir} = \sigma(\tilde{D}^{-\frac{1}{2}} \tilde{A}^\top D^{-\frac{1}{2}} X_T W_{Td}) \tag{7}$$

where $\tilde{A} = A + I$, D and $\tilde{D}$ are out-degree and in-degree matrices, respectively, $Z_{R,dir} \in \mathbb{R}^{n \times d_h}$ is the hidden state matrix that aggregates the information of direct neighbors.

Finally, RDGCN fuses $Z_{R,hop}$ and $Z_{R,dir}$ to obtain the output embeddings. The fusion method is to concat the two embeddings, and the calculation process is as follows:

$$H_R = Concat(Z_{R,hop}, Z_{R,dir}) \tag{8}$$

H_R is the final output node embedding of RDGCN. It extracted asymmetric structural features and preserved the asymmetric transitivity of dynamic digraphs.

3.2   Long Short-Term Temporal Attention Network

To comprehensively mine the evolution patterns of dynamic graphs, we propose LSTAN extract both long-term and short-term temporal features into node embeddings. LSTAN is an attention network that employs a recurrent structure. It divides all snapshots into multiple short-term attention blocks (ST-blocks), each containing w consecutive snapshots. The node states within the ST-block are then summarized as short-term information. LSTAN can effectively preserve and update the long-term state of nodes by recurrently transmitting hidden states across different blocks. Furthermore, it can adaptively combine the long-term and short-term temporal features using the attention network.

Specifically, suppose that we have an ST-block $\mathcal{B}^i = \{\mathcal{G}^{t-w+1}, ..., \mathcal{G}^t\}$. After processing the RDGCN, we obtain the embedding sequences of $\mathcal{B}^i$, which is $\{H_R^{t-w+1}, ..., H_R^t\}$ $R \in \{S, R\}$. For each node v in $\mathcal{B}^i$, we define the input as $\mathcal{I}_{R,v}^i = \{M_{R,v}^{i-1}, H_{R,v}^{t-w+1}, ... , H_{R,v}^t\}$, where $H_{R,v}^t$ is the embedding of node v in $\mathcal{G}^t$. $M_{R,v}^{i-1}$ is the long-term state of node v from previous block.

Before inputting the sequence into the multi-head attention network, we need to encode the positional information into the sequence using learned positional encoding [5] and pack it to a matrix as the input of the attention network. We denote the matrix as $\tilde{\mathcal{I}}_v^i$, and it can be formalized as:

$$\tilde{\mathcal{I}}_{R,v}^i = pack(PE(\mathcal{I}_{R,v}^i)) \tag{9}$$

$$PE(\mathcal{I}_{R,v}^i) = \{M_{R,v}^{i-1} + p^1, H_{R,v}^{t-w+1} + p^2, ..., H_{R,v}^t + p^{w+1}\} \tag{10}$$

where $p^i \in \mathbb{R}^{d_h}$ denotes the positional embedding of relative position i, and $\tilde{\mathcal{I}}_{R,v}^i \in \mathbb{R}^{(w+1) \times d_h}$.

Then $\tilde{\mathcal{I}}_{R,v}^i$ is input into the multi-head attention to get the output representation sequence $\mathcal{O}_{R,v}^i$, and it can be formalized as follows:

$$\mathcal{O}_{R,v}^i = \{M_{R,v}^i, O_{R,v}^{t-w+1}, ..., O_{R,v}^t\} = MultiHead(\tilde{\mathcal{I}}_{R,v}^i) \tag{11}$$

$$MultiHead(\tilde{\mathcal{I}}_{R,v}^i) = Concat(head_{R,1}, ..., head_{R,h})W_R^O \tag{12}$$

where $O_{R,v}^t$ is the output representation of node v in $\mathcal{G}^t$, $W_R^O \in \mathbb{R}^{hd_z \times d_o}$ is the learnable parameter. d_o is the dimension of the output representation of multi-head attention. d_z is the dimension of the output representation of single-head attention. $head_{R,j} \in \mathbb{R}^{(w+1) \times d_z}$ is the output of a single layer attention. h is the number of heads. A single layer attention is defined as follows:

$$head_{R,j} = Attention_{R,j}(\tilde{\mathcal{I}}_{R,v}^i) = softmax(\frac{Q_j K_j^\top}{\sqrt{d_z}})V_j \tag{13}$$

$$\begin{cases} Q_j = \tilde{\mathcal{I}}_{R,v}^i W_{R,j}^Q \\ K_j = \tilde{\mathcal{I}}_{R,v}^i W_{R,j}^K \\ V_j = \tilde{\mathcal{I}}_{R,v}^i W_{R,j}^V \end{cases} \tag{14}$$

where $W_{R,j}^Q \in \mathbb{R}^{d_h \times d_k}, W_{R,j}^K \in \mathbb{R}^{d_h \times d_k}$ and $W_{R,j}^V \in \mathbb{R}^{d_h \times d_z}$ are the learnable parameters. d_k is the dimension of keys and values.

3.3   Anomaly Detector

Anomalous Score for Edges. For each node $v_i \in \mathcal{V}$, we have its source embedding $O_{S,i}$ and target embedding $O_{T,i}$. Now, we define the anomalous score function $f(e)$ to detect if an edge is anomalous or not, which can be computed as:

$$f(e) = f((v_i, v_j)) = \sigma(Conncat(O_{S,i}, O_{T,i})W_a + b) \tag{15}$$

where $\sigma(\cdot)$ is the $Sigmod(\cdot)$ activation function, $W_a \in \mathbb{R}^{2d_o \times 1}$ and b are the weights and bias parameters of fully connected neural network, respectively.

Negative Sampling in Dynamic Directed Graph. Most existing negative sampling strategies neglect the anomaly patterns of directed edges, resulting in suboptimal performance in detecting anomalies in directed dynamic graphs. To address this issue, we constructs a reverse probability distribution based on the in-degree and out-degree of each edge. Specifically, for edge $v_i \rightarrow v_j \in \mathcal{E}$, if edge $v_j \rightarrow v_i$ does not exist, we sample $v_j \rightarrow v_i$ as anomalous edge with probability $\frac{d_{i,in} + d_{j,out}}{d_i + d_j}$, where $d_{i,in}$ and $d_{i,out}$ are the in-degree and out-degree of node v_i respectively, $d_i = d_{i,in} + d_{i,out}$. If edge $v_j \rightarrow v_i$ exist or it is not sampled as negative sample, we apply the strategy proposed in AddGraph [20] to generate negative samples, which replace node v_i with other unconnected nodes according to probability $\frac{d_i}{d_i + d_j}$. Intuitively, for an edge in the digraph, if its source node has a larger out-degree and its target node has a larger in-degree, we think that its reverse edge is more likely to be an anomalous edge.

Loss Function. We employ the cross-entropy loss function to train our model. the loss function for snapshot $\mathcal{G}^t$ can be computed as:

$$\mathcal{L}^t = -\sum_{e \in \mathcal{E}^t} log(f(e)) + log(1 - f(e_{neg})) + \lambda \mathcal{L}_{L2} \tag{16}$$

where e_{neg} is the negative sample of e.

4   Experiment

4.1   Datasets and Baseline

We compare our methods with other 6 benchmark datasets. The details of the datasets is shown in Table 1. The **DRAPA** [12], **Reddit Hyperlink** [7], and **Epinions** [10] datasets have ground-truth anomaly data, while **UCI Messages** [14], **Digg** [4] and Cit-HepPh [11] datasets do not. Therefore, inspired by NERD [6] to inject negative samples for directed link prediction tasks, We injected three types of anomaly data into the datasets, each accounting for 10% of the total data: (1) undirected abnormal injection, where all injected abnormal edges come from two previously unconnected vertices, (2) 50% of anomaly data derived from edge reversal if the reverse edge does not exist in the original data, and (3) 100% of anomaly data derived from edge reversal.

Table 1. Statistics of Datasets

Dataset	Nodes	Edges	Avg. Degree	Snapshots
UCI	1,899	13,838	14.57	58
Digg	30,360	85,155	5.61	84
Cit-HepPh	34,546	421,578	24.41	36
DRAPA	25,525	4,554,344	12.62	63
Reddit Hyperlink	55,863	858,490	30.74	30
Epinions	131,828	841,372	12.77	32

We compare our method with five state-of-the-art baselines, including two classical anomaly detection methods (**CM-Sketch** [16]), and four deep learning-based anomaly detection methods (**DSEDN** [1], **NetWalk** [19], **StrGNN** [3], **AddGraph** [20]).

Table 2. The AUC results on dataset with ground-truth anomaly data

Datasets	CM-Sketch	Netwalk	DSEDN	StrGNN	AddGraph	DyGRL
DRAPA	0.676	0.733	0.795	0.771	0.784	**0.902**
Reddit Hyperlink	0.604	0.622	0.703	0.657	0.723	**0.827**
Epinions	0.653	0.668	0.726	0.743	0.711	**0.848**

4.2 Experimental Setup

For each dataset, DyGRL sets the number of hop k to 3, the number of attention heads h to 4, and the block-size w to 6. The dimension of the representation vector d_f and d_o is set to 32, and d_h is set to 16. DyGRL uses the area under the curve (AUC) score to measure the anomaly detection performance of all methods. The method performs better when the AUC is higher.

Table 3. The AUC results on dataset injected with anomaly data

Method	UCI Message			Digg			Cit-HepPh		
	0%	50%	100%	0%	50%	100%	0%	50%	100%
CM-Sketch	0.684	0.623	0.591	0.636	0.621	0.586	0.627	0.586	0.538
Netwalk	0.722	0.662	0.611	0.684	0.626	0.584	0.723	0.677	0.611
DSEDN	0.811	0.746	0.677	0.813	0.743	0.704	0.803	0.724	0.674
StrGNN	0.796	0.702	0.635	0.827	0.724	0.685	**0.886**	0.751	0.724
ADyGRLraph	0.768	0.682	0.624	**0.837**	0.786	0.723	0.781	0.713	0.658
DyGRL	**0.848**	**0.836**	**0.792**	0.834	**0.821**	**0.778**	0.842	**0.811**	**0.791**

4.3   Experimental Results

The Overall AUC Result. Table 2 shows that DyGRL outperforms other baseline methods on all three datasets. Specifically, it achieves an improvement of 13.5%, 14.3%, and 14.1% over the best baseline method on DRAPA, Reddit Hyperlink, and Epinions datasets, respectively. The results demonstrate that DyGRL has better performance in detecting anomalies in directed graphs.

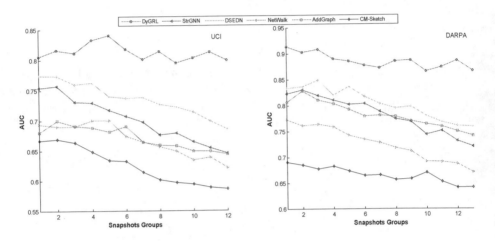

Fig. 4. The AUC results of each snapshot

Table 3 presents the AUC results of the dataset injected with anomaly data. According to the table, detecting directed anomaly data is generally more difficult than detecting undirected anomaly data. DyGRL outperforms other methods on directed dynamic graphs and still performs well in detecting undirected anomaly data

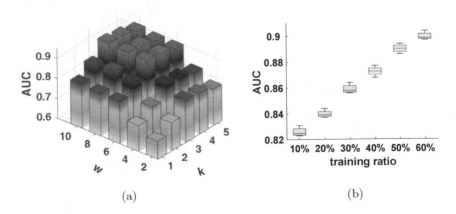

(a)   (b)

Fig. 5. Parameter Sensitivity in darpa

The Experimental Results of Each Snapshot. Figure 4 shows the AUC results of each snapshot in UCI and DARPA datasets. DyGRL outperforms all baseline methods in each timestamp, with only a slight degradation in performance over time. In contrast, baseline methods show a significant downward trend as the snapshot increases. Comparing the average AUC of the first 30% snapshots to the last 30% snapshots, we find that the best baseline method's performance drops by 8.9% and 9.1% on UCI and DARPA datasets, respectively. These results suggest that DyGRL is better at preserving and extracting temporal features of dynamic graphs for improved anomaly detection performance.

Parameter Sensitivity. This section evaluates the impact of various hyperparameters of DyGRL on the AUC results, including the number of hops k in RDGCN, the size of the ST-block w, and training percentage. Figure 5a presents the results of parameter sensitivity analysis. The AUC increases significantly as w grows from 2 to 6, and it remains stable when $w > 6$. DyGRL is trained with training percentages ranging from 10% to 60%. The experimental results in Fig. 5b show that with an increasing training ratio, the AUC score of DyGRL shows an upward trend. Even when the training ratio is low, such as 10% or 20%, DyGRL still exhibits relatively good performance.

5   Conclusion

In this paper, we propose DyGRL, an end-to-end deep anomaly detection framework to solve the problem of anomaly detection in directed dynamic graphs. We extract the structural and temporal features by RDGCN and LSTAN. RDGCN aggregates different neighbors' information to obtain the node embeddings, which can make DyGRL better extract the structural features of dynamic digraphs. And the LSTAN extracts the temporal features of nodes by considering both the long-term and short-term evolution patterns. Finally, we compare our model with five state-of-the-art baselines on six real-world datasets, and the experimental results show that DyGRL performs better than other anomaly detection methods.

Acknowledgement. The authors would like to thank Mr. Leming Ma and Ziming Luo for his discussion regarding the implementation. This work was supported by the National Key R&D Program of China: Research on the applicability of port food risk traceability, early warning and emergency assessment models (No.: 2019YFC160 5504).

References

1. Bansal, M., Sharma, D.: Density-based structural embedding for anomaly detection in dynamic networks. Neurocomputing **500**, 724–740 (2022)
2. Bhatia, S., Hooi, B., Yoon, M., Shin, K., Faloutsos, C.: MIDAS: microcluster-based detector of anomalies in edge streams. In: AAAI, vol. 34, no. 04, pp. 3242–3249 (2020)

3. Cai, L., et al.: Structural temporal graph neural networks for anomaly detection in dynamic graphs. In: CIKM, pp. 3747–3756 (2021)
4. De Choudhury, M., Sundaram, H., John, A., Seligmann, D.D.: Social synchrony: predicting mimicry of user actions in online social media. In: CSE, vol. 4, pp. 151–158 (2009)
5. Devlin, J., Chang, M., Lee, K., Toutanova, K.: BERT: pre-training of deep bidirectional transformers for language understanding. CoRR abs/1810.04805 (2018). http://arxiv.org/abs/1810.04805
6. Khosla, Megha, Leonhardt, Jurek, Nejdl, Wolfgang, Anand, Avishek: Node representation learning for directed graphs. In: Brefeld, Ulf, Fromont, Elisa, Hotho, Andreas, Knobbe, Arno, Maathuis, Marloes, Robardet, Céline. (eds.) ECML PKDD 2019. LNCS (LNAI), vol. 11906, pp. 395–411. Springer, Cham (2020). https://doi.org/10.1007/978-3-030-46150-8_24
7. Kumar, S., Hamilton, W.L., Leskovec, J., Jurafsky, D.: Community interaction and conflict on the web. In: WWW, pp. 933–943. International World Wide Web Conferences Steering Committee (2018)
8. Kumar, S., Hooi, B., Makhija, D., Kumar, M., Faloutsos, C., Subrahmanian, V.: REV2: fraudulent user prediction in rating platforms. In: WSDM, pp. 333–341 (2018)
9. Kumar, S., Spezzano, F., Subrahmanian, V., Faloutsos, C.: Edge weight prediction in weighted signed networks. In: ICDM, pp. 221–230 (2016)
10. Leskovec, J., Huttenlocher, D., Kleinberg, J.: Signed networks in social media. In: Proceedings of the SIGCHI Conference on Human Factors in Computing Systems, pp. 1361–1370 (2010)
11. Leskovec, J., Kleinberg, J., Faloutsos, C.: Graphs over time: densification laws, shrinking diameters and possible explanations. In: Proceedings of the Eleventh ACM SIGKDD International Conference on Knowledge Discovery in Data Mining, pp. 177–187 (2005)
12. Lippmann, R., et al.: Results of the DARPA 1998 offline intrusion detection evaluation. In: Recent Advances in Intrusion Detection, vol. 99, pp. 829–835 (1999)
13. Ma, X., et al.: A comprehensive survey on graph anomaly detection with deep learning. TKDE **abs/2106.07178**, 1 (2021)
14. Opsahl, T., Panzarasa, P.: Clustering in weighted networks. Soc. Netw. **31**(2), 155–163 (2009)
15. Ou, M., Cui, P., Pei, J., Zhang, Z., Zhu, W.: Asymmetric transitivity preserving graph embedding. In: SIGKDD, pp. 1105–1114 (2016)
16. Ranshous, S., Harenberg, S., Sharma, K., Samatova, N.F.: A scalable approach for outlier detection in edge streams using sketch-based approximations. In: SIAM, pp. 189–197 (2016)
17. Ranshous, S., Shen, S., Koutra, D., Harenberg, S., Faloutsos, C., Samatova, N.F.: Anomaly detection in dynamic networks: a survey. Wiley Interdiscip. Rev. Comput. Stat. **7**(3), 223–247 (2015)
18. Wang, L., Yu, Z., Xiong, F., Yang, D., Pan, S., Yan, Z.: Influence spread in geo-social networks: a multiobjective optimization perspective. IEEE Trans. Cybern. **51**(5), 2663–2675 (2021)
19. Yu, W., Cheng, W., Aggarwal, C.C., Zhang, K., Chen, H., Wang, W.: NetWalk: a flexible deep embedding approach for anomaly detection in dynamic networks. In: SIGKDD, pp. 2672–2681 (2018)
20. Zheng, L., Li, Z., Li, J., Li, Z., Gao, J.: AddGraph: anomaly detection in dynamic graph using attention-based temporal GCN. In: IJCAI, pp. 4419–4425 (2019)

Anomaly-Based Insider Threat Detection via Hierarchical Information Fusion

Enzhi Wang[1,2], Qicheng Li[1(✉)], Shiwan Zhao[3], and Xue Han[4]

[1] College of Computer Science, Nankai University, Tianjin, China
`liqicheng@nankai.edu.cn`
[2] Shanxi University, Taiyuan, China
[3] Beijing, China
[4] China Mobile Research Institute, Beijing, China
`hanxueai@chinamobile.com`

Abstract. Insider threats can cause serious damage to organizations and insider threat detection has received increasing attention from research and industries in recent years. Anomaly-based methods are one of the important approaches for insider threat detection. Existing anomaly-based methods usually detect anomalies in either the entire sample space or the individual user space. However, we argue that whether the behavior is anomalous depends on the corresponding contextual information and the context scope can have more granularities. Overall normal behavior may be anomalous within a specific department, while normal behavior within a department may be anomalous for a specific person. To this end, in this paper, we propose a novel insider threat detection method that explicitly models anomalies with hierarchical context scopes (i.e., organization, department, and person) and fuses them to compute anomaly scores. Comparisons with the unsupervised state-of-the-art approaches on the CMU CERT dataset demonstrate the effectiveness of the proposed method. Our method won the first prize in the CCF-BDCI competition.

Keywords: insider threat detection · anomaly detection · hierarchical fusion

1 Introduction

Insider threats seriously jeopardize an organization's data security and cause severe financial and reputational damage to the organization. With the continued adoption of information technology, organizations generate more and more data in their operation and management activities, resulting in more opportunities

---

[1] https://pages.securonix.com/rs/179-DJP-142/images/2019-Insider-Threat-Report-Securonix.pdf.

S. Zhao—Independent Researcher.

for insiders to access sensitive data, exacerbating the seriousness of the insider threat problem. The 2019 Securonix Insider Threat Report[1] indicates that 68% of organizations feel moderate to extremely vulnerable to insider attacks and 73% of organizations confirm that insider attacks are becoming more frequent.

The anomaly-based technique [15] is one of the important approaches for insider threat detection [21] because the insider threat sample size is usually small and hidden among a large number of normal samples. Anomaly-based insider threat detection first performs feature extraction on log data (e.g., IP address, switch port, time, PC, etc.), and then feeds the features into an anomaly detection model to output an anomaly score for each behavior data as a criterion for judging the malicious level. Compared with supervised learning algorithms [19,20], unsupervised machine learning algorithms are more often used for insider threat detection due to the following three reasons. First, log data is often unlabeled, and manual labeling consumes a lot of resources. Second, the scale of malicious activities is usually small compared to normal samples, and the problem of sample imbalance will lead to performance degradation of supervised learning. Third, unsupervised algorithms can automatically discover a small amount of data that deviates from the data center as potential possible anomalies, identifying new anomalies and uncovering unknown risks.

Current anomaly-based methods usually apply the anomaly detection model to either the entire sample space or the individual user space, without considering the impact of more context scopes on anomaly detection. We argue that whether the behavior is anomalous depends on the scope of the corresponding contextual information and the context scope can have more granularities. For example, the behavior of accessing source code repositories is normal in general but abnormal within the sales department. Furthermore, the normal behavior of downloading product specifications within a sales department may be anomalous for a particular person who is in the sales department but is responsible for products in another line of business.

To solve the aforementioned problem, we propose a novel insider threat detection method that explicitly models anomalies with hierarchical context scopes (i.e., organization, department, and person) and fuses them to compute anomaly scores. Specifically, we first obtain organization anomalies by modeling the entire training sample space and get suspicious departments and users according to their organization anomaly scores. And then, the department and user anomalies are computed in the context of the suspicious departments and users, respectively. Finally, the three scores are fused as the predicted anomaly scores. We employ the classical anomaly detection algorithm Isolation Forest [9] based on statistical machine learning and AutoEncoder [11] based on deep learning as the baselines to conduct comparison experiments on the CMU CERT dataset [4]. The results show that the performance of the proposed method has been significantly improved.

In summary, the main contributions of our paper are threefold:

- We propose a novel unsupervised learning approach for insider threat detection which defines anomalies under hierarchical context scopes, and carry out implicit and explicit fusion strategies.
- Experimental results show that our approach outperforms anomaly-based detection baselines such as Isolated Forests and AutoEncoder.
- We participated in the CCF-BDCI[2] competition and won the first prize, proving that our method is effective in real industrial scenarios.

Reproducibility: Our code and datasets are publicly available at https://github.com/Summer-Enzhi/Fusion-Insider-threat-detection.

2   Related Work

Unsupervised anomaly-based insider threat detection methods fall into two main categories according to their contextual scope: the entire sample space and the individual user space. The former models the entire sample space and determines whether a sample is a malicious activity based on how much it deviates from the overall data. Le et al. [7] explore data representation methods with different temporal granularities and integrate four unsupervised anomaly detection models with different principles, including Isolation Forest, Local Outlier Factor (LOF), Lightweight On-line Detector of Anomalies (LODA), and AutoEncoder. Aldairi et al. [1] use the unsupervised Isolation Forest and one-class SVM to obtain the anomaly value of behavior and define a trust score for each user based on the anomaly value of the current time period, which is used for judging the anomaly in the latter time period. Liu et al. [10] use a graph neural network with activities as nodes, relationships between activities as edges, and the completed node graph is fed to a clustering algorithm that outputs malicious activities.

The latter models each individual user for anomaly detection. Le et al. [6] take each user's historical behavioral data as a sequence and input it into the unsupervised hidden Markov model to judge the degree of deviation of each behavior. Lu et al. [12] propose a system based on Long Short-Term Memory (LSTM) to model each user's system logs as a naturally structured sequence. A similar work [22] designs a two-layer LSTM network to capture information for each user's intra-session and inter-session time range, respectively. Tuor et al. [18] propose a stream-based online learning approach that builds RNN models for each user and implements parameter sharing among each RNN. Sun et al. [16] use a tree-structure-based approach to represent each user's log data, and later the unsupervised anomaly detection method is used to identify malicious users. In this work, we model anomalies with three hierarchical context scopes and fuse them together to compute the anomaly scores.

---

[2] https://www.datafountain.cn/competitions/520.

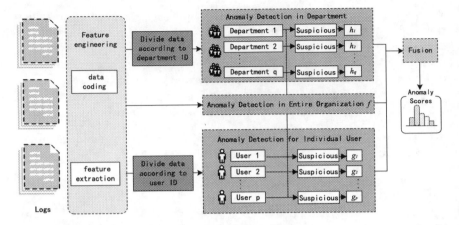

Fig. 1. The overall framework of hierarchical information fusion for insider threat behavior detection.

3   Method

3.1   Problem Statement

Formally, given a set of n user behaviors $D = \{d_1, d_2, ..., d_n\}$, each behavior instance $d_i = [d_i^1, d_i^2, ..., d_i^t]$ has t fields, where each field d_i^m can be categorical (e.g. Group) or numerical (e.g. network port). The task is to calculate the anomaly scores $Q = \{q_1, q_2, ..., q_n\}$ for every behavior.

3.2   Framework

In general, unsupervised insider threat detection methods learn the probability density distribution of the data, with anomalies located in low probability density regions and normal points in high probability density regions. Whether the behavior is abnormal or not depends on the probability density distribution function, which in turn depends on the context scope. For example, a behavior is considered normal when it is located in a high probability density region of the entire space, whereas it is abnormal from the perspective of a particular department or user because the behavior is located in a low probability density area of that department or user space. In this paper, we detect anomalies considering three hierarchical context scopes, i.e., organization, department, and user. To facilitate the explanation of the details of our algorithm, we first introduce the definitions of the three anomalies.

Organization Anomaly. The model learns the probability density distribution f of the entire data space $D = \{d_1, d_2, ..., d_n\}$ by extracting multidimensional features during training, and the point d_i is anomalous if it is located in the low probability density regions of f.

Algorithm 1. Anomaly Score Calculation via hierarchical Information Fusion

---

Input: User behavior dataset D, proportion of suspicious users K, proportion of suspicious departments L, user threshold μ, department threshold λ, fusion strategy Φ

Output: The anomaly score $Q = \{q_1, q_2, ..., q_n\}$ for every behavior

1: Construct organization anomaly detection model f on the whole dataset D. Get organization anomaly score $f(D) = Q_{global} = \{q_{global,1}, q_{global,2}, ..., q_{global,n}\}$

2: Collect all department IDs T and all user IDs R.

3: **for** c in T **do**

4:     Compute department anomaly score q_c using Eq. (1)

5: **for** u in R **do**

6:     Compute individual user anomaly score q_u using Eq. (2)

7: Get the suspicious departments T_S with its anomaly scores q_c in the top L percent of T.

8: Get the suspicious users R_S with its anomaly scores q_u in the top K percent of R.

9: **for** c in T_S **do**

10:     Get department's behavior data set $D_c = \{d_i | d_i^C = c, 1 \le i \le n\}$

11:     **if** $|D_c| > \lambda$ **then**

12:         Construct department anomaly detection model h_c on D_c

13:         Get department anomaly score $h_c(D_c) = \{q_{department,i} | d_i^C = c\}$

14: **for** u in R_S **do**

15:     Get user's behavior data set $D_u = \{d_i | d_i^U = u, 1 \le i \le n\}$

16:     **if** $|D_u| > \mu$ **then**

17:         Construct user anomaly detection model g_u on D_u

18:         Get user anomaly score $g_u(D_u) = \{q_{user,i} | d_i^U = u\}$

19: **while** $i < n$ **do**

20:     $q_{set} = \{q_{global,i}\} \cup \{q_{department,i}\} \cup \{q_{user,i}\}$

21:     $q_{fusion,i} = \Phi(q_{set})$

22:     $Q \leftarrow Q \cup \{q_{fusion,i}\}$

23: **return** Q

Department Anomaly. Suppose d_i^C is the field of department ID, then we denote $D_c = \{d_i | d_i^C = c, 1 \le i \le n\}$ as all behavior instances within the department c. The model first learns the probability density distribution function h_c of the department, and the anomalies are those behaviors located in the low probability density regions of h_c. If a user's behavior deviates from the historical behavior patterns of the department to which the user belongs, it can be identified as a candidate for anomalous behavior in the department.

User Anomaly. Similarly, d_i^U is the field of user ID, and we denote $D_u = \{d_i | d_i^U = u, 1 \le i \le n\}$ as all behavior instances of the user u. The model first learns the probability density distribution function g_u of D_u, and then the anomalies are located in the low probability density regions of g_u. Users usually have fixed job responsibilities and their behaviors have certain regularity. If a behavior deviates from the user's own historical pattern, it can be identified as a candidate for anomalous behavior.

The overall framework of hierarchical information fusion for insider threat behavior detection is shown in Fig 1 and Algorithm 1. First, the whole dataset D is fed into the anomaly detection model which outputs the global organization anomaly scores for all behavior data (Line 1 in algorithm 1). Then the anomaly score of each department and user is calculated according to Eq. (1) and Eq. (2), where E in the formula refers to calculating the average of the elements in the set. The formula (1) means that the global anomaly score for all data with department ID c is formed into a set and the average of the set is calculated as the anomaly score for this department. The user anomaly score is similar. Then the top K and top L percent of users and departments are selected as suspicious users and suspicious departments (Lines 2–8). For each suspicious department, the department-level anomalies are computed for all its behavioral data (Lines 9–13). Similarly, for each suspicious user, user anomaly modeling is further performed within it to obtain the user anomaly value of all its behavioral data (Lines 14–18). Finally, for each behavioral data d_i, the final score is obtained according to the fusion strategy Φ (Lines 19–23). The fusion strategy Φ includes average, maximum or weighted value.

$$q_c = E(\{q_{global,i}|d_i^C = c\}) \tag{1}$$

$$q_u = E(\{q_{global,i}|d_i^U = u\}) \tag{2}$$

3.3   Anomaly Detection Algorithm

The models f, g_u, and h_c in the above framework have the following two options:

(1) **Isolation Forest:** As an integration-based unsupervised anomaly detection algorithm, it has been widely used in the field of anomaly detection because of its low linear time complexity, parallelizability [5], and proven high effectiveness [17]. The algorithm constructs a collection of isolation trees from random subsets of data and aggregates the anomaly score from each tree to produce a final anomaly score.

(2) **Deep Autoencoder:** A deep neural network-based method that first encodes data into a latent representation with dimensionality reduction, and then decodes the latent representation to reconstruct the data. The reconstruction error obtained between the original and the decoded data is used to measure whether any behavior is anomalous or not [11].

3.4   Fusion Strategy

Implicit Fusion: Suspicious Department and Suspicious User. If insider threat behaviour occurs frequently within a user, in other word, the user has some bad "record", it is more likely that new insider threat behaviour will occur within the user, so the user can be defined as a suspicious user and deserves to be modeled and judged further. The judging mechanism here can be considered as an implicit fusion strategy. So we take all the data with the same user ID as a set, calculate the average of the whole organization-level anomaly scores within this set, and take the top K percent as the suspicious users. The same is true within departments, for example, if a department has sensitive data or a high turnover of personnel, the suspicious department can be defined similarly. The detailed calculation process is shown in the above Eq. (1) and Eq. (2).

Explicit Fusion. Limited by the unsupervised method adopted, we cannot train more regression classifiers to determine the weights for fusion. So the explicit fusion strategy Φ includes averaging, weighting, or maximizing. For each data d_i, first compute the $q_{set} = \{q_{global,i}\} \cup \{q_{department,i}\} \cup \{q_{user,i}\}$, and the final anomaly score $q_{fusion,i}$ is ten calculated depending on the combination strategy Φ. The specific calculation is as follows:

$$q_{fusion,i} = \text{maximum}(q_{set}) \qquad (\Phi = \text{MAX}) \qquad (3)$$

$$q_{fusion,i} = \text{average}(q_{set}) \qquad (\Phi = \text{MEAN}) \qquad (4)$$

For the weighted fusion strategy, the variance of a set of data can reflect the information entropy. Therefore, for all organization anomaly scores Q_{global}, the abnormal score using the weighted fusion strategy is calculated according to formula Eq.(5). The variance of the other two scores is similar. Finally, for data i, the fusion score is $\sigma^2_{global}q_{global,i} + \sigma^2_{department}q_{department,i} + \sigma^2_{user}q_{global,i}$.

$$\sigma^2_{global} = E[(Q_{global} - E(Q_{global}))^2] \qquad (5)$$

4   Empirical Experiments

4.1   Datasets

We experiment with the CMU CERT insider threat detection dataset [4], which is widely used in the field of insider threat detection. The dataset has many versions and the most used version is R4.2. In CERT R4.2, there are 1000 employees, 70 malicious insiders, and 32,770,227 activities generated by these users, of which there are 7323 malicious activities. Since data preprocessing is not the focus of this study, we use the data preprocessing method [8] and aggregate the data by day to get the activity behavior data of each user on all PCs per day.

4.2   Baseline Models

Firstly, the two algorithms Isolation Forest (IS) and Autoencoder (AE), mentioned in Sect. 3.4 are modeled on the whole dataset respectively, and the anomalous values output by the algorithms are used as the basis for determining whether they are malicious behaviors or not. And then, the two algorithms are sequentially used as the anomaly detection models in the framework proposed in this paper to perform insider threat detection by fusing hierarchical information, corresponding to Fusion-IS and Fusion-AE respectively, in order to evaluate the enhancement effect of the proposed framework.

Table 1. Comparison between our method and baseline models on CERT R4.2 dataset for daily auditing.

Approach	Algorithm	AUC
Baseline Models	Isolation Forest [9]	0.846
	Autoencoder [11]	0.774
	Hidden Markov model [14]	0.830
	Hidden Markov model [6]	0.858
	Periodic-based model [1]	0.890
	Ensemble model [7]	0.909
Our Fusion Models	Fusion-IS($\Phi = MEAN$)	0.915
	Fusion-IS($\Phi = MAX$)	0.914
	Fusion-IS($\Phi = Weight$)	0.926
	Fusion-AE($\Phi = MEAN$)	0.941
	Fusion-AE($\Phi = MAX$)	0.945
	Fusion-AE($\Phi = Weight$)	**0.947**

Secondly, the state-of-the-art unsupervised insider threat detection approaches are selected as the baseline for a side-by-side comparison experiment to evaluate our approach performance. The first approach uses the hidden Markov model [6,14] to learn what constitutes normal, and then detect significant deviations from that behavior. The second approach is a periodic-based model [1] that applies an unsupervised algorithm in a periodic manner and produces an anomaly score for each active user in every period. The third approach is an ensemble-based model [7] that represents the data with temporal information, then combines Autoencoder, Isolation Forest, LODA, and Local outlier Factor to get performance enhancement.

4.3 Experimental Setup

For the Isolated Forest algorithm, the number of isolated trees is set to 100, which is the optimal parameter in the original paper [9]. For the AE algorithm, a neural network of $256 \rightarrow 128 \rightarrow 64 \rightarrow 32 \rightarrow 16 \rightarrow 8 \rightarrow 4 \rightarrow 4 \rightarrow 8 \rightarrow 16 \rightarrow 32 \rightarrow 64 \rightarrow 128 \rightarrow 256$ is used, the activation function is $ReLU$, the optimizer is $Adam$, and a total of 150 epochs are trained. In the proposed framework, the user ID attribute U is "user" in the R4.2 dataset, and the department ID attribute C is "team". For the hyperparameter settings, the top K percentage of suspicious users is set to 40%, the top L percentage of suspicious departments is set to 40%, the minimum threshold for modeling within the user μ is 50, and the minimum threshold for modeling within the department λ is 1000.

4.4 Results

The results of the comparison experiments on CERT R4.2 dataset for daily auditing are shown in Table 1. First, Fusion-IS under the proposed framework improves 8.15%, 8.03% and 9.45% over IS under the three combined strategies Φ, and Fusion-AE improves 21.58%, 22.10% and 22.35% over AE under the three combined strategies, respectively, which is a significant improvement. Second, Fusion-AE scores 0.947, outperforming other state-of-the-art insider threat detection approaches.

A comparison of the ROCs between the methods in our framework and the baseline models is shown in Fig. 2. The corresponding curves of our method are always above the baseline model. Our method always has a higher TPR than the baseline model for the same FPR, which means that our method always gets a higher detection rate at the cost of a lower false positive rate for different thresholds, thus indicating the better robustness of our method. And it can also be seen that when the combined strategy Φ is average, maximum or weighted combination, the three ROCs are very close and they all have good performance. In addition, the best performance is the weight fusion strategy.

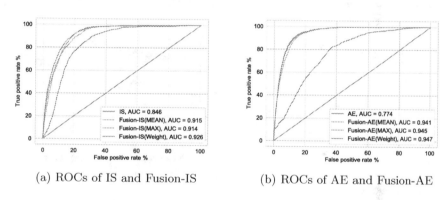

(a) ROCs of IS and Fusion-IS   (b) ROCs of AE and Fusion-AE

Fig. 2. Comparison of ROCs Between Our Methods and the base Models.

4.5 Ablation Study

The proportion of suspicious users K and the proportion of suspicious departments L are the most important parameters in the framework. As a result, to examine their effects on model performance, we increase K and L from 0 to 1 and observe their effects on AUC, as shown in Fig. 3. The x-axis of this figure represents L, the y-axis represents K, and each grid represents the AUC score. The redder color means a higher AUC score, and the bluer color means a lower AUC score. Figure 3.(a) shows Fusion-IS, and Fig. 3.(b) shows Fusion-AE, which are combined with the strategy of taking the arithmetic mean.

The color difference between rows in the figure is larger than the color difference between columns, implying that the parameter K has a more significant impact on the model performance. And it can also be seen that when the parameter K is 0, it is equivalent to applying only the global organization anomaly detection model without hierarchical fusion. So when the parameter K converges to 0, the AUC score also converges to the AUC score of the base model. Although the percentage of malicious users itself is low (7% of malicious users in the CMU CERT dataset), using the global organization anomaly score alone is not very reliable because of the hidden and disguised nature of some malicious users, and then taking a value for K close to the actual percentage of malicious users in the dataset (e.g., 7%) would deprive the model of the opportunity to perform local anomaly detection within a larger number of possible potential malicious users, making the framework of hierarchical scope fusion lose its greater usefulness. So when the proportion of suspicious users K takes a larger value than the actual proportion of malicious users, individual user anomalies can be used to detect malicious users and malicious behavior, and the framework will perform better. As shown in the figure, K takes the highest value of AUC when it is between 0.3 and 0.6. Also, it can be seen that Fusion-IS has an AUC score range of 0.85 to 0.92, while Fusion-AE has an AUC score range of 0.73 to 0.95, which means that Fusion-IS has better stability than Fusion-AE.

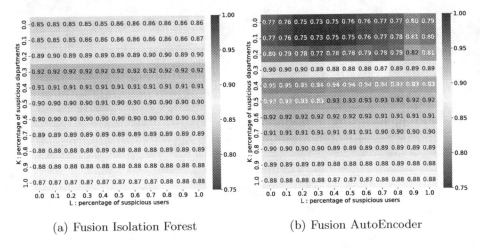

(a) Fusion Isolation Forest   (b) Fusion AutoEncoder

Fig. 3. Heat map of the effect of parameters K and L on model performance. X-axis represents L, y-axis represents K, and each grid represents the AUC score.

5   Case Study

We attend the CCF Big Data and Computational Intelligence Competition, which has become one of the most influential activities in the field of big data and artificial intelligence in China. We verify our approach on the track: UEBA-based Analysis of Users' Abnormal Internet Behavior. This track's task is to use artificial intelligence methods to build the user online behavior model and determine behavior deviation.

5.1   Datasets

The data is extracted from the log database of the terminal anti-leakage product, mainly involving the logs of users' online behavior within the enterprise, including more than 520,000 pieces of data from 2021/4/30 to 2021/6/9.

5.2   Baseline Models and Experimental Setup

For the comparison experiments, classical anomaly detection methods such as Local Outlier Factor (LOF) [3], Rotation-based Outlier Detection (ROD) [2], Lightweight On-line Detector of Anomalies (LODA) [13], Isolated Forest [9], and AutoEncoder [11] are selected as baseline models. The parameters for the experiments are set as follows. In the LOF algorithm, the number of neighbors is set to 500, and the distance between neighbors is calculated using the Minkowski distance. In the IS algorithm, the number of iTrees is set to the optimal value of 100 in the original paper. In the AE algorithm, a neural network with 6 hidden layers is used and the activation function is $ReLU$. In the Fusion-IS and Fusion-AE algorithms proposed in this paper, μ is set to 500, λ is set to 50, K is set to 40%, L is set to 40%.

Table 2. Model Performance and Time Comparison on CCF BDCI Dataset

Algorithm	RMSE	R2_score	Time(s)		
			Train	Test	Total
LOF	0.337	−1.357	132.8	56.9	189.7
ROD	0.289	−0.733	17.5	3.3	20.8
LODA	0.212	0.068	2.5	2.7	5.2
IS	0.2	0.179	25.7	6.4	32.1
AE	0.201	0.161	107.9	9.6	117.5
Fusion-IS	**0.182**	**0.312**	105.9	19.6	125.5
Fusion-AE	0.193	0.23	338.2	19.2	357.4

5.3   Results

The measurement of this competition is root-mean-square error (RMSE) which lower one is better and R2_score which higher one is better. A comparison of the performance and elapsed time of each algorithm is shown in Table 2. The performance of IS and AE is basically the same, and they are better than other similar models; while in the model that fuses hierarchical information, the detection accuracy is improved over the original model, with Fusion-IS improving the most, performing the best, and taking the shortest time; the running time of the fusion model is about three times that of the original model and is the same complexity level as the original algorithm.

6   Conclusions

In this work, we propose a novel insider threat behavior detection method, which improves the accuracy of anomaly detection by fusing anomaly detection models hierarchically in three context scopes: the entire organization, the department, and the individual user. We present an empirical experiment and the results show that our framework significantly outperforms the baselines. We introduce the industry case study about CCF Big Data and Computational Intelligence Competition and we win the first prize, which proves that our method is effective in real industrial scenarios.

References

1. Aldairi, M., Karimi, L., Joshi, J.: A trust aware unsupervised learning approach for insider threat detection. In: 2019 IEEE 20th International Conference on Information Reuse and Integration for Data Science (IRI), pp. 89–98 (2019). https://doi.org/10.1109/IRI.2019.00027
2. Almardeny, Y., Boujnah, N., Cleary, F.: A novel outlier detection method for multivariate data. IEEE Transactions on Knowledge and Data Engineering (2020)
3. Breunig, M.M., Kriegel, H.P., Ng, R.T., Sander, J.: LOF: identifying density-based local outliers. In: Proceedings of the 2000 ACM SIGMOD international conference on Management of data, pp. 93–104 (2000)
4. Glasser, J., Lindauer, B.: Bridging the gap: a pragmatic approach to generating insider threat data. In: 2013 IEEE Security and Privacy Workshops, pp. 98–104. IEEE (2013)
5. Hariri, S., Kind, M.C.: Batch and online anomaly detection for scientific applications in a kubernetes environment. In: Proceedings of the 9th Workshop on Scientific Cloud Computing. ScienceCloud'18, Association for Computing Machinery, New York, NY, USA (2018). DOI: https://doi.org/10.1145/3217880.3217883, https://doi.org/10.1145/3217880.3217883D
6. Le, D.C., Zincir-Heywood, A.N.: Evaluating insider threat detection workflow using supervised and unsupervised learning. In: 2018 IEEE Security and Privacy Workshops (SPW), pp. 270–275 (2018). https://doi.org/10.1109/SPW.2018.00043
7. Le, D.C., Zincir-Heywood, N.: Anomaly detection for insider threats using unsupervised ensembles. IEEE Trans. Netw. Serv. Manage. **18**(2), 1152–1164 (2021). https://doi.org/10.1109/TNSM.2021.3071928
8. Le, D.C., Zincir-Heywood, N., Heywood, M.I.: Analyzing data granularity levels for insider threat detection using machine learning. IEEE Trans. Netw. Serv. Manage. **17**(1), 30–44 (2020). https://doi.org/10.1109/TNSM.2020.2967721
9. Liu, F.T., Ting, K.M., Zhou, Z.H.: Isolation-based anomaly detection. ACM Trans. Knowl. Disc. from Data (TKDD) **6**(1), 1–39 (2012)
10. Liu, F., Wen, Y., Zhang, D., Jiang, X., Xing, X., Meng, D.: Log2vec: a heterogeneous graph embedding based approach for detecting cyber threats within enterprise. In: Proceedings of the 2019 ACM SIGSAC Conference on Computer and Communications Security, pp. 1777–1794 (2019)
11. Liu, L., De Vel, O., Chen, C., Zhang, J., Xiang, Y.: Anomaly-based insider threat detection using deep autoencoders. In: 2018 IEEE International Conference on Data Mining Workshops (ICDMW), pp. 39–48. IEEE (2018)

12. Lu, J., Wong, R.K.: Insider threat detection with long short-term memory. In: Proceedings of the Australasian Computer Science Week Multiconference, pp. 1–10 (2019)

13. Pevný, T.: Loda: Lightweight on-line detector of anomalies. Mach. Learn. **102**(2), 275–304 (2016)

14. Rashid, T., Agrafiotis, I., Nurse, J.R.: A new take on detecting insider threats: exploring the use of hidden markov models. In: Proceedings of the 8th ACM CCS International workshop on managing insider security threats, pp. 47–56 (2016)

15. Sanzgiri, A., Dasgupta, D.: Classification of insider threat detection techniques. In: Proceedings of the 11th annual cyber and information security research conference, pp. 1–4 (2016)

16. Sun, X., Wang, Y., Shi, Z.: Insider threat detection using an unsupervised learning method: COPOD. In: 2021 International Conference on Communications, Information System and Computer Engineering (CISCE), pp. 749–754 (2021). https://doi.org/10.1109/CISCE52179.2021.9445898

17. Susto, G.A., Beghi, A., McLoone, S.: Anomaly detection through on-line isolation forest: an application to plasma etching. In: 2017 28th Annual SEMI Advanced Semiconductor Manufacturing Conference (ASMC), pp. 89–94 (2017). https://doi.org/10.1109/ASMC.2017.7969205

18. Tuor, A., Kaplan, S., Hutchinson, B., Nichols, N., Robinson, S.: Deep learning for unsupervised insider threat detection in structured cybersecurity data streams. In: Workshops at the Thirty-First AAAI Conference on Artificial Intelligence (2017)

19. Vinay, M., Yuan, S., Wu, X.: Contrastive learning for insider threat detection. In: International Conference on Database Systems for Advanced Applications. pp. 395–403. Springer (2022)

20. Yuan, F., Cao, Y., Shang, Y., Liu, Y., Tan, J., Fang, B.: Insider threat detection with deep neural network. In: International Conference on Computational Science. pp. 43–54. Springer (2018)

21. Yuan, S., Wu, X.: Deep learning for insider threat detection: Review, challenges and opportunities. Comput. Secur. **104**, 102221 (2021)

22. Yuan, S., Zheng, P., Wu, X., Li, Q.: Insider threat detection via hierarchical neural temporal point processes. In: 2019 IEEE International Conference on Big Data (Big Data), pp. 1343–1350. IEEE (2019)

CSEDesc: CyberSecurity Event Detection with Event Description

Gaosheng Wang[1,2], Peipei Liu[1,2], Jintao Huang[1,2], Shuaizong Si[2], Hongsong Zhu[1,2(✉)], and Limin Sun[1,2]

[1] School of Cyber Security, University of Chinese Academy of Sciences, Beijing, China
{wanggaosheng,liupeipei,huangjintao,zhuhongsong,sunlimin}@iie.ac.cn
[2] Institute of Information Engineering, Chinese Academy of Sciences, Beijing, China
sishuaizong@iie.ac.cn

Abstract. Cybersecurity event detection enables security operators to clearly know the occurrence of network threats, thereby improving the efficiency of security analysis. However, previous approaches considered it as a trigger classification task, which has limitations in accurately locating triggers, especially for long phrases commonly used in the cybersecurity domain. Additionally, tagging triggers is often time-consuming and unnecessary. To address these issues, we propose **CyberSecurity Event Detection with event Description** (**CSEDesc**), which encodes sentence representations based on event description information to detect cybersecurity events without triggers. Our approach is divided into three modules. Firstly, we introduce context-dependent and independent word embeddings, as well as character-level word embeddings, to effectively represent domain words in the context encoding module. Additionally, we employ an attention mechanism to fuse sentences with event information and obtain description-aware embeddings. Secondly, in the syntactic graph convolutional networks module, we use GCNs to encode the sentence, which exploits sentence structure information and improves the robustness of sentence representation. Finally, we perform binary classification for each instance. Experiments on two cybersecurity event detection datasets, CASIE and CySecED, show that our method achieves new state-of-the-art F1-score of 88.2 and 58.3, respectively.

Keywords: cybersecurity · event detection · attention · gcn

1 Introduction

Cyberattacks occur every day, affecting not only people's network activities but also their social lives (e.g., attacks on IoT or critical infrastructure). In general, attacks soar after the first public disclosure of a vulnerability, as hackers usually attempt to exploit the unpatched weakness [6]. For example, according to [2], more than 70,000 attacks occurred after the first disclosure of log4j vulnerability in a week. Cybersecurity events including attacks and vulnerabilities

© The Author(s), under exclusive license to Springer Nature Switzerland AG 2023
L. Iliadis et al. (Eds.): ICANN 2023, LNCS 14256, pp. 26–38, 2023.
https://doi.org/10.1007/978-3-031-44213-1_3

are widely discussed on the internet producing a lot of text data (e.g., reports, news, comments, etc.). Such text data contains rich threat information that is very important for operators. Early detection of relevant cybersecurity events before attacking your system will contribute to targeted defense deployment, which could mitigate the impact of the attack or prevent the occurrence of the attack. For this reason, we aim to detect cybersecurity events in this work.

Event detection is a sub-task of information extraction aiming to detect the occurrence of events and categorize them into specific types. Most previous works consider event detection as a word classification task that first recognizes the event triggers (a word or phrase that most clearly expresses the event occurrence) and then classifies them into specific types since event triggers usually contain rich semantics of an event [3,13]. However, event triggers extraction is not necessary for event detection whose goal is to recognize and categorize events [12]. Moreover, event triggers in cybersecurity domain are often multi-words bringing difficulties to locate them accurately. As attacks grow fast and are often accompanied by new types, tagging event types without extra triggers could save more time and improve research efficiency. So, in this paper, we propose to detect cybersecurity events without triggers.

Without trigger recognition, it's intuitive to convert this task to text classification. There are three challenges in this task: 1) Trigger absence problem. Previous works have demonstrated the importance of event triggers and have explicitly exploited annotated trigger words that provide significant clues about specific events. Without trigger semantic information, it's challenging to classify a sentence into the correct category. 2) Multi-type events problem. As a sentence may contain multiple events, it's challenging to classify a sentence without triggers into multiple types. 3) Domain-specific problem. There are professional terms and strings with specific meanings in the field of cybersecurity, which makes generalized semantics difficult to represent words.

To solve the problems mentioned above, we propose a novel paradigm called **CyberSecurity Event Detection with event Description** (i.e., **CSEDesc**). The event description should embody crucial characteristics of an event, such as the definition of an event or a set of keywords that could represent the event. Typically, it contains rich event semantic information. In this work, we choose event definition as event description for convenience, as each dataset provides a definition of an event. Integrating event description information into the sentence can help us judge whether the text relates to such an event type. To capture the semantic information of a specific event for a sentence, we design an input pattern called "Sentence and Description" (i.e., SD) and make a binary classification for each SD. A given sentence s attached to each pre-defined event description forms an instance, which is expected to be labeled with 0 or 1. For each sentence, we generate X instances, where X equals the number of event types in the dataset. In this paradigm, one sentence that carries each event description will generate all possible cases. In this example "No customer account information was touched by the phishing attack.", "was touched" is the trigger of the Attack.Databreach event and "the phishing attack" triggers Attack.Phishing event. Also, it can solve the multi-type problem where a sentence contains multiple events through binary classification.

To utilize our proposed paradigm for cybersecurity event detection, we have developed an end-to-end model as shown in Fig. 1. In the context encoding module, we first fine-tune the pretrained language model on the cybersecurity event detection dataset and then introduce the context-independent domain-word2vec and char-level lstm to augment word embeddings, which could address the domain-specific problem. Furthermore, we introduce an attention mechanism to capture interactions between the sentence and event description to incorporate the sentence with event semantic information and get the description-aware word representations. In the syntactic graph convolution networks module, we employ graph convolutional networks to produce sentence representation in order to utilize the syntactic structure features. Because sentences are sequential, the semantic role and structural semantics of words in sentences are ignored. The syntactic structure which provides model with such ignored information can thus enhance the robustness of sentence representation. In the classifier module, we perform binary classification for each sentence representation to determine whether the sentence belongs to such an event.

We have evaluated our approach on two public cybersecurity event detection datasets: CASIE [16] and CySecED [18]. The results show that our approach outperforms all the compared baselines, and achieves new state-of-the-art F1-score 88.2 and 58.3 separately. Our work makes three main contributions:

- We propose a new paradigm for cybersecurity event detection with event description, which helps to save annotation work and improve researcher's efficiency.
- We propose to combine context-dependent word embeddings, context-independent word embeddings and char-level word embeddings to augment word representation in the cybersecurity domain.
- We validate our approach on both public cybersecurity event detection datasets, and results show that our method achieves new state-of-the-art performance.

2   Related Work

Previous works detect cybersecurity events from multiple sources, such as social media, reports, news, etc. The early work is based on keywords and machine learning. [7] proposes a dynamic typed query expansion approach to detect cybersecurity events from social media based on weakly supervised learning which learns to map a small set of event triggers to specific event-related text. SONAR [9] detects cybersecurity events based on a taxonomy of cybersecurity events and a set of seed keywords describing the type of events. It designs a self-learned keywords mechanism based on word embedding to discover new relevant keywords. CySecAlert [15] uses a supervised classifier based on active learning to filter cybersecurity-related text and cluster the relevant text according to event topics where each cluster represents an event candidate. In keywords-based methods, the recall score is affected by the dictionaries they use. With the rapid development of deep learning, researchers began to study the application of deep learning to cybersecurity event detection. CAISE [16] uses different deep neural networks approaches with attention to extract cybersecurity events. It utilizes rich linguistic features (e.g., POS, entity types, syntax dependency relations, etc.) and word embeddings, which can improve the performance of the model. Facing the problem of missing annotation datasets, they label about 1,000 newswire articles related to cybersecurity events and make them public. CySecED [18] introduces a dataset for event detection in cybersecurity text. Compared to CASIE, CySecED defines more fine-grained event types including 30 subevent types totally, and considers the document-level information which can only be detected by combining multiple sentence information in the document. In addition, CySecED evaluates the advanced models on it and CASIE and compares the F1 performance. Also, we compare our method with them on both CySecED and CASIE datasets.

3 Methods

CSEDesc takes the pair of sentence data and event description as the input and incorporates event semantic information into the sentence to determine whether the sentence belongs to such an event. Our model is illustrated in Fig. 1. In the following sections, we will first introduce the formulation of inputs for CSEDesc and then demonstrate each component in detail.

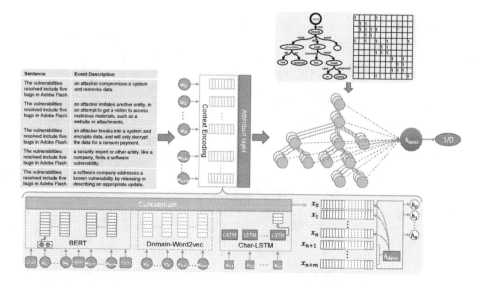

Fig. 1. Architecture of CSEDesc. CSEDesc contains 3 core components: context encoding, syntactic graph convolutional networks, and binary classifier.

3.1 Inputs Formulating

To integrate event information into sentences, CSEDesc takes both a sentence and its corresponding event description as input. The event description contains critical characteristics of an event and effectively represents it. To construct the input, we concatenate a sentence and an event description. Specifically, given a sentence $W = \{w_0, w_1, ..., w_n\}$ and an event description $D = \{w_{n+1}^t, w_{n+2}^t, ..., w_{n+m}^t\}$, the formulated input is:

$$C = \{s_0, w_0, w_1, ..., w_n, s_1, w_{n+1}^t, w_{n+2}^t, ..., w_{n+m}^t, s_2\} \tag{1}$$

where $w_{0:n}$ is the sentence token, $w_{n+1:n+m}^t$ is the description token, t is the type of an event, s_i is the special token for the pretrained language model. If pretrained model is not applicable, the special tokens are not needed.

3.2 Context Encoding

Considering domain characteristics, we adopt three embedding methods and an additional attention mechanism for the embedding fusion as shown in Fig. 1: 1) contextual word representations; 2) domain-specific word representations; 3) char-level word representations; 4) description-aware word representations.

Contextual Word Representations. The pretrained language model has been demonstrated to be powerful for representing words and it enables users to fine-tune the model to adapt to the downstream task. We use the pretrained BERT model [5] to obtain contextual embeddings for each SD and fine-tune it in our neural networks. Because it is context-dependent, the same word has different representation vectors. That's to say when a sentence carries different event descriptions, the word representations are different and the event description information will be integrated into the word in the sentence. As the BERT uses WordPiece tokenization, which may break a word into a few tokens and generate different embeddings for each token. In CSEDesc, we only adopt the first token as the word embeddings $b_i \in \mathbb{R}^{d_b}$.

Domain-Specific Word Representations. Since BERT is trained on a general corpus with limited cybersecurity domain knowledge, incorporating domain-related embeddings for semantic augmentation would be beneficial. While in-domain words typically have consistent meanings, context-free embeddings can still be used. For CSEDesc, we follow [16] to adopt the non-contextual embedding, domain-word2vec, which uses 100-dimension randomly initialized vectors and required words to occur at least twice in the corpus. In this way, We obtain the word embedding $v_i \in \mathbb{R}^{d_v}$.

Character-Level Word Representations. Cybersecurity text often contains unseen words causing the out-of-vocabulary (OOV) words problem. Moreover, such OOV words may convey crucial information. For example, misspelled email addresses (like xxx@docusgn.com, whose correct spelling is xxx@docusign.com) and malicious domains (e.g., googledocs.g-docs.win, googledocs.g-docs.pro) are often associated to phishing attacks, because the phishing attack arrives as an e-mail with a malicious URL or documents. Previous studies have demonstrated the usefulness of character-level word embeddings in dealing with unseen words and OOV words [11]. These embeddings are effective in capturing OOV word features and can thus improve the performance of cybersecurity event detection task. In CSEDesc, we employ a two-layers character-level LSTM (char-lstm) encoder to learn the representation of each word and finally output the last $c_i \in \mathbb{R}^{d_c}$ as the word embeddings.

When obtaining all the 3 kinds of embeddings, we will concatenate them all as the final word representation for text features extraction:

$$x_i = [b_i; v_i; c_i] \tag{2}$$

Description-Aware Word Representations. Each event description contains critical features that are essential for detecting and categorizing events. Incorporating such features into the sentence is helpful to distinguish whether the sentence pertains to such an event. To achieve this, we propose an attention-based method for capturing the interactions between the concatenated text embeddings and event description embeddings. Specifically, we first compute event description representation h_{desc} using mean pooling, and then calculate cosine similarity between h_{desc} and x_i. Finally, obtain the description-aware word representation h_i by:

$$h_i = \cos(x_i, h_{desc}) \cdot x_i \tag{3}$$

3.3 Syntactic Graph Convolutional Networks

The token sequence only contains the sequence semantics of the sentence, in which the semantic role and structural semantics are missing. The syntactic tree structure and syntactic relations are helpful to enhance sentence representation [17]. To leverage such structural characteristics, we adopt Graph Convolution Networks [8] to compute the sentence representation. Given the dependency tree of a sentence, we first transform it into a graph by representing each word as a node and each syntactic relation between words as an edge [4]. For a graph with n nodes, we employ a symmetric adjacency matrix $A \in \mathbb{R}^{n \times n}$ to represent the graph, where $A_{ij} = 1$ if there is a dependency edge between node i and node j, otherwise $A_{ij} = 0$.

As the node in the dependency tree never connects to itself, the information in h_i^{l-1} will never be delivered to h_i^l, causing loss of information. So, we add self-loops to each node in the graph, and the graph convolution operation in layer l could be written as:

$$H^l = ReLU(\tilde{A}WH^{l-1}) \tag{4}$$

where $\tilde{A} = A + I$, I is the identity matrix. We obtain the final output vector representation of each node after the L-layer GCN. In order to generate the sentence vector, we employ a max pooling function to aggregate the node vectors as follows:

$$h_{sent} = f_{max}(H^L) \tag{5}$$

3.4 Classifier

After aggregating each node representation in the graph, we obtain the sentence representation h_{sent}. We then feed this representation into a fully-connected network, which is followed by a sigmoid function to predict the probability of a binary variable:

$$o = \sigma(U \cdot h_{sent}) \tag{6}$$

where $U \in \mathbb{R}^{d1}$. Given an instance I, the model assign it a label $\tilde{y}$ according to the following equation:

$$\tilde{y} = \begin{cases} 0, o < 0.5 \\ 1, otherwise \end{cases} \tag{7}$$

3.5 Focal Loss Function

In the CSEDesc paradigm, one sentence with each event description generates all possible instances meaning that it will produce many extra negative samples. For example, there are 30 subevent types in CySecED, if a sentence only contains one event, it will generate 29 negative samples and 1 positive sample. Though some sentences contain more than one event, the number of negative samples still far exceeds the number of positive samples. The imbalance of positive and negative samples will affect the training effect. To give higher weight to positive samples, we use the focal loss function [10] to optimize our model:

$$loss(\tilde{y}) = -\alpha_t(1 - \tilde{y})^\gamma \log(\tilde{y}) \tag{8}$$

where α is used to adjust the proportion between positive and negative sample loss, and γ is used to enlarge the focus of ambiguous samples.

4 Experiments

In this section, we will introduce the datasets we evaluate on and conduct a series of experiments to demonstrate the effectiveness of our method.

4.1 Datasets

Our experiments are conducted on two public cybersecurity event detection datasets, CASIE [16] and CySecED [18]:

CASIE [16] is the first dataset for cybersecurity event extraction. It defines two major types of events: Attack and Vulnerability, and further subcategorized them into 5 event subtypes. CySecED [18] is a large dataset for cybersecurity event detection. It categorizes 30 subevent types into 4 event types (Discover, Patch, Attack, Impact) based on the four stages of a cyber attack. Notably, CySecED contains ambiguous triggers whose type can only be predicted with the help of document context, which is not considered in this work.

In this work, we focus on detecting events without triggers on sentence-level. We remove the trigger annotations from the corpus and employ Stanford CoreNLP Toolkit to split each article into sentences and generate dependency trees. To satisfy our need, we convert each original sample to sentence-description instance and label it with 1/0 according to its original label. Ultimately, we will generate 5 and 30 instances for a sentence in CASIE dataset and CySecED dataset, separately.

Table 1 illustrates the statistics for CASIE and CySecED. Although CySecED contains more samples than CASIE, it has fewer positive samples. In trigger-based word classification methods, negative examples refer to non-trigger words, while positive examples are the annotated trigger words. However, this work does not use triggers but constructs sentences with event descriptions as instances. In CSEDesc, sentences belonging to such events are positive instances, and others are negative instances. Thus, our method naturally has fewer positive samples. Furthermore, when a sentence contains multiple triggers belonging to the same event, it is considered as multiple positive samples in the trigger-based classification method, but as one positive sample in our method. Such cases are common in the CySecED dataset, which contributes to the lower number of positive samples in our dataset.

Table 1. Statistics for CASIE and CySecED Datasets

	CASIE	CySecED
# event types	5	30
# positive examples	8,470	8,014
# negative examples	240,682	282,220
# positive instances (CSEDesc)	3,809	4,671
# negative instances (CSEDesc)	77,311	176,550
# sentences per document (average)	16.69	24.94

4.2   Hyper Parameters

A grid search was used to select appropriate hyperparameters. In the context encoding module, we use the pretrained bert-base-uncase model [1] for fine-tuning, and we set the dimension of word2vec embedding as 100, the dimension of char-lstm embedding as 100. In the GCN module, we use a four-layer GCN, and the activate function is ReLU. The gcn-dim is set as 512. We try mean-pooling, max-pooing, sum-pooling to aggregate node embeddings and finally we choose the best max-pooing strategy. In the focal loss function, we set α as 0.3, γ as 2. The batch size is 40 in our experiments. We optimize our model with adam optimizer, and the learning rate is set to 1e-5. In addition, we have the learning rate scheduler with cosine strategy, and the weight decay is set to 1e-5.

4.3   Main Results and Analysis

We compare our methods with some state-of-the-art event detection systems. Here we give a brief introduction of them as follows:

- CNN [13] utilizes CNN without complicated feature engineering to detect events.
- DMCNN [3] is a dynamic multi-pooling CNN model capturing more sentence-level features and solving the multi-type event problem.
- GCN [14] converts dependency trees into graphs and proposes a pooling method based on entity mention to perform event detection.
- MOGANED [19] proposes to use a dependency tree based graph convolution network with attention to model multi-order syntactic representations for event detection.
- CyberLSTM(CASIE) [16] is a cybersecurity event extraction system and presents the CASIE dataset publicly. The model employs a biLSTM network with an attention layer for event detection. The model uses several linguistic features including POS, NER, Dependency, etc.

Table 2. The Performance (F1-score) of the Models

Model	Dataset	
	CASIE	CySecED
CNN	83.8	43.0
DMCNN	84.0	42.7
GCN	85.4	48.9
MOGANED	86.5	56.5
CyberLSTM (CASIE)	82.3	34.5
CSEDesc (Ours)	**88.2**	**58.3**

Table 2 presents the F1 performance of different methods and the ablation results are from [18]. These results demonstrate the effectivenesses of our method which incorporates the event description information and multiple embeddings. CSEDesc can reach the best performance on both datasets. We can see that CSEDesc achieves the best 88.2 and 58.3 performance on CASIE and CySecED dataset, respectively. It is obvious that the performance on CySecED dataset is generally lower than that on CASIE dataset. The reason for this is that certain event types in CySecED dataset require document-level information for their determination, which may necessitate the aggregation of information across multiple sentences to enable more complex long text reasoning. Results show that GCN-based methods are better than CNN-based methods, highlighting the importance of structural semantics. In the graph-based methods, both CSEDesc and the GCN methods utilize first-order syntactic relations and CSEDesc improves by 2.8 compared to the GCN method. The F1-score of CSEDesc is still higher than MOGANED, though MOGANED uses both first-order and high-order syntactic relations. It's because of that event descriptions contain more event features and CSEDesc could fuse such features. Notably, CSEDesc outperforms the CyberLSTM by 5.9 in the case that it not only uses multiple embeddings but also uses rich syntactic features and additional features. We observe that CSEDesc outperforms all sentence-level models and achieves a new state-of-the-art. And We do not compare our method with HBTNGMA and DEEB-RNN methods mentioned in [18] because they are document-level event detection methods.

Table 3. Ablation study

Module	CASIE			CySecED		
	P	R	F1	P	R	F1
CSEDesc	**86.9**	89.5	**88.2**	**57.4**	59.2	**58.3**
-char_lstm	83.5	**90.8**	87.0	54.7	**59.5**	57.0
-word2vec	83.1	88.9	85.9	51.9	54.8	53.3
-word2vec&char_lstm	82.6	87.7	85.1	51.0	52.8	51.9

4.4 Ablation Study

To understand the contribution of different embeddings to our model, we conduct an ablation study where we removed each embedding individually, as well as both word2vec and char-lstm embeddings.

The experimental results presented in Table 3 reveal that the removal of any embedding leads to a decrease in model performance. The lowest F1-score is observed when both the word2vec and char_lstm embeddings are removed. These findings suggest that both embeddings significantly contribute to the model's performance. We find that the domain-word2vec embedding method has more effects on the model. This is due to the fact that domain-word2vec captures lexical semantic features specific to the cybersecurity domain, and as a result, when it is removed the F1-score drops a lot, especially in CySecED dataset. The char_lstm embedding could also improve the word representation but contributes to the model less than domain-word2vec. This may be attributed to the fact that char_lstm is better suited for handling abbreviations and OOV words, which are relatively rare in the dataset.

5   Conclusion

In this paper, we propose a new cybersecurity event detection paradigm, CSEDesc, which leverages event descriptions to improve the accuracy of event detection. To enhance word representations in the cybersecurity domain, we introduce three different word embedding methods. First, we fine-tune BERT on cybersecurity datasets, then introduce domain-word2vec embeddings and character-level word embeddings. To capture cybersecurity event information and exploit syntactic structure information, we apply an attention mechanism and a GCN, respectively. Finally, we employ binary classification to identify if a sentence relates to such a cybersecurity event. Our experiments on two cybersecurity event detection datasets demonstrate the effectiveness of our approach.

Acknowledgment. This research was supported in part by National Key R&D Program of China (Grant No.2022YFB3103904), National Natural Science Foundation of China (Grant No.61931019), and National Natural Science Young Foundation of China (Grant No.62002342). Any opinions, findings, and conclusions in this paper are those of the authors and do not necessarily reflect the views of the funding agencies.

References

1. https://huggingface.co/bert-base-uncased
2. Chen, R.: Day 10: where we are with log4j from honeypot's perspective (2021)
3. Chen, Y., Xu, L., Liu, K., Zeng, D., Zhao, J.: Event extraction via dynamic multi-pooling convolutional neural networks. In: Proceedings of the 53rd Annual Meeting of the Association for Computational Linguistics and the 7th International Joint Conference on Natural Language Processing. vol. 1: Long Papers, pp. 167–176 (2015)
4. Cui, S., Yu, B., Liu, T., Zhang, Z., Wang, X., Shi, J.: Edge-enhanced graph convolution networks for event detection with syntactic relation. arXiv preprint arXiv:2002.10757 (2020)
5. Devlin, J., Chang, M.W., Lee, K., Toutanova, K.: BERT: Pre-training of deep bidirectional transformers for language understanding. arXiv preprint arXiv:1810.04805 (2018)

6. Kerner, S.M.: Log4j explained: Everything you need to know. https://www.techtarget.com/whatis/feature/Log4j-explained-Everything-you-need-to-know (2022)
7. Khandpur, R.P., Ji, T., Jan, S., Wang, G., Lu, C.T., Ramakrishnan, N.: Crowdsourcing cybersecurity: cyber attack detection using social media. In: Proceedings of the 2017 ACM on Conference on Information and Knowledge Management, pp. 1049–1057 (2017)
8. Kipf, T.N., Welling, M.: Semi-supervised classification with graph convolutional networks. arXiv preprint arXiv:1609.02907 (2016)
9. Le Sceller, Q., Karbab, E.B., Debbabi, M., Iqbal, F.: SONAR: automatic detection of cyber security events over the twitter stream. In: Proceedings of the 12th International Conference on Availability, Reliability and Security, pp. 1–11 (2017)
10. Lin, T.Y., Goyal, P., Girshick, R., He, K., Dollár, P.: Focal loss for dense object detection. In: Proceedings of the IEEE International Conference on Computer Vision, pp. 2980–2988 (2017)
11. Liu, P., Li, H., Wang, Z., Liu, J., Ren, Y., Zhu, H.: Multi-features based semantic augmentation networks for named entity recognition in threat intelligence. arXiv preprint arXiv:2207.00232 (2022)
12. Liu, S., Li, Y., Zhang, F., Yang, T., Zhou, X.: Event detection without triggers. In: Proceedings of the 2019 Conference of the North American Chapter of the Association for Computational Linguistics: Human Language Technologies. vol. 1 (Long and Short Papers), pp. 735–744 (2019)
13. Nguyen, T.H., Grishman, R.: Event detection and domain adaptation with convolutional neural networks. In: Proceedings of the 53rd Annual Meeting of the Association for Computational Linguistics and the 7th International Joint Conference on Natural Language Processing. vol. 2: Short Papers), pp. 365–371. Association for Computational Linguistics, Beijing, China (2015). https://doi.org/10.3115/v1/P15-2060, https://aclanthology.org/P15-2060
14. Nguyen, T.H., Grishman, R.: Graph convolutional networks with argument-aware pooling for event detection. In: Proceedings of the Thirty-Second AAAI Conference on Artificial Intelligence and Thirtieth Innovative Applications of Artificial Intelligence Conference and Eighth AAAI Symposium on Educational Advances in Artificial Intelligence. AAAI2018/IAAI2018/EAAI2018, AAAI Press (2018)
15. Riebe, T., et al.: CySecAlert: an alert generation system for cyber security events using open source intelligence data. In: Gao, D., Li, Q., Guan, X., Liao, X. (eds.) ICICS 2021. LNCS, vol. 12918, pp. 429–446. Springer, Cham (2021). https://doi.org/10.1007/978-3-030-86890-1_24
16. Satyapanich, T., Ferraro, F., Finin, T.: CASIE: extracting cybersecurity event information from text. In: Proceedings of the AAAI Conference on Artificial Intelligence. vol. 34, pp. 8749–8757 (2020)
17. Sun, K., Zhang, R., Mensah, S., Mao, Y., Liu, X.: Aspect-level sentiment analysis via convolution over dependency tree. In: Proceedings of the 2019 Conference on Empirical Methods in Natural Language Processing and the 9th International Joint Conference on Natural Language Processing (EMNLP-IJCNLP), pp. 5679–5688. Association for Computational Linguistics, Hong Kong, China (2019). https://doi.org/10.18653/v1/D19-1569, https://aclanthology.org/D19-1569

18. Trong, H.M.D., Le, D.T., Veyseh, A.P.B., Nguyễn, T., Nguyen, T.H.: Introducing a new dataset for event detection in cybersecurity texts. In: Proceedings of the 2020 Conference on Empirical Methods in Natural Language Processing (EMNLP), pp. 5381–5390 (2020)
19. Yan, H., Jin, X., Meng, X., Guo, J., Cheng, X.: Event detection with multi-order graph convolution and aggregated attention. In: Proceedings of the 2019 Conference on Empirical Methods in Natural Language Processing and the 9th International Joint Conference on Natural Language Processing (EMNLP-IJCNLP), pp. 5766–5770. Association for Computational Linguistics, Hong Kong, China (2019). https://doi.org/10.18653/v1/D19-1582, https://aclanthology.org/D19-1582

GanNeXt: A New Convolutional GAN for Anomaly Detection

Bowei Pu[1], Shiyong Lan[1(✉)], Wenwu Wang[2], Caiying Yang[1], Wei Pan[1], Hongyu Yang[1], and Wei Ma[1]

[1] College of Computer Science, Sichuan University, Chengdu 610065, China
lanshiyong@scu.edu.cn
[2] University of Surrey, Guildford GU2 7XH, UK

Abstract. Anomaly detection refers to the process of detecting anomalies from data that do not follow its distribution. In recent years, Transformer-based methods utilizing generative adversarial networks (GANs) have shown remarkable performance in this field. Unlike traditional convolutional architectures, Transformer structures have advantages in capturing long-range dependencies, leading to a substantial improvement in detection performance. However, transformer-based models may be limited in capturing fine-grained details as well as the inference speed. In this paper, we propose a scalable convolutional Generative Adversarial Network (GAN) called GanNeXt. Our design incorporates a new convolutional architecture that utilizes depthwise convolutional layers and pointwise convolutional layers as extension layers. In addition, we introduce skip connections to capture multi-scale local details. Experiments demonstrate that our proposed method achieves a 58% reduction in floating-point operations per second (FLOPs), while outperforming state-of-the-art Transformer-based GAN baselines on CIFAR10 and STL10 datasets. The codes will be available at https://github.com/SYLan2019/GanNeXt.

Keywords: Anomaly Detection · CNN · Generative Adversarial Network

1 Introduction

Anomaly detection is an increasingly important area in the field of computer vision, and has been widely studied in numerous application domains, such as video surveillance, risk management, and damage detection. Currently, the advanced methods in this field are based on deep learning, as shown in [5,9,17]. However, the performance of these methods is limited by the lack of labeled data. On one hand, collecting abnormal images is challenging due to the imbalanced distribution between normal and abnormal data. On the other hand, defining

This work was funded by 2035 Innovation Pilot Program of Sichuan University, China.

L. Iliadis et al. (Eds.): ICANN 2023, LNCS 14256, pp. 39–49, 2023.
https://doi.org/10.1007/978-3-031-44213-1_4

abnormal data is difficult. In contrast, unsupervised learning algorithms are commonly used to learn the distribution of normal data. They are trained only on normal data and then tested on both normal and abnormal data. If a given data point is significantly different from the learned distribution based on a predefined threshold, it will be classified as an abnormal object.

In the field of computer vision, anomaly detection is a challenging task that aims to detect abnormal data caused by environmental changes, device damage or human interference. In recent years, unsupervised learning methods based on Generative Adversarial Networks (GANs) [1] have made significant progress in anomaly detection. In these methods, the generator aims to generate data by learning the normal data distribution, while the discriminator tries to distinguish the generated data from the original data. Among these methods, AnoGAN [14] is the first GAN-based anomaly detection representation learning method. To overcome the limitations of GANs, many researchers have proposed improved GAN models, such as GANomaly [1] that uses an encoder-decoder-encoder network, Skip-GANomaly [2] that uses a U-Net structure, and SAGAN [11] that uses attention modules. In recent years, with the emergence of Vision-Transformer [4], attention modules have been used to improve GAN models such as AnoTrans [20], thus further improving the accuracy of the model. However, due to the use of the transformer-based autoregressive model in its inference stage, the inference speed of the attention-based model is limited.

ConvNeXt [13,18] is a convolutional neural network architecture that draws inspiration from the ideas of Vision Transformer [4] and Swin Transformer [12], utilizing attention mechanisms and window partitioning to learn long-range spatial dependencies within images. In addition, it retains the characteristics of ResNet [6] by using residual connections and group convolutions to enhance feature representation and reduce computational complexity. Through this design, ConvNeXt not only achieves faster inference speed than Vision Transformer and Swin Transformer under the same amount of computations but also achieves higher accuracy on tasks such as image classification, object detection, and semantic segmentation.

In this paper, we propose a new framework for anomaly detection. Inspired by ConvNeXt, we design a purely convolutional network called GanNeXt with a U-shaped architecture that combines the advantages of long range information modeling by using Transformer structures and the higher inference speed of CNN networks. In addition, the special module design allows for different numbers of modules to be used at different depths of the U-Net, enabling a fine-grained network design to improve the capture of image features with deep networks. Notably, to address the issue of long-term dependencies, we propose a special skip-connection mechanism that enhances the reconstruction ability of the U-shaped network.

The experimental results show that the proposed method outperforms the state-of-the-art anomaly detection methods on external tasks such as CIFAR10 [10], STL10 [15], as well as on datasets such as LBOT [11]. The main contributions of this paper are summarized as follows:

- Our paper introduces a novel anomaly detection framework named GanNeXt. The proposed framework combines ConvNeXt modules with existing GAN-based methods, aiming to overcome the limitations of CNN encoders in GAN-based modeling.
- Our experimental results on three datasets, namely CIFAR10, STL10, and LBOT, demonstrate that our proposed approach outperforms the state-of-the-art CNN-based methods in detecting anomalies. Moreover, our approach requires significantly fewer FLOPs compared to the most advanced methods, with a reduction of up to 58%.
- We design a new Skip-Connect method to improve the reconstruction capability of the decoder.

2 Proposed Method

2.1 Model Overview

The ConvNeXt [13,18] block inherits many important design choices from Transformers, designed to limit computational cost while increasing the receptive field width to learn global features, demonstrating performance improvements over standard ResNets [6]. By leveraging these advantages to improve the inference speed while maintaining high accuracy, we propose GanNeXt (as shown in Fig. 1), based on the general design of ConvNeXt [13], with AnoTran [20] and Skip-Gan Normaly [2]. In addition, we introduce a new type of skip connection for the CNN networks, using GanNeXt blocks (similar to ConvNeXt blocks) to replace self-attention modules, similar to the skip-attention introduced by

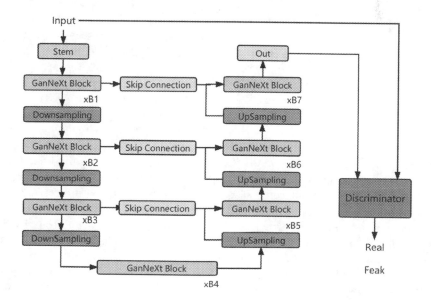

Fig. 1. The structure of our proposed model

AnoTran [20] , to enhance the feature representation of the input images. The experiment shows that compared to the skip-attention based on self-attention modules, this skip connection is more efficient. We added batch normalization at the beginning of the input, which reduces the overall shift in each batch of the input data, improving the representation learning of normal data in the generator.

As shown in Fig. 1, our model consists of a generator and a discriminator. The performance improvement of our model is due to the deep separable convolution based on the Transformer design, which will be described in Sect. 2.2. In the downsampling module, we design parallel downsampling modules to improve feature representation, as described in Sect. 2.3. We introduce an improved skip connection module based on GanNeXt blocks, as described in Sect. 2.4. The loss function and the standard for computing anomaly scores used in our model will be described in Sects. 2.6 and 2.7, respectively. In our model, we use the same discriminator as AnoTran to distinguish the label of the extracted potential representation of input images.

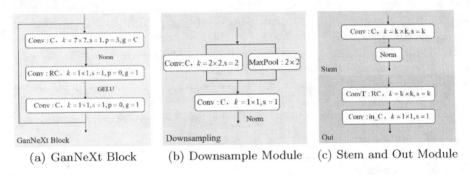

| (a) GanNeXt Block | (b) Downsample Module | (c) Stem and Out Module |

Fig. 2. Three important modules of our proposed model

2.2 GanNeXt Block

In GanNeXt Block (see Fig. 2(a)), the first layer consists of a deep convolution layer containing a kernel size of $k \times k$, followed by normalization and with C output channels. Different normalization methods are used for different tasks, including LayerNorm [3] and BatchNorm [8]. The performance of these two methods varies greatly across different tasks, which will be discussed in Sect. 3.3. The deep convolution enables large convolution kernels to achieve the large attention window effect of Swin-Transformers [12] while limiting computation, thereby delegating important computational tasks to the expansion layer. The expansion layer uses a dilation rate of R and is activated by GELU [7], similar to the design of the Feedforward layer [16] in Transformers. This allows the network to expand in width and effectively separate kernel size expansion from width expansion in the previous layer.

2.3   DownSampling Module

The downsampling operation is often used to reduce the size and number of parameters in feature maps, in order to decrease computational cost while maintaining model performance. In this paper, we selected parallel MaxPooling and convolution kernels of 2×2 with a stride of 2 for downsampling (see Fig. 2(b)). Downsampling through convolution enables the learning of more diversified feature representations, while max pooling emphasizes the feature representation in the feature map. We parallelized these two methods and then used a 1×1 convolution to restore the number of channels, enabling our model to learn richer and more accurate feature representations, which is beneficial for image restoration by the decoder. Similar to GanNeXt Block, the normalization method can also be replaced.

2.4   Stem and Out

In the Stem Module (Fig. 2(c)), we employed a strategy similar to that used in [4,12]. Specifically, we used convolution with the same stride and kernel size, followed by normalization with a replaceable Norm layer.

In the Out Module (Fig. 2(c)), we designed a structure similar to the extension layers. We first performed transposed convolution to restore the output image size to match the input size. Next, we increased the channel number according to a given ratio. Finally, we used 1×1 convolution to restore the channel number to match the input.

2.5   Skip Connection

In Unet, skip connections can be used to directly transfer low-level feature map information to high-level feature maps, helping the network capture features at different scales effectively. This can improve model performance and accuracy, while mitigating the problems arising from gradient vanishing and overfitting due to information loss. AnoTran [20] found the U-Generator to be ineffective in capturing some critical local information in feature representation, and proposed the Skip Attention Connection to further improve performance. Inspired by AnoTran and SAGAN [11], we designed skip connections using GanNeXt Block (see Fig. 2(a)) in our method. Our approach is a pure convolutional structure that does not require transformations (such as reshape operation and convolution) as performed in the CBAM [19], allowing direct convolution operations. Via the GanNeXt block in the skip connections (GSC), the generator can obtain fine-grained feature representations and reduce noise and irrelevant information by preserving the original feature map information, making the model more stable and robust.

2.6   Loss Function

We employed the same loss functions Lcon, Llat, and Ladv as used in Skip-GANomaly [2] , which are formulated as follows:

$$L_{adv} = \mathbb{E}_{x \sim p_x}[\log D(x)] + \mathbb{E}_{x \sim p_z}[\log(1 - D(G(x)))] \tag{1}$$

$$L_{lat} = \mathbb{E}_{x \sim p_x} \|D(x) - D(G(x))\|_2 \tag{2}$$

$$L_{con} = \mathbb{E}_{x \sim p_x} \|x - G(x)\|_1 \tag{3}$$

The adversarial loss, denoted as L_{adv}, is a commonly used loss function in GANs for optimizing the generator G and discriminator D. The goal is to make the generated images as realistic as possible through the classification results provided by the discriminator.

The content loss, denoted as L_{con}, is employed to improve the realism of the generated image $G(x)$. It aims to preserve contextual information in the image. The latent loss, denoted as L_{lat}, captures the difference between the latent representations of the input image x and the generated image $G(x)$. It measures the consistency between the latent representations of x and $G(x)$, denoted as $z = D(x)$ and $\hat{z} = D(G(x))$, respectively.

$$L = \lambda_{adv}L_{adv} + \lambda_{con}L_{con} + \lambda_{lat}L_{lat} \tag{4}$$

The overall objective function L is a weighted sum of L_{adv}, L_{con}, and L_{lat}, where the weights λ_{adv}, λ_{con}, and λ_{lat} are chosen empirically in our experiments.

2.7 Anomaly Scores

We compute the anomaly scores of the test images using the methods in [2, 20]. The anomaly score of a test image x, denoted as $A(x)$, is calculated as $\lambda R(x) + (1 - \lambda)L(x)$. Here, $R(x)$ is the reconstruction score calculated based on x and its generated image x', and $L(x)$ represents the difference between the latent representations of x and x' obtained from the discriminator. The weight λ controls the relative importance of $R(x)$ and $L(x)$ in the calculation of $A(x)$.

$$A(x) = \lambda R(x) + (1 - \lambda)L(x) \tag{5}$$

$$A'(x) = \frac{A(x) - \min(A)}{\max(A) - \min(A)} \tag{6}$$

We calculate the original anomaly scores of all the test samples in the test set and represent the set of anomaly scores as a vector A. Then, we standardize each anomaly score to the range $[0, 1]$ using the same method as in [20]. Specifically, the final anomaly score $A'(x)$ of a single test sample x is computed as $(A(x) - \min(A))/(\max(A) - \min(A))$.

3   Experiment

We evaluated our model using a "leave-one-class-out" anomaly detection method with CIFAR10 [10], STL10 [15] and [11] datasets. The area under the Receiver Operating Characteristic (ROC) curve (AUC) was used as the performance metric in the evaluation. AnoTran, SAGAN, and Skip-Anomaly were used as baseline methods for performance comparison (Fig. 3).

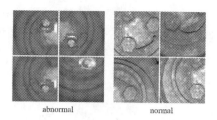

(a) Some image examples from the LBOT dataset, the red box contains abnormal data, which includes bolts that are either damaged or missing.

(b) Examples of the CIFAR-10 dataset.

Fig. 3. Examples in the dataset.

3.1 Dataset

CIFAR-10: Both Skip-GANomaly [2] and AnoTran [20] used the CIFAR-10 dataset and formulated a leave-one-class-out anomaly detection problem. For comparison purposes, we also utilized this dataset. Similar to [2,11,20], we divided the CIFAR-10 dataset into eight distinct categories, each of which contains 45,000 normal training samples, 9,000 normal testing samples, and 6,000 abnormal testing samples. One of the categories was defined as the anomaly class, while the remaining categories were defined as the normal classes.

STL10: The STL-10 dataset is an image recognition dataset used for developing unsupervised feature learning, deep learning, and self-supervised learning algorithms. As with CIFAR-10, the difference between them lies in the fact that STL-10 has less labeled training data per class. In addition, the images in STL-10 are of a resolution of 96×96 pixels. The training methodology used on the STL-10 dataset is similar to that used on CIFAR-10.

LBOT: The LBOT dataset, as reported by reference [11], is an image dataset used for the detection of train axle bolts in railway systems. A total of 5,000 image patches were extracted using the 128×128 overlapping sliding window method to determine the state of the train axle bolts. The dataset was divided into 4,000 training images and 1,000 test images, among which 1,000 test images comprised of 500 normal bolt images and 500 abnormal bolt images.

3.2 Training Detail

We trained the model on a server with an NVIDIA GeForce RTX 3090 GPU and 24GB memory. The Adam optimization algorithm was used with an initial learning rate of $2e-4$, momentum parameters of $\beta_1=0.5$ and $\beta_2=0.999$, and a λ value of 0.9 for computing anomaly scores. In the loss function, we set λ_{adv},

λ_{con}, and λ_{lat} to 1, 50, and 1, respectively. The number of blocks per layer is discussed in Sect. 3.4. We used BatchNorm for training on the CIFAR10 and STL10 datasets and LayerNorm for LBOT.

3.3 Experimental Analysis

In this paper, we compare our proposed method with GANomaly [1], Skip-GANomaly [2], SAGAN [11], and AnoTran [20] models on CIFAR10, STL10 and LBOT datasets. Furthermore, we compare the effectiveness of the skip connection module, and the results show that using the GanNeXt Block with skip connections performs better on average.

Table 1. The AUC results on the CIFAR10 dataset.

Model	frog	bird	cat	deer	dog	horse	ship	truck	airplane	automobile	Average
GANomaly [1]	0.512	0.523	0.466	0.467	0.502	0.387	0.534	0.579	0.789	0.786	0.555
Skip-GANomaly [2]	0.955	0.611	0.670	0.845	0.706	0.666	0.909	0.857	0.748	0.790	0.776
SAGAN [11]	0.996	0.957	0.951	0.998	0.975	0.891	0.990	0.980	**1.000**	0.979	0.971
AnoTran [20]	**1.000**	0.944	0.960	0.999	0.968	0.949	0.999	0.990	1.000	**0.999**	0.980
Proposed w/o GSC	1.000	0.969	**0.999**	1.000	0.985	0.999	**1.000**	**0.996**	1.000	0.987	0.994
Proposed with GSC	1.000	**0.983**	0.992	**1.000**	**0.996**	**1.000**	1.000	0.996	1.000	0.997	**0.996**

Table 2. The AUC results on the STL10 dataset.

Model	bird	car	cat	deer	dog	horse	monkey	ship	truck	airplane	Average
GANomaly [1]	0.588	0.902	0.556	0.664	0.581	0.726	0.590	0.568	0.770	0.748	0.669
Skip-GANomaly [2]	0.929	**1.000**	0.963	0.996	0.859	0.947	0.979	**0.999**	0.998	0.879	0.955
SAGAN [11]	0.916	0.999	0.937	0.991	0.821	0.922	0.938	0.993	0.997	**1.000**	0.951
AnoTran [20]	0.966	1.000	0.985	0.998	0.942	0.975	0.980	0.999	0.997	1.000	0.984
Proposed w/o GSC	**0.968**	1.000	0.988	0.999	0.967	0.969	0.994	0.999	0.999	1.000	0.988
Proposed with GSC	0.964	1.000	**0.989**	**1.000**	**0.978**	**0.981**	**0.995**	0.999	**1.000**	1.000	**0.991**

On the CIFAR10 dataset, as shown in Table 1, our GanNeXt model outperforms the attention-based and traditional CNN models in all metrics. Notably, for three anomalous classes where the AUC is not 1.000, our method achieves a score of 1.000, and for bird, cat, and dog classes, we improve over the baseline method by more than 3%, with an average AUC improvement of 2%.

On the STL10 dataset, as shown in Table 2, our proposed method outperforms the baseline method in all classes except for bird anomalies. For the truck class, the AUC reaches 1.000. Our method outperforms the baseline on both the CIFAR10 and STL10 datasets, which is attributed to the fact that Transformer-based networks lack the inductive bias towards visual data and require more training data to learn image features. Our method combines the advantages of deep separable convolution and expansion layers to retain the long-term dependencies brought by the Transformer while preserving the bias dependencies brought by the convolutional layers, resulting in better performance without pretraining. By comparing different skip connection methods, we find that using the GanNeXt Block connection performs better on most datasets, demonstrating the effectiveness of our skip connection method.

Table 3 presents the results of our approach applied to the LBOT dataset, demonstrating that our method achieved comparable results to the state-of-the-art and surpassed all convolution-based models.

3.4   Computational Efficiency

We compared our method with Skip-GAnomaly, SAGAN, and AnoTran models, in terms of their computational efficiency. The FLOPs were calculated using a 32 × 32 × 3 input, and as shown in Table 4, our model reduced the FLOPs by 58% compared to the baseline methods. We believe that the local connectivity and parameter sharing of the CNN network enables efficient utilization of computational resources while reducing the computational complexity of the network in image processing. Conversely, Transformer-based CV networks require global self-attention mechanisms at each pixel position, resulting in significantly higher FLOPs compared to CNN networks, requiring more computational resources and time.

Table 3. The AUC results on the LBOT dataset.

Model	AUC
GANomaly [1]	0.900
Skip-GANomaly [2]	0.840
SAGAN [11]	0.960
AnoTran [20]	**0.996**
Proposed	0.985

Table 4. FLOPs of the models.

Model	FLOPs/M
Skip-GANomaly	226
SAGAN	708
AnoTran	283
Proposed	**121**

3.5   Ablation Study

To analyse the effectiveness of the various components of our proposed model, we compare the performance on the STL10 dataset with the different number of blocks in our model. The results are shown in Table 5, in which the "Num of Block" column indicates the number of GanNeXt Blocks in each layer. In addition, we set the same number of GanNeXt blocks for the decoder and generator at the same depth. For example, [2,2,6,4] denotes that the number of GanNeXt blocks of first layer in Fig. 1 is 2 (i.e., $B1 = B7 = 2$), similarly, $B2 = B6 = 2$, $B3 = B5 = 6$, $B4 = 4$. Based on this ablation experiment, we use the settings [2,2,6,4] as the default configuration of our proposed model.

Table 5. GanNeXt results of different number of blocks on the STL10 dataset.

Num of Blocks	bird	car	cat	deer	dog	horse	monkey	ship	truck	airplane	Average	FLOPs
[2,2,6,4]	0.964	1.000	0.989	0.999	**0.978**	**0.981**	0.995	**1.000**	1.000	1.000	**0.991**	121M
[1,1,3,2]	**0.967**	1.000	0.987	**0.999**	0.972	0.967	0.994	1.000	1.000	**1.000**	0.989	71M
[4,4,4,4]	0.959	1.000	**0.992**	0.999	0.964	0.976	0.994	1.000	1.000	1.000	0.988	126M
[3,3,3,3]	0.953	1.000	0.991	0.999	0.967	0.971	0.994	0.999	0.999	1.000	0.987	102M
[2,2,2,2]	0.956	1.000	0.99	0.999	0.97	0.98	0.994	1.000	0.999	1.000	0.989	78M
[1,1,1,1]	0.947	**1.000**	0.986	0.998	0.955	0.97	**0.995**	**1.000**	0.999	0.999	0.985	54M

4 Conclusion

In this paper, we have proposed a CNN-based image anomaly detection method that outperforms previous CNN and attention-based methods. Our method employs deep separable convolution and expansion layers to acquire long-term dependencies, similar to attention methods, while simultaneously reducing FLOPs by 58%. Furthermore, we demonstrate the effectiveness of our skip connection in mining multi-scale information. Our experiments reveal that different normalization methods have a significant impact on various tasks, and we plan to explore their effects on representation enhancement in future research.

References

1. Akcay, S., Atapour-Abarghouei, A., Breckon, T.P.: GANomaly: semi-supervised anomaly detection via adversarial training. In: Jawahar, C.V., Li, H., Mori, G., Schindler, K. (eds.) ACCV 2018. LNCS, vol. 11363, pp. 622–637. Springer, Cham (2019). https://doi.org/10.1007/978-3-030-20893-6_39
2. Akçay, S., Atapour-Abarghouei, A., Breckon, T.P.: Skip-GANomaly: skip connected and adversarially trained encoder-decoder anomaly detection. In: 2019 International Joint Conference on Neural Networks (IJCNN), pp. 1–8. IEEE (2019)
3. Ba, J.L., Kiros, J.R., Hinton, G.E.: Layer normalization. arXiv preprint arXiv:1607.06450 (2016)
4. Dosovitskiy, A., et al.: An image is worth 16×16 words: Transformers for image recognition at scale. arXiv preprint arXiv:2010.11929 (2020)
5. Esteva, A., et al.: Dermatologist-level classification of skin cancer with deep neural networks. Nature **542**(7639), 115–118 (2017)
6. He, K., Zhang, X., Ren, S., Sun, J.: Deep residual learning for image recognition. In: Proceedings of the IEEE Conference on computer Vision and Pattern Recognition, pp. 770–778 (2016)
7. Hendrycks, D., Gimpel, K.: Gaussian error linear units (GELUs). arXiv preprint arXiv:1606.08415 (2016)
8. Ioffe, S., Szegedy, C.: Batch normalization: Accelerating deep network training by reducing internal covariate shift. In: International Conference on Machine Learning, pp. 448–456. pmlr (2015)
9. LeCun, Y., Bengio, Y., Hinton, G., et al.: Deep learning. Nature **521**(7553), 436–444(2015)
10. Li, H., Liu, H., Ji, X., Li, G., Shi, L.: CIFAR10-DVS: an event-stream dataset for object classification. Front. Neurosci. **11**, 309 (2017)

11. Liu, G., Lan, S., Zhang, T., Huang, W., Wang, W.: Sagan: skip-attention GAN for anomaly detection. In: 2021 IEEE International Conference on Image Processing (ICIP), pp. 2468–2472. IEEE (2021)
12. Liu, Z., et al.: Swin transformer: hierarchical vision transformer using shifted windows. In: Proceedings of the IEEE/CVF International Conference on Computer Vision, pp. 10012–10022 (2021)
13. Liu, Z., Mao, H., Wu, C.Y., Feichtenhofer, C., Darrell, T., Xie, S.: A convnet for the 2020s. In: Proceedings of the IEEE/CVF Conference on Computer Vision and Pattern Recognition, pp. 11976–11986 (2022)
14. Schlegl, T., Seeböck, P., Waldstein, S.M., Schmidt-Erfurth, U., Langs, G.: Unsupervised anomaly detection with generative adversarial networks to guide marker discovery. In: Niethammer, M., et al. (eds.) IPMI 2017. LNCS, vol. 10265, pp. 146–157. Springer, Cham (2017). https://doi.org/10.1007/978-3-319-59050-9_12
15. Singh, H., Swagatika, S., Venkat, R.S., Saxena, S.: Justification of STL-10 dataset using a competent CNN model trained on CIFAR-10. In: 2019 3rd International Conference on Electronics, Communication and Aerospace Technology (ICECA), pp. 1254–1257. IEEE (2019)
16. Vaswani, A., et al.: Attention is all you need. In: Advances in Neural Information Processing Systems. vol. 30 (2017)
17. Wang, M., Deng, W.: Deep face recognition: a survey. Neurocomputing **429**, 215–244 (2021)
18. Woo, S., et al.: ConvNeXt V2: Co-designing and scaling convnets with masked autoencoders. arXiv preprint arXiv:2301.00808 (2023)
19. Woo, S., Park, J., Lee, J.-Y., Kweon, I.S.: CBAM: convolutional block attention module. In: Ferrari, V., Hebert, M., Sminchisescu, C., Weiss, Y. (eds.) ECCV 2018. LNCS, vol. 11211, pp. 3–19. Springer, Cham (2018). https://doi.org/10.1007/978-3-030-01234-2_1
20. Yang, C., et al.: A Transformer-based GAN for anomaly detection. In: Pimenidis, E., Angelov, P., Jayne, C., Papaleonidas, A., Aydin, M. (eds.) Artificial Neural Networks and Machine Learning-ICANN 2022. ICANN 2022. Lecture Notes in Computer Science. vol. 13530. Springer, Cham (2022). https://doi.org/10.1007/978-3-031-15931-2_29

K-Fold Cross-Valuation for Machine Learning Using Shapley Value

Qiangqiang He, Mujie Zhang, Jie Zhang, Shang Yang, and Chongjun Wang[✉]

State Key Laboratory for Novel Software Technology, Nanjing University, Nanjing, China
{qqh,mujiezhang,iip_zhangjie,yangshang}@smail.nju.edu.cn,
chjwang@nju.edu.cn

Abstract. Research on data valuation using Shapley value has recently garnered significant attention. Existing approaches typically estimate the value of the training set by using the model's performance on a validation set as a utility function. However, since the validation set is often a small subset of the complete dataset, a dataset shift between the training and validation sets may lead to biased data valuation. To address this issue, this paper proposes a k-fold cross-validation method based on the Shapley value. Specifically, the dataset is divided into k subsets, and each subset is employed in turn as a validation set to evaluate the valuation of the training set composed of the remaining $k-1$ subsets by using the Shapley value. The average of $k-1$ valuations of each data instance is taken as the valuation result. Given the exponential correlation between the Shapley value's computation overhead and the volume of data, we propose the Monte Carlo permutation, incremental learning, and batch data valuation methodologies. This approach aids in approximating the true Shapley value as precisely as possible while simultaneously reducing computation time. Extensive experiments have demonstrated the effectiveness of our method, especially in the presence of noise and outliers in the validation set.

Keywords: Shapley value · Machine learning · K fold cross-valution · Data valuation

1 Introduction

Data-driven machine learning methods have propelled the rapid development of computer vision and have achieved impressive performance in tasks such as object detection [1,2], pneumonia detection [3], face recognition [4], and human pose estimation [5]. However, this progress has been limited by the availability of high-quality training data. While datasets like ImageNet [6] have been instrumental in advancing the field, not all tasks have access to large, accurately labeled datasets. For example, in the medical image domain, where accurate annotation requires significant time and cost due to the need for domain expertise. To achieve strong performance on a range of tasks, models need to integrate data from diverse sources, which can introduce noise such as inaccurate labels

© The Author(s), under exclusive license to Springer Nature Switzerland AG 2023
L. Iliadis et al. (Eds.): ICANN 2023, LNCS 14256, pp. 50–61, 2023.
https://doi.org/10.1007/978-3-031-44213-1_5

or measurement errors. Therefore, developing methods to estimate data value is critical to ensure model performance and robustness.

Shapley value [7] well satisfies the group rationality, fairness and additivity of equitable data valuation, so it is widely used in the data valuation for machine learning. We treat the n instances in the training set as the n players of a cooperative game, where the value of each instance is similar to the reward of each player. x_i and y_i are the features and the label of instance i. Learning algorithm $\mathcal{A}$ takes the training set as input and outputs a trained model. The model's performance on the validation set is adopted as a utility function to estimate the data value of the training set. For example, $\mathcal{A}$ could be the empirical risk minimization where it solves $\theta^* = \text{argmin}_\theta \sum l\left(f\left(x_i; \theta\right), y_i\right)$, where θ, $f(x_i; \theta)$ and l are the model parameters, the prediction and the loss. The negative of the loss in the validation set can be used as a utility function, which makes lower losses correspond to higher utility scores.

Despite its popularity, using the Shapley value for data valuation has limitations. In particular, the current approach estimates the value of the training set by solely relying on the model's performance on the validation set (e.g., loss, accuracy) without considering the issues that may exist in the validation set. Since the validation set is often a small subset of the entire dataset, problems such as noise and outliers in the training set may also appear in the validation set, potentially impacting the results of data valuation. The dataset shift [8,9] can also affect data valuation outcomes. Unlike overfitting, the dataset shift occurs when the training and validation sets come from different distributions, causing the model to perform well on the training set but poorly on the validation set. For instance, if the validation set has more positive and fewer negative instances compared to the training set, which leads to a biased data valuation.

To address the aforementioned challenges, this paper proposes a k-fold cross-valuation method (KF-Shapley). We divide the dataset into k subsets that are identically distributed. Each subset is employed in turn as a validation set to evaluate the valuation of the training set composed of the remaining $k-1$ subsets by using the Shapley value. The average of $k-1$ valuations of each data instance is taken as the valuation result. Given the exponential correlation between the Shapley value's computation overhead and the volume of data, we propose the Monte Carlo permutation, incremental learning, and batch data valuation methodologies. This approach aids in approximating the true Shapley value as precisely as possible while simultaneously reducing computation time. Our contributions are summarized as follows:

- We propose a k-fold cross-valuation method based on the Shapley value, effectively overcoming estimation bias due to the dataset shift and noise in the validation set.
- We propose the Monte Carlo permutation, incremental learning and batch data valuation methods that can effectively reduce the time overhead without affecting the valuation results.
- Extensive experiments on multiple datasets validate the effectiveness of our method, especially in the presence of noise and outliers in the validation set.

2   Related Work

2.1   Shapley Value

Shapley value is derived from the cooperative game, which aims to distribute the benefits of cooperation among individuals in a team. The additivity, fairness and group rationality of the Shapley value make it widely used in data valuation [10–12], feature selection [13,14], federated learning [15,16], and interpretability [17,18]. Let D denote the set of players in a cooperative game. S is a subset of D and represents a coalition of players. V is the utility function and $V(S)$ represents the overall reward obtained by S for cooperation. Then the payment of player i is obtained by the following formula:

$$\phi_i = \frac{1}{n} \sum_{S \subseteq D - \{i\}} \frac{V(S \cup \{i\}) - V(S)}{\binom{n-1}{|S|}} \tag{1}$$

where n represents the number of players in D, and ϕ_i represents the payment of the i-th player. ϕ has the following properties:

- **Group rationality**. The profits of the coalition are completely assigned to all players in the coalition.
- **Fairness**. If player i and player j have $V(S \cup \{i\}) = V(S \cup \{j\})$ for $\forall S \subseteq D \setminus \{i,j\}$, then $\phi_i = \phi_j$. A player who contributes 0 to all sub-coalition in D gets 0 rewards. That is, for all S, $V(S \cup \{i\}) = V(S)$ then $\phi_i = 0$.
- **Additivity**. If the overall utility is the sum of M individual utilities, the player's reward is the sum of M utilities. For example, for two utility functions V and W, $\phi_i(V + W) = \phi_i(V) + \phi_i(W)$

Group rationality states that players expect to divide the total payoff of their team among themselves. The fairness property requires that a player's personal information should not affect the payoff they receive, and their payoff should only be dependent on the utility function's response to the player's presence. Additivity allows for the decomposition of a given utility function into the sum of multiple utility functions, thereby making computation more transparent and decentralized.

2.2   Data Valuation

Each data instance corresponds to a player when using the Shapley value to estimate data value. The utility function, which represents the contribution of the data instances to model performance, is typically defined as the model's loss, accuracy, or other relevant metrics in the validation set. Let $D = \{x_i, y_i\}_1^n$ denote the training set consisting of n data instances, where x_i and y_i are the features and the label of the i-th instance. A learning algorithm $\mathcal{A}$ takes an arbitrary training set $S \subseteq D$ as input and outputs a trained model. The model's performance on the validation set is the overall benefit of S.

There are various methods to estimate data value in addition to the Shapley value, such as function utility [19], leave-one-out [20], and core sets [21] that have been used in previous studies. However, these methods do not fully meet the requirements of fairness. Ghorbani [11] proposed a framework that employs the Shapley value in a data-sharing system. Jia [10] improved this approach by developing more effective methods for estimating the Shapley value. Kwon [22] argued that this calculation time could be reduced with approximation techniques tailored for specific machine learning models. However, recent studies have not considered the effect of the validation set quality and the dataset shift on data valuation. In the next section, we will present our proposed method.

3   Method

Computing the Shapley value of a data instance in Eq. (1) necessitates the computation of its marginal contribution on all subsets $S \subseteq D$, which exhibits an exponential relationship with the number of instances. Moreover, training a model on S can be time-consuming and expensive, rendering direct application of the Shapley value for data valuation unfeasible. To address this challenge, we utilize three approaches to approximate the data Shapley.

3.1   Approximating Data Shapley

Monte Carlo Permutation Sampling. We express the uniform permutation of n data instances as Π, which allows us to obtain an equivalent formulation of Eq. (1).

$$\phi_i = \mathbb{E}_{\pi \sim \Pi} \left[V \left(S_\pi^i \cup \{i\} \right) - V \left(S_\pi^i \right) \right] \tag{2}$$

where S_π^i is the set of instances of the first i (excluding i) elements of permutation π. If i is the first element $S_\pi^i = \emptyset$.

Equation (2) transforms the Shapley value computation into an expectation calculation problem. In each iteration, a random permutation π of the data instances is sampled, and the permutation is scanned sequentially from the first element. The marginal contribution of the new element is calculated by adding it to S. The average marginal contribution of multiple iterations of the data instances is employed as its valuation. Castro et al. [23] provide asymptotic error limits for this approximation method based on the central limit theorem when the variance of the marginal contributions is known. Maleki et al. [24] expand the analysis of this sampling method by providing error bounds using Chebyshev's and Hoeffding's inequalities when either the variance or the range of the marginal contributions is known. Ghorbani's work [11] shows that the data estimation generally converges with under $3n$ Monte Carlo permutations.

Value of a Batch of Data Instances. Quantifying the value of an individual instance in deep learning scenarios is exceptionally challenging due to the large training set size, where the impact of a single instance on the model is

---

Algorithm 1. K-Fold Cross-Valuation

1: **Input:** Parametrized and differentiable loss function $\mathcal{L}(.;\theta)$, dataset $D = \{d_1, ..., d_{nk}\}$, k-fold dataset $D_i = \{d_{i,j} | 1 \leq j \leq n, i \in \{1, ..., k\}\}$, learning algorithm $\mathcal{A}$, utility function $V(\theta)$.
2: **Output:** Shapley value of $\phi_1, ..., \phi_{nk}$
3: Initialize $\phi_i = 0$ for $i = 1, \ldots, nk$ and $t = 0$
4: **while** Does not meet the convergence criteria **do**
5:     $t \leftarrow t + 1$
6:     $\theta_{ori}^t \leftarrow$ Random parameters
7:     **for** $i \in \{1, \ldots, k\}$ **do**
8:         $D_{val} \leftarrow D_i$
9:         $\pi^t \leftarrow$ Random permutation of D
10:        $\theta_0^t \leftarrow copy(\theta_{ori}^t)$
11:        $\theta_1^t \leftarrow \theta_0^t - \alpha \frac{1}{|\pi^t[0]|} \sum_{d \in \pi^t[0]} \nabla_\theta \mathcal{L}(d; \theta_0)$
12:        $v_1^t \leftarrow V\left(\theta_1^t, D_{val}\right)$
13:        **for** $j \in \{2, \ldots, nk\}$ **do**
14:            **if** $\pi^t[j] \subseteq D_{val}$ **then**
15:                **continue**
16:            **end if**
17:            **while** θ_j^t does not meet convergence
                  criteria on $\pi^t[j]$ **do**
18:                $\theta_j^t \leftarrow \theta_{j-1}^t - \alpha \frac{1}{|\pi^t[j]|} \sum_{d \in \pi^t[j]} \nabla_\theta \mathcal{L}(d; \theta_{j-1})$
19:            **end while**
20:            $v_j^t \leftarrow V\left(\theta_j^t, D_{val}\right)$
21:            $\phi_{\pi^t[j]} = \frac{t-1}{(k-1)t} \phi_{\pi^{t-1}[j]} + \frac{1}{(k-1)t}\left(v_j^t - v_{j-1}^t\right)$
22:        **end for**
23:    **end for**
24: **end while**

---

negligible. Furthermore, stochastic gradient descent for single-instance training is susceptible to local optima and outlier interference. To mitigate these issues, we quantify the value of a batch of data rather than an individual instance by dividing the data into non-overlapping batches. Batch processing can significantly reduce computing time. Our setup uses a typical batch size of 16 for deep learning. Note that our batch method is different from the grouping method proposed by Ghorbani [11]. Our batch method is combined with batch gradient descent, so if data needs to be grouped on top of the batch, the size of each group must be a multiple of the batch size. In addition, when sampling permutations, the instances within the same batch are randomly shuffled to reduce the impact of the order of instances on the estimation.

Incremental Learning. Despite batching the data, training a new model on S_π^i remains computationally expensive. We propose an incremental learning method to reduce the computational overhead further, which allows the model to process the current batch multiple times before processing the next batch.

While sequentially scanning the i-th batch of the permutation π, we perform multiple batch gradient descents on the current batch until the model performance converges on this, such as when the loss does not decrease or the accuracy does not change. The performance improvement of the model on the validation set is then considered as the marginal contribution of the i-th batch. Deep models can easily overfit the training set. In our experiments, every batch with a size of 16 can achieve 99.5% accuracy by performing an average of six batch gradient descents. Incremental learning makes the first batch in permutation π significantly impact the model's performance, resulting in higher estimation. Therefore, in each random permutation π, we skip the estimation of the first batch and set it to zero.

3.2 K-Fold Cross-Valuation

In this paper, we utilize the k-fold cross-validation method to mitigate estimation errors caused by low quality and dataset shift issues in the validation set. Given a complete dataset D_{full}, we randomly sample a portion of the data as the holdout set D_h, which is used to compare the results of various data valuation methods. The remaining data $D = \{d_1, ..., d_{nk}\}$ is equally divided into k mutually exclusive and identically distributed subsets, denoted as $D_i = \{d_{i,j} | 1 \leq j \leq n, i \in 1, ..., k\}$. During a round of k-fold cross-validation, each subset is employed as a validation set to estimate the data value of the training set consisting of the remaining subsets. After a round of cross-validation, the average of the $k - 1$ valuations for each batch is used as the current round valuation. The batch valuation gradually converges after many iterations. Please refer to Algorithm 1 for more details.

4 Experiments

In this section, we present extensive experiments conducted on multiple datasets to demonstrate the advantageous properties of KF-Shapley. Firstly, our experiments in Sect. 4.2 reveal that the model's performance is highly reliant on high-value instances, while low-value instances have an adverse effect on the model's performance. Next, we perform G-Shapley in Sect. 4.3 by utilizing validation sets with varying valuations, which poses a significant shift in the valuation of the training set instances. Finally, in Sect. 4.4, we introduce outliers into the training and validation sets and observe that KF-Shapley exhibits superior robustness to these.

In our experiments, we compare the performance of KF-Shapley and G-Shapley and leave-one-out (LOO). G-Shapley uses online learning to estimate the data value. Specifically, G-Shapley utilizes a gradient descent to approximate the estimation of a batch in one iteration, which means that during a Monte Carlo permutation process, the model is trained for only one epoch on the training set. LOO is computed as the difference between the performance on the validation set of a model trained with and without the instances of interest on the entire training set.

In all experiments, we train a resnet-50 [25] model to classify images. The trained optimizer is SGD with a learning rate of 0.005 and a momentum of 0.9. The consine scheduler is employed to update the learning rate. The convergence criterion of KF-Shapley is $\frac{1}{n} \sum_{i=1}^{n} min(\frac{|\phi_i^t - \phi_i^{t-100}|}{|\phi_i^t|}, 5) \leq 0.05$. The convergence criterion of the model parameters in a batch is that its accuracy reaches above 99.5% in this batch. All experiments are conducted on two Telsa V100 graphics cards, and the experimental environment is pytorch1.10. It should be noted that the k-fold cross-validation process is highly parallelizable, enabling us to accelerate calculations by adding more machines.

4.1   KF-Shapley for Medical Data

In this section, we estimate the data values of the COVIDx [27] and CT-KIDNEY [28] datasets. COVIDx comprises 30,386 chest X-ray images from 16,648 patients for detecting patients as positive for Covid-19, including 14,192 negative images and 16,194 positive images. We select 4,786 images from the COVIDx dataset as the holdout set, and the remaining images are divided into five subsets, each containing 320 batches of data with a batch size of 16. The CT-KIDNEY dataset contains 12,446 kidney images. The kidney states include tumor, cyst, normal, and stone, corresponding to 3709, 5077, 1377, and 2283 images, respectively. We randomly sample 926 images from the CT-KIDNEY dataset as the hold set, and the remaining images are used in the same configuration as the COVIDx dataset. Note that in the k-fold cross-validation, each subset is used as a validation set to estimate the value of the remaining subsets. In contrast, in the G-Shapley and LOO methods, the fifth subset is used as the validation set to calculate the valuation of the first four subsets, leaving the fifth subset not estimated in these two methods.

After calculating the valuation of the batches using KF-Shapley, G-Shapley, and LOO, we sequentially remove batches starting from the most valuable to the least valuable, as estimated by the corresponding methods. After removing each batch, we retrain a model and validate its performance on the holdout set. Figure 1(a) and (b) show the change in model performance when high-value data is discarded. The model performance degrades as the number of training set decreases, irrespective of the valuation method used. The accuracy degradation rate corresponds to the removed batch's true value. After removing the most valuable 40% of the batches estimated by the KF-Shapley method, the model performance decreases from 98.71% (COVIDx) and 99.32% (CT-KIDNEY) to 93.33% and 94.72%, respectively, indicating that KF-Shapley outperforms the other three methods. Figure 1(c) and (d) illustrate the opposite operation, i.e., removing batches from the least valuable to the most valuable. KF-Shapley assigns negative valuation to approximately 24% of the batches in the two datasets, indicating that these data are usually detrimental to the model's performance. Removing them can improve the model's performance. Overall, KF-Shapley slightly outperforms G-Shapley, while both outperform LOO and

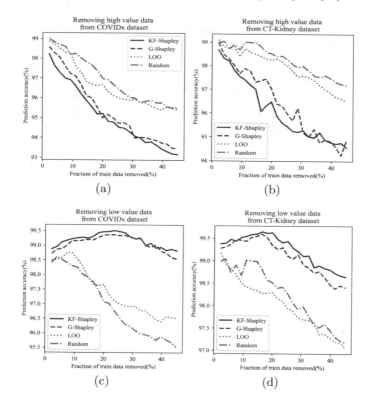

Fig. 1. In (a) and (b), we remove the batches from the most valuable to the least valuable, as ranked by KF-Shapley, G-Shapley, LOO. We do the opposite operation in (c) and (d), removing the least valuable batches from the training set.

random methods. We will explain the defects of G-Shapley and the need for KF-Shapley in the next section.

4.2   Impact of the Validation Set Quality

In this section, we investigate the impact of the validation set quality on data valuation and identify the flaw of G-Shapley. In Fig. 1, the performance of G-Shapley is close to that of KF-Shapley. Hence we adopt the holdout set as the validation set and employ G-Shapley to estimate the valuation of batches in the training set. We then sort the batches based on their valuations in ascending order and divide them equally into five subsets, where subset 0 has the lowest valuation and subset 4 has the highest valuation. We sequentially use a subset as the validation set and estimate the valuations of the remaining subsets using G-Shapley. Tables 1 and 2 display the valuations of the subsets under different validation sets. The experimental results show two interesting observations. Firstly, when subset 0, with a negative average valuation, is used as the validation set, all the other four high-value subsets are estimated as negative, leading

Table 1. Different subsets are utilized as validation sets to estimate the value of the remaining subsets on the COVIDx dataset. The valuation of the subset is the average valuation of the batches contained in this subset.

Validation set	Subset 0	Subset 1	Subset 2	Subset 3	Subset 4
Holdout set	−0.00315	0.00274	0.00328	0.00356	0.00377
Subset 0		−0.00179	−0.00195	−0.00227	−0.00248
Subset 1	−0.00281		0.00347	0.00344	0.00369
Subset 2	−0.00268	0.00304		0.00357	0.00363
Subset 3	−0.00349	0.00273	0.00334		0.00417
Subset 4	−0.00296	0.00187	0.00317	0.00382	

to significant errors in data valuation. Secondly, we observe that selecting a validation set with a similar valuation to the current subset can result in the highest valuation for that subset. For example, the validation set that makes subset 3 obtain the highest valuation is generally subset 2 or subset 4. We hypothesize that the closer the dataset distribution is to the validation set, the higher its valuation. We leave the proof of this conjecture to future research.

4.3 Capture Outliers

In this section, we demonstrate that KF-Shapley is more effective in detecting outliers compared to other methods. We conduct experiments on two datasets: the IMDB movie review dataset, which is a binary review classification dataset with 25,000 positive and 25,000 negative examples, and the CIFAR-10 [28] dataset, which contains 10 different categories of approximately 6,000 color images each. We randomly select 5,000 samples from each dataset and divide them into 5 subsets of identical distribution. We intentionally change the labels of 15% of instances in each subset to create outliers in both training and validation sets. G-Shapley, LOO and random methods use the fifth subset as the validation set, while KF-Shapley uses each subset in turn as the validation set.

Table 2. Different subsets are utilized as validation sets to estimate the value of the remaining subsets on the CT−KIDNEY dataset.

Validation set	Subset 0	Subset 1	Subset 2	Subset 3	Subset 4
Holdout set	−0.00291	0.00380	0.00396	0.00425	0.00479
Subset 0		−0.00183	−0.00199	−0.00219	−0.00218
Subset 1	−0.00186		0.00375	0.00399	0.00420
Subset 2	−0.00288	0.00399		0.00402	0.00414
Subset 3	−0.00304	0.00386	0.00397		0.00491
Subset 4	−0.00343	0.00343	0.00388	0.00386	

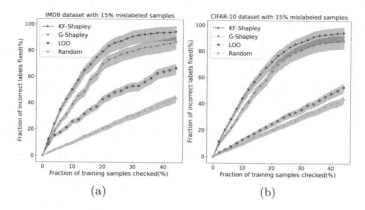

Fig. 2. We sort the valuations calculated by the corresponding method from low to high and fix the mislabeled samples.

FastText [29] and resnet-50 [25] with a batch size of 1 are employed as the models for the two datasets. We sort the training set consisting of the first four subsets from lowest to highest valuation and examine each sample to fix outliers. The experimental results in Fig. 2(a) and 2(b) show that KF-Shapley can more accurately and efficiently detect outliers compared to other methods. After examining 30% of the samples, KF-Shapley notices 90% of the outliers.

5   Conclusion

We propose a k-fold cross-validation approach for machine learning using the Shapley value in this work. Our method divides the dataset into k subsets and uses one of the subsets as the validation set in turn to estimate the value of the training set composed of the remaining subsets. This approach estimates the data value based on all other data rather than just a small validation set, thus addressing the estimation error caused by the validation set's quality and the dataset shift problems. We employ the Monte Carlo permutation, batch data valuation, and incremental learning methods to approximate the Shapley value. Our experiments demonstrate that KF-Shapley outperforms other methods and better captures outliers in the dataset. Furthermore, our experiments provide two interesting insights. Firstly, a low-quality validation set can cause devastating errors in data valuation, and we conjecture that the closer the dataset distribution is to the validation set, the higher its valuation. Secondly, KF-Shapley can be used to identify low-value and incorrectly labeled instances for downstream tasks.

Acknowledgement. This paper is supported by the National Natural Science Foundation of China (Grant No. 62192783, U1811462), the Collaborative Innovation Center of Novel Software Technology and Industrialization at Nanjing University.

References

1. Wang, W., et al.: Internimage: Exploring large-scale vision foundation models with deformable convolutions. arXiv preprint arXiv:2211.05778 (2022)
2. Liu, Z., et al.: Swin transformer v2: Scaling up capacity and resolution. In: Proceedings of the IEEE/CVF Conference on Computer Vision and Pattern Recognition, pp. 12009–12019 (2022)
3. Varshni, D., Thakral, K., Agarwal, L., Nijhawan, R., Mittal, A.: Pneumonia detection using CNN based feature extraction. In: 2019 IEEE International Conference on Electrical, Computer and Communication Technologies (ICECCT), pp. 1–7. IEEE (2019)
4. Chrysos, G.G., Moschoglou, S., Bouritsas, G., Panagakis, Y., Deng, J., Zafeiriou, S.: P-nets: Deep polynomial neural networks. In: Proceedings of the IEEE/CVF Conference on Computer Vision and Pattern Recognition, pp. 7325–7335 (2020)
5. Sun, K., Xiao, B., Liu, D., Wang, J.: Deep high-resolution representation learning for human pose estimation. In: Proceedings of the IEEE/CVF Conference on Computer Vision and Pattern Recognition, pp. 5693–5703 (2019)
6. Russakovsky, O., et al.: Imagenet large scale visual recognition challenge. Int. J. Comput. Vision **115**, 211–252 (2015)
7. Winter, E.: The shapley value. In: Handbook of game theory with economic applications, 3, pp. 2025–2054 (2002)
8. Quinonero-Candela, J., Sugiyama, M., Schwaighofer, A., Lawrence, N.D., (eds.).: Dataset shift in machine learning. In: Mit Press (2008)
9. Park, C., Awadalla, A., Kohno, T., Patel, S.: Reliable and trustworthy machine learning for health using dataset shift detection. Adv. Neural Inform. Process. Syst. **34**, 3043–3056 (2021)
10. Jia, R., et al.: Towards efficient data valuation based on the shapley value. In: The 22nd International Conference on Artificial Intelligence and Statistics, pp. 1167–1176. PMLR (2019)
11. Ghorbani, A., Zou, J.: Data shapley: Equitable valuation of data for machine learning. In: International Conference on Machine Learning, pp. 2242–2251. PMLR (2019)
12. Tang, S., et al.: Data valuation for medical imaging using Shapley value and application to a large-scale chest X-ray dataset. Sci. Reports **11**(1), 1–9 (2021)
13. Sun, X., Liu, Y., Li, J., Zhu, J., Liu, X., Chen, H.: Using cooperative game theory to optimize the feature selection problem. Neurocomputing **97**, 86–93 (2012)
14. Koh, P.W., Liang, P.: Understanding black-box predictions via influence functions. In: International Conference on Machine Learning, pp. 1885–1894. PMLR (2017)
15. Liu, Z., Chen, Y., Yu, H., Liu, Y., Cui, L.: Gtg-shapley: Efficient and accurate participant contribution evaluation in federated learning. ACM Trans. Intell. Syst. Technol. (TIST), **13**(4), 1–21 (2022)
16. Song, T., Tong, Y., Wei, S.: Profit allocation for federated learning. In: 2019 IEEE International Conference on Big Data (Big Data), pp. 2577–2586. IEEE (2019)
17. Chen, J., Song, L., Wainwright, M.J., Jordan, M.I.: L-shapley and c-shapley: Efficient model interpretation for structured data. arXiv preprint arXiv:1808.02610 (2018)
18. Ancona, M., Oztireli, C., Gross, M.: Explaining deep neural networks with a polynomial time algorithm for shapley value approximation. In: International Conference on Machine Learning, pp. 272–281. PMLR (2019)

19. Sharchilev, B., Ustinovskiy, Y., Serdyukov, P., Rijke, M.: Finding influential training samples for gradient boosted decision trees. In: International Conference on Machine Learning, pp. 4577–4585. PMLR (2018)
20. Cook, R.D.: Detection of influential observation in linear regression. Technometrics **42**(1), 65–68 (2000)
21. Dasgupta, A., Drineas, P., Harb, B., Kumar, R., Mahoney, M.W.: Sampling algorithms and coresets for _p regression. SIAM J. Comput. **38**(5), 2060–2078 (2009)
22. Kwon, Y., Rivas, M.A., Zou, J.: Efficient computation and analysis of distributional shapley values. In: International Conference on Artificial Intelligence and Statistics, pp. 793–801. PMLR (2021)
23. Castro, J., Gómez, D., Tejada, J.: Polynomial calculation of the Shapley value based on sampling. Comput. Oper. Res. **36**(5), 1726–1730 (2009)
24. Maleki, S., Tran-Thanh, L., Hines, G., Rahwan, T., Rogers, A.: Bounding the estimation error of sampling-based Shapley value approximation. arXiv preprint arXiv:1306.4265 (2013)
25. He, K., Zhang, X., Ren, S., Sun, J.: Deep residual learning for image recognition. In: Proceedings of the IEEE Conference on Computer Vision and Pattern Recognition, pp. 770–778 (2016)
26. Wang, L., Lin, Z.Q., Wong, A.: Covid-net: A tailored deep convolutional neural network design for detection of Covid-19 cases from chest x-ray images. Sci. Reports **10**(1), 1–12 (2020)
27. Islam, M.N., Hasan, M., Hossain, M.K., Alam, M.G.R., Uddin, M., Soylu, A.: Vision transformer and explainable transfer learning models for auto detection of kidney cyst, stone and tumor from CT-radiography. Sci. Reports **12**(1), 11440 (2022)
28. Krizhevsky, A., Hinton, G.: Learning multiple layers of features from tiny images. 7 (2009)
29. Joulin, A., Grave, E., Bojanowski, P., Douze, M., Jégou, H., Mikolov, T.: Fasttext. zip: Compressing text classification models. arXiv preprint arXiv:1612.03651 (2016)

Malicious Domain Detection Based on Self-supervised HGNNs with Contrastive Learning

Zhiping Li[1,2], Fangfang Yuan[1(✉)], Cong Cao[1], Majing Su[3], Yuhai Lu[1], and Yanbing Liu[1,2]

[1] Institute of Information Engineering, Chinese Academy of Sciences, Beijing, China
{lizhiping,yuanfangfang,caocong,luyuhai,liuyanbing}@iie.ac.cn
[2] School of Cyber Security,
University of Chinese Academy of Sciences, Beijing, China
[3] The 6th Research Institute of China Electronic Corporations, Beijing, China
sumj@ncse.com.cn

Abstract. The Domain Name System (DNS) facilitates access to Internet devices, but is also widely used for various malicious activities. Existing detection methods are mainly classified into statistical feature-based methods and graph structure-based methods. However, highly hidden malicious domains can bypass statistical feature-based methods, and graph structure-based methods have limited performance in the case of extremely sparse labels. In this paper, we propose a malicious domain detection method based on self-supervised HGNNs with contrastive learning, which can make full use of unlabeled domain data. Specifically, we design a hierarchical attention mechanism and a cross-layer message passing mechanism in the encoder for discovering more hidden malicious domains. Then, we construct a node-level contrastive task and graph-level similarity task to pre-train high-quality domain representations. Finally, we classify domains by fine-tuning the model with a small number of domain labels. Extensive experiments are conducted on the real DNS dataset and the results show that our method outperforms the state-of-the-art methods.

Keywords: Malicious Domain Detection · Self-supervised Learning · Contrastive Learning

1 Introduction

DNS provides mapping between domains and IP addresses, making it convenient for people to use Internet devices. At the same time, it is widely used in various malicious activities such as malware, botnets, phishing sites, etc. However, with the development of the Internet, domains are growing in scale, which makes malicious domain detection become a challenging task.

At present, there are many studies devoted to the task of malicious domain detection. They can be roughly divided into two categories: statistical

L. Iliadis et al. (Eds.): ICANN 2023, LNCS 14256, pp. 62–73, 2023.
https://doi.org/10.1007/978-3-031-44213-1_6

feature-based methods and graph structure-based methods. For statistical feature-based methods, they rely on extracting domain features to train machine learning classifiers. For example, Antonakakis et al. [2] exploits network, zone, and evidence features to build a dynamic reputation system to find malicious domains. Schüppen et al. [17] extracts 21-dimensional features by monitoring non-existent domain responses to train SVM or Random Forest classifiers. Despite their high detection accuracy, attackers can bypass these detection methods by adding features commonly used by benign domains. Recently, graph structure-based methods [11,18] have emerged with better performance since the relationships between entities in the DNS are difficult to tamper with. For example, Sun et al. [18] designs a GCN model on a heterogeneous graph to infer the category of domains. Li et al. [11] uses the BERT [4] model to analyze characters and uses a hierarchical graph attention mechanism to detect malicious domains. These methods usually utilize labeled domains as supervised signals to ensure detection performance. However, domain labeling is time-consuming and costly, and it cannot provide sufficient labels for the large-scale domains in real world. Therefore, how to make full use of the information of unlabeled domains to detect malicious domains is a pressing need.

In this paper, we propose a malicious domain detection method based on self-supervised HGNNs with contrastive learning, named DoDe-CL. Specifically, we first model the domains, clients, IP addresses and their relationships as a DNS heterogeneous graph. Then, we design a hierarchical attention mechanism and a cross-layer message passing mechanism in the encoder for learning information of higher-order neighbors. Finally, we propose a self-supervised contrastive learning strategy to fully learn the information of unlabeled domains. In particular, we design a node-level contrastive task and a graph-level similarity task to pre-train the high-quality domain representations. Then, we fine-tune the model in the malicious domain detection task by a small number of labeled domains. Experimental results show that our method significantly outperforms the state-of-the-art methods, especially on the real datasets with extremely sparse labels.

The main contributions of this paper are summarized as follows:

- We propose a malicious domain detection method based on self-supervised HGNNs with contrastive learning. We model domains, clients, IP addresses and their relationships as a DNS heterogeneous graph.
- We design an encoder to discover more hidden malicious domains. Particularly, we propose a self-supervised contrastive learning strategy on malicious domain detection to fully learn the information of unlabeled domains.
- We extensively evaluate the proposed DoDe-CL on the real DNS dataset and the results demonstrate that our method outperforms the state-of-the-art methods.

2   Related Work

2.1   Heterogeneous Graph Neural Networks

Recently, heterogeneous graph neural networks [5,8,22] have been proposed for modeling complex entities and rich relationships in various applications and have achieved rapid development. Wang et al. [20] proposes a hierarchical graph attention mechanism consisting of node-level and semantic-level structures. Hu et al. [7] designs a heterogeneous graph transformer model for web-scale heterogeneous graphs. Zhao et al. [25] exploits the network schema of heterogeneous graphs to mine the information of graph. However, the above methods cannot utilize supervised signals to learn node embeddings from the data itself.

2.2   Contrastive Learning

Contrastive learning is the most popular paradigm of self-supervised learning by distinguishing between positive and negative samples. Here, we introduce some excellent contrastive learning models in heterogeneous graph neural networks. Park et al. [13] creates pretext tasks by maximizing global and local mutual information. Wang et al. [21] designs a cross-view contrastive learning task consisting of a network schema view and a meta-path view. Yin et al. [23] designs an automatic learnable view generator to generate perturbed views. Kim et al. [9] utilizes edit distance to accurately represent the differences between views. However, simply applying the above methods to malicious domain detection does not achieve a good performance because of the sensitivity and the community of domain relationships.

2.3   Malicious Domain Detection

Malicious domain detection has gradually developed from the early rule-based and statistical feature-based methods to graph structure-based methods. For rule-based methods, Sato et al. [16] uses the relationships of domains to find unknown malicious domains. For feature-based methods, Antonakakis et al. [2] proposes a dynamic reputation system by exploiting network, zone and evidence features. Schüppen et al. [17] extracts 21-dimensional features including domain structure features, language features and statistical features to train machine learning classifiers. For graph structure-based methods, Sun et al. [18] designs a GCN model on a heterogeneous graph to infer the category of domains. Li et al. [11] uses the BERT model to analyze characters, and then uses a hierarchical graph attention mechanism to mine heterogeneous graph information. However, the above methods utilize labeled domains as supervised signals, which means that their performance often relies on accurate labels and cannot make full use of the information of unlabeled data.

3   Preliminary

Definition 1. *Heterogeneous Graph.* *A Heterogeneous graph is defined as a graph $\mathcal{G} = (\mathcal{V}, \mathcal{E}, \mathcal{A}, \mathcal{R})$, where $\mathcal{V}$ and $\mathcal{E}$ denote the sets of nodes and edges. It is also associated with a node type mapping function $\phi : \mathcal{V} \to \mathcal{A}$ and an edge type mapping function $\varphi : \mathcal{E} \to \mathcal{R}$. $\mathcal{A}$ and $\mathcal{R}$ denote the sets of node types and the sets of edge types, where $|\mathcal{A}| + |\mathcal{R}| > 2$.*

Definition 2. Meta-path. *A meta path is defined as a path in the form of* $\mathcal{A}_1 \xrightarrow{\mathcal{R}_1} \mathcal{A}_2 \xrightarrow{\mathcal{R}_2} \cdots \xrightarrow{\mathcal{R}_l} \mathcal{A}_{l+1}$, *which can also be described as* $\mathcal{A}_1 \mathcal{A}_2 \cdots \mathcal{A}_{l+1}$ *or* $\mathcal{R}_1 \circ \mathcal{R}_2 \circ \cdots \mathcal{R}_l$, *where* $\circ$ *is defined as a combination operator on relations.*

4   The System Description of DoDe-CL

In this section, we introduce DoDe-CL in detail. It consists of three main modules: construction of heterogeneous graph, pre-training and fine-tuning. Figure 1 shows the overview of DoDe-CL.

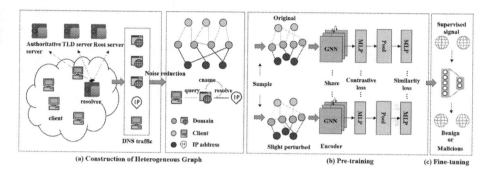

Fig. 1. The system architecture of DoDe-CL.

4.1   Construction of Heterogeneous Graph

A large amount of data is generated in the process of domain resolution, including DNS traffic, DNS log, etc. We extract the necessary data from DNS traffic: domains, clients, IP addresses and corresponding relationships.

Noise Reduction. Since the collected DNS traffic contains a lot of dirty and useless data, such as popular domains, large clients, etc. We need to perform noise reduction. The rules for noise reduction are as follows:

- **Popular domains.** In most cases, popular domains that are queried by a large fraction of clients are usually benign, otherwise, there will be a significant attack event and it is easy to be detected by the security management department. Hence, we remove domains queried by more than $K_1\%$ of clients.
- **Large clients.** There are some "large" clients that query a large number of domains, but they are often some DNS forwarders or large proxies. Therefore, we remove clients that query more than K_2 domains.
- **Inactive clients.** Clients with fewer domain queries will have a smaller effect in the graph and may even bring large computational overhead, so we remove the clients that query less than K_3 domains.
- **Rare IPs.** For the same reasons as inactive clients, we remove the IP addresses that map to one domain.

Graph Construction. After we get the filtered data, we construct them as a heterogeneous graph. The graph includes three types of nodes: domains, clients, and IP addresses, three types of edges: query, resolve, and cname, and three meta-paths: domain-client-domain, domain-IP address-domain, and domain-domain. Figure 1(a) are a heterogeneous graph instance and its network schema.

4.2   Pre-training

Augmentations. We have observed the fact that benign domains will not resolve to "malicious" IP addresses, and the cname of benign domains will not be malicious domains. Once a random perturbation is introduced in the graph (such as adding an edge between a benign domain and a "malicious" IP address), it may make the benign domain become malicious domain, which leads to a change in the semantic of the domain itself. That means, there is a strong sensitivity to the domain relationship. Therefore, the choice of data augmentation in our multi-view contrastive learning is very important. Specifically, we introduce the perturbation to generate a slightly perturbed graph of the original graph (such as adding or deleting a part of the edge) at the data level and use the random mask of dropout to introduce a certain perturbation at the model level.

Encoder. We give a description of the encoder: aggregation and combination.

$$h_i^l \leftarrow \text{Combine}^l \left(\text{Aggregate}^l \left(h_j^{l-1} \right), h_i^{l-1} \right), \tag{1}$$

where $\text{Aggregate}^l (\cdot)$ is the function to aggregate information of domain neighbors in layer l, $\text{Combine}^l (\cdot)$ is the function to combine the messages in layer l, h_j^{l-1} is the embedding of node j in layer $l-1$, node j is the neighbor of node i.

During the aggregation process, we adopt a hierarchical attention mechanism to learn the importance of different neighbors and the importance of different meta-paths. The node-level attention mechanism is formulated as follows:

$$\alpha_{ij}^P = \frac{\exp \left(\sigma \left(a_P^T \cdot [h_i^{l-1} || h_j^{l-1}] \right) \right)}{\sum_{k \in \mathcal{N}_i^P} \exp \left(\sigma \left(a_P^T \cdot [h_i^{l-1} || h_k^{l-1}] \right) \right)}, \tag{2}$$

$$z_i^P = \sigma \left(\sum_{j \in \mathcal{N}_i^P} \alpha_{ij}^P \cdot h_j^{l-1} \right), \tag{3}$$

where a_P is the attention vector of the meta-path P, $||$ is the concatenate operation, σ is the activation function, $\mathcal{N}_i^P$ is the set of neighbors of node i under the meta-path P, α_{ij}^P is the importance of neighbor j, z_i^P is the representation of node i aggregated under meta-path P.

Then, to exploit the contributions of different semantics, we introduce a meta-path-level attention mechanism to fuse the learned domain representations:

$$w_P = \frac{1}{|\mathcal{V}|} \sum_{i \in \mathcal{V}} q^T \cdot \tanh \left(W_q \cdot z_i^P + b \right), \tag{4}$$

$$\beta_P = \frac{\exp\left(w_P\right)}{\sum_{l=0}^{M} \exp\left(w_l\right)}, \tag{5}$$

$$\tilde{h}_i^l = \sum_{P=0}^{M} \beta_P \cdot z_i^P, \tag{6}$$

where w_P is the importance of meta-path P, W_q is the weight matrix, β_P is the weight of meta-path P, M is the number of meta-paths, $\tilde{h}_i^l$ is the learned embedding of node i in layer l.

During the combination process, we stack multiple layers of our graph neural network to capture high-order neighbor information. In order to preserve the messages of each layer as much as possible, we introduce a cross-layer message passing mechanism. The combination process is formulated as follows:

$$h_i^l = h_i^{l-1} + \tilde{h}_i^l, \tag{7}$$

where h_i^l is the output embedding of node i in layer l.

Node-Level Contrastive Task. Contrastive learning is to build self-supervised learning by pulling positive samples closer and pushing negative samples farther away in the feature space. In our model, we feed the same feature to the encoder in two different views respectively. In this way, we introduce random dropout at the model level and slight perturbations at the data level to protect the semantic invariance of domain nodes. Specifically, we use the same nodes in two views as positive samples and other nodes in a batch as negative samples. In this way, we can encourage the model to distinguish the difference between domains, and intend to embed domains into uniformly distributed points in the feature space to maintain their own information.

Before the contrastive learning task, we feed the learned domain embeddings into a MLP to project them into the contrastive space:

$$z_i = W_2 \cdot \sigma\left(W_1 \cdot h_i^L + b_1\right) + b_2. \tag{8}$$

For the loss function, we use infoNCE loss, the formula is as follows:

$$\mathcal{L}_n = -\sum_{i=1}^{2N} \log \frac{\exp(\mathrm{sim}(z_{i,\mathcal{G}}^{D_i}, z_{i,\mathcal{G}'}^{D_i'})/\tau)}{\sum_{j=1}^{N} \mathbb{K}_{[j \neq i]}\exp(\mathrm{sim}(z_{i,\mathcal{G}}^{D_i}, z_{j,\mathcal{G}}^{D_j})/\tau) + \sum_{j=1}^{N} \exp(\mathrm{sim}(z_{i,\mathcal{G}}^{D_i}, z_{j,\mathcal{G}'}^{D_j'})/\tau)}, \tag{9}$$

where τ is a temperature parameter, $\mathrm{sim}(z_1, z_2)$ is the cosine similarity $\frac{z_1^{\mathrm{T}} \cdot z_2}{||z_1|| \cdot ||z_2||}$, $z_{i,\mathcal{G}}^{D_i}$ and $z_{i,\mathcal{G}'}^{D_i'}$ is the embeddings of node i with different dropout D_i in graph $\mathcal{G}$ and D_i' in graph $\mathcal{G}'$, $\mathbb{K}_{[\cdot]}$ is the indicator function, N is the batch size.

Graph-Level Similarity Task. We have observed the fact that IP owners usually reuse IP addresses due to the high cost and clients usually query a large number of malicious domains due to attacks. Hence, most of the benign (malicious) domains in the graph will cluster on the same IP address or client, which means that the domain shows a strong community.

Contrastive learning mining local information ignores the learning of the global representation [6], but the globality of the graph needs to be paid attention to because of the strong community of domains. Therefore, we introduce a graph-level similarity loss function to learn the global information of the sampled graph. We obtain a global embedding representation of a subgraph through a readout function, encouraging the model to maximize the similarity. Therefore, the original graph and the perturbed graph are still consistent under slight perturbations. The formula is as follows:

$$\mathcal{L}_{\mathcal{G}} = -\text{sim}(h_{\mathcal{G}}, h_{\mathcal{G}'}), \tag{10}$$

$$h_{\mathcal{G}} = W_2' \cdot \sigma \left(W_1' \cdot \sum_{i=1}^{N} h_{i,\mathcal{G}}^{L} + b_1' \right) + b_2', \tag{11}$$

where $h_{\mathcal{G}}$ is the graph embedding obtained by the readout function and MLP, we use the sum function for the readout function, and sim is the cosine similarity, $h_{i,\mathcal{G}}^{L}$ is the encoder output in graph $\mathcal{G}$. Finally, our overall learning objectives are described as:

$$\mathcal{L} = \mathcal{L}_n + \mathcal{L}_{\mathcal{G}}. \tag{12}$$

4.3   Fine-Tuning

For fine-tuning in supervised learning, we use a small number of labeled domains as supervised signals. We chose a simple linear layer for binary classification to verify the quality of domain representations learned by our pre-training model.

5   Experiments

5.1   Experimental Setup

Dataset. We collect the real DNS traffic of the university for two weeks from 2020-08-01 to 2020-08-14. From the DNS traffic, we extract the necessary data including domains, clients and IP addresses. Through the reduction operation described in Sect. 4.1, we remove unhelpful data and construct a DNS heterogeneous graph. The target nodes are domains, which are divided into two categories: benign and malicious.

Since the model will employ a small number of labeled domains as supervised signals in the downstream task, we need to label a portion of domains. We collect domains from the top 1M of alexa [1] as a whitelist and from malwaredomains [15], phishtank [12] and cybercrime [3] as a blacklist, which is used to label domains in DNS heterogeneous graph. In order to construct a sparsely labeled scenario, we only use a very small number of labeled domains for the model training. The validation set and the test set we divide in a ratio of about 9:1. The detailed descriptions are summarized in Table 1.

Table 1. The description of experimental dataset.

DNS Heterogeneous Graph		
#Clients	#Domains	#IP addresses
1,639	320,481	50,164
#Domain-Client	#Domain-Domain	#Domain-IP address
78,167	61,347	324,926
Split of the Dataset		
#Training set	#Validation set	#Test set
20 or 40 or 60	117,704	13,000

Baselines. We compare our method with two categories of methods: statistical feature-based methods, graph structure-based methods to demonstrate the effectiveness of our method.

- **FANCI** [17]. It manually extracts structural features, linguistic features and statistical features of domains, which are used to train machine learning classifiers such as SVM and Random Forest.
- **GAMD** [24]. It constructs a node-type and edge-type aware attention mechanism to aggregate neighbors of node, which aims to learn fine-grained domain node representations.
- **HANDom** [11]. It utilizes BERT to analyze domain character features, and then designs a heterogeneous graph hierarchical attention mechanism to fuse neighbor information.
- **DeepWalk** [14]. It utilizes the random walk to generate node sequences and learns node representations on homogeneous graphs.
- **Mp2vec** [5]. It uses the meta-path based random walk to generate node sequences, and then uses a skip-gram model to learn node representations on heterogeneous graphs.
- **GCN** [10]. It uses convolution operations on the graph to aggregate information of high-order neighbors in the spectral domain.
- **GAT** [19]. It uses an attention mechanism on the graph to learn the importance of different neighbors to aggregate information.

Implementation Details. For heterogeneous graph construction, we remove useless data by setting $K_1 = 70$, $K_2 = 30$, $K_3 = 4$. For DoDe-CL, we set the pre-training learning rate to 5e−5, set the patience to 30, set the dimension of the hidden embedding to 64, set the dropout to 0.5, set the τ to 0.3, set the layer to 3 and set the fine-tuning learning rate to 5e−4, randomly initialize the domain features. For baselines, we set parameters according to the original paper and made several modifications, such as setting the dropout to 0.5, the dimension of embeddings to 64. For fairness, we keep the dimensions of the hidden embeddings the same and the meta-paths consistent. We set the walk length to 20 for DeepWalk and Mp2vec. For DeepWalk, GCN and GAT, we ignore the heterogeneity of graph nodes.

5.2   Comparison Results

After model pre-training, we get the learned domain node embeddings. Then, we design a linear classifier in the fine-tuning stage, and feed the learned domain node embeddings to the classifier to predict their labels. In order to construct a scene with extremely few labels, we selected 20, 40, and 60 labeled domain nodes as the training set, 117,704 nodes as the verification set, and 13,000 nodes as the test set. Finally, we evaluated the performance of each method. The experimental results are shown in Table 2.

From Table 2, we can see that our proposed DoDe-CL achieves the best performance. Comparing DeepWalk with Mp2vec, we can see that Mp2vec outperforms DeepWalk, demonstrating the benefit of graph heterogeneity. Comparing DoDe-CL with GAMD, HANDom, GCN and GAT, we can see that our proposed self-supervised learning method outperforms the semi-supervised learning method when the labels are extremely sparse, which demonstrates the positive impact of mining unlabeled information. The better performance of DoD-CL compared to FANCI also demonstrates the superiority of the self-supervised learning method. In summary, the performance of DoDe-CL is the best, because it makes full use of unlabeled data and fine-tunes with a small amount of labeled domain, making the domain representation fully suitable for the malicious domain detection task.

Table 2. Comparison results ($\%\pm\sigma$) of DoDe-CL with baselines.

Metrics	Macro-F1			Micro-F1		
Split	20	40	60	20	40	60
FANCI	85.20±0.4	85.52±0.4	85.48±0.4	85.90±0.4	86.17±0.4	86.13±0.4
GAMD	59.73±0.5	60.83±0.4	64.73±0.4	60.57±0.5	61.63±0.4	66.11±0.4
HANDom	71.78±0.5	75.66±0.7	72.41±0.6	74.37±0.5	77.05±0.7	73.01±0.6
DeepWalk	58.95±0.9	60.51±0.7	61.60±0.7	59.89±0.9	62.45±0.7	63.32±0.7
Mp2vec	66.98±1.1	71.49±0.9	73.06±0.9	67.09±1.1	72.25±0.9	73.64±0.9
GCN	64.60±0.4	66.82±0.4	68.85±0.5	65.07±0.4	67.11±0.4	69.07±0.5
GAT	65.18±0.6	67.93±0.6	70.11±0.5	65.34±0.6	68.32±0.6	70.62±0.5
DoDe-CL	**90.66±1.1**	**93.37±0.8**	**94.02±0.7**	**90.82±1.1**	**93.48±0.8**	**94.10±0.7**

5.3   Variant Analysis

To verify the effectiveness of the components in DoDe-CL, we propose four variants of DoDe-CL, as follows:

- w/o cross layer. To demonstrate the effectiveness of our cross-layer message passing mechanism, we remove the cross-layer message passing mechanism and train the model directly by stacking the same layers.
- w/o pre-training. To demonstrate the effectiveness of our pre-training, we remove the pre-training module and directly fine-tune model.
- w/o $\mathcal{L}_{\mathcal{G}}$. To demonstrate the effectiveness of our graph-level similarity task, we remove the graph-level similarity task and only use the node-level contrastive task to pre-train model.
- w/o $\mathcal{L}_n$. To demonstrate the effectiveness of our node-level contrastive task, we remove the node-level contrastive task and only use the graph-level similarity task to pre-train model.

From Fig. 2, we observe that DoDe-CL outperforms the w/o cross layer, which demonstrate that the model preserving as much information of each layer as possible can contribute to the performance improvement. Compared with w/o pre-training, DoDe-CL has better performance, which prove that high-quality domain embeddings obtained through pre-training are more suitable for malicious domain detection after fine-tuning. Compared with w/o $\mathcal{L}_{\mathcal{G}}$, DoDe-CL performs better, which proves the necessity of mining domain community characteristics in DNS scenarios. Compared with w/o $\mathcal{L}_n$, the performance of DoDe-CL is superior. This is because the lack of a node-level contrastive learning task may result in the failure to learn discriminative domain embeddings.

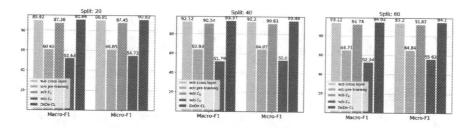

Fig. 2. Performance comparisons of DoDe-CL with its variants.

5.4 Parameter Analysis

In order to analyze the effect of parameters, we conduct a sensitivity analysis on the number of layer l of the model. l are taken from 1 to 5 for the experiments, and the experimental results of the sensitivity analysis are shown in Fig. 3.

From Fig. 3, we can see that the model performance is a gradual increase as l increases from 1 to 3, indicating that mining higher-order neighbor information can bring positive effects to the model. The model performance is the best when l is 3. However, as l increases, the model performance decreases, which is because the more layers there are, the more irrelevant noise feeds into the domain nodes, which leads to the degradation of the model.

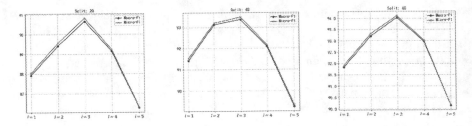

Fig. 3. Parameter sensitivity analysis of DoDe-CL

6   Conclusion

In this paper, we propose a malicious domain detection method based on self-supervised HGNNs with contrastive learning. Specifically, we first model domains, clients, IP addresses and their relationships as a DNS heterogeneous graph. Then, we design a hierarchical attention mechanism and a cross-layer message passing mechanism in the encoder for discovering more hidden malicious domains. Finally, we design a node-level contrastive task and graph-level similarity task to pre-train the high-quality representations of domains and classify domains by fine-tuning with a small number of domain labels. Extensive experimental results show that our proposed DoDe-CL outperforms the state-of-the-art methods on the DNS dataset.

Acknowledgements. This work is supported by Key Research and Development Program Projects of Xinjiang (No. 2022B03010-2), Strategic Priority Research Program of the Chinese Academy of Sciences (No.XDC02030400).

References

1. ALEXA: Alexa top 1 million (2022). www.aws.amazon.com/cn/alexa-top-sites/
2. Antonakakis, M., Perdisci, R., Dagon, D., Lee, W., Feamster, N.: Building a dynamic reputation system for DNS. In: USENIX Security Symposium, pp. 273–290 (2010)
3. cybercrime: cybercrime-tracker (2022). www.cybercrime-tracker.net/
4. Devlin, J., Chang, M.W., Lee, K., Toutanova, K.: BERT: pre-training of deep bidirectional transformers for language understanding. arXiv preprint arXiv:1810.04805 (2018)
5. Dong, Y., Chawla, N.V., Swami, A.: metapath2vec: scalable representation learning for heterogeneous networks. In: Proceedings of the 23rd ACM SIGKDD International Conference on Knowledge Discovery and Data Mining, pp. 135–144 (2017)
6. Hassani, K., Khasahmadi, A.H.: Contrastive multi-view representation learning on graphs. In: International Conference on Machine Learning, pp. 4116–4126. PMLR (2020)
7. Hu, Z., Dong, Y., Wang, K., Sun, Y.: Heterogeneous graph transformer. In: Proceedings of the Web Conference 2020, pp. 2704–2710 (2020)
8. Ji, H., Wang, X., Shi, C., Wang, B., Yu, P.: Heterogeneous graph propagation network. IEEE Trans. Knowl. Data Eng. (2021)

9. Kim, D., Baek, J., Hwang, S.J.: Graph self-supervised learning with accurate discrepancy learning. arXiv preprint arXiv:2202.02989 (2022)
10. Kipf, T.N., Welling, M.: Semi-supervised classification with graph convolutional networks. arXiv preprint arXiv:1609.02907 (2016)
11. Li, Z., Yuan, F., Liu, Y., Cao, C., Fang, F., Tan, J.: Heterogeneous graph attention network for malicious domain detection. In: Pimenidis, E., Angelov, P., Jayne, C., Papaleonidas, A., Aydin, M. (eds.) ICANN 2022. LNCS, vol. 13530, pp. 506–518. Springer, Cham (2022). https://doi.org/10.1007/978-3-031-15931-2_42
12. OPENDNS: Phishtank (2022). www.phishtank.com
13. Park, C., Kim, D., Han, J., Yu, H.: Unsupervised attributed multiplex network embedding. In: Proceedings of the AAAI Conference on Artificial Intelligence, vol. 34, pp. 5371–5378 (2020)
14. Perozzi, B., Al-Rfou, R., Skiena, S.: Deepwalk: online learning of social representations. In: Proceedings of the 20th ACM SIGKDD International Conference on Knowledge Discovery and Data Mining, pp. 701–710 (2014)
15. Riskanalytics: Malware domain block list (2022). www.malwaredomains.com
16. Sato, K., Ishibashi, K., Toyono, T., Hasegawa, H., Yoshino, H.: Extending black domain name list by using co-occurrence relation between DNS queries. IEICE Trans. Commun. **95**(3), 794–802 (2012)
17. Schüppen, S., Teubert, D., Herrmann, P., Meyer, U.: {FANCI}: feature-based automated nxdomain classification and intelligence. In: 27th {USENIX} Security Symposium ({USENIX} Security 18), pp. 1165–1181 (2018)
18. Sun, X., Tong, M., Yang, J., Xinran, L., Heng, L.: Hindom: a robust malicious domain detection system based on heterogeneous information network with transductive classification. In: 22nd International Symposium on Research in Attacks, Intrusions and Defenses ({RAID} 2019), pp. 399–412 (2019)
19. Veličković, P., Cucurull, G., Casanova, A., Romero, A., Lio, P., Bengio, Y.: Graph attention networks. arXiv preprint arXiv:1710.10903 (2017)
20. Wang, X., et al.: Heterogeneous graph attention network. In: The World Wide Web Conference, pp. 2022–2032 (2019)
21. Wang, X., Liu, N., Han, H., Shi, C.: Self-supervised heterogeneous graph neural network with co-contrastive learning. In: Proceedings of the 27th ACM SIGKDD Conference on Knowledge Discovery and Data Mining, pp. 1726–1736 (2021)
22. Wu, Z., Pan, S., Chen, F., Long, G., Zhang, C., Philip, S.Y.: A comprehensive survey on graph neural networks. IEEE Trans. Neural Netw. Learn. Syst. **32**(1), 4–24 (2020)
23. Yin, Y., Wang, Q., Huang, S., Xiong, H., Zhang, X.: AutoGCL: automated graph contrastive learning via learnable view generators. In: Proceedings of the AAAI Conference on Artificial Intelligence, vol. 36, pp. 8892–8900 (2022)
24. Zhang, S., et al.: Attributed heterogeneous graph neural network for malicious domain detection. In: 2021 IEEE 24th International Conference on Computer Supported Cooperative Work in Design (CSCWD), pp. 397–403. IEEE (2021)
25. Zhao, J., Wang, X., Shi, C., Liu, Z., Ye, Y.: Network schema preserving heterogeneous information network embedding. In: International Joint Conference on Artificial Intelligence (IJCAI) (2020)

Time Series Anomaly Detection with Reconstruction-Based State-Space Models

Fan Wang[1(✉)], Keli Wang[2,3], and Boyu Yao[1]

[1] Novo Nordisk A/S, Beijing, China
{fqxw,uqby}@novonordisk.com
[2] Postgraduate Department, China Academy of Railway Sciences, Beijing, China
keli_wang@126.com
[3] China Railway Test and Certification Center Limited, Beijing, China

Abstract. Recent advances in digitization have led to the availability of multivariate time series data in various domains, enabling real-time monitoring of operations. Identifying abnormal data patterns and detecting potential failures in these scenarios are important yet rather challenging. In this work, we propose a novel anomaly detection method for time series data. The proposed framework jointly learns the observation model and the dynamic model, and model uncertainty is estimated from normal samples. Specifically, a long short-term memory (LSTM)-based encoder-decoder is adopted to represent the mapping between the observation space and the state space. Bidirectional transitions of states are simultaneously modeled by leveraging backward and forward temporal information. Regularization of the state space places constraints on the states of normal samples, and Mahalanobis distance is used to evaluate the abnormality level. Empirical studies on synthetic and real-world datasets demonstrate the superior performance of the proposed method in anomaly detection tasks.

Keywords: Time series · Neural networks · Anomaly detection · State-space models

1 Introduction

Anomaly detection of time series data has wide applications in areas such as finance, health care, and manufacturing. An anomaly is usually an important sign of critical events, such as faulty operation and health deterioration, and thus capturing such signs from a data perspective is of key interest. Time series data in real life often exhibit complex patterns, which pose challenges to the methodology of anomaly detection algorithms. Particularly, high dimensionality increases the difficulty of extracting meaningful features, which is essential to algorithm performance; Highly non-linear dynamics further complicate the identification of system states.

Detecting anomalies on a set of measurements over time has always been an active research area [3]. It typically consists of two phases: in the training phase, one models historical data to learn the temporal pattern of time series, and in the testing phase, one evaluates whether each observation follows a normal or abnormal pattern. Since real-world datasets usually lack labeled anomalies, and anomalies can exhibit unpredictable data behavior, the training set may only consist of data from normal operations in these scenarios. Anomaly detection methods can be categorized into clustering-based, distance-based, density-based, isolation-based, and hybrid methods. Traditional machine learning methods such as one-class support vector machines [15], isolation forest [14], etc. face challenges as data collected from real-world scenarios show ever-increasing dimensionality and complexity in dynamics. These methods can fail to achieve competitive performance due to the curse of dimensionality and failure to comprehend temporal relationships. In the meantime, deep learning-based approaches are drawing much attention due to their capability to model complex patterns [4,6].

2   Related Work

With enhanced expressiveness, deep learning-based methods use neural networks to model the dynamics behind data and can outperform traditional machine learning methods. For example, Deep Support Vector Data Description [20] is a one-class classification model which shares a similar ideology with one-class support vector machines. For distance-based models, which are more commonly used in practice, the level of abnormality can be determined by the difference between observation and estimation. For example, one can use Long Short-Term Memory (LSTM) neural network [8] to predict future observations based on past observations, and the prediction error indicates whether the temporal relationship of normal data is violated.

In recent years, the reconstruction-based state-space model has been a popular topic. One such attempt is to jointly learn the non-linear mapping between observations and hidden states and non-linear transition in state space; The learned model is then used for inference. For example, authors in [17] proposed for time series data, using an encoder to obtain the hidden state, a transition function to model state evolution, and a decoder to transform the hidden state to observation space. The method additionally learns an observer function that forwards the state, control, and observation to the next state. Although the framework is used for model predictive control, it can be extended for filtering purposes. Authors in [5] proposed Neural System Identification and Bayesian Filtering (NSIBF), which adopts a similar encoder-transition-decoder architecture for anomaly detection purposes. In the testing phase, the method leverages the Bayesian filtering scheme to recursively estimate hidden states over time, where the measurement function and state transition function are represented by the learned neural networks. Compared to fully connected neural networks used as encoder-decoder in the above methods, recurrent neural networks (RNNs), such as LSTM, can capture the temporal relationship within time series. Bidirectional RNN can further learn jointly for both directions of time series and provide a more comprehensive representation of the underlying dynamics. Finally, proper regularization of state space behavior and consistent definition of anomaly level are essential for anomaly detection performance.

3   Method

3.1   Problem Statement

Let $\{x^{(1)}, x^{(2)} \dots x^{(\tau)}\}$ denote a time series of signals variables, and $\{u^{(1)}, u^{(2)} \dots u^{(\tau)}\}$ be the corresponding control variables. Since anomalies often reflect at sequence level as a violation of temporal relationship, we consider a time window of xl at time t:

$$x_t = \{x^{(t-xl+1)} \dots x^{(t-1)}, x^{(t)}\}, \tag{1}$$

and similarly, the corresponding control sequence of window size ul is

$$u_t = \{u^{(t-ul+1)} \dots u^{(t-1)}, u^{(t)}\}, \tag{2}$$

The original sequence is thus transformed into windows of signal sequence $X = \{x_1, x_2, \dots x_T\}$ and control sequence $U = \{u_1, u_2, \dots u_T\}$, in both training and testing phase. Each sample x_t ($t = 1 \dots T$) is labeled by a binary variable $y_t \in \{0, 1\}$, indicating normal ($y_t = 0$) or abnormal ($y_t = 1$). We consider the scenario where no abnormal data is available in the training phase, and a model is trained on normal samples of the above form. In the testing phase, for a previously unseen sample $x_{t'}$, one labels it with $\hat{y}_{t'} = 0$ or 1 based on an anomaly score by applying the trained model.

For a dynamic system, a hidden state is typically assumed to be a compressed representation of an observation in a lower dimension. Thus modeling such a system includes mapping between observations and hidden states, and transition within state space over time, i.e.,

$$\begin{aligned} s_t &= \Phi(s_{t-1}, u_{t-1}) + w_t \\ x_t &= \Theta(s_t) + v_t, \end{aligned} \tag{3}$$

where $\Phi(.,.)$, $\Theta(.)$ are the state transition and measurement functions, and w_t, v_t are the corresponding noises with zero mean at time t. s_t is the hidden state at time t, which is a compact representation of x_t. When $\Phi(.,.)$, $\Theta(.)$ are linear mappings and w_t, v_t follow Gaussian distributions, Model (3) becomes the widely used Kalman filter [11].

3.2   Bidirectional Dynamic State-Space Model

The overall architecture of the proposed model is illustrated in Fig. 1, and the anomaly detection pipeline consists of three phases[1] In the training phase, the model learns the mapping between the observation space and the state space by an LSTM-based encoder-decoder, and jointly learns forward and backward

---

[1] Code available at https://github.com/DeepTSAD/BDM.

state transition functions by leveraging Bidirectional LSTM ($BiLSTM$) [7]. Concretely, system dynamics is modeled as follows:

$$
\begin{aligned}
s_t &= E(\boldsymbol{x}_t) \\
\boldsymbol{x}_t &= D(\boldsymbol{s}_t) \\
s_{t+1} &= F(\boldsymbol{s}_t, \boldsymbol{u}_t) = (f(\boldsymbol{s}_t) + \boldsymbol{u}_t+)/2 \\
s_{t-1} &= B(\boldsymbol{s}_t, \boldsymbol{u}_t) = (f(\boldsymbol{s}_t) + \boldsymbol{u}_t-)/2 \\
\boldsymbol{u}_t+, \boldsymbol{u}_t- &= BiLSTM(\boldsymbol{u}_t),
\end{aligned}
\tag{4}
$$

where $\boldsymbol{x}_t$, $\boldsymbol{u}_t$ and $\boldsymbol{s}_t$ are the observed signal sequence and control sequence, and the hidden state vector at time t. The loss function for model training is

$$
L = \sum_{t=2}^{T-1} \alpha_1 \|\boldsymbol{x}_{t-1} - \hat{\boldsymbol{x}}_{t-1}\|^2 + \alpha_2 \|\boldsymbol{x}_t - \hat{\boldsymbol{x}}_t\|^2 + \alpha_3 \|\boldsymbol{x}_{t+1} - \hat{\boldsymbol{x}}_{t+1}\|^2
\tag{5}
$$

$$
+ \beta_1 \|\boldsymbol{s}_{t-1} - \hat{\boldsymbol{s}}_{t-1}\|^2 + \beta_2 \|\boldsymbol{s}_t\|^2 + \beta_3 \|\boldsymbol{s}_{t+1} - \hat{\boldsymbol{s}}_{t+1}\|^2,
$$

$$
\begin{aligned}
\boldsymbol{s}_t &= E(\boldsymbol{x}_t); \hat{\boldsymbol{s}}_{t-1} = B(\boldsymbol{s}_t, \boldsymbol{u}_t); \hat{\boldsymbol{s}}_{t+1} = F(\boldsymbol{s}_t, \boldsymbol{u}_t) \\
\hat{\boldsymbol{x}}_{t-1} &= D(\hat{\boldsymbol{s}}_{t-1}); \hat{\boldsymbol{x}}_t = D(\boldsymbol{s}_t); \hat{\boldsymbol{x}}_{t+1} = D(\hat{\boldsymbol{s}}_{t+1}),
\end{aligned}
\tag{6}
$$

where $\alpha_1, \alpha_2, \alpha_3, \beta_1, \beta_2, \beta_3 > 0$ represent the weights of the terms. $E(\boldsymbol{x}_t)$ is the encoding function, realized as an LSTM encoder. $D(\boldsymbol{s}_t)$ is the decoding function, realized as an LSTM decoder [16]. $F(\boldsymbol{s}_t, \boldsymbol{u}_t)$ and $B(\boldsymbol{s}_t, \boldsymbol{u}_t)$ are the forward and backward transition functions, which are jointly learned as follows. Similar to [5], for the rest of the paper, the control sequence $\boldsymbol{u}_t$ represents the union of signal variables and control variables of a sliding window with length ul. $BiLSTM(\boldsymbol{u}_t)$ jointly learns $\boldsymbol{u}_t+$ and $\boldsymbol{u}_t-$, hidden vectors for forward and backward directions; $f(\boldsymbol{s}_t)$ is realized as a fully connected neural network; Finally $F(\boldsymbol{s}_t, \boldsymbol{u}_t)$ and $B(\boldsymbol{s}_t, \boldsymbol{u}_t)$ are realized as $(f(\boldsymbol{s}_t) + \boldsymbol{u}_t+)/2$ and $(f(\boldsymbol{s}_t) + \boldsymbol{u}_t-)/2$ respectively, where $f(.)$ and $BiLSTM(.)$ share the same activation function.

The first three terms in (5) are the reconstruction errors in the observation space. Note that $\hat{\boldsymbol{x}}_{t-1}$ and $\hat{\boldsymbol{x}}_{t+1}$ are the results of encoder-decoder as well as transition functions. This attempts to avoid errors of $F(.,.)$ and $B(.,.)$ being amplified by the decoder. Since dynamics of both directions are considered, the encoder-decoder pair learns a unified representation and tends to be more robust. The fourth and sixth terms in (5) are the prediction errors in state space, and the fifth term aims to shrink the state estimates. This regularization term forces states of normal samples to be close to the origin, which stabilizes the training process by avoiding the unexpected distribution of hidden states; It also benefits the anomaly detection process since abnormal samples with states far from the origin will lead to large reconstruction errors.

In the validation phase, for each signal pair $(\boldsymbol{x}_{t-1}, \boldsymbol{x}_t)$ and control $\boldsymbol{u}_{t-1}$ in validation data D_{val}, we calculate the reconstruction error as follows:

$$
\begin{aligned}
\boldsymbol{s}_{t-1} &= E(\boldsymbol{x}_{t-1}) \\
\boldsymbol{e}_t &= \boldsymbol{x}_t - D(F(\boldsymbol{s}_{t-1}, \boldsymbol{u}_{t-1})).
\end{aligned}
\tag{7}
$$

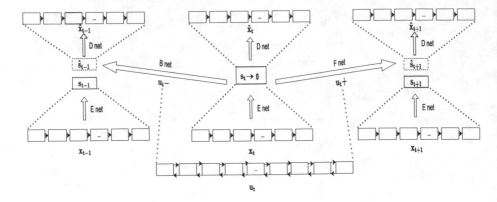

Fig. 1. The architecture of the proposed network

The covariance of such reconstruction errors is empirically calculated, denoted as Σ.

In the testing phase, at time t', with signal pair $(\boldsymbol{x}_{t'-1}, \boldsymbol{x}_{t'})$ and control $\boldsymbol{u}_{t'-1}$, the anomaly score is defined by Mahalanobis distance [19] as follows:

$$
\begin{aligned}
\boldsymbol{s}_{t'-1} &= E(\boldsymbol{x}_{t'-1}) \\
\boldsymbol{\mu}_{t'} &= D(F(\boldsymbol{s}_{t'-1}, \boldsymbol{u}_{t'-1})) \\
\text{anomaly score} &= \sqrt{(\boldsymbol{x}_{t'} - \boldsymbol{\mu}_{t'})^T \boldsymbol{\Sigma}^{-1}(\boldsymbol{x}_{t'} - \boldsymbol{\mu}_{t'})},
\end{aligned}
\tag{8}
$$

and a high anomaly score indicates a possible anomaly. Note that Mahalanobis distance takes into account the scales of variables compared to vanilla reconstruction error, i.e., the magnitude of error is assessed relative to its baseline covariance instead of by its own.

4   Results

In this section, we compare the proposed method with several state-of-the-art anomaly detection approaches in synthetic and real-world datasets. Throughout the paper, we use the same network structure for the proposed method, where $E(.)$ has one LSTM layer with dimension 4, so is the hidden state; $D(.)$ has one LSTM layer of dimension 4, followed by a fully connected layer of dimension 4; $BiLSTM(.)$ has two Bidirectional LSTM layers of dimension 4, and $f(.)$ has two fully connected layers of dimension 4. Throughout the paper, we apply min-max normalization to continuous variables and one-hot encoding to discrete variables. We use 3/4 of the training data for training the proposed model, and the rest 1/4 of the training data for validation. α_1, α_2, α_3, β_1, β_2, β_3 in (5) are fixed as 1, 1, 1, 0.1, 0.1, 0.1 for all the experiments, as we find it usually achieves desirable results.

4.1 Baseline Methods

We consider the following anomaly detection approaches as baselines:

- Isolation Forest (IF) [14] is an isolation-based method by learning a tree-based architecture
- AutoEncoder (AE) [13] consists of an encoder and a decoder of fully connected layers, and uses reconstruction error as the anomaly score
- LSTM AutoEncoder (LSTM AE) [16] consists of an encoder and a decoder implemented as LSTM networks, and uses reconstruction error as the anomaly score
- Deep Autoencoding Gaussian Mixture Model (DAGMM) [21] jointly learns a deep autoencoder and a Gaussian mixture model to calculate the likelihood of observations
- Neural System Identification and Bayesian Filtering (NSIBF) [5] jointly learns the encoder, decoder and state transition function, and uses Bayesian filtering to recursively update the state estimates
- UnSupervised Anomaly Detection (USAD) [2] adversarially trains an autoencoder model to amplify the reconstruction errors of abnormal samples

4.2 Synthetic Data Example

In this section, we compare our proposed method to the above state-of-the-art anomaly detection approaches using a simulated time series scenario. We consider the normal samples generated from below simple dynamic model in the training phase. For $t = 1, 2, ...T$:

$$
\begin{aligned}
u^{(t)} &= \lceil \frac{t - 1000 \times \lfloor \frac{t-1}{1000} \rfloor}{100} \rceil \\
s^{(t)} &= sin(t-1) + sin(u^{(t)}) + w^{(t)} \\
x^{(t)} &= s^{(t)} + v^{(t)},
\end{aligned}
\tag{9}
$$

where $T = 10000$, $w^{(t)} \sim N(0, 0.5^2)$, and $v^{(t)} \sim N(0, 1)$. In the testing phase, another $T' = 10000$ samples are generated using the same dynamic, except anomalies are injected with $w^{(t)} \sim N(0, 1)$ and $v^{(t)} \sim N(0, 2^2)$ for the last 100 samples of every 1000 samples. xl and ul are chosen to be 8 and 16 for constructing signal and control sequences, respectively.

Below are the Receiver Operating Characteristic (ROC) curves of candidate methods and corresponding Area Under Curve (AUC) values [9] to assess their ranking performance. As shown in Fig. 2, our method achieves the best AUC of 0.95, followed by IF, AE, USAD, and LSTM AE, with a higher true positive rate when controlling the false positive rate to be small. Notably, in this synthetic example with simple dynamics, the traditional machine learning method IF achieves the second-best ranking performance compared to other deep learning-based approaches, with an AUC of 0.935. NSIBF and DAGMM have similar ranking performance, less competitive compared to others.

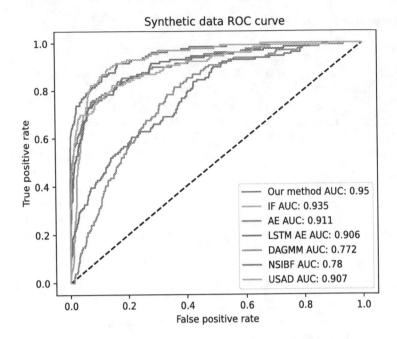

Fig. 2. ROC curves of the synthetic dataset (Color figure online)

4.3 Real-World Examples

In this section, we evaluate the proposed method using real-world datasets. Such datasets with proper labeling of underlying anomalies are scarce in practice, and we use two datasets generated from water treatment plants, $SWaT$ [18] and $WADI$ [1], where anomalies are labeled by domain experts based on simulated attack scenarios. The two datasets are originally generated from fully functional testbeds, which aim to mimic the dynamics of real industrial facilities. The datasets consist of sensor measurements (signal variables) as well as actuator states (control variables) as time series.

– $SWaT$ testbed is a scaled-down industrial water purification plant. Data collected from this testbed consists of every second for 11 days, and in the last four days, attack scenarios were simulated and are reflected in the dataset. Following [5], we downsample the data to have one sample every five seconds. Following [12], the following variables are removed from the dataset based on the similarity of probability distributions between training and testing data: AIT201, AIT202, AIT203, P201, AIT401, AIT402, AIT501, AIT502, AIT503, AIT504, FIT503, FIT504, PIT501, PIT502 and PIT503. After processing, there are 11 signal variables and 25 control variables.
– $WADI$ testbed is a scaled-down industrial water distribution system. The training data consists of every second of 14 days of normal working conditions. In the last two days of the operation, various attack scenarios were

simulated. Following [5], we downsample the data to have one sample every five seconds and remove actuators with a constant value in training data. Data from the last day is ignored due to the distribution shift caused by the change of operational mode. Following [12], the following variables are removed from the dataset based on the similarity of probability distributions between training and testing data: 1_AIT_001_PV, 1_AIT_003_PV, 1_AIT_004_PV, 1_AIT_005_PV, 2_LT_001_PV, 2_PIT_001_PV, 2A_AIT_001_PV, 2A_AIT_003_PV, 2A_AIT_004_PV, 2B_AIT_001_PV, 2B_AIT_002_PV, 2B_AIT_003_PV, 2B_AIT_004_PV, and 3_AIT_005_PV. After processing, there are 53 signal variables and 26 control variables.

In our experiment, xl is set to be 16 for the SWaT dataset and 8 for WADI; ul is set to be 32 for the SWaT dataset and 16 for WADI. After obtaining anomaly scores of each method, we enumerate all possible anomaly thresholds to obtain the best F1 score as the evaluation metric. We also report the corresponding precision and recall. The results are summarized in Table 1. We see that our method has the best F1 scores for both datasets, achieving 2.4% and 18.2% improvements compared to the second-best methods for SWaT and WADI, respectively. Traditional machine learning approach IF has inferior relative performance in both datasets, indicating its difficulty in capturing complex temporal patterns in high dimensional settings. AE and LSTM AE have similar performance and might be affected by the fact that their reconstruction errors ignore the scales of different variables. DAGMM has competitive performance in the SWaT dataset but the worst in WADI dataset, and this may be due to its difficulty in inferring likelihood in high dimensional settings. NSIBF has a similar F1 score as USAD in the WADI dataset and better in the SWaT dataset; NSIBF is the only method that does not support batch processing in the testing phase due to its filtering scheme, which can take more time when analyzing historical data.

Table 1. Comparison of anomaly detection performance on SWaT and WADI datasets

Method	SWaT			WADI		
	Precision	Recall	Best F1	Precision	Recall	Best F1
IF	1.0	0.567	0.723	0.180	0.455	0.258
AE	0.995	0.613	0.759	0.220	0.537	0.312
LSTM AE	0.997	0.598	0.748	0.492	0.220	0.304
DAGMM	0.957	0.643	0.769	0.904	0.131	0.228
NSIBF	0.892	0.712	0.792	0.234	0.496	0.318
USAD	0.995	0.629	0.771	0.243	0.462	0.319
Our method	0.991	0.685	0.811	0.276	0.593	0.377

4.4   Additional Investigations

We analyze the property of the proposed definition of anomaly measure. Both NSIBF and our method use Mahalanobis distance to measure the level of abnormality. In the testing phase, NSIBF assumes the hidden state follows Gaussian distribution, and recursively applies the unscented Kalman filter [10] to update state distribution, based on measurement function and transition function realized as neural networks. Since neural networks are highly non-linear, a small change in input could significantly alter the output. Thus when they are applied to samples from state distribution (e.g., sigma points as in [5]), those far from the actual state may cause unexpected behavior of Mahalanobis distance. Below we revisit the synthetic data example in Sect. 4.2, and Fig. 3 compares the anomaly scores generated by NSIBF and the proposed method. We can see that both methods in general give higher anomaly scores to those anomaly periods, but NSIBF has fluctuating behavior in normal periods, while our method has more stable anomaly scores. Thus it can better distinguish between normal and abnormal samples.

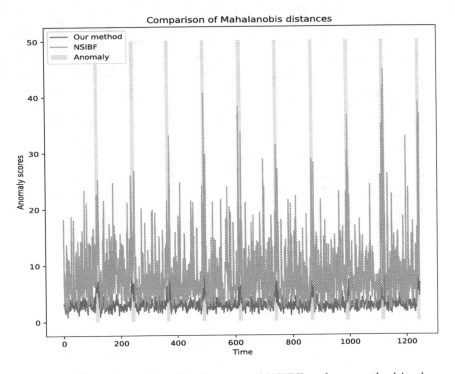

Fig. 3. Comparison of Mahalanobis distances of NSIBF and our method in the synthetic example from Sect. 4.2. Red shadows mark the anomaly periods (Color figure online)

Similar to [5], the proposed model can be combined with a Bayesian filtering scheme for state identification. Moreover, since the forward and backward transition functions are jointly learned, one can make inferences based on the dynamics of both directions.

We use the synthetic data example from Sect. 4.2, except in both training and testing phases, the noise levels are set to be small, with $w^{(t)} \sim N(0, 0.1^2)$ and $v^{(t)} \sim N(0, 0.1^2)$. The ground truth is defined as the observations from the noiseless process with $w^{(t)} = v^{(t)} = 0$, and the goal is reconstruction based on noisy data to recover the ground truth. We combine the proposed model with the unscented Kalman filter scheme presented by [5], except we have the transition functions and corresponding error covariance estimates for both directions. We conduct the filtering (forward pass) recursively to reconstruct the signal sequence x_t by $\hat{x}_t$, from the state estimate s_t^f. i.e.,

$$s_{t-1}^f \sim N(\hat{s}_{t-1}^f, \hat{P}_{t-1}^f) \xrightarrow[D(.)]{F(.,.)} s_t^f \sim N(\hat{s}_t^f, \hat{P}_t^f)$$
$$\hat{x}_t = D(\hat{s}_t^f), \tag{10}$$

where $\hat{s}_t^f$ and $\hat{P}_t^f$ are the mean and covariance estimates of the updated state distribution from forward pass at time t. In comparison, we reconstruct the signal sequence x_t by $\hat{x}_t'$, from the state estimate of backward pass s_t^b, by applying the backward transition function on the state estimate from the forward pass. i.e.,

$$s_{t+1}^f \sim N(\hat{s}_{t+1}^f, \hat{P}_{t+1}^f) \xrightarrow[D(.)]{B(.,.)} s_t^b \sim N(\hat{s}_t^b, \hat{P}_t^b)$$
$$\hat{x}_t' = D(\hat{s}_t^b), \tag{11}$$

where $\hat{s}_t^b$ and $\hat{P}_t^b$ are the mean and covariance estimates of the updated state distribution from the backward pass at time t. Figure 4 compares reconstructions of the forward pass and the backward pass. With additional information from future observation, the backward pass in general has a smaller reconstruction error. This is particularly true during the transition phase of the underlying dynamics, as illustrated here around time $t = 180$ (mean squared reconstruction errors across all samples for the forward pass and the backward pass are 0.0020 and 0.00056, respectively).

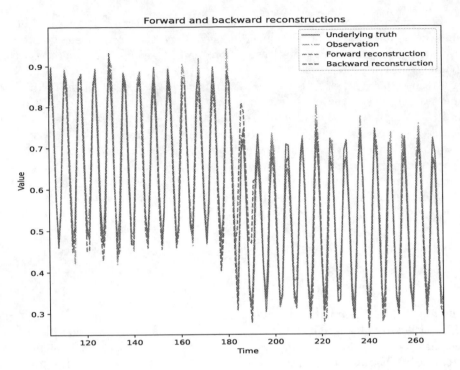

Fig. 4. Comparison of forward and backward reconstructions in the low-noise simulation study (selected period). Ground truth is presented by blue solid lines; Observations are presented by orange dashed lines; Forward and backward reconstructions are presented by green and red dashed lines, respectively (Color figure online)

5   Conclusion

In this paper, we introduce a novel deep learning-based state-space model for anomaly detection of time series data. We use an LSTM encoder-decoder to learn the hidden representation of time series in state space and its mapping to observation space. The model jointly learns the transition functions of both directions by leveraging Bidirectional LSTM on time sequence. Regularization is applied to the state space to make the learning process more stable and informative. Anomaly score is defined to adaptively take scales of variables into account. Both synthetic and real-world data experiments show improvements in anomaly detection metrics compared to several state-of-the-art approaches. The model also enjoys the benefit of easy implementation and the potential of combining with a Bayesian filtering scheme. One interesting topic to investigate further is, when jointly modeling observation space and state space, how to systematically balance the two to achieve optimal overall performance.

References

1. Ahmed, C.M., Palleti, V.R., Mathur, A.P.: WADI: a water distribution testbed for research in the design of secure cyber physical systems. In: Proceedings of the 3rd International Workshop on Cyber-Physical Systems for Smart Water Networks, pp. 25–28. Association for Computing Machinery (2017). https://doi.org/10.1145/3055366.3055375
2. Audibert, J., Michiardi, P., Guyard, F., et al.: USAD: unsupervised anomaly detection on multivariate time series. In: Proceedings of the 26th ACM SIGKDD International Conference on Knowledge Discovery and Data Mining, pp. 3395–3404. Association for Computing Machinery (2020). https://doi.org/10.1145/3394486.3403392
3. Chandola, V., Banerjee, A., Kumar, V.: Anomaly detection: a survey. ACM Comput. Surv. **41**(3), 15:1–15:58 (2009)
4. Darban, Z.Z., Webb, G.I., Pan, S., et al.: Deep learning for time series anomaly detection: a survey. arXiv e-prints (2022). https://doi.org/10.48550/arxiv.2211.05244
5. Feng, C., Tian, P.: Time series anomaly detection for cyber-physical systems via neural system identification and Bayesian filtering. In: Proceedings of the 27th ACM SIGKDD Conference on Knowledge Discovery and Data Mining, pp. 2858–2867. Association for Computing Machinery (2021). https://doi.org/10.1145/3447548.3467137
6. Garg, A., Zhang, W., Samaran, J., et al.: An evaluation of anomaly detection and diagnosis in multivariate time series. IEEE Trans. Neural Netw. Learn. Syst. **33**, 2508–2517 (2021)
7. Graves, A., Schmidhuber, J.: Framewise phoneme classification with bidirectional LSTM and other neural network architectures. Neural Netw. **18**(5), 602–610 (2005). https://doi.org/10.1109/IJCNN.2005.1556215
8. Hochreiter, S., Schmidhuber, J.: Long short-term memory. Neural Comput. **9**(8), 1735–1780 (1997)
9. Huang, J., Ling, C.X.: Using AUC and accuracy in evaluating learning algorithms. IEEE Trans. Knowl. Data Eng. **17**(3), 299–310 (2005). https://doi.org/10.1109/TKDE.2005.50
10. Julier, S.J., Uhlmann, J.K.: Unscented filtering and nonlinear estimation. Proc. IEEE **92**(3), 401–422 (2004). https://doi.org/10.1109/JPROC.2003.823141
11. Kalman, R.E.: A new approach to linear filtering and prediction problems. J. Basic Eng. **82**(1), 35–45 (1960)
12. Kravchik, M., Shabtai, A.: Efficient cyber attack detection in industrial control systems using lightweight neural networks and PCA. IEEE Trans. Depend. Secure Comput. **19**(04), 2179–2197 (2022). https://doi.org/10.1109/TDSC.2021.3050101
13. LeCun, Y., Bengio, Y., Hinton, G.E.: Deep learning. Nature **521**(7553), 436–444 (2015). https://doi.org/10.1038/nature14539
14. Liu, F.T., Ting, K.M., Zhou, Z.H.: Isolation forest. In: 2008 Eighth IEEE International Conference on Data Mining, pp. 413–422. IEEE (2008)
15. Ma, J., Perkins, S.: Time-series novelty detection using one-class support vector machines. In: Proceedings of the International Joint Conference on Neural Networks, vol. 3, pp. 1741–1745 (2003). https://doi.org/10.1109/IJCNN.2003.1223670
16. Malhotra, P., Ramakrishnan, A., Anand, G., et al.: LSTM-based encoder-decoder for multi-sensor anomaly detection. arXiv e-prints (2016). https://doi.org/10.48550/arxiv.1607.00148

17. Masti, D., Bemporad, A.: Learning nonlinear state-space models using autoencoders. Automatica **129**, 109666 (2021). https://doi.org/10.1016/j.automatica.2021.109666
18. Mathur, A.P., Tippenhauer, N.O.: SWaT: a water treatment testbed for research and training on ICS security. In: 2016 International Workshop on Cyber-Physical Systems for Smart Water Networks, pp. 31–36 (2016). https://doi.org/10.1109/CySWater.2016.7469060
19. McLachlan, G.J.: Mahalanobis distance. Resonance **4**, 20–26 (1999)
20. Ruff, L., Vandermeulen, R., Goernitz, N., et al.: Deep one-class classification. In: Proceedings of the 35th International Conference on Machine Learning. Proceedings of Machine Learning Research, vol. 80, pp. 4393–4402 (2018)
21. Zong, B., Song, Q., Min, M.R., et al.: Deep autoencoding Gaussian mixture model for unsupervised anomaly detection. In: International Conference on Learning Representations (2018)

ReDualSVG: Refined Scalable Vector Graphics Generation

Shannan Yan[✉]

School of Computer Science, Wuhan University, Wuhan, China
`shannany0606@whu.edu.cn`

Abstract. Vector graphics generation is a critical task in computer vision. However, existing approaches suffer from several limitations, such as lack of extensibility, inadequate consideration of both image and sequence modalities, and the issue of location change. To address these challenges, we present ReDualSVG, a refined scalable vector graphics generation method based on dual-modality information. ReDualSVG overcomes these problems through a hierarchical, transformer-based design that effectively distinguishes high-level shapes from the low-level instructions encoding the shape itself. Our method capitalizes on dual-modality data by fully utilizing the information present in both image and sequence modalities, offering richer insights from global and local perspectives. Additionally, we tackle the issue of location change by employing a differentiable rasterizer for further refinement. Finally, we conducted qualitative and quantitative experiments on a publicly available dataset, which demonstrated that ReDualSVG achieves high-quality synthesis results in the applications of image reconstruction and interpolation, outperforming other alternatives.

Keywords: Hierarchical transformer · Dual Modality · Differentiable Rasterizer · Scalable Vector Graphics

1 Introduction

Generating vector graphics is a crucial and challenging task within the realm of computer vision. Although recent advancements have been made in raster image generation, the creation of high-quality vector graphics still poses an unsolved problem. Scalable Vector Graphics (SVG) has become the predominant standard for online animations and digital graphics due to their scale-invariant properties, which grant them superiority over raster images.

Raster images are typically represented as a rectangular grid of pixels, each assigned a shade or color value. Convolutional neural networks (CNNs) have contributed significantly to the success of deep learning applied to these images by learning powerful representations that capitalize on inherent translational invariance. Nonetheless, three key issues hinder the production of aesthetically pleasing vector graphics.

L. Iliadis et al. (Eds.): ICANN 2023, LNCS 14256, pp. 87–98, 2023.
https://doi.org/10.1007/978-3-031-44213-1_8

The first issue arises from the fact that many studies fail to extend their methods from font generation to image generation. DeepVecFont [18] utilizes techniques from image synthesis, sequence modeling, and differentiable rasterization to generate high-quality vector fonts while managing both raster and boundary representation modalities. Given the similarities between vector font generation and image generation, these techniques serve as an inspiration for our work.

The second issue is that most previous endeavors only consider one type of feature during encoding, such as image representation [10] or sequence representation [1]. When presented with a vector graphic, the image modality provides a general impression of its shape, while the sequence modality or drawing instructions offer specific structural details and a scale-invariant representation. In this study, we investigate optimal methods to fully harness the information available in both image and sequence modalities.

The third issue involves disregarding location change. While Mixture Distribution Models (MDN) seem capable of addressing uncertainty during model training by combining multiple distributions, they often result in positional alterations to image outlines. Moreover, RNNs face difficulties in connecting various drawing stages due to the vanishing gradient problem. Consequently, the generated vector images are unable to align precisely with the ground truth, unlike image synthesis tasks. To address this, we employ an accurate rasterizer [9] based on Monte Carlo sampling for further refinement to produce our final synthesized vector graphics.

In this paper, we address the challenge of developing generative models for vector graphics. To tackle this problem, we propose a hierarchical, transformer-based architecture that effectively distinguishes high-level shapes from low-level instructions encoding the shape itself. Specifically, we first encode each shape separately, after which we obtain the latent vector for image reconstruction and interpolation. Our decoder subsequently predicts a set of shape representations and their associated properties in a single forward pass. The resulting SVG is created by concatenating a series of draw command sequences generated from these vectors. Lastly, we employ a differentiable rasterizer to enhance the quality of the output SVG, referring to the corresponding raster image.

In summary, our contributions include:

- Introducing ReDualSVG, a generative model for the reconstruction and interpolation of vector graphics that exploits dual-modality data and builds upon hierarchical transformers and autoencoders.
- Developing a dual-modality learning approach that leverages both image-aspect and sequence-aspect features of images.
- Proposing a practical technique for improving SVG quality by employing a differentiable rasterizer.

2   Related Work

2.1   Glyph Image Generation

Deep convolutional neural networks have gained significant attention in recent years within the domain of visual image synthesis. Various studies have advocated the use of Variational Auto-encoders (VAEs) [7] and Generative Adversarial Networks (GANs) [3] to convey styles of glyph shapes [4] or glyph texture effects [20]. STEFANN [15] accomplished scene text transformation in two steps, utilizing structure and color transfer. Wang et al.'s [17] research on controlled font generation through descriptive features also allows novice users to intuitively create their own fonts. However, image-based approaches are more susceptible to blurring and ghosting irregularities, as the structural information of glyphs is often lost during rasterization and cannot be scaled to arbitrary resolutions.

2.2   Vector Font Generation

The design of vector fonts presents a common challenge in computer graphics. One of the earliest deep learning-based endeavors, SVG-VAE [10], utilized sequential generative modeling to generate latent representations for the SVG format and subsequently applied the model to fonts. Given a latent code encoded from the rasterized input, Im2Vec [12] predicted a set of ordered closed vector paths using RNN, and DiffVG [9] compared the rasterized output it produced to the input for supervision during training. In the pursuit of high-quality vector fonts, DeepVecFont [18] addressed both boundary and raster representation modalities, treating vector font production as a sequence generation issue.

2.3   Differentiable Rasterization

In order to mimic the rasterization process and render it differentiable, neural approximations of rasterization employ neural networks [5]. More recently, Li et al. [9] developed a differentiable rasterizer, made possible by two distinct anti-aliasing approaches. The first method involves Monte Carlo sampling, while the second technique employs an estimated analytical prefilter based on the signed distance to the nearest curve. They also demonstrated how their approach could further refine SVGs by minimizing the L1 distance between an SVG's rasterized image and the corresponding ground-truth image.

3   Methodology

3.1   Data Structure

To develop deep neural networks capable of encoding and predicting vector graphics, we first necessitate a clearly defined and straightforward representation of the input. We achieve this by adopting the SVG format with the following simplifications. We employ the following three commands:

- **Move**(x_1, y_1). This command moves the cursor to the endpoint (x_1, y_1) without drawing anything.
- **Line**(x_1, y_1). This command draws a line to the point (x_1, y_1).
- **CubicBeziers**$(q_{x1}, q_{y1}, q_{x2}, q_{y2}, x_1, y_1)$. This command generates a cubic Bezier curve with control points $(q_{x1}, q_{y1}), (q_{x2}, q_{y2})$, and end-point (x_1, y_1).

In practice, the expressivity is not significantly limited, as other basic shapes can be converted into a series of Bezier curves and lines. We regard a vector graphics image $V = \{P_1, \cdots, P_{N_P}\}$ as a set of N_P paths P_i. Assuming $S_i = (C_i^1, \cdots, C_i^{N_C})$ encompasses a sequence of N_C commands C_i^j and $v_i \in \{0, 1\}$ indicates the path's visibility. Each path is then specified as S_i. The command $C_i^j = (c_i^j, X_i^j)$ itself is characterized by its type $c_i^j \in \{Move, Line, CubicBeziers\}$ and parameters, as previously discussed. To facilitate the parallel processing, we employ a fixed-length argument list $X_i^j = (q_{x_1,i}^j, q_{y_1,i}^j, q_{x_2,i}^j, q_{y_2,i}^j, x_{1,i}^j, y_{1,i}^j) \in \mathbb{R}^6$, where any unused argument is assigned a value of -1.

3.2   Model Overview

In this section, we use the Hierarchical Generative Network architecture of DeepSVG [1] as the foundation for our model ReDualSVG, aimed at advanced vector graphics generation and interpolation. Our network is a Variational Auto-Encoder (VAE) [7], consisting of the image encoder, the image decoder, the sequence encoder, and the sequence decoder.

Inspired by the success of transformer-based architectures in a wide range of tasks [2,8,14], we integrate them as the fundamental components of our network. Both the encoders and decoders are based on transformer architectures. These networks are designed by examining the hierarchical representation of an SVG image, which consists of a collection of paths, with each path representing a series of instructions. Detailed information about the architectures of ReDualSVG can be found in Fig. 1.

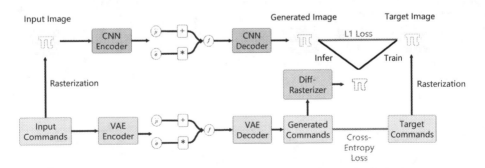

Fig. 1. A comprehensive overview of our proposed model ReDualSVG. Given a vector image, our model receives its drawing commands as input and generates the drawing commands of the same image. Diff-Rasterizer refers to the Differentiable Rasterizer. In the training and inference stages, the outputs of the Differentiable Rasterizer are refined by the target image and the generated image respectively via L1 distance.

3.3   Path Prediction

In our approach, we predict the N_C instructions $\left(\hat{c}_i^j, \hat{X}_i^j\right)$ for each path using a purely feed-forward method, in contrast to the autoregressive technique employed in prior works [10], which constructs a model that forecasts subsequent commands based on previous ones. Consequently, our generative model is factorized as follows:

$$p\left(\hat{V}|z,\theta\right) = \prod_{i=1}^{N_P} p\left(\hat{v}_i|z,\theta\right) \prod_{j=1}^{N_C} p\left(\hat{c}_i^j|z,\theta\right) p\left(\hat{X}_i^j|z,\theta\right),\tag{1}$$

where z represents the latent vector and $p\left(\hat{X}_i^j|z,\theta\right)$ further factorizes into individual arguments.

3.4   Image Encoder

Generally, a single image may not adequately represent the style of the associated icon. Consequently, we use N reference images to stabilize the image feature statistics extracted by both the image encoder and the sequence encoder. The image encoder is designed using a Convolutional Neural Network (CNN). Owing to the parallel computation of each feature channel in CNNs, we concatenate all reference images along the channel dimension and obtain the latent code f_{img}:

$$f_{img} = CNN([X_{s_1}; X_{s_2}; \cdots ; X_{s_{N_r}}]).\tag{2}$$

3.5   Image Decoder

Using the learned latent code f_{img}, we proceed to synthesize the target raster images. The image decoder is a Deconvolutional Neural Network (DCNN). We input f_{img} into the image decoder:

$$\hat{X}_t = DCNN(f_{img}).\tag{3}$$

In contrast to SVG-VAE [10], we employ L1 loss instead of Cross-Entropy loss for image reconstruction, as the L1 loss results in much sharper images. Additionally, we adopt the perceptual loss [6] as an extra term for calculating the image reconstruction loss L_{rec}:

$$L_{rec} = ||\hat{X}_t - X_t||_1 + L_{per}(\hat{X}_t, X_t).\tag{4}$$

The perceptual loss is defined by the feature distance in different layers of the VGG Network [16], which helps preserve more details in the generated images.

3.6   Sequence Encoder

To maintain the permutation invariance property of the path set $\{P_i\}_1^{N_P}$, we individually encode each path P_i using the sequence path encoder E_1. Specifically, E_1 takes the embeddings $(e_i'^j)_{j=1}^{N_C}$ as input and returns vectors $(e_i'^j)_{j=1}^{N_C}$ with the same dimension. We apply average pooling to the output vectors along the sequential dimension to obtain the single path encoding u_i. The N_P path encodings $\{u_i\}_1^{N_P}$ are then input into the sequence encoder E_2, which outputs the parameters of a Gaussian distribution $\hat{\mu}$ and $\hat{\sigma}$ after pooling along the set-dimension. The index embedding in vector e_i^j enables E_1 to reason about the sequential nature of its input, while E_2 preserves the permutation invariance of the input paths. The latent vector is eventually obtained via the reparametrization trick [7] as $\hat{z} = \hat{\mu} + \hat{\sigma} \cdot \epsilon$, where $\epsilon \sim \mathcal{N}(0, I)$.

3.7   Sequence Decoder

The decoder's architecture reflects the encoder's two-stage design. At each transformer block, the sequence decoder D_2 continuously takes the latent vector z as input and generates a representation for every shape in the image. In contrast to its corresponding encoder stage, permutation invariance is not desired for D_2 as its objective is to produce the shapes present in the image. This is achieved by using a learned index embedding as input for the decoder, resulting in distinct embeddings for each path and breaking symmetry during the generation process. Following the decoder, a Multilayer Perceptron (MLP) predicts the path encoding $\hat{u}_i$ and visibility $\hat{v}_i$ for each index $1 \leq i \leq N_p$.

We incorporate the Cross-Entropy loss as an additional term for calculating the image visibility loss L_{vis}:

$$L_{vis} = w_{vis} C(v_i, \hat{v}_i). \tag{5}$$

More importantly, the losses for commands and arguments are determined by:

$$L_{args} = C(x_{1,\hat{i}}^j, \hat{x}_{1,i}^j) + C(y_{1,\hat{i}}^j, \hat{y}_{1,i}^j) + \sum_{k \in \{1,2\}} \left[C(q_{x_k,\hat{i}}^j, \hat{q}_{x_k,i}^j) + C(q_{y_k,\hat{i}}^j, \hat{q}_{y_k,i}^j) \right], \tag{6}$$

$$L_{cmd} = v \cdot \sum_{j=1}^{N_C} \left(w_{cmd} C\left(c_i^j, \hat{c}_i^j\right) + w_{args} L_{args} \right). \tag{7}$$

Here, C denotes the Cross-Entropy loss. Each term's impact is controlled by its weight w. The losses for commands and arguments are masked when the ground-truth path is not visible.

In a manner similar to the encoder, the vectors $\{\hat{u}_i\}_1^{N_p}$ are decoded by the sequence decoder D_1 into the final output path representations $\left\{ \left(\hat{C}_i^1, \cdots, \hat{C}_i^{N_C} \right) \right\}_1^{N_p}$. Analogous to D_2, we employ learned constant embeddings as input and an MLP to predict the command and argument logits. This approach ensures that the decoder generates accurate and distinct path representations, contributing to the overall efficacy of the model in synthesizing target vector images.

3.8   Loss Function

The comprehensive loss function for our ReDualSVG model, encompassing both predicted and ground-truth paths is formulated as follows:

$$L_{total} = L_{rec} + L_{vis} + L_{args} + L_{cmd}. \tag{8}$$

In this expression, the primary term represents image reconstruction, while the subsequent terms pertain to sequence reconstruction. It is worth mentioning that the weight assigned to each term, derived from experimental selection, has been omitted from the equation for the sake of brevity.

3.9   Differentiable Rasterizer

The integration of MDN inherently introduces spatial discrepancies, leading to seemingly disorganized vector images. This phenomenon is primarily attributed to the absence of a comprehensive understanding of glyph structures during the optimization of Cross-Entropy and MDN loss functions. To address this challenge, we adopt the approach presented by Li et al. [9], which utilizes a rasterizer to establish a direct correlation between the image generated from the anticipated drawing commands and the corresponding ground truth throughout the training process.

4   Experiments

4.1   Dataset

Prevailing vector graphics datasets primarily concentrate on font generation [10], thereby constraining their utility in tackling the challenges associated with generating complex vector graphics, as investigated in this study. As a result, we employed the SVG-Icons8 dataset [1], consisting of SVG icons obtained from https://icons8.com/icons. In our experiments, to simplify the icon synthesis problem, we assign the arguments of the filling attribute in all SVGs to 0.

4.2   Implementation Details

We make use of the AdamW [11] optimization algorithm, starting with a learning rate of 10^{-3}. A dropout rate of 0.1 is implemented across all transformer layers, and gradient clipping is set at 1.0. Our models undergo training for a total of 100 epochs with a comprehensive batch size of 64, running on a single 4090 GPU, and requiring approximately one day to complete.

4.3   Image Rasterization

Initially, the SVG digital instructions from the SVG-Icons8 dataset are employed to generate vector-based images. We developed code to convert these images into rasterized representations. Consequently, the images are transformed into Portable Network Graphics (PNG) format. A detailed visualization of the results can be observed in Fig. 2.

Fig. 2. Examples from the results of the rasterization process

4.4 Image Reconstruction

The accuracy of a model in reconstructing its input is a crucial metric for assessing its representational capabilities. In this study, we train the model to reconstruct input vector images at a resolution of 128×128 pixels. The same configuration is applied to DeepSVG [1], VAE [7], Im2Vec [12] and multi-implicits [13] for a fair comparison. We evaluate the performance using structural similarity (SSIM) [19] and L1 distance between the reconstructed and original images. Our model achieves the highest accuracy, as shown in Table 1, and its commendable performance is further demonstrated in Fig. 3.

Table 1. Quantitative comparison of DeepSVG, VAE, Im2Vec, multi-implicits and our model in the image reconstruction experiments.

Method	SSIM↑	L1↓
DeepSVG [1]	0.8564	0.0229
VAE [7]	0.7808	0.0325
Im2Vec [12]	0.8823	0.0169
Multi-implicits [13]	0.8754	0.0174
ReDualSVG(Ours)	**0.9458**	**0.0128**

As is shown in Fig. 3, our representation achieves remarkable reconstruction, characterized by distinct boundaries, intricate details, and sharp corners, at times indistinguishable from the original images. The aforementioned evidence supports the superiority of our model over the previous models.

4.5 Random Sampling and Interpolation

Leveraging the normalization training applied to the latent spaces, our model demonstrates the ability to interpolate vector images between diverse instances by manipulating their associated latent codes. Given two images, A and B, and assuming that $\lambda \in [0, 1]$, the interpolated feature $f(C)$ can be computed as:

$$f(C) = (1 - \lambda) \cdot f(A) + \lambda \cdot f(B). \tag{9}$$

Fig. 3. A comparison of original images (odd rows) and reconstructed images (even rows).

Subsequently, $f(C)$ is fed into the sequence decoder within our model, resulting in the generation of interpolated vector images. Figure 4 shows the model's proficiency in achieving smooth interpolation across similar vector icons.

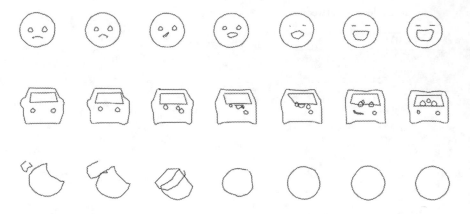

Fig. 4. Interpolation between similar vector icons in the latent space of ReDualSVG. From left to right, $\lambda = 0, 0.2, 0.4, 0.5, 0.6, 0.8, 1$ in each column respectively.

4.6   Ablation Study

To verify the effectiveness of the Differentiable Rasterizer (DR), we assess performance variations in the vector image generation task under different configurations. The qualitative results are shown in Fig. 5, while the quantitative results are illustrated in Table 2.

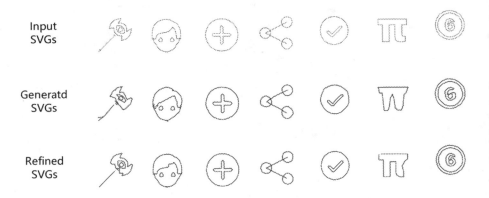

Fig. 5. Performance of our model under different configurations (without or with the refinement process). The leftmost input SVG has an ID of 1, the next SVG to the right has an ID of 2, and this pattern continues for all subsequent images in the same row.

Drawing from both qualitative and quantitative results, it is evident that refined SVGs demonstrate a greater degree of similarity to input SVGs in comparison to their generated counterparts. The refinement process contributes to curves presenting a more natural appearance, straight lines showcasing improved linearity, and inaccurately generated parts being generally corrected. As the gen-

Table 2. L1 losses between input SVGs and corresponding generated SVGs.

Input SVG's ID	1	2	3	4	5	6	7	average
without DR (Generated SVGs)	0.0210	0.0215	0.0178	0.0185	0.0153	0.0198	0.0315	0.0208
with DR (Refined SVGs)	0.0117	0.0123	0.0117	0.0099	0.0089	0.0115	0.0159	0.0117

erated SVGs can be regarded as the output of our benchmark model, DeepSVG, these aforementioned enhancements underscore the superiority of our model over DeepSVG.

5 Conclusion

In this study, we present ReDualSVG, an advanced model capable of generating high-quality vector graphics by effectively utilizing pertinent and synergistic information derived from two distinct image modalities: raster images and vector outlines. This approach facilitates the automatic generation of aesthetically appealing vector images, yielding exceptional outcomes that surpass the generation results of previous models including DeepSVG, VAE, Im2Vec, and multi-implicits.

Future research directions include broadening our approach to tackle more complex image synthesis and interpolation problems and producing even higher-quality vector graphics. Furthermore, although ReDualSVG was specifically developed for the natural representation of Scalable Vector Graphics, our architecture demonstrates versatility for tasks involving data represented as a set of sequences. Consequently, our approach can be adapted to a wide range of tasks, including but not limited to multi-instrument audio generation and multi-human motion trajectory generation.

References

1. Carlier, A., Danelljan, M., Alahi, A., Timofte, R.: DeepSVG: a hierarchical generative network for vector graphics animation. Adv. Neural. Inf. Process. Syst. **33**, 16351–16361 (2020)
2. Child, R., Gray, S., Radford, A., Sutskever, I.: Generating long sequences with sparse transformers. arXiv preprint arXiv:1904.10509 (2019)
3. Creswell, A., White, T., Dumoulin, V., Arulkumaran, K., Sengupta, B., Bharath, A.A.: Generative adversarial networks: an overview. IEEE Signal Process. Mag. **35**(1), 53–65 (2018)
4. Hayashi, H., Abe, K., Uchida, S.: GlyphGAN: style-consistent font generation based on generative adversarial networks. Knowl.-Based Syst. **186**, 104927 (2019)
5. Huang, Z., Heng, W., Zhou, S.: Learning to paint with model-based deep reinforcement learning. In: Proceedings of the IEEE/CVF International Conference on Computer Vision, pp. 8709–8718 (2019)

6. Johnson, J., Alahi, A., Fei-Fei, L.: Perceptual losses for real-time style transfer and super-resolution. In: Leibe, B., Matas, J., Sebe, N., Welling, M. (eds.) ECCV 2016. LNCS, vol. 9906, pp. 694–711. Springer, Cham (2016). https://doi.org/10.1007/978-3-319-46475-6_43

7. Kingma, D.P., Welling, M.: Auto-encoding variational Bayes. arXiv preprint arXiv:1312.6114 (2013)

8. Li, G., Zhu, L., Liu, P., Yang, Y.: Entangled transformer for image captioning. In: Proceedings of the IEEE/CVF International Conference on Computer Vision, pp. 8928–8937 (2019)

9. Li, T.M., Lukáč, M., Gharbi, M., Ragan-Kelley, J.: Differentiable vector graphics rasterization for editing and learning. ACM Trans. Graph. (TOG) **39**(6), 1–15 (2020)

10. Lopes, R.G., Ha, D., Eck, D., Shlens, J.: A learned representation for scalable vector graphics. In: Proceedings of the IEEE/CVF International Conference on Computer Vision, pp. 7930–7939 (2019)

11. Loshchilov, I., Hutter, F.: Decoupled weight decay regularization. arXiv preprint arXiv:1711.05101 (2017)

12. Reddy, P., Gharbi, M., Lukac, M., Mitra, N.J.: Im2Vec: synthesizing vector graphics without vector supervision. In: Proceedings of the IEEE/CVF Conference on Computer Vision and Pattern Recognition, pp. 7342–7351 (2021)

13. Reddy, P., Zhang, Z., Wang, Z., Fisher, M., Jin, H., Mitra, N.: A multi-implicit neural representation for fonts. Adv. Neural. Inf. Process. Syst. **34**, 12637–12647 (2021)

14. Ribeiro, L.S.F., Bui, T., Collomosse, J., Ponti, M.: Sketchformer: transformer-based representation for sketched structure. In: Proceedings of the IEEE/CVF Conference on Computer Vision and Pattern Recognition, pp. 14153–14162 (2020)

15. Roy, P., Bhattacharya, S., Ghosh, S., Pal, U.: STEFANN: scene text editor using font adaptive neural network. In: Proceedings of the IEEE/CVF Conference on Computer Vision and Pattern Recognition, pp. 13228–13237 (2020)

16. Simonyan, K., Zisserman, A.: Very deep convolutional networks for large-scale image recognition. arXiv preprint arXiv:1409.1556 (2014)

17. Wang, Y., Gao, Y., Lian, Z.: Attribute2Font: creating fonts you want from attributes. ACM Trans. Graph. (TOG) **39**(4), 1–69 (2020)

18. Wang, Y., Lian, Z.: DeepVecFont: synthesizing high-quality vector fonts via dual-modality learning. ACM Trans. Graph. (TOG) **40**(6), 1–15 (2021)

19. Wang, Z., Bovik, A.C., Sheikh, H.R., Simoncelli, E.P.: Image quality assessment: from error visibility to structural similarity. IEEE Trans. Image Process. **13**(4), 600–612 (2004)

20. Yang, S., Liu, J., Wang, W., Guo, Z.: TET-GAN: text effects transfer via stylization and destylization. In: Proceedings of the AAAI Conference on Artificial Intelligence, vol. 33, pp. 1238–1245 (2019)

Rethinking Feature Context in Learning Image-Guided Depth Completion

Yikang Ding[✉], Pengzhi Li, Dihe Huang, and Zhiheng Li

Tsinghua University, Beijing, China
{dyk20,lpz21,hdh20}@mails.tsinghua.edu.cn, zhhli@mail.tsinghua.edu.cn

Abstract. Depth completion (DC) is a classical computer vision task, which aims to estimate the 3D structure of the observed scene by utilizing the sparse depth from the Lidar and the RGB image from the camera. Treating DC as a regression task, most recent papers ignore the importance of feature representation. In this paper, we discuss the feature context in image-guided depth completion and propose a novel dual-arch feature extractor that includes a CNN branch and transformer branch. By combining the efficient CNN layers and effective transformer blocks, our proposed method achieves significant improvement compared with the baseline network. Experimental results and ablation study show the proposed approach can help existing DC methods perform better with limited extra computation.

Keywords: Depth completion · Feature context · Transformer

1 Introduction

Estimating the 3D structure of the real world is critical to creating high-quality 3D multimedia applications in metaverse, robotics and autonomous driving. As RGB images are widely used in these applications, one of the basic problems to forecast the structure of the real world is to predict the dense maps which correspond to the RGB images. Recently, using the single RGB image [27,40], stereo images [2,14] and multi-view images [38,39] have achieve great performance in predicting dense depth. However, the aforementioned works utilize only RGB images and thus suffer from inaccurate and unstable estimations. With the popularization of depth sensors (e.g., the commonly used Lidar sensors), combining the reliable depth prior from such devices could help strengthen the dense depth prediction. Under such circumstances, image-guided depth completion (DC) aims to estimate the dense depth map by fusing the sparse depth from the Lidar and the dense RGB image from the camera.

Most recent learning-based works [12,16,18–20,29,30] treat DC as a regression problem and use CNN networks to extract and fuse the deep features of sparse depth maps and RGB images, which will be fed into the decoder network to output the dense predicted depth. Based on this paradigm, some following works [4,25] combine spatial propagation networks (SPN) with the CNN backbone networks and achieve promising performance. However, previous

L. Iliadis et al. (Eds.): ICANN 2023, LNCS 14256, pp. 99–110, 2023.
https://doi.org/10.1007/978-3-031-44213-1_9

works mainly focus on the propagation layers [3,4,25,37] or novel training losses [23,34,35], few works have paid attention to explore the feature representation. Typically, the convolution shallow networks work well in various vision tasks but are still subject to the limited receptive field and local feature context. To handle this problem in down-stream tasks, some works extend convolution networks to extremely large kernel [9,26] to enlarge the feature context, while others work to replace the CNN backbone with the popular transformer network [32] to capture global feature information. Though such practice achieves superior performance to traditional CNN networks in image classification, semantic segmentation, and monocular depth estimation tasks, few experiments have explored how the feature representation affects the DC results as the DC networks need to handle multi-modal input data (which is different from the aforementioned vision tasks).

In this paper, we first discuss the feature context in image-guided depth completion. As the commonly used convolution nets tend to produce deep features with regular and limited context, important global feature information can not be captured. As for RGB images input that contains rich and dense circumstance information, global feature modeling has been verified to be beneficial for dense prediction [5,6,10,33,36], and we believe it would be critical for DC task. However, simply using only the transformers to extract the features of images and sparse depths would suffer from heavy computation as the attention mechanism needs a lot of calculation. Based on the aforementioned insight, we propose a novel dual-arch feature extractor as the backbone network for DC. Specifically, we make use of the traditional CNN-based residual network as a base extractor since the local feature from convolution layers is computed efficiently and effectively. To perform long-range context aggregation and interaction, we additionally combine a lightweight transformer-like branch and use it as the global supplement to CNN branch. By applying this extractor to our implemented baseline network, we introduce a dual-arch depth completion network, named DDCNet. With limited extra computation, the dual-arch backbone helps DDCNet predict the more accurate dense depth and achieves comparable performance compared to the recent state-of-the-art methods. We also apply our designed dual-arch backbone to the off-the-shelf DC networks, experimental results indicate that our proposed method could help improve the performance of existing methods. Our main contributions can be summarized as:

- We first discuss and explore the influence of the feature context in image-guided depth completion task.
- We introduce DDCNet with a novel dual-arch feature extractor which includes a CNN-based branch and a lightweight transformer branch.
- Experimental results indicate that our method achieves comparable performance to the existing state-of-art methods and can be easily applied to the existing DC methods.

2   Related Works

2.1   Depth Completion

Depth completion (DC) is a classical computer vision task, which is akin to monocular depth estimation (MDE). The difference between DC and MDE is that the sparse depth information could provide accurate and reliable prior for DC methods to strengthen the dense depth prediction.

For the input image and sparse depth, some methods fuse multimodal data at the front of the model. The usual approach is to directly concatenate the visual image and sparse depth in the channel dimension at the very first phase [8,24], or use the first CNN layers to fuse multimodal features of the image and sparse depth before inputting them into subsequent models [17,22]. [18] first proposes a deep completion network based on a dual-encoder structure. After two independent encoder networks extract multimodal features, the features of each intermediate layer are concatenated in the channel dimension and input into the decoder network. [28] changes the aggregation of intermediate features from channel splicing to element addition, and achieves superior performance. [42] proposes to guide multimodal feature aggregation by calculating the correlation between image features and sparse depth. Though many recent depth completion methods have made impressive progress, few works pay attention to efficient global feature learning.

2.2   Vision Transformers

Due to its excellent performance on vision challenges, the transformer, which was originally designed for natural language processing (NLP), has caught the interest of the computer vision community [32]. Inspire by the transformer's success, ViT [11] directly applies transformer architecture as the backbone for image classification and achieves state-of-the-art performance. While ViT requires pre-training on its large dataset, DeiT [1] introduces several training strategies that enable ViT to perform well on the smaller dataset. balabala However, Transformers are difficult to be applied in dense prediction tasks due to the computational complexity of full attention. With a hierarchical architecture represented by shifted windows, Swin Transformers [21] achieves excellent performance in a variety of computer vision tasks while just requiring linear processing complexity. In this paper, we follow and extend Swin Transformers to a 3D version and use it to perform global feature aggregation.

3   Methodology

As shown in Fig. 1, given a pair of input data including an RGB image and a sparse depth map, image-guided DC networks aim to fuse the multi-modal data and predict the dense depth map corresponding to the image. The common design of DC networks includes a feature extractor and a feature decoder, we

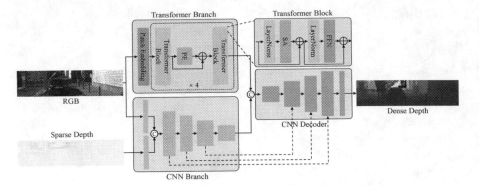

Fig. 1. Network overview. Given a pair of input data including an RGB image and a sparse depth map, DDCNet first extracts the deep features using the dual-arch backbone network, which includes a CNN branch and a Transformer branch. The CNN decoder takes as input the extracted features and produces the dense depth estimations.

follow this paradigm and propose a dual-arch feature extractor that consists of a CNN branch and a transformer branch. The CNN decoder takes the extracted features as input and produces the final dense depth estimation. The whole network is trained end-to-end. In the following sections, we first introduce the preliminaries of the attention mechanism and vision transformer in Sect. 3.1, then illustrate the architecture of the whole network in Sect. 3.2, depict the loss functions and training data in Sect. 3.3.

3.1 Preliminary

Transformers [32] together with the attention mechanism are first proposed in natural language processing (NLP) task. The core part of transformers is multi-head self-attention (MSA), which is designed for sequence input and is able to model the global information among all the tokens. To employ transformers in computer vision tasks (e.g., image classification), ViT [11] and DeiT [1] divide the input images into different patches to form a sequence data, which will be fed into the classical transformer blocks to extract deep features. To compute the attention in each transformer block, the input features will be grouped as query $\mathbf{Q}$, key $\mathbf{K}$ and value $\mathbf{V}$. The attention computation in each layer can be formally denoted as

$$Attention(\mathbf{Q}, \mathbf{K}, \mathbf{V}) = softmax(\mathbf{Q}\mathbf{K}^\top)\mathbf{V}. \tag{1}$$

This dot-product attention model the feature similarity between $\mathbf{Q}$ and $\mathbf{K}$, the $softmax(\mathbf{Q}\mathbf{K}^\top)$ plays a role similar to the weight which retrieves information from $\mathbf{V}$.

As for dense prediction tasks (e.g., semantic segmentation and depth estimation), the computation complexity of vanilla attention grows rapidly for the high-resolution input image. To handle this problem, Twins [5] and CPVT [6] introduce the spatially separable self-attention (SSSA). Following these works [5, 6], we use the SSSA-based transformer block to construct the transformer branch. Specifically, the SSSA can be written as

$$\hat{\mathbf{z}}_{ij}^{l} = \text{LSA}\left(\text{LayerNorm}\left(\mathbf{z}_{ij}^{l-1}\right)\right) + \mathbf{z}_{ij}^{l-1}, \tag{2}$$

$$\mathbf{z}_{ij}^{l} = \text{FFN}\left(\text{LayerNorm}\left(\hat{\mathbf{z}}_{ij}^{l}\right)\right) + \hat{\mathbf{z}}_{ij}^{l}, \tag{3}$$

$$\hat{\mathbf{z}}^{l+1} = \text{GSA}\left(\text{LayerNorm}\left(\mathbf{z}^{l}\right)\right) + \mathbf{z}^{l}, \tag{4}$$

$$\mathbf{z}^{l+1} = \text{FFN}\left(\text{LayerNorm}\left(\hat{\mathbf{z}}^{l+1}\right)\right) + \hat{\mathbf{z}}^{l+1}, \tag{5}$$

where LSA and GSA indicate the locally-grouped self-attention within a sub-window and the global sub-sampled attention, more details can be found in [5]. We also use the conditional positional encoding [6] instead of the absolute positional encoding to encode position information.

3.2   Network Architecture

Transformer Branch. The transformer branch mainly consists of 2 stages and each stage includes a patch embedding layer and 4 transformer blocks, the details of the transformer block are illustrated in Fig. 1 and Sect. 3.1. In the first stage, we divide the input features into embedded partitions of 1/4 resolution, and further divide the partitions into 1/8 resolution in the second stage. As a result, the transformer branch finally produces deep features with the shape of $256 \times \frac{h}{8} \times \frac{w}{8}$, where the h and w indicate the resolution of the input image.

CNN Branch. Following the common practice of CNN-based DC methods, we implement the CNN branch as ResNet-like [15] encoder. Specifically, we first use two separate convolution layers with a kernel size of 3 to process RGB images and sparse depth accordingly. Then the aforementioned features will be concatenated in channel dimension and fed into the following CNN layers, each layer interacts with CNN decoder via the residual connection. More details can be found in Table 1.

CNN Decoder. The CNN decoder takes as input the concatenated features of the transformer branch and CNN branch and produces the final dense depth of the same spatial resolution as the input image. More details can be found in Table 1.

3.3   Loss Function and Training Data

In this paper we focus on the supervised image-guided depth completion task, thus we assume that the ground truth dense depth labels are available.

Table 1. Structure of CNN branch and CNN decoder. Each layer in the CNN branch uses the vanilla convolution layer with kernel size set to 3 and padding set to 1. The transposed convolution layers in the CNN decoder also use the kernel size=3. Each layer consists of batch normalization and ReLU.

Layer	Description	Output Dim
enc1-RGB	(stride = 1) × 1	(B, 48, H, W)
enc1-Dep	(stride = 1) × 1	(B, 48, H, W)
enc2	(stride = 1) × 6	(B, 64, H, W)
enc3	(stride = 2) × 1, (stride = 1) × 5	(B, 128, H/2, W/2)
enc4	(stride = 2) × 1, (stride = 1) × 9	(B, 256, H/4, W/4)
enc5	(stride = 2) × 1, (stride = 1) × 5	(B, 512, H/8, W/8)
enc6	(stride = 2) × 1	(B, 512, H/16, W/16)
dec1	(Conv-T, stride = 2) × 1	(B, 256, H/8, W/8)
dec2	(Conv-T, stride = 2) × 1	(B, 128, H/4, W/4)
dec3	(Conv-T, stride = 2) × 1	(B, 64, H/2, W/2)
dec4	(Conv-T, stride = 2) × 1	(B, 64, H, W)
out	(Conv, stride=1) × 2	(B, 1, H, W)

Loss Function. We mainly use the $\ell 1$ and $\ell 2$ loss to train the network, with the loss wights w_1 and w_2, the total training loss can be written as:

$$\mathcal{L} = \frac{1}{|\mathcal{V}|} \sum_{p \in \mathcal{V}} w_1 |d_p - \hat{d}_p| + w_2 |d_p - \hat{d}_p|^2, \tag{6}$$

where $\mathcal{V}$ indicate the valid pixels with ground truth depth d_p, $\hat{d}_p$ is the estimated depth.

Training Data. Following the common practice of image-guided depth completion task, we use the KITTI-DC dataset [31] to train and evaluate our method. KITTI-DC includes more than 90K pairs of RGB images and a Lidar sparse depth map, we use the official training set to train our model and use the validation set and test set for evaluation.

4   Experiments

In this section, we describe our implementation details and evaluation metrics in Sect. 4.1, and conduct experiments to verify the effectiveness of our method in Sect. 4.2, and show the ablation study results in Sect. 4.3.

4.1   Implementation Details and Metrics

We implement DDCNet with Pytorch and train it using 8 NVIDIA RTX 2080Ti GPUs on KITTI-DC training set, and we ignore the areas without Lidar projection and bottom-crop the raw input into patches of 1216 × 256 for training.

Table 2. Quantitive results on KTTI-DC benchmark [31]. **Bold** indicates the best result, <u>underline</u> indicates the second best.

Method	RMSE ↓	MAE ↓	iRMSE ↓	iMAE ↓
DFuseNet [30]	1206.66	419.93	3.62	1.79
CSPN [4]	1019.64	279.46	2.93	1.15
pNCNN [12]	960.05	251.77	3.37	1.05
DFineNet [41]	943.89	301.17	3.21	1.39
Spade-RGBsD [18]	917.64	234.81	2.17	0.95
TWISE [16]	840.20	**195.58**	**2.08**	**0.82**
SSGP [29]	838.22	244.70	2.51	1.09
NConv-CNN [13]	829.98	233.26	2.60	1.03
CrossGuidance [19]	807.42	253.98	2.73	1.33
BAGC [20]	<u>799.31</u>	232.98	2.44	1.05
DDCNet (Ours)	**788.18**	<u>213.44</u>	<u>2.15</u>	<u>0.91</u>

For all the experiments, we adopt the Adam optimizer with $\beta_1 = 0.9$, $\beta_2 = 0.999$ and training for 20 epochs with the initial learning rate of 0.001. Typically, with batch size set to 1, the training phase takes about 2 days. By following the common practice, we use the official metrics of KITTI-DC dataset [31] to evaluate our method. Specifically, $RMSE$ is defined as $\sqrt{\frac{1}{|\mathcal{V}|} \sum_{p \in \mathcal{V}} |d_p - \hat{d}_p|^2}$, MAE is defined as $\frac{1}{|\mathcal{V}|} \sum_{p \in \mathcal{V}} |d_p - \hat{d}_p|$, while the $iMASE$ and $iMAE$ are defined as $\sqrt{\frac{1}{|\mathcal{V}|} \sum_{p \in \mathcal{V}} |1/d_p - 1/\hat{d}_p|^2}$ and $\frac{1}{|\mathcal{V}|} \sum_{p \in \mathcal{V}} |1/d_p - 1/\hat{d}_p|$.

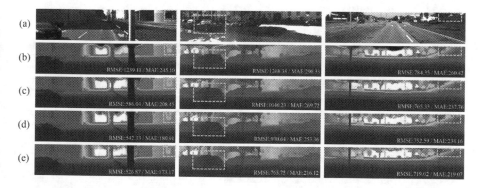

Fig. 2. Depth completion results on the KITTI-DC test set [31]. (a) RGB image, (b) CSPN [4], (c) SSGP [29], (d) BAGC [20], (e) Ours. We also report the RMSE and MAE results of above methods in bottom-right corner.

Table 3. Alation study results on KTTI-DC [31] validation set. TR.B. is the abbreviation of the transformer branch, P.T. indicates pre-train the transformer branch on ImageNet [7]. Mem. is the total GPU memory consumption during inference phase.

Base Net	Settings		Results		Mem.	Time
	TR.B.	P.T.	RMSE	MAE		
[25]*			871.2	231.8	4314M	0.278 s
	✓		**856.9**	227.9	4420M	0.291 s
	✓	✓	869.8	**226.5**	4420M	0.291 s
Ours			900.5	234.4	2860M	0.268 s
	✓		**875.8**	**229.8**	2998M	0.281 s
	✓	✓	895.8	250.8	2998M	0.281 s

4.2 Experimental Results

As done in previous works [4,25], we evaluate our proposed network and compare our results with the existing methods on the KITTI-DC benchmark [31]. The quantitive results are shown in Table 2. In terms of the official metrics, our method achieves comparable performance compared to the existing state-of-art works, especially in the RMSE(mm) metric. The qualitative comparison is visualized in Fig. 2. We compare and visualize the predicted dense depth results of our method, CSPN [4], SSGP [29], BAGC [20], and we report the corresponding RMSE and MAE results in the bottom-right corner. Compared with the aforementioned methods, our method achieves superior performance in various scenarios, e.g., remote detailed objects in the right column of Fig. 2.

4.3 Ablation Study

To analyze the effectiveness of our proposed method, we perform ablation study on the KITTI-DC validation set. We choose two different networks (our DDCNet and the CNN-based NLSPN [25]) as the base model for the ablation study. As shown in Table 3, TR.B. indicates the transformer branch in feature extractor, P.T means whether pre-train the transformer branch on ImageNet dataset [7]. In all the settings, we keep the training hyper-parameters the same and fixed (e.g., use 8 GPUs for training 20 epochs with batch size set to 1.) According to the results, the transformer branch helps [25] and our network gets better results with limited extra memory consumption ($\sim$100 MB) and runtime ($\sim$0.12 s). It is noteworthy that pre-training on ImageNet makes the transformer harder to fit into the depth completion task, and might affect the final results with only 20 epochs for training. In Fig. 3, we visualize the extracted features from the CNN branch and transformer branch (after pre-trained on ImageNet), where the features of the transformer highlight the detailed regions and capture more long-range context, leaving a noticeable domain difference between features from transformer branch and CNN branch.

(a) RGB   (b) Transformer Branch Feature   (c) CNN Branch Feature

Fig. 3. Visualization of extracted features by the proposed dual-arch extractor.

5 Conclusion

In this paper, we discuss the feature context in image-guided depth completion and propose a novel dual-arch feature extractor as the backbone network for DC. We utilize the traditional CNN-based residual network as a base extractor and additionally combine a lightweight transformer branch as the global supplement to the CNN branch to perform long-range context aggregation and interaction. With limited extra computation, the dual-arch backbone helps DDCNet predict the more accurate dense depth and achieves comparable performance compared to the recent state-of-the-art methods. Experimental results show that our proposed method could help improve the performance of the baseline network by applying the dual-arch feature extractor to the existing methods.

References

1. Carion, N., Massa, F., Synnaeve, G., Usunier, N., Kirillov, A., Zagoruyko, S.: End-to-end object detection with transformers. In: Vedaldi, A., Bischof, H., Brox, T., Frahm, J.-M. (eds.) ECCV 2020. LNCS, vol. 12346, pp. 213–229. Springer, Cham (2020). https://doi.org/10.1007/978-3-030-58452-8_13
2. Chang, J.R., Chen, Y.S.: Pyramid stereo matching network. In: Proceedings of the IEEE Conference on Computer Vision and Pattern Recognition, pp. 5410–5418 (2018)
3. Cheng, X., Wang, P., Guan, C., Yang, R.: CSPN++: learning context and resource aware convolutional spatial propagation networks for depth completion. In: Proceedings of the AAAI Conference on Artificial Intelligence, vol. 34, pp. 10615–10622 (2020)
4. Cheng, X., Wang, P., Yang, R.: Depth estimation via affinity learned with convolutional spatial propagation network. In: Proceedings of the European Conference on Computer Vision (ECCV), pp. 103–119 (2018)
5. Chu, X., et al.: Twins: revisiting the design of spatial attention in vision transformers. Adv. Neural. Inf. Process. Syst. **34**, 9355–9366 (2021)
6. Chu, X., et al.: Conditional positional encodings for vision transformers. arXiv preprint arXiv:2102.10882 (2021)

7. Deng, J., Dong, W., Socher, R., Li, L.J., Li, K., Fei-Fei, L.: ImageNet: a large-scale hierarchical image database. In: 2009 IEEE Conference on Computer Vision and Pattern Recognition, pp. 248–255. IEEE (2009)

8. Dimitrievski, M., Veelaert, P., Philips, W.: Learning morphological operators for depth completion. In: Blanc-Talon, J., Helbert, D., Philips, W., Popescu, D., Scheunders, P. (eds.) ACIVS 2018. LNCS, vol. 11182, pp. 450–461. Springer, Cham (2018). https://doi.org/10.1007/978-3-030-01449-0_38

9. Ding, X., Zhang, X., Han, J., Ding, G.: Scaling up your kernels to 31×31: revisiting large kernel design in CNNs. In: Proceedings of the IEEE/CVF Conference on Computer Vision and Pattern Recognition, pp. 11963–11975 (2022)

10. Ding, Y., et al.: TransMVSNet: global context-aware multi-view stereo network with transformers. In: Proceedings of the IEEE/CVF Conference on Computer Vision and Pattern Recognition, pp. 8585–8594 (2022)

11. Dosovitskiy, A., et al.: An image is worth 16×16 words: transformers for image recognition at scale. arXiv preprint arXiv:2010.11929 (2020)

12. Eldesokey, A., Felsberg, M., Holmquist, K., Persson, M.: Uncertainty-aware CNNs for depth completion: uncertainty from beginning to end. In: Proceedings of the IEEE/CVF Conference on Computer Vision and Pattern Recognition, pp. 12014–12023 (2020)

13. Eldesokey, A., Felsberg, M., Khan, F.S.: Confidence propagation through CNNs for guided sparse depth regression. IEEE Trans. Pattern Anal. Mach. Intell. **42**(10), 2423–2436 (2019)

14. Gu, X., Fan, Z., Zhu, S., Dai, Z., Tan, F., Tan, P.: Cascade cost volume for high-resolution multi-view stereo and stereo matching. In: Proceedings of the IEEE/CVF Conference on Computer Vision and Pattern Recognition, pp. 2495–2504 (2020)

15. He, K., Zhang, X., Ren, S., Sun, J.: Deep residual learning for image recognition. In: Proceedings of the IEEE Conference on Computer Vision and Pattern Recognition, pp. 770–778 (2016)

16. Imran, S., Liu, X., Morris, D.: Depth completion with twin surface extrapolation at occlusion boundaries. In: Proceedings of the IEEE/CVF Conference on Computer Vision and Pattern Recognition, pp. 2583–2592 (2021)

17. Imran, S., Long, Y., Liu, X., Morris, D.: Depth coefficients for depth completion. In: 2019 IEEE/CVF Conference on Computer Vision and Pattern Recognition (CVPR), pp. 12438–12447. IEEE (2019)

18. Jaritz, M., De Charette, R., Wirbel, E., Perrotton, X., Nashashibi, F.: Sparse and dense data with CNNs: depth completion and semantic segmentation. In: 2018 International Conference on 3D Vision (3DV), pp. 52–60. IEEE (2018)

19. Lee, S., Lee, J., Kim, D., Kim, J.: Deep architecture with cross guidance between single image and sparse lidar data for depth completion. IEEE Access **8**, 79801–79810 (2020)

20. Liu, K., Li, Q., Zhou, Y.: An adaptive converged depth completion network based on efficient RGB guidance. Multimed. Tools Appl. **81**(25), 35915–35933 (2022)

21. Liu, Z., et al.: Swin transformer: hierarchical vision transformer using shifted windows. In: Proceedings of the IEEE/CVF International Conference on Computer Vision, pp. 10012–10022 (2021)

22. Long, Y., Yu, H., Liu, B.: Depth completion towards different sensor configurations via relative depth map estimation and scale recovery. J. Vis. Commun. Image Represent. **80**, 103272 (2021)

23. Ma, F., Cavalheiro, G.V., Karaman, S.: Self-supervised sparse-to-dense: self-supervised depth completion from lidar and monocular camera. In: 2019 International Conference on Robotics and Automation (ICRA), pp. 3288–3295. IEEE (2019)

24. Ma, F., Karaman, S.: Sparse-to-dense: depth prediction from sparse depth samples and a single image. In: 2018 IEEE International Conference on Robotics and Automation (ICRA), pp. 4796–4803. IEEE (2018)

25. Park, J., Joo, K., Hu, Z., Liu, C.-K., So Kweon, I.: Non-local spatial propagation network for depth completion. In: Vedaldi, A., Bischof, H., Brox, T., Frahm, J.-M. (eds.) ECCV 2020. LNCS, vol. 12358, pp. 120–136. Springer, Cham (2020). https://doi.org/10.1007/978-3-030-58601-0_8

26. Peng, C., Zhang, X., Yu, G., Luo, G., Sun, J.: Large kernel matters-improve semantic segmentation by global convolutional network. In: Proceedings of the IEEE Conference on Computer Vision and Pattern Recognition, pp. 4353–4361 (2017)

27. Ranftl, R., Bochkovskiy, A., Koltun, V.: Vision transformers for dense prediction. In: Proceedings of the IEEE/CVF International Conference on Computer Vision, pp. 12179–12188 (2021)

28. Ryu, K., Lee, K.I., Cho, J., Yoon, K.J.: Scanline resolution-invariant depth completion using a single image and sparse lidar point cloud. IEEE Robot. Autom. Lett. 6(4), 6961–6968 (2021)

29. Schuster, R., Wasenmuller, O., Unger, C., Stricker, D.: SSGP: sparse spatial guided propagation for robust and generic interpolation. In: Proceedings of the IEEE/CVF Winter Conference on Applications of Computer Vision, pp. 197–206 (2021)

30. Shivakumar, S.S., Nguyen, T., Miller, I.D., Chen, S.W., Kumar, V., Taylor, C.J.: DFuseNet: Deep fusion of RGB and sparse depth information for image guided dense depth completion. In: 2019 IEEE Intelligent Transportation Systems Conference (ITSC), pp. 13–20. IEEE (2019)

31. Uhrig, J., Schneider, N., Schneider, L., Franke, U., Brox, T., Geiger, A.: Sparsity invariant CNNs. In: 2017 international conference on 3D Vision (3DV), pp. 11–20. IEEE (2017)

32. Vaswani, A., et al.: Attention is all you need. Adv. Neural Inf. Process. Syst. 30 (2017)

33. Wang, W., et al.: Pyramid vision transformer: a versatile backbone for dense prediction without convolutions. In: Proceedings of the IEEE/CVF International Conference on Computer Vision, pp. 568–578 (2021)

34. Wong, A., Cicek, S., Soatto, S.: Learning topology from synthetic data for unsupervised depth completion. IEEE Robot. Autom. Lett. 6(2), 1495–1502 (2021)

35. Wong, A., Soatto, S.: Unsupervised depth completion with calibrated backprojection layers. In: Proceedings of the IEEE/CVF International Conference on Computer Vision, pp. 12747–12756 (2021)

36. Xie, E., Wang, W., Yu, Z., Anandkumar, A., Alvarez, J.M., Luo, P.: SegFormer: simple and efficient design for semantic segmentation with transformers. Adv. Neural. Inf. Process. Syst. 34, 12077–12090 (2021)

37. Xu, Z., Yin, H., Yao, J.: Deformable spatial propagation networks for depth completion. In: 2020 IEEE International Conference on Image Processing (ICIP), pp. 913–917. IEEE (2020)

38. Yao, Y., Luo, Z., Li, S., Fang, T., Quan, L.: MVSNet: depth inference for unstructured multi-view stereo. In: Proceedings of the European Conference on Computer Vision (ECCV), pp. 767–783 (2018)

39. Yao, Y., Luo, Z., Li, S., Shen, T., Fang, T., Quan, L.: Recurrent MVSNet for high-resolution multi-view stereo depth inference. In: Proceedings of the IEEE/CVF Conference on Computer Vision and Pattern Recognition, pp. 5525–5534 (2019)
40. Yin, W., et al.: Learning to recover 3D scene shape from a single image. In: Proceedings of the IEEE/CVF Conference on Computer Vision and Pattern Recognition, pp. 204–213 (2021)
41. Zhang, Y., et al.: DFineNet: ego-motion estimation and depth refinement from sparse, noisy depth input with RGB guidance. arXiv preprint arXiv:1903.06397 (2019)
42. Zhong, Y., Wu, C.Y., You, S., Neumann, U.: Deep RGB-D canonical correlation analysis for sparse depth completion. Adv. Neural Inf. Process. Syst. **32** (2019)

Semantic and Frequency Representation Mining for Face Manipulation Detection

Jihao Cao[ID], Jinsheng Deng, Xiaoqing Yin[✉], Zhichao Zhang, and Hui Chen

National University of Defense Technology, Changsha 410073, Hunan, China
{jhcao_cs,jsdeng,yinxiaoqing,zhangzhichao11,chenhui19}@nudt.edu.cn

Abstract. Face manipulation technologies pose a great threat to the current digital media. Although previous methods have achieved excellent detection performance, they tend to focus on specific artifacts and lead to overfitting. Erasing-based augmentations can alleviate this issue, but they still suffer from high randomness and fixed shapes. Therefore, we propose a novel face masking method named Landmarks Based Erasing (LBE), which exploits the geometric information of the face and forgery attention map to perform erasure, thereby forcing the network to mine discriminative features from other face regions. Furthermore, Wavelet Packet with Attention (WPA) mechanism module is designed to extract multi-level frequency features, providing a complementary perspective to LBE module. Finally, we employ a score fusion strategy to fuse two types of complementary feature information for forgery detection. Extensive experiments on three large public datasets demonstrate that our proposed method achieves state-of-the-art detection performance and exhibits good generalization ability.

Keywords: Face manipulation detection · Landmarks based erasing · Wavelet packets · Attention mechanism

1 Introduction

Face manipulation refers to the use of certain forgery techniques to tamper with the facial attributes of a source image. In recent years, the rapid progress of deep learning technologies have fueled a series of face manipulation methods, including Deepfake [1], Faceswap [2], StyleGAN [14], PGGAN [13] etc. The fake images forged by these methods are becoming increasingly realistic, making it challenging for human eyes to differentiate between real and fake faces. Therefore, it is of significant importance to develop reliable forensic models for detecting manipulated faces.

Due to the powerful representation ability of Convolutional Neural Network (CNN), many scholars have employed it to construct forgery detectors for mitigating the toll caused by manipulation technologies. Although vanilla CNN-based detectors have achieved acceptable detection performance, they tend to focus on a limited region of face, which can lead to overfitting to specific forgery

L. Iliadis et al. (Eds.): ICANN 2023, LNCS 14256, pp. 111–122, 2023.
https://doi.org/10.1007/978-3-031-44213-1_10

artifacts and poor generalization ability on unseen datasets [8]. To achieve better detection performance, the classification network should focus on representative features related to forgery techniques, rather than overfitting the limited face region which are mainly useful in minimizing the classification loss function [25]. Based on this, a direct solution is to occlude the sensitive region of face, forcing the network to explore discriminative features from other face regions, so as to enhance the detection performance to a extent. However, previous erasing methods have the following limitations: lack of utilization of face structure information, irregular shape of erased area. Moreover, it is insufficient to rely solely on semantic information for forgery detection, recent studies have shown that the artifacts of image synthesised based on GANs are easier to capture in the frequency domain, while most of the existing methods only employ the semantic information, and features related to the frequency domain have not been effectively exploited.

In this paper, we propose a Landmarks Based Erasing (LBE) method that exploits facial landmarks information and Forgery Attention Map (FAM) for facial erasure. Compared with previous erasing methods, LBE can perform more reasonable erasure on the facial area that the network pays attention to, thus enabling the network to explore features from wider face regions. Besides, we present a novel frequency-domain feature extraction module, which combines Wavelet Packets with Attention mechanism (WPA) to extract discriminative features. We further fuse these two types of cross-domain representations to improve detection performance. The main contributions of our work can be summarized as follows:

- We propose a novel facial mask algorithm named LBE that can utilize facial landmarks and FAM to erase sensitive areas, thereby alleviating the overfitting problems and improving the generalization ability of the forensic models.
- We further design a frequency domain feature extraction module that employs wavelet packets to extract multi-level frequency features, and introduce an attention mechanism to assign different weights to features, allowing the network to selectively focus on important information.
- We fuse the above two complementary data features for face manipulation detection, which achieves state-of-the-art detection performance on three public datasets. Ablation studies and visualizations further validate the effectiveness and feasibility of our proposed method.

2   Related Work

2.1   Face Manipulation Detection

Since the rise of deepfake technologies, researchers have proposed various face forgery detection methods, and most of them formulate face manipulation detection as a binary classification task. In the early stage of face forgery detection research, Afchar et al. [4] design a compact network called MesoNet for video forgery detection, which mainly focuses on the mesoscopic properties in forged videos. Since then, a quantity of face forgery detection methods combined with deep learning technology have emerged. Rssler et al. [21] propose a benchmark dataset FaceForensics++, and adopt Xception [7] network as the baseline. Face X-ray [18] aims to detect the blending boundary introduced in general manipulation processes, which does not rely on any prior knowledge about forgery traces and shows good generalization ability on unseen datasets. However, the performance of Face X-ray drops significantly when detecting images without blended boundaries. In addition, the performance of most detection models is susceptible to compression and noise interference, so recent work mainly focus on the robustness and generalization of models.

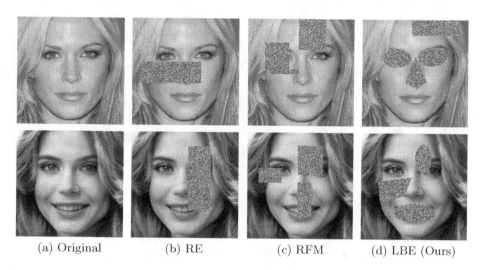

| (a) Original | (b) RE | (c) RFM | (d) LBE (Ours) |

Fig. 1. Examples of face images masked by RE, RFM, and our proposed LBE. Compared with RE and RFM, LBE can effectively utilize the geometric information of face for masking, and its masking shapes are more diverse. Obviously, the masking effect of LBE is more reasonable and flexible, which leads to better detection performance and generalization ability.

2.2   Data Augmentation

Data Augmentation is an effective way to alleviate model overfitting problems, among which Random Flipping [16], Random Cropping [23] on the original image are commonly used augmentation methods. At present, there also exists other augmentation strategies involve Random Erasing (RE) [27] and RFM [25]. As shown in Fig. 1(b), RE generates a random-sized rectangular block on the face area to complete the masking operation. RFM shown in Fig. 1(c) tracks and selectively masks the Top-N sensitive facial regions, encouraging the model to mine more representative forgery cues. However, these methods fail to utilize the geometric information of the face, resulting in irregular masking shapes and randomness. Face-Cutout [10] exploits the facial landmarks information and pre-calculated difference mask to cut out regions of an image, but introduces additional computational overhead. Therefore, we propose a novel face masking method LBE that utilizes the geometry and gradient information of face for more efficient data augmentation.

2.3   Frequency Domain Features

Frequency-domain features provide a brand-new perspective to semantic features, and Frank et al. [11] demonstrate that artifacts of GAN-synthesized fake images are easier to capture in the frequency domain. Qian et al. [20] propose two complementary frequency domain feature extraction modules to capture subtle forgery artifacts, which have achieved superior detection performance on compressed datasets. Chen et al. [6] combine multi-scale semantic information with DFT-transformed frequency domain features for forgery detection and achieve ideal detection performance. Unlike previous methods of obtaining frequency features through DCT or DFT, Wolter et al. [26] employ wavelet packets to extract multi-level frequency information and retain spatial information to a degree. Inspired by their work, we employ wavelet packets to obtain decomposed frequency features.

3   Method

3.1   Overview

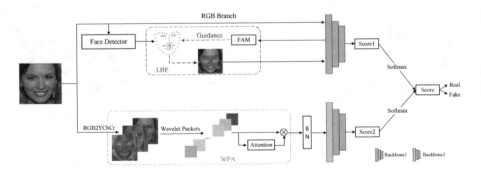

Fig. 2. The framework of our proposed method, where Backbone1 is the Xception network, and Backbone2 is modified Resnet18 network.

In this section, we propose a dual-stream framework to process semantic features and frequency features respectively, and its overall structure is shown in Fig. 2. The semantic features branch utilizes facial landmarks information and gradient value of the network backpropagation to complete the face masking, and then feeds the masked image into backbone again to learn more representative information. The other module employs the wavelet packets to extract the decomposed frequency features and introduces an attention mechanism to locate discriminative representations. The specific details of LBE and WPA will be introduced in the following text.

3.2   Landmarks Based Erasing

Previous masking methods have certain limitations such as fixed rectangular masking shape and random position. Based on this observation, we employ facial landmarks information and Fogery Attention Map (FAM) values to achieve more reasonable face masking. As shown in the upper part of Fig. 2, for each image in mini-batch, we first use Dlib [15] to obtain the coordinates of its face landmarks, and then calculate the FAM values according to the gradient value of the network backpropagation, the formula of FAM is defined as follows:

$$FAM = \max\left(\nabla_I\left(abs\left(O_{fake} - O_{real}\right)\right)\right) \tag{1}$$

where O_{fake} and O_{real} represent the predicted values after the detection model receives the input data respectively, and ∇_I denotes the gradient value of the input. Note that $\max(\cdot)$ and $abs(\cdot)$ are commonly used mathematical functions, each value in FAM indicates the sensitivity value of the detector at that pixel.

After obtaining the facial landmarks coordinates and FAM values, we divide the face into two areas: special areas including eyes, nose, cheek and mouth; and general areas containing other parts of the face. This allows us to make full use of the geometric information of the face. We then sort FAM values in descending order, select the current maximum FAM value and calculate the corresponding coordinate position. If the calculated coordinate is located in the special area that is not occluded, it will be occluded directly based on the facial landmarks points. Otherwise, it will be masked with probability using a rectangle, ellipse or adjacent landmarks points. Note that the area masked by adjacent landmarks points is not counted in the number of erasing blocks because its masked area is small. The detailed procedure of LBE is shown in Algorithm 1, and its erasing example is presented in Fig. 1(d).

3.3   Wavelet Packets with Attention Mechanism

The Wavelet Packets with Attention (WPA) mechanism module is designed to mine complementary frequency features, and its pipeline is presented in the lower part of Fig. 2. Instead of taking RGB image as input directly, we convert it into YCbCr color sapce to avoid redundant information, which is more conducive to the extraction of frequency features. The distribution of artifacts introduced by different types of forgery techniques is distinct in the frequency domain, and traditional Fourier-based frequency feature extraction methods are not sufficient

---

Algorithm 1. Landmarks Based Erasing

Input: Input image I, Image size H and W, 68 facial landmarks $L[68]$;
   Forgery Attention map Map, Erasing Block count N;
   Erasing probability P;
   Probability of Rectangular occlusion R_p and Elliptical occlusion E_p;
   Max erase size H_{max} and W_{max}, Number of adjacent points N_1;
Output: Erased Image I^*
Initialization: $P_1 \leftarrow Rand(0,1)$; Special Area: $S_a : \{eyes \dots mouth\} \leftarrow L[68]$.
1: **if** $P_1 \leq P$ **then**
2: $count = 0$
3: **while** $count < N$ **do**
4:   $[i, j]$ = coordinate of the ind^{th} largest value in Map;
5:   **if** $[i, j]$ has not been occluded **then**
6:    **if** $[i, j] \in S_a$ **then**
7:     $S_a \leftarrow Rand(0, 255)$;
8:    **end if**
9:    **if** $[i, j] \notin S_a$ **then**
10:     $P_2 = Rand(0, 1)$;
11:     **if** $P_2 \leq R_p$ **then**
12:      $H = Rand(1, H_{max})$; $W = Rand(1, W_{max})$;
13:      $Rectangle[i, j, H, W] \leftarrow Rand(0, 255)$
14:     **else if** $P_2 \leq R_p + E_p$ **then**
15:      $L_{radius} = Rand(1, H_{max})/2$; $S_{radius} = Rand(1, W_{max})/2$;
16:      $Ellipse[i, j, L_{radius}, S_{radius}] \leftarrow Rand(0, 255)$;
17:     **else**
18:      $points \leftarrow$ Find N_1 points in L[68] that are adjacent to $[i, j]$;
19:      $Ploygon[points] \leftarrow Rand(0, 255)$; // Not counted.
20:     **end if**
21:    **end if**
22:    $count \leftarrow count + 1$;
23:   **end if**
24: **end while**
25: **end if**
26: $I^* \leftarrow I$;
27: **return** I^*;

---

for mining high-frequency information. Therefore, we adopt wavelet packets to acquire the decomposed frequency features, and conduct a more detailed exploration of the forged traces in different frequency bands.

For each input image, let F^c represents the decomposed features of each channel, and its feature decomposition process can be expressed as:

$$F^c = Coiflet\{f_a, f_h, f_v, f_d\} \quad \text{s.t. } c \in \{0, 1, 2\}$$
$$F = Concatenate([F^0, F^1, F^2]) \tag{2}$$

In the above formula, f represents a filter vector. In the two-dimensional case, a, h, v and d denote approximation coefficients, horizontal coefficients, vertical coefficients, and diagonal coefficients respectively. We apply Coiflet wavelet transform to decompose the input data of three color channels and then concatenate these vectors along the channel axis to obtain the complete frequency features. However, the large amount of decomposed feature blocks are adverse for network training, so we introduce the GCNet [5] to dynamically adjust the weight of each feature block. Which can help the network locate forgery-related clues and improve detection performance.

3.4   Fusion Strategy

We employ a score fusion strategy to combine the classification information of two complementary modules. The score value of each module is the output result of the last linear layer. Let S_1 represents the score of the LBE module, and S_2 represents the score of the WPA module. The final score value S of the model can be defined as follows:

$$S = W_1 \cdot Softmax(S_1) + W_2 \cdot Softmax(S_2) \tag{3}$$

where W_1 and W_2 denote the weight values of the two modules respectively. To optimize the performance after fusion, we can dynamically adjust the weights of the two modules based on their detection performance. Since face manipulation detection is defined as a binary classification task, $Softmax(S_1)$ is a 1 * 2 vector, which respectively represent the probability values that the input data is predicted to be real or fake.

4   Experiment

4.1   Experimental Settings

Datasets. In this work, we evaluate our proposed method by conducting experiments on three well-known datasets: DFFD [9], FaceForensics++ (FF++) [21], and Celeb-DF [19]. DFFD dataset contains fake images synthesized by various GAN techniques such as classic StyleGAN [14]and PGGAN [13], which greatly enrich the diversity of the dataset. The FF++ dataset consists of 1000 pristine videos and 5000 fake videos generated with five forgery methods. Celeb-DF dataset is composed of 590 real videos and 5639 fake videos, and its visual quality is closer to the videos circulated online.

Implementation Details. For video datasets, we first extract image frames and then crop the face regions. For FF++ dataset, we sample 60 frames per video. While for the Celeb-DF dataset, we extract its keyframes for forgery detection and divide 20% of the training samples into the validation set. Each image is then resized to a 256×256 shape and randomly flipped with a probability of 0.5. We employ Xception as the Backbone1, and the modified Resnet18 [12] is adopt as Backbone2. All detectors are trained by using Adam optimizer with an initial learning rate of 0.0004. The size of mini-batch is set to 16, and each mini-batch consists of 8 pristine and 8 forged images. We adopt cross-entropy as the loss function and employ an early stopping strategy with a patience value of 10. The hyperparameters N, R_p, E_p, and N_1 of the LBE algorithm are set to 3, 0.5, 0.5, and 4, respectively. And the score fusion parameters W_1 and W_2 are set to 0.5 by default. Following [25], other parameters P, H_{max}, W_{max} are set to 1.0, 120, 120, respectively.

Evaluation Metrics. We adopt Area Under Curve (AUC), True Detect Rate (TDR) at False Detect Rate (FDR) of 0.01% (denoted as $TDR_{0.01\%}$) and 0.1% (denoted as $TDR_{0.1\%}$) as the evaluation metrics of detection performance.

4.2   Ablation Study

In this section, we conducted extensive ablation studies on three public datasets to verify the effectiveness of our proposed module. The LBE algorithm is based on facial landmarks, so the training data used in the experiment has been filtered by Dlib. To ensure the fairness of the experiment, all inputs are kept with the same settings.

Table 1. Comparison of LBE and existing masking methods on DFFD. ($TDR_{0.1\%}$).

Methods	SG_{celeba}	SG_{ffhq}	FaceAPP	PG_{v1}	PG_{v2}	Average
Resnet18 (CVPR2016) [12]	99.85	96.54	81.12	99.96	99.94	95.48
Xception (CVPR2017) [7]	99.58	95.04	84.53	99.93	99.81	95.77
+ RE (AAAI2020) [27]	99.98	99.51	84.59	99.98	100.00	96.81
+ RFM (CVPR2021) [25]	99.75	98.66	84.82	100.00	99.96	96.63
+ LBE (Ours)	99.95	98.55	**93.50**	99.89	99.84	**98.34**
+ LBE & Resnet18 (Ours)	99.96	99.55	94.58	100.00	99.98	98.81
+ LBE & WPA (Ours)	99.73	99.46	**96.91**	99.97	99.98	**99.21**

StyleGAN (SG), PGGAN (PG).

Comparison with Well-Known Erasing Methods. We first compare our proposed method with existing masking strategies on the DFFD dataset, and the results are shown in Table 1. As can be seen from the table, LBE has increased by 8.91% $TDR_{0.1\%}$ and 8.68% $TDR_{0.1\%}$ respectively on FaceAPP [3] when compared with RE and RFM. The overall performance has been improved by 1.53% $TDR_{0.1\%}$ and 1.71% $TDR_{0.1\%}$, respectively. Moreover, we compare the performance of WPA with its backbone network. The integration of LBE and WPA is 2.33% $TDR_{0.1\%}$ ahead of the backbone network on FaceAPP, with an average increase of 0.4% $TDR_{0.1\%}$. This experimental result shows that the WPA module can mine feature information complementary to the LBE module, thereby further improving detection performance.

Table 2. Quantitative comparison results on FF++ and Celeb-DF datasets.

Methods	FF++ (HQ)		FF++ (LQ)		Celeb-DF	
	AUC	$\text{TDR}_{0.1\%}$	AUC	$\text{TDR}_{0.1\%}$	AUC	$\text{TDR}_{0.1\%}$
Meso-Inception4 (WIFS2018) [4]	82.62	30.82	77.08	15.31	95.79	56.90
Face X-ray (CVPR2020) [18]	94.41	53.02	82.02	22.40	98.43	70.60
EfficientNet-B0 (ICML2019) [24]	96.82	63.18	87.24	28.56	99.58	91.80
Xception (CVPR2017) [7]	97.91	77.66	87.01	26.68	99.45	88.48
+ RE (AAAI2020) [27]	98.02	82.95	85.74	27.33	99.55	89.56
+ RFM (CVPR2021) [25]	97.93	81.59	<u>87.54</u>	**35.12**	99.70	92.71
F^3-Net (ECCV2020) [20]	<u>98.28</u>	<u>83.48</u>	86.32	28.24	**99.77**	**95.69**
Ours	**98.39**	**84.59**	**87.83**	<u>29.01</u>	<u>99.75</u>	<u>94.66</u>

Note: FaceShifter [17] is included in FF++.

Comparison with State of the Art. We also conduct experiments on FF++ and Celeb-DF to compare our proposed method with the state of the art methods. As shown in Table 2, compared with the baseline Xception network, the detection performance on the FF++ and Celeb-DF datasets has been improved after applying RE and RFM masking, which indicates the effectiveness of the masking strategies. What's more, our proposed method achieves state-of-the-art detection performance and outperforms the baseline network Xception by a large margin on the $\text{TDR}_{0.1\%}$ metric. Specifically, we achieve 0.48% AUC, 6.93% $\text{TDR}_{0.1\%}$ gains under HQ quality settings and 0.82% AUC, 2.33% $\text{TDR}_{0.1\%}$ gains under LQ quality settings. Compression has an impact on the detection of face landmarks, so our method achieves suboptimal performance on Celeb-DF dataset. However, it still outperforms existing erasing methods by improving 0.3% AUC and 6.18% $\text{TDR}_{0.1\%}$ compared to the baseline, which is comparable to the best performance.

Table 3. Probability parameters.

R_p	E_p	N_p	AUC	$\text{TDR}_{0.1\%}$	$\text{TDR}_{0.01\%}$
0.5	0.5	0.0	**99.89**	**98.62**	**91.31**
0.45	0.45	0.1	99.71	95.87	72.80
0.4	0.4	0.2	99.73	95.94	86.28
0.35	0.35	0.3	99.80	96.71	89.11
0.3	0.3	0.4	99.74	96.11	87.83

Table 4. Number of masking blocks.

N_1	AUC	$\text{TDR}_{0.1\%}$	$\text{TDR}_{0.01\%}$
1	99.77	96.21	84.17
2	99.86	97.83	**92.17**
3	**99.89**	**98.62**	91.31
4	99.74	95.74	86.41
5	99.76	96.15	87.81

Ablation Study with Different Hyperparameters. We further explore the impact of different hyperparameters on detection performance. As shown in Table 3, we study the detection performance for different values of masking probability on the DFFD dataset, where N_p denotes the probability of applying adjacent landmarks points occlusion. We find that the detection performance is optimal when the R_p and E_p values are 0.5, indicating that rectangular masking and elliptical masking perform better on the DFFD dataset.

Table 5. Ablation study of cheek masking ($TDR_{0.1\%}$).

cheek_mask	DFFD	FF++(HQ)	FF++ (LQ)	Celeb-DF
✓	**99.21**	81.30	26.49	93.63
	99.06	**84.59**	**29.01**	**94.66**

In addition, we investigate the relationship between the number of masked blocks and detection performance. As shown in Table 4, detection performance improved when the number of masked blocks is set to 3. This experimental result demonstrates that the number of masking blocks should be set appropriately; otherwise, it will cause performance degradation. In the end, we have verified the effect of cheek masking on three datasets. The results in Table 5 show that cheek masking works well on DFFD dataset but not on FF++ and Celeb-DF datasets.

Cross-Dataset Evaluations. In this part, we evaluate the generalization ability of our proposed method, which is trained on FF++ (HQ) with five forgery methods but tested on the Celeb-DF dataset. For the Celeb-DF dataset, we sample its keyframes to compute the frame-level AUC scores. As shown in Table 6, our proposed method outperforms all other methods on both datasets, which firmly verifies the good transferability of the proposed method.

Table 6. Cross-dataset evaluations on Celeb-DF dataset by training on FF++ (AUC).

Methods	FF++ (HQ) (%)	Celeb-DF (%)
Meso-Inception4 (WIFS2018) [4]	82.62	52.18
Xception (CVPR2017) [7]	97.91	54.21
+ RE (AAAI2020) [27]	98.02	55.26
+ RFM (CVPR2021) [25]	97.93	57.45
F^3-Net (ECCV2020) [20]	98.28	59.44
Face X-ray (CVPR2020) [18]	94.41	60.17
Ours	**98.39**	**62.64**

4.3   Visual Analysis

To further demonstrate the feasibility of the LBE algorithm, we visualize the features extracted by Grad-CAM [22]. As shown in Fig. 3, while the baseline tends to focus on a limited area of the face, the network after LBE masking can explore a wider range of facial areas to mine more forgery clues. This visualization fits with the idea of our LBE algorithm, which is to mask the attention region of the network and force it to learn features from other regions.

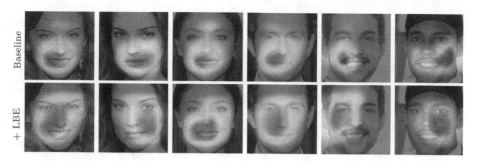

Fig. 3. The Grad-CAM visualization of Baseline and our proposed LBE method.

5   Conclusion

In this work, we propose a novel face masking method (LBE) that exploits facial landmarks and forgery attention map to achieve more efficient erasure. This enables the network learn features from a broader facial region and alleviates the overfitting problem of the model. We also designed a module that combines wavelet packets with attention mechanism to extract complementary features in the frequency domain. Extensive experiments on three public datasets demonstrate the effectiveness of our proposed method, and we further explain its feasibility through visual analysis.

Acknowledgements. This work was supported by the National Natural Science Foundation of China (62001493), the Hunan Provincial Postgraduate Scientific Research Innovation Project (QL20220009).

References

1. Deepfakes (2018). www.github.com/deepfakes/faceswap
2. FaceSwap (2018). www.github.com/MarekKowalski/FaceSwap/
3. FaceApp (2019). www.faceapp.com/app
4. Afchar, D., Nozick, V., Yamagishi, J., Echizen, I.: MesoNet: a compact facial video forgery detection network. In: 2018 IEEE International Workshop on Information Forensics and Security (WIFS) (2018)
5. Cao, Y., Xu, J., Lin, S., Wei, F., Hu, H.: GCNet: non-local networks meet squeeze-excitation networks and beyond. In: Proceedings of the IEEE/CVF International Conference on Computer Vision Workshops (2019)
6. Chen, Z., Yang, H.: Manipulated face detector: joint spatial and frequency domain attention network. arXiv preprint arXiv:2005.02958 **1**(2), 4 (2020)
7. Chollet, F.: Xception: deep learning with depthwise separable convolutions. In: 2017 IEEE Conference on Computer Vision and Pattern Recognition (CVPR) (2017)
8. Dai, Y., Fei, J., Wang, H., Xia, Z.: Attentional local contrastive learning for face forgery detection. In: Pimenidis, E., Angelov, P., Jayne, C., Papaleonidas, A., Aydin, M. (eds.) ICANN 2022, Part I. LNCS, vol. 13529, pp. 709–721. Springer, Cham (2022). https://doi.org/10.1007/978-3-031-15919-0_59

9. Dang, H., Liu, F., Stehouwer, J., Liu, X., Jain, A.: On the detection of digital face manipulation (2019)
10. Das, S., Seferbekov, S., Datta, A., Islam, M., Amin, M., et al.: Towards solving the deepfake problem: an analysis on improving deepfake detection using dynamic face augmentation. In: Proceedings of the IEEE/CVF International Conference on Computer Vision, pp. 3776–3785 (2021)
11. Frank, J., Eisenhofer, T., Schnherr, L., Fischer, A., Kolossa, D., Holz, T.: Leveraging frequency analysis for deep fake image recognition (2020)
12. He, K., Zhang, X., Ren, S., Sun, J.: Deep residual learning for image recognition. In: Proceedings of the IEEE Conference on Computer Vision and Pattern Recognition, pp. 770–778 (2016)
13. Karras, T., Aila, T., Laine, S., Lehtinen, J.: Progressive growing of GANs for improved quality, stability, and variation. arXiv preprint arXiv:1710.10196 (2017)
14. Karras, T., Laine, S., Aila, T.: A style-based generator architecture for generative adversarial networks. In: Proceedings of the IEEE/CVF Conference on Computer Vision and Pattern Recognition, pp. 4401–4410 (2019)
15. King, D.E.: Dlib-ml: a machine learning toolkit. J. Mach. Learn. Res. **10**, 1755–1758 (2009)
16. Krizhevsky, A., Sutskever, I., Hinton, G.E.: ImageNet classification with deep convolutional neural networks. Commun. ACM **60**(6), 84–90 (2017)
17. Li, L., Bao, J., Yang, H., Chen, D., Wen, F.: FaceShifter: towards high fidelity and occlusion aware face swapping. arXiv preprint arXiv:1912.13457 (2019)
18. Li, L., et al.: Face X-ray for more general face forgery detection. In: Proceedings of the IEEE/CVF Conference on Computer Vision and Pattern Recognition, pp. 5001–5010 (2020)
19. Li, Y., Yang, X., Sun, P., Qi, H., Lyu, S.: Celeb-DF: a large-scale challenging dataset for deepfake forensics. In: 2020 IEEE/CVF Conference on Computer Vision and Pattern Recognition (CVPR) (2020)
20. Qian, Y., Yin, G., Sheng, L., Chen, Z., Shao, J.: Thinking in frequency: face forgery detection by mining frequency-aware clues. In: Vedaldi, A., Bischof, H., Brox, T., Frahm, J.-M. (eds.) ECCV 2020. LNCS, vol. 12357, pp. 86–103. Springer, Cham (2020). https://doi.org/10.1007/978-3-030-58610-2_6
21. Rssler, A., Cozzolino, D., Verdoliva, L., Riess, C., Thies, J., Niener, M.: FaceForensics++: learning to detect manipulated facial images (2019)
22. Selvaraju, R.R., Cogswell, M., Das, A., Vedantam, R., Parikh, D., Batra, D.: Grad-CAM: visual explanations from deep networks via gradient-based localization. In: Proceedings of the IEEE International Conference on Computer Vision, pp. 618–626 (2017)
23. Simonyan, K., Zisserman, A.: Very deep convolutional networks for large-scale image recognition. arXiv preprint arXiv:1409.1556 (2014)
24. Tan, M., Le, Q.: EfficientNet: rethinking model scaling for convolutional neural networks. In: International Conference on Machine Learning, pp. 6105–6114. PMLR (2019)
25. Wang, C., Deng, W.: Representative forgery mining for fake face detection (2021)
26. Wolter, M., Blanke, F., Heese, R., Garcke, J.: Wavelet-packets for deepfake image analysis and detection. Mach. Learn. **111**, 1–33 (2022)
27. Zhong, Z., Zheng, L., Kang, G., Li, S., Yang, Y.: Random erasing data augmentation. In: Proceedings of the AAAI Conference on Artificial Intelligence, vol. 34, pp. 13001–13008 (2020)

Single Image Dehazing Network Based on Serial Feature Attention

Yan Lu[1,2], Miao Liao[1,2(✉)], Shuanhu Di[3], and Yuqian Zhao[4]

[1] School of Computer Science and Engineering,
Hunan University of Science and Technology, Xiangtan 411201, China
`liaomiaohi@163.com`
[2] Hunan Key Laboratory for Services Computing and Novel Software,
Hunan University of Science and Technology, Xiangtan 411201, China
[3] College of Intelligence Science and Technology, National University of Defense
Technology, Changsha 410073, China
[4] School of Automation, Central South University, Changsha 410083, China

Abstract. Images captured under hazy weather conditions often show significant degradation, limiting their applications in military reconnaissance, traffic monitoring, and other fields. To obtain clear and haze free images, the paper proposes a dehazing network based on serial feature attention. The network adaptively captures the inter-dependency between features from channel and spatial perspectives, respectively, learns the weights of features, and uses long and short jump connections to make the network more focused on the important information of haze concentration to improve the network dehazing performance. Extensive experiments are conducted on synthetic and real scene datasets, and the results show that the proposed method recovers haze image with natural colors and high image quality.

Keywords: Image dehazing · Attention mechanism · Deep learning · Feature fusion

1 Introduction

In hazy environments, suspended particles such as fog and haze in the atmosphere have a scattering and absorption effect on visible light. Images acquired by outdoor imaging equipment in this environment often suffer from colour distortion, loss of detail, visual artefacts and low contrast, resulting in less external information being obtained visually through the images and making subsequent processing and analysis of the images difficult. Therefore, how to quickly and effectively implement image dehazing has become a current research hotspot in the field of image processing and computer vision, with important research value and practical significance.

Supported by Hunan Provincial Natural Science Foundation of China (Grant 2021JJ30275) and National Natural Science Foundation of China (Grant 62272161).

Based on the atmospheric scattering model [12–14] and by observational analysis of a large number of haze-free images, He et al. [7] found that some of the pixels in the non-sky regions of the images had pixel values close to zero in at least one colour channel. Based on this discovery, the dark channel a priori dehazing method is proposed. Zhu et al. [19] proposed a method for haze removal based on a colour attenuation prior by assuming that the difference between luminance and saturation is positively correlated with haze concentration. This type of image dehazing algorithm, based on traditional methods, relies on a priori knowledge. Therefore, in some scenarios where the a priori knowledge does not establish, the estimated transmittance will be biased, resulting in poor dehazing results.

With the rapid development of deep learning in the field of computer vision, many scholars have proposed dehazing methods based on convolutional neural networks. Cai et al. [2] built a convolutional neural network model to learn the mapping relationship between the haze image and the transmittance. Ren et al. [16] used a multi-scale convolutional neural network to estimate and refine the transmittance. This type of method makes better use of features by learning the mapping relationship between the haze image and the clear image, resulting in a more realistic dehazed image. Despite the many advantages of CNN-based dehazing methods, there are still some problems, such as small reception fields and poor dehazing of large haze areas.

To address some of the problems of image dehazing, we propose an image dehazing network based on serial feature attention (SFA-Net). This dehazing network adaptively captures the interdependencies between features and learns the weights of features from the perspective of channels and space, respectively. It is also fused with the output features of the feature attention group structure to enhance the valuable features. In addition, we use long and short jump to make the network more focused on important information in dense haze regions and enhancing the dehazing performance of the dehazing network, resulting in high quality and clear dehazed images.

The proposed method, SFA-Net, exhibits the following advantages.

- An image dehazing network based on serial feature attention is proposed for image dehazing, which can remove haze interference while maintaining image colour to obtain haze free images with rich detail and high contrast.
- To enhance the network features, we propose a serial feature attention module, which recalibrates the feature image by serial channel attention and spatial attention.
- By constructing multiple serial feature attention modules and attention group structures, a larger receptive domain is obtained and multiple layers of features are fused.
- Extensive experimental analyses of synthetic and real scene haze image were carried out, and quantitative and qualitative comparisons were made with traditional and deep learning haze removal methods, showing that the proposed method is more effective in removing haze.

2 Related Work

Currently, existing dehazing methods are divided into two main categories: traditional methods and deep learning methods.

2.1 Image Dehazing Based on Traditional Methods

Image dehazing based on traditional methods includes two categories: image enhancement and image restoration. Image enhancement based dehazing algorithms usually do not take into account the formation of haze and the causes of image degradation, but only process images from the perspective of improving visual effects. Haidi et al. [8] use a histogram equalisation algorithm to balance the histogram distribution of the image and expand the dynamic range of the image. This is used to enhance the contrast of the image and to achieve improved image quality. However, the method is less effective at dehazing images where the haze is not uniformly distributed. As a result, many scholars have improved the histogram equalisation algorithm. Stark et al. [17] proposed an adaptive histogram equalisation algorithm to improve the contrast of images. Because the root cause of the image degradation is not considered, but only the contrast of the image is enhanced, the quality of the recovered hazed image is poor. As a result, image restoration based dehazing methods are proposed. This method constructs a physical model of fog map imaging by studying and analysing the causes of image quality degradation, and obtains a clear image by inverse solving. Berman et al. [1] found that pixels with similar colours in real scenes have a linear distribution of their colours in the haze image and used the Hough transform and clustering to estimate atmospheric light and transmittance in an atmospheric scattering model. Zhu et al. [19] proposed a colour attenuation prior based dehazing algorithm by observing a large number of blurred haze images. The algorithm takes advantage of the phenomenon that the colour saturation of pixels in the image attenuates with the depth of the scene to construct a linear model of colour versus scene depth, so as to estimate the scene transmittance and recover a clear image without haze. Methods based on image restoration are prone to over dehazing when performing dehazing, resulting in distorted restored images.

2.2 Image Dehazing Based on Deep Learning Methods

In recent years, many scholars have proposed the use of deep learning methods to deal with the degradation of haze images. Dong et al. [4] proposed a multi-scale enhanced dehazing network based on dense feature fusion to develop a simple and effective enhanced decoder for progressive image recovery by adding an enhancement strategy of "enhancement-operation-subtraction" to the decoder. Zhang et al. [18] proposed a Guided Generative Adversarial Dehazing Network which verifies each layer of the generator's network by adding a bootstrap module to the generator to enhance the detail of the image. Dong et al. [5] proposed

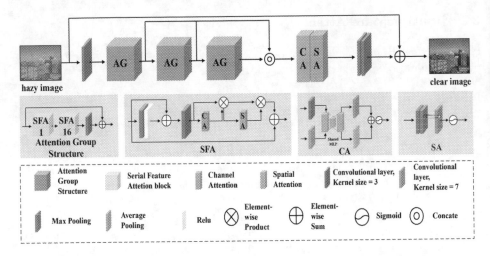

Fig. 1. The architecture of SFA-Net.

a fusion discriminative network model using frequency information as an additional prior, which introduces high and low frequency prior information from clear haze-free images to constrain the generative adversarial network while generating haze-free images to obtain better colour recovery. Deep learning methods for dehazing can learn the complex mapping relationships between haze and clear images directly, without the need to acquire additional prior knowledge. As a result, errors caused by separate estimates of atmospheric light and transmittance can be avoided and clear, haze-free images with true colours and rich detail can be obtained.

3   Method

3.1   SFA-Net Architecture

To obtain a clear haze-free image, we propose the Serial Feature Attention Network (SFA-Net). As shown in Fig. 1, the SFA-Net first passes the input raw haze image to the shallow feature extraction module to extract the features of the image, and then inputs them to the three Feature Attention Group Structure (FAG). Each FAG structure contains a long jump connection and 16 Serial Feature Attention (SFA) modules. Next, the weights of the features are learned adaptively by using Channel Attention (CA) and Spatial Attention (SA) in series in the Serial Feature Attention module, and the weights are fused with the output features of the FAG structure. The features are then further optimised using the channel and spatial attention modules in turn, making the serial feature attention network more focused on dense haze and high frequency texture regions. Finally, clear, haze-free images are obtained by convolutional layers and long jump connections.

3.2 Serial Feature Attention Module

Most image dehazing networks do not take into account that the distribution of haze in natural scenes is uneven and continue to process features equally across channels and spaces. As a result, the recovered dehazed images suffer from the problem of uneven and incomplete dehazing. Based on this, a serial feature attention module is constructed in this paper to enhance the features of the images. The attention mechanism is a common feature enhancement method in computer vision to enhance valuable features and suppress non-valuable features in the image from the channel and spatial perspectives respectively. The serial feature attention module assigns different weights to each channel and spatial feature according to the validity of the image information, enabling recalibration of channel features and spatial features.

As shown in Fig. 1, the serial feature attention module consists of short-hop connections, channel attention and spatial attention. The module uses short-hop connections to skip over unimportant parts of the information such as mist and low frequencies, allowing the main network to pay more attention to the important information. The channel attention module is used to calculate the weights of each channel in the input image, giving more attention to channels containing critical information. Based on the orientation of the channels, the spatial attention module is used to find the regions where the most information is gathered, thus improving the representativeness of the features.

Channel Attention Module. After the convolution operation, the features of different channels represent different information and their importance should be different. Therefore, we propose a channel attention mechanism that adaptively assigns different weights to channel features according to their importance, thus reinforcing important features and suppressing unimportant ones.

First, global pooling and averaging pooling operations are used in the spatial dimension to aggregate the information in the input feature image. Two different channel descriptors are generated: F_{avg}^c and F_{max}^c, denoting the average pooled and maximum pooled features respectively, facili-tate the learning of the channel features later.

$$F_{avg}^c = P_a\left(F\right) = \frac{1}{H \times W} \sum_{i=1}^{H} \sum_{j=1}^{W} x_k\left(i, j\right) \tag{1}$$

$$F_{max}^c = P_m\left(F\right) = \sum_{i=1}^{H} \sum_{j=1}^{W} \max\left(x_k\left(i, j\right)\right) \tag{2}$$

where $x_k(i, j)$ denotes the value of the k-th feature at position (i, j). P_a denotes the average pooling function, P_m denotes the maximum pooling function.

Secondly, the results of the global and average pooling are fed into a shared network that is used to learn the features and importance of the channel dimensions. This shared network consists of a Multi-Layer Perceptron (MLP) with two convolutional layers and a hidden layer. To reduce the parameter overhead, the size of the activation function ReLU for the hidden layer is set to $R^{c/r \times 1 \times 1}$, where r represents the reduction ratio. Then, the output features of the multi-layer perceptron (MLP) are fused by element-wise sum and a sigmoid activation function is used to generate the final channel attention feature image, i.e. $M_c(F)$

$$\begin{aligned} M_c(F) &= \sigma\left(MLP\left(AvgPool\left(F\right)\right) + MLP\left(MaxPool\left(F\right)\right)\right) \\ &= \sigma\left(W_1\left(W_0\left(F^c_{avg}\right)\right) + W_1\left(W_0\left(F^c_{\max}\right)\right)\right) \end{aligned} \tag{3}$$

$$MLP\left(AvgPool\left(F\right)\right) = Conv\left(\delta\left(Conv\left(F^c_{avg}\right)\right)\right) \tag{4}$$

$$MLP\left(MaxPool\left(F\right)\right) = Conv\left(\delta\left(Conv\left(F^c_{\max}\right)\right)\right) \tag{5}$$

where, σ denotes the sigmoid function, δ denotes the ReLU function, $W_0 \in R^{c/r \times c}$, $W_1 \in R^{c \times c/r}$ and the input features F^c_{avg} and $F^c_{\max}$ can share weights W_0 and W_1. Finally, by multiplying the input feature F with the channel attention feature image $M_c(F)$ by element, the output feature F_c is obtained after the channel attention process.

$$F_c = F \otimes M_c(F) \tag{6}$$

Spatial Attention Module. Since the haze concentration is not always consistent throughout the haze image, we use the spatial relationships between features to generate a spatial attention feature image, allowing the network model to focus more on the parts of the image where information is clustered, for example, the dense haze areas and some high frequency texture areas containing rich detail.

First, the feature descriptions are generated by aggregating the channel information of the input features over the channel space using maximum pooling and average pooling operations: F^s_{avg} and $F^s_{\max}$. This compresses the size of the channels and facilitates subsequent learning of the spatial features.

$$F^s_{avg} = P_a\left(F_c\right) = \frac{1}{H \times W} \sum_{i=1}^{H} \sum_{j=1}^{W} x_k\left(i, j\right) \tag{7}$$

$$F^s_{\max} = P_m\left(F_c\right) = \sum_{i=1}^{H} \sum_{j=1}^{W} \max\left(x_k\left(i, j\right)\right) \tag{8}$$

Next, the aggregated features are stitched together by convolutional layers and sigmoid functions to generate a spatially noticed feature image, i.e. $M_s(F)$.

$$\begin{aligned} M_s(F_c) &= \sigma\left(f^{7\times7}\left(\left[AvgPool\left(F_c\right); MaxPool\left(F_c\right)\right]\right)\right) \\ &= \sigma\left(f^{7\times7}\left(\left[F^s_{avg}; F^s_{\max}\right]\right)\right) \end{aligned} \tag{9}$$

where, $f^{7\times7}$ denotes a convolution operation with a filter size of 7×7. Finally, the spatially attended output feature F_s is obtained by multiplying the input feature F with the spatially attended feature map $M_s(F_c)$ by element.

3.3   Attention Group Architecture

The attention group structure consists of 16 serial feature attention modules and long jump connections. The continuous serial feature attention module improves the depth and expressiveness of the feature attention network and enables the network to fit the features better. The long jump connection better solves some complex problems encountered during the training of the serial feature attention network, such as gradient disappearance. It also helps to backpropagate the gradient, speed up the training process, and improve the efficiency of the network.

4   Loss Function

Currently, the majority of loss functions used for image deblurring are $L2$ loss functions, which have many advantages but also many limitations. For example, when using the $L2$ loss function, it needs to be assumed that the noise effects are independent of the local area of the image and are not affected by the local area. In contrast, the sensitivity of the human visual system (HVS) to noise depends on the brightness and contrast of the local area. Therefore, the $L2$ loss function has a poor correlation with the quality of images perceived by humans. lim et al. [11], after extensive experimental analysis, pointed out that better image quality was obtained using the $L1$ loss function during training for many image recovery tasks. On this basis, we used a simple L1 loss function to calculate the loss value between the defogged image and the true clear image obtained by the model.

$$L^{l_1}(x) = \frac{1}{N} \sum_{x=1}^{N} \parallel I_{gt}^x - CSP(I_{hazy}^x) \parallel \qquad (10)$$

where, I_{gt} represents the real scene image and I_{hazy} represents the input hazed image.

5   Experimental Results and Analysis

5.1   Dataset

In this paper, synthetic haze images and their corresponding clear haze-free images from the outdoor training set (OTS) of the RESIDE public dataset [10] were selected as the training set. The 500 synthetic outdoor haze images and clear images from the synthetic object test set (SOTS) of the RESIDE public dataset, and 500 fog images of real scenes collected from Google and Bing were selected as the test set. And, the images are in JPEG format.

5.2   Evaluation Indicator

To further confirm the effectiveness of the method, we use Information Entropy (IE), Peak Signal to Noise Ratio (PSNR) and Structural Similarity (SSIM) to

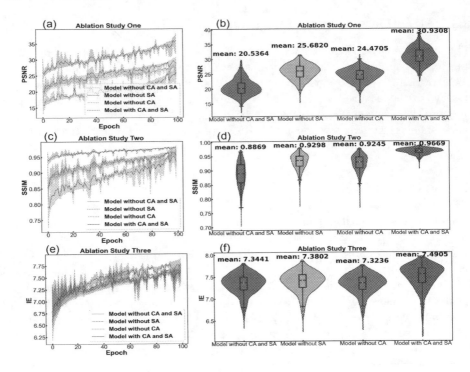

Fig. 2. Ablation study of SFA-Net.

quantitatively evaluate the dehazed images. The information entropy represents the average amount of information in an image. When the pixels are evenly distributed, the image has the most detail and the corresponding IE is the highest, and conversely, when the pixels are concentrated in a narrow interval, the corresponding IE is lower. The PSNR indicates the difference in greyscale between the dehazed image and the true clear reference image, with smaller values indicating more serious image distortion. SSIM is a composite measure of image similarity in terms of brightness, contrast and structural information, respectively, and takes values in the range [0,1], a higher value indicates less distortion in the image.

5.3   Ablation Study

In this section, to further validate the effectiveness of our proposed network, we conduct ablation experiments by considering different attentional modules of our proposed network. We designed the network in four ways: (1) with neither channel nor spatial attention modules, (2) with only spatial attention modules, (3) with only channel attention modules, and (4) with both channel and spatial attention modules. These four networks were then quantitatively analysed on the SOTS test set using three image quality evaluation metrics, IE, PSNR and

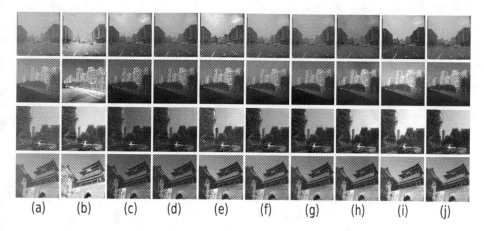

(a)   (b)   (c)   (d)   (e)   (f)   (g)   (h)   (i)   (j)

Fig. 3. Comparison of the results of dehazing using different dehazing methods on the OTS dataset. (a) Haze image, (b) [6], (c) [7], (d) [19], (e) [1], (f) [2], (g) [9], (h) [3], (i) [15], and (j) Ours.

Table 1. Performance comparison of dehazing using different methods on OTS datasets (mean value).

Indicators	[6]	[7]	[19]	[1]	[2]	[9]	[3]	[15]	Ours
IE	7.40	7.30	7.42	7.47	7.48	7.38	7.35	7.51	7.72
PSNR	16.13	19.18	21.10	18.86	23.23	23.62	25.14	29.18	31.16
SSIM	0.83	0.88	0.87	0.86	0.91	0.88	0.94	0.96	0.97

SSIM. The evaluation results are shown in Fig. 2. It can be seen that the values of IE, PSNR and SSIM of our proposed dehazing network containing both channel and spatial attention modules are significantly higher than those of the other two networks, indicating that both the channel attention module and the spatial attention module play a crucial role in the network performance, further validating the rationality and effectiveness of our proposed dehazing network.

5.4 Results Analysis

Comparison of the Dehazing Effect of Synthetic Haze Images. To verify the dehazing effect of the algorithm in this paper, we selected eight classical methods to compare the dehazing effect of the synthetic haze images in the OTS dataset, where column (a) is the original hazed image, and columns (b) to (j) are the [1–3,6,7,9,15,19], and the method in this paper respectively. Some of the image dehazing results are shown in Fig. 3. The dehazed images obtained by the methods of [2,6,9,15] all suffer from incomplete dehazing. The images from [7,19] are darker overall. The dehazed images from [1,3,6] suffer from oversaturation and colour shift in some sky areas. Our method effectively overcomes these problems by effectively removing the haze while maintaining the colour of

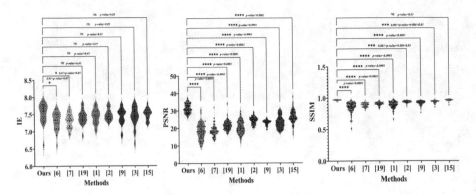

Fig. 4. Comparative analysis of significant differences between our proposed method and the comparison method on IE, PSNR and SSIM indicators.

Table 2. Performance comparison of dehazing using different methods in real scenarios (mean value).

Indicators	[6]	[7]	[19]	[1]	[2]	[9]	[3]	[15]	Ours
IE	6.81	7.02	7.23	7.31	7.06	6.85	7.20	7.34	7.64

the image, resulting in a more detailed and realistic dehazed image. The visual effect of the image is significantly better than other dehazing methods.

In addition, the information entropy (IE), peak signal-to-noise ratio (PSNR) and structural similarity (SSIM) were used to quantitatively evaluate the dehazed images, and the mean values obtained are shown in Table 1. It can be seen that the IE of the dehazed images obtained by this method is higher than that of other methods, with a mean value of 7.72. This indicates that the dehazed images obtained by this method are richer in colour and detail and more informative. The PSNR and SSIM of the images processed by this method are also significantly higher than those of other methods, with mean values of 31.16 and 0.97 respectively, indicating that the dehazed images obtained by this method are closer to the real haze-free images, and the distortion of the images is smaller. To make the evaluated metrics statistically significant, we compared statistical differences in mean of the indicators between methods using One-Way ANOVA. As shown in Fig. 4, the statistics of different methods on PSNR and SSIM indicators are obviously different (p-value<0.0001), whereas on IE indicator, this difference is not obvious. This indicates that the PSNR and SSIM indicators can reflect the defogging performance of the algorithms in a large extent.

Comparison of the Dehazing Effect of Real Scene Haze Images. For the practical application environment of image dehazing, we give a comparison of the effectiveness of various algorithms to dehaze real scene haze images. As

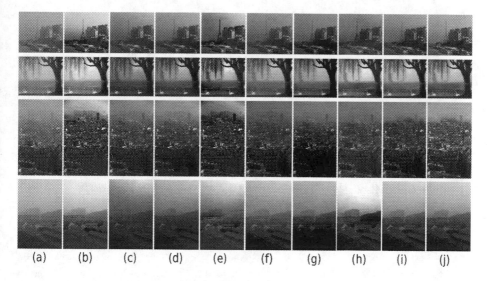

(a)   (b)   (c)   (d)   (e)   (f)   (g)   (h)   (i)   (j)

Fig. 5. Comparison of the results of dehazing using different dehazing methods in real scenarios. (a) Haze image, (b) citefattal2008single, (c) [7], (d) citezhu2015fast, (e) [1], (f) [2], (g) [9], (h) [3], (i) [15], and (j) Ours.

shown in Fig. 5, where (a) is the original hazed image and (b) to (i) are the dehazing results of the [1–3, 6, 7, 9, 15, 19], and this paper's methods, respectively. The dehazed images obtained by the methods of [1, 7, 9] all have halo, noise and colour shift. The dehazed images obtained by the methods of [1, 7, 19] suffer from colour oversaturation in the sky region. After the method of [9], the overall colour of the image is dark and the details are not clear. The dehazed images obtained by [2, 15] are not as bright and clear as those in this paper.

In addition, we used information entropy (IE) to quantitatively evaluate the four images in Fig. 5 and the 500 haze images of real scenes obtained from Google and Bing for the dehazing images, and the results are shown in Table 2. It can be seen that the IE calculated by the method in this paper are higher than the dehazing method shown in the paper. This indicates that the clear images obtained using the method in this paper contain more information and have better dehazing effects.

6   Conclusion

In order to obtain high quality clear images, we propose a SFA-Net, which can effectively process images containing different weight information by means of serial channels and spatial attention mechanism. And a large number of experiments are conducted on public datasets and natural scene haze images. The results show that the algorithm in this paper can effectively remove the interference of haze in images, overcome the problems of colour bias, halation, artefacts and noise in the images after the dehazing process, and obtain clear and natural haze-free images with rich details and high colour fidelity.

References

1. Berman, D., Treibitz, T., Avidan, S.: Single image dehazing using haze-lines. IEEE Trans. Pattern Anal. Mach. Intell. **42**(3), 720–734 (2018)
2. Cai, B., Xu, X., Jia, K., Qing, C., Tao, D.: Dehazenet: an end-to-end system for single image haze removal. IEEE Trans. Image Process. **25**(11), 5187–5198 (2016)
3. Chen, D., et al.: Gated context aggregation network for image dehazing and deraining. In: 2019 IEEE Winter Conference on Applications of Computer Vision (WACV), pp. 1375–1383. IEEE (2019)
4. Dong, H., et al.: Multi-scale boosted dehazing network with dense feature fusion. In: Proceedings of the IEEE/CVF Conference on Computer Vision and Pattern Recognition, pp. 2157–2167 (2020)
5. Dong, Y., Liu, Y., Zhang, H., Chen, S., Qiao, Y.: FD-GAN: generative adversarial networks with fusion-discriminator for single image dehazing. In: Proceedings of the AAAI Conference on Artificial Intelligence, vol. 34, pp. 10729–10736 (2020)
6. Fattal, R.: Single image dehazing. ACM Trans. Graph. (TOG) **27**(3), 1–9 (2008)
7. He, K., Sun, J., Tang, X.: Single image haze removal using dark channel prior. IEEE Trans. Pattern Anal. Mach. Intell. **33**(12), 2341–2353 (2010)
8. Ibrahim, H., Kong, N.S.P.: Brightness preserving dynamic histogram equalization for image contrast enhancement. IEEE Trans. Consum. Electron. **53**(4), 1752–1758 (2007)
9. Li, B., Peng, X., Wang, Z., Xu, J., Feng, D.: AOD-Net: all-in-one dehazing network. In: Proceedings of the IEEE International Conference on Computer Vision, pp. 4770–4778 (2017)
10. Li, B., et al.: Benchmarking single-image dehazing and beyond. IEEE Trans. Image Process. **28**(1), 492–505 (2018)
11. Lim, B., Son, S., Kim, H., Nah, S., Mu Lee, K.: Enhanced deep residual networks for single image super-resolution. In: Proceedings of the IEEE Conference on Computer Vision and Pattern Recognition Workshops, pp. 136–144 (2017)
12. McCartney, E.J.: Optics of the atmosphere: scattering by molecules and particles. New York (1976)
13. Narasimhan, S.G., Nayar, S.K.: Chromatic framework for vision in bad weather. In: Proceedings IEEE Conference on Computer Vision and Pattern Recognition, CVPR 2000 (Cat. No. PR00662), vol. 1, pp. 598–605. IEEE (2000)
14. Narasimhan, S.G., Nayar, S.K.: Vision and the atmosphere. Int. J. Comput. Vision **48**(3), 233 (2002)
15. Qin, X., Wang, Z., Bai, Y., Xie, X., Jia, H.: FFA-Net: feature fusion attention network for single image dehazing. In: Proceedings of the AAAI Conference on Artificial Intelligence, vol. 34, pp. 11908–11915 (2020)
16. Ren, W., Liu, S., Zhang, H., Pan, J., Cao, X., Yang, M.-H.: Single image dehazing via multi-scale convolutional neural networks. In: Leibe, B., Matas, J., Sebe, N., Welling, M. (eds.) ECCV 2016. LNCS, vol. 9906, pp. 154–169. Springer, Cham (2016). https://doi.org/10.1007/978-3-319-46475-6_10
17. Stark, J.A.: Adaptive image contrast enhancement using generalizations of histogram equalization. IEEE Trans. Image Process. **9**(5), 889–896 (2000)

18. Zhang, J., Dong, Q., Song, W.: GGADN: guided generative adversarial dehazing network. Soft. Comput. **27**(3), 1731–1741 (2023)
19. Zhu, Q., Mai, J., Shao, L.: A fast single image haze removal algorithm using color attenuation prior. IEEE Trans. Image Process. **24**(11), 3522–3533 (2015)

Single Image Super-Resolution with Sequential Multi-axis Blocked Attention

Bincheng Yang[✉] and Gangshan Wu

Nanjing University, Nanjing 210023, Jiangsu, People's Republic of China
yangbincheng@hotmail.com, gswu@nju.edu.cn
http://mcg.nju.edu.cn/en/index.html

Abstract. Single image super-resolution is an ill-posed inverse problem which has no unique solution because the low resolution image can be mapped to many different undegraded high resolution images. Previous methods based on deep neural networks try to utilize non-local attention mechanisms to leverage self-similarity prior in natural images in order to tackle the ill-posedness of SISR and improve the performance for SISR. However, because non-local attention has a quadratic order computation complexity with respect to the number of attention locations and the very big spatial sizes of feature maps of SISR networks, the non-local attention mechanisms utilized in current methods can not achieve a good trade-off between global modelling capability of self-similarity to improve performance and lower computation complexity to be efficient and scalable. In this paper, we propose to utilize a sequential multi-axis blocked attention (S-MXBA) mechanism in a deep neural network (MXBASRN) to achieve a good trade-off between performance and efficiency for SISR. S-MXBA splits the input feature map into blocks of appropriate size to balance the size of each block and the number of all the blocks, then does non-local attention inside each block followed by non-local attention to the same relative locations across all blocks. In this way, MXBASRN both improves global modelling capability of self-similarity to boost performance and decreases computation complexity to sub-quadratic order to be more efficient and scalable. Experiments demonstrate MXBASRN works effectively and efficiently for SISR compared to state-of-the-art methods. Especially, MXBASRN achieves comparable performance to recent non-local attention based SISR methods of NLSN and ENLCN with about one-third parameters of them. Code will be available at https://github.com/yangbincheng/MXBASRN.

Keywords: Single image super-resolution · Multi-axis blocked attention · Deep neural network

---

Supported by Nanjing University.

L. Iliadis et al. (Eds.): ICANN 2023, LNCS 14256, pp. 136–148, 2023.
https://doi.org/10.1007/978-3-031-44213-1_12

1   Introduction

Singe image super-resolution (SISR) is the task of reconstructing a high resolution (HR) image from only one low resolution (LR) input image. There are many applications such as satellite and aerial imaging, security and surveillance, and medical image for SISR. It is an ill-posed inverse problem because there are many different HR images that can be degraded to the input LR image. How to use different image priors is the key to tackle the ill-posedness of SISR.

Since the pioneer work of Dong *et al.* [2] uses a three layer convolutional neural network (SRCNN) to solve SISR problem, deep convolutional neural network based methods have been studied extensively to boost performance for SISR. The re-occurrences of small patches in the same image are demonstrated as a strong image prior in natural images [19], which is so-called self-similarity prior. Non-local attention mechanisms can be used in deep convolutional neural networks to model self-similarity in input LR image to improve reconstruction performance for SISR [1, 8–10, 15, 18].

Although non-local attention mechanisms have been utilized in deep neural networks to leverage self-similarity prior to make progress for SISR, current methods have some drawbacks. Because the computation complexity of non-local attention is asymptotic quadratic order with respect to the number of attention locations and the feature maps in SISR networks have very big spatial sizes, various non-local attention mechanisms have been studied for SISR. One category of methods, such as RNAN [15], SAN [1] and CSNLN [10], apply non-local attention to all the spatial locations of feature maps to leverage self-similarity globally and fully, they have an asymptotic quadratic complexity with respect to the spatial size of feature map to be inefficient and unscalable. Another category of methods, such as NLRN [8], utilize a large local window of constant size to do non-local attention to lower computation complexity to asymptotic linear order with respect to the spatial size of feature map, but they lose global modelling capability of self-similarity. Except these two categories, recent methods IGNN [18] and NLSN [9] constrain non-local attention to a constant number of spatial locations either to k nearest neighbors of query feature or to a constant number of features with similar locality sensitive hashing codes to the query feature respectively. Although they achieve global modelling capability of self-similarity approximately and reduce non-local attention operations alone to asymptotic linear complexity with respect to the spatial size of feature map, because the complexity to compute k nearest neighbors of whole feature map or the complexity of compute all the locality sensitive hashing codes of whole feature map are asymptotic quadratic order with respect to the spatial size of feature map, they still have total complexity of asymptotic quadratic order with respect to the spatial size of feature map. To sum up, current non-local attention based SISR networks can not achieve a good trade-off between global modelling capability of self-similarity to improve performance and a lower computation complexity to be efficient and scalable for SISR.

To overcome these drawbacks, we propose to utilize a sequential multi-axis blocked attention (S-MXBA) mechanism in a deep convolutional neural network

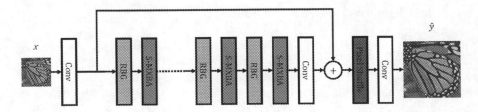

Fig. 1. The architecture of MXBASRN.

(MXBASRN) for single image super-resolution task. S-MXBA is inspired by HiT [17], which uses a parallel multi-axis blocked attention mechanism in a transformer for image generation task from an input random vector. S-MXBA first splits the input feature map into non-overlapping blocks of appropriate size to balance the size of each block and the number of all blocks, then utilizes sequential mixing of attentions on two axes, i.e., block attention and grid attention. Block attention performs non-local attention among locations inside each block separately, while grid attention performs non-local attention among the same relative locations across all blocks. In this way, S-MXBA can achieve better global modelling capability of self-similarity to improve performance while having an asymptotic sub-quadratic computation complexity with respect to the spatial size of feature map to be more efficient and scalable. In order to make training of network more stable, layer normalization and residual connection are used for block attention and grid attention. Multiple S-MXBA modules are used in the MXBASRN so that block attention and grid attention are executed alternately to strengthen information interaction and global modelling capability of self-similarity.

In summary, our main contributions are as follows:

- We propose to utilize a sequential multi-axis blocked attention (S-MXBA) mechanism in a deep neural network (MXBASRN) for SISR, which achieves a good trade-off between global modelling capability of self-similarity to improve performance and an asymptotic sub-quadratic complexity with respect to the spatial size of feature map to be more efficient and scalable.
- Ablation studies investigate various ways of using attention mechanisms and demonstrate effectiveness of proposed S-MXBA for SISR.
- Experiments show proposed MXBASRN works effectively and efficiently for SISR on standard benchmark data sets compared to state-of-the-art methods.

2   Method

2.1   Network Structure

Our proposed MXBASRN is shown in Fig. 1. In order to demonstrate the effectiveness of S-MXBA for SISR, we construct a Baseline model which is the model

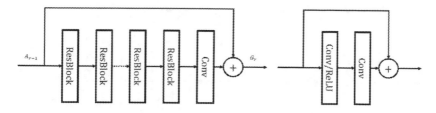

Fig. 2. The structure of RBG (left) and ResBlock (right).

of RCAN [14] with channel attention removed. Then we insert a S-MXBA module after each Residual Block Group (RBG) in the Baseline Model to form MXBASRN. The Residual Block Group (RBG) and Residual Block (ResBlock) are illustrated in Fig. 2 for completeness.

Let's denote x as the LR input of the network, $\widehat{y}$ as the HR output of the network and y as the ground truth HR image.

At first, a 3×3 convolution layer is used to extract low level features from network input x,

$$A_0 = F_0 = Conv(x), \tag{1}$$

where $Conv$ denotes a 3×3 convolution layer, F_0 denotes the extracted features to be sent to the first RBG.

Secondly, R RBGs and R S-MXBA modules are stacked alternately to extract rich convolutional features by modelling global self-similarity efficiently,

$$G_r = f_{RBG,r}(A_{r-1}), r = 1, 2, ..., R, \tag{2}$$

$$A_r = f_{S-MXBA,r}(G_r), r = 1, 2, ..., R, \tag{3}$$

where $f_{RBG,r}$ and G_r denote the function and output of r-th RBG, $f_{S-MXBA,r}$ and A_r denote the function and output of r-th S-MXBA module.

Next, the rich features output by the final S-MXBA module (denoted as A_R) are processed by a 3×3 convolution layer, then the output is added to the output of the first convolution layer in the network (denoted as F_0),

$$F_{Recon} = F_0 + Conv(A_R). \tag{4}$$

Finally, F_{Recon} is used to reconstruct high resolution image by a pixel shuffle layer [12] and a 3×3 convolution layer,

$$\widehat{y} = Conv(f_{PS}(F_{Recon})), \tag{5}$$

where f_{PS} denotes the function of the pixel shuffle layer.

2.2 Sequential Multi-axis Blocked Non-local Attention

Current non-local attention based SISR networks either attend to a local window of constant size to lower computation complexity therefore impede global modelling capability of self-similarity, or try to enforce global modelling capability

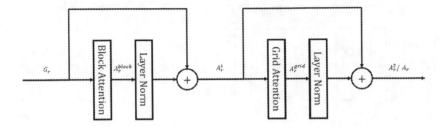

Fig. 3. The structure of S-MXBA.

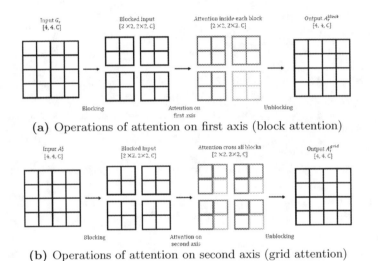

(a) Operations of attention on first axis (block attention)

(b) Operations of attention on second axis (grid attention)

Fig. 4. Illustration of operations of block attention and grid attention. Attention is performed between the locations with the same color.

of self-similarity but have quadratic order computation complexity to be inefficient and unscalable for SISR. Inspired by parallel multi-axis blocked attention [17], which is originally used in a transformer for image generation task from an input random vector, we propose to use a sequential multi-axis blocked attention (S-MXBA) mechanism as shown in Fig. 3 in a deep neural network to improve global modelling capability of self-similarity prior more efficiently.

Assuming the input feature map has the spatial dimensions of (H, W) and the spatial size of $S = H \times W$. S-MXBA first pads the input feature map to $(\lceil\sqrt{H}\rceil^2, \lceil\sqrt{W}\rceil^2)$ by zeros, and splits the input feature map into blocks of spatial size $(\lceil\sqrt{H}\rceil, \lceil\sqrt{W}\rceil)$ without overlapping. The relative locations in each block are numbered from 1 to $\lceil\sqrt{H}\rceil \times \lceil\sqrt{W}\rceil$ in the same way, all the blocks are also numbered from 1 to $\lceil\sqrt{H}\rceil \times \lceil\sqrt{W}\rceil$. Then S-MXBA performs attention on two different axes sequentially. The attention on first axis of S-MXBA performs non-local attention among all locations inside each block separately, we call it "block attention", and the attention on second axis of S-MXBA performs non-local attention among the same relative locations across all blocks, we call it "grid attention". The interaction between block attention and grid attention helps to improve global modelling capability of self-similarity. In order to ease information flow and make optimization stable, we use a layer normalization layer and a residual connection for block attention and grid attention inside S-MXBA. The proposed S-MXBA for SISR can be formulated as follows:

$$A_{r,b,l}^{block} = \Sigma_{m:m\in L}\frac{exp(\phi_r^1(G_{r,b,l})^T\phi_r^1(G_{r,b,m}))}{\Sigma_{n:n\in L}exp(\phi_r^1(G_{r,b,l})^T\phi_r^1(G_{r,b,n}))}\psi_r^1(G_{r,b,m}), \qquad (6)$$

$$A_r^1 = G_r + LN(A_r^{block}), \qquad (7)$$

$$A_{r,b,l}^{grid} = \Sigma_{c:c\in B}\frac{exp(\phi_r^2(A_{r,b,l}^1)^T\phi_r^2(A_{r,c,l}^1))}{\Sigma_{d:d\in B}exp(\phi_r^2(A_{r,b,l}^1)^T\phi_r^2(A_{r,d,l}^1))}\psi_r^2(A_{r,c,l}^1), \qquad (8)$$

$$A_r = A_r^2 = A_r^1 + LN(A_r^{grid}), \qquad (9)$$

where $r \in \{1, 2, ..., R\}$ which denotes the set of the indices for RBGs or S-MXBA modules, $b \in B = \{1, 2, ..., \lceil\sqrt{H}\rceil \times \lceil\sqrt{W}\rceil\}$, $l \in L = \{1, 2, ..., \lceil\sqrt{H}\rceil \times \lceil\sqrt{W}\rceil\}$, B denotes the set of indices for all the blocks, L denotes the set of all the relative locations in each block, LN denotes the function of layer normalization, $G_{r,b,l}$ denotes the feature at the l-th relative location in the b-th block of G_r, the meaning of subscripts for $A_{r,b,l}^{block}$, $A_{r,b,l}^1$, $A_{r,b,l}^{grid}$, $A_{r,b,l}^2$ and $A_{r,b,l}$ is the same, ϕ_r^1 and ϕ_r^2 denote linear transforms for queries with keys of block attention and grid attention in r-th S-MXBA module respectively, ψ_r^1 and ψ_r^2 denote linear transforms for values of block attention and grid attention in r-th S-MXBA module respectively. The operations of 6 and 8 are illustrated in Fig. 4(a) and Fig. 4(b) respectively.

It is worth noting that the proposed S-MXBA has an asymptotic $O(\sqrt{S}S)$ complexity because the way of splitting input feature map into non-overlapping blocks of appropriate size to balance the size of each block and the number of all blocks following the strategy in HiT [17]. The size of each block will be $(\lceil\sqrt{H}\rceil \times \lceil\sqrt{W}\rceil \approx \sqrt{S})$ and there will be $(\lceil\sqrt{H}\rceil \times \lceil\sqrt{W}\rceil \approx \sqrt{S})$ blocks. So the complexity of attention on each axis will all be $(O(\sqrt{S}\sqrt{S}\sqrt{S}) = O(\sqrt{S}S))$.

2.3 Training Loss

Given a set of training image pairs $\{x_{(n)}, y_{(n)}\}_{n=1}^N$, the following Mean Absolute Error (MAE) loss is minimized for MXBASRN:

$$J(\Theta) = \frac{1}{N}\sum_{n=1}^N ||y_{(n)} - \widehat{y_{(n)}}||_1, \qquad (10)$$

where Θ is the parameters of MXBASRN.

Table 1. Average PSNR/SSIM metrics of various strategies of mixing block attention, grid attention and channel attention for ablation study. Best is in red, and second best is in blue.

Method	Scale	Set5		Set14		B100		Urban100		Manga109	
		PSNR	SSIM	PSNR	SSIM	PSNR	SSIM	PSNR	SSIM	PSNR	SSIM
Baseline	×2	38.20	0.9611	34.03	0.9217	32.36	0.9020	32.99	0.9361	39.21	0.9779
Baseline+CA	×2	38.26	0.9615	34.05	0.9215	32.37	0.9022	33.16	0.9373	39.33	0.9784
Baseline+BA	×2	38.22	0.9613	33.99	0.9215	32.38	0.9022	33.14	0.9375	39.36	0.9781
baseline+GA	×2	38.27	0.9616	34.09	0.9216	32.40	0.9026	33.24	0.9384	39.45	0.9787
Baseline+PBG	×2	38.27	0.9616	34.10	0.9226	32.40	0.9025	33.29	0.9386	39.49	0.9785
Baseline+SGB	×2	38.25	0.9616	34.22	0.9230	32.41	0.9026	33.34	0.9389	39.56	0.9789
Baseline+SBG	×2	38.30	0.9617	34.22	0.9236	32.41	0.9027	33.41	0.9393	39.57	0.9786
Baseline+SBG+CA	×2	38.29	0.9617	34.06	0.9217	32.42	0.9028	33.41	0.9396	39.55	0.9786

3   Experiments

3.1   Datasets and Evaluation Metrics

We use DIV2K as training set, five standard benchmark data sets, Set5, Set14, BSD100, Urban100 and Manga109, for performance evaluation. HR images and corresponding LR images downsampled using bicubic interpolation are provided in DIV2K dataset. Two kinds of data augmentation during training are used: 1) Rotate the images of 90, 180, 270°; 2) Flip the images vertically. Peak signal-to-noise ratio (PSNR) and structural similarity index (SSIM) are used as evaluation metrics. The networks are trained using all three RGB channels and tested from Y channel of YCbCr color space of images.

3.2   Implementation Details

The MXBASRN used in experiments has 6 RBGs, and 6 S-MXBA modules with one S-MXBA module after each RBG. Each RBG has 8 ResBlocks. The width of network is set to 128, except that the last 3×3 convolutional layer outputs reconstructed HR color image, that the ϕ^1 and ϕ^2 linear transformation layers in S-MXBA modules output 32 features to compute similarities and attention scores and that the pixel shuffle layers in upsampling head output 64 features. All layers use 3×3 convolutional kernels except that the ψ^1 and ψ^2 linear transformation layers in S-MXBA modules use 1×1 kernels to transform features before fusion using attention scores. Mini-batch size is set to 16 due to memory limit. We use 64×64 LR image patches and corresponding HR image patches for ×2, ×3, ×4 scale factors to train our models. At each iteration of training MXBASRN for each scale factor, we first sample an image pair from all pairs of corresponding HR and LR images uniformly, then we sample a training patch pair from the sampled image pair uniformly. Adam optimizer [5] is used to train the network weights, learning rate is initialized to 1×10^{-4}. We train our network for 1×10^6 iterations for each scale factor, the learning rate is step-decayed by 2 after 2×10^5 iterations. We implement MXBASRN with PyTorch framework.

Table 2. Average PSNR/SSIM metrics of compared methods for scale factors ×2, ×3, ×4 on benchmark datasets. Best is in red, and second best is in blue.

Method	Scale	Set5		Set14		B100		Urban100		Manga109	
		PSNR	SSIM	PSNR	SSIM	PSNR	SSIM	PSNR	SSIM	PSNR	SSIM
EDSR [7]	×2	38.11	0.9602	33.92	0.9195	32.32	0.9013	32.93	0.9351	39.10	0.9773
D-DBPN [3]	×2	38.09	0.9600	33.85	0.9190	32.27	0.9000	32.55	0.9324	38.89	0.9775
RDN [16]	×2	38.24	0.9614	34.01	0.9212	32.34	0.9017	32.89	0.9353	39.18	0.9780
RCAN [14]	×2	38.27	0.9614	34.12	0.9216	32.41	0.9027	33.34	0.9384	39.44	0.9786
MSRN [6]	×2	38.08	0.9605	33.74	0.9170	32.23	0.9013	32.22	0.9326	38.82	0.9868
NLRN [8]	×2	38.00	0.9603	33.46	0.9159	32.19	0.8992	31.81	0.9249	-	-
RNAN [15]	×2	38.17	0.9611	33.87	0.9207	32.32	0.9014	32.73	0.9340	39.23	0.9785
SAN [1]	×2	38.31	0.9620	34.07	0.9213	32.42	0.9028	33.10	0.9370	39.32	0.9792
OISR-RK3 [4]	×2	38.21	0.9612	33.94	0.9206	32.36	0.9019	33.03	0.9365	-	-
IGNN [18]	×2	38.24	0.9613	34.07	0.9217	32.41	0.9025	33.23	0.9383	39.35	0.9786
HAN [11]	×2	38.27	0.9614	34.16	0.9217	32.41	0.9027	33.35	0.9385	39.46	0.9785
NLSN [9]	×2	38.34	0.9618	34.08	0.9231	32.43	0.9027	33.42	0.9394	39.59	0.9789
ENLCN [13]	×2	38.37	0.9618	34.17	0.9229	32.49	0.9032	33.56	0.9398	39.64	0.9791
MXBASRN (Ours)	×2	38.30	0.9617	34.22	0.9236	32.41	0.9027	33.41	0.9393	39.57	0.9786
MXBASRN+ (Ours)	×2	38.36	0.9619	34.37	0.9246	32.46	0.9032	33.60	0.9407	39.75	0.9791
EDSR [7]	×3	34.65	0.9280	30.52	0.8462	29.25	0.8093	28.80	0.8653	34.17	0.9476
RDN [16]	×3	34.71	0.9296	30.57	0.8468	29.26	0.8093	28.80	0.8653	34.13	0.9484
RCAN [14]	×3	34.74	0.9299	30.65	0.8482	29.32	0.8111	29.09	0.8702	34.44	0.9499
NLRN [8]	×3	34.27	0.9266	30.16	0.8374	29.06	0.8026	27.93	0.8453	-	-
RNAN [15]	×3	34.66	0.9290	30.52	0.8462	29.26	0.8090	28.75	0.8646	34.25	0.9483
SAN [1]	×3	34.75	0.9300	30.59	0.8476	29.33	0.8112	28.93	0.8671	34.30	0.9494
OISR-RK3 [4]	×3	34.72	0.9297	30.57	0.8470	29.29	0.8103	28.95	0.8680	-	-
IGNN [18]	×3	34.72	0.9298	30.66	0.8484	29.31	0.8105	29.03	0.8696	34.39	0.9496
HAN [11]	×3	34.75	0.9299	30.67	0.8483	29.32	0.8110	29.10	0.8705	34.48	0.9500
NLSN [9]	×3	34.85	0.9306	30.70	0.8485	29.34	0.8117	29.25	0.8726	34.57	0.9508
MXBASRN (Ours)	×3	34.83	0.9305	30.68	0.8485	29.34	0.8115	29.15	0.8708	34.66	0.9510
MXBASRN+ (Ours)	×3	34.91	0.9310	30.80	0.8502	29.41	0.8125	29.35	0.8737	34.98	0.9524
EDSR [7]	×4	32.46	0.8968	28.80	0.7876	27.71	0.7420	26.64	0.8033	31.02	0.9148
D-DBPN [3]	×4	32.47	0.8980	28.82	0.7860	27.72	0.7400	26.38	0.7946	30.91	0.9137
RDN [16]	×4	32.47	0.8990	28.81	0.7871	27.72	0.7419	26.61	0.8028	31.00	0.9151
RCAN [14]	×4	32.63	0.9002	28.87	0.7889	27.77	0.7436	26.82	0.8087	31.22	0.9173
MSRN [6]	×4	32.07	0.8903	28.60	0.7751	27.52	0.7273	26.04	0.7896	30.17	0.9034
NLRN [8]	×4	31.92	0.8916	28.36	0.7745	27.48	0.7306	25.79	0.7729	-	-
RNAN [15]	×4	32.49	0.8982	28.83	0.7878	27.72	0.7421	26.61	0.8023	31.09	0.9149
SAN [1]	×4	32.64	0.9003	28.92	0.7888	27.78	0.7436	26.79	0.8068	31.18	0.9169
OISR-RK3 [4]	×4	32.53	0.8992	28.86	0.7878	27.75	0.7428	26.79	0.8068	-	-
IGNN [18]	×4	32.57	0.8998	28.85	0.7891	27.77	0.7434	26.84	0.8090	31.28	0.9182
HAN [11]	×4	32.64	0.9002	28.90	0.7890	27.80	0.7442	26.85	0.8094	31.42	0.9177
NLSN [9]	×4	32.59	0.9000	28.87	0.7891	27.78	0.7444	26.96	0.8109	31.27	0.9184
ENLCN [13]	×4	32.67	0.9004	28.94	0.7892	27.82	0.7452	27.12	0.8141	31.33	0.9188
MXBASRN (Ours)	×4	32.67	0.9000	28.89	0.7888	27.75	0.7432	26.88	0.8098	31.36	0.9189
MXBASRN+ (Ours)	×4	32.76	0.9015	28.99	0.7907	27.84	0.7450	27.07	0.8136	31.73	0.9219

3.3   Ablation Study

To validate effectiveness of proposed S-MXBA for SISR, we do ablation study for various strategies of mixing block attention, grid attention and channel attention. Baseline (no attention) refers to modified MXBASRN model with S-MXBA modules removed. Baseline+CA (channel attention) is the model with channel attention inserted after the second convolution layer of each ResBlock of Baseline model, which is the same model as RCAN [14]. Baseline+BA (block attention) refers to modified MXBASRN model with grid attention in S-MXBA replaced by block attention. Baseline+GA (grid attention) refers to modified MXBASRN model with block attention in S-MXBA replaced by grid attention. Baseline+PBG (parallel block attention and grid attention) refers to modified MXBASRN model with the S-MXBA replaced by a parallel block attention and grid attention structure, which is formed by parallel block attention and grid attention, then an 1×1 fusion convolution layer followed by layer normalization and residual connection. Baseline+SGB (sequential grid attention and block attention) refers to modified MXBASRN model with the order of block attention and grid attention in S-MXBA reversed. Baseline+SBG (sequential block attention and grid attention, i.e., S-MXBA) refers to our MXBASRN. Baseline+SBG+CA (sequential block attention and grid attention with channel attention) refers to modified MXBASRN model with channel attention inserted after the second convolution layer of each ResBlock of MXBASRN model.

Fig. 5. The image from Manga109 with an upscaling factor 3.

The results are shown in Table 1. The following facts can be observed. First, Baseline+SBG (S-MXBA) has the best performance compared to other mixing strategies of block and grid attention. Second, Baseline+SBG (S-MXBA) improves the Baseline model significantly and is better than Baseline+CA which uses channel attention mechanism. Finally, Baseline+SBG+CA which combines Baseline-SBG and channel attention does not improve the performance of Baseline+SBG. So we choose Baseline+SBG as our model and name it as MXBASRN in this paper.

We also investigate the effect of number of S-MXBA modules to performance for SISR. The S-MXBA modules are added from the last RBG to the first RBG step by step. As shown in Fig. 7, more S-MXBA modules will achieve better performance.

3.4 Comparison with State-of-the-Art Methods

We compare our method with EDSR [7], D-DBPN [3], RDN [16], RCAN [14], MSRN [6], NLRN [8], RNAN [15], SAN [1], OISR-RK3 [4], IGNN [18], HAN [11], NLSN [9] and ENLCN [13] which also base on convolutional neural networks to validate effectiveness and efficiency of MXBASRN. We also adopt self-ensemble strategy [7] to improve MXBASRN following the literature and MXBASRN with self-ensemble strategy is denoted as MXBASRN+.

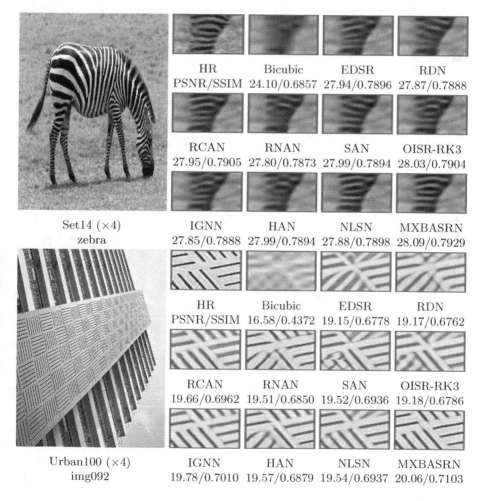

Fig. 6. The images from Set14 and Urban100 with an upscaling factor 4.

The peak signal-to-noise ratio (PSNR) and the structural similarity index measure (SSIM) evaluation metrics of compared methods on five benchmark datasets are shown in Table 2. Our method is on par with other state-of-the-art methods on different combinations of scale factors and benchmark datasets.

Figure 5 and Fig. 6 show visual comparisons. As shown in *zebra* from Set14, *img*092 from Urban100 and *Hamlet* from Manga109, our method reconstructs clearer edges, more textures, less artifacts, less blurring of images than other state-of-the-art methods.

We also investigate performance and number of parameters of compared methods. As shown in Fig. 8, our method achieves a good trade-off between performance and number of parameters compared with other state-of-the-art methods. It is worth noting our method achieves comparable performance to recent non-local attention based SISR methods of NLSN [9] and ENLCN [13] with about one-third parameters of them.

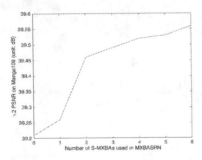

Fig. 7. The effect of different number of S-MXBAs to performance.

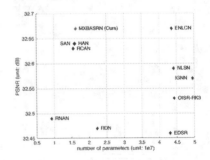

Fig. 8. Comparison for ×4 PSNR on Set5 and number of parameters.

4   Conclusion

In this work, we propose to utilize a sequential multi-axis blocked attention (S-MXBA) mechanism in a deep neural network (MXBASRN) for SISR, which has the benefits of both good global modelling capability of self-similarity to improve performance and an asymptotic $O(\sqrt{S}S)$ complexity to be more efficient and scalable (S is the spatial size of feature map). Ablation studies demonstrate effectiveness of the proposed sequential multi-axis blocked attention (S-MXBA) for SISR and experiments show our MXBASRN works effectively and efficiently for SISR compared to state-of-the-art methods.

References

1. Dai, T., Cai, J., Zhang, Y., Xia, S., Zhang, L.: Second-order attention network for single image super-resolution. In: 2019 IEEE/CVF Conference on Computer Vision and Pattern Recognition (CVPR), pp. 11057–11066 (2019)

2. Dong, C., Loy, C.C., He, K., Tang, X.: Image super-resolution using deep convolutional networks. IEEE Trans. Pattern Anal. Mach. Intell. **38**(2), 295–307 (2016)
3. Haris, M., Shakhnarovich, G., Ukita, N.: Deep back-projection networks for super-resolution. In: Proceedings of the IEEE Conference on Computer Vision and Pattern Recognition, pp. 1664–1673 (2018)
4. He, X., Mo, Z., Wang, P., Liu, Y., Yang, M., Cheng, J.: ODE-inspired network design for single image super-resolution. In: IEEE Conference on Computer Vision and Pattern Recognition, CVPR 2019, Long Beach, CA, USA, 16–20 June 2019, pp. 1732–1741. Computer Vision Foundation/IEEE (2019)
5. Kingma, D.P., Ba, J.: Adam: a method for stochastic optimization. In: Bengio, Y., LeCun, Y. (eds.) 3rd International Conference on Learning Representations, ICLR 2015, San Diego, CA, USA, 7–9 May 2015, Conference Track Proceedings (2015)
6. Li, J., Fang, F., Mei, K., Zhang, G.: Multi-scale residual network for image super-resolution. In: Proceedings of the European Conference on Computer Vision (ECCV), pp. 517–532 (2018)
7. Lim, B., Son, S., Kim, H., Nah, S., Mu Lee, K.: Enhanced deep residual networks for single image super-resolution. In: Proceedings of the IEEE Conference on Computer Vision and Pattern Recognition Workshops, pp. 136–144 (2017)
8. Liu, D., Wen, B., Fan, Y., Loy, C.C., Huang, T.S.: Non-local recurrent network for image restoration. In: Bengio, S., Wallach, H.M., Larochelle, H., Grauman, K., Cesa-Bianchi, N., Garnett, R. (eds.) Advances in Neural Information Processing Systems 31: Annual Conference on Neural Information Processing Systems 2018, NeurIPS 2018, 3–8 December 2018, Montréal, Canada, pp. 1680–1689 (2018)
9. Mei, Y., Fan, Y., Zhou, Y.: Image super-resolution with non-local sparse attention. In: Proceedings of the IEEE/CVF Conference on Computer Vision and Pattern Recognition, pp. 3517–3526 (2021)
10. Mei, Y., Fan, Y., Zhou, Y., Huang, L., Huang, T.S., Shi, H.: Image super-resolution with cross-scale non-local attention and exhaustive self-exemplars mining. In: 2020 IEEE/CVF Conference on Computer Vision and Pattern Recognition, CVPR 2020, Seattle, WA, USA, 13–19 June 2020, pp. 5689–5698. Computer Vision Foundation/IEEE (2020)
11. Niu, B., et al.: Single image super-resolution via a holistic attention network. In: Vedaldi, A., Bischof, H., Brox, T., Frahm, J.-M. (eds.) ECCV 2020. LNCS, vol. 12357, pp. 191–207. Springer, Cham (2020). https://doi.org/10.1007/978-3-030-58610-2_12
12. Shi, W., et al.: Real-time single image and video super-resolution using an efficient sub-pixel convolutional neural network. In: Proceedings of the IEEE Conference on Computer Vision and Pattern Recognition, pp. 1874–1883 (2016)
13. Xia, B., Hang, Y., Tian, Y., Yang, W., Liao, Q., Zhou, J.: Efficient non-local contrastive attention for image super-resolution. In: Thirty-Sixth AAAI Conference on Artificial Intelligence, AAAI 2022, Thirty-Fourth Conference on Innovative Applications of Artificial Intelligence, IAAI 2022, The Twelveth Symposium on Educational Advances in Artificial Intelligence, EAAI 2022 Virtual Event, 22 February–1 March 2022, pp. 2759–2767. AAAI Press (2022)
14. Zhang, Y., Li, K., Li, K., Wang, L., Zhong, B., Fu, Y.: Image super-resolution using very deep residual channel attention networks. In: Proceedings of the European Conference on Computer Vision (ECCV), pp. 286–301 (2018)
15. Zhang, Y., Li, K., Li, K., Zhong, B., Fu, Y.: Residual non-local attention networks for image restoration. In: 7th International Conference on Learning Representations, ICLR 2019, New Orleans, LA, USA, 6–9 May 2019. OpenReview.net (2019)

16. Zhang, Y., Tian, Y., Kong, Y., Zhong, B., Fu, Y.: Residual dense network for image super-resolution. In: Proceedings of the IEEE Conference on Computer Vision and Pattern Recognition, pp. 2472–2481 (2018)

17. Zhao, L., Zhang, Z., Chen, T., Metaxas, D.N., Zhang, H.: Improved transformer for high-resolution GANs. In: Ranzato, M., Beygelzimer, A., Dauphin, Y.N., Liang, P., Vaughan, J.W. (eds.) Advances in Neural Information Processing Systems 34: Annual Conference on Neural Information Processing Systems 2021, NeurIPS 2021, 6–14 December 2021, virtual, pp. 18367–18380 (2021)

18. Zhou, S., Zhang, J., Zuo, W., Loy, C.C.: Cross-scale internal graph neural network for image super-resolution. In: Larochelle, H., Ranzato, M., Hadsell, R., Balcan, M., Lin, H. (eds.) Advances in Neural Information Processing Systems 33: Annual Conference on Neural Information Processing Systems 2020, NeurIPS 2020, 6–12 December 2020, virtual (2020)

19. Zontak, M., Irani, M.: Internal statistics of a single natural image. In: Proceedings of the 2011 IEEE Conference on Computer Vision and Pattern Recognition, CVPR 2011, pp. 977–984. IEEE Computer Society, USA (2011)

SS-Net: 3D Spatial-Spectral Network for Cerebrovascular Segmentation in TOF-MRA

Chaozhi Yang[1], Yachuan Li[1], Yun Bai[1], Qian Xiao[1], Zongmin Li[1(✉)] (iD),
Hongyi Li[2](iD), and Hua Li[3](iD)

[1] College of Computer Science and Technology, China University of Petroleum
(EastChina), Qingdao 266580, China
lizongmin@upc.edu.cn
[2] Beijing Hospital, Institute of Geriatric Medicine,
Chinese Academy of Medical Science, Beijing 100730, China
[3] Key Laboratory of Intelligent Information Processing, Institute of Computing
Technology, Chinese Academy of Sciences, Beijing 100190, China

Abstract. The extraction of cerebrovascular structure plays a pivotal role in the diagnosis and analysis of various cerebrovascular diseases. However, cerebrovascular segmentation from time-of-flight magnetic resonance angiography (TOF-MRA) volumes remains a challenging task due to the complex topology, slender contour, and noisy background. This paper proposes a 3D SS-Net that combines the spatial and spectral domain features to accurately segment the cerebral vasculature. The SS-Net is based on an end-to-end autoencoder architecture, which incorporates both spatial and a spectral encoders. The spectral encoder branch applies 3D fast Fourier convolution (FFC) to extract global features and frequency domain features in the shallow layers of the network. Furthermore, we introduce cerebrovascular edge supervised information, which enables the network to model the high-frequency variations and distribution patterns of cerebrovascular edges more effectively. Experimental results show that the SS-Net delivers outstanding performance, achieving the DSC of 71.14% on a publicly available dataset and outperforming other 3D deep-learning-based approaches. Code: github.com/y8421036/SS-Net.

Keywords: Cerebrovascular segmentation · Fast Fourier Convolution · 3D U-Net · Edge supervision · TOF-MRA

1 Introduction

Cerebrovascular diseases, such as intracranial aneurysms, arteriovenous malformations, and stenoses, are a significant threat to human health for high incidence, mortality, and disability rates [8]. Time-of-flight magnetic resonance angiography

L. Iliadis et al. (Eds.): ICANN 2023, LNCS 14256, pp. 149–159, 2023.
https://doi.org/10.1007/978-3-031-44213-1_13

is a non-invasive imaging technique routinely used for evaluating vascular abnormalities without administering contrast. The accurate extraction of the vascular system allows clinicians to support early diagnosis, optimal treatment, and neurosurgery planning. However, automatic cerebrovascular segmentation from TOF-MRA is challenging due to anatomical variations, sophisticated geometry and shape, and data sparseness (artifacts, noises, low signal-to-noise ratio).

In the last two decades, there have been many model-driven vessel segmentation methods proposed, including active contours [18], tractography [2], shape model [10,22], Hessian matrix filtering [7], and symmetry filtering [21]. These algorithms need detailed design and rely on complicated manual parameter adjustments.

With the rapid development of deep learning technology, data-driven segmentation methods achieve better performance. Phellan et al. [13] utilized the 2D convolutional neural network (CNN) to segment the cerebral vessel slices. Sanchesa et al. [14] proposed the Uception segmentation model that combines inception [16] and 3D U-Net [5]. Wang et al. [17] constructed a joint convolutional embedding space where computed joint cerebrovascular probabilities. Mou et al. [12] presented a generic and unified CNN for segmentating curvilinear structures, including 2D and 3D vasculatures. Chen et al. [3] proposed a GAN-based method that maps the TOF-MRA images to cerebral vessels. However, the above methods neglect to prioritize the extraction of cerebrovascular edges that are essential for vessel connectivity. Although several studies [1,20] focus on edge information, they leave out practical features in the spectral domain, which existing spatial neural networks may not extract.

The high-frequency variations of cerebrovascular edges in TOF-MRA images make edge features suitable to be extracted in the spectral domain. In this paper, we combine the spatial and spectral features to segment the brain vessels. First, we design a spectral encoder as another branch of 3D U-Net to extract frequency domain features and process global information. Cerebrovascular edge labels are then introduced as additional supervision, allowing the SS-Net to focus more on edge features in both the spatial and spectral domains. The contributions of this paper are summarized as follows:

1. To our knowledge, SS-Net is the first 3D cerebrovascular segmentation network combining spatial and spectral domain features.
2. We introduce edge supervision to improve the spectral encoder's ability to learn the cerebrovascular edges' frequency domain features.
3. Experimental results on a public dataset demonstrate that the SS-Net outperforms other deep learning methods quantitatively and qualitatively.

2   Method

2.1   The Overall Framework of SS-Net

The proposed SS-Net consists of several components: a spatial encoder, a spectral encoder, a spatial decoder, skip connections, and double-task head. The core unit

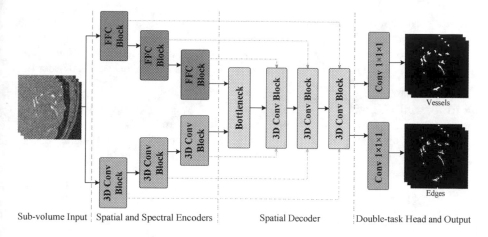

Fig. 1. Overview of the proposed SS-Net.

of the proposed spectral encoder is the Fast Fourier Convolution [4,6,15], which learns cerebrovascular features from the frequency domain and processes global features that the spatial convolution may miss. The overall framework of SS-Net is shown in Fig. 1.

3D Spatial Encoder. Our spatial encoder contains the same skip connections as 3D U-Net's encoder to complement the details lost by downsampling. The number of downsampling operations and 3D convolution blocks is both 3. A $3 \times 3 \times 3$ convolutional kernel, a 3D Batch Normalization (BN), and an activation function (ReLU) are sequentially combined to form a 3D convolution block in our spatial encoder. The downsampling operation adopts a 3D Max Pooling (MP), and the kernel size of the MP is 2. The input of the first 3D convolution block is a cropped sub-volume from the original image, and the output is fed to the next block.

3D Spectral Encoder. Similar to the spatial encoder, the spectral encoder has skip connections, downsampling, and sub-volume input. Three FFC blocks process the input to obtain the output. Each FFC block contains regular convolutions for processing local information and the spectral transform for processing global information. The core of the spectral transform is the Fast Fourier Transform (FFT) and the inverse Fast Fourier Transform (IFFT). The FFT converts image features into frequency domain features. The IFFT does the opposite. Updating a single value affects all the original data globally in the frequency domain transformed by FFT. Therefore, this gives the FFC-generated features image-wide receptive fields even in the shallow layers of the network.

3D Spatial Decoder. The spatial decoder contains a bottleneck layer and three 3D convolution blocks. The bottleneck layer concatenates the output features of the two encoders and learns the semantic features using a $3 \times 3 \times 3$ convolutional kernel. The new features are upsampled and passed to a 3D convolutional block similar to the spatial encoder. Each 3D convolutional block fuses features from previous decoder blocks with features from skip connections to learn higher-level features. In order to restore the feature map to the size of the sub-volume input, the spatial decoder employs three upsampling operations based on transpose convolution.

Double-Task Head. The output of the decoder is processed by the double-task head to obtain a vessel segmentation map and an edge segmentation map, respectively. Both task heads have the same architectural design, consisting of a $1 \times 1 \times 1$ convolution kernel and an activation function (sigmoid).

2.2   3D Spectral Encoder Components

3D FFC Block. As shown in Fig. 2(a), the FFC Block divides the input equally into two parts by the number of channels and feeds to two inter-connected paths. In the first FFC block, since the input is a sub-volume of the original image, the number of channels of the global path is set to 0. The local path conducts ordinary convolution, and the global path uses the spectral transform to operate in the spectral domain. Since each path captures complementary information with a different receptive field, the two paths exchange information through multi-scale fusion. Then the features are fed into a 3D BN, a ReLU, and a 3D MP. Finally, the features of the two paths are concatenated at the channel level and used as the output of the FFC Block.

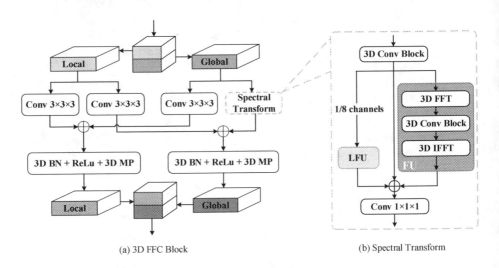

(a) 3D FFC Block   (b) Spectral Transform

Fig. 2. The design of fast Fourier convolution.

Spectral Transform. Spectral transform extracts frequency domain features and allows the network to account for the global context starting from the shallow layer. In Fig. 2(b), after the input features are applied to a 3D convolutional block with a kernel size of 1, the new features are passed to three paths: i) Fourier

Unit (FU), ii) residual connection, and iii) Local Fourier Unit (LFU). Note that the LFU path requires only one-eighth of the channels. The outputs of the three paths are fused and fed to a $1 \times 1 \times 1$ convolution kernel.

FU and LFU. The FU first utilizes FFT to convert spatial features into real and imaginary parts. These two parts are stacked and fed to a 3D convolutional block with a kernel size of 1. The generated features are split into two parts as real and imaginary. They are then converted back to image features by IFFT. The FFT can be applied only to real-valued signals, and the IFFT ensures that the output is real valued. To capture semi-local information, we devise LFU, whose pipeline is shown in Fig. 3. The key difference between LFU and FU is a split-concatenate-repeat step, which halves three spatial dimensions of input feature maps and processes eight small feature maps. Standard FU is then applied to stacked feature maps. The generated features are shifted and repeated to restore to the initial resolution.

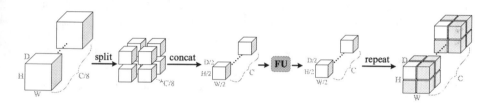

Fig. 3. Illustration of the computational pipeline of local Fourier unit.

2.3   Loss Function

Three different loss functions train the vessel and edge segmentation tasks. For the cerebrovascular segmentation task, the loss function $L_{cere} = L_{BCE} + \lambda_1 L_{dice}$ is defined as the combination of the Binary Cross-Entropy (BCE) loss and the dice coefficient loss:

$$L_{dice} = 1 - \frac{2 \sum_{j=1}^{N} p_j g_j + \epsilon}{\sum_{j=1}^{N} p_j + \sum_{j=1}^{N} g_j + \epsilon} \tag{1}$$

$$L_{BCE} = -\frac{1}{N} \sum_{j=1}^{N} g_j log(p_j) + (1 - g_j)log(1 - p_j) \tag{2}$$

where p_j and g_j indicate the predicted probability and ground truth of the j-th voxel within an input volume patch. N is the number of voxels. The parameter ϵ (set as 1) is the Laplace smoothing factor that guarantees numerical stability. The λ_1 is the weight balance parameter between L_{dice} and L_{BCE}, which is empirically set as 1.

For the edge segmentation task, due to the problem of severe class imbalance, the well-known focal loss is used, defined as follows:

$$L_{edge} = L_{focal} = \frac{1}{N} \sum_{j=1}^{N} -\alpha(1 - p_j)^\gamma log(p_j) \tag{3}$$

where α and γ are adjustable factors and are set to 0.25 and 2, respectively. Therefore, the proposed SS-Net can be jointly optimized by minimizing the joint loss $L = L_{cere} + \lambda_2 L_{edge}$ in an end-to-end manner. The hyper-parameter λ_2 controls the influence of the edge part and is empirically set to 0.5.

3   Experimental Results

3.1   Datasets and Pre-processing

We conduct our experiments on the MIDAS[1] dataset. The MIDAS contains 42 TOF-MRA volumes of different subjects, acquired by a Siemens Allegra head-only 3T MR system. The intra-cranial vessel annotations are obtained via the TubeTK toolkit. The voxel spacing for the MRA images is $0.5 \times 0.5 \times 0.8$ mm^3 with a volume size of $448 \times 448 \times 128$ voxel.

We apply the BET [9] of the MR-based skull-stripping algorithm to extract the pure brain region from each volumetric data. To reduce the difference of intensity distribution among volumes, each TOF-MRA volume is normalized by min-max scaling. A 6-neighborhood filter generates the one-voxel-thick cerebrovascular edge labels given the ground-truth volume G of the input TOF-MRA volume I. The $N(i)$ denotes the 6-neighbor voxels of i. We define the set of voxels E on the cerebrovascular edge as:

$$E_i = \{i \mid g_i = 1, \exists x \in N(i), g_x = 0\} \tag{4}$$

3.2   Implementation Details

In this work, we randomly extract training sub-volumes with a specified size of $96 \times 96 \times 96$ for each case. The sliding window strategy of no overlapping is employed during testing. It is worth noting that we combine the predicted values of all sub-volumes for evaluation. The MIDAS dataset's random training/validation/testing case split is $36/2/4$.

The proposed network adopts the Adam optimizer with an initial learning rate of 0.0005 with 0.5 as the learning decay factor. The network is implemented on PyTorch with an NVIDIA GeForce GTX TITAN X GPU (12G RAM). Following previous work [19], we adopted the poly learning rate method with a power of 0.9.

We compare with other deep learning segmentation models, including U-ception [14], RE-Net [20] and CS^2-Net [12] for 3D cerebrovascular segmentation, and two state-of-the-art 3D FCNs for medical volume segmentation, such as 3D UNet [5] and V-Net [11].

---

[1] https://public.kitware.com/Wiki/TubeTK/Data.

For evaluating the segmentation performance of our network, some well-known metrics were introduced: Dice Similarity Coefficient (DSC), Sensitivity (SE), Specificity (SP), Precision (PR), and Accuracy (ACC). Since the above metrics are insensitive to the foreground edge, the 95th Hausdorff Distance (HD95) and the Average Hausdorff Distance (AHD) were adopted better to evaluate the segmentation results of the cerebral vasculature. The HD95 is the 95 percentile of the Hausdorff distance (HD). These metrics are defined as follows:

$$
\begin{cases}
DSC = \frac{2TP}{FP+2TP+FN} \\
SE = \frac{TP}{TP+FN} \\
SP = \frac{TN}{FP+TN} \\
PR = \frac{TP}{TP+FP} \\
ACC = \frac{TP+TN}{TP+TN+FP+FN} \\
HD = \max\{\max_{p\in P}\min_{g\in G}||p-g||, \max_{g\in G}\min_{p\in P}||g-p||\} \\
AHD = \frac{1}{2}\{\frac{1}{\#P}\sum_{p\in P}\min_{g\in G}||p-g|| + \frac{1}{\#G}\sum_{g\in G}\min_{p\in P}||g-p||\}
\end{cases}
\tag{5}
$$

in which TP, FP, FN, and TN are true positive, false positive, false negative, and true negative in the confusion matrix. The P and G denote the voxel sets of prediction and ground truth, respectively. The # represents the number of voxels in a set. The symbol of $||\cdot||$ is taken as the Euclidean distance between two voxels.

3.3 Ablation Study

The main contribution of our network is to design the 3D spectral encoder and introduce the edge auxiliary task for improving cerebrovascular segmentation accuracy. To verify the efficacy of these modules, we conduct ablation experiments on the MIDAS dataset. Note that the baseline is 3D U-Net. In addition, we compare the performance of triple downsampling and quadruple downsampling based on SS-Net.

The results of the ablation experiment are summarized in Table 1. Introducing any of the two modules achieves better performance than the baseline. In terms of the DSC indicator, adding the 3D spectral decoder alone improved the score by 5.28%, and introducing the edge task alone improved it by 3.64%. The SS-Net achieves the highest scores in most metrics by incorporating both modules. Specifically, SS-Net improved by 6.04% and 1.91mm in DSC and $HD95$, respectively, compared with the baseline network. We believe that the edge segmentation assistance task helps to enhance the vessel edge features and reduce the effect of background noise. Moreover, based on our proposed framework, better results are obtained using three times downsampling.

3.4 Quantitative and Qualitative Analysis

To qualitatively compare the segmentation results of the proposed method with other deep learning vessel segmentation methods, Fig. 4 shows the segmentation

Table 1. Effect of modular ablation experiments on segmentation index of the cerebral vasculature. Bold denotes the best results.

Methods	SE(%)↑	SP(%)↑	DSC(%)↑	HD95(mm)↓	AHD(mm)↓
Baseline	65.97 ± 3.96	99.83 ± 0.02	65.10 ± 3.31	10.26 ± 2.37	1.2560 ± 0.25
Baseline + Spectral Encoder	66.61 ± 2.54	99.90 ± 0.02	70.38 ± 2.91	9.32 ± 2.48	1.0601 ± 0.18
Baseline + Edge Task	66.37 ± 2.59	99.84 ± 0.03	68.74 ± 2.71	10.39 ± 2.01	1.2045 ± 0.28
SS-Net with 4 downsampling	64.23 ± 2.38	99.90 ± 0.02	68.32 ± 2.81	10.57 ± 2.04	1.1243 ± 0.17
SS-Net	**67.92 ± 2.66**	**99.91 ± 0.01**	**71.14 ± 2.76**	**8.35 ± 2.18**	**1.0416 ± 0.23**

examples of 3D views on the test set. The 3D U-Net has poor segmentation performance. The V-Net generates more false negative errors. The amount of detached false positive errors produced by SS-Net is apparently less than that of other compared methods. The SS-Net performs well in segmenting multi-size vessel branches and maintaining the continuity of the vessels. Overall, SS-Net

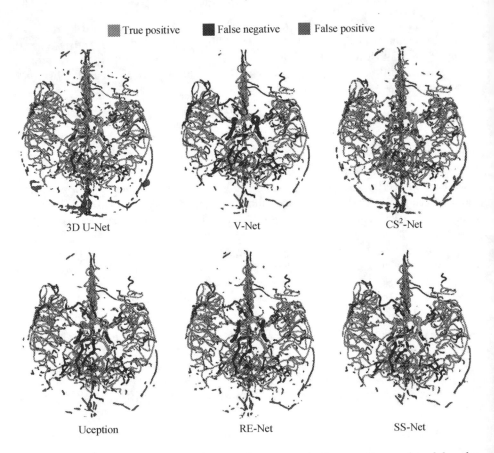

Fig. 4. Visual comparison of cerebrovascular segmentation results produced by the SS-Net and other deep-learning methods from a 3D view.

yields more complete segmentation of the whole cerebrovascular structure. We believe that better performance comes from the contribution of vessel edges and global features.

The evaluation scores in Table 2 reinforce the above findings. In terms of DSC metrics, SS-Net is 6.04%, 9.11%, 5.7%, 8.36%, and 4.37% higher than 3D U-Net, V-Net, CS^{2}Net, Uception, and RE-Net, respectively. It can be seen that the proposed SS-Net outperformed the other methods and achieved the highest scores in all metrics. Overall, the proposed SS-Net excels in cerebral vascular segmentation from 3D TOF-MRA volumes.

Table 2. Segmentation results obtained by different methods.

Metrics	3D U-Net [5]	V-Net [11]	CS^2-Net [12]	Uception [14]	RE-Net [20]	SS-Net
SE(%)↑	65.97 ± 3.96	60.35 ± 3.33	66.17 ± 1.80	56.39 ± 4.64	64.51 ± 4.40	**67.92 ± 2.66**
SP(%)↑	99.83 ± 0.02	99.90 ± 0.01	99.79 ± 0.02	99.89 ± 0.02	99.89 ± 0.01	**99.91 ± 0.01**
PR(%)↑	67.36 ± 3.09	69.32 ± 3.06	57.60 ± 4.57	70.82 ± 3.23	67.77 ± 4.04	**74.70 ± 3.15**
ACC(%)↑	99.75 ± 0.02	99.73 ± 0.03	99.70 ± 0.02	99.75 ± 0.01	99.75 ± 0.02	**99.79 ± 0.03**
DSC(%)↑	65.10 ± 3.31	62.03 ± 2.70	65.44 ± 3.25	62.78 ± 2.22	66.77 ± 3.13	**71.14 ± 2.76**
HD95(mm)↓	10.26 ± 2.37	9.53 ± 0.14	10.46 ± 1.76	10.00 ± 0.79	9.50 ± 0.88	**8.35 ± 2.18**
AHD(mm)↓	1.2560 ± 0.25	1.2526 ± 0.17	1.3358 ± 0.28	1.1990 ± 0.16	1.0676 ± 0.12	**1.0416 ± 0.23**

4 Conclusion

In this work, we have proposed a 3D convolution network, SS-Net, to segment cerebrovascular structure from TOF-MRA volumes. Our FFC-based spectral encoder obtains global information more quickly and efficiently than an encoder containing ordinary convolution. In addition, by introducing cerebral vascular edge supervision, the spectral encoder can model the distribution of cerebrovascular edge, improving vascular connectivity. Our SS-Net combines image and frequency domain features to extract more accurate cerebrovascular structure. Experimental results based on publicly available datasets show that the proposed method significantly improves the accuracy of cerebrovascular segmentation.

Acknowledgements. This work is partly supported by National Key R&D Program of China (Grant no. 2019YFF0301800), National Natural Science Foundation of China (Grant no. 61379106, 61806199), the General Research Projects of Beijing Educations Committee in China (Grant no. KM201910005013), the Shandong Provincial Natural Science Foundation (Grant nos. ZR2015FM011).

References

1. Banerjee, S., Toumpanakis, D., Dhara, A.K., Wikström, J., Strand, R.: Topology-aware learning for volumetric cerebrovascular segmentation. In: 2022 IEEE 19th International Symposium on Biomedical Imaging, pp. 1–4 (2022). https://doi.org/10.1109/ISBI52829.2022.9761429

2. Cetin, S., Demir, A., Yezzi, A., Degertekin, M., Unal, G.: Vessel tractography using an intensity based tensor model with branch detection. IEEE Trans. Med. Imaging **32**(2), 348–363 (2013). https://doi.org/10.1109/TMI.2012.2227118

3. Chen, Z., et al.: Generative adversarial network based cerebrovascular segmentation for time-of-flight magnetic resonance angiography image. Neurocomputing **488**, 657–668 (2022)

4. Chi, L., Jiang, B., Mu, Y.: Fast fourier convolution. In: Larochelle, H., Ranzato, M., Hadsell, R., Balcan, M., Lin, H. (eds.) Advances in Neural Information Processing Systems, vol. 33, pp. 4479–4488. Curran Associates, Inc. (2020)

5. Çiçek, Ö., Abdulkadir, A., Lienkamp, S.S., Brox, T., Ronneberger, O.: 3D U-Net: learning dense volumetric segmentation from sparse annotation. In: Ourselin, S., Joskowicz, L., Sabuncu, M.R., Unal, G., Wells, W. (eds.) MICCAI 2016. LNCS, vol. 9901, pp. 424–432. Springer, Cham (2016). https://doi.org/10.1007/978-3-319-46723-8_49

6. Farshad, A., Yeganeh, Y., Gehlbach, P., Navab, N.: Y-net: a spatiospectral dual-encoder network for medical image segmentation. In: Wang, L., Dou, Q., Fletcher, P.T., Speidel, S., Li, S. (eds.) MICCAI 2022. LNCS, vol. 13432, pp. 582–592. Springer, Cham (2022). https://doi.org/10.1007/978-3-031-16434-7_56

7. Frangi, A.F., Niessen, W.J., Vincken, K.L., Viergever, M.A.: Muliscale vessel enhancement filtering. In: International Conference on Medical Image Computing and Computer-Assisted Intervention (1998)

8. Han, H., et al.: Reduction of cerebral blood flow in community-based adults with subclinical cerebrovascular atherosclerosis: a 3.0T magnetic resonance imaging study. NeuroImage **188**, 302–308 (2019). https://doi.org/10.1016/j.neuroimage.2018.12.021

9. Jenkinson, M., Pechaud, M., Smith, S., et al.: BET2: MR-based estimation of brain, skull and scalp surfaces. In: Eleventh Annual Meeting of the Organization for Human Brain Mapping, Toronto, vol. 17, p. 167 (2005)

10. Liao, W., Rohr, K., Wörz, S.: Globally optimal curvature-regularized fast marching for vessel segmentation. In: Mori, K., Sakuma, I., Sato, Y., Barillot, C., Navab, N. (eds.) MICCAI 2013. LNCS, vol. 8149, pp. 550–557. Springer, Heidelberg (2013). https://doi.org/10.1007/978-3-642-40811-3_69

11. Milletari, F., Navab, N., Ahmadi, S.A.: V-net: fully convolutional neural networks for volumetric medical image segmentation. In: 2016 Fourth International Conference on 3D Vision, pp. 565–571. IEEE (2016)

12. Mou, L., et al.: CS2-Net: deep learning segmentation of curvilinear structures in medical imaging. Med. Image Anal. **67**, 101874 (2021)

13. Phellan, R., Peixinho, A., Falcão, A., Forkert, N.D.: Vascular segmentation in TOF MRA images of the brain using a deep convolutional neural network. In: Cardoso, M.J., et al. (eds.) LABELS/CVII/STENT -2017. LNCS, vol. 10552, pp. 39–46. Springer, Cham (2017). https://doi.org/10.1007/978-3-319-67534-3_5

14. Sanchesa, P., Meyer, C., Vigon, V., Naegel, B.: Cerebrovascular network segmentation of mra images with deep learning. In: 2019 IEEE 16th International Symposium on Biomedical Imaging, pp. 768–771. IEEE (2019)

15. Suvorov, R., et al.: Resolution-robust large mask inpainting with fourier convolutions. In: 2022 IEEE/CVF Winter Conference on Applications of Computer Vision, pp. 3172–3182 (2022). https://doi.org/10.1109/WACV51458.2022.00323

16. Szegedy, C., Ioffe, S., Vanhoucke, V., Alemi, A.A.: Inception-v4, inception-resnet and the impact of residual connections on learning. In: Thirty-First AAAI Conference on Artificial Intelligence (2017)

17. Wang, Y., et al.: JointVesselNet: joint volume-projection convolutional embedding networks for 3D cerebrovascular segmentation. In: Martel, A.L., et al. (eds.) MICCAI 2020. LNCS, vol. 12266, pp. 106–116. Springer, Cham (2020). https://doi.org/10.1007/978-3-030-59725-2_11

18. Yang, X., Cheng, K.T., Chien, A.: Geodesic active contours with adaptive configuration for cerebral vessel and aneurysm segmentation. In: 2014 22nd International Conference on Pattern Recognition, pp. 3209–3214 (2014). https://doi.org/10.1109/ICPR.2014.553

19. Zhang, H., et al.: Context encoding for semantic segmentation. In: Proceedings of the IEEE Conference on Computer Vision and Pattern Recognition, pp. 7151–7160 (2018)

20. Zhang, H., et al.: Cerebrovascular segmentation in MRA via reverse edge attention network. In: Martel, A.L., et al. (eds.) MICCAI 2020. LNCS, vol. 12266, pp. 66–75. Springer, Cham (2020). https://doi.org/10.1007/978-3-030-59725-2_7

21. Zhao, Y., et al.: Automatic 2-D/3-D vessel enhancement in multiple modality images using a weighted symmetry filter. IEEE Trans. Med. Imaging **37**(2), 438–450 (2018). https://doi.org/10.1109/TMI.2017.2756073

22. Zhou, S., et al.: Statistical intensity- and shape-modeling to automate cerebrovascular segmentation from TOF-MRA data. In: Shen, D., et al. (eds.) MICCAI 2019. LNCS, vol. 11765, pp. 164–172. Springer, Cham (2019). https://doi.org/10.1007/978-3-030-32245-8_19

STAN: Spatio-Temporal Alignment Network for No-Reference Video Quality Assessment

Zhengyi Yang, Yuanjie Dang, Jianjun Xiang, and Peng Chen[✉]

Zhejiang University of Technology, Hangzhou 310000, China
chenpeng@zjut.eud.cn

Abstract. With the rapid development of multimedia user-generated content (UGC), the number of videos characterized by multiple resolutions and frame rates has increased. The development of efficient no-reference video quality assessment (NR-VQA) models for UGC with these features is a challenging task. Although previous studies have proposed solutions that combine multi-scale spatial and multi-rate motion information, existing NR-VQA models simply connect multi-attribute features obtained separately, often leading to information loss and distortion. In this study, we developed a spatiotemporal alignment network addressing the limitations of existing methods. Our model includes two modules, one for multi-rate motion feature alignment and the other for multi-scale spatial feature alignment. Moreover, by introducing a Lagrangian multi-rate and multi-scale attention-based alignment mechanism, multiple features can be effectively processed without incurring in unwanted information conflict or loss. By associating spatial and time-series information, our attention-based feature-alignment module enhances low-quality spatial regions around subject objects, thus, improving the performance of the model significantly. Our experimental results demonstrated that the proposed model outperforms other existing methods on several benchmark datasets, proving its effectiveness and generalizability. Code will be available at: https://github.com/945402003/STAN-VQA.

Keywords: video quality assessment · UGC videos · human visual system · spatio-temporal alignment

1 Introduction

The popularity of user-generated content (UGC), particularly videos, has recently increased. With millions of UGC videos uploaded daily, relying solely on the human visual system (HVS) for quality assessment would be ineffective. Therefore, to ensure high-quality video services, developing reliable video quality assessment (VQA) models is essential.

This work was supported in part by the Natural Science Foundation of China under Grant U1909203, 62036009, the Zhejiang Provincial Natural Science Foundation of

L. Iliadis et al. (Eds.): ICANN 2023, LNCS 14256, pp. 160–171, 2023.
https://doi.org/10.1007/978-3-031-44213-1_14

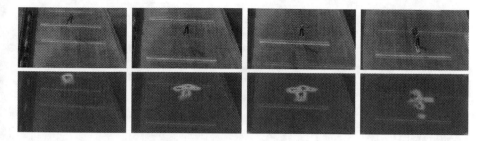

Fig. 1. Visualization of the attention-based feature alignment module. First row: original image. Second row: effect map with attention guidance.

Objective VQA can be categorized into three types: full-reference VQA (FR-VQA), reduced-reference VQA (RR-VQA), and no-reference VQA (NR-VQA). Since in-the-wild UGC videos lack a reference video, only NR-VQA models are suitable for their quality evaluation. Several existing NR-VQA methods leverage single-attribute features for regression prediction of quality scores, including hand-crafted [14,17,18] and deep-learning features [8,10]. Recently, with the availability of large UGC VQA databases, such as KoNViD-1k [6] and YouTube-UGC [19], several studies [2,9,16] have considered multi-attribute features, including multi-rate and multi-scale features. Based on the assumption that multi-attribute features are derived from tightly aligned feature spaces, these methods directly concatenate the obtained features.

However, multi-attribute features often exhibit different resolutions and granularities in both time and space, thus, a direct features splicing may lead to information bias. Previous research has demonstrated that the absence of feature alignment in the spatial dimension can affect the ability of the model to capture the relationships between different regions. Similarly, ineffective feature alignment in the time domain may prevent the model from learning the temporal relationships between data from different time series [1].

To address these limitations, in this study, we developed the multi-feature alignment model illustrated in Fig. 2, which comprises a multi-rate motion feature alignment module (MMFA) and a multi-scale spatial feature alignment module (MSFA). These modules enable our network to align features effectively from different sources, addressing important limitations of existing methods. Generally, attention-based methods can be used to align only motion features with the same sampling frequency in the time domain. To overcome this limitation, in the proposed model, we introduced a Lagrangian multi-rate interpolation method to align motion features with different sampling rates effectively. Moreover, to align multi-scale spatial features, we developed a multi-scale channel attention model that aggregates contextual information at different scales along the channel dimension, thus, simultaneously emphasizing both the global

China under Grant LQ22F020007, the Zhejiang Postdoctoral Science Foundation under Grant ZY21191190003, and the Ten Thousand Talent Program of Zhejiang Province.

spatial distribution of subjects and local spatial details. Our contributions can be summarized as follows:

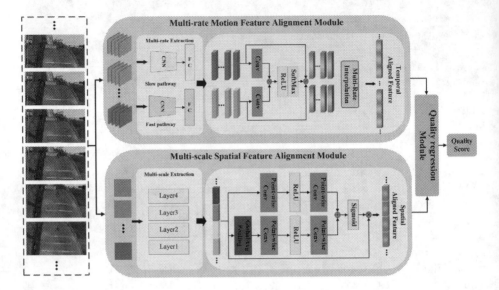

Fig. 2. Schematic of the proposed VQA model including the multi-rate motion feature alignment, multi-scale spatial feature alignment, and quality regression modules.

- We developed a spatio-temporal alignment network for multi-attribute feature alignment in NR-VQA to address information bias during feature fusion.
- We developed an effective attention-based feature alignment mechanism that enables the association of spatial and time-series information, especially emphasizing low-quality regions around subject objects.
- We conducted extensive experiments on four benchmark datasets, demonstrating that the proposed model outperforms state-of-the-art methods.

2   Related Work

Hand-Crafted Feature-Based NR-VQA Models: Traditional NR-VQA approaches [7,14,17,18]employed hand-crafted features leveraging a set of generic quality-aware characteristics in combination with no-reference image quality assessment (IQA) methods to predict quality scores using regression techniques. NR-VQA methods focus both on temporal and spatial features because the spatial and temporal domains are key attributes of VQA tasks. For instance, V-BLIINDS [14] uses natural scene statistics to measure frame differences and motion coherency in videos. The two-level video quality model (TLVQM) [7] extracts spatiotemporal features at high and low complexity levels. VIDEVAL [17] uses features from typical no-reference image/video quality assessment (NR-I/VQA) methods to train a support vector regression (SVR) model that can accurately predict video quality measures.

Deep Learning-Based NR-VQA Models: Recent studies have proposed convolutional neural network (CNN) models that extract temporal and spatial domain information for VQA tasks more effectively. For instance, CNN-TLVQM [8] uses the hand-crafted statistical temporal features of TLVQM [7] augmented with spatial features obtained by IQA transfer learning. Li et al. [11] developed a NR-VQA model using a three-dimensional (3D) shearlet transform to extract features at different spatial and temporal scales from videos. Liu et al. [12] proposed a multi-task blind VQA model called V-MEON consisting of a 3D CNN that performs simultaneous spatial and temporal information extraction for quality assessment. In the VSFA model [10], content and temporal memory were integrated for the first time into an NR-VQA model using a gated recurrent unit (GRU) for long-term temporal feature extraction. Xu et al. [21] used a pre-trained IQA model and graph convolution to enhance spatial features and integrate them with motion features extracted in the optical flow domain using a bidirectional long short-term memory network. Subsequent studies focused on improving the details of the features in both spatial and temporal domains. You et al. [23] used a 3D convolution network to extract local spatiotemporal features from small video clips. Ying et al. [22] introduced the concept of global and local information by combining the spatial features of a two-dimensional (2D)CNN model with the motion features of a 3D CNN network. Li et al. [9] implemented a knowledge transfer from two distinct sources: authentically distorted IQA databases and large-scale action recognition datasets, which include several motion patterns. Recent research has increasingly focused on multi-scale issues in spatiotemporal domain. For instance, RIRNet [3] exploits motion information extracted considering multi-scale frequencies in the time domain for video quality assessment. GSTVQA [2] imposes a Gaussian distribution constraint on quality features to resolve resolution issues. Sun et al. [16] proposed an efficient end-to-end model that uses a multi-scale quality fusion strategy to solve the VQA problem at various spatial resolutions.

3   Proposed Model

In this study, we focused on aligning multi-rate and multi-scale features. Therefore, we developed two-feature alignment networks that improve the ability of the model to capture temporal and spatial information effectively.

3.1   Overview of the Proposed Model

Figure 2 shows the structure of the proposed model, which includes the following parts: the MMFA and MSFA modules, and the quality regression module. First, the input video is processed in two separate domains to obtain spatial and motion features, which represent the two types of information used by HVS as confirmed by several studies [9]. Subsequently, the input video is split V into N_k continuous clips contained in the vector $p = \{p_i\}_{i=1}^{N_k}$. Each clip p_i includes N_f frames: $p_i = \{f_{i,j}\}$. A keyframe $f_{i,1}$ is selected in each chunk to extract the spatial features; the motion features of each chunk are extracted using all the frames in p_i. The feature extraction module captures multi-rate motion and multi-scale spatial features that convey semantic information at various depths and levels. Subsequently, the features that encode different semantic information are fed into the feature alignment module to obtain spatial and motion information aligned across time and space. Finally, the two-way features are fused and the resulting quality-aware features are mapped into quality scores using a quality regression module.

3.2   Multi-rate Motion Feature Alignment Module

Traditional single-rate motion features are limited in capturing the different dynamics and temporal relationships of slow and fast motion in videos. The MMFA module extracts multi-rate motion features including both slow and fast motion information. However, owing to differences in their temporal characteristics, the alignment of these multi-rate motion features is required before further processing.

Multi-rate Motion Feature Extraction. We used a pre-trained slow-fast action recognition model [4] to obtain the motion features for each video clip. The slow-fast model extracts spatial and motion information through slow and fast branches, respectively, so that the feature representation of the action recognition network can reflect the motion information of the video effectively. Therefore, given a video clip $p_i(i \in \{1, 2, 3, \ldots, N_c\})$, using the motion recognition network, we obtain the slow and fast features μ_i^s and μ_i^f, respectively. By connecting these features, we obtain two feature sets, one with slow features $X_{slow} = \{\mu_1^s, \mu_2^s, \mu_3^s, \ldots, \mu_I^s\}$ and one with fast features $X_{fast} = \{\mu_1^f, \mu_2^f, \mu_3^f, \ldots, \mu_I^f\}$.

Multi-rate Motion Feature Alignment. The MMFA module adaptively aligns motion features at multiple rates by learning attention weights and performing the weighted summation of multiple motion features. We applied an attention mechanism to the input features at different motion rates X_{slow}, X_{fast} to obtain the respective frame features F^s, F^t using different weights:

$$W_{att} = Softmax\left(ReLu\left(Conv1\left(X_{slow}\right) + Conv2\left(X_{fast}\right)\right)\right) \quad (1)$$

$$F^{s,t} = X_{slow,fast} \otimes W_{att} \quad (2)$$

where $Conv1()$ and $Conv2()$ are two 2D CNNs with unitary kernel size, $ReLu()$ and $Softmax()$ are activation functions, and W_{att} is the attention weight. To obtain data with the same size and sampling rate in the time dimension, we used a multi-rate interpolation method for interpolation and alignment. For each timestamp t, we interpolated and aligned the processed features F^s, F^t to obtain the resulting features at that timestamp:

$$F_t^{s,f} = \sum_{i \in s,f} v_i\left(t\right) F_{\lfloor \frac{t}{r_i} \rfloor r_i}^i \quad (3)$$

where $F_t^{s,f}$ is the feature extracted by the slow-fast network at the video frame t, s and f represent the slow and fast paths, respectively, r_i is the time sampling rate of the i-th frame of the path, and $\lfloor \frac{t}{r_i} \rfloor \cdot r_i$ represents the timestamp closest to t in the i-th path. $v_i(t)$ is the interpolation coefficient obtained by linear or nearest neighbor interpolation as follows:

$$v_i(t) = \frac{\prod_{j=0, j \neq i}^{N} (t - t_j)}{\prod_{j=0, j \neq i}^{N} (t_i - t_j)} \qquad (4)$$

Finally, the aligned features of the slow and fast path are fused using a certain ratio α to obtain the final video feature representation:

$$F_{motion} = \alpha F_t^s + (1 - \alpha) F_t^f \qquad (5)$$

3.3   Multi-scale Spatial Feature Alignment Module

Features extracted from images or data at different scales exhibit distinct properties in terms of resolution and contextual information. Therefore, they require proper alignment before the subsequent processing steps are performed to ensure the accuracy and effectiveness of the model.

Multi-scale Spatial Feature Extraction. Using a pre-trained ResNet [5] model to extract spatial features, we obtained a feature representation with robust generalization capabilities to single-frame spatial resolutions [10,24]. Spatial-domain convolutions of different sizes and depths can capture different types of semantic information. Prior research [2] has demonstrated that, compared to high-level features, low-level features are characterized by higher resolution, and greater location and more detailed information, but lower semantic content and higher noise levels. By contrast, high-level features offer strong semantic information at a low resolution and with poor detail awareness. They prioritize content-aware information and reflect global distortions in videos. Considering the input frames p_i and stage characteristics X_s, we defined $X_s = CNN_s(X_{s-1})$ as the multi-scale output of the CNN model at the stage

Multi-scale Spatial Feature Alignment. To effectively align features that present different semantics and scales, we used a multi-scale channel attention module (MS-CAM). This module aligns features at different scales using channel attention at multiple scales obtained by varying the spatial pooling size. To ensure computational efficiency, we opted for pointwise convolution to implement local contextual aggregation, which only leverages pointwise channel interactions at each spatial location. Given a multi-scale feature $X = \{X_1, X_2, X_3, X_4\}$, the output of the MS-CAM is defined as follows:

$$X' = X \otimes \sigma(L(X) \oplus G(X)), \qquad (6)$$

where $L(X)$ and $G(X)$ denote the local and global channel contexts used by MS-CAM, respectively, $\oplus$ denotes broadcasting addition, $\otimes$ represent elementwise multiplication, and σ is a *sigmoid* activation function. The attention weights $L(X)$ and $G(X)$ are defined as follows:

$$G(X) = \mathcal{B}\left(W^{(3)}\delta\left(\mathcal{B}\left((W^{(4)}\mathcal{P}(X))\right)\right)\right) \tag{7}$$

where $W^{(1)}$, $W^{(2)}$, $W^{(3)}$, and $W^{(4)}$ are the learnable weights of the four convolutional layers, δ denotes the ReLU activation function, $\mathcal{B}$ represents batch normalization, and $\mathcal{P}(X) = \frac{1}{H \times W}\sum_{i=1}^{H}\sum_{i=1}^{W} X_{[:,i,j]}$ is the global average pooling.

3.4   Quality Regression Module

Once we have obtained perceptual feature representations using the feature extraction model, these are mapped onto quality regression models using a multi-layer perceptron (MLP) to calculate the corresponding quality scores. The features obtained from the MMFA and MSFA modules are fed into the quality regression module defined as follows:

$$Q_{final} = MLP\left(Concat\left(F_{motion}, X^{'}\right)\right), \tag{8}$$

where Q_{final} represents the predicted score. By combining motion and spatial domain information, the input of the final quality regression layer of our model includes the two main information streams characterizing the human perception of video content:

3.5   Loss Functions

We used two loss functions to optimize the performance of the proposed model, namely, the mean absolute error (MAE) loss and RANK loss [20] defined as follows:

$$L_{MAE} = \frac{1}{N}\sum_{i=1}^{N}\left|Q_i - \hat{Q}_i\right| \tag{9}$$

$$L_{RANK}^{ij} = \max\left(0, \left|\hat{Q}_i - \hat{Q}_j\right| - e\left(\hat{Q}_i, \hat{Q}_j\right) \cdot (Q_i - Q_j)\right) \tag{10}$$

where i and j are the indices identifying a video in the batch , N is the number of videos in the batch, and $e\left(\hat{Q}_i, \hat{Q}_j\right)$ is defined as follows:

$$e\left(\hat{Q}_i, \hat{Q}_j\right) = \begin{cases} 1, & Q_i > Q_j \\ -1, & otherwise \end{cases} \tag{11}$$

Table 1. Details of the four VQA benchmark datasets

DATASET	Videos	Scenes	Resolution	Time Duration	Annotation Range
CVD2014 [13]	234	5	480p, 720p	10–25 s	[−6.50, 93.38]
KoNViD-1k [6]	1200	1200	540p	8 s	[1.22, 4.64]
LIVE-VQC [15]	585	585	240p-1080p	10 s	[6.2237, 94.2865]
YouTube-UGC [19]	1,142	1,142	360p-4k	20 s	[1.242, 4.698]

Subsequently, L_{RANK} is calculated as follows:

$$L_{RANK} = \frac{1}{N \cdot N} \sum_{i=1}^{N} \sum_{j=1}^{N} L_{RANK}^{ij}. \tag{12}$$

Finally, the loss function is obtained by summation:

$$L = L_{MAE} + \lambda \cdot L_{RANK}, \tag{13}$$

where λ is a hyperparameter that balances the MAE and RANK losses.

4 Experiments

4.1 Experimental Setups

Databases. We used four recent UGC-VQA databases to evaluate the performance of the proposed model: CVD2014 [13], KoNViD-1k [6], LIVE-VQC [15], and YouTube-UGC [19]. The details of these databases are summarized in Table 1.

Performance Metrics. We used two common metrics to test the performance of the model: the Spearman correlation coefficient (SRCC) to evaluate monotonicity, and the Pearson linear correlation coefficient (PLCC) to evaluate the prediction accuracy of the experimental results.

Comparison Methods. We compared the proposed method with the following no-reference models: 1) hand-crafted models: V-BLIINDS [14], TLVQM [7], VIDEVAL [17]; 2)CNN-based models: RAPIQUE [18], VSFA [10]; 3)spatio-temporal features-based models: GSTVQA [2], BVQA [9], SimpleVQA [16].

Implementation Details. In our study, we used pre-trained CNN-based models, such as ResNet-50 and VGG-16, and others networks to extract spatial features. We used fine-tuned pre-trained slow-fast models on the Kinetics-400 dataset to extract motion features. In the spatial branch of our model, the input frames were randomly cropped at a resolution of 448×448; in the temporal

Table 2. Median SRCC and PLCC values for CVD2014, KoNViD-1k, LIVE-VQC, and YouTube-UGC under a single training setup. The best performing model in each metric is highlighted in bold.

DATASET	CVD2014		KoNViD-1k		YouTube-UGC		LIVE-VQC	
Method	SRCC	PLCC	SRCC	PLCC	SRCC	PLCC	SRCC	PLCC
V-BLIINDS [14]	0.8048	0.8126	0.7085	0.7499	0.5688	0.5643	0.6969	0.7367
TLVQM [7]	0.7850	0.7880	0.7644	0.7607	0.6697	0.665	0.7698	0.813
VIDEVAL [17]	0.8251	0.8292	0.7857	0.7925	0.7857	0.7925	0.7530	0.7935
RAPIQUE [18]	0.8015	0.8024	0.8044	0.8094	0.7664	0.7736	0.7591	0.7998
VSFA [10]	0.8499	0.8478	0.7824	0.7867	0.7618	0.7819	0.7338	0.7711
GSTVQA [2]	0.8276	0.838	0.8107	0.8009	-	-	0.7103	0.7320
BVQA [9]	0.8634	0.8618	0.8335	0.8401	0.8330	0.8334	0.8228	0.8198
SimpleVQA [16]	**0.8663**	0.8646	0.8505	0.8492	0.8471	**0.8494**	0.8367	0.8355
Proposed	0.8658	**0.8658**	**0.8581**	**0.8546**	**0.8538**	0.8488	**0.8466**	**0.8411**

Table 3. SRCC results of the cross-database evaluation.

Training	LIVE-VQC		KoNViD-1k		YouTube-UGC	
Testing	KoNViD-1k	YouTube-UGC	LIVE-VQC	YouTube-UGC	LIVE-VQC	KoNViD-1k
BVQA [9]	0.7382	0.6025	0.6949	0.7799	0.6887	**0.7847**
Proposed	**0.7489**	**0.6450**	**0.7153**	**0.7901**	**0.7074**	0.7815

branch, the resolution of video clips was resized to 224×224. We used Adam as the optimizer with an initial learning rate of 0.00001 and batch size of 8, with the relevant settings following [16]. We trained the proposed model using a server with four NVIDIA RTX2080Ti. The hyper-parameters λ and α were set to 1 and 0.4, respectively; both values were determined experimentally. For KoNViD-1k, YouTube-UGC, LIVE-VQC, and CVD2014, we randomly split these databases into the training setwith 80% videos and the test set with 20% videos for 10 times, and report the median values of SRCC and PLCC.

4.2   Performance Comparison

Table 2 presents the performance results of the proposed VQA model evaluated on KoNViD-1k, YouTube-UGC, CVD2014, and LIVE-VQC datasets. Our model significantly outperforms the compared methods on the three UGC VQA databases. The improvement on the CVD2014 dataset was moderate possibly owing to its limited number of scenes and videos, which may restrict the access of the model to spatial and temporal features, thus, affecting the accuracy of predictions. The performance improvement of our model on the KoNViD-1k dataset was also limited owing to the absence of multi-resolution data, which prevented the proposed feature alignment module from contributing significantly.

Hand-crafted NR-VQA methods, such as V-BLIINDS, TLVQM, and VIDE-VAL, showed promising results on simple datasets by combining spatial and

Table 4. Ablation experiments of the proposed module.

DATASET	LIVE-VQC		KoNViD-1k		YouTube-UGC	
Method	SRCC	PLCC	SRCC	PLCC	SRCC	PLCC
STAN-VQA w/o MMFA & MSFA	0.7901	0.7874	0.8007	0.7893	0.8115	0.8104
STAN-VQA w/o MMFA	0.8153	0.8056	0.827	0.8292	0.8342	0.8351
STAN-VQA w/o MSFA	0.8213	0.8352	0.8352	0.8327	0.8411	0.8468
STAN-VQA	0.8466	0.8411	0.8581	0.8546	0.8538	0.8488

temporal quality features. However, their performance deteriorated significantly on more complex and diverse datasets. On such datasets, deep learning-based VQA methods showed an improved performance. Since VSFA extracts spatial features from a pre-trained image recognition model without considering video quality, its performance was relatively poor. GSTVQA and BVQA combine relevant features in the spatial and temporal domains, thus, their performance was significantly enhanced compared to that of the previous methods. SimpleVQA achieved impressive outcomes on large datasets including data at multiple resolutions and frame rates owing to the combination of multi-scale and multi-rate aligned features. Similarly, the proposed model realized multi-scale and multi-rate feature alignments based on spatial and time-series relationship information. This alignment process led to significant improvements in the performance of our model on large datasets.

4.3   Cross-Database Evaluation

UGC videos can encompass several distortions and contents, many of which may not be present in a single training set. Therefore, the ability of UGC VQA models to generalize is critical. For this reason, we performed cross-dataset tests to demonstrate the strong generalization ability of the proposed method. In addition, we trained the quality prediction models on one of the three experimental datasets (KoNViD-1k, LIVE-VQC, and YouTube-UGC) and used the remaining two datasets for testing, considering the same conditions used by BVQA [9]. The experimental results listed in Table 3 confirm the significantly improved performance of the proposed model in cross-database evaluation tasks, showing both effectiveness and generalizability.

4.4   Ablation Study

Ablation experiments were conducted to assess the impact of the proposed MMFA and MSFA modules on the performance of the system. We jointly removed these two modules from the proposed model structure and directly performed feature splicing in the feature extraction stage (STAN-VQA w/o MMFA & MSFA experiment). The results presented in Table 4 indicate that relying solely on spatio-temporal features significantly affects the performance of the model on complex VQA tasks. The addition of both MMFA and MSFA modules results in an improvement in the performance higher than that obtained by adding each module separately, thus, confirming the importance of the synergic contribution of the MMFA and MSFA modules. In addition, as evidenced by the attention maps depicted in Fig. 1, the combined MMFA and MSFA modules successfully identify low-quality regions located at the edges of the target objects and in the background.

5   Conclusion

In this study, we developed a STAN model for NR-VQA that performs combined multi-rate motion and multi-scale spatial feature alignment, implemented by the MMFA and MSFA modules, respectively. By integrating Lagrangian multi-rate and multi-scale attention-based alignment mechanisms into our network architecture, we developed a model that handles multiple features efficiently without information loss or conflict issues. Moreover, the addition of an attention-based feature alignment module enables the association of time-series and spatial information, thus, enhancing low-quality regions around subject objects and ultimately delivering superior outcomes. The proposed model was evaluated on various benchmark datasets, showing superior performance compared with that of existing methods and demonstrating the effectiveness of our combined approach. This study shows that overcoming the challenges of UGC problems is a complex task with several constraints. However, these challenges can be addressed by efficiently aligning spatial and temporal aspects at different resolutions and frame rates. Our results confirmed that combining feature alignment approaches using attention mechanisms represents a promising solution to address current limitations of NR-VQA methods.

References

1. Caspi, Y., Irani, M.: Spatio-temporal alignment of sequences. IEEE Trans. Pattern Anal. Mach. Intell. **24**(11), 1409–1424 (2002)
2. Chen, B., Zhu, L., Li, G., Lu, F., Fan, H., Wang, S.: Learning generalized spatial-temporal deep feature representation for no-reference video quality assessment. IEEE Trans. Circuits Syst. Video Technol. **32**(4), 1903–1916 (2021)
3. Chen, P., Li, L., Ma, L., Wu, J., Shi, G.: Rirnet: recurrent-in-recurrent network for video quality assessment. In: Proceedings of the 28th ACM International Conference on Multimedia, pp. 834–842 (2020)
4. Feichtenhofer, C., Fan, H., Malik, J., He, K.: Slowfast networks for video recognition. In: Proceedings of the IEEE/CVF International Conference on Computer Vision, pp. 6202–6211 (2019)
5. He, K., Zhang, X., Ren, S., Sun, J.: Deep residual learning for image recognition. In: Proceedings of the IEEE Conference on Computer Vision and Pattern Recognition, pp. 770–778 (2016)
6. Hosu, V., et al.: The Konstanz natural video database (KoNViD-1k). In: 2017 Ninth International Conference on Quality of Multimedia Experience (QoMEX), pp. 1–6. IEEE (2017)

7. Korhonen, J.: Two-level approach for no-reference consumer video quality assessment. IEEE Trans. Image Process. **28**(12), 5923–5938 (2019)
8. Korhonen, J., Su, Y., You, J.: Blind natural video quality prediction via statistical temporal features and deep spatial features. In: Proceedings of the 28th ACM International Conference on Multimedia, pp. 3311–3319 (2020)
9. Li, B., Zhang, W., Tian, M., Zhai, G., Wang, X.: Blindly assess quality of in-the-wild videos via quality-aware pre-training and motion perception. IEEE Trans. Circuits Syst. Video Technol. **32**(9), 5944–5958 (2022)
10. Li, D., Jiang, T., Jiang, M.: Quality assessment of in-the-wild videos. In: Proceedings of the 27th ACM International Conference on Multimedia, pp. 2351–2359 (2019)
11. Li, Y., et al.: No-reference video quality assessment with 3D shearlet transform and convolutional neural networks. IEEE Trans. Circuits Syst. Video Technol. **26**(6), 1044–1057 (2016). https://doi.org/10.1109/TCSVT.2015.2430711
12. Liu, W., Duanmu, Z., Wang, Z.: End-to-end blind quality assessment of compressed videos using deep neural networks. In: ACM Multimedia, pp. 546–554 (2018)
13. Nuutinen, M., Virtanen, T., Vaahteranoksa, M., Vuori, T., Oittinen, P., Häkkinen, J.: CVD 2014-a database for evaluating no-reference video quality assessment algorithms. IEEE Trans. Image Process. **25**(7), 3073–3086 (2016)
14. Saad, M.A., Bovik, A.C., Charrier, C.: Blind prediction of natural video quality. IEEE Trans. Image Process. **23**(3), 1352–1365 (2014). https://doi.org/10.1109/TIP.2014.2299154
15. Sinno, Z., Bovik, A.C.: Large-scale study of perceptual video quality. IEEE Trans. Image Process. **28**(2), 612–627 (2018)
16. Sun, W., Min, X., Lu, W., Zhai, G.: A deep learning based no-reference quality assessment model for UGC videos. In: Proceedings of the 30th ACM International Conference on Multimedia, pp. 856–865 (2022)
17. Tu, Z., Wang, Y., Birkbeck, N., Adsumilli, B., Bovik, A.C.: UGC-VQA: benchmarking blind video quality assessment for user generated content. IEEE Trans. Image Process. **30**, 4449–4464 (2021)
18. Tu, Z., Yu, X., Wang, Y., Birkbeck, N., Adsumilli, B., Bovik, A.C.: Rapique: rapid and accurate video quality prediction of user generated content. IEEE Open J. Signal Process. **2**, 425–440 (2021)
19. Wang, Y., Inguva, S., Adsumilli, B.: Youtube UGC dataset for video compression research. In: 2019 IEEE 21st International Workshop on Multimedia Signal Processing (MMSP), pp. 1–5. IEEE (2019)
20. Wen, S., Wang, J.: A strong baseline for image and videoquality assessment. In: arXiv preprint arXiv:2111.07104 (2021)
21. Xu, J., Li, J., Zhou, X., Zhou, W., Wang, B., Chen, Z.: Perceptual quality assessment of internet videos. In: Proceedings of the 29th ACM International Conference on Multimedia, pp. 1248–1257 (2021)
22. Ying, Z., Mandal, M., Ghadiyaram, D., Bovik, A.: Patch-VQ: 'patching up' the video quality problem. In: Proceedings of the IEEE/CVF Conference on Computer Vision and Pattern Recognition, pp. 14019–14029 (2021)
23. You, J., Korhonen, J.: Deep neural networks for no-reference video quality assessment. In: 2019 IEEE International Conference on Image Processing (ICIP), pp. 2349–2353. IEEE (2019)
24. Zhang, W., Ma, K., Yan, J., Deng, D., Wang, Z.: Blind image quality assessment using a deep bilinear convolutional neural network. IEEE Trans. Circuits Syst. Video Technol. **30**(1), 36–47 (2018)

Style Expansion Without Forgetting for Handwritten Character Recognition

Jie Ruan(iD), Zhenyu Weng(iD), Jian Zhang(iD), Yuqing Wang(iD), Longhui Yu, Qiankun Gao, and Yuesheng Zhu(✉)(iD)

School of Electronic and Computer Engineering, Peking University, Beijing, China
{ruanjie,wyq,yulonghui,gqk}@stu.pku.edu.cn,
{zhangjian.sz,wzytumbler,zhuys}@pku.edu.cn

Abstract. Handwritten character recognition (HCR) is still a challenging task due to diverse writing styles. In existing works, the recognition models for recognizing handwritten characters are usually trained with limited handwriting styles. However, there are always some new styles that are not included in the training sets in practical applications, degrading the recognition performance. Re-training the models with updated training sets containing new styles would increase the computational cost and complexity. In this paper, a new **Style Expansion Learning HCR** (StyleEL-HCR) problem is formulated to characterize this issue and a novel **Reliable Prototype Augmentation** (RePA) framework is developed for StyleEL-HCR. The RePA is composed of Soft Knowledge Distillation with replay (SKD), Character Prototype Augmentation (CPA), and Strict Gate Mechanism (SGM). SKD memorizes knowledge from old styles through distillation and replay, CPA learns representative information by memorizing character-representative prototypes and augmenting them in new learning phases to better distinguish different characters when the replay data is limited, and SGM augments the prototypes in a reliable way to improves the reliability of the recognition model. Adopting distillation and replay together with reliable prototype augmentation, RePA has the ability to learn new styles as well as preserve knowledge of old styles. Our experimental results have shown that the RePA can obtain better recognition performance for handwritten English, Chinese and digit characters compared to other methods, particularly when the handwritten Chinese character categories scale is large.

Keywords: Handwritten character recognition · Style expansion learning · Knowledge distillation

1 Introduction

Handwritten character recognition (HCR) aims to convert handwritten characters to digital characters to make handwritten text ready for convenient use in practical application [26]. Research on HCR is challenging because the writing styles are diverse and increasing when the styles of training data are limited.

L. Iliadis et al. (Eds.): ICANN 2023, LNCS 14256, pp. 172–184, 2023.
https://doi.org/10.1007/978-3-031-44213-1_15

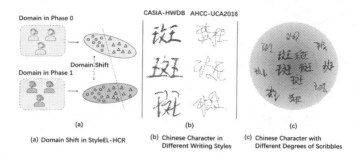

Fig. 1. (a) Domain shift problem in StyleEL-HCR. (b) Chinese characters in different writing styles. (c) Chinese characters with different degrees of scribbles.

Moreover, the scale of character categories in some languages is large, such as Chinese, making handwritten character recognition more challenging [15,32].

Modern deep-learning-based HCR methods [5,9,20,28–31,33] mainly use a limited number of writing styles and assume styles in the existing dataset can cover most of the styles in reality. Several works [3,16] use domain adaptation to reduce the mismatch between training and test data. However, it had become apparent that these models tend to over-fit the captured styles or cause domain drift during domain adaptation, which causes forgetting knowledge learned before. Moreover, considering that different people have different handwriting styles (as shown in Fig. 1(b)), there are always new people who produce new handwriting styles. Therefore, it is necessary to improve the recognition ability in the case of increasing handwriting styles in network training.

In this paper, we formulate a new **Style Expansion Learning HCR** (StyleEL-HCR) problem. In a low-resource environment, the HCR model is trained on existing data to learn the knowledge of existing styles. When new-style data arrive, we hope to update the HCR model with only the train data in new styles, so that the model can remember the learned knowledge and absorb new knowledge. The goal is to make the model have good performance in recognizing both existing-style data and new-style data. The general motivation behind the recently proposed incremental learning [24,25] matches ours. However, getting it to work with HCR has its challenges, and to our knowledge has not been tackled before in the literature. The main challenges come from the large scale of character categories in some languages and the increasing styles of handwritten characters. Specifically, some handwriting styles are rather sloppy (as shown in Fig. 1(c)), which can cause the model to suffer from these outliers when only a small amount of knowledge can be replayed, resulting in catastrophic forgetting.

In order to solve the catastrophic forgetting caused by domain shift in the StyleEL-HCR problem, we propose a new framework namely **Reliable Prototype Augmentation** (RePA). RePA is composed of three modules, namely Soft Knowledge Distillation with replay (SKD), Character Prototype Augmentation (CPA), and Strict Gate Mechanism (SGM). SKD memorizes knowledge learned from old styles through soft knowledge distillation and replay methods. Meanwhile, considering that the scale of character categories in some languages may be large, the CPA module memorizes one character-representative prototype for each learned character and learns augmented prototypes in the new training phases. Moreover, we propose SGM that reliably augments prototypes to reduce the impact of outliers on the overall performance of the system.

The main contributions are as follows: 1) We formulate the problem of StyleEL-HCR, where the model needs to maintain recognition performance on characters of both the new and old styles while only learning characters of the new style in the new phase. 2) We propose RePA to tackle this problem by introducing reliable prototype augmentation with a gate mechanism to enable the model better review the learned knowledge and reduce the impact of scribbled characters. 3) Experimental results on handwritten English, Chinese and digit character recognition show RePA can better tackle the forgetting problem in StyleEL-HCR, especially when the scale of Chinese character categories is large.

2 Related Works

Incremental learning is one of the most challenging problems in neural networks which suffers from catastrophic forgetting. Researchers have proposed methods to solve this forgetting dilemma. Those methods can be divided into three main categories, namely architectural strategies, regularisation strategies, and rehearsal strategies. **Architectural strategies** design specific architecture to deal with catastrophic forgetting [24,25]. **Regularisation strategies** put regularisation terms into the loss function to promote selective consolidation of significant past weights, as done by EWC [14] and RW [6]. **Rehearsal strategies**, which are a kind of solutions to forgetting, are based on absorbing past information and replaying it to the model in new training phases to strengthen connections for memories. For example, Meta-Experience Replay [23] proposed a replay method by using meta-learning techniques to maximize transfer and minimize interference. Wang et al. [27] proposed memory replay with data compression to improve the efficiency of utilizing the old samples in a limited buffer.

Recently, DER [4] is a strong baseline for the general domain continual learning setting by replaying network responses instead of ground truth labels. However, DER does not consider the influence brought by sloppy handwriting styles, which is not suitable for StyleEL-HCR. PASS [34] memorizes one class-representative prototype for each old class and adopts prototype augmentation in the deep feature space to maintain the decision boundary of previous tasks, which is similar to CPA. However, PASS is designed to solve the catastrophic forgetting problem in class increment learning where the model needs to continuously learn new classes from the data stream. Since the number of classes of the StyleEL-HCR task does not vary with the input of the data, PASS is not suitable for solving the StyleEL-HCR problem. To our knowledge, there is no incremental learning work designed for the task of HCR currently.

3 Methodology

3.1 Problem Statement

The StyleEL-HCR problem is split into T learning phases in total, i.e., one initial phase and $T-1$ incremental phase where the domain is changing in each phase

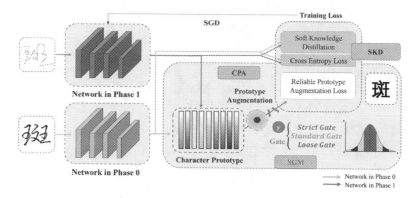

Fig. 2. The proposed framework RePA for StyleEL-HCR.

$t \in \{0, ..., T-1\}$. In the initial phase, input samples x together with their labels y, which satisfies i.i.d distribution D_t, is available to train the model f with parameters θ. Incremental learning systems have strict memory space limitations, so in later phases, only a small subset of data in the previous phases can be saved in the exemplar and used to replay in later phases. Specifically, in the current phase t_c, exemplar data from old phases together with all data from the new phase are used to train the model. Then data from both old and new domains are evaluated on the trained model. The objective is to classify data from any of the previous phases up to the current one $t \in \{0, ...t_c\}$: $\text{argmin}_{\theta} \sum_{t=0}^{t_c} \mathcal{L}_t$, where $\mathcal{L}_t \cong \mathbb{E}_{(x,y)\sim D_t} [L_{ce}(y, f_\theta(x))]$ and L_{ce} is the cross-entropy loss.

3.2 Overview of Framework

As shown in Fig. 2, RePA is composed of three modules, namely Soft Knowledge Distillation with replay (SKD), Character Prototype Augmentation (CPA), and Strict Gate Mechanism (SGM). SKD memorizes knowledge learned from old styles through soft knowledge distillation and replay methods to solve catastrophic forgetting. CPA module memorizes one character-representative prototype for each learned character and learns augmented prototypes in the new training phases to solve the problem of large-scale Chinese character categories. SGM only resamples reliable samples with representative and transferable features when the prototype is augmented to reduce the impact of outliers and improve reliability.

In the initial phase, samples with their labels in the same domain are used to train the 0-th phase network. A small subset of the data is saved as exemplars and several prototypes where each prototype represents a character in a training phase are memorized. Then in the new phase, only new data, exemplars, and prototypes in the old phases are accessible to the training network which not only distills knowledge learned in the old phase but also trains accessible data in the current phase. During training, each prototype is augmented with certain disturbances. Moreover, SGM samples characters near the class center, which excludes the influence of outliers on the overall performance. Data from both new and old phases will be tested in each phase.

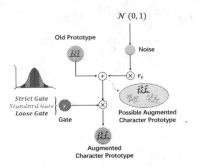

Fig. 3. Reliable prototype augmentation: CPA with SGM.

The overall objective of the proposed RePA is as follows:

$$\mathcal{L}_{RePA} = \mathcal{L}_{SKD} + w\mathcal{L}_{CPA\&SGM}, \tag{1}$$

where w is a balance factor.

3.3   Soft Knowledge Distillation with Replay (SKD)

RePA aims to learn new knowledge in the new phase while preserving knowledge learned in the old phase. To better preserve knowledge learned before and inspired by knowledge distillation and replay methods [4,13,17,22], we seek to minimize the following objective:

$$\mathcal{L}_{SKD} = \mathcal{L}_{t_c} + \alpha\mathbb{E}_{(x',z')}\left[D_{KL}\left(\text{softmax}(z')\|f_\theta(x')\right)\right] + \beta\mathbb{E}_{(x',y')}\left[L_{ce}\left(y', f_\theta\left(x'\right)\right)\right], \tag{2}$$

where x' and y' are data and labels in the buffer. α and β are to balance terms. The output logits is $z' \cong h_\theta(x')$, where $f_\theta(x') \cong \text{softmax}\left(h_\theta(x')\right)$.

3.4   Character Prototype Augmentation (CPA)

Since there are various handwriting styles and a large number of categories of handwritten characters in languages like Chinese, the model needs to memorize more representative information to have better performance. Therefore, RePA remembers the general feature of each character. In this way, the model can recall the knowledge learned before in the new stage through the general feature information of these character categories. However, only learning class feature information in the new stage is not enough. By augmenting the category features, the model can review more information learned before in the new stage. In short, the CPA module learns representative information by memorizing character-representative prototypes and augmenting them in new learning phases.

Firstly, CPA learns typical category information. In order to reduce the distortion of the feature space when training data in the new domain, we calculate and store one prototype for each class k in each phase t:

$$\mu_{t,k} = \frac{\sum_{n=1}^{N_{t,k}} F_{\theta_t}(x_{n,t,k})}{N_{t,k}}, \tag{3}$$

where $N_{t,k}$ represents the number of labeled training samples in t-th phase. F_{θ_t} is the feature extractor of t-th phase. During the new phase, the prototypes from each class in the old phases are augmented in this way:

$$F_{t,k} = \mu_{t,k} + o \times r_t, \tag{4}$$

where $o \sim \mathcal{N}(0,1)$ is the Gaussian noise and $F_{t,k}$ is the augmented prototype of class k in the t-th phase. r_t is a scale to control the uncertainty of the augmented prototypes which can be computed as the average variance of prototypes in the t-th phase. In this way, the model can recover more information about category features. r is calculated as:

$$r_t = \sqrt{r_{t-1}^2 + \frac{1}{K} \sum_{k=1}^{K} \frac{\text{tr}\,(\Sigma_{t,k})}{R}}, \tag{5}$$

where K is the number of classes and R represents the dimension of the feature space. $\Sigma_{t,k}$ indicates the covariance matrix for the features from class k at phase t and tr operation computes the trace of matrix $\Sigma_{t,k}$. r_t adaptively updated by data from each class in new phases in Eq. 5 which means when domain shifts, r_t can be updated adaptively.

3.5 Strict Gate Mechanism (SGM)

There are various styles for handwritten characters (as shown in Fig. 1(c)). Most of the characters written by people are quite satisfactory, such as the words in the dashed box near the center of the category in Fig. 1(c). However, a small number of people wrote more scribbled words, such as the words outside the dotted line in Fig. 1(c). We hope to reduce the impact of outliers when we can only recall previous knowledge by replaying a limited number of samples. In order to select reliable exemplars to represent knowledge learned in old phases and reduce the impact of outliers, we propose a gate mechanism, which keeps unreliable samples out of the door and allows reliable samples be selected. The gate mechanism is shown in Fig. 3. Specifically, a gate γ is to control the augmentation process:

$$F_{t,k} = \gamma \times (\mu_{t,k} + o \times r_t), \tag{6}$$

where γ represents three states of the gate namely strict state, standard state, and loose state inspired by standard deviations in the Gaussian distribution.

When the gate is in a strict state, only samples in the range of one-fold variance near the prototype can enter the experience replay stage in new phases, which means 68.27% samples can be resampled by the prototype augmentation process. Standard gata allows samples in the range of $\mu \pm 2\delta$ to be replayed. The loose gate allows samples in the range of $\mu \pm 3\delta$ to be resampled, which means it only excludes 0.26% samples that are outliers to be replayed.

The loss function of the CPA module and SGM module is as follows:

$$\mathcal{L}_{CPA\&SGM} = \sum_{t=0}^{T-1} L_{ce}\left(y, f_{\theta_t}(F_t)\right), \tag{7}$$

where F_t is the features augmented for all the classes in the t-th phase. Intuitively, prototypes augmented with soft variance together with new data are fed to the model to maintain discrimination and make a balance between different domains during new phases.

4 Experiments

To evaluate the performance of RePA, we conduct experiments on the challenging style expansion handwritten Chinese character recognition task (StyleEL-HCCR) with large character scale and the style expansion handwritten English character recognition (StyleEL-HECR) and digit character recognition (StyleEL-HDCR) tasks. Extensive ablation experiments are conducted to investigate the role of each module of our model and the influence of some parameters.

4.1 Datasets and Comparison Methods

Datasets. We conduct StyleEL-HCCR experiments on CASIA-HWDB1.1 (as shown in Fig. 1(b)) [16] and AHCC-UCAS2016 (as shown in Fig. 1(b)) [21]. CASIA-HWDB consists of data in normal writing style and AHCC-UCAS2016 is an in-air handwritten Chinese character dataset. We select 3755 common classes, each class has 70 training samples and 30 test samples at each stage. The incremental learning method is first trained in dataset CASIA-HWDB1.1 and tested on dataset CASIA-HWDB1.1 in the initial phase. In the new phase, the model is trained on the dataset from a different domain such as AHCC-UCAS2016. The model needs to have good recognition performance on data from all datasets that have been trained. Experiment on StyleEL-HDCR is conducted on Permuted MNIST (P-MNIST) [14] and Rotated MNIST (R-MNIST) [19]. P-MNIST uses a random permutation to the pixels and R-MNIST rotates the image by a random angle in the interval $[0, \pi]$. Experiments on StyleEL-HECR are conducted on datasets Permuted EMNIST (P-EMNIST) and Rotated EMNIST (R-EMNIST), which use the same transform method as P-MNIST [14] and R-MNIST [19] to process a handwritten English character dataset EMNIST [10]. All MNIST-based and EMNIST-based experiments consist of 20 steps. Each step contains all classes.

Comparison Approaches. For the StyleEL-HCCR experiment, RePA is compared with several popular incremental learning methods namely LUCIR [13], AANET-iCaRL [17,22], AANET-LUCIR [13,17] and DER [4]. We also compare RePA with traditional joint training. For the StyleEL-HDCR experiment, we conduct the experiment on seven related methods (ER [23], GEM [19], A-GEM [8], FDR [2], GSS [1], HAL [7], DER [4]). Due to the large performance gap between DER [4] and other methods, the handwritten English character recognition experiment only compares with DER [4].

Table 1. Experiment results of accuracy in StyleEL-HCCR. Overall represents the overall performance of all stages of the model. GAP1 represents the difference between the baseline method LUCIR vs the current method in Phase 1. GAP2 represents the overall performance gap between the baseline method LUCIR vs the current method. RePA* represents RePA runs under a large buffer size.

Method	Phase 0 (%)	Phase 1 (%)	GAP1 (%)	Overall (%)	GAP2 (%)
JOINT	-	90.75%	29.66%	90.75%	13.20%
LUCIR	94.02%	61.09%	-	77.56%	-
AANET-iCaRL	94.13%	64.78%	3.69%	79.46%	1.90%
AANET-LUCIR	93.87%	64.78%	3.69%	79.33%	1.77%
DER	91.82%	70.93%	9.84%	81.38%	3.82%
RePA (ours)	92.68%	**78.92%**	**17.83%**	**85.80%**	**8.24%**
RePA* (ours)	93.55%	**91.99%**	**30.90%**	**92.77%**	**15.22%**

4.2   Implementation Details

To provide a fair comparison among all methods, we use ResNet-34 [12] as the backbone for all methods on StyleEL-HCCR tasks and ResNet-18 on StyleEL-HECR and StyleEL-HDCR tasks. Changing the backbone will improve the performance in Phase 0. All the models are trained with Stochastic Gradient Descent (SGD) optimizer. Following replay setting in methods [11,13,18,22], LUCIR [13], AANET-iCaRL [17,22] and AANET-LUCIR [13,17], we store 20 exemplars for each old class. We iterate 160 epochs per phase. As RePA uses the reservoir sampling method, we use a smaller buffer than their method to explore the performance of our method in a limited storage space, which stores 200 samples, only 5% of the classes at most in the HCCR experiment, handwritten English character and digit recognition experiments. We also explore the performance of our model with the same storage space as other comparison method, which is 75100 samples in the HCCR experiment. Moreover, random crops and horizontal flips are used for both streaming data and buffer examples in our method. The batch size of the HCCR experiment is 256 and RePA iterates 100 epochs per phase. The batch size of handwritten digit recognition and handwritten English character recognition experiments is 128 and we iterate one epoch per phase. We set $\alpha = \beta = 1$ for the experiment on P-MNIST and P-EMNIST, $\alpha = 1$ and $\beta = 0.5$ for experiment on R-MNIST and R-EMNIST, and $\alpha = 0.1$ and $\beta = 0.5$ for HCCR experiment. We use $w = 1$ in the StyleEL-HCCR experiment and $w = 10$ in the StyleEL-HECR and StyleEL-HDCR experiments.

4.3 Performance Evaluation

Handwritten Chinese Character Recognition Task. Experiment results are shown in Table 1. It is obvious that RePA outperforms other methods when storing only 200 samples, which confirms that RePA is able to memorize more effective knowledge and can better tackle catastrophic forgetting as well as style incremental problems. Take the results of Phase 1 as example, our method works better than other methods and outperforms the popular incremental learning method LUCIR with a gap of 17.83%. In addition, the overall performance of RePA is 8.24% better than LUCIR.

We further explore the performance of RePA on a larger buffer size and find RePA* outperforms joint training when using a buffer size of 75100 which is

Table 2. Results for four benchmarks namely P-MNIST, R-MNIST, P-EMNIST, and R-EMNIST, averaged across 5 runs. † indicates experiment results from paper [4]. Acc denotes the recognition accuracy of the last phase. GAP represents the accuracy of improvement between the current method and the worst performing method.

Method	P-MNIST		R-MNIST	
	Acc (%)	GAP (%)	Acc (%)	GAP (%)
JOINT †	94.33 ± 0.17		95.76 ± 0.04	
GSS †	63.72 ± 0.70	-	79.50 ± 0.41	-
GEM †	66.93 ± 1.25	3.21	80.80 ± 1.15	1.3
A-GEM †	66.42 ± 4.00	2.7	81.91 ± 0.76	2.41
ER †	72.37 ± 0.87	8.65	85.01 ± 1.90	5.51
FDR †	74.77 ± 0.83	11.05	85.22 ± 3.35	5.72
HAL †	74.15 ± 1.65	10.43	84.02 ± 0.98	4.52
DER †	83.58 ± 0.59	19.86	90.43 ± 1.87	10.93
DER	83.71 ± 1.14	19.99	89.17 ± 1.84	9.67
RePA (ours)	$\mathbf{84.20 \pm 0.60}$	**20.48**	$\mathbf{90.58 \pm 3.20}$	**11.08**
Method	P-EMNIST		R-EMNIST	
	Acc (%)	GAP (%)	Acc (%)	GAP (%)
DER	89.76 ± 0.25	-	89.69 ± 0.24	-
RePA (ours)	$\mathbf{89.85 \pm 0.22}$	**0.09**	$\mathbf{89.78 \pm 0.28}$	**0.09**

28.6% of the samples. This is the same buffer size as LUCIR, AANET-iCaRL and AANET-LUCIR. The result shows RePA can use less computing power and memory space to achieve better results than the traditional joint training method. The reason why RePA* outperforms joint training is that the reliable prototype augmentation method enables the model to learn more effective pattern knowledge of handwritten Chinese characters.

Handwritten Digit and English Character Recognition Tasks. We also conduct experiments on four style expansion handwritten digit and English character recognition tasks. Results are shown in Table 2. After twenty domain incremental phases, RePA achieves higher accuracy than all other comparison methods except for the joint training method in the incremental handwritten digit recognition experiment, which shows that RePA can better tackle the style expansion learning handwritten digit recognition problem. Take the results of the experiment on the benchmark P-MNIST as an example, RePA outperforms the baseline GSS with a gap of 20.48%. On the incremental handwritten English character recognition problem, RePA also achieves better performance than the strong comparison method DER, which shows the potential of our method in solving style expansion learning handwritten English character recognition problem. Experiment results show the ability of RePA to solve the problem of style expansion learning handwritten character recognition.

4.4 Ablation Study

RePA Component Ablation. The proposed method RePA is comprised of three components: SKD, CPA, and SGM. We analyze the isolated effect of each component on RePA by adding modules on the basic component SKD on the challenging StyleEL-HCCR problem. The backbone is ResNet-18. From the isolation experiment in Table 3, we can observe that: (1) Fundamental component SKD reaches an accuracy at 70.93% in the first stage and 81.38% overall. It is obvious that Knowledge distillation with soft logit together with the experiment replay method is important for RePA. (2) When adding the prototype augmentation component, the method is 7.06% better than the original SKD component in the first phase. The reason why the performance of the model is improved is that the prototype augmentation method allows the model to learn more representative information about characters. (3) Gate mechanism successfully selects reliable samples to train in the new phase and achieves better results than Case 2. By employing character prototype augmentation and the strict gate mechanism in SKD, the network can memorize more representative and transferable features about styles for new HCR tasks.

Table 3. Effectiveness of components in RePA.

Case	SKD	CPA	SGM	Phase 0 (%)	Phase 1 (%)	Overall (%)
1	√			91.82%	70.93%	81.38%
2	√	√		92.74%	77.99%	85.37%
3	√	√	√	92.68%	78.92%	85.80%

Table 4. RePA with different gate restrictions.

Range	Phase 0 (%)	Phase 1 (%)	Overall (%)
$\mu \pm \delta$	92.68%	**78.92%**	**85.8%**
$\mu \pm 2\delta$	92.68%	78.43%	85.56%
$\mu \pm 3\delta$	92.62%	78.36%	85.49%
w/o **Gate**	92.74%	77.99%	85.37%

Gate Hyperparameter Selection. We propose a multi-gate mechanism to limit the impact of outliers on the system. There are three kinds of gates, namely strict gate, standard gate, and loose gate, which represent sampling data in the range of $\mu \pm \delta$, $\mu \pm 2\delta$, and $\mu \pm 3\delta$ respectively. Here μ represents the mean of each class and δ represents the variance of each class. As shown in Table 4, RePA without gate mechanism reaches an accuracy at 77.99% in the 1-*st* phase and 85.37% overall. Table 4 demonstrates that when selecting 68.37%, 95.45% and 99.74% samples in the Gaussian distribution, our method achieve an accuracy rate of 78.92%, 78.43% and 78.36% in the 1-*st* phase respectively. Here we find strict gate mechanism outperforms other gates in our experiment setting as it selects the samples close to the center of each class in the new training phase, which allows it to ensure the overall performance of the model and eliminate the influence of interfering data. Therefore, we adopt the strict gate mechanism.

5   Conclusion

In this paper, we first formulate StyleEL-HCR: a Style Expansion Learning Handwritten Character Recognition problem. And we propose a novel baseline, RePA, for writing style expansion handwritten character recognition. RePA uses reliable prototype augmentation with a gate mechanism for retaining handwritten character knowledge learned before as well as improving the robustness of the model and therefore avoiding catastrophic forgetting due to domain shift. Extensive experiments on style expansion learning handwritten English, Chinese and digit character recognition demonstrate that RePA outperforms other approaches in learning new styles as well as preserving knowledge of old styles, which confirms that RePA can better memorize and review the reliable knowledge learned before. In future work, unsupervised StyleEL-HCR or few-shot StyleEL-HCR will be further explored.

Acknowledgement. This work was supported in part by the National Innovation 2030 Major S&T Project of China under Grant 2020AAA0104203, in part by the Nature Science Foundation of China under Grant 62006007.

References

1. Aljundi, R., Lin, M., Goujaud, B., Bengio, Y.: Gradient based sample selection for online continual learning. In: NeurIPS, vol. 32 (2019)
2. Benjamin, A.S., Rolnick, D., Kording, K.: Measuring and regularizing networks in function space. arXiv preprint arXiv:1805.08289 (2018)
3. Bhunia, A.K., Ghose, S., Kumar, A., Chowdhury, P.N., Sain, A., Song, Y.Z.: MetaHTR: towards writer-adaptive handwritten text recognition. In: CVPR, pp. 15830–15839 (2021)
4. Buzzega, P., Boschini, M., Porrello, A., Abati, D., Calderara, S.: Dark experience for general continual learning: a strong, simple baseline. In: NeurIPS (2020)
5. Cao, Z., Lu, J., Cui, S., Zhang, C.: Zero-shot handwritten Chinese character recognition with hierarchical decomposition embedding. Pattern Recogn. **107**, 107488 (2020)
6. Chaudhry, A., Dokania, P.K., Ajanthan, T., Torr, P.H.: Riemannian walk for incremental learning: understanding forgetting and intransigence. In: ECCV, pp. 532–547 (2018)
7. Chaudhry, A., Gordo, A., Dokania, P.K., Torr, P., Lopez-Paz, D.: Using hindsight to anchor past knowledge in continual learning. arXiv preprint arXiv:2002.08165 (2020)
8. Chaudhry, A., Ranzato, M., Rohrbach, M., Elhoseiny, M.: Efficient lifelong learning with a-gem. arXiv preprint arXiv:1812.00420 (2018)
9. Chen, J., Li, B., Xue, X.: Zero-shot chinese character recognition with stroke-level decomposition. arXiv:2106.11613 (2021)
10. Cohen, G., Afshar, S., Tapson, J., van Schaik, A.: EMNIST: an extension of MNIST to handwritten letters. arXiv preprint arXiv:1702.05373 (2017)
11. Douillard, A., Cord, M., Ollion, C., Robert, T., Valle, E.: PODNet: pooled outputs distillation for small-tasks incremental learning. In: Vedaldi, A., Bischof, H., Brox, T., Frahm, J.-M. (eds.) ECCV 2020. LNCS, vol. 12365, pp. 86–102. Springer, Cham (2020). https://doi.org/10.1007/978-3-030-58565-5_6
12. He, K., Zhang, X., Ren, S., Sun, J.: Deep residual learning for image recognition. In: CVPR, pp. 770–778 (2016)
13. Hou, S., Pan, X., Loy, C.C., Wang, Z., Lin, D.: Learning a unified classifier incrementally via rebalancing. In: CVPR, pp. 831–839 (2019)
14. Kirkpatrick, J., et al.: Overcoming catastrophic forgetting in neural networks. Proc. Natl. Acad. Sci. **114**(13), 3521–3526 (2017)
15. Li, Z., Wu, Q., Xiao, Y., Jin, M., Lu, H.: Deep matching network for handwritten Chinese character recognition. Pattern Recogn. **107**, 107471 (2020)
16. Liu, C.L., Yin, F., Wang, D.H., Wang, Q.F.: Online and offline handwritten Chinese character recognition: benchmarking on new databases. Pattern Recogn. **46**(1), 155–162 (2013)

17. Liu, Y., Schiele, B., Sun, Q.: Adaptive aggregation networks for class-incremental learning. In: CVPR, pp. 2544–2553 (2021)
18. Liu, Y., Su, Y., Liu, A.A., Schiele, B., Sun, Q.: Mnemonics training: multi-class incremental learning without forgetting. In: CVPR, pp. 12245–12254 (2020)
19. Lopez-Paz, D., Ranzato, M.: Gradient episodic memory for continual learning. In: NeurIPS, vol. 30 (2017)
20. Luo, C., Zhu, Y., Jin, L., Li, Z., Peng, D.: Slogan: handwriting style synthesis for arbitrary-length and out-of-vocabulary text. IEEE Trans. Neural Netw. Learn. Syst. (2022)
21. Qu, X., Wang, W., Lu, K., Zhou, J.: Data augmentation and directional feature maps extraction for in-air handwritten Chinese character recognition based on convolutional neural network. Pattern Recogn. Lett. **111**, 9–15 (2018)
22. Rebuffi, S.A., Kolesnikov, A., Sperl, G., Lampert, C.H.: ICARL: incremental classifier and representation learning. In: CVPR, pp. 2001–2010 (2017)
23. Riemer, M., et al.: Learning to learn without forgetting by maximizing transfer and minimizing interference. arXiv preprint arXiv:1810.11910 (2018)
24. Rusu, A.A., et al.: Progressive neural networks. arXiv preprint arXiv:1606.04671 (2016)
25. Schwarz, J., et al.: Progress & compress: a scalable framework for continual learning. In: ICML 2018, pp. 4528–4537. PMLR (2018)
26. Shi, B., Yang, M., Wang, X., Lyu, P., Yao, C., Bai, X.: Aster: an attentional scene text recognizer with flexible rectification. TPAMI **41**(9), 2035–2048 (2018)
27. Wang, L., et al.: Memory replay with data compression for continual learning. arXiv preprint arXiv:2202.06592 (2022)
28. Wang, T.Q., Yin, F., Liu, C.L.: Radical-based Chinese character recognition via multi-labeled learning of deep residual networks. In: ICDAR, vol. 1, pp. 579–584. IEEE (2017)
29. Wu, C., Fan, W., He, Y., Sun, J., Naoi, S.: Handwritten character recognition by alternately trained relaxation convolutional neural network. In: 2014 14th International Conference on Frontiers in Handwriting Recognition, pp. 291–296. IEEE (2014)
30. Yang, W., Jin, L., Tao, D., Xie, Z., Feng, Z.: Dropsample: a new training method to enhance deep convolutional neural networks for large-scale unconstrained handwritten Chinese character recognition. Pattern Recogn. **58**, 190–203 (2016)
31. Yang, X., He, D., Zhou, Z., Kifer, D., Giles, C.L.: Improving offline handwritten Chinese character recognition by iterative refinement. In: ICDAR, vol. 1, pp. 5–10. IEEE (2017)
32. Zhang, X.Y., Bengio, Y., Liu, C.L.: Online and offline handwritten Chinese character recognition: a comprehensive study and new benchmark. Pattern Recogn. **61**, 348–360 (2017)
33. Zhang, X.Y., Yin, F., Zhang, Y.M., Liu, C.L., Bengio, Y.: Drawing and recognizing Chinese characters with recurrent neural network. TPAMI **40**(4), 849–862 (2017)
34. Zhu, F., Zhang, X.Y., Wang, C., Yin, F., Liu, C.L.: Prototype augmentation and self-supervision for incremental learning. In: CVPR, pp. 5871–5880 (2021)

TransVQ-VAE: Generating Diverse Images Using Hierarchical Representation Learning

Chuan Jin[1]([✉])[ID], Anqi Zheng[1], Zhaoying Wu[2], and Changqing Tong[1]

[1] School of Sciences, Hangzhou Dianzi University, Hangzhou 310018, China
{j_chuan,211070104,tongchangqing}@hdu.edu.cn
[2] Southeast-Monash Joint Graduate School, Southeast University, Suzhou 210096, China
zwuu0079@student.monash.edu

Abstract. Understanding how to learn feature representations for images and generate high-quality images under unsupervised learning was challenging. One of the main difficulties in feature learning has been the problem of posterior collapse in variational inference. This paper proposes a hierarchical aggregated vector-quantized variational autoencoder, called TransVQ-VAE. Firstly, the multi-scale feature information based on the hierarchical Transformer is complementarily encoded to represent the global and structural dependencies of the input features. Then, it is compared to the latent encoding space with a linear difference to reduce the feature dimensionality. Finally, the decoder generates synthetic samples with higher diversity and fidelity compared to previous ones. In addition, we propose a dual self-attention module in the encoding process that uses spatial and channel information to capture distant texture correlations, contributing to the consistency and realism of the generated images. Experimental results on MNIST, CIFAR-10, CelebA-HQ, and ImageNet datasets show that our approach significantly improves the diversity and visual quality of the generated images.

Keywords: Image generation · Unsupervised learning · Variational autoencoder · Hierarchical representation · Dual self-attention

1 Introduction

Deep generative models have rapidly evolved and garnered widespread attention in recent years for their applications in various fields, including image [7,13], speech [4], and video [5]. These models utilize an encoder-decoder architecture and typically employ emerging approaches, such as generative adversarial networks (GAN) [6] and variational autoencoders (VAE) [12], which combine reconstruction and adversarial loss during training. The generated samples produced by these models are challenging to distinguish from real data without careful examination.

Supported by the National Social Science Fund of China (21BTJ071).

L. Iliadis et al. (Eds.): ICANN 2023, LNCS 14256, pp. 185–196, 2023.
https://doi.org/10.1007/978-3-031-44213-1_16

Training generative models have always been a challenge in machine learning. Most of the standard techniques suffer from the following three serious drawbacks: (1) constraints must be placed on the model structure; (2) approximations to the data distribution are required; and (3) potentially relying on expensive computing inference processes like Markov Chain Monte Carlo (MCMC). Since the discovery of backpropagation, training convolutional neural networks (CNN) has become readily available in recent years. Some work [8,14,16] have trained CNN as powerful function approximators via backpropagation.

We compared two primary types of generative models: hidden variable-based models, such as GANs, and likelihood function-based models, like VAEs. The former generates images by mapping random noise to images through a neural generator network, optimizing the objects. The discriminator defines the loss function of the generator by classifying the samples as true or false. However, the samples generated by these models cannot fully capture the diversity of the actual distribution. In contrast, the likelihood-based approach optimizes the training data's negative log-likelihood (NLL). This allows for model comparison and generalization to unseen data while maximizing the probability that the model can be assigned to all examples in the training set. In principle, the likelihood-based model covers all possibilities of the data without the pattern collapse and lack of diversity issues often found in GANs [20].

Despite these advantages, their usefulness depends on the application for which the features are used and highly susceptible to posterior collapse for different tasks. Nevertheless, good generative models should not be computationally complex but have solid decoding capabilities. We aim to implement a model that preserves the critical features of the data in the latent space while optimizing for maximum likelihood. Our contributions can thus be summarised as follows:

1. Our model's feature extraction process relies exclusively on the Transformer. This powerful tool enables the capture of global dependencies through dynamic receptive fields. The Transformer's inherent serial correlation also allows for exceptional feature matching within a predefined embedding space.
2. We use hierarchical representation learning to reconstruct features. It can enhance the model's generalization performance and effectively alleviate the posterior collapse problem of variational inference during feature learning.
3. We propose a dual self-attention module in encoding process, leveraging spatial and channel information to capture long-range texture correlations effectively, significantly enhances the fidelity and consistency of the images.

2   Related Work

Unlike traditional autoencoders (denoising autoencoder [1,25], sparse autoencoder [18], and shrinkage autoencoder [21]), the VAE is rooted in variational Bayes and graph model approach and gives an explicit solution to the problem of how to define the hidden variable z and deal with the integration over z [11].

VAE [12] uses Kullback-Leibler (KL) divergence to quantify the distance between the approximation distribution $q_\phi(z|x)$ and the true distribution

$p_\theta(z|x)$. The objective is to minimize $D_{KL}(q_\phi(z|x)||p_\theta(z|x))$ with respect to the parameter ϕ, defined in Eq. 1:

$$
\begin{aligned}
D_{KL}(q_\phi(z|x)||p_\theta(z|x)) = {} & \log p_\theta(x) + D_{KL}(q_\phi(z|x)||p_\theta(z)) \\
& - E_{z \sim q_\phi(z|x)} \log p_\theta(x|z)
\end{aligned}
\tag{1}
$$

Maximize the likelihood of generating true data (log-likelihood $\log p_\theta(x)$) and minimize the difference between the actual distribution and the estimated posterior distribution $D_{KL}(q_\phi(z|x)||p_\theta(z|x))$. Define the loss function for training as defined in Eq. 2:

$$
\begin{aligned}
\mathcal{L}_{\mathrm{VAE}}(\theta, \phi) &= -\log p_\theta(x) + D_{KL}(q_\phi(z|x)||p_\theta(z|x)) \\
&= -E_{z \sim q_\phi(z|x)} \log p_\theta(x|z) + D_{KL}(q_\phi(z|x)||p_\theta(z)) \\
\theta^*, \phi^* &= \operatorname*{argmin}_{\theta, \phi} \mathcal{L}_{\mathrm{VAE}}
\end{aligned}
\tag{2}
$$

where the KL divergence was always non-negative. Therefore, minimizing the loss function can maximize the lower bound on the probability of generating an actual data sample.

VQ-VAE [24] learns discrete hidden variables through an encoder, similar to the k-nearest neighbor (KNN), that maps samples to a prime vector with a minimum Euclidean distance. By defining $e \in \mathbb{R}^{K \times D}$ as the potential embedding space in VQ-VAE, where K is the number of potential variable categories, and D is the dimensionality of the embedding vector. A single embedding vector $e_i \in \mathbb{R}^D, i = 1, 2, \cdots, K$.

The encoder output $\mathbb{E}(x) = z_e$ matches the embedding vector in K by the nearest neighbor lookup, and this matched code vector subsequently becomes the input to the decoder $\mathbb{D}(\cdot)$, as seen in Eq. 3:

$$
z_q(x) = \mathrm{Quantize}(\mathbb{E}(x)) = e_k, \quad \text{where} \quad k = \operatorname*{argmin}_{i} ||\mathbb{E}(x) - e_i||_2
\tag{3}
$$

However, the argmin function is not differentiable on the discrete space, hence the additional optimization of the VQ loss (L_2 loss between the embedding space and the encoder output) and the commitment loss (encouraging the encoder output to be closer to the embedding space). The optimized overall VQ-VAE loss function as defined in Eq. 4:

$$
\mathcal{L}_{VQ-VAE} = \underbrace{||x - \mathbb{D}(e_k)||_2^2}_{\text{reconstruction loss}} + \underbrace{||\mathrm{sg}[\mathbb{E}(x)] - e_k||_2^2}_{\text{VQ loss}} + \underbrace{\beta ||\mathbb{E}(x) - \mathrm{sg}[e_k]||_2^2}_{\text{commitment loss}}
\tag{4}
$$

where β is the adjustment coefficient, and $\mathrm{sg}[\cdot]$ refers to stop gradient, which truncates the gradient information and is used to solve the integrability problem of the argmin function on discrete spaces during backpropagation.

With the popularity of VAE in generative models, several interesting works have emerged. For example, PixelSNAIL [3] uses powerful autoregressive models with multi-head self-attention layer enhancements to capture prior distributions.

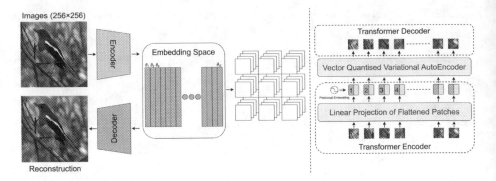

Fig. 1. Overall structural representation of the model. Left: encoding the input sequence in the embedding space and decoding the output image. Right: image split and reorganisation based entirely on the Transformer structure.

β-VAE [2,10] improves on VAE with an emphasis on discovering the underlying factors of the solution. VQ-VAE-2 [20] is the two-level hierarchical autoregressive VQ-VAE model incorporating a self-attention mechanism. RQ-VAE [15] performs residual quantization on the embedding space, effectively generating high-resolution images while reducing computational costs. SQ-VAE [23] extends the standard VAE with new stochastic de-quantization and vectorization to efficiently use the embedding space.

3   Method

The image generation model constructed based on VAE has to solve the posterior collapse problem in variational inference [12]. In VAE, we usually assume that both $q_\phi(z|x)$ and $p_\theta(z)$ follow a Gaussian distribution and hence can obtain the solution $D_{KL}(q_\phi(z|x)||p_\theta(z))$ analytic solution. Equation 1 is equivalent as defined in Eq. 5:

$$\mathbb{E}_{p_\theta(x)}[\mathbb{E}_{q_\phi(z|x)}[\log p_\theta(x|z)] - D_{KL}(q_\phi(z|x)||p_\theta(z))] \tag{5}$$

The log-likelihood can thus be expressed as defined in Eq. 6:

$$\begin{aligned}
\log p_\theta(x) = \;&\mathbb{E}_{p_\theta(x)}[D_{KL}(q_\phi(z|x)||p_\theta(z))] \\
&- \mathbb{E}_{p_\theta(x)}[D_{KL}(q_\phi(z|x)||q_\phi(z))] - D_{KL}(q_\phi(z)||p_\theta(z))
\end{aligned} \tag{6}$$

the posterior collapse is when the KL divergence value in Eq. 5 gradually vanishes, i.e., $q_\phi(z|x) \approx p_\theta(z)$, equivalently with $D_{KL}(q_\phi(z|x)||p_\theta(z))$ tends to 0. The hidden variable z becomes independent of x and cannot reflect any information from the data.

3.1   Overview

Figure 1 illustrates our approach, which comprises three components: an embedding space for the quantized vectors, a hierarchical Transformer encoder, and a

---

Algorithm 1. Training Stage for TransVQ-VAE

Input: real sample images x from the original dataset X
Output: images that are similar but not identical to the original dataset
 1: set initialize parameters θ, ϕ, iterations T, embedding space e_j
 2: $x \rightarrow z_e(x) = \text{encoder}(x) \rightarrow z_q(x) = \text{Quantize}(z_q(x)) \rightarrow x' = \text{decoder}(z_q(x'))$
 3: **while** number of iterations **do**
 4:     **for** $i = 1, \cdots, T$ **do**
 5:         input x through the encoder to output $z_e(x)$
 6:         **if** $k = \text{argmin}_j \|z_e(x) - e_j\|_2$ **then**
 7:            $q_\phi(z = k|x) = 1$
 8:         **else**
 9:            $q_\phi(z = k|x) = 0$
10:         **end if**
11:         $z_q(x) = e_k$, where $k = \text{argmin}_j \|z_e(x) - e_j\|_2$
12:     **end for**
13:     $x' = \text{decoder}(z_q(x))$
14:     calculate the loss function:
15:     $\mathcal{L}(\theta, \phi, e) = -\mathbb{E}_{z \sim q_\phi(z|x)} \log p_\theta(x|z) + \text{D}_{\text{KL}}(q_\phi(z|x)\|p_\theta(z)) + \|\text{sg}[\mathbb{E}(x)] - e_k\|_2^2 +$
      $\beta\|\mathbb{E}(x) - \text{sg}[e_k]\|_2^2$, the prior $p_\theta(z)$ is a uniform multiclass distribution
16: **end while**

Transformer decoder for texture generation. In the embedding space, the codebook vector generated automatically is compared with the feature vector using linear interpolation to reduce feature dimensionality. The hierarchical encoder separates the true object's discrete structural and texture features, while the decoder produces the reconstructed image. Algorithm 1 shows the overall flow.

3.2   Hierarchical Representation Learning

In the context of Bayes theory, the issue of "vanishing gradient" or "exploding gradient" in neural networks has been replaced by the concept of "posterior collapse". A model must acquire information from each new sample and update itself accordingly. Specifically, the hidden variable z is now generated independently of the model encoder, allowing it to output one or more patterns summarizing most of the samples. This means that the model now depends solely on the autoregressive properties of the decoder.

When the posterior distribution does not collapse, the dth dimension z_d of the latent variables can be obtained from $q_\phi(z|x) = N(\mu_d, \sigma_d^2)$ samples. The μ_d and σ_d^2 are fitting functions obtained through training a neural network on the input x. The encoder part of the network extracts valid information from x and produces μ_d and σ_d^2. However, when the posterior distribution collapses, the values of μ_d and σ_d^2 become almost unrelated to the input x, and the number of samples decreases. In other words, μ_d and σ_d^2 converge to constant values a and b, respectively. This results in a signal being fed to the decoder different from the input x, rendering the sampled z value useless. Ultimately, the decoder tries

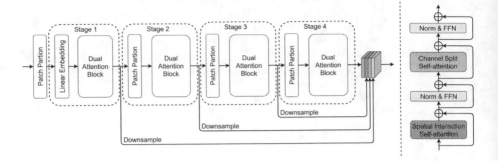

Fig. 2. The structure of Transformer-based hierarchical feature learning. Left: extraction and aggregation of feature information from different resolution layers using dual self-attention. Right: the dual self-attention block.

to reconstruct x by ignoring the irrelevant z value sampled from the collapsed posterior distribution $N(a, b)$.

It is essential to enrich the available information to enhance image generation, particularly for self-encoders. Achieving a balance between inference and generation is crucial in such cases. Recently studies [17] have shown that one practical approach to addressing the problem of posterior collapse is to increase the complexity of the latent variable z rather than relying on a single Gaussian distribution. Our approach is to strengthen the encoder and infer complex latent variables from the input decoders' sequence instead of weakening them. To this end, we propose a hierarchical feature aggregation method to model the hidden variables, as illustrated in Fig. 2.

Our encoder consists of four stages, each beginning with a patch embedding layer. In each stage, we include dual self-attention and halve the image feature resolution while keeping the feature dimensionality constant. To enhance the encoder's feature extraction ability, we concatenate the feature information from different stages by downsample. Our optimization objective function is expressed as Eq. 7:

$$\mathcal{L}_{TransVQ-VAE}(\theta, \phi) = -\log p_\theta(x) + D_{KL}(q_\phi(z_i|x)||p_\theta(z_i|x))$$
$$+ ||\text{sg}[\mathbb{E}(x)] - e_k||_2^2 + \beta||\mathbb{E}(x) - \text{sg}[e_k]||_2^2$$
$$= -E_{z_i \sim q_\phi(z_i|x)}\log p_\theta(x|z_i) + D_{KL}(q_\phi(z_i|x)||p_\theta(z_i)) \quad (7)$$
$$+ ||\text{sg}[\mathbb{E}(x)] - e_k||_2^2 + \beta||\mathbb{E}(x) - \text{sg}[e_k]||_2^2$$
$$\theta^*, \phi^* = \underset{\theta, \phi}{\arg\min} \mathcal{L}_{TransVQ-VAE}$$

where $z_i(i = 1, 2, 3, 4)$ represents mutually independent Gaussian distributions, each stage predicts a Gaussian distribution independent of the others. Since the sum of independent Gaussian distributions is also a Gaussian distribution, we can use an encoder to directly determine the distribution parameters μ^* and σ^{*2} after splicing and summation.

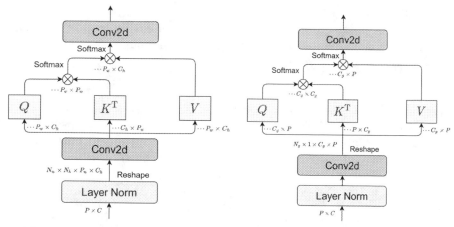

(a) Spatial Interaction Self-attention   (b) Channel Split Self-attention

Fig. 3. The dual self-attention structure that captures feature information in both spatial and channel dimensions schematically.

3.3 Dual Self-attention

In this section, we will introduce the concept of dual self-attention. This module is a simple yet effective method for extracting texture features that can capture global context while maintaining computational efficiency, as illustrated in Fig. 3. This module considers all spatial locations to compute the attention score between channels, allowing it to naturally capture global interactions and representations. Additionally, spatial attention is employed to refine local representations by performing fine-grained interactions at spatial locations, which in turn helps model the worldwide channel attention information. Using "spatial tokens" and "channel tokens", this module can capture fine-grained structural patterns and global interactions, providing the decoder with the necessary texture information to generate high-quality images.

Assume an $\mathbb{R}^{P \times C}$ dimensional visual feature, where P is the number of pixels and C is the number of channels. Simply apply the standard global self-attention, which is defined by the Eq. 8:

$$\text{Attention}(Q, K, V) = \text{softmax}\left(\frac{QK^{\mathrm{T}}}{\sqrt{d_k}}\right) V$$

$$\text{MultiHead}(Q, K, V) = \text{Concat}(\text{head}_1, \text{head}_2, \cdots, \text{head}_h)W^O$$

$$(8)$$

the query matrix Q, the key matrix K, and the value matrix V are each mapping of features, i.e., sequences are matched to extract semantic dependencies between their parts. d_k is the channel dimension, $\text{head}_i = \text{Attention}(QW_i^Q, KW_i^K . VW_i^V)$, $W_i^O \in \mathbb{R}^{hd_v \times d_{model}}$, W_i^Q and $W_i^K \in \mathbb{R}^{d_{model} \times d_k}$, $W_i^V \in \mathbb{R}^{d_{model} \times d_v}$.

Spatial interaction self-attention is calculated for the current batch, as shown in Fig. 3a. The images are divided uniformly in a non-overlapping manner. Assuming that there are N_w distinct batches containing P_w patches, $P = N_w \times P_w$. This can be expressed as Eq. 9:

$$\text{Attention}_{\text{Spatial}}(Q, K, V) = \{\text{Attention}(Q_i, K_i, V_i\}_{i=1}^{N_w} \tag{9}$$

where $Q_i, K_i, V_i \in \mathbb{R}^{P_w \times C_h}$ are the local query, key, and value matrix.

Self-attention in existing vision work typically defines markers with pixels or patches and captures feature information along the spatial dimension. We attempt to collect information on the transposition of patch markers. To obtain global information in the spatial dimension, we set the number of heads to 1, as shown in Fig. 3b. In this way, it is possible to interact with image-level tokens in the same batch of channels. Let N_g denote the number of batches and C_g denote the number of channels in each batch. This is defined as Eq. 10:

$$\text{Attention}_{\text{Channel}} = \{\text{Attention}_{\text{batch}}(Q_i, K_i, V_i)^{\text{T}}\}_{i=1}^{N_b}$$

$$\text{Attention}_{\text{batch}}(Q_i, K_i, V_i)^{\text{T}} = \text{softmax}\left(\frac{Q_i^{\text{T}} K_i}{\sqrt{C_g}}\right) V_i^{\text{T}} \tag{10}$$

where $Q_i, K_i, V_i \in \mathbb{R}^{P \times C_{\hat{g}}}$ are image-level matrices grouped by channel. Considering that the number of spatial patches varies with image size, the above design ensures that our model can be generalized to arbitrary image sizes.

4   Experiments

4.1   Datasets

We experimented on four datasets with different resolutions (MNIST, CIFAR-10, CelebA-HQ, ImageNet) to validate the effectiveness of the proposed method.

MNIST: contains 70,000 images and labels, with 60,000 images and labels in the training set and 10,000 images and labels in the test set. Each image is a 28×28 pixel point image of a grey matter handwritten number with labels 0 to 9, with white text on a black background.

CIFAR-10: a colour image dataset of near-universal objects. It contains a total of 10 categories of RGB colour images. Each image has a size of 32×32, and there are 6000 images in each category. There are 50,000 training images and 10,000 test images in the dataset.

CelebA-HQ: consisting of high-resolution face images and associated attribute labels. It contains over 30,000 high-resolution (1024×1024) face images from over 1,000 celebrities. The CelebA-HQ dataset is primarily used for high-resolution face generation and super-resolution reconstruction tasks.

ImageNet: encompasses over 10 million images, each manually labelled with a category covering most of the categories in life. The dataset has more images, higher resolution and extraneous noise and variation in the images, making it more challenging to generate high-quality images.

4.2   Experimental Details

Our model was implemented in Pytorch 1.12 and trained on an NVIDIA Tesla A100 with 40 GB of memory. The batch size was 64, and the dimensions of the embedding space for four datasets were 256, 512, 1024, and 2048, respectively. The training was performed using the Adam optimizer with an initial learning rate of 0.005. The image size was kept constant for MNIST and CIFAR-10. CelebA-HQ's training images were downsampled to 256×256, and data enhancement was applied. ImageNet's training images were instead randomly cropped to 256×256.

4.3   Experimental Results and Analysis

For the generated images, two main aspects are considered: (1) Quality. Whether the generated image is clear, complete, and realistic in content. (2) Diversity. The images generated by the final generator need to be diverse and not just one or a few types of images. Therefore, we consider the number of images generated by the model in terms of the Classification Accuracy Score (CAS) [19], Frechet Inception Distance (FID) [9], and Inception Score (IS) [22] evaluation metrics.

We know that the NLL on the train and validation sets allows us to detect the model's fit while providing an objective generalization criterion. Other commonly used performance metrics, such as FID and IS, only provide a proxy for the samples' quality and diversity but ignore the retained images' generalization performance. Using the same pretrained VQ-VAE, the NLL values for the top and bottom priors were compared, as presented in Table 1. The NLL values for train and validation are very close, indicating no risk of overfitting the model.

Table 1. The top and bottom predefined NLL results on the train and validation sets demonstrate no risk of overfitting the model.

	Train NLL	Val NLL	Train MSE	Val MSE
Top prior	3.28	3,30	–	–
Bottom prior	3,41	3,41	–	–
TransVQ-VAE Decoder	–	–	0.0035	0.0041

CAS: The score requires training the ImageNet classifier on samples of candidate models, evaluating its classification accuracy on actual images from the validation set, thus measuring sample quality and diversity. The results of our evaluation of this metric on the ImageNet dataset are shown in Table 2. TransVQ-VAE builds complex encoders through hierarchical representation learning, which can close the field gap and achieve a high CAS for multi-category datasets.

FID and IS: The most common evaluation metrics for comparing GANs. FID measures the distance between the feature vectors of the actual image and the generated image. It measures the similarity between the two sets of images in

Table 2. Comparison of the CAS results of our method with VQ-VAEs on the ImageNet dataset. Our method's two types of accuracy are closer to the real data.

	Top-1 Accuracy	Top-5 Accuracy
VQ-VAE	54.83	77.59
VQ-VAE after reconstructing	58.74	80.98
VQ-VAE-2	60.32	82.31
TransVQ-VAE	62.85	83.88
Real data	73.09	91.47

terms of the statistical similarity of the computer visual features of the original image, as calculated using the Inception v3 image classification model. The lower score means that the two sets of images are more similar or that the statistics of the two are more similar. IS uses Inception v3, pretrained on ImageNet as a classification network, to input the images generated by the generator into the Inception v3 Network and to statistically analyze the output values (the categories to which the images belong) of the network. The higher the score, the higher the diversity of the generated images. The FID and IS values were calculated on the four datasets, as presented in Table 3.

Table 3. Comparison of FID and IS results with the standard generative models. The lower the FID value, the better. The higher the IS value, the better.

Methods	MNIST		CIFAR-10		CelebA-HQ		ImageNet	
	FID↓	IS↑	FID↓	IS↑	FID↓	IS↑	FID↓	IS↑
VAE	32.19	–	35.73	1.36	96.14	–	38.49	83.46
CVAE	28.62	–	33.85	1.83	89.30	–	34.62	92.73
β-VAE	25.13	–	29.67	2.74	75.21	–	27.48	112.37
VQ-VAE	17.93	–	22.15	4.11	50.49	–	21.85	137.38
VQ-VAE-2	14.31	–	18.64	5.80	38.71	–	14.68	184.59
TransVQ-VAE	7.62	–	16.45	7.63	22.79	–	8.34	228.71

The visualization of the proposed method on the four datasets is shown in Fig. 4, and it can be seen that the generated images have high diversity and conservation rates compared to the original datasets.

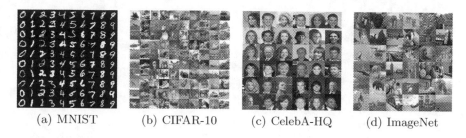

| (a) MNIST | (b) CIFAR-10 | (c) CelebA-HQ | (d) ImageNet |

Fig. 4. Visualization of experimental results. The capability to produce images of high visual quality similar to the original datasets.

5   Conclusion

In this work, we propose a new variational inference-based generative model, called TransVQ-VAE, to generate diverse and high-quality images through VQ-VAE. At first, our approach extracts the feature information of the images from a multi-layer Transformer and generates diverse structures using an autoregressive distribution to alleviate the posterior collapse problem in variational inference through complex distributions. Then a dual self-attention module is proposed to capture the global contextual information of the image in both spatial and channel dimensions to ensure that the texture features of each structure synthesized by the decoder are consistent with the generated structures. Experimental results show that the proposed hierarchical representation model alleviates the problem of a posterior collapse and improves the quality and diversity of the generated images.

Although high-quality images can be generated by the Transformer's global, dynamic receptive field, and natural sequence correlation, large-scale training still faces challenges as the size of the model and training dataset grows. Therefore, we will explore improving training efficiency on large-scale datasets.

References

1. Bengio, Y., Laufer, E., Alain, G., Yosinski, J.: Deep generative stochastic networks trainable by backprop. In: International Conference on Machine Learning, vol. 32, pp. 226–234 (2014)
2. Burgess, C.P., et al.: Understanding disentangling in β-VAE. arXiv preprint arXiv:1804.03599 (2018)
3. Chen, X., Mishra, N., Rohaninejad, M., Abbeel, P.: Pixelsnail: an improved autoregressive generative model. In: International Conference on Machine Learning, pp. 864–872 (2018)
4. Chien, J.T., Wang, C.W.: Hierarchical and self-attended sequence autoencoder. IEEE Trans. Pattern Anal. Mach. Intell. **44**(9), 4975–4986 (2021)
5. Finn, C., Goodfellow, I., Levine, S.: Unsupervised learning for physical interaction through video prediction. Adv. Neural. Inf. Process. Syst. **29**, 64–72 (2016)
6. Goodfellow, I., et al.: Generative adversarial nets. Adv. Neural. Inf. Process. Syst. **27**, 2674–2780 (2014)

7. Gregor, K., Besse, F., Jimenez Rezende, D., Danihelka, I., Wierstra, D.: Towards conceptual compression. Adv. Neural. Inf. Process. Syst. **29**, 3549–3557 (2016)
8. He, K., Zhang, X., Ren, S., Sun, J.: Deep residual learning for image recognition. In: Proceedings of the IEEE Conference on Computer Vision and Pattern Recognition, pp. 770–778 (2016)
9. Heusel, M., Ramsauer, H., Unterthiner, T., Nessler, B., Hochreiter, S.: GANs trained by a two time-scale update rule converge to a local nash equilibrium. Adv. Neural. Inf. Process. Syst. **30**, 6626–6637 (2017)
10. Higgins, I., et al.: Beta-VAE: learning basic visual concepts with a constrained variational framework. In: International Conference on Learning Representations (2016)
11. Hinton, G.E., Salakhutdinov, R.R.: Reducing the dimensionality of data with neural networks. Science **313**(5786), 504–507 (2006)
12. Kingma, D.P., Welling, M.: Auto-encoding variational bayes. arXiv preprint arXiv:1312.6114 (2013)
13. Kingma, D.P., Salimans, T., Jozefowicz, R., Chen, X., Sutskever, I., Welling, M.: Improved variational inference with inverse autoregressive flow. Adv. Neural. Inf. Process. Syst. **29**, 4743–4751 (2016)
14. Krizhevsky, A., Sutskever, I., Hinton, G.E.: Imagenet classification with deep convolutional neural networks. Adv. Neural. Inf. Process. Syst. **25**, 1097–1105 (2012)
15. Lee, D., Kim, C., Kim, S., Cho, M., Han, W.S.: Autoregressive image generation using residual quantization. In: Proceedings of the IEEE/CVF Conference on Computer Vision and Pattern Recognition, pp. 11523–11532 (2022)
16. Liu, W., et al.: SSD: single shot MultiBox detector. In: Leibe, B., Matas, J., Sebe, N., Welling, M. (eds.) ECCV 2016. LNCS, vol. 9905, pp. 21–37. Springer, Cham (2016). https://doi.org/10.1007/978-3-319-46448-0_2
17. Lucas, J., Tucker, G., Grosse, R.B., Norouzi, M.: Don't blame the ELBO! A linear VAE perspective on posterior collapse. Adv. Neural. Inf. Process. Syst. **32**, 9408–9418 (2019)
18. Makhzani, A., Frey, B.: K-sparse autoencoders. arXiv preprint arXiv:1312.5663 (2013)
19. Ravuri, S., Vinyals, O.: Classification accuracy score for conditional generative models. Adv. Neural. Inf. Process. Syst. **32**, 12268–12279 (2019)
20. Razavi, A., Van den Oord, A., Vinyals, O.: Generating diverse high-fidelity images with VQ-VAE-2. Adv. Neural. Inf. Process. Syst. **32**, 14866–14876 (2019)
21. Rifai, S., Vincent, P., Muller, X., Glorot, X., Bengio, Y.: Contractive auto-encoders: explicit invariance during feature extraction. In: Proceedings of the 28th International Conference on International Conference on Machine Learning, pp. 833–840 (2011)
22. Salimans, T., Goodfellow, I., Zaremba, W., Cheung, V., Radford, A., Chen, X.: Improved techniques for training GANs. Adv. Neural. Inf. Process. Syst. **29**, 2234–2242 (2016)
23. Takida, Y., et al.: SQ-VAE: variational Bayes on discrete representation with self-annealed stochastic quantization. In: International Conference on Machine Learning, pp. 20987–21012 (2022)
24. Van Den Oord, A., Vinyals, O., Kavukcuoglu, K.: Neural discrete representation learning. Adv. Neural. Inf. Process. Syst. **30**, 6306–6315 (2017)
25. Vincent, P., Larochelle, H., Bengio, Y., Manzagol, P.A.: Extracting and composing robust features with denoising autoencoders. In: Proceedings of the 25th International Conference on Machine Learning, pp. 1096–1103 (2008)

UG-Net: Unsupervised-Guided Network for Biomedical Image Segmentation and Classification

Zhiqiang Li[1,2], Xiaogen Zhou[1,2], and Tong Tong[1,2,3(✉)]

[1] College of Physics and Information Engineering, Fuzhou University, Fuzhou, China
ttraveltong@gmail.com
[2] Fujian Key Lab of Medical Instrumentation and Pharmaceutical Technology,
Fuzhou University, Fuzhou, China
[3] Imperial Vision Technology, Fujian, China

Abstract. Biomedical image segmentation and classification are two critical components in computer-aided diagnosis systems. However, various deep convolutional neural networks are trained by a single task, ignoring the potential contribution of mutually performing multiple tasks. In this paper, we propose an unsupervised-guided network for automated white blood cell (WBC) and skin lesion segmentation and classification called UG-Net. UG-Net consists of an unsupervised-based strategy (US) module, an enhanced segmentation network, and a mask-guided classification network. On the one hand, the proposed US module produces coarse masks that provide a prior localization map for the proposed segmentation network to enhance it in locating and segmenting a target object accurately. On the other hand, the enhanced coarse masks predicted by the proposed segmentation network are then fed into the proposed classification network for accurate classification. Moreover, a novel contextual encoding module is presented to capture high-level information and preserve spatial information. Meanwhile, a hybrid loss is defined to alleviate the imbalance training problem. Experimental results show that our approach achieves state-of-the-art segmentation performance on two public biomedical image datasets.

Keywords: Skin lesion segmentation and classification · White blood cell segmentation and classification · Unsupervised-guided network

1 Introduction

Skin cancers and acute lymphoblastic leukaemia are two diseases with a very high incidence. Skin disease is one of the most pervasive threats to human health globally, among which skin cancers cause serious harm to humans and can lead to death [2]. For instance, melanoma ranks top in skin cancers, whose five-year survival rate is less than 15%. Melanocytes are one of the scarce cells

---

Supported by National Natural Science Foundation of China under Grant 62171133.

that are naturally coloured and visible in human eyes, which allows doctors to diagnose using clinical images. Dermoscopy has been widely employed as a non-invasive imaging instrument to analyze skin lesions and their surrounding areas. However, manual annotation of dermoscopic images for quantitative diagnosis is time-consuming work. In addition, acute lymphoblastic leukaemia (ALL) is a condition of unrestricted cell growth in the human body and is among the deadliest diseases globally. Preliminary diagnostic validation of ALL is based on the count and appearance of WBC. Higher accuracy examinations for the identification of leukaemia include cytochemistry, immuno-histochemistry, and flow cytometry which are based on the reaction of staining chemicals with the proteins of human WBCs. However, a computer-aided diagnosis (CAD) [16] system can free doctors from time-consuming work and improve the accuracy and efficiency of skin cancer and ALL diagnosis. Biomedical image segmentation and

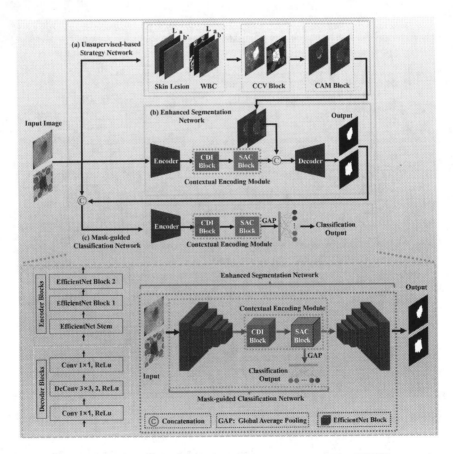

Fig. 1. An overview of the proposed UG-Net architecture. The UG-Net consists of an unsupervised-based strategy module, a segmentation network, and a classification network. Moreover, a novel contextual encoding module is presented to capture high-level information.

diagnosis are essential for modern CAD systems. Thus, accurate segmentation and classification of WBC and skin lesion from biomedical images are essential steps in guiding clinical applications, such as disease diagnosis and further treatment. There are two basic tasks for building a CAD system of blood diseases and skin cancer: WBC and skin lesion segmentation and classification. Recently, deep convolutional neural networks (DCNNs) have shown a strong ability in biomedical image diagnosis and segmentation [4,6,8,9,12,14,15]. However, most existing DCNN-based models are trained by a single task [5,7,13], ignoring the potential contribution of mutually performing multiple tasks. To alleviate this issue, we propose an unsupervised enhanced CNN framework for WBC and skin lesion segmentation and classification, called UG-Net, which is driven by both the segmentation and classification tasks. On the one hand, the unsupervised method transfers hand-crafted features to the segmentation network to help it accurately segment. On the other hand, the segmentation network also provides localization information to the classification network for accurate classification.

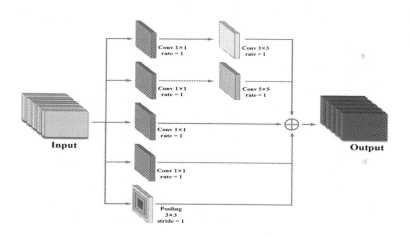

Fig. 2. Illustration of the cascaded densely inception block.

2   Methods

Unsupervised-Based Strategy (US) Module: Our proposed US module is an unsupervised method for extracting hand-crafted features, which contains a colour channel volume (CCV) block and a colour activation mapping (CAM) block. The details of our US module are illustrated as follows.

Colour Channel Volume Block: The colour channel volume (CCV) [17] block is a hand-crafted colour feature extractor built upon the *Lab* colour space transformation. The CCV block is constructed by combining L, a, and b channels in the *Lab* colour space to highlight the ROI of targets and suppress its image

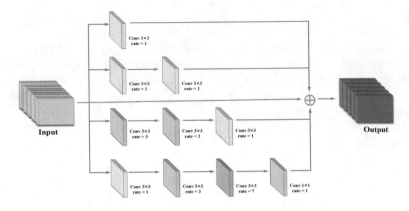

Fig. 3. Illustration of the stacked atrous convolutional block.

background. Our proposed CCV is defined as:

$$CCV = \frac{1}{2}\pi L \times a \times (N_a + b),\tag{1}$$

where L, a, and b are the channels of the *Lab* colour space, and N_a is normalized by the channel a.

Colour Activation Mapping Block: Furthermore, a weighted mean attention map is presented to extract a refined saliency map from the extracted CCV block results. First, we perform the colour name volume (CNV) to yield $C_i (i \in [1, 11])$, where each CNV channel C_i has a range of values $[0, 1]$. Thus, for the resized RGB image I, the colour representation of each pixel is mapped from a 3-dimensional value to a probabilistic 11-dimensional vector which sums up to 1. Each C_i is normalized to $[0, 255]$ for the subsequent thresholding operation. Then, we binarize each C_i to n $(n \in [1, 11])$ boolean maps (BM) using the following function

$$BM_i^j = Threshold(C_i, T_j), |T_j \in [0, 1]\tag{2}$$

where each threshold T_j $(j \in [1, 11])$ is obtained by the adaptive thresholding strategy [1]. The above function generates a boolean map BM_i^j. After that, we perform some morphological operations on the BM_i^j, including closing operation, hole-filling operation, and foreground regions connected, to obtain an attention map A_i^j. The same processing steps are also employed for the complement map of the A_i^j, denoted $\bar{A}_i^j$. Further, we compute the mean attention map named $A_m(i)$ from the A_i^j and $\bar{A}_i^j$. Finally, we combine the mean attention map $A_m(i)$ and the colour channel volume CCV to produce a colour activation mapping (CAM). The mean attention map $A_m(i)$ and the colour activation mapping (CAM) can be calculated via the following equations:

$$A_m(i) = \frac{1}{2n}\sum_{j=1}^{n}(A_i^j + \bar{A}_i^j),\tag{3}$$

$$CAM = \frac{1}{11} \sum_{i=1}^{11} A_m(i) \times CCV. \tag{4}$$

Enhanced Segmentation Network: In our UG-Net, the EfficientNet [11] blocks are exploited as the encoder backbone of our segmentation network as shown in Fig. 4. Our proposed segmentation network is a simple yet effective compound coefficient by uniformly scaling all dimensions of depth/width/resolution. Each EfficientNet block consists of several MBConv blocks [10], which are formed by several 1 × 1 convolutional layers, batch normalization, swish activate layers, and squeeze excitation (SE) blocks. Thus, our proposed segmentation network can achieve remarkable performance with the same parameters by uniformly scaling the network of depth/width/resolution in a fixed proportion.

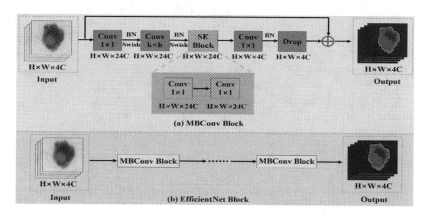

Fig. 4. The illustration of the MBConv block and the EfficientNet block.

Mask-Guided Classification Network: An enhanced segmentation mask predicted by the proposed segmentation network can improve the classification network's object localization and discrimination ability. Our proposed classification network has four components: an encoder flow, a CDI block, a SAC block, and a global average pooling (GAP). Our proposed classification network architecture is shown in Fig. 1. In our proposed classification network structure, each encoder flow performs an EfficientNet block with a filter to generate a set of encoder feature maps. The ReLU activation function is also used. Then, the CDI block and the SAC block are used to encode high-level semantic features. Finally, the GAP is performed to yield feature maps and fed into a new fully connected layer with class number neurons, followed by a softmax activation function.

Contextual Encoding Module: Figure 1 shows an overview of the proposed contextual encoding module architecture, which is integrated by a novel cascaded densely inception (CDI) block and stacked atrous convolutional (SAC) block to encode the high-dimensional information. The details of our CDI block and SAC block are illustrated as follows.

Cascaded Densely Inception (CDI) Block: The CDI block is proposed to extract rich spatial representation. As shown in Fig. 2, The CDI block is composed of 3×3 max pooling, 1×1 convolutional layer, 1×1 and 5×5 convolutional layers with a dilated rate of 1, and 1×1 and 3×3 convolutional layers with a dilated rate of 1.

Stacked Atrous Convolutional (SAC) Block: A novel SAC block is presented to capture high-level semantic features. As shown in Fig. 3, The SAC block consists of four cascaded branches with the gradual increment of the number of the dilated convolutional layers from 1 to 1, 3, and 7, then the receptive field (RF) of each branch is 3, 7, 9 and 23. In each dilated convolutional layer branch followed a rectified linear activation. Finally, we directly add the original feature maps with other feature maps.

Hybrid Loss Strategy: We train the proposed UG-Net with a hybrid loss strategy, which is presented by jointly integrating the Dice loss $\mathcal{L}_{dice}$ with the cross-entropy loss $\mathcal{L}_{ce}$ in the training stage to alleviate the class imbalance training issues. The hybrid loss is defined as follows:

$$\mathcal{L}_{hybrid} = \lambda \mathcal{L}_{ce} + \mu \mathcal{L}_{dice}, \tag{5}$$

where λ and μ are two weighting factors that control the contribution of $\mathcal{L}_{ce}$ and $\mathcal{L}_{dice}$, respectively.

3   Experiments

ISIC-2017 Dataset: The 2017 International Skin Imaging Collaboration (ISIC) dataset [18] is associated with a disease type and manual segmentation of the lesion for each image. There are 2000 images for training, 150 images for validation and 600 images for testing. Each image is paired with an expert manual segmentation as the ground truth (GT) for the segmentation task and two types of skin lesion, including melanoma and keratosis for the classification task.

BCISC Dataset: The blood cell images segmentation and classification dataset, called BCISC [3]. There are 185 training samples, 53 validation samples, and 30 testing samples. Each blood smear image is paired with an expert manual segmentation as the GT labelled by pathologists for the segmentation task and five types of WBC, including basophil, eosinophil, lymphocyte, monocyte, and neutrophil for the classification task.

Training Phase and Testing Phase: Our UG-Net was trained on the training dataset using pixel-level labels. First, to reduce the risk of overfitting, we enlarged the training dataset with online data augmentation processing. The adam optimizer with a batch of 16 was used to optimize the UG-Net. We set the initialized learning rate to 0.0001. To improve the robustness of the UG-Net, we also utilized the data augmentation strategy for the testing dataset. All baseline approaches adopt the same strategy during testing. To evaluate the segmentation and classification performance of our UG-Net, we used the Specificity, Sensitivity, Accuracy, and mean intersection-over-union (mIoU) as measurements for WBC and skin lesion segmentation and classification.

Table 1. Segmentation performance of our method and other methods on two biomedical image datasets.

Dataset	Methods	Accuracy	mIoU	Specificity
ISIC-2017 dataset	U-Net [9]	92.99	82.37	97.48
	AG-Net [14]	92.7	82.08	96.69
	AttU-Net [8]	92.9	82.22	97.68
	M-Net [4]	92.91	82.31	97.37
	U-Net++ [15]	93.1	82.81	97.43
	U-Net3+ [7]	93.15	82.71	97.53
	MB [12]	92.75	82.1	98.24
	Ours	**93.96**	**84.31**	**98.4**
BCISC dataset	U-Net [9]	96.13	87.1	96.63
	AG-Net [14]	96.78	89.39	98.9
	AttU-Net [8]	97.06	90.79	98.51
	M-Net [4]	97.56	91.84	98.68
	U-Net++ [15]	96.8	89.23	98.86
	U-Net3+ [7]	97.09	89.93	98.99
	MB [12]	96.27	87.36	98.3
	Ours	**97.7**	**92.28**	**99.7**

Segmentation Results: We compared the proposed segmentation network with several WBC and skin lesion segmentation approaches in Table 1, including U-Net [9], AG-Net [14], AttU-Net [8], M-Net [4], U-Net++ [15], U-Net3+ [7], MB [12]. Three metrics were used, including Accuracy, mIoU, and Specificity, to evaluate those methods' skin lesion and WBC segmentation performance. A quantitative comparison is shown in Table 1. As can be seen, our proposed segmentation network achieves the best performance on both datasets. On the ISIC-2017 dataset for skin lesion segmentation, our model achieves 0.9396, 0.8431, and 0.984 in Accuracy, mIoU, and Specificity, more accurate than other methods. On the BCISC dataset for WBC segmentation, our model achieves 0.977, 0.9228, and 0.997 in Accuracy, mIoU, and Specificity, more accurate than other methods, which demonstrates that the proposed CDI block, SAC block, and the US module are effective for skin lesion and WBC segmentation.

Classification Results: We compared our proposed classification network with several skin lesion and WBC classification approaches: ARL-Net [13], Dermaknet [5], and MB-DCNN [12]. A quantitative comparison is shown in Table 2. As can be seen, our proposed classification network achieves a comparable classification

Table 2. Classification performance of our UG-Net and other methods on two biomedical image datasets.

Dataset	Type	Metric	ARL-Net	Dermaknet	MB-DCNN	Ours
ISIC-2017 dataset	Melanoma	Accuracy	88.17	84.5	86.33	**86.83**
		Sensitivity	85.11	86.62	90.32	**91.56**
		Specificity	90.59	89.61	92.24	**92.55**
	Keratosis	Accuracy	81.67	82.83	80.67	**86.5**
		Sensitivity	92.72	82.82	89.34	**93.92**
		Specificity	90.27	**94.63**	90.68	88.45
BCISC dataset	Basophil	Accuracy	93.52	92.5	**98.1**	97.65
		Sensitivity	97.55	93.5	97.5	**98.34**
		Specificity	94.37	93.7	91.7	**97.82**
	Eosinophil	Accuracy	96.67	94.4	97.6	**98.22**
		Sensitivity	95.48	94.8	**98.8**	95.85
		Specificity	95.83	96.48	98.36	**98.58**
	Lymphocyte	Accuracy	96.67	93.1	97.1	**97.64**
		Sensitivity	93.33	94.1	**98.64**	98.15
		Specificity	95.52	95.2	97.33	**98.33**
	Monocyte	Accuracy	96.31	93.1	97.62	**97.92**
		Sensitivity	98.31	94.14	98.2	**98.7**
		Specificity	95.53	95.35	95.8	**97.8**
	Neutrophil	Accuracy	95.66	95.66	96.6	**97.8**
		Sensitivity	96.53	95.32	96.8	**98.4**
		Specificity	97.43	94.32	**97.5**	95.8

performance on both datasets. On the ISIC-2017 dataset, there were two types of skin lesion classification. In the melanoma classification, our model achieves the highest Accuracy, Sensitivity, and Specificity scores. In the keratosis classification, our model achieves a remarkably higher Accuracy than the MB-DCNN [12] (from 0.8067 to 0.865), the highest Sensitivity of 0.9392, and a comparable Specificity of 0.8845, which demonstrates that our proposed classification network has a competitive classification ability. Our model achieves remarkable WBC segmentation performance on the BCISC dataset for five types of WBC classification, demonstrating that the proposed CDI block and the SAC block are beneficial for WBC classification.

Table 3. Ablation studies of our segmentation network on the BCISC dataset.

Methods				Metrics		
Base	CDI block	SAC block	US module	Accuracy	mIoU	Specificity
✓				95.6	91.5	98.07
✓	✓			96.01	91.77	99.63
✓	✓	✓		97.06	92.15	98.33
✓	✓	✓	✓	**97.7**	**92.28**	**99.7**

Ablation Studies of Segmentation Network: The ablation studies (see Table 3) were conducted to show the effectiveness of each component of our proposed segmentation network on the BCISC dataset. We can see from Table 3 that, in each experimental setting, the one with those strategies of the CDI block or the SAC block produces more notable performance than the one without those strategies. This suggests that each block is useful for improving the segmentation performance. Moreover, our UG-Net with the unsupervised-based strategy (US) module generates better segmentation performance than those without it. This indicates that adding the US module can improve segmentation performance.

Table 4. Skin lesion classification performance of our proposed classification network with or without using segmentation network to boost classification network strategy on the ISIC-2017 dataset.

Methods	Melanoma	Keratosis
	Accuracy	Accuracy
Ours (w/o segmentation network boost classification network)	85.23	85.3
Ours (w/ segmentation network boost classification network)	**86.83**	**86.5**

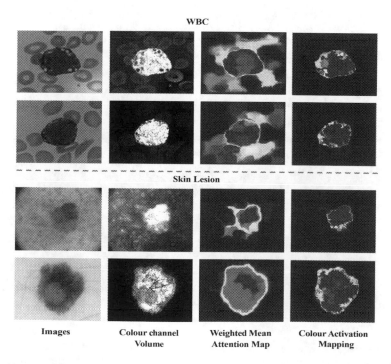

Fig. 5. Examples of WBC and skin lesion results was generated by our proposed US module.

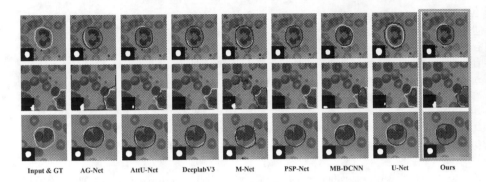

Fig. 6. Visualization of WBC segmentation results was obtained by our proposed method and the other methods on the BCISC dataset. We used yellow boxes to highlight our results. (Color figure online)

Ablation Studies of Classification Network: In the proposed classification network, we concatenate the images and the corresponding segmentation masks predicted by the proposed segmentation network as the input of the proposed classification network, aiming to exploit the results of skin lesion segmentation to facilitate skin lesion classification. To evaluate the effectiveness of this strategy, we compared the skin lesion classification performance obtained on the ISIC-2017 dataset with or without using the coarse lesion masks produced by the proposed segmentation network in Table 4. Compared to the strategy without the segmentation boost classification strategy, our proposed classification network with the segmentation boost classification strategy increases the Accuracy by 1.6% and 1.2% in the melanoma and keratosis classification, respectively. **Visualization of unsupervised-based strategy module results:** In this section, we provided processing details of the unsupervised-based (US) strategy module. Figure 5 illustrates the US module procedure for generating a colour

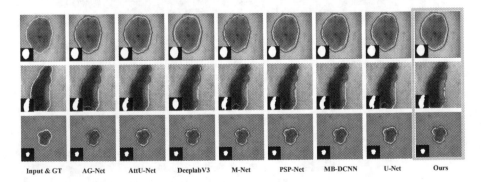

Fig. 7. Visualization of skin lesion segmentation results was generated by our proposed method and the other methods on the ISIC-2017 dataset. We used yellow boxes to highlight our results. (Color figure online)

activation mapping (CAM) block. From the second column of Fig. 5, we can see that our colour channel volume (CCV) block may highlight the region of interest (ROI) of WBC and skin lesion and suppress its image background and distractions. In the third column of Fig. 5, the weighted mean attention map can highlight the foreground and boundary information using an attention mechanism. The fourth column of Fig. 5 shows that our proposed CAM block may further indicate discriminative image regions of WBC/skin lesion, which is helpful in improving segmentation and classification tasks. **Visualization of WBC and skin lesion segmentation results:** We provided visualization of skin lesion and WBC segmentation results in our experiments. Figure 6 shows the visualization of WBC segmentation results obtained by our proposed method and the other methods on the BCISC dataset. Figure 7 shows the visualization of skin lesion segmentation results obtained by our proposed method and the other methods on the ISIC-2017 dataset. It is obvious that the results obtained by our proposed method have higher accuracy and fewer false-positive regions than other comparison methods.

4   Conclusions

In this paper, we proposed a novel UG-Net for automated medical image segmentation and classification. Specially, we proposed an unsupervised-based strategy, which can bring better information fusion. In addition, UG-Net can capture more high-level information and preserve spatial information by integrating a cascaded densely inception block and a stacked atrous convolutional block. Experiments on two biomedical image datasets have demonstrated the effectiveness of our UG-Net. As a powerful biomedical image analysis approach in computer-aided diagnosis systems, UG-Net has excellent potential to provide guidelines for subsequent surgery and significant clues to assist doctors in diagnosing and treating skin cancer or acute lymphoblastic leukaemia early. Future work will focus on semi-supervised segmentation for 3D multimodal images.

References

1. Bobin, J., Starck, J.L., Fadili, J.M., Moudden, Y., Donoho, D.L.: Morphological component analysis: an adaptive thresholding strategy. IEEE Trans. Image Process. **16**(11), 2675–2681 (2007)
2. DeSantis, C.E., Miller, K.D., Goding Sauer, A., Jemal, A., Siegel, R.L.: Cancer statistics for African Americans, 2019. CA Cancer J. Clin. **69**(3), 211–233 (2019)
3. Fan, H., Zhang, F., Xi, L., Li, Z., Liu, G., Xu, Y.: Leukocytemask: an automated localization and segmentation method for leukocyte in blood smear images using deep neural networks. J. Biophotonics **12**(7), e201800488 (2019)
4. Fu, H., Cheng, J., Xu, Y., Wong, D.W.K., Liu, J., Cao, X.: Joint optic disc and cup segmentation based on multi-label deep network and polar transformation. IEEE Trans. Med. Imaging **37**(7), 1597–1605 (2018)
5. Gonzalez-Diaz, I.: Dermaknet: incorporating the knowledge of dermatologists to convolutional neural networks for skin lesion diagnosis. IEEE J. Biomed. Health Inform. **23**(2), 547–559 (2018)

6. Gu, Z., et al.: CE–Net: context encoder network for 2D medical image segmentation. IEEE Trans. Med. Imaging **38**(10), 2281–2292 (2019)

7. Huang, H., et al.: UNet 3+: a full-scale connected UNet for medical image segmentation. In: ICASSP 2020–2020 IEEE International Conference on Acoustics, Speech and Signal Processing (ICASSP), pp. 1055–1059. IEEE (2020)

8. Oktay, O., et al.: Attention U-Net: learning where to look for the pancreas. arXiv preprint arXiv:1804.03999 (2018)

9. Ronneberger, O., Fischer, P., Brox, T.: U-Net: convolutional networks for biomedical image segmentation. In: Navab, N., Hornegger, J., Wells, W.M., Frangi, A.F. (eds.) MICCAI 2015. LNCS, vol. 9351, pp. 234–241. Springer, Cham (2015). https://doi.org/10.1007/978-3-319-24574-4_28

10. Sandler, M., Howard, A., Zhu, M., Zhmoginov, A., Chen, L.C.: Mobilenetv 2: inverted residuals and linear bottlenecks. In: Proceedings of the IEEE Conference on Computer Vision and Pattern Recognition, pp. 4510–4520 (2018)

11. Tan, M., Le, Q.: Efficientnet: rethinking model scaling for convolutional neural networks. In: International Conference on Machine Learning, pp. 6105–6114. PMLR (2019)

12. Xie, Y., Zhang, J., Xia, Y., Shen, C.: A mutual bootstrapping model for automated skin lesion segmentation and classification. IEEE Trans. Med. Imaging **39**(7), 2482–2493 (2020)

13. Zhang, J., Xie, Y., Xia, Y., Shen, C.: Attention residual learning for skin lesion classification. IEEE Trans. Med. Imaging **38**(9), 2092–2103 (2019)

14. Zhang, S., et al.: Attention guided network for retinal image segmentation. In: Shen, D., et al. (eds.) MICCAI 2019. LNCS, vol. 11764, pp. 797–805. Springer, Cham (2019). https://doi.org/10.1007/978-3-030-32239-7_88

15. Zhou, Z., Rahman Siddiquee, M.M., Tajbakhsh, N., Liang, J.: UNet++: a nested U-Net architecture for medical image segmentation. In: Stoyanov, D., et al. (eds.) DLMIA/ML-CDS -2018. LNCS, vol. 11045, pp. 3–11. Springer, Cham (2018). https://doi.org/10.1007/978-3-030-00889-5_1

16. Zhou, X., et al.: H-Net: a dual-decoder enhanced FCNN for automated biomedical image diagnosis. Inf. Sci. **613**, 575–590 (2022)

17. Zhou, X., et al.: Cuss-net: a cascaded unsupervised-based strategy and supervised network for biomedical image diagnosis and segmentation. IEEE J. Biomed. Health Inform. **27**(5), 2444–2455 (2023)

18. Codella, N.C., et al.: Skin lesion analysis toward melanoma detection: a challenge at the 207 international symposium on biomedical imaging (ISBI), hosted by the international skin imaging collaboration (ISIC). In: 2018 IEEE 15th International Symposium on Biomedical Imaging (ISBI 2018), pp. 168–172. IEEE (2018)

Unsupervised Shape Enhancement and Factorization Machine Network for 3D Face Reconstruction

Leyang Yang[1], Boyang Zhang[1], Jianchang Gong[1], Xueming Wang[1(✉)], Xiangzheng Li[2], and Kehua Ma[1]

[1] School of Information Engineering, Ningxia University, Yinchuan 750021, China
wangxm@nxu.edu.cn
[2] Ningxia Normal University, Guyuan, China
82021011@nxnu.edu.cn

Abstract. Existing unsupervised methods are often unable to capture accurate 3D shapes due to the ambiguity of shapes and albedo maps, limiting their applicability to downstream tasks. Therefore, this article proposes an unsupervised shape enhancement and decomposition machine network for 3D facial reconstruction. Specifically, we design a shape enhancement network, further combining global and local features, which can restore more complete and realistic albedo images without introducing additional supervision, so as to obtain higher-quality 3D faces. Secondly, based on the principle of decomposition machines, we design a decomposition module. By decomposing large matrices, the network learns to infer better results, while reducing the number of network parameters further improving the accuracy of our model. Extensive experiments on BFM and CelebA data demonstrate the effectiveness of our methods.

Keywords: 3D face reconstruction · Unsupervised · Channel Information Enhancement · Factorization

1 Introduction

In recent years, the application of face analysis techniques in computer vision has become increasingly widespread, such as 3D scanning in medicine, 3D face modeling in animation production and face attribute editing in film production and many other application scenarios. Among them, the three-dimensional face reconstruction application prospect is very broad, it also has an important position in computer vision. 3D face reconstruction from a single view is

This work was supported by the Ningxia Graduate Education and Teaching Reform Research and Practice Project 2021, in part by National Natural Science Foundation of China under Grant 62062056, and in part by the Ningxia Natural Science Foundation under Grant 2022AAC03327.

a long-standing problem. Its potential applications include biometric recognition and face digitization. The proposed 3D Morphable Model [1] enables people to realize reconstruction by regression of face model parameters [2]. With the rapid development of deep learning, many methods have been used to improve 3DMM parameters or nonlinear from 2D images [3–6]. At the same time, due to the limited information that a single view can provide, some jobs provide the use of multi-view consistency to rebuild a three-dimensional face model [7,8]. Recently, the new three-dimensional face model Flame [9] has greatly promoted the development of three-dimensional face reconstruction [10–12]. However, due to prior model constraints, it is difficult for them to work well on identity, facial detail reconstruction, and so on. The latest work Unsup3d [13] unsupervised face reconstruction based on symmetry constraints, decoupling the face into intrinsic factors such as albedo, depth, light, and viewpoint. However, due to the low resolution of the image and inaccurate light prediction, the reconstructed face shape is blurred, or wrinkles and other details are incorrectly reconstructed, as shown in the albedo image and reconstruction mesh in Fig. 1. We note that the amount of network parameters have a crucial impact on the overall performance of the network.With the development of deep separable convolution [14,15], we can reduce the number of network parameters while capturing information. Matrix decomposition [16,17] has been widely used by many people as an existing method to reduce the number of network parameters.

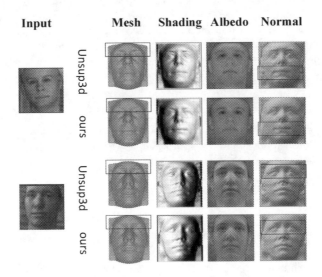

Fig. 1. Qualitative comparison between our method and Unsup3d [13]. Our results show better face shape, finer detail, and less noise.

Based on the above observations, this paper first proposes a new shape enhancement network. By transforming the number and scale of channels in the input image, the network uses the complementarity of the local field of view of depth convolution and the global field of view of self attention to achieve more accurate albedo map prediction and further improve the accuracy of the reconstructed image. In addition, a network based on factorization machine is proposed to replace the common down-sampling encoder structure. The network greatly reduces the number of network parameters and improves the accuracy of 3D reconstruction through the learnable method of splitting matrices and weighted recombination. We achieved better results and higher quality reconstruction than state-of-the-art methods, as shown in Fig. 1. In general, our main contributions are as follows:

1. We propose a Shape Enhanced Network (ShapeENet) that captures the details required for albedo well. At the same time, it filters out some of the noise and, in combination with shape and light, reconstructs a three-dimensional face that is rich in detail and reasonably shaped.
2. We design a factorization machine network. By disassembling the large matrix operation, using the results of small matrices and replacing the results of large matrix operation, the network parameter quantity is significantly reduced while the model accuracy is also improved to a certain extent.
3. Experimental results on BFM dataset and CelebA dataset show that our method has improved significantly. Finally, we have provided an ablation experiment that has proved the effectiveness of our method.

2   Method

In this chapter, we will detail our architecture of shape enhancement and factorization machine. The shape enhancement network consists of the bottom sampling channel information enhancement module and the feature refinement module. The overall network architecture is shown in Fig. 2.

First, given a collection of unrestricted face images, our main purpose is to learn a model. The input to the model is a face image, which is then broken down into 3D shapes, albedo, light, and viewpoints. Finally, these factors are precisely modeled. To predict 3D faces without the 3DMM hypothesis, we followed the frame design of the photo geometry self-encoder in Unsup3d [13].

For an image $I \in R^{3 \times H \times W}$, we want to map image I through a function F with four factors (d, a, v, l), d is the depth map, a is the albedo map, v is the viewpoint, and l is the light. The image is eventually reconstructed by these four factors.

$$\hat{I} = \Phi(d, a, v, l) = \Pi(\Lambda(d, a, l), d, v) \tag{1}$$

Here Λ performs shading with albedo a, depth map d, and light direction l, while Π performs viewpoint change and generates the image viewed from the viewpoint v.

To constrain the canonical view of d and a to represent the full front, we built the loss function based on the symmetry hypothesis.

$$\hat{\mathbf{I}}' = \Pi\left(\Lambda\left(a', d', l\right), d', w\right) \tag{2}$$

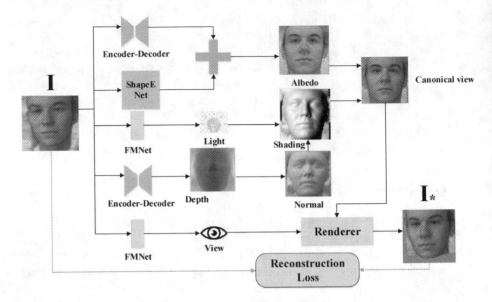

Fig. 2. This is the overall architecture of our network. Our network decomposes the input image into albedo, light, depth, and viewpoint. In the albedo diagram section, the network is enhanced through our channel shape, the global feature and local feature are fused, the more refined albedo diagram is extracted, and the face detail is clearly displayed. In the light and viewpoint network, our factorization machine network is used to improve prediction accuracy while reducing the number of network parameters. Finally, the final face model is generated from the four components we predict, and the corresponding 2D images are rendered. The entire network operates under unsupervised conditions.

where a' and d' are flipped versions of a, d, so that $\hat{I}$ is as similar to $\hat{I}'$ as possible. The viewpoint w is the image perspective of network prediction. This results in an unsupervised three-dimensional face reconstruction of the image without the 3DMM hypothesis.

2.1 Shape Enhancement Network

Although the original albedo map has a rough outline, it is still not clear and accurate enough. This will cause distortion in the reconstructed 3D facial shape. So we propose a shape enhancement network, as shown in Fig. 3. Our shape enhancement network has two main modules, the downsampling channel information enhancement module (CIEM) and the feature optimization module (FRM). Next, we will introduce these two parts in detail.

CIEM: As shown in Fig. 4, CIEM is also a dual-branched encoder that realizes the feature extraction part of face albedo image sampling. In the global feature extraction section, 1 * 1 convolution is used to increase dimensionality and reduce the size of the feature map, thereby enhancing the feature expression

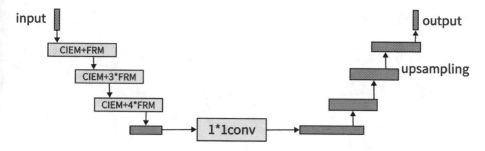

Fig. 3. This is a schematic diagram of our enhanced network of channel shape. The two core components are the channel information enhancement module and the feature refinement module respectively. Our high-quality albedo graph is obtained by combining two modules.

space. Subsequently, channel-by-channel convolution is used to extract features while reducing computational complexity. The added attention block provides more contextual information as a supplement, and finally uses point-by-point convolution to weight in the depth direction to strengthen the global feature space connection. In the local feature extraction section, we use max pooling to extract the largest feature in the graph with a small increase in parameter size. Finally, we fuse the features of the upper and lower parts to obtain the final downsampling result.

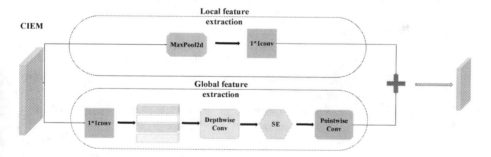

Fig. 4. This is the architecture of our channel information enhancement module. It is divided into upper and lower branches, the upper branch is responsible for extracting global features, and the lower branch is responsible for extracting detailed local features. The feature diagrams of the last two branches are fused to get the results we want.

FRM: FRM is the global feature extraction module of CIEM, but it does not perform downsampling operations. Secondly, we introduce residuals in the output to ensure that the feature extraction is refined in the correct direction. The purpose of the FRM block is to further aggregate the albedo map information and enhance the global information on the albedo map. A CIEM may be followed by multiple FRM blocks, enabling strong aggregation of feature information.

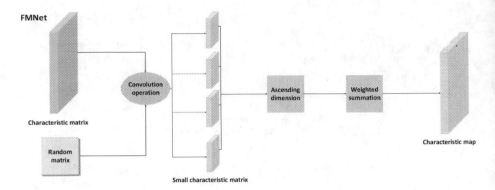

Fig. 5. This is the factorization machine network (FMNet) architecture. The characteristic matrix is convoluted with multiple randomly generated matrices (reducing the number of channels) to obtain multiple small matrices. Small matrices become new characteristic matrices after weighted summation through ascending dimensional operation.

2.2   Factorization Machine Network

It can be seen from Fig. 2 that the predicted illumination affects the rendering performance of the shape and final albedo diagram, and the viewpoint network determines the angle of view accuracy of the final rendering result. As a result, both networks also have a critical impact on rebuilding results. In past practice, little research has been done on this segment. We believe that the existing predictive network formed by sampling under ordinary convolution has a significant effect on the final convergence and accuracy of the network due to a large amount of training data and increasing computational volume. To solve this problem, we propose a factorization machine network(FMNet) to replace the original two predictive subnets As shown in Fig. 5.

The basic idea of our FMNet comes from Factor Machine, and we want to be able to extract the most important potential features from existing raw data while minimizing the number of operations. We first randomly initialize k matrices Q, multiply the characteristic diagrams we enter with matrix Q, and get K matrices P. The matrix P transforms the number of channels by convolution into the number we need to output. Finally, k matrices P are weighted and added by adding learnable weight parameters through the results of convolution. Through subsequent experiments, we proved the validity of our method and greatly reduced the number of network parameters. Here we will give an algorithmic process for our network:

$$Q_{1...k} = Rand(torch.Tensor(cin, d)) \tag{3}$$

$$P_i(N, H * W, C) = F(N, H * W, C) * Q_i \tag{4}$$

$$P_i^* = P_i(N, H * W, C) * Conv \tag{5}$$

$$F_* = \sum_{i=1\ldots k}^{i=1} P_i^* * W_i \tag{6}$$

where F is the input feature diagram, N is the batch size, H and W are the length and width of the feature map, cin is the number of channels we enter, and d is a hyperparameter we set to reduce the number of channels to reduce calculations. W_i is a learnable weight and the final output is F_*.

3   Experiments

3.1   Setup

Datasets: We tested our approach on two face datasets: CelebA [18] and BFM [19]. CelebA is a rich face dataset with 20,2599 pictures of 10,177 celebrity identities, each marked with features, including a face box markup box, 5 face feature point coordinates, and 40 property markers. BFM is a data set built from a 3DMM model that contains 3D scanning data for 100 men and 100 women, and marks expression coefficients, texture coefficients, coordinates for 68 key points, and 7 coefficients for the camera. We use it to evaluate the quality of 3D reconstruction (because field data sets lack real data).

Metrics: We evaluated our reconstruction results on the BFM and CelebA datasets. We evaluate the effectiveness of our reconstruction using Scale Invariant Depth Error (SIDE) [20] and the Mean Angular Deviation (MAD) between the calculated normals of the true and predicted depths on the ground.

Implementation Details: We used Adam to train images with batch size 64, and we entered a picture size of 64 * 64, training a total of 30 epochs. For visualization, we sampled depth maps and so on to 256 * 256 for easy display. We set the dimension d of the four-layer partition used in FMNet to (4,8,8,4) based on our experience.

3.2   Comparison with the State-of-the-Art

Quantitative Comparison. We compare our approach to the most advanced unsupervised approach. Specifically, we trained and tested our algorithms on the BFM dataset, and others did the same as we did. The reconstruction of depth and normal is measured using the scale-invariant depth error (SIDE) and average angle deviation (MAD), as shown in Table 1. We can see that we are far ahead of the most advanced methods, Unsup3d [13], LeMul [21], Gan2Shape [22] and G-SCR [23], in both metrics, showing that we have rebuilt a better three-dimensional structure with better detail clarity. As far as we know, our current average angle deviation (MAD) on BFM [19] data is the best of the unsupervised methods. Meanwhile, in the last column, we also displayed the changes in the corresponding network parameters after applying FMNet, and it can be seen that our parameter count has decreased by 95%.

Table 1. We have quantitative comparisons with other methods on the BFM dataset.

No	Method	SIDE($\times 10^{-2}$ $\downarrow$)	MAD(deg.)$\downarrow$	L/V Parameter
(1)	Unsup3d [13]	0.793 ± 0.1403	16.51 ± 1.56	1.739264
(2)	LeMul [21]	0.834 ± 0.169	15.49 ± 1.50	1.739264
(3)	Gan2Shape [22]	0.756 ± 0.156	15.35 ± 1.49	1.739264
(4)	G-SCR [23]	0.859 ± 0.215	15.17 ± 1.92	-
(5)	Ours	**0.734 ± 0.139**	**14.01 ± 1.45**	**0.086336**

For FMNet, we also compared the memory and model size of FLOPs, MAdd, and runtime, and found that the runtime memory occupied by FMNet was significantly reduced, which can support a larger batch size at once and assist in the operation of downstream tasks. At the same time, it can significantly reduce the computational complexity of FLOPs and MAdd, making the model size smaller and making its future applications possible. The results are shown in Table 2.

Table 2. Multiplication and addition operations, computational complexity, running memory, and model size changes.

Method	MAdd(M)	FLOPs(M)	Runtime Memory(MB)	Model size(MB)
Unsup3d [13]	55.58	27.85	5269	425
LeMul [21]	55.58	27.85	6295	455
Gan2Shape [22]	216.01	108.13	11614	470
FMNet	**8.42**	**4.27**	**5151**	**387**

Qualitative Evaluation. Figure 6 visualizes the results of our approach on BFM. It can be seen that the three-dimensional model, shape, and albedo diagrams reconstructed by our method are significantly superior to other methods. Compared to Unsup3d [13] and LeMul [21], our method has significant improvements in the eyes and mouth, and there is no abnormal bulging of the eyeballs. Compared with Gan2Shape [22], our method can reconstruct better 3D facial shapes. These are all thanks to our proposed shape enhancement network. At the same time, we tested our methods on the CelebA dataset to see that our methods s shown in Fig. 7. We can see that the albedo diagram extracted by our method has a more accurate complexion and a more realistic human face. This proves the effectiveness of our method. In this way, we can restore a more refined 3D face model.

3.3   Ablation Study

In this section, we mainly test the influence of shape enhancement network and factorization convolution module on model performance, mainly relying on

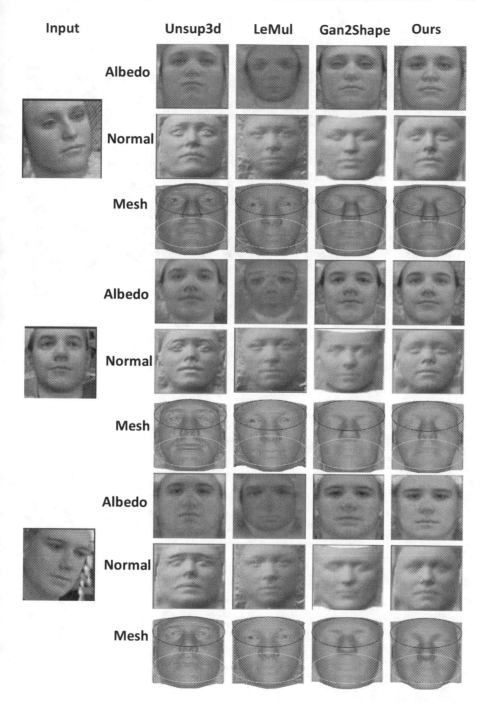

Fig. 6. Qualitative comparison of our method with Unsup3d [13], LeMul [21], and Gan2Shape [22] on the BFM dataset. It can be seen that our method can better reconstruct the overall shape and details. The effect on the eyes, forehead, and mouth is significantly better than other methods.

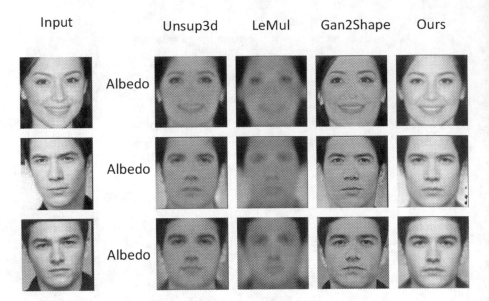

Fig. 7. Qualitative comparison of our method with Unsup3d [13], LeMul [21], and Gan2Shape [22] on CelebA dataset. We highlight the excellent performance of our methods for albedo graphs. As you can see, the diagram we get in the method contains more accurate skin tones and more realistic face shapes.

Table 3. Ablation study.

No	Method	SIDE($\times 10^{-2}$ ↓)	MAD(deg.)↓
(1)	w/o CIEM	0.748 ± 0.137	15.01 ± 1.47
(2)	w/o FRM	0.745 ± 0.137	15.03 ± 1.48
(3)	w/o ShapeENet(CIEM+FRM)	0.772 ± 0.141	15.23 ± 1.50
(4)	w/o FMNet	0.749 ± 0.150	14.70 ± 1.41
(5)	Ours full	$\mathbf{0.734 \pm 0.139}$	$\mathbf{14.01 \pm 1.45}$

intuitive quantitative results on the BFM data set, including scale invariant depth error (SIDE) and average angle deviation (MAD). As shown in Table 3, we demonstrate the impact of these two major components on model performance. Finally, we also provided the selection experiment of FMNet hyperparameter d, and we ultimately used the configuration of the last row, as shown in Table 4.

Table 4. Quantitative Case of FMNet Different Settings on a BFM Data Set

Method	SIDE($\times 10^{-2}$ $\downarrow$)	MAD(deg.)$\downarrow$	L/V Parameter
Unsup3d [13]	0.793	16.51	1.739264
FMNet(4,8,4,4)	0.799	16.04	0.066882
FMNet(4,4,4,2)	0.797	15.80	0.046912
FMNet(8,8,8,8)	0.782	16.00	0.111681
FMNet(4,4,4,4)	0.774	15.71	0.057152
FMNet(4,8,8,4)	**0.772**	**15.23**	0.086336

4   Conclusion

This paper proposes a shape enhancement network to solve the problem of face albedo map prediction under an unconstrained environment, which improves the accuracy of albedo map, further improves the accuracy of 3D face reconstruction, and smoothes the irregular reconstruction part. While improving the reconstruction accuracy, we also considered the potential impact of increasing network parameters. Therefore, we further design a factorization machine network, which can reduce the number of partial branch network parameters and improve the overall performance of the network. Numerous quantitative and qualitative experiments have shown that our method outperforms state-of-the-art methods.

References

1. Blanz, V., Vetter, T., Rockwood, A.: A morphable model for the synthesis of 3D faces. In: ACM SIGGRAPH, pp. 187–194 (2002)
2. Yang, M., et al.: Self-supervised High-fidelity and Re-renderable 3D Facial Reconstruction from a Single Image (2021)
3. Zhou, Y., et al.: Dense 3D face decoding over 2500FPS: joint texture & shape convolutional mesh decoders. In: Proceedings of the IEEE/CVF Conference on Computer Vision and Pattern Recognition (2019)
4. Zhu, X., et al.: Beyond 3DMM: Learning to Capture High-fidelity 3D Face Shape (2022)
5. Bao, L., et al.: High-Fidelity 3D Digital Human Head Creation from RGB-D Selfies. ACMPUB27, New York, NY (2022)
6. Jiang, D., et al.: Sphere Face Model: A 3D Morphable Model with Hypersphere Manifold Latent Space (2021)
7. Rahim, J.A., et al.: Deep facial non-rigid multi-view stereo. In: Conference on Computer Vision and Pattern Recognition (2020)
8. Yoon, J.S., et al.: Self-Supervised Adaptation of High-Fidelity Face Models for Monocular Performance Tracking (2019)
9. Li, T., et al.: Learning a model of facial shape and expression from 4D scans. ACM Trans. Graph. (TOG) (2017)
10. Feng, Y., et al.: Learning an animatable detailed 3D face model from in-the-wild images. ACM Trans. Graph. **40**(4), 1–13 (2021)

11. Danecek, R., Black, M.J., Bolkart, T.: EMOCA: Emotion Driven Monocular Face Capture and Animation (2022)
12. Zielonka, W., Bolkart, T., Thies, J.: Towards metrical reconstruction of human faces. In: Avidan, S., Brostow, G., Cissé, M., Farinella, G.M., Hassner, T. (eds.) ECCV 2022. LNCS, vol. 13673, pp. 250–269. Springer, Cham (2022). https://doi.org/10.1007/978-3-031-19778-9_15
13. Wu, S., Rupprecht, C., Vedaldi, A.: Unsupervised learning of probably symmetric deformable 3D objects from images in the wild. In: 2020 IEEE/CVF Conference on Computer Vision and Pattern Recognition (CVPR) (2020)
14. Shaheed, K., et al.: Finger-vein presentation attack detection using depthwise separable convolution neural network. Expert Syst. Appl. **198**, 116786 (2022)
15. Li, G., et al.: Efficient depthwise separable convolution accelerator for classification and UAV object detection. Neurocomputing **490**, 1–16 (2022)
16. Zhou, K., et al.: High-quality gene/disease embedding in a multi-relational heterogeneous graph after a joint matrix/tensor decomposition. J. Biomed. Inform. **126**, 103973 (2022)
17. Huang, L., et al.: Context-aware road travel time estimation by coupled tensor decomposition based on trajectory data. Knowl.-Based Syst. **245**, 108596 (2022)
18. Liu, Z., et al.: Deep learning face attributes in the wild. IEEE (2016)
19. Paysan, P., et al.: A 3D face model for pose and illumination invariant face recognition. In: 2009 Sixth IEEE International Conference on Advanced Video and Signal Based Surveillance (AVSS). IEEE (2009)
20. Eigen, D., Puhrsch, C., Fergus, R.: Depth Map Prediction from a Single Image using a Multi-Scale Deep Network. MIT Press, Cambridge (2014)
21. Ho, L.N., et al.: Toward Realistic Single-View 3D Object Reconstruction With Unsupervised Learning From Multiple Images (2021)
22. Pan, X., et al.: Do 2D GANs Know 3D Shape? Unsupervised 3D Shape Reconstruction from 2D Image GANs (2021)
23. Liu, W.: Structural causal 3D reconstruction. In: Avidan, S., Brostow, G., Cissé, M., Farinella, G.M., Hassner, T. (eds.) ECCV 2022. LNCS, vol. 13661, pp. 140–159. Springer, Cham (2022). https://doi.org/10.1007/978-3-031-19769-7_9

Visible-Infrared Person Re-identification via Modality Augmentation and Center Constraints

Qiang Chen⬤, Guoqiang Xiao$^{(\boxtimes)}$⬤, and Jiahao Wu

College of Computer and Information Science, Southwest University,
Chongqing, China
{cq0907,a948246605}@email.swu.edu.cn, gqxiao@swu.edu.cn

Abstract. Visible-infrared person re-identification (VI-ReID) is a tricky cross-modality retrieval problem, where main challenge is the significant modality discrepancy. Existing methods mainly focus on bridging the relation between modalities by shared representation learning in the common embedding space. However, due to the outliers, these methods often struggle to build compact clustering subspaces. Besides, these methods also suffer from modality imbalance problem caused by more visible (VIS) modality images than infrared (IR) modality images, which induces the features of IR modality have to face an extra modality bias during the test phase. In this paper, we propose a novel modality augmentation and center constraints (MACC) framework, where grayscale channel joint random patch is adopted to generate semantic-rich images that are more similar to IR modality images in style, which reduces the modality discrepancy and, to some extent, alleviates the modality imbalance problem. In addition, based on the idea of partition, we design a fine-grained feature mining module (FFMM) to mine nuanced but discriminative information within each part, which is benefit to further alleviate the modality discrepancy. Meanwhile, to encourage more compact clustering, we propose a novel compact center clustering (C^3) loss to achieve intra-modality and inter-modality compact clustering. Apart from C^3 loss, we also introduce the center distribution consistencies (CDC) loss to align the feature vectors and prediction logits by optimizing the standard deviation and JS divergence, respectively. Extensive experiments on two public datasets demonstrate that our method achieves new state-of-the-art performance. The code will be available at https://github.com/cq0907/MACC.

Keywords: Cross-modality retrieval · Modality augmentation · Feature mining · Center clustering · Center alignment

1 Introduction

Person re-identification (Re-ID) is a single-modality retrieval task, which aims at retrieving a specific pedestrian image from a gallery set captured only by

Supported by organization Southwest University.

visible (VIS) cameras. It has been widely studied because of its importance in various video surveillance systems. However, VIS camera in low-light conditions works badly, e.g., at night. For better 24-hour surveillance, infrared (IR) camera is applied to capture the target in low-illumination environment due to it rarely depends on VIS light. Accordingly, visible-infrared person re-identification (VI-ReID), that is, given a VIS/IR modality image matches the corresponding IR/VIS modality images with same identity, has aroused extensive research.

The major challenge in VI-ReID lies in the significant modality discrepancy, as shown in Fig. 1(a), followed by the modality imbalance problem. The former is caused by the data heterogeneity of different spectrum cameras. The latter stems from training samples imbalance, i.e., more VIS modality images captured by VIS cameras. Therefore, two main types of frameworks, metric learning and generative adversarial networks [5] (GANs), are proposed to overcome the above challenges. Benefiting from the powerful feature extraction capability of convolutional neural networks [6] (CNNs), metric-based learning methods [22,24,28] can extract the shared features of different modality images with same identity and then enforce a higher similarity by the constraint of well-designed objective function. Although these methods usually achieve encouraging performance with the end-to-end optimization strategy, they are often difficult to form compact clusters due to the outliers. Another line of approaches is GANs-based methods [4,19,20]. The purpose of GANs-based methods can be summarized in two-fold: (1) Reducing the color discrepancy of different modality images and thereby narrowing the modality gap. (2) Enlarging the diversity of the training samples and then alleviating the modality imbalance problem, as shown in Fig. 1(b). This kind of methods tends to achieve better performance in terms of robustness. However, due to the introduce of extra noise, the semantic correspondence between modalities could be not well learned.

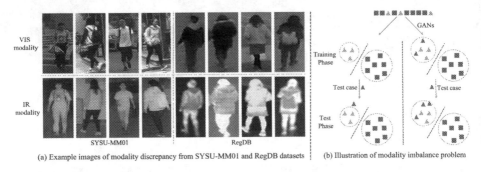

(a) Example images of modality discrepancy from SYSU-MM01 and RegDB datasets   (b) Illustration of modality imbalance problem

Fig. 1. The challenges in VI-ReID. (a) Modality discrepancy between VIS and IR modality images on two datasets. (b) Modality imbalance problem. Triangles and squares represent different modalities.

To overcome the drawbacks of above methods, we propose a novel modality augmentation and center constraints (MACC) framework to achieve the interclass separability and intra-class compactness without introducing extra noise.

Specifically, MACC is composed of two core modules: random grayscale patch module (RGPM) and fine-grained feature mining module (FFMM). Inspired by [2,25], we use RGPM to generate intermediate modality image by mixing grayscale VIS modality image and random patch from IR modality image. In this way, the intermediate modality image contain not only the structural information of VIS and IR modality images, but also is more similar to IR modality image in style. Thus, the RGPM benefits VI-ReID task in two aspects: (1) Different from the methods based on GANs, all pixels of the intermediate modality images are taken from the original VIS and IR modality images, which is beneficial for minimizing the introduction of extra noise. (2) The semantic-rich images generated by RGPM contribute to alleviate the modality discrepancy and imbalance problem. The FFMM aims to mine nuanced but discriminative information from local features. Since the global feature maps are distractive, we split the global feature maps into multiple parts and mine fine-grained information within each part. In addition, to encourage compact clustering, a novel compact center clustering (C^3) loss is designed to enforce each sample clustering towards homo-modality intra-class center, and per identity center clustering towards cross-modality intra-class center. Meanwhile, from the perspective of alignment, we propose center distribution consistencies (CDC) loss to align the feature vectors and prediction logits. We first align the feature vectors by minimizing/maximizing the intra-class/inter-class standard deviation, and then align the prediction logits via minimizing JS divergence.

Overall, our main contributions can be summarized in four-fold: (1) A random grayscale patch module (RGPM) is proposed to generate semantic-rich intermediate modality images which are beneficial for reducing the modality discrepancy and alleviating the modality imbalance problem. (2) A fine-grained feature mining module (FFMM) is designed to mine nuanced but discriminative information within part-level features. (3) we propose a novel compact center clustering (C^3) loss to achieve intra-modality and inter-modality compact clustering. Besides, we introduce the center distribution consistencies (CDC) loss to align the intra-class feature vectors and prediction logits. (4) On the public SYSU-MM01 and RegDB datasets, our approach achieves new the state-of-the-art performance.

2   Proposed Method

In this section, we first describe the overview of the proposed framework (Sect. 2.1), and then make a description of random grayscale patch module (RGPM, Sect. 2.2) and fine-grained feature mining module (FFMM, Sect. 2.3) in detail. Finally, the objective functions (Sect. 2.4) used in our method will be introduced.

2.1   Overview

The overview of the proposed framework is illustrated in Fig. 2(a). We adopt a two-stream network as our backbone which consists of pre-trained ResNet-50,

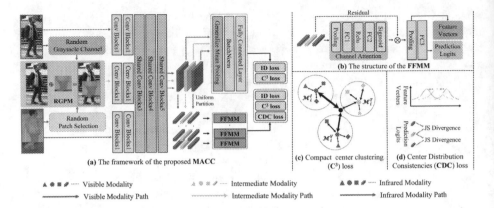

Fig. 2. (a)The framework of the proposed MACC. (b) The structure of Fine-grained feature mining module (FFMM). (c) Compact center clustering (C^3) loss. The thickness of the black (red) arrows indicate intra-modality (inter-modality) different penalties. (d) The schematic diagram of center distribution consistencies (CDC) loss. The gray arrows represents mutual alignment. (Color figure online)

where the first and second convolution blocks are weight-specific for extracting modality-specific features, and the others are weight-shared in order to learn fused features and then obtain discriminative shared features. Followed by this commonly-adopted backbone [11,12], we design two branches to explore the shared features from global and local perspectives. Global branch uses generalize mean pooling (GMP) and fully connected layer (FC) to generate feature vectors and prediction logits of each modality image. Concurrently, based on the idea of partition [18], local branch divides per feature map horizontally into multiple parts, and then mines nuanced but discriminative information within each part by channel attention [21]. Similar to global branch, after pooling and classifying, we can obtain the part-level feature vectors and prediction logits. To further cluster and align the distribution, we put forward two kinds of losses: compact center clustering (C^3) loss and center distribution consistencies (CDC) loss. Both of them enforce the inter-class separability and intra-class compactness.

2.2 Random Grayscale Patch Module

To alleviate the modality discrepancy and imbalance problem, current some works [8,10,25] take account of introducing intermediate modality. Inspired by these works, we propose a novel random grayscale patch module (RGPM) which is composed of random grayscale channel and random patch selection.

As shown in Fig. 2(a), given a pair of VIS and IR modality images, denoted by x^V and x^I, we construct the intermediate modality image x^T by mixing the grayscale x^V and random patch from x^V. In theory, the RGPM benefits cross-modality learning from two aspects: (1) the x^T not only contains the structural information of x^V and x^I, but also is more similar x^I in terms of color style, which reduces the color discrepancy between modalities and alleviates the modality imbalance problem. (2) Due to the location and size of the patch is adjustable and all pixels of x^T are taken from x^V and x^I, we can generate a lot of semantic-rich x^T without importing additional noise, which enhances the robustness of model.

2.3   Fine-Grained Feature Mining Module

Following the PCB model [18], some researchers [11,30,31] focus on learning local features to address the distraction problem of global feature maps. However, insufficient mining of nuanced but discriminative information within local feature maps limits the improvement of performance. Hence we proposed a fine-grained feature mining module (FFMM) to further mine local feature maps, illustrated in Fig. 2(b).

As we all known, the representation learning is distractive, which induces many discriminative information, such as clothing and shoes logos, package, face, etc., have not been fully mined. Inspired by [11,21], we introduce the channel attention on the basis of uniform partition, which guides the model to focus on important information within each part. Given the output feature maps of the convolution blocks-5 as Z, we first divide the Z horizontally into N parts, denoted by $\{Z_i | i = 1, \cdots, N\}$. Sequentially, channel attention module is used to mine important channel information, which is calculated by:

$$m_i^c = \phi(\boldsymbol{W_2}\delta(\boldsymbol{W_1}f_{avg}(Z_i)) + \boldsymbol{W_2}\delta(\boldsymbol{W_1}f_{max}(Z_i))), \qquad (1)$$

where $f_{avg}(\cdot)$ and $f_{max}(\cdot)$ denote the average- and max-pooling operations. $\boldsymbol{W_1}$ and $\boldsymbol{W_2}$ are learnable parameters. $\phi(\cdot)$ and $\delta(\cdot)$ refer to ReLU and sigmoid activation functions, respectively. Afterwards, the m_i^c is applied on Z_i by a residual operation to emphasize the learned important information. Followed by a GMP layer and FC layer, we can obtain the part-level feature vectors and prediction logits, denoted by F_i^f and F_i^p. In general, the overall computation process can be summarized as:

$$F_i^f = f_{gmp}(m_i^c \otimes Z_i), \qquad (2)$$

$$F_i^p = \boldsymbol{W_3}(P_i^f), \qquad (3)$$

where $\otimes$ denotes the element-wise multiplication, $f_{gmp}(\cdot)$ represents generalize mean pooling operation, and $\boldsymbol{W_3}$ is the learnable parameters of FC layer.

2.4   Objective Function

Aside from the generic identity (ID) loss, compact center clustering (C^3) loss and center distribution consistencies (CDC) loss are proposed to jointly optimize the whole network. Assume that we randomly select P person identities and K corresponding images. Through the RGPM, a mini-batch contains $P \times K$ VIS modality images, $P \times K$ IR modality images and $P \times K$ intermediate modality images, i.e., a total of $3 \times P \times K$ images are used for each iteration.

ID Loss ($\mathcal{L}_{ID}$). Given an arbitrary modality image x with corresponding identity label y, ID loss aims to increase the probability that x belongs to class y. A *softmax* function is used to calculate the probability $p_l(y|x)$ and $p_g(y|x)$, formulated as:

$$p_l(y|x) = \frac{exp(F_{l,y}^p)}{\sum_{k=1}^{C} exp(F_{l,k}^p)}, \quad p_g(y|x) = \frac{exp(F_{g,y}^p)}{\sum_{k=1}^{C} exp(F_{g,k}^p)}, \tag{4}$$

where $F_{l,y}^p$ ($F_{l,k}^p$) and $F_{g,y}^p$ ($F_{g,k}^p$) represent the probability score of local and global prediction logits at position y (k). C is the total number of identities. With the calculated probabilities, we use cross-entropy loss to optimize the local and global prediction logits, denoted by:

$$\mathcal{L}_{ID} = -\frac{1}{n} \sum_{j=1}^{n} log(p_g(y_j|x_j)) - \frac{1}{n*N} \sum_{j=1}^{n} \sum_{i=1}^{N} p_l(y_{j,i}|x_{j,i}) \tag{5}$$

where $x_{j,i}$ represents the ith part of sample x_j. N is the number of parts. n refers to the number of samples at each mini-batch, denoted by $n = 3 \times P \times K$.

C³ Loss ($\mathcal{L}_{C^3}$). To achieve compact clustering, we encourage each sample clustering towards the homo-modality intra-class center and per identity center clustering towards cross-modality intra-class center. Accordingly, we design a compact center clustering (C³) loss to achieve intra-modality and inter-modality compact clustering, as shown in Fig. 2(c). Meanwhile, based on the property of triplet loss [16], we also push the inter-class distance between cross-modality centers. In the following, we describe the basic idea of intra- and inter-modality clustering without distinguishing between local and global branches. Firstly, we calculate the intra-modality identity center of feature vectors by:

$$c^V = \frac{1}{K} \sum_{k=1}^{K} F_k^{V,f}, \quad c^T = \frac{1}{K} \sum_{k=1}^{K} F_k^{T,f}, \quad c^I = \frac{1}{K} \sum_{k=1}^{K} F_k^{I,f}, \tag{6}$$

where $F_k^{V,f}$, $F_k^{I,f}$ and $F_k^{T,f}$ denote the kth feature vector of VIS, IR and intermediate modalities of each identity, respectively. With the intra-modality centers, we can compute the intra-class distance between each sample and corresponding homo-modality center, denoted by:

$$\mathcal{L}_{C^3}^{s2c} = \frac{1}{3 \times P \times K} \sum_{j=1}^{P} \sum_{k=1}^{K} \left\| F_{j,k}^{V,f} - c_j^V \right\|_2 + \left\| F_{j,k}^{T,f} - c_j^T \right\|_2 + \left\| F_{j,k}^{I,f} - c_j^I \right\|_2, \tag{7}$$

where $\| \cdot \|_2$ computes the Euclidean distance. To optimize the inter-modality distance of all positive and negative center pairs. Following [7], we adopt a *softplus* function for the optimization. The mathematical form is denoted by:

$$\mathcal{L}_{C^3}^{c2c} = \frac{1}{P} \sum_{u=1}^{P} log(1 + exp(\sum_{v=1}^{P} w_{u,v}^{pos} d_{u,v}^{pos} - w_{u,w}^{neg} d_{u,w}^{neg})),$$

$$w_{u,v}^{pos} = \frac{exp(d_{u,v}^{pos})}{\sum_{d_{u,v}^{pos} \in \mathcal{P}_u} exp(d_{u,v}^{pos})}, \quad w_{u,v}^{neg} = \frac{exp(-d_{u,w}^{neg})}{\sum_{d_{u,w}^{neg} \in \mathcal{N}_u} exp(-d_{u,w}^{neg})}, \tag{8}$$

where (u, v, w) represent a triplet in the mini-batch. For the anchor center c_u. $d_{u,v}^{pos}$ and $d_{u,w}^{neg}$ are the Euclidean distance between anchor center and positive center, and anchor center and negative center, respectively, denoted by $d_{u,v}^{pos} = \|c_u - c_v\|_2$ and $d_{u,w}^{neg} = \|c_u - c_w\|_2$. $\mathcal{P}_u$ and $\mathcal{N}_u$ denote the positive and negative sets for the anchor center c_u. In short, C^3 loss achieves intra- and inter-modality compact clustering from two aspects: (1) Pulling the intra-class distance between each sample and homo-modality center, and per identity center and cross-modality center. (2) Pushing the inter-class distance between cross-modality negative center pairs. The final form is denoted by:

$$\mathcal{L}_{C^3} = \mathcal{L}_{C^3}^{s2c} + \mathcal{L}_{C^3}^{c2c}. \tag{9}$$

CDC Loss ($\mathcal{L}_{DC}$). As shown in Fig. 2(d), we align the intra-class feature vectors and prediction logits by center distribution consistencies (CDC) loss. To constrain the feature vectors, our basic idea is to minimize the standard deviation between intra-class centers and maximize the standard deviation between inter-class centers, calculated by:

$$\mathcal{L}_{CDC}^{Feat} = max[\rho + \sqrt{\frac{1}{P}\sum_{u=1}^{P}\sigma_u^{pos}} - \sqrt{\frac{1}{P}\sum_{u=1}^{P}\sigma_u^{neg}}, 0],$$

$$\sigma_u^{pos} = \|c_u - \frac{1}{\mathcal{C}(\mathcal{P}_u)}\sum_{c_v\in\mathcal{P}_u} c_v\|_2^2, \quad \sigma_u^{neg} = \|c_u - \frac{1}{\mathcal{C}(\mathcal{N}_u)}\sum_{c_w\in\mathcal{N}_u} c_w\|_2^2, \tag{10}$$

here $\mathcal{C}(\cdot)$ returns the cardinality of a set. ρ is the least margin among centers. Concurrently, we align prediction logits by minimizing JS divergence, which can be formulated as:

$$c_u^{VT} = \frac{c_u^V + c_u^T}{2}, \qquad c_u^{IT} = \frac{c_u^I + c_u^T}{2},$$

$$\mathcal{L}_{CDC}^{Pred} = \frac{1}{2}(\sum_{u=1}^{P} c_u^V \log\frac{c_u^V}{c_u^{VT}} + \sum_{u=1}^{P} c_u^T \log\frac{c_u^T}{c_u^{VT}})+$$

$$\frac{1}{2}(\sum_{u=1}^{P} c_u^I \log\frac{c_u^I}{c_u^{IT}} + \sum_{u=1}^{P} c_u^T \log\frac{c_u^T}{c_u^{IT}}), \tag{11}$$

where c_u^V, c_u^I and c_u^T represent the VIS, IR and intermediate modality centers of identity u, respectively. Combining $\mathcal{L}_{CDC}^{Feat}$ and $\mathcal{L}_{CDC}^{Pred}$, the CDC loss is defined as:

$$\mathcal{L}_{CDC} = \mathcal{L}_{CDC}^{Feat} + \mathcal{L}_{CDC}^{Pred}. \tag{12}$$

Note that we optimize the global branch only with ID loss and C^3 loss, and optimize the local branch with ID loss, C^3 loss and CDC loss. Accordingly, we design the following overall objective function:

$$\mathcal{L} = (\mathcal{L}_{ID} + \mathcal{L}_{C^3})_g + (\mathcal{L}_{ID} + \mathcal{L}_{C^3} + \mathcal{L}_{CDC})_l. \tag{13}$$

3 Experiments

3.1 Datasets and Settings

Dataset. There are two available benchmark datasets for evaluating the performance of our approach: SYSU-MM01 [22] and RegDB [14]. The former is captured by six cameras. 22258 VIS and 11909 IR modality images with 395 identities are used for training and 301 VIS and 3803 IR modality images with 96 identities are utilized for testing. The latter is collected by dual camera systems, it contains in total 412 identities, half for training and half for testing. For both datasets, Rank-1 accuracy, mean Average Precision (mAP), and mean Inverse Negative Penalty (mINP) are adopted as the evaluation protocol.

Settings. Following the classic methods of VI-ReID, all VIS and IR modality person images are resized to 288×144. The total epoch is 60 and we use SGD optimizer with momentum 0.9 and weight decay 5e-4 to optimize our model. The initial learning rate is 0.1, which will decay by a factor of 10 at the 20th and 50th epoch. The hyper-parameters in the formula are set as: $\lambda_N = 6$, $P=8$, $K=8$ and $\rho = 0.3$. We implement the proposed method with PyTorch and use single Geforce RTX 3090 GPU for acceleration.

3.2 Comparison with State-of-the-Art Methods

We compare our MACC with the state-of-the-art methods for VI-ReID, including Zero-Padding [22], cmGAN [4], D^{2}RL [20], Xmodal [9], DDAG [26], Hi-CMD [3], AGW [27], LbA [15], CAJ [25], SPOT [1], DCLNet [30], MPANet [23], FMCNet [29] and MAUM [13].

As shown in Table 1, we conduct a quantitative comparison between MACC and the state-of-the-art methods on the SYSU-MM01 and RegDB datasets. The results show that our approach outperforms existing SOTAs on three main evaluation metrics. In the challenging *all-search* mode of SYSU-MM01 dataset, MACC exceeds the CAJ by 3.32% in Rank-1 accuracy, 2.57% in mAP and 1.65% in mINP. In the *indoor-search* mode of SYSU-MM01 dataset, MACC obtains the improvement of 3.96% Rank-1 accuracy, 2.38% mAP and 2.24% mINP over CAJ, respectively. Meanwhile, compared with CAJ in *visible2infrared/infrared2visible* mode of RegDB dataset, the Rank-1 accuracy, mAP and mINP are significantly improved by 9.83%/8.79%, 10.16%/10.31% and 12.76%/14.01%. In short, quantitative comparison demonstrates the superiority of MACC over SOTAs. Note that, we don't use the re-ranking algorithms as post-processing.

3.3 Ablation Study

To verify the effectiveness of each component in MACC, we conduct ablation studies under the *all-search* mode of SYSU-MM01 dataset. The experimental results are shown in Table 2.

Baseline. We adopt a two-stream network with ID loss and hetero-center triplet (HCT) loss [11] as baseline.

Table 1. Comparison with state-of-the-art methods on SYSU-MM01 and RegDB datasets. Rank-1 accuracy (%), mAP (%) and mINP (%) are reported.

Method	Venue	SYSU-MM01						RegDB					
		All-Search			Indoor-Search			Visble2Thermal			Thermal2Visible		
		Rank-1	mAP	mINP	Rank-1	mAP	mINP	Rank-1	mAP	mINP	Rank-1	mAP	mINP
Zero-Padding	ICCV17	14.80	15.95	-	20.58	26.92	-	14.80	18.90	-	16.63	17.82	-
cmGAN	IJCAI18	26.97	27.80	-	31.63	42.19	-	-	-	-	-	-	-
D^{2}RL	CVPR19	28.90	29.20	-	-	-	-	26.97	44.10	-	-	-	-
Xmodal	AAAI20	49.9	50.7	-	-	-	-	62.21	60.18	-	-	-	-
DDAG	ECCV20	54.75	53.02	-	61.02	67.98	-	69.34	63.46	-	68.06	61.80	-
Hi-CMD	CVPR20	34.94	35.94	-	-	-	-	70.93	66.04	-	-	-	-
AGW	TPAMI21	47.50	47.65	35.30	54.17	62.97	59.23	70.05	66.37	50.19	70.49	65.90	51.24
LbA	ICCV21	55.41	54.14	-	58.46	66.33	-	74.17	67.64	-	72.43	65.46	-
CAJ	ICCV21	69.88	66.89	53.61	76.26	80.37	76.79	85.03	79.14	65.33	84.75	77.82	61.56
MPANet	CVPR21	70.58	68.24	-	76.74	80.95	-	83.7	80.9	-	82.8	80.7	-
SPOT	TIP22	65.34	62.25	48.86	69.42	74.63	70.48	80.35	72.46	56.19	79.37	72.26	56.06
DCLNet	MM22	70.6	66.9	-	-	76.2	79.6	-	91.6	84.1	-	87.5	80.5	-
FMCNet	CVPR22	66.34	62.51	-	68.15	74.09	-	89.12	84.43	-	88.38	83.86	-
MAUM	CVPR22	71.68	68.79	-	76.97	81.94	-	87.87	85.09	-	86.95	84.34	-
MACC(Ours)	-	**73.20**	**69.46**	**55.26**	**80.22**	**82.75**	**79.03**	**94.86**	**89.30**	**78.09**	**93.54**	**88.13**	**75.57**

Effectiveness of FFMM. When mining part-level features upon the baseline, the performance is improved by 2.48%, 2.24% and 2.19% on Rank-1 accuracy, mAP and mINP, respectively, which demonstrates the effectiveness of FFMM on mining fine-grained important information.

Effectiveness of RGPM. The RGPM aims to alleviate the modality discrepancy and imbalance problem. We can see that the performance achieves the improvement of 3.27% Rank-1 accuracy, 3.08% mAP and 8.16%mINP. Note that the result fluctuation between training and test phase becomes smaller after introducing RGPM. Both prove the RGPM can effectively narrow the gap of modalities and alleviate modality imbalance.

Effectiveness of C^3 Loss. Based on the above ablation experiments, we replace the HCT loss with C^3 loss. We observe that the Rank-1 accuracy, mAP and mINP are increased by 4.15%, 3.94% and 3.52%.

Effectiveness of CDC Loss. Combining both C^3 loss and CDC loss, as shown in last row of Table 2, the Rank-1 accuracy, mAP and mINP are respectively boosted by 2.76%, 2.88% and 0.85%, thanks to that CDC loss further aligns the feature vectors and prediction logits.

Table 2. Ablation studies on the SYSU-MM01 dataset

Baseline	FFMM	RGPM	$\mathcal{L}_{C^3}$	$\mathcal{L}_{CDC}$	Rank-1	mAP	mINP
$\checkmark$					60.54	57.32	40.54
$\checkmark$	$\checkmark$				63.02	59.56	42.73
$\checkmark$	$\checkmark$	$\checkmark$			66.29	62.64	50.89
$\checkmark$	$\checkmark$	$\checkmark$	$\checkmark$		70.44	66.58	54.41
$\checkmark$	$\checkmark$	$\checkmark$	$\checkmark$	$\checkmark$	**73.20**	**69.46**	**55.26**

3.4   Visualization

In this subsection, we conduct qualitative analysis to validate the effectiveness of our approach by visualizing the class activation mapping (CAM) [17] and cosine similarity distribution.

Visualized CAM. As shown in Fig. 3(a), the highlighted areas show that our model focuses on discriminative features, such as face, clothing and shoes logos, package, etc., which are distinctive characters of one identity.

Visualized Distribution. We randomly select 9600 inter-modality positive and intra-modality negative matching pairs from the test set of SYSU-MM01 to calculate the cosine similarity scores. As illustrated in Fig. 3(b), our method can effectively increase the cosine similarity of positive sample pairs and reduce the cosine similarity of negative sample pairs, which demonstrates that our method achieves inter-class separability and intra-class compactness.

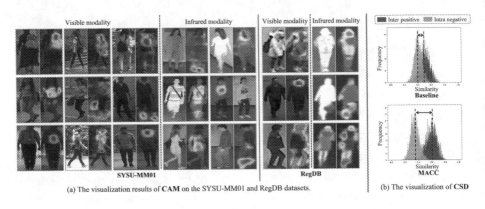

(a) The visualization results of **CAM** on the SYSU-MM01 and RegDB datasets.   (b) The visualization of **CSD**

Fig. 3. The visualization results of the class activation mapping (CAM) and cosine similarity distribution (CSD).

4   Conclusion

In this paper, a modality augmentation and center constraints (MACC) framework is proposed for VI-ReID, where a random grayscale patch module (RGPM) is designed to alleviate the modality discrepancy and imbalance problem. To fully explore the nuanced but discriminative information, we introduce a fine-grained feature mining module (FFMM) to mine local important information. Besides, to constrain the feature vectors and prediction logits, we propose two kinds of losses: compact center clustering (C^3) loss and center distribution consistencies (CDC) loss. The former encourages intra- and inter-modality compact clustering. The latter aligns the feature vectors and prediction logits via optimizing the standard deviation and JS divergence. Extensive experiment results have validated the effectiveness of MACC compared with other SOTAs.

References

1. Chen, C., Ye, M., Qi, M., Wu, J., Jiang, J., Lin, C.W.: Structure-aware positional transformer for visible-infrared person re-identification. IEEE Trans. Image Process. **31**, 2352–2364 (2022)
2. Chen, M., Wang, Z., Zheng, F.: Benchmarks for corruption invariant person re-identification. arXiv preprint arXiv:2111.00880 (2021)
3. Choi, S., Lee, S., Kim, Y., Kim, T., Kim, C.: Hi-CMD: hierarchical cross-modality disentanglement for visible-infrared person re-identification. In: Proceedings of the IEEE/CVF Conference on Computer Vision and Pattern Recognition, pp. 10257–10266 (2020)
4. Dai, P., Ji, R., Wang, H., Wu, Q., Huang, Y.: Cross-modality person re-identification with generative adversarial training. In: IJCAI, vol. 1, p. 6 (2018)
5. Goodfellow, I., et al.: Generative adversarial networks. Commun. ACM **63**(11), 139–144 (2020)
6. He, K., Zhang, X., Ren, S., Sun, J.: Deep residual learning for image recognition. In: Proceedings of the IEEE Conference on Computer Vision and Pattern Recognition, pp. 770–778 (2016)
7. Hermans, A., Beyer, L., Leibe, B.: In defense of the triplet loss for person re-identification. arXiv preprint arXiv:1703.07737 (2017)
8. Huang, Z., Liu, J., Li, L., Zheng, K., Zha, Z.J.: Modality-adaptive mixup and invariant decomposition for RGB-infrared person re-identification. In: Proceedings of the AAAI Conference on Artificial Intelligence, vol. 36, pp. 1034–1042 (2022)
9. Li, D., Wei, X., Hong, X., Gong, Y.: Infrared-visible cross-modal person re-identification with an X modality. In: Proceedings of the AAAI Conference on Artificial Intelligence, vol. 34, pp. 4610–4617 (2020)
10. Ling, Y., Zhong, Z., Luo, Z., Rota, P., Li, S., Sebe, N.: Class-aware modality mix and center-guided metric learning for visible-thermal person re-identification. In: Proceedings of the 28th ACM International Conference on Multimedia, pp. 889–897 (2020)
11. Liu, H., Tan, X., Zhou, X.: Parameter sharing exploration and hetero-center triplet loss for visible-thermal person re-identification. IEEE Trans. Multimedia **23**, 4414–4425 (2020)
12. Liu, H., Ma, S., Xia, D., Li, S.: Sfanet: a spectrum-aware feature augmentation network for visible-infrared person reidentification. IEEE Trans. Neural Netw. Learn. Syst. (2021)
13. Liu, J., Sun, Y., Zhu, F., Pei, H., Yang, Y., Li, W.: Learning memory-augmented unidirectional metrics for cross-modality person re-identification. In: Proceedings of the IEEE/CVF Conference on Computer Vision and Pattern Recognition, pp. 19366–19375 (2022)
14. Nguyen, D.T., Hong, H.G., Kim, K.W., Park, K.R.: Person recognition system based on a combination of body images from visible light and thermal cameras. Sensors **17**, 605 (2017)
15. Park, H., Lee, S., Lee, J., Ham, B.: Learning by aligning: visible-infrared person re-identification using cross-modal correspondences. In: Proceedings of the IEEE/CVF International Conference on Computer Vision, pp. 12046–12055 (2021)
16. Schroff, F., Kalenichenko, D., Philbin, J.: Facenet: a unified embedding for face recognition and clustering. In: Proceedings of the IEEE Conference on Computer Vision and Pattern Recognition, pp. 815–823 (2015)

17. Selvaraju, R.R., Cogswell, M., Das, A., Vedantam, R., Parikh, D., Batra, D.: Grad-cam: visual explanations from deep networks via gradient-based localization. In: ICCV, pp. 618–626 (2017)
18. Sun, Y., Zheng, L., Yang, Y., Tian, Q., Wang, S.: Beyond part models: person retrieval with refined part pooling (and a strong convolutional baseline). In: Proceedings of the European Conference on Computer Vision (ECCV), pp. 480–496 (2018)
19. Wang, G., Zhang, T., Cheng, J., Liu, S., Yang, Y., Hou, Z.: RGB-infrared cross-modality person re-identification via joint pixel and feature alignment. In: Proceedings of the IEEE/CVF International Conference on Computer Vision, pp. 3623–3632 (2019)
20. Wang, Z., Wang, Z., Zheng, Y., Chuang, Y.Y., Satoh, S.: Learning to reduce dual-level discrepancy for infrared-visible person re-identification. In: Proceedings of the IEEE/CVF Conference on Computer Vision and Pattern Recognition, pp. 618–626 (2019)
21. Woo, S., Park, J., Lee, J.Y., Kweon, I.S.: CBAM: convolutional block attention module. In: Proceedings of the European Conference on Computer Vision (ECCV), pp. 3–19 (2018)
22. Wu, A., Zheng, W.S., Yu, H.X., Gong, S., Lai, J.: RGB-infrared cross-modality person re-identification. In: Proceedings of the IEEE International Conference on Computer Vision, pp. 5380–5389 (2017)
23. Wu, Q., et al.: Discover cross-modality nuances for visible-infrared person re-identification. In: Proceedings of the IEEE/CVF Conference on Computer Vision and Pattern Recognition, pp. 4330–4339 (2021)
24. Ye, M., Lan, X., Li, J., Yuen, P.: Hierarchical discriminative learning for visible thermal person re-identification. In: Proceedings of the AAAI Conference on Artificial Intelligence, vol. 32 (2018)
25. Ye, M., Ruan, W., Du, B., Shou, M.Z.: Channel augmented joint learning for visible-infrared recognition. In: Proceedings of the IEEE/CVF International Conference on Computer Vision, pp. 13567–13576 (2021)
26. Ye, M., Shen, J., J. Crandall, D., Shao, L., Luo, J.: Dynamic dual-attentive aggregation learning for visible-infrared person re-identification. In: Vedaldi, A., Bischof, H., Brox, T., Frahm, J.-M. (eds.) ECCV 2020. LNCS, vol. 12362, pp. 229–247. Springer, Cham (2020). https://doi.org/10.1007/978-3-030-58520-4_14
27. Ye, M., Shen, J., Lin, G., Xiang, T., Shao, L., Hoi, S.C.: Deep learning for person re-identification: a survey and outlook. IEEE Trans. Pattern Anal. Mach. Intell. **44**(6), 2872–2893 (2021)
28. Ye, M., Wang, Z., Lan, X., Yuen, P.C.: Visible thermal person re-identification via dual-constrained top-ranking. In: IJCAI, vol. 1, p. 2 (2018)
29. Zhang, Q., Lai, C., Liu, J., Huang, N., Han, J.: FMCNet: feature-level modality compensation for visible-infrared person re-identification. In: Proceedings of the IEEE/CVF Conference on Computer Vision and Pattern Recognition, pp. 7349–7358 (2022)
30. Zhang, Y., Yan, Y., Lu, Y., Wang, H.: Towards a unified middle modality learning for visible-infrared person re-identification. In: Proceedings of the 29th ACM International Conference on Multimedia, pp. 788–796 (2021)
31. Zhao, Z., Liu, B., Chu, Q., Lu, Y., Yu, N.: Joint color-irrelevant consistency learning and identity-aware modality adaptation for visible-infrared cross modality person re-identification. In: Proceedings of the AAAI Conference on Artificial Intelligence, vol. 35, pp. 3520–3528 (2021)

Water Conservancy Remote Sensing Image Classification Based on Target-Scene Deep Semantic Enhancement

Xin Wang[✉], Guangyue Zuo, Ke Li, Li Li, and Aiye Shi

School of Computer and Information, Hohai University, Nanjing 211100, China
wang_xin@hhu.edu.cn

Abstract. Water conservancy remote sensing image classification is an important task for water conservancy image interpretation, which provides indispensable analysis results for the applications of water conservancy remote sensing images. However, in the high-resolution remote sensing images of water conservancy, the objects and water bodies are usually diverse, and the image semantics are fuzzy, leading to poor classification performance. To handle it, this paper proposes a novel classification method based on target-scene deep semantic enhancement for high-resolution remote sensing images of water conservancy, which consists of two key branches. The upper branch is an improved ResNet18 network based on dilated convolution, which is used to extract scene-level features of images. The lower branch is a novel multi-level semantic-understanding based Faster R-CNN, which is used to extract the target-level features of images. The experimental results show that the features extracted by the proposed method contain more discriminative scene-level information as well as more detailed target-level information, which can effectively help generate better classification performance.

Keywords: Remote sensing · Image classification · Deep semantic enhancement · Water conservancy

1 Introduction

China is one of the countries with the most complex and prominent water problems in the world, including but not limited to more people and less water, serious water pollution, diverse spatiotemporal distributions of water resources, which have seriously affected the construction of water ecological civilization in China. The traditional water quality and environmental monitoring technologies are not practical and perfect, but currently the advanced remote sensing techniques can make up for the disadvantages of traditional monitoring approaches [1,2]. Therefore, it is of great theoretical significance and practical value to study remote sensing image classification technologies for water conservancy deeply.

In recent years, with the continuous improvement of spatial resolutions of water conservancy remote sensing images, complex background interferences and

L. Iliadis et al. (Eds.): ICANN 2023, LNCS 14256, pp. 233–245, 2023.
https://doi.org/10.1007/978-3-031-44213-1_20

variable water structures in the images become more and more serious, which brings severe challenges to the classification of water conservancy remote sensing images [3,4].

At present, deep learning, due to its powerful feature extraction ability, has become a very useful and important solution to water conservancy remote sensing image classification. However, there are still two vital problems for the deep learning-based remote sensing image classification methods. First, the resolutions of feature maps extracted by the traditional deep convolutional neural networks (CNNs) are not high enough. When a convolutional neural network extracts features for water conservancy remote sensing images, it usually performs a down-sampling operation. In this process, the spatial resolutions of feature maps gradually decrease, making the spatial structure information of images destroyed [5]. Second, the semantic information obtained by CNNs with scene-level labels is not very strong [6,7]. A single scene label of an image only provides the overall understanding of images and ignores the influence of correlations between targets in images, hardly providing the target-level understanding [8].

Therefore, to handle the above two issues, in this paper, we propose a novel remote sensing image classification method based on target-scene deep semantic enhancement. Our main contributions are as follows. First, an improved ResNet18 network based on dilated convolution is proposed, which is used to extract the scene-level features of images. Second, a novel multi-level semantic understanding based Faster R-CNN is proposed, which is used to extract the target-level features of images. Experimental results demonstrate that, compared to single level, i.e., target-level or scene-level, features, our combined target-scene level features can greatly boost the classification performance.

2   Proposed Method

2.1   The Overall Framework

Here we propose a water conservancy remote sensing image classification method based on target-scene level deep semantic enhancement, which extracts image features in both scene and target levels. The overall framework is shown in Fig. 1. It mainly consists of four parts.

First, to cope with the low resolutions of feature maps extracted by the traditional CNNs, an improved dilated convolutional ResNet (referred to as DCR) is proposed as the upper branch.

Second, to further enhance the semantics of targets, the lower branch is constructed based on the multi-level semantic understanding based Faster R-CNN, so as to extract important features of various targets in images.

Third, we combine the scene-level and target-level features together, so that the fused features will contain stronger semantic information for scenes as well as richer spatial information for targets, which can more comprehensively represent the whole water conservancy remote sensing images.

Finally, the fused target-scene deep features are fed into the classifier to get the final classification results.

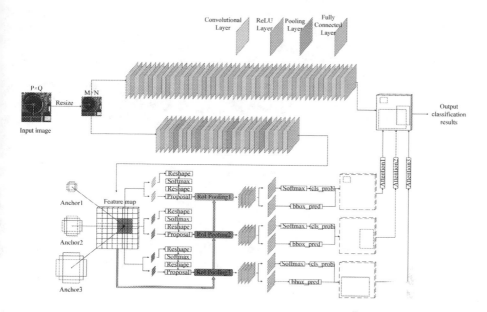

Fig. 1. The overall framework of the proposed method.

2.2 Dilated Convolution Based ResNet18 for Scene-Level Feature Extraction

Dilated Convolution. Dilated convolution proposed by Fisher Yu and Vladlen Koltun [5], is hardly affected by image scaling, and thus beneficial to multi-scale context information extraction without resolution lose. Dilated convolution can increase the receptive fields by embedding a series of weights into the convolution kernels, and thus the receptive fields can grow exponentially after only one convolution operation.

The operation process of a standard discrete convolution can be expressed as:

$$(F * k)(p) = \sum_{s+t=p} F(s)k(t) \tag{1}$$

where $F : \mathbb{Z}^2 \to \mathbb{R}$ is the discrete function; assuming that $\Omega_r = [-r, r]^2 \cap \mathbb{Z}^2$, $k : \Omega_r \to \mathbb{R}$ is the standard discrete convolution filter of size $(2r + 1)^2$.

When the dilation factor is d, the dilated convolution operator $*_d$ is expressed as:

$$(F *_d k)(p) = \sum_{s+dt=p} F(s)k(t) \tag{2}$$

The receptive field of the convolution kernel is given as follows:

$$F_{i+1} = F_i *_{2^i} k_i, i = 0, 1, \cdots, n - 2 \tag{3}$$

where F_{i+1} is the size of the receptive field of the $i + 1$ layer and i is the number of layers.

Finally, the 1-dilated, 2-dilated and 4-dilated convolutions are shown in Fig. 2.

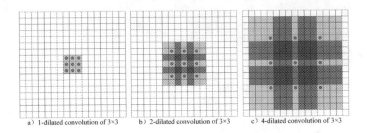

a) 1-dilated convolution of 3×3   b) 2-dilated convolution of 3×3   c) 4-dilated convolution of 3×3

Fig. 2. Dilated convolution with different expansion factors.

Improved ResNet18 Network Based on Dilated Convolution. Although ResNet18 can be used as a backbone, after downsampling, the length and width of the feature map will be reduced to half of the original, and the resolutions of feature maps will gradually decrease. In order to improve the receptive fields without reducing the resolutions of feature maps, we introduce the dilated convolution [9] into ResNet18. As a result, the sizes of the output feature maps of the improved ResNet18 will be eight times of the input feature maps in each dimension, effectively improving the feature resolutions.

Specifically, we first eliminate the downsampling of the last two groups of convolutional layers, i.e., group5 G^5 and group6 G^6 in ResNet18, as shown in Fig. 3, to make the resolution consistent. Then, the expansion factor of the subsequent dilated convolution is set to 2:

$$\left(G_i^5 *_2 f_i^5\right)(p) = \sum_{a+2b=p} G_i^5(a) f_i^5(b) \tag{4}$$

Next, the receptive field of the subsequent layers is reduced by 4 times:

$$\left(G_i^6 *_4 f_i^6\right)(p) = \sum_{a+4b=p} G_i^6(a) f_i^6(b) \tag{5}$$

In addition, to reduce the "Degridding" [9], we delete the pooling layer in ResNet18 and add the convolutional layer after group6, gradually reducing the expansion factors of dilated convolution.

Finally, the overall architecture of our improved ResNet18 network based on dilated convolution (DCR) is shown in Fig. 3, where the convolution in the same color represents that the output feature maps of the convolution have the same size. It is worth pointing out that we don't apply dilated convolution to groups 1–4, for the improvement of feature resolutions needs to sacrifice memory and computing power.

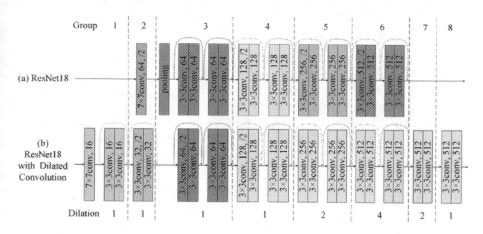

Fig. 3. Improved ResNet18 network based on dilated convolution.

2.3 Multi-level Semantic Understanding Based Faster R-CNN for Target-Level Feature Extraction

Faster R-CNN [10] is a target detection network proposed by Ross Girshick on the basis of both R-CNN [11] and Fast R-CNN [12]. In Faster R-CNN, the region proposal network (RPN) was proposed, which has improved the accuracy and speed for target detection tasks. Therefore, here we design a multi-level semantic understanding based Faster R-CNN for target-level feature extraction. It includes four crucial components: feature extraction layer, RPN layer based on multi-level semantics, RoI pooling layer and classification layer.

Feature Extraction Layer. This layer consists of 13 convolutional layers, 13 ReLU layers, and 4 maximum pooling layers. The specific structure is given in Table 1.

RPN Layer Based on Multi-level Semantics. RPN is a fully convolutional network. The input feature map can be any size and the output is a group of rectangular candidate regions. The input feature map is fed into two networks: one is a classification network for classifying the object categories in the candidate regions, and the other is a regression network for detecting the object positions in the candidate regions.

Candidate regions with different sizes can be generated on each anchor [13]. The classification layer outputs a score, which represents the probability that each candidate region is an object or a non-object. The regression layer outputs four values, representing the four vertices of the candidate regions. We use IoU to measure the accuracy of candidate regions: when $IoU \geq 0.7$, the anchor is judged as a positive sample; when $IoU \leq 0.3$, the anchor is judged as a negative sample; when $0.3 < IoU < 0.7$, the anchor is discarded.

Table 1. Architecture of feature extraction layer.

Operation	Output(Width, Height, Channel)	Name
inputs	(256, 256, 3)	Inputs
resize	(600, 600, 3)	Resize
convolution+ BN+ReLU	(600, 600, 64)	conv1_1
convolution+ BN+ReLU	(600, 600, 64)	conv1_2
max-pooling	(300, 300, 64)	pool1
convolution+ BN+ReLU	(300, 300, 128)	conv2_1
convolution+ BN+ReLU	(300, 300, 128)	conv2_2
max-pooling	(150, 150, 128)	pool2
convolution+ BN+ReLU	(150, 150, 256)	conv3_1
convolution+ BN+ReLU	(150, 150, 256)	conv3_2
convolution+ BN+ReLU	(150, 150, 256)	conv3_3
max-pooling	(75, 75, 256)	pool3
convolution+ BN+ReLU	(75, 75, 512)	conv4_1
convolution+ BN+ReLU	(75, 75, 512)	conv4_2
convolution+ BN+ReLU	(75, 75, 512)	conv4_3
max-pooling	(38, 38, 512)	pool4
convolution+ BN+ReLU	(38, 38, 512)	conv5_1
convolution+ BN+ReLU	(38, 38, 512)	conv5_2
convolution+ BN+ReLU	(38, 38, 512)	conv5_3

Through the continuous regression of candidate regions, the RPN layer reduces the loss function and finally obtains more accurate candidate regions. The loss function of the RPN layer is defined as follows:

$$L\left(\{p_i\}, \{t_i\}\right) = \frac{1}{N_{cls}} \sum_i L_{cls}\left(p_i, p_i^*\right) + \lambda \frac{1}{N_{reg}} \sum_i p_i^* L_{reg}\left(t_i, t_i^*\right) \qquad (6)$$

where i is the index of the anchor and p_i is the probability of whether the anchor contains the target. If the area contains a target, then $p_i^* = 1$; otherwise, $p_i^* = 0$. t_i is the vector related to the regression of candidate regions and t_i^* is the vector related to the anchor labeled as positive samples. N_{cls} and N_{reg} are the normalized parameters. λ is the balance parameter to make the weights of classification and regression items roughly equal. $L_{cls}(p_i, p_i^*)$ is the classification function of candidate regions. $L_{reg}\left(t_i, t_i^*\right)$ is the regression function of candidate regions. $\{p_i\}$ and $\{t_i\}$ are the output sets of classification layer and regression layer, respectively.

If all anchors in an image are used to optimize the loss function, the results will be biased to negative samples. In the training of RPN for calculating the loss function, 256 anchors will be selected in an image to participate in the calculation, in which the proportion of positive samples and negative samples is 1:1.

There are three types of anchors: 128^2, 256^2 and 512^2, and three types of aspect ratio: 1:2, 1:1 and 2:1. In each type of anchor, 43 positive samples and 43 negative samples are selected for training. In the training process, to reduce the redundancy, non-maximum suppression is adopted according to the classification score of candidate regions [10], which can greatly reduce the number of candidate regions without reducing the final classification accuracy.

RoI Pooling Layer and Classification Layer. As seen in Fig. 1, for each PRN layer, there is a RoI pooling layer corresponding to it. Each RoI pooling layer first extracts the prediction regions by anchors from the original feature maps, and then scales them to different sizes. After a fully connected layer, the target category of each prediction region is determined and its position in the image is corrected. Then, it is classified by softmax. Finally, considering the different contribution degrees of different semantic level objects, each RoI pooling layer output is given by an attention matrix, and then fused with the feature maps extracted by the feature extraction layer to get the feature maps with outstanding target features.

2.4   Target-Scene Level Feature Fusion

The scene-level and target-level features are fused to enhance the image representations. Since the size of the feature maps extracted from the upper branch is $28 \times 28 \times 512$ and the size of the feature maps extracted by the lower branch is $38 \times 38 \times 512$, the feature maps of the lower branch are scaled to the same size as those of the upper branch. Besides, the features of different semantic levels extracted from the lower branch are given different attention matrices, and then embedded in the corresponding parts of feature maps in the upper branch. Assuming that the scene-level feature is F_s and the target-level feature is F_o, feature fusion module connects the two kinds of features along the channel dimension, and the final fused feature can be expressed as:

$$F_C = concat\,(F_S, F_O) \tag{7}$$

3   Experimental Results and Analysis

3.1   Experimental Settings

The experimental image data sets used in this paper are manually selected and annotated from some publicly available remote sensing image data sets, including DIOR [14], AID [15], RSI-CB [16], WHU-RS19 [17], PatternNet [18], UC Merced Land-Use [19], and NWPU-RESISC45 [20]. We set a total of 17 labels of water conservancy related scenes: beach, bridge, dam, farmland, forest, harbor, hirst, lake, lakeshore, pond, river, sea, sea-ice, stream, terrace, wastewater treatment plant, and wetland.

Besides scene-level labels for overall understanding, we also give target-level labels to represent the important objects. We set 15 labels for typical targets:

beach, bridge, dam, farmland, habor, hirst, lake, lakeshore, pond, river, sea-ice, stream, terrace, wastewater treatment plant, and wetland.

The experiments are implemented on a server with Ubuntu 14 system, Tesla k40c GPU, and 11g video memory. Batch size is set to 16. Also, 100 epochs are trained, and the learning rate is set to 0.0001.

To evaluate the proposed method, both qualitative and quantitative results are provided. Further, four evaluation indexes, including confusion matrix, classification accuracy, error rate and Kappa coefficient, are employed.

3.2 Results and Analysis

Target-Level Feature Extraction Results. Figure 4 shows the labeled objects of each type and the objects detected by our proposed multi-level semantics based Faster R-CNN. It can be seen that our approach can detect the key targets in each kind of scene images, and classify them accurately. Especially, for objects such as forest and sand that are irregular and can't be accurately framed by boxes, our regression positions of candidate regions can still cover more than 80% of their target regions.

Scene-Level Feature Extraction Results. The confusion matrix for the 17-class scene classification is shown in Fig. 5. Figure 5(a) shows the confusion matrix by the original ResNet18. It can be seen that there are serious errors in some categories, such as beach, dam, and river. Beach is easy to be misclassified as sea, dam is easy to be misclassified as bridge, and river is easy to be misclassified as bridge. On the contrary, Fig. 5(b) shows the confusion matrix of our proposed method. It can be seen that for the serious classification errors in Fig. 5(a), our proposed method improves the results, while for the higher classification categories in Fig. 5(a), our proposed method obtains even higher classification accuracy of these categories.

Comparison with Other Networks. We compares the proposed method with some existing methods. The comparison networks includes VGG16 [21], VGG19, ResNet18 [22], and ResNet34. Table 2 shows the comparison results of them. It can be seen that the proposed method has the highest accuracy and Kappa coefficient. For instance, compared with VGG16, the proposed method has improved by 0.1135 in accuracy, and increased by 0.1168 in Kappa coefficient. Compared with ResNet18, the proposed method improves accuracy by 0.0823 and increases the Kappa coefficient by 0.0855.

3.3 Discussion

Network Stability Analysis. In this section, five different loss functions are used: RPN cls loss, RPN loc loss, RoI cls loss, RoI loc loss, and total loss, where cls loss represents the classification performance and loc loss represents the regression performance.

The five loss curves are shown in Fig. 6. In Fig. 6, the horizontal axis represents the number of iterations where a total of 15 epochs are trained, and the

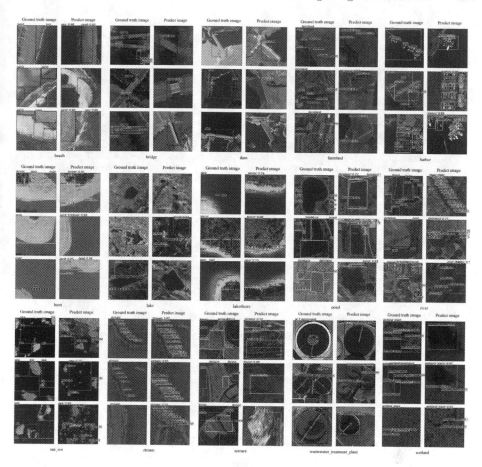

Fig. 4. Target-level feature extraction results.

Table 2. Comparison between the proposed method and other methods.

Network	Acc	Kappa	Error
VGG16	0.7423	0.7314	0.2577
VGG19	0.7718	0.7602	0.2282
ResNet18	0.7735	0.7627	0.2265
ResNet34	0.7916	0.7814	0.2084
Our method	0.8558	0.8482	0.1442

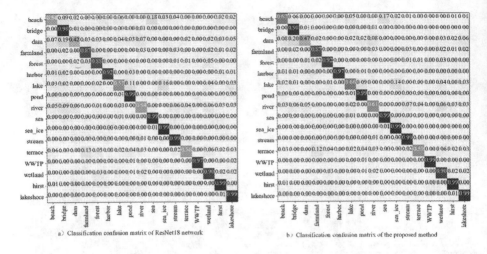

a) Classification confusion matrix of ResNet18 network   b) Classification confusion matrix of the proposed method

Fig. 5. Confusion matrix of different methods.

vertical axis represents the actual value of each loss. It can be seen that when the training reaches the third epoch, there is a sharp drop in the RPN_cls_loss and RoI_cls_loss. When the training reaches the 13th epoch, each loss tends to be stable and the network tends to converge.

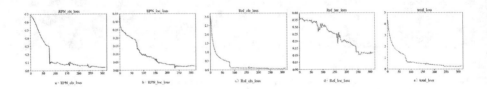

Fig. 6. Loss curves of our multi-level semantic understanding based Faster R-CNN.

Ablation Experiment for Upper Branch. Table 3 shows the accuracy and Kappa coefficient based on three classification networks: standard ResNet18, standard ResNet34, and our ResNet18 based on dilated convolution. It can be seen that the accuracy and Kappa coefficient of ResNet18 are the lowest, while the accuracy and Kappa coefficient of our ResNet18 based on dilated convolution are the highest. Benefiting from the dilated convolution, the accuracy is improved by 0.0538 and the Kappa coefficient is improved by 0.0558, compared to the standard ResNet18.

Ablation Experiment for Lower Branch. Table 4 shows the classification performance of different methods for the lower branch. According to Table 3 and

Table 3. Comparison of several models for upper branch.

Network	Acc	Kappa
ResNet18	0.7735	0.7627
ResNet34	0.7916	0.7814
our ResNet18 with Dilated Convolution	0.8273	0.8185

Table 4, the lower branch can effectively improve the performance, that is, it improves accuracy by 0.0285 and Kappa coefficient by 0.0297.

Table 4. Comparison of several classification methods for lower branch.

Network	Acc	Kappa
ResNet18+Faster R-CNN based on multi-level semantics	0.8023	0.7925
ResNet34+Faster R-CNN based on multi-level semantics	0.8356	0.8271
The proposed method	0.8558	0.8482

Table 5. Comparison of several classification methods for lower branch.

Network	mAP
ResNet18+Faster R-CNN based on multi-level semantics	0.7923
ResNet34+Faster R-CNN based on multi-level semantics	0.8047
The proposed method	0.8325

Addition, Table 5 shows the mAP comparison for some methods in the lower branch. It can be seen that among the three methods, the mAP of our method is the highest.

Based on the above results, we can find that, our DCR can effectively improve the classification performance for water conservancy remote sensing images. Also, the combination of our upper branch and lower branch can further boost the classification effects. Consequently, our proposed water conservancy remote sensing image classification method based target-scene deep semantic enhancement is superior to some existing methods.

4   Summary

This paper proposes a new water conservancy remote sensing image classification method based on target-scene deep semantic enhancement. The method consists of two key branches: one is the DCR with dilated convolution that is used to improve the resolutions of scene semantic feature maps; the other is the

Faster R-CNN based on multi-level semantics that is used to classify the objects with different semantic levels in the images. The experimental results show that the proposed method achieves good results on real-world data sets, and improves the classification performance for water conservancy remote sensing images compared with some existing models.

References

1. Gómez-Chova, L., Tuia, D., Moser, G., Camps-Valls, G.: Multimodal classification of remote sensing images: a review and future directions. Proc. IEEE **103**(9), 1560–1584 (2015)
2. Ran, Q., et al.: The status and influencing factors of surface water dynamics on the Qinghai-Tibet plateau during 2000–2020. IEEE Trans. Geosci. Remote Sens. **61**, 1–14 (2022)
3. Kadapala, B.K.R., Hakeem, A.: Region-growing-based automatic localized adaptive thresholding algorithm for water extraction using sentinel-2 MSI imagery. IEEE Trans. Geosci. Remote Sens. **61**, 1–8 (2023)
4. Xiang, D., Zhang, X., Wu, W., Liu, H.: Denseppmunet-a: a robust deep learning network for segmenting water bodies from aerial images. IEEE Trans. Geosci. Remote Sens. **61**, 1–11 (2023)
5. Yu, F., Koltun, V.: Multi-scale context aggregation by dilated convolutions. arXiv preprint arXiv:1511.07122 (2015)
6. Chaudhuri, B., Demir, B., Chaudhuri, S., Bruzzone, L.: Multilabel remote sensing image retrieval using a semisupervised graph-theoretic method. IEEE Trans. Geosci. Remote Sens. **56**(2), 1144–1158 (2017)
7. Hua, Y., Mou, L., Zhu, X.X.: Relation network for multilabel aerial image classification. IEEE Trans. Geosci. Remote Sens. **58**(7), 4558–4572 (2020)
8. Hua, Y., Mou, L., Zhu, X.X.: Recurrently exploring class-wise attention in a hybrid convolutional and bidirectional LSTM network for multi-label aerial image classification. ISPRS J. Photogramm. Remote. Sens. **149**, 188–199 (2019)
9. Yu, F., Koltun, V., Funkhouser, T.: Dilated residual networks. In: Proceedings of the IEEE Conference on Computer Vision and Pattern Recognition, pp. 472–480 (2017)
10. Ren, S., He, K., Girshick, R., Sun, J.: Faster R-CNN: towards real-time object detection with region proposal networks. In: Advances in Neural Information Processing Systems, vol. 28 (2015)
11. Girshick, R., Donahue, J., Darrell, T., Malik, J.: Rich feature hierarchies for accurate object detection and semantic segmentation. In: Proceedings of the IEEE Conference on Computer Vision and Pattern Recognition, pp. 580–587 (2014)
12. Girshick, R.: Fast R-CNN. In: Proceedings of the IEEE International Conference on Computer Vision, pp. 1440–1448 (2015)
13. Wang, J., Chen, K., Yang, S., Loy, C.C., Lin, D.: Region proposal by guided anchoring. In: Proceedings of the IEEE/CVF Conference on Computer Vision and Pattern Recognition, pp. 2965–2974 (2019)
14. Li, K., Wan, G., Cheng, G., Meng, L., Han, J.: Object detection in optical remote sensing images: a survey and a new benchmark. ISPRS J. Photogramm. Remote. Sens. **159**, 296–307 (2020)
15. Xia, G.S., et al.: AID: a benchmark data set for performance evaluation of aerial scene classification. IEEE Trans. Geosci. Remote Sens. **55**(7), 3965–3981 (2017)

16. Li, H., et al.: RSI-CB: a large-scale remote sensing image classification benchmark using crowdsourced data. Sensors **20**(6), 1594 (2020)
17. Dai, D., Yang, W.: Satellite image classification via two-layer sparse coding with biased image representation. IEEE Geosci. Remote Sens. Lett. **8**(1), 173–176 (2010)
18. Zhou, W., Newsam, S., Li, C., Shao, Z.: Patternnet: a benchmark dataset for performance evaluation of remote sensing image retrieval. ISPRS J. Photogramm. Remote. Sens. **145**, 197–209 (2018)
19. Yang, Y., Newsam, S.: Bag-of-visual-words and spatial extensions for land-use classification. In: Proceedings of the 18th SIGSPATIAL International Conference on Advances in Geographic Information Systems, pp. 270–279 (2010)
20. Cheng, G., Han, J., Lu, X.: Remote sensing image scene classification: benchmark and state of the art. Proc. IEEE **105**(10), 1865–1883 (2017)
21. Simonyan, K., Zisserman, A.: Very deep convolutional networks for large-scale image recognition. arXiv preprint arXiv:1409.1556 (2014)
22. He, K., Zhang, X., Ren, S., Sun, J.: Deep residual learning for image recognition. In: Proceedings of the IEEE Conference on Computer Vision and Pattern Recognition, pp. 770–778 (2016)

A Partitioned Detection Architecture for Oriented Objects

Shuyang Zhang$^{(\boxtimes)}$ and Yuntao Wei

University of Science and Technology of China, Hefei, China
{zhangsy2023,yuntaowei}@mail.ustc.edu.cn

Abstract. Rotated object detection aims to identify and locate objects in images with oriented angles. In this case, the detection scenario varies a lot in multi-dimensions. Besides, multiple oriented objects always exist within a single image, which increase the complexity for angle prediction. Although representing the angle by an extra regression branch can enhance precision in rotated box detector, it's more plausible to optimize the prediction process in a global view including feature-extraction, detection field partition and angle regression branch. In this paper, we introduced a partitioned detection architecture to identify objects which are at different scales, corresponding to different feature levels of the network. Inspired by Vision Transformer, a series of novel attention layers are embedded seamlessly for extracting necessary features from different scales and regions. We also conducted a short-term diffusion process to produce Gaussian noise in original image considering generalizability. As is shown, our detectors show a significant improvement of mAP and balance between performance and accuracy in two challenging aerial detection task, DOTA and HRSC2016.

Keywords: Oriented Object Detection · Cross-layer Attention · Decoupled Head

1 Introduction

Rotated object detection is emerging as an important research topic in recent years for its potential value in applications. It has become one of the most common image interpretation steps for tasks such as traffic planning, industrial detects detection and remote sensing [1]. However, rotated object detection still remains a challenging problem. Different from generic object detection, where detection boxes and the ground truth are aligned with image axes, objects in oriented detection scenarios are presented with arbitrary orientation. Besides, some extra characteristics of detection targets such as large aspect ratios and large scale variations (Fig. 1), also appear to be difficulties in detection tasks.

Considerable improvements are achieved in recent years to address challenges above. To predict the oriented angle of objects in an image, an extra prediction branch is embedded into the detection head to regress direction loss [2,3] and

© The Author(s), under exclusive license to Springer Nature Switzerland AG 2023
L. Iliadis et al. (Eds.): ICANN 2023, LNCS 14256, pp. 246–257, 2023.
https://doi.org/10.1007/978-3-031-44213-1_21

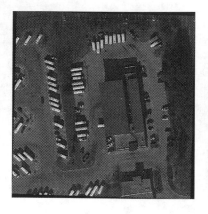

Fig. 1. Comparision between rotated object detection (left) and general object detection (right). It's obvious that rotated object detection is more challenging considering the irregular distribution of objects.

the design of more suitable loss functions for representing these objects has been widely explored [4,5]. Since the connection between neck and head of the detector always has an effect, mechanisms of representing bonding box and label assignment strategies are also considered [7,8]. At the same time, it's proved that the improvement of backbone also works [9]. Encouraged by the progress of instance segmentation and semantic segmentation, horizontal box annotation-based oriented object detector is proposed with semi-supervised method [10]. As is mentioned above, most of current work aims to partly design and redefine the detector itself, while little effort has been made considering the characteristics of images and the distribution of boxes in real scenarios. So we believe that building more reliable detector for oriented objects needs synergy from global view.

Concretely, when dealing a detection task, the size of targets varies a lot, which means objects in different size are assigned to the corresponding level of feature maps. During multi layers of pooling and sampling, feature maps may loss partial features, result in general missing for tiny objects. To alleviate the influence of variety in scale, a more reliable spatial assignment tragedy is applied by dividing the origin image into different patches with parts of overlap. For detection cases like aerial or remote sensing, spatial distribution of objects is uneven, often along with specific blocks or axis, then the feature density of different fields in an image is different, thus we propose a novel attention mechanism to merge information from spatial and channel branch between layers based on our newly designed pipeline. Besides, our method is extensive and reusable to applications. We conduct experiments on DOTA [14] and HRSC2016 [15] dataset with the angle branch, demonstrating the superiority of our method.

The contributions of our work can be summarized as follows:

1) We construct a partitioned detector with parts of spatial overlap, which can alleviate feature missing for scale diversity while approving the detection accuracy of tiny objects.
2) A newly designed attention mechanism aggregating features between layers is applied to adjust feature density in image.
3) We added Gaussian noise by short-term diffusion while keeping main features constant, which can enhance generalizability to detect objects vary in clarity.

The remainder of this paper is organized as follows: In Sect. 2, we reviewed the related work. The details of our design is introduced in Sect. 3. Experiments and alalyses are described in Sect. 4, followed by a summarize in Sect. 5.

2   Related Work

Oriented Object Detection. Considering wide range of application scenarios, oriented object detection has developed rapidly. Most of these detectors take the loss of angle branch into account. For instance, CSL [16] converted the angle regression to classification to solve boundary discontinuity problem, KLD [17] and G-rep [18] represented arbitrary-oriented objection as an Gaussian distribution. Another way to achieve accurate orientation is regressing the set of points rather than bounding box orientations like oriented reppoints [7]. Improvements for label assignment in oriented cases are also proposed such as AutoAssign [8] and GGHL [19].

Attention in Feature Extraction. Attention mechanism is applied in our architecture to alleviate the diversity of information density in different scenarios. Previous work like BAM [12], CBAM [13] and DRN [26] are basic paradigms of attention layers in CNN-based network. Generally speaking, attention module in convolution layers always includes channel branch and spatial module, designed to extract information in different aspects, but the organization and structure varies a lot.

Object Detection by Partition. In a wide range of application scenarios, small objects are widely distributed but hard to detect. For instance, target objects like pedestrians are very small in terms of pixels, making them hard to be distinguished from surrounding background, and targets are sparsely distributed, making the detection inefficient. To address these difficulties, Clustered Detection (ClusDet) network that unifies object cluster and detection in an end-to-end framework is proposed [20]. However, few of them cares about the overlap of different fields and the processing for tiny objects alongside the edge of clusters.

3   Method

The architecture of the detector we designed is initially presented in this section. Then we described our components, such as partition tragedies, weighted attention modules, and the distinction between our system and a conventional pipeline's decoupled prediction head.

3.1 An Overview of Our Architecture

The general architecture of our detector is concise. By dividing the input image by the stride parameter, we ensured overlap fields to be controlled by the field under various thresholds for information fusion. In order to connect the backbone and Feature Pyramid Network (FPN), we also construct spatial and channel attention branches and share attention feature vectors between layers. Our decoupled head is consisted of four parts: a classification predictor ($H \times W \times C$), where C is the number of classes, a position branch ($H \times W \times 4$) showing the position coordinates for boxes, a KFIoU branch [11] merges the loss of each positive sample ($H \times W \times 1$) and its oriented angle within $0°$–$180°$ for an input image sized $H \times W$. Enlighted by diffusion model, we add Gaussian noise (optional) to enhance generalizability of our detector.

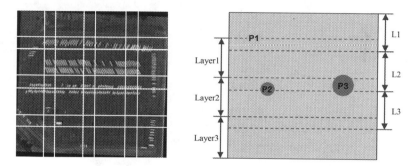

Fig. 2. Illustration of partition for objects with different size, for clarity, we only show the dimension of height. Layer1 Layer3, L1 L3 are the spatial blocks. The figure shows the overlap fields of different layers

3.2 Partition Tragedy

Suppose the full-scale of an input image is $W \times H$, representing the width and height, separately. Two sets of configure parameters are obtained, namely, (w, h) and $(\Delta w, \Delta h)$, determining the width, height of a block and the stride for sliding windows via different axes. Now we can infer an approximate number of blocks by calculating steps in width and height:

$$s1 = \left\lfloor \frac{W - w}{\Delta w} \right\rfloor + 1$$
$$s2 = \left\lfloor \frac{H - h}{\Delta h} \right\rfloor + 1 \tag{1}$$

as general, the original size of the image can't be divided as blocks as shown above, so we consider resizing a picture $W \times H$:

$$W' = \begin{cases} s1 \cdot w - (s1-1)\Delta w, & W - (s1-1)\Delta w - w < \frac{w}{2} \\ (s1+1) \cdot w - s1\Delta w, & otherwise \end{cases} \tag{2}$$

and the resize for height is similar. In this way, the image after resize can be exactly divided by scale parameters (w, h) and stride parameters $(\Delta w, \Delta h)$.

Partition method above performs exceptionally well with small items, especially for objects whose size is 1–2 orders of magnitude less than the original image. When the size of targets exceeding this range while still hard to be focused without partition, omission appears to be a main problem.

Algorithm 1: Fuzzy matching for objects in intersection area.

Φ: A set of objects in intersection area

Ψ: Output array, initialized as null

for *element in Φ* **do**

Set a lower classification confidence ε for intersection area than global confidence ϵ

Set a selection confidence ε_0 which is lower than ε

Maintain an array ν where keeps prediction of the *element* for each overlap field

Here, $\nu_i = (x_1, x_2, y_1, y_2, cls, conf)$ represents the coordinate, class and confidence based on local perception

Set $cls, conf$ as the maximum **for** each $cls, conf$ in ν_i

if $conf < \varepsilon$: **then**

$\quad\vert$ Recognize the union area for each ν_i as background

else

$\quad\vert$ Set the bbox area as the union area **for** each ν_i where $conf_i > \varepsilon_0$

Perform a detection pipeline without partition, if the object can be captured, then use the outcome of global detector as a replace

Append the detection outcome $(bbox, cls, conf)$ to the output array Ψ

Figure 2 shows the distribution of three objects, namely, P1, P2, P3. In our partition tragedy, P1 and P2 are detected by L1 and L2 separately. However, target P3 can't be recognized entirely by any layer, even it's associated with Layer2 and L2. For this case, we conduct a fuzzy matching method for image blocks, which can mix the information among layers to infer a appropriate outcome as is shown in Algorithm 1. In the algorithm proposed, we perform a filtration process by confidence threshold, makes the boxes remained have relevantly high confidence. Moreover, we compare the outcome with a detector without partition to ensure the detection priority.

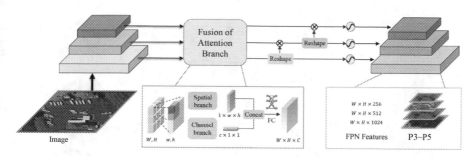

Fig. 3. Structure of Fusion attention mechanism for connection between backbone and FPN.

3.3   Attention with Fusion for Feature Extraction

Considering the imbalance of information density, attention mechanism is involved in our pipeline. We first divide the input image $I \in \mathbb{R}^{C \times H \times W}$ into $F \in \mathbb{R}^{C \times h \times w}$. The basic block has two branches: spatial branch and channel branch, which is shown in Fig. 3. For a given input feature map, the refined feature map is obtained by:

$$F^{'} = F + F \otimes M(F) \tag{3}$$

where $\otimes$ denotes element-wise multiplication, $M(F) \in \mathbb{R}^{C \times H \times W}$ consists a channel attention branch $M_c(F) \in \mathbb{R}^C$ and a spatial attention branch $M_s(F) \in \mathbb{R}^{H \times W}$:

$$M(F) = \sigma(M_c(F) + M_s(F)) \tag{4}$$

where σ is a sigmoid function. Now we expand this paradigm to a fusion pattern. Suppose $F_3^{'}, F_4^{'}, F_5^{'}$ are feature maps after BAM layers, $\mathcal{R}(F_i^{'})$ outputs a feature map $F_i^{''}$ sized as same as $F_{i-1}^{'}$ and $\mathcal{N}$ represents a normalization operator. Inspired by Eq. (3), we perform a fusion function which combines the feature information between layers so as to avoid loss of important features by downsampling:

$$F_i^{'} = F_i^{'} + F_i^{'} \otimes \mathcal{N}(F_{i-1}^{''}) \tag{5}$$

The feature pyramid network is generated after feature fusion and activation specifically. Figure 4 shows the feature map within the process. Experiments show a well performance in our architecture proposed above.

3.4   Decoupled Head for Oriented Targets

We extended conventional detector by modifying the decoupled head. We replaced the box-IoU branch by KFIoU branch, which takes a Gaussian-based loss to represent both position and angle of a box. In default case, detected rectangle is represented by four parameters (x, y, w, h) and an extra classification

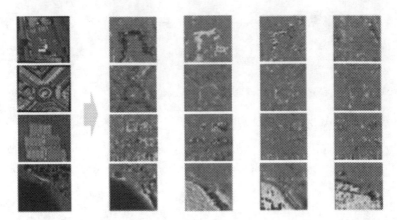

Fig. 4. Feature map of the FPN period after fusion attention mechanism. Figures from left to right represent feature maps in different layers. We added the original picture for comparison.

parameter cls, where (x, y) represents the coordinate of center, (w, h) represents the width, height and classification outcome of an anchor. In our implement, we represent a rotated bounding box by a 5-tuple: (x, y, w, h, θ) where θ is the angle within the range of $0°$–$180°$ while maintain the classification branch. Figure 5 shows the pipeline of detection neck and decoupled head of our architecture comparing with traditional detector.

Additionally, we add Gaussian noise to interfere the pixels of feature map so as to improve the generalizability of detector. We can easily interfere the original pixel by:

$$p_\epsilon(\mathbf{x}'|\mathbf{x}) := \mathcal{N}(\mathbf{x}; \mu_\epsilon(x), \sigma^2 \mathbf{I}) \qquad (6)$$

where $\mathbf{x}$ and $\mathbf{x}$' represent the pixels before and after process. $\mu_\epsilon(x)$ and σ^2 are parameters relevant to Gussian distribution. In our implementation, we simply set the array to $(0, 1)$ as default.

4   Experiments

In this section, we analyze the results of experiments on two publicly available and challenging datasets, DOTA [14] and HRSC2016 [15], separately, to check the performance of our method. Details of datasets, implementation settings, evaluation metrics and results are introduced in the following sections.

4.1   Datasets

DOTA is a publicably available, large-scale dataset in aerial scene with OBB annotations for oriented targets. 2,806 aerial images collected from different sensors and platforms with the size of each image ranges from 800×800 to 4000×4000 pixels are contained in the DOTA dataset. There are 188,282 fully

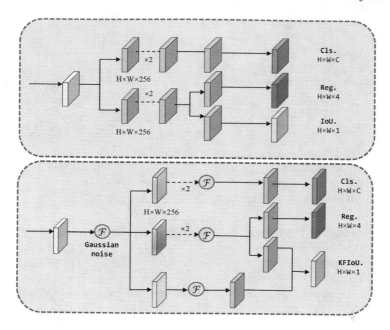

Fig. 5. General structure of our decoupled head. Comparing with generic detector, we represent the IoU branch to fit for rotated situation and involve Gaussian noise by short-term diffusion.

annotated images with 15 common target categories, half of the original images are randomly selected as the training set, 1/4 as the validation set, and 1/4 as the testing set. Considering the large size of images, we divided all images to 640×640 sub-images with an overlap of 160 pixels during training and inference, hence we have about 18,000 training and 9,000 validation patches.

HRSC2016 contains images from two scenarios with inshore and offshore ships. The training, validation and test sets include 436 images, 181 images and 444 images range from 300×300 to 1500×900 pixels. We also resized these images to 640×640 blocks with an overlap of 160 pixels during training and inference.

4.2   Implementation Details

We implemented our proposed approach based on ResNet101 [21] as our backbone. We train the models for 200 epochs on DOTA and 160 epochs on HRSC-2016. We use stochastic gradient descent (SGD) optimizer for training. The initial learning rate is set to $lr \times BatchSize/64$ with an initial setting for $lr = 0.001, BatchSize = 64$ by default. The weight decay is 0.0005 and the SGD momentum is 0.9. Learning rate is reduced smoothly to hDalf of the initial value after 100 epochs. L1-loss is involved in last 15 epochs. For experiments on DOTA and HRSC2016, our network is trained with four NVIDIA A40 GPUs (48 GB Memory) with 64 images per batch. We use mean Average Precision(mAP) with IoU threshold 0.5 to evaluate the accuracy of detectors and frames per second (fps) to evaluate the inference speed.

4.3 Ablation Study and Comparison

We conduct a series of ablative experiments with DOTA dataset based on our architecture, which is shown in Table 1. Mentioned methods all take the same backbone. We designed our baseline by adding a decoupled head and an extra box-IoU branch for angle prediction on traditional detector, which is illustrated in Fig. 5. The methods column shows the result of different tragedies. In comparison, 'att.' means additional attention modules between layers, 'KF.', 'Gau' means using KFIoU and adding Gaussian noise, separately.

Table 1. More detailed mAP results of ablation experiments on the DOTA Dataset. The best result is highlighted in bold.

Methods	PL	BD	BR	GTF	SV	LV	SH	TC	BC	ST	SBF	RA	HA	SP	HC	mAP (%)
Baseline	82.60	80.06	38.70	62.54	69.33	72.40	85.99	90.24	74.14	72.09	32.69	52.21	64.14	61.98	48.60	65.85
Baseline(Partitioned)	86.76	84.57	48.86	65.10	72.53	74.05	87.29	90.36	76.97	78.82	45.12	57.85	64.28	67.66	53.20	70.23
Part.+att	86.81	84.56	49.72	66.04	74.39	74.43	87.48	90.24	77.65	79.03	46.57	59.41	65.08	69.64	54.14	71.31
Part.+att.+KF	87.06	85.28	51.24	**66.17**	74.32	**75.35**	87.66	90.41	78.84	**80.97**	46.32	62.05	66.08	71.14	54.56	71.82
Part.+att.+KF.+Gau	**87.20**	**85.33**	**51.54**	66.04	**74.79**	75.30	**87.83**	**90.54**	79.05	80.84	**47.20**	**62.54**	**66.12**	**71.16**	**55.01**	**72.03**

Table 2. Results of mAP (%) on different diffusion steps. Experiments are performed on baseline setting in Table 1.

Step(s)	mAP(Small)	mAP(Medium)	mAP(Large)	Average
0	57.54	59.09	67.36	61.33
1	62.36	61.73	70.12	64.73
2	**63.49**	63.40	70.67	**65.85**
3	63.20	**63.45**	70.69	65.78
4	62.95	63.43	**70.72**	65.70
5	61.07	61.84	69.04	63.98

For better generalizability, we apply a short-term diffusion process to make pixel-level disturbance. Table 2 shows the relationship between step of forward diffusion process and performance (average mAP on Baseline). We compared the accuracy and precision of our architecture to a number of conventional and cutting-edge techniques. An absolutely fair comparison is difficult to make because of variations in experiment settings, hardware situations, and other situations. We simply apply the methods-proposed strategies and adapt them to rotated detection by including an angle branch utilizing KFIoU in a comparable manner. On DOTA and HRSC2016, Table 3 and Table 4 compare performance using several state-of-the-art methodologies, including anchor-based methods and anchor-free methods individually.

Table 3. Performance comparison with different state-of-the-art methods on DOTA dataset. HG104 means Hourglass 104. * indicates ResNet101 backbone. The best result is highlighted in black and red bold in anchor-based and anchor-free method, respectively.

Methods	Backbone	PL	BD	BR	GTF	SV	LV	SH	TC	BC	ST	SBF	RA	HA	SP	HC	mAP (%)	fps
Anchor-based Methods:																		
CenterMap-Net [4]	Res50	89.02	80.56	49.41	61.98	77.99	74.19	83.74	89.44	78.01	83.52	47.64	65.93	63.68	67.07	61.59	71.59	-
SCRDet [2]	Res101	**89.98**	80.65	52.09	68.36	68.36	60.32	72.41	**90.85**	**87.94**	86.86	65.02	66.68	66.25	68.24	65.21	72.61	9.5
Gliding-Ver. [6]	Res101	89.64	**85.00**	52.26	77.34	73.01	73.14	86.82	90.74	79.02	86.81	59.55	**70.91**	72.94	70.86	57.32	75.02	13.1
R³Det [6]	Res50	89.02	75.47	43.86	65.84	75.83	73.44	86.03	90.57	81.11	82.84	55.57	59.10	56.57	70.31	50.45	70.40	-
S²A-Net [23]	Res50	89.11	82.84	48.37	71.11	78.11	78.39	87.25	90.83	84.90	85.64	60.36	62.60	65.26	69.13	57.94	74.12	17.6
S²A-Net*	Res101	88.89	83.60	**57.74**	**81.95**	**79.94**	**83.19**	**89.11**	90.78	84.87	**87.81**	**70.30**	68.25	**78.30**	**77.01**	**69.58**	**79.42**	17.6
Anchor-free Methods:																		
PIoU [24]	DLA34	80.90	69.70	24.10	60.20	38.30	64.40	64.80	90.90	77.20	70.40	46.50	37.10	57.10	61.90	64.00	60.50	-
ATSS [25]	Res50	88.47	80.05	47.27	60.65	79.85	78.86	87.41	90.75	77.37	85.24	43.22	60.80	66.52	70.95	41.82	70.61	-
DRN [26]	HG104	88.91	80.22	43.52	63.35	73.48	70.69	84.94	90.14	83.85	84.11	50.12	58.41	67.62	68.60	52.50	70.70	-
O²-DNet [27]	HG104	89.31	82.14	47.33	61.21	71.32	74.03	78.62	90.76	82.23	81.36	60.93	60.17	58.21	66.98	64.03	71.04	-
Our Method	Res50	86.94	84.21	47.79	64.92	75.72	75.45	86.92	90.27	79.17	78.16	46.09	62.07	66.93	70.09	55.21	71.33	26.7
Our Method*	Res101	87.20	85.33	51.54	66.04	74.79	75.30	87.83	90.54	79.05	80.84	47.20	62.54	66.12	71.16	55.01	72.93	25.4

Table 4. Performance comparison with different state-of-the-art methods on the HRSC2016 dataset. The best result is highlighted in bold.

Methods	Backbone	mAP$_{07}$ (%)	mAP$_{12}$ (%)
***Anchor-based** Methods*			
R²PN [28]	VGG16	79.6	-
RoI-Transformer [29]	Res101	86.2	-
Gliding-Ver. [6]	Res101	88.2	-
DAL [30]	Res50	**88.6**	-
CenterMap-Net [4]	Res50	-	**92.8**
***Anchor-free** Methods*			
RC2 [31]	VGG16	75.7	-
Axis-Learning [32]	Res101	78.2	-
TOSO [33]	Res101	79.3	-
DRN [26]	H104	-	92.7
Our Method	Res101	**88.9**	**92.8**

5 Conclusion

In this paper, we presented a novel detector for oriented objects. Different from previous methods, we draw more attention on characteristics of image, hence partition tragedy and attention between layers were proposed. The proposed improvements aforementioned can be embedded into multiple detection architecture, which is convenient to transfer and apply to more general senses with an optional angle regression branch, and achieves comparable performance while keeping reasonable accuracy. Experiment results verity that our detector can achieve a significant improvement of mAP and a balanced result between performance and accuracy.

References

1. Zaidi, S.S.A., et al.: A survey of modern deep learning based object detection models. Digit. Signal Process. **126**, 103514 (2022)
2. Yang, X., et al.: SCRDet: towards more robust detection for small, cluttered and rotated objects. In: Proceedings of the IEEE/CVF International Conference on Computer Vision, pp. 8232–8241 (2019)
3. Wang, X., et al.: PP-YOLOE-R: An Efficient Anchor-Free Rotated Object Detector. arXiv preprint arXiv:2211.02386 (2022)
4. Wang, J., et al.: Learning center probability map for detecting objects in aerial images. IEEE Trans. Geosci. Remote Sens. **59**(5), 4307–4323 (2020)
5. Wang, H., et al.: Multigrained angle representation for remote-sensing object detection. IEEE Trans. Geosci. Remote Sens. **60**, 1–13 (2022)
6. Yang, X., et al.: R3Det: refined single-stage detector with feature refinement for rotating object. In: Proceedings of the AAAI Conference on Artificial Intelligence, pp. 3163–3171 (2021)
7. Li, W., et al.: Oriented reppoints for aerial object detection. In: Proceedings of the IEEE/CVF Conference on Computer Vision and Pattern Recognition, pp. 1829–1838 (2022)
8. Zhu, B., et al.: Autoassign: differentiable label assignment for dense object detection. arXiv preprint arXiv:2007.03496 (2020)
9. Newell, A., Yang, K., Deng, J.: Stacked hourglass networks for human pose estimation. In: Leibe, B., Matas, J., Sebe, N., Welling, M. (eds.) ECCV 2016. LNCS, vol. 9912, pp. 483–499. Springer, Cham (2016). https://doi.org/10.1007/978-3-319-46484-8_29
10. Yang, X., et al.: H2RBox: Horizonal Box Annotation is All You Need for Oriented Object Detection. arXiv preprint arXiv:2210.06742 (2022)
11. Yang, X., et al.: The KFIoU loss for rotated object detection. arXiv preprint arXiv:2201.12558 (2022)
12. Park, J., Woo, S., Lee, J.Y., Kweon, I.S.: BAM: bottleneck attention module. In: British Machine Vision Conference (2018)
13. Woo, S., Park, J.C., Lee, J.-Y., Kweon, I.: CBAM: convolutional block attention module. In: 15th European Conference, Munich, Germany, 8–14 September 2018, Part VII (2018). https://doi.org/10.1007/978-3-030-01234-2-1
14. Xia, G.-S., et al.: DOTA: a large-scale dataset for object detection in aerial images. In: Proceedings of the IEEE Conference on Computer Vision and Pattern Recognition, pp. 3974–3983 (2018)
15. Liu, Z., et al.: A high resolution optical satellite image dataset for ship recognition and some new baselines. In: ICPRAM, pp. 324–331 (2017)
16. Yang, X., Yan, J.: Arbitrary-oriented object detection with circular smooth label. In: Vedaldi, A., Bischof, H., Brox, T., Frahm, J.-M. (eds.) ECCV 2020. LNCS, vol. 12353, pp. 677–694. Springer, Cham (2020). https://doi.org/10.1007/978-3-030-58598-3_40
17. Yang, X., et al.: Learning high-precision bounding box for rotated object detection via kullback-leibler divergence. In: Advances in Neural Information Processing Systems, vol. 34, pp. 18381–18394 (2021)
18. Hou, L., Lu, K., Yang, X., Li, Y., Xue, J.: G-Rep: gaussian representation for arbitrary-oriented object detection. Remote. Sens. **15**, 757 (2022)
19. Guan, J., et al.: EARL: An Elliptical Distribution aided Adaptive Rotation Label Assignment for Oriented Object Detection in Remote Sensing Images. arXiv preprint arXiv:2301.05856 (2023)

20. Yang, F., Fan, H., Chu, P., Blasch, E., Ling, H.: Clustered object detection in aerial images. In: 2019 IEEE/CVF International Conference on Computer Vision (ICCV), Seoul, Korea (South), pp. 8310–8319 (2019). https://doi.org/10.1109/ICCV.2019.00840
21. He, K., et al.: Deep residual learning for image recognition. In: Proceedings of the IEEE Conference on Computer Vision and Pattern Recognition (2016)
22. Ge, Z., et al.: Yolox: exceeding yolo series in 2021. arXiv preprint arXiv:2107.08430 (2021)
23. Han, J., et al.: Align deep features for oriented object detection. IEEE Trans. Geosci. Remote Sens. **60**, 1–11 (2021)
24. Chen, Z., et al.: PIoU loss: towards accurate oriented object detection in complex environments. In: Vedaldi, A., Bischof, H., Brox, T., Frahm, J.-M. (eds.) ECCV 2020. LNCS, vol. 12350, pp. 195–211. Springer, Cham (2020). https://doi.org/10.1007/978-3-030-58558-7_12
25. Zhang, S., et al.: Bridging the gap between anchor-based and anchor-free detection via adaptive training sample selection. In: Proceedings of the IEEE/CVF Conference on Computer Vision and Pattern Recognition, pp. 9759–9768 (2020)
26. Pan, X., et al.: Dynamic refinement network for oriented and densely packed object detection. In: Proceedings of the IEEE/CVF Conference on Computer Vision and Pattern Recognition, pp. 11207–11216 (2020)
27. Wei, H., et al.: Oriented objects as pairs of middle lines. ISPRS J. Photogramm. Remote. Sens. **169**, 268–279 (2020)
28. Jiang, Y., et al.: R2CNN: rotational region CNN for orientation robust scene text detection. arXiv preprint arXiv:1706.09579 (2017)
29. Ding, J., et al.: Learning ROI transformer for oriented object detection in aerial images. In: Proceedings of the IEEE/CVF Conference on Computer Vision and Pattern Recognition, pp. 2849–2858 (2019)
30. Ming, Q., et al.: Dynamic anchor learning for arbitrary-oriented object detection. In: Proceedings of the AAAI Conference on Artificial Intelligence, pp. 2355–2363 (2021)
31. Liu, Z., et al.: Rotated region based CNN for ship detection. In: 2017 IEEE International Conference on Image Processing (ICIP), pp. 900–904. IEEE (2017)
32. Xiao, Z., Qian, L., Shao, W., Tan, X., Wang, K.: Axis learning for orientated objects detection in aerial images. Remote Sens. **12**, 908 (2020)
33. Feng, P., et al.: TOSO: Student'sT distribution aided one-stage orientation target detection in remote sensing images. In: ICASSP 2020–2020 IEEE International Conference on Acoustics, Speech and Signal Processing (ICASSP), pp. 4057–4061. IEEE (2020)

A Personalized Federated Multi-task Learning Scheme for Encrypted Traffic Classification

Xueyu Guan, Run Du, Xiaohan Wang, and Haipeng Qu[✉]

School of Computer Science and Technology, Ocean University of China,
Qingdao, China
quhaipeng@ouc.edu.cn

Abstract. Traffic classification is a crucial technology for ensuring Quality of Service (QoS) in network services and network security management. Deep learning has shown great promise in this area, particularly for classifying encrypted traffic. However, the significant number of samples required for training models presents a challenge. In this paper, we propose a multi-task learning and Federated Learning approach for training multi-task models for encrypted traffic classification in a privacy-protected, multi-enterprise setting. Our proposed two-stage federated multi-task learning scheme, pFedDAMT, aims to address data heterogeneity by first obtaining a global multi-task model that performs well for all tasks and then personalizing and fine-tuning the model with each enterprise's dataset to generate personalized models. Our experiments demonstrate that pFedDAMT improves prediction accuracy by an average of 1.58% compared to other schemes.

Keywords: Encrypted Traffic Classification · Federated Learning · Multi-Task Learning · Personalized Federated Learning

1 Introduction

Traffic classification is crucial for network services and security management. However, the prevalence of encrypted traffic has brought about significant challenges, given the content invisibility and feature uncertainty it presents. Deep learning has replaced statistical machine learning in this field, owing to its high efficiency and ability to bypass complex feature engineering.

The predictive power of models is limited by sample size, necessitating multi-task learning. This approach leverages related task samples to compensate for single-task sample scarcity, enhance model generalization, and produce results for multiple tasks simultaneously. Federated Learning (FL) has also been applied to meet the demands of large-scale sample requirements, given its privacy preserving and distributed collaborative training capabilities. Several efforts combine FL and multi-task learning to collaboratively train high-quality models.

L. Iliadis et al. (Eds.): ICANN 2023, LNCS 14256, pp. 258–270, 2023.
https://doi.org/10.1007/978-3-031-44213-1_22

However, data heterogeneity remains a pressing issue that can significantly impact the accuracy of the training model in FL. Personalized FL algorithms like pFedMe [15] and Per-FedAvg [4] are the current dominant solutions to this problem, offering localized personalized models tailored to each client's data distribution. Nonetheless, when multi-task learning is introduced, data heterogeneity takes on a new form, i.e., task heterogeneity. This poses a challenge to traditional FL frameworks, as local multi-task models trained by different enterprises focus on different tasks, resulting in task imbalance. Additionally, existing personalized FL algorithms are usually only suitable for single-task learning or multi-task learning without task heterogeneity. For a certain enterprise, irrelevant knowledge can also affect the performance of its personalized model.

To address these challenges, this paper proposes a two-stage federated multi-task learning scheme, pFedDAMT, to improve personalized model performance. In the first stage, pFedDAMT constructs a global multi-task model with good generalization on all tasks. In the second stage, the model is fine-tuned on each enterprise's dataset to generate a personalized model that fits its data distribution. The main contributions of this paper are summarized as follows.

- In the first stage, to address the task imbalance problem caused by task heterogeneity, we modify the model aggregation process of federated learning, thus making the prediction ability of the global multi-task model for each task affected by the task weights. In addition, a new dynamic task weighting algorithm is designed in this paper to dynamically adjust the task weights according to the sample size and current training status.
- In the second stage, to mitigate model performance degradation due to data heterogeneity, we proposes a new personalized FL algorithm, pFMTL, which is suitable when multi-task learning is introduced. By introducing multiple penalty term objectives to the local optimization objectives, pFMTL enables each enterprise to obtain a personalized model that fits its data distribution.
- The public encrypted traffic datasets USTC-TFC [18], ISCX VPN-NonVPN [3], and CSTNET-TLS1.3 [8] are classified according to two data distributions with reference to the FL experimental standard. And on this basis, a set of simulation experiments is designed to verify the effectiveness of the proposed scheme. The experimental results show that pFedDAMT is able to improve the prediction accuracy by 1.58% on average compared with FMTL (FedAvg), FedProx, Per-FedAvg, and pFedMe.

2   Related Works

2.1   Encrypted Traffic Classification

According to [14], user behavior, operating systems, and network conditions can influence statistical characteristics. Deep learning (DL) is widely used in encrypted traffic classification, with Wang [17] proposing a 1D-CNN based scheme for malware traffic detection, Liu et al. [10] proposing FS-Net using BiGRU for feature learning, and Lotfollahi et al. [12] proposing DeepPacket for packet-level classification using 1D-CNN and SAE. Lin et al. [8] introduced BERT [16] and proposed ET-BERT, which pre-trains on unlabeled data and fine-tunes on a small amount of labeled data for traffic classification. Recently, multi-task learning (MTL) has been introduced in this area, with Huang et al. [5] using a 2D-CNN to handle multiple tasks and Zhao et al. [21] combining MTL, FL, and encrypted traffic classification in MT-DNN-FL, but ignoring data heterogeneity.

2.2   Federated Learning

FedAvg [13] is the first algorithm of Federated Learning, introduced by Google in 2016 to address the "data silo" problem and provide privacy protection while reducing communication burden. However, the prevalence of real-life data heterogeneity makes it challenging to apply FL in practice. To address this issue, Li et al. [7] proposed FedProx, which uses proximal gradient descent to reduce the deviation between local and global models and accelerate convergence.

Personalized FL has been introduced in recent years to generate models that fit the distribution of clients' own data. For example, Fallah et al. proposed Per-FedAvg [4], borrowing from the idea of model agnostic meta-learning (MAML). Dinh [15] introduced pFedMe, which employs Moreau Envelope to solve the computational problem in Per-FedAvg. However, when multi-task learning is added, the above personalized algorithms still suffer from performance deficits of the multi-task model due to the neglect of task heterogeneity.

3   Problem Formulation

Suppose the set of all tasks is T, and the set of enterprises (hereafter called "client") is S, $|S| = N$. Suppose the set of tasks of client i be T_i, and its dataset be D_i, $|D_i| = n_i$. The set of samples for task t in D_i is D_i^t, $|D_i^t| = n_i^t$. The set of clients that satisfy the condition of having task t in its taskset T_i is C^t. Thus, $\bigcup_{t \in T_i} D_i^t = D_i$. FedAvg require server to solve:

$$\min_{\omega \in \mathbb{R}^d} f(\omega) = \sum_{i \in S} p_i \cdot f_i(\omega), \text{ where } f_i(\omega) = \frac{1}{n_i} \sum_{(x,y) \in D_i} \ell(x, y; \omega) \tag{1}$$

where p_i is the weight of client i in the global. Typically, $p_i = \frac{n_i}{\sum_{i \in S} n_i}$ or $p_i = \frac{1}{N}$. $f_i(\cdot)$ denotes the expected loss over client i's dataset D_i. $\ell(x, y; \omega)$ is the loss value predicted by the model ω for the sample (x, y) in the dataset D_i. FedAvg minimizes the global objective $f(\omega)$ by optimizing the local objective $f_i(\omega)$. When multi-task learning is introduced, the local optimization objective will become weighted by the optimization objectives of multiple tasks, i.e.

$$f_i(\omega) = \sum_{t \in T_i} \zeta_i^t \cdot f_i^t(\omega) = \sum_{t \in T_i} \frac{1}{n_i^t} \sum_{(x,y) \in D_i^t} \ell(x, y; \omega) \tag{2}$$

where $\zeta_i^t = \frac{n_i^t}{n_i}$. And $f_i^t(\cdot)$ is the expected loss over D_i^t.

In the classic FL framework, when task heterogeneity occurs, (i.e. for any client i and j, T_i is different from T_j), the shared layers of each client's local multi-task model are very different. This is because, different clients have different tasks, their local shared layers will then tend to be different. This will make the aggregated models diverge and favor tasks with larger sample sizes.

For ease of exposition, assume that for any multi-task model,

$$
\omega = \omega[s] \odot \begin{cases} \dots \\ \omega[t] \, , \\ \dots \end{cases} \qquad \omega(x) = \begin{cases} \dots \\ \omega[t]\,(\omega[s](x)) \\ \dots \end{cases} \tag{3}
$$

where x is the sample and $\omega[s]$ is the shared layers of the multi-task model. $\omega[t]$ is the task-specific layers of the multi-task model. $\odot$ is the linkage symbol between the shared layer and the task-specific layer. $\omega(\cdot)$ represents the output of the model ω, and $\omega[t](\cdot)$ and $\omega[s](\cdot)$ do the same. The above equation shows that the multi-task model consists of shared layers (shared by all tasks) and task-specific layers (unique to a certain task).

4   Proposed Scheme

pFedDAMT consists of two stages, where the first stage accelerates the convergence speed of the global model on all tasks by modifying the model aggregation. And the second stage introduces multiple regularization penalty terms that enable each client to train a personalized model that fits its own dataset. The detailed flow and overview of pFedDAMT are shown in Algorithm 1 and Fig. 1.

4.1   The First Stage: FedDAMT

The local training process of the first stage of pFedDAMT (named FedDAMT) is consistent with the traditional FL framework, as shown in lines 4 to 13 in Algorithm 1. However, in the model aggregation on the server, FedDAMT splits the multi-task model uploaded by the client into a shared layer and a task-specific layer, and follows the following steps for the aggregation process:

1. For each task t, aggregate the local shared layers and local task-specific layers into the global shared layers and global task-specific layers of that task, respectively, as shown in line 14 and line 15 in Algorithm 1.
2. Aggregate each task's global shared layers into the shared layers of the final global multi-task model, as shown in line 16 in Algorithm 1.
3. Reassemble $\omega^k[s]$ and $\omega^k[t]$, i.e. $\omega^k = \omega^{k,t}[s] \odot \omega^k[t]$.

In contrast, FedDAMT first aggregates the local shared layers of all clients into a global shared layer for each task during aggregation. Note that the global shared layer for task t will tend to task t. Then, FedDAMT aggregates the final global shared layer according to the task weights. This shows that FedDAMT can adjust the final global shared layer's tendency for each task by task weights, thus achieving task balance in the multi-task model and accelerating the convergence of the global model over all tasks.

Algorithm 1. pFedDAMT

Input: *taskset T, client set S, the global rounds of FedDAMT and pFMTL: K and K', the local rounds E, learning rate η, initial model ω^0, ε*

1: **for** $k = 1$ to K **do**   /**Stage 1**/
2:     $S_k \leftarrow$ random set of m clients in S
3:     Server sends ω^{k-1} to clients in S_k , $S_k \in S$
4:     **for** client $i \in S_k$ **in parallel do**
5:         compute $f_i^t(\omega^{k-1}) = \frac{1}{n_i^t} \sum_{(x,y) \in D_i^t} \ell\left(\omega[t] \odot \omega[s](x), y\right)$

6:         $\omega_{i,0}^k = \omega^{k-1}$
7:         **for** $e = 1$ to E **do**
8:             $\omega_{i,e}^k = \omega_{i,e-1}^k - \eta \nabla f_i(\omega_{i,e-1}^k)$
9:         sends $\omega_i^k = \omega_{i,E}^k$ and $f_i^t(\omega^{k-1})$ to Server
10:     **for** $t \in T$ **do**   /**Server do**/
11:         $f^t(\omega^{k-1}) = \frac{1}{\sum_{i \in S_k} n_i^t} \sum_{i \in S_k} n_i^t f_i^t(\omega^{k-1})$
12:         compute $r^t(k), \rho^t(k), \upsilon^t(k)$ as in definition
13:         compute γ^t as in Eq. (5) with $\rho^t(k), \upsilon^t(k)$
14:         $\omega^k[t] = \frac{1}{\sum_{i \in C^t} n_i^t} \sum_{i \in C^t} n_i^t \cdot \omega_i^k[t], \omega^{k,t}[s] = \frac{1}{\sum_{i \in C^t} n_i^t} \sum_{i \in C^t} n_i^t \cdot \omega_i^k[s]$
15:     update $\omega^k[s] = \sum_{t \in T} \gamma^t \cdot \omega^{k,t}[s]$
16: **for** $t \in T$ **do**   /**Stage 2**/
17:     $\omega^{0,t} = \omega^K$ // Model initialization of Stage 2
18: **for** $k' = 1$ to K' **do**
19:     Server sends $\{\omega^{k'-1,t}|t \in T_i\}$ to client $i \in S_{k'}$
20:     **for** client $i \in S_{k'}$ **in parallel do**
21:         $\theta_{i,0}^{k'}[t] := \omega^{k'-1,t}[t], \theta_{i,0}^{k'}[s] := \sum_{t \in T_i} \zeta_i^t \cdot \omega^{k'-1,t}[s]$
22:         **for** $e = 1$ to E **do**
23:             $\theta_{i,e}^{k'} = \theta_{i,e-1}^{k'} - \eta \nabla h_i(\theta_i; \tilde{\omega}_{T_i})$
24:         $\theta_i^{k',t} = \theta_{i,E}^{k',t}, \forall t \in T_i$
25:     sends $\{\theta_i^{k',t}|t \in T_i\}$ to Server
26:     **for** $t \in T$ **do**   /**Server do**/
27:         $\omega^{k',t}[s] = \frac{1}{\sum_{i \in C^t} n_i^t} \sum_{i \in C^t} n_i^t \cdot \theta_i^{k'}[s], \omega^{k'}[t] = \frac{1}{\sum_{i \in C^t} n_i^t} \sum_{i \in C^t} n_i^t \cdot \theta_i^{k'}[t]$
28: **return** $\{\theta_i^{K'}|i \in S\}$

For the calculation of the task weights γ^t, we first give the following definition:

$$r^t(k) = \frac{f^t(\omega^{k-1})}{f^t(\omega^0)}, \rho^t(k) = \frac{|T| \cdot r^t(k)}{\sum_{t \in T} r^t(k)}, \upsilon^t(k) = \frac{\sum_{i \in C^t} n_i^t}{\sum_{t' \in T}\sum_{i \in C^{t'}} n_i^{t'}} \quad (4)$$

where $r^t(k)$ is the ratio of the global loss of the current round to the initial global loss for task t, which measures the current reverse training speed of task t. $\rho^t(k)$

represents the relative reverse training speed of task t in the k-th round. $v^t(k)$ denotes the sample share of of task t in the k-th round. According to the above definition, the global task weights γ^t are calculated as follows.

$$\gamma^t = \frac{\beta^{\rho^t(k)-1} \cdot v^t(k)}{\sum_{t' \in T} \beta^{\rho^{t'}(k)-1} \cdot v^{t'}(k)} \tag{5}$$

where β is the training speed focus constant. The larger β is, the higher is the degree of focus for the training speed. When $\beta = 1$, $\gamma^t = v^t(k)/\sum_{t \in T} v^t(k)$. This represents that γ^t is only determined by the sample size share of task t, which is the same as the traditional FL scheme. From Eq. (9), it is clear that both the sample size share and the relative speed of training are considered when deciding γ^t. Further, $\rho^t(k)$ is placed in the exponential position, indicating that training speed is considered to be a more important metric than sample size share here.

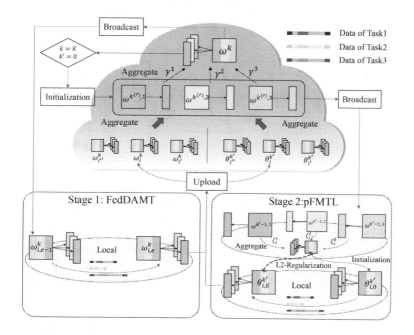

Fig. 1. Overview of pFMTL.

For most multi-task models like Shared-Bottom, we only need to identify the shared layers and task-specific layers. However, for MMoE, suppose

$$\omega(x) = \omega[t]\left(\omega[g]^{t,1}(x) \cdot \omega[s]^1(x) + \ldots + \omega[g]^{t,n}(x) \cdot \omega[s]^N(x)\right) \tag{6}$$

where $\omega[s]^n$ is the n-th Expert of ω, $\omega[g]^t$ is the Gate Layer of ω for task t and $\omega[g]^{t,n}(x)$ is the n-th element of the output vector. Locally, FedDAMT requires clients to count the gate output value $g_i^{t,n} = \frac{1}{E \cdot n_i^t} \sum_{e=1}^{E} \sum_{(x,y) \in D_i^t} \omega_{i,e}^k[g]^{t,n}(x)$.

In addition, the aggregation of Gate Layers are the same as Task-Specific Layers, as shown in Eq. (6). But for the aggregation of n-th Expert, it follows

$$\omega^k[s]^n = \sum_{t \in T} \gamma^{t,n} \cdot \omega^{k,t}[s]^n, \quad \omega^{k,t}[s]^n = \frac{1}{\sum_{i \in C^t} g_i^{t,n} \cdot n_i^t} \sum_{i \in C^t} g_i^{t,n} \cdot n_i^t \cdot \omega_i^k[s]^n \quad (7)$$

where $\gamma^{t,n}$ is the task weight of task t for n-th Expert. Moreover, $\gamma^{t,n}$ follows

$$\gamma^{t,n} = \frac{\beta^{\rho^t(k)-1} \cdot \upsilon^{t,n}(k)}{\sum_{t' \in T} \beta^{\rho^{t'}(k)-1} \cdot \upsilon^{t',n}(k)}, \quad \text{where } \upsilon^{t,n}(k) = \frac{\sum_{i \in C^t} n_i^t \cdot g_i^{t,n}}{\sum_{t' \in T} \sum_{i \in C^{t'}} n_i^{t'} \cdot g_i^{t',n}} \quad (8)$$

This is done because, for a given task t, some experts may not be involved or have little involvement in the prediction of that task. And the extent of involvement is determined by the output value of the Gate Layers. Therefore, unlike Eq. (6), here we include the gate output values in the weight calculation.

4.2   The Second Stage: pFMTL

In the second stage of pFedDAMT (pFMTL), the server will maintain a global single-task model for each task instead of a global multi-task model.

Specifically, at the beginning of the k'-th round, the server will send $|T_i|$ global models ($\{\omega^{k'-1,t} | t \in T_i\}$) to each client according to its taskset T_i. Locally, client i will initialize its personalized multi-task model as shown in line 22 in Algorithm 1, where $\zeta_i^t = \frac{n_i^t}{n_i}$. In pFMTL, the client's local optimization goal becomes:

$$\min_{\theta_i \in \mathbb{R}^d} h_i(\theta_i; \tilde{\omega}_{T_i}) = \sum_{t \in T_i} \zeta^t \cdot h_i^t(\theta_i; \omega^t) = f_i(\theta_i) + \sum_{t \in T_i} \frac{\varepsilon \cdot \zeta^t}{2} ||\theta_i - \omega^t||^2 \quad (9)$$

Here $\tilde{\omega}_{T_i}^{k-1} = \{\omega^{k-1,t} | t \in T_i\}$. Then, the client will train to obtain the approximate optimal solution of Eq. (9) by gradient descent. After E local rounds, the personalized model will fit client i's local data, and simultaneously approximates to multiple global task models by the restriction of multiple regularization penalty terms (instead of a single penalty term, such as pFedMe [15]), thus obtaining useful knowledge from them. By this way, pFMTL allows one's personalized model to be free from the interference of unrelated tasks, and to approach and draw knowledge only from the global models of his owned tasks.

When the local training process is finished, each client will upload the personalized model θ_i^k ($\theta_i^k = \theta_{i,E}^k$). On the server side, the aggregation process of pFMTL is the same as the first step in the FedDAMT aggregation process, which is to aggregate a global single-task model for each task, as shown in line 28.

It is worth noting that, according to the gradient formula,

$$\nabla h_i(\theta_i; \tilde{\omega}_{T_i}) = \nabla f_i(\theta_{i,e-1}^k) + \varepsilon(\theta_{i,e-1}^k - \sum_{t \in T_i} \zeta_i^t \cdot \omega^{k-1,t}) \quad (10)$$

which shows that $\sum_{t \in T_i} \zeta_i^t \cdot \omega^{k-1,t}$ can be involved in the computation instead of $\omega^{k-1,t}$ during training. Thus, the server can directly send $\sum_{t \in T_i} \lambda^t \cdot \omega^{k-1,t}$ to each client i. This greatly reduces the amount of communication for model.

4.3   Analysis

Unlike many personalized algorithms, such as pFedMe [15] and Per-FedAvg [4], we first train a relatively good global model, i.e. the first stage of pFedDAMT, before personalization. Because in a task heterogeneous environment, if personalization is performed directly, the gap between $\omega^{k,t}$ and the optimal solution at the beginning of the FL process is too large. Thus it is difficult for client i to obtain a personalized model with higher accuracy level through training. And it will lead to difficulty in convergence of the model in a task heterogeneous environment, which was verified in the experiments, as shown in Sect. 5.

When the first stage is over, there will be a fairly good global multi-task model ω^K for all tasks, i.e. $\left\|\omega^K - \omega^{t*}\right\|^2 \leqslant \epsilon$, where $\epsilon \to 0$. This means that the distance between ω^K and the global optimal solution for each task is fairly small after the first stage. Therefore, in the second stage, clients are able to make the personalized model generalize better over his own dataset by local training.

5   Experiment and Evaluation

In this section, three typical traffic datasets USTC-TFC [18], ISCX-VPN [3] and CSTNET-TLS1.3 [8] (hereafter referred to as TLS1.3) are divided into four classification tasks to demonstrate the performance pFedDAMT.

5.1   Experiment Setting

Data Partition. In our experiments, we divided the dataset into four tasks: binary classification for VPN/non-VPN (Task 1), 12-classification for applications (Task 2), 20-classification for USTC-TFC (Task 3), and 10-classification for TLS1.3 (Task 4). To simulate a non-independent homogeneous data environment, we used three data distribution settings: "IID", "Label Imbalance", and "Dirichlet Distribution". We set up 25 enterprises, with No. 13–24 containing samples of Task 2 and Task 1, No. 0–19 containing data of Task 3, and No. 5–14 containing data of Task 4. Under "IID", each enterprise has data of all classes for tasks it owns. While under "Label Imbalance", each enterprise has data for only some of the classes (1 or 2 classes of Task 1, 4 classes of Task 2, 5 classes of Task 3 and 5 classes of Task 4). And under "Dirichlet", dataset of each enterprise follows the Dirichlet distribution (parameter $\alpha = 0.3$).

Network Structure. TextCNN and DPCNN are used as prediction models with shared layers of sizes (60005, 200) and 256x(2, 3, 4) for embedding and convolutional layers, respectively. Task-specific layers are implemented using fully-connected layers. MMoE, CGC, and MTAN are among the multi-task models used, with MMoE having 4 experts, CGC having one expert per task and one expert for sharing, and MTAN using only DPCNN as the prediction model.

Parameters. $m = 15$, $E = 5$, $\eta = 0.001$, $K = 200$ ($K = 180, K' = 20$ for pFedDAMT), and $BatchSize = 32$. And $\varepsilon = 1$ is used for all FL algorithms.

Table 1. Comparison of the highest accuracy of all schemes when using DPCNN (%)

Multi-task model	Algorithm	Label Imbalance/Dirichlet Distribution			
		Task 1	Task 2	Task 3	Task 4
Shared-Bottom	FMTL	99.63/99.70	97.93/98.10	97.72/98.26	95.98/95.46
	FedDAMT	99.68/99.69	97.92/97.97	97.77/98.44	96.30/96.10
	FedProx	99.76/**99.77**	98.26/98.12	97.76/98.37	95.56/94.49
	Per-FedAvg	90.44/95.04	70.04/67.07	75.18/96.35	44.65/71.03
	pFedMe	98.90/98.84	95.62/94.57	97.42/98.39	79.58/90.47
	pFMTL	99.89/98.82	91.28/94.73	98.82/98.91	89.74/91.03
	pFedDAMT	**99.78**/99.73	**98.45/98.13**	**99.72/99.98**	**96.54/97.06**
MMoE	FMTL	98.23/99.01	96.98/97.13	95.21/95.81	91.01/92.10
	FedDAMT	99.76/99.72	97.01/98.09	97.37/98.73	96.31/96.90
	FedProx	99.76/99.73	97.88/**98.30**	95.66/96.59	91.06/92.62
	Per-FedAvg	90.77/89.67	64.22/70.97	70.74/96.53	40.19/71.22
	pFedMe	99.55/97.46	93.48/93.05	96.66/97.64	74.49/89.17
	pFMTL	**99.83**/97.31	92.85/90.61	89.84/96.49	89.59/93.66
	pFedDAMT	99.76/**99.74**	**98.06**/98.17	**99.77/99.98**	**96.81/97.24**
CGC	FMTL	99.79/99.62	98.21/98.14	97.89/98.71	96.00/95.66
	FedDAMT	99.67/**99.77**	98.39/98.33	97.85/98.59	97.19/96.93
	FedProx	99.72/99.76	98.33/**98.40**	97.74/98.74	97.14/94.94
	Per-FedAvg	91.72/96.16	77.74/67.53	74.04/76.14	42.48/44.17
	pFedMe	99.80/98.63	93.59/92.64	97.47/97.60	78.75/88.84
	pFMTL	**99.89**/99.34	85.60/91.20	98.12/99.39	90.41/93.72
	pFedDAMT	99.76/99.69	**98.51**/98.23	**99.81/99.99**	**97.70/97.17**
MTAN	FMTL	99.91/99.78	97.47/97.01	97.22/97.67	87.81/88.19
	FedDAMT	**99.99**/99.71	98.33/97.15	97.36/97.31	89.62/91.21
	FedProx	**99.99**/99.85	98.53/97.57	97.30/97.56	88.57/90.60
	Per-FedAvg	92.15/94.31	81.71/66.61	80.86/95.01	41.10/63.55
	pFedMe	99.54/95.57	83.02/82.29	93.19/93.48	50.69/79.69
	pFMTL	99.64/97.88	92.60/85.38	93.78/96.59	67.74/79.41
	pFedDAMT	**99.99/99.89**	**98.54/97.69**	**99.11/99.90**	**90.19/93.62**

5.2 Performance Comparison

All schemes include FMTL (the classic federated multi-task learning framework), FedDAMT, FedProx, Per-FedAvg, pFedMe, pFMTL and pFedDAMT. Table 2 and Table 1 shows the highest accuracy of all schemes for each task. From Table 2, we can see that the accuracy of pFedDAMT is improved in all tasks. This shows that it can effectively cope with the challenge of model performance degradation in this heterogeneous data distribution.

In contrast, Per-FedAvg, pFedMe and pFMTL have worse results. Among these three algorithms, the accuracy pFMTL is the highest, which also verifies the effectiveness of the proposed personalized algorithm pFMTL. However, all three algorithms are much lower than FedAvg and FedProx. The reasons for this are mentioned in Sect. 4.4, i.e. the above three algorithms can only work when the gap is pretty small, otherwise they will hinder the model updating process

Table 2. Comparison of the highest accuracy of all schemes when using TextCNN (%)

Multi-task model	Algorithm	Label Imbalance/Dirichlet Distribution			
		Task 1	Task 2	Task 3	Task 4
Shared-Bottom	FMTL	99.49/99.56	97.63/97.62	97.13/97.69	93.53/92.24
	FedDAMT	99.69/99.74	97.80/97.87	97.13/97.68	93.85/92.46
	FedProx	99.51/99.64	97.66/97.73	97.27/97.29	93.55/92.40
	Per-FedAvg	82.27/81.94	61.07/51.34	73.52/91.82	42.91/70.98
	pFedMe	99.04/93.45	92.79/87.58	96.42/96.99	67.28/87.12
	pFMTL	98.91/95.04	90.73/86.88	97.12/98.86	80.69/87.32
	pFedDAMT	**99.93/99.79**	**98.57/98.77**	**99.79/99.97**	**96.02/96.27**
MMoE	FMTL	99.27/99.14	97.27/96.93	94.53/94.81	91.01/91.10
	FedDAMT	99.75/99.73	97.71/98.05	96.69/98.20	94.52/93.77
	FedProx	99.72/99.70	97.31/97.69	94.67/95.21	91.17/92.02
	Per-FedAvg	85.52/88.32	54.78/38.63	71.96/88.68	41.66/70.73
	pFedMe	97.50/91.63	87.64/84.58	94.45/95.29	59.35/85.65
	pFMTL	99.22/96.67	87.21/86.67	96.41/98.85	77.42/85.99
	pFedDAMT	**99.95/99.77**	**98.71/98.63**	**97.56/99.97**	**94.90/95.02**
CGC	FMTL	99.68/99.70	97.99/97.90	97.75/97.97	94.53/92.65
	FedDAMT	99.78/**99.77**	98.16/98.12	97.78/98.12	94.53/93.33
	FedProx	99.76/99.51	98.02/97.80	97.63/98.11	94.39/93.60
	Per-FedAvg	82.23/88.39	57.38/53.45	77.94/92.95	45.41/69.99
	pFedMe	98.61/91.12	90.49/85.76	95.21/96.20	62.16/85.34
	pFMTL	99.22/98.21	87.21/85.82	96.41/96.93	77.42/90.06
	pFedDAMT	**99.91/99.73**	**98.68/98.58**	**99.81/99.95**	**94.94/95.91**

of federated learning. In the experiments, the above three algorithms show poor performance as a result. To address such problems, we proposes the integrated two-stage federated multi-task learning algorithm pFedDAMT. And its accuracy gains can effectively validate the effectiveness.

5.3   Ablation Experiments

The accuracy improvement of pFMTL over pFedMe and Per-FedAvg has proven its effectiveness at the personalization level. For the first stage of pFedDAMT (FedDAMT), we compare multiple task balancing techniques in multi-task learning to verify whether FedDAMT can speed up the average convergence of multi-task models. In this paper, multiple task balancing techniques are used for comparison. The task balancing techniques used include Equal Weighting (EW), UW [6], GradNorm [1], PCGrad [20], GradVac [19], CAGrad [9], GradDrop [2] and DWA [11]. The number of rounds required to reach the target task-averaged accuracy is used as a criterion for each scheme's effectiveness in alleviating task imbalance. Figure 2 shows the experimental results. There are two columns, which are the results when TextCNN and DPCNN are used as prediction models. As can be seen, FedDAMT reaches the target task-averaged accuracy as fast as possible

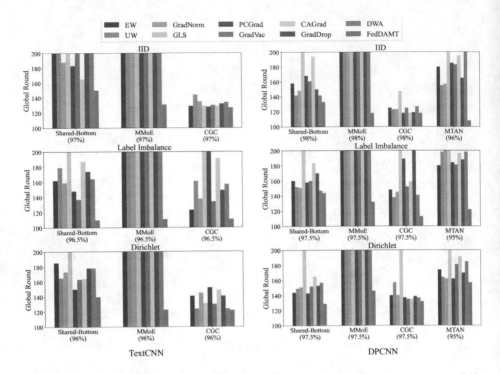

Fig. 2. Global communication rounds required to reach the average accuracy of the target task for all schemes.

in all data distribution. Specifically, FedDAMT is more effective on MMoE. This is because FedDAMT makes a special treatment for aggregation of MMoE.

6   Conclusion

To help enterprises with heterogeneous encrypted traffic data to efficiently collaborate training and build high-performance multi-task models, we propose a two-stage personalized federated multi-task learning scheme (pFedDAMT). The experimental results show that our proposed algorithms pFedDAMT can effectively deal with the data heterogeneity problem. Later we will continue to try to extend the proposed scheme to adapt to pre-trained models such as BERT.

References

1. Chen, Z., Badrinarayanan, V., Lee, C.Y., Rabinovich, A.: Gradnorm: gradient normalization for adaptive loss balancing in deep multitask networks. In: International Conference on Machine Learning, pp. 794–803. PMLR (2018)
2. Chen, Z., et al.: Just pick a sign: optimizing deep multitask models with gradient sign dropout. Adv. Neural. Inf. Process. Syst. **33**, 2039–2050 (2020)

3. Draper-Gil, G., Lashkari, A.H., Mamun, M.S.I., Ghorbani, A.A.: Characterization of encrypted and VPN traffic using time-related. In: Proceedings of the 2nd International Conference on Information Systems Security and Privacy (ICISSP), pp. 407–414 (2016)

4. Fallah, A., Mokhtari, A., Ozdaglar, A.: Personalized federated learning: a meta-learning approach. arXiv preprint arXiv:2002.07948 (2020)

5. Huang, H., Deng, H., Chen, J., Han, L., Wang, W.: Automatic multi-task learning system for abnormal network traffic detection. Int. J. Emerg. Technol. Learn. **13**(4) (2018)

6. Kendall, A., Gal, Y., Cipolla, R.: Multi-task learning using uncertainty to weigh losses for scene geometry and semantics. In: Proceedings of the IEEE Conference on Computer Vision and Pattern Recognition, pp. 7482–7491 (2018)

7. Li, T., Sahu, A.K., Zaheer, M., Sanjabi, M., Talwalkar, A., Smith, V.: Federated optimization in heterogeneous networks. Proc. Mach. Learn. Syst. **2**, 429–450 (2020)

8. Lin, X., Xiong, G., Gou, G., Li, Z., Shi, J., Yu, J.: ET-BERT: a contextualized datagram representation with pre-training transformers for encrypted traffic classification. In: Proceedings of the ACM Web Conference 2022, pp. 633–642 (2022)

9. Liu, B., Liu, X., Jin, X., Stone, P., Liu, Q.: Conflict-averse gradient descent for multi-task learning. In: Beygelzimer, A., Dauphin, Y., Liang, P., Vaughan, J.W. (eds.) Advances in Neural Information Processing Systems (2021)

10. Liu, C., He, L., Xiong, G., Cao, Z., Li, Z.: FS-Net: a flow sequence network for encrypted traffic classification. In: IEEE INFOCOM 2019-IEEE Conference on Computer Communications, pp. 1171–1179. IEEE (2019)

11. Liu, S., Johns, E., Davison, A.J.: End-to-end multi-task learning with attention. In: Proceedings of the IEEE/CVF Conference on Computer Vision and Pattern Recognition, pp. 1871–1880 (2019)

12. Lotfollahi, M., Jafari Siavoshani, M., Shirali Hossein Zade, R., Saberian, M.: Deep packet: a novel approach for encrypted traffic classification using deep learning. Soft Comput. **24**(3), 1999–2012 (2020)

13. McMahan, B., Moore, E., Ramage, D., Hampson, S., Arcas, B.A.: Communication-efficient learning of deep networks from decentralized data. In: Artificial Intelligence and Statistics, pp. 1273–1282. PMLR (2017)

14. Rezaei, S., Liu, X.: Deep learning for encrypted traffic classification: an overview. IEEE Commun. Mag. **57**(5), 76–81 (2019)

15. T Dinh, C., Tran, N., Nguyen, J.: Personalized federated learning with moreau envelopes. In: Advances in Neural Information Processing Systems, vol. 33, pp. 21394–21405 (2020)

16. Vaswani, A., et al.: Attention is all you need. In: Advances in Neural Information Processing Systems, vol. 30 (2017)

17. Wang, W., Zhu, M., Wang, J., Zeng, X., Yang, Z.: End-to-end encrypted traffic classification with one-dimensional convolution neural networks. In: 2017 IEEE International Conference on Intelligence and Security Informatics (ISI), pp. 43–48. IEEE (2017)

18. Wang, W., Zhu, M., Zeng, X., Ye, X., Sheng, Y.: Malware traffic classification using convolutional neural network for representation learning. In: 2017 International Conference on Information Networking (ICOIN), pp. 712–717. IEEE (2017)

19. Wang, Z., Tsvetkov, Y., Firat, O., Cao, Y.: Gradient vaccine: investigating and improving multi-task optimization in massively multilingual models. In: International Conference on Learning Representations (2021)

20. Yu, T., Kumar, S., Gupta, A., Levine, S., Hausman, K., Finn, C.: Gradient surgery for multi-task learning. Adv. Neural. Inf. Process. Syst. **33**, 5824–5836 (2020)
21. Zhao, Y., Chen, J., Wu, D., Teng, J., Yu, S.: Multi-task network anomaly detection using federated learning. In: Proceedings of the Tenth International Symposium on Information and Communication Technology, pp. 273–279 (2019)

Addressing Delays in Reinforcement Learning via Delayed Adversarial Imitation Learning

Minzhi Xie, Bo Xia, Yalou Yu, Xueqian Wang$^{(\boxtimes)}$, and Yongzhe Chang

Shenzhen International Graduate School, Tsinghua University,
Shenzhen 518000, China
xiemz21@mails.tsinghua.edu.cn, wang.xq@sz.tsinghua.edu.cn

Abstract. Observation and action delays occur commonly in many real-world tasks which violate Markov property and consequently degrade the performance of Reinforcement Learning methods. So far, there have been several efforts on delays in RL. Model-based methods train forward models to predict unknown current information while model-free approaches focus on state-augmentation to define new Markov Decision Processes. However, previous works suffer from difficult model fine-tuning and the curse of dimensionality that prevent them from solving delays. Motivated by the advantage of imitation learning, a novel idea is introduced that a delayed policy can be trained by imitating undelayed expert demonstrations. Based on the idea, we propose an algorithm named Delayed Adversarial Imitation Learning (DAIL). In DAIL, a few undelayed expert demonstrations are utilized to generate a surrogate delayed expert and a delayed policy is trained by imitating the surrogate expert using adversarial imitation learning. Moreover, a theoretical analysis of DAIL is presented to validate the rationality of DAIL and guide the practical design of the approach. Finally, experiments on continuous control tasks demonstrate that DAIL achieves much higher performance than previous approaches in solving delays in RL, where DAIL can converge to high performance with an excellent sample efficiency, even for substantial delays, while previous works cannot due to the divergence problems.

Keywords: Reinforcement Learning · Delays · Adversarial Imitation Learning

1 Introduction

Reinforcement Learning (RL) is based on Markov Decision Process (MDP). However, undesirable observation, action and reward delays break Markov property which consequently poses huge challenge to RL in many real-world problems such as robots control [1], remote control [2] and communication network design [3].

In recent years, there have been many efforts to solve delays in the RL domain, which can be divided into two main categories, model-based and model-free approaches. Model-based methods train delayed policies by the learned forward models. [4] develops a delay-aware model-based RL framework to incorporate multi-step delays into a learned system model without learning. [5] endows agents with a neural predictive model of the environment which "undoes" the delay inherent in their environment. For model-free methods, solutions are much different. [6] proposes two novel temporal difference (TD) methods, d-Q and d-SARSA to address delays. Another important work is [7] which generates actual on-policy sub-trajectories from off-policy samples by partially resampling and proposes DCAC that results good performance in many continuous control tasks.

However, there are significant shortcomings in previous approaches. In detail, model-free methods suffer from the curse of dimensionality that deteriorates the performance with the increasement of delay. On the other hand, it is necessary for model-based methods to design and fine-tune fragile forward models which is nearly impossible when facing delays.

In real-world tasks, it is simple to get expert demonstrations in an undelayed environment. Therefore, learning a delayed policy from undelayed expert demonstrations by Imitation Learning (IL) could be a promising solution to delays. Researches on IL have been broadly classified under the twin fields of Behavioral Cloning (BC) and Inverse Reinforcement Learning (IRL). Delayed BC (DBC) [8] introduces BC [9,10] to deal with delays. However, DBC struggles in continuous control problems, encounters compounding errors and needs a huge amount of demonstrations. IRL algorithms, especially Adversarial Imitation Learning (AIL) [11] which is the combination of IRL [12] and GAN [13], can overcome the distribution drift BC experiences and derive more robust policies. Therefore, AIL is a potential method to deal with delays.

In this work, we introduce Adversarial Imitation Learning to address delays so that the agent can learn how to act in a delayed environment from undelayed expert demonstrations. Based on the idea, we propose the first AIL algorithm to address delays, named Delayed Adversarial Imitation Learning (DAIL). The algorithm DAIL consists of two steps: generating a surrogate delayed expert from undelayed demonstrations and imitating the surrogate expert to learn a delayed policy by AIL. Additionally, a theoretical analysis is provided to illustrate why delays can be solved by DAIL. With the analysis, the modules of DAIL are designed practically. Finally, we empirically show that DAIL converges to high performance with an excellent sample efficiency in several continuous control tasks. More specifically, the contribution of this work can be summarized as follow:

- Introducing adversarial imitation learning to address delays and propose Delayed Adversarial Imitation Learning (DAIL).
- Providing a theoretical analysis that there is an upper bound of the performance difference between the undelayed optimal policy and the delayed policy trained by DAIL.
- Illustrating that DAIL outperforms other methods by a huge margin and overcomes substantial delays, by performing experiments on several continuous control tasks.

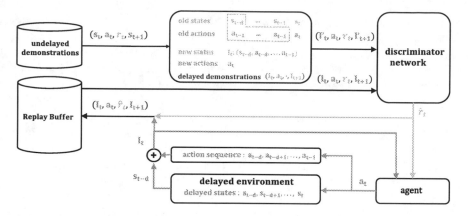

Fig. 1. Delayed Adversarial Imitation Learning: the delayed demonstrations are generated from the demonstrations in an environment without delay and a delayed policy is learned by Adversarial Imitation Learning.

2 Related Work

Adversarial Imitation Learning. Adversarial Imitation Learning(AIL) is the mixture of IRL and GAN which utilizes cost learning in GAN to recover unknown reward function to perform IRL. GAIL [14] extracts the policy directly from the demonstrations and learns the discriminator reward. AIRL [15] modifies GAIL framework and trains a reward network to solve the reward ambiguity problem. **Augmented Reinforcement Learning.** Augmented Reinforcement Learning takes the augmented state as input to address delay issues. RTAC [16] avoids the problems associated with conventional off-policy methods with real-time interaction and merged actor and critic. DCAC [7] proposes an off-policy method that turns the off-policy demonstrations into the on-policy ones. DBC [8] trains a delayed policy by imitating the undelayed one. In our work, we propose DAIL which absorbs the strengths of AIL framework and augmented RL methods to remove the constraints of other algorithms above.

3 Methodology

In this section, Delayed Markov Decision Process is introduced to model the delays and DAIL is proposed to deal with delays. To put it simply, there are three efforts in DAIL: (1) rearrangement of undelayed demonstrations to model a surrogate delayed expert, (2)preprocessing of samples to overcome reward bias, (3)imitation by AIL to train a delayed policy. More details are presented below.

3.1 Delayed Markov Decision Process

In real-world tasks, kinds of delays damage the performance of RL methods for violating Markov property. There are three kinds of delays in Markov Decision

Process: observation, action and reward delay. To avoid unnecessary redundancy, the following discussion will be based on the observation delay. It is worth noting that it does not compromise the generalization of our approach in such a specific problem setting [17]. In an environment with observation delay of d timesteps, the current state s_t of the environment is observed by the agent at step $t + d$.

Augmented Reinforcement Learning method is one of the most popular solutions to delays which introduces an augmented state called information state [3] to MDP and formulates Delayed Markov Decision Process (DMDP) to analyze delays. In an environment with observation delay of d timesteps, the information state I_t at step t is defined as $(s_{t-d}, a_{t-d+1}, \ldots, a_{t-1})$ which is the information necessary for optimal action a_t selection. Therefore, Delayed Markov Decision Process can be defined by a tuple $(\mathcal{I}, \mathcal{A}, \boldsymbol{\rho}, \boldsymbol{p}, \boldsymbol{r}, \gamma)$:

(1) information state space $\mathcal{I} = \mathcal{S} \times \mathcal{A}^d$, (2) action space $\mathcal{A}$,
(3) initial information state distribution $\boldsymbol{\rho} : \mathcal{I} \to \mathbb{R}$,
(4) transition distribution $\boldsymbol{p} : \mathcal{I} \times \mathcal{I} \times \mathcal{A} \to \mathbb{R}$,
(5) reward function $\boldsymbol{r} : \mathcal{I} \times \mathcal{A} \to \mathbb{R}$, (6) discount factor γ.

There is a connection between DMDP and MDP that MDP $(\mathcal{S}, \mathcal{A}, \rho, p, r, \gamma)$ with the observation delay of d timesteps can be reduced to DMDP $(\mathcal{I}, \mathcal{A}, \boldsymbol{\rho}, \boldsymbol{p}, \boldsymbol{r}, \gamma)$ where $\mathcal{I} = \mathcal{S} \times \mathcal{A}^d$ and $\boldsymbol{r}_t = r_{t-d}$. Based on the above conclusion, we can conclusively deal with intractable delays in the new DMDP setting.

In this work, we propose DAIL, a kind of augmented RL methods, which trains a policy that takes the information state as input to make decisions. At the same time, DAIL is equipped with off-policy module that reduce the agent-environment interactions by a large margin which solves the sampling inefficiency. As a result, with only a few undelayed demonstrations, DAIL outperforms other methods in solving delays.

3.2   Delayed Adversarial Imitation Learning

The challenges faced by previous methods to address delays can be largely reduced by imitation learning. Besides, demonstrations in undelayed environments are easy to obtained by existing methods. Hence we introduce a novel idea that a delayed agent can be trained by imitating the undelayed demonstrations.

Motivated by the shortcomings of previous methods and the novel idea above, we present a novel method to deal with delays by Adversarial Imitation Learning. We first rearrange and preprocess the undelayed trajectories into the augmented form as the surrogate delayed expert. And then, the agent imitates the surrogate delayed expert using augmented RL methods to deal with delays. The imitation process is under the AIL framework to make the best of the undelayed expert.

Though one of the most powerful AIL frameworks, there are some drawbacks of GAIL in addressing delays. First, the numerous agent-environment interactions hinder the policy learning. At the same time, GAIL learns a biased discriminator reward which prevents it to generalize different environments.

To overcome the limitations of GAIL, off-policy discriminator and RL method are introduced to reduce the interactions. Besides, absorbing state is added to the framework. Absorbing state is a state whose next state is itself which achieves the absorption. It is proved that [18] making the absorbing state as the next state of the terminal state can deal with credit assignment problem and make sure the convergence. Besides, the reward function of AIRL [15] $logD(s,a) - log(1 - D(s,a))$ is used for all of the environments that improves the generalization of the method. Therefore, we propose the first AIL approach - DAIL to address delays whose framework of DAIL is shown in Fig. 1. Details about three steps of DAIL are presented as follow.

Rearrangement. In this step, we do some rearrangements to combine the state s_{t-d} with the action sequence $(a_{t-d}, a_{t-d+1}, \ldots, a_{t-1})$ to form the information state I_t and generate a new transition (I_t, a_t, r_t, I_{t+1}) for DMDP. However, by standard rearrangement, there are no complete action sequences for the information state in the last d steps. For the efficiency in the use of demonstrations, we generate imaginary actions for the last d steps using zero actions. The idea of the rearrangement step is that the rearranged demonstrations can represent the delayed expert trajectories based on the theoretical analysis which will be presented later. Therefore, rearrangement can simulate a good surrogate delayed expert which provides a strong support to DAIL.

Preprocessing. After the rearrangement, the on-policy samples and augmented demonstrations will be preprocessed to overcome the reward bias. Before the training, the absorbing state is added to the terminal of every trajectory and an indicative dimension is introduced to each information state to show whether it is an absorbing state. After the preprocessing, the transitions are put into the Expert Buffer $\mathcal{R}_{\mathcal{E}}$. During the training, on-policy transitions (I_t, a_t, r_t, I_{t+1}) are sampled from the delayed environment. Once a trajectory finished, an absorbing state is added and Replay Buffer $\mathcal{R}$ is updated with the preprocessed transitions.

Imitation. DAIL imitates the delayed expert to train a delayed agent by AIL. During the training, after certain rounds of the agent-environment interactions and the real-time preprocessing, we first do mini-batch sampling from $\mathcal{R}_{\mathcal{E}}$ and $\mathcal{R}$. And then, the discriminator is updated with GAN with the loss function $logD(I_t, a_t) - log(1 - D(I'_t, a'_t)) - \lambda H(\pi)$ using the off-policy transitions (I_t, a_t, r_t, I_{t+1}) and the rearranged demonstrations $(I'_t, a'_t, r_t, I'_{t+1})$. Next, the reward function is updated with another mini-batch off-policy samples using $\hat{r}_t = logD(I_t, a_t) - log(1 - D(I_t, a_t))$ for each transition. Until now, each off-policy transition $(I_t, a_t, \hat{r}_t, I_{t+1})$ is composed of the information states I_t, I_{t+1}, the current action a_t and the current reward estimation $\hat{r}_t$. Finally, the delayed policy is updated with the final transitions. It is noticed that DAIL is updated with an off-policy RL method TD3 to deal with the sample inefficiency of GAIL. Later, we will discuss how DAIL can work in addressing delays theoretically.

4   Theory

DAIL utilizes a few expert demonstrations in an undelayed environment to train a delayed policy. To support DAIL, a theoretical analysis will be provided by bounding the performance difference between the undelayed optimal policy and the delayed policy trained by DAIL. In this section, different superscripts and subscripts are used to tell which kind the policy belongs to. π^* and π_E represent the optimal policy and the expert policy in an undelayed environment while π_D and π_I correspond to the surrogate expert policy and the imitation policy trained by DAIL in a delayed environment. Consequently, the total performance difference we would like to analyse can be written simply as $V^*(s) - V^{\pi_I}(I)$.

4.1   The Total Performance Difference

In this work, we introduce the transition distribution $q(s|I)$ and the surrogate delayed expert policy can be written as $\pi_D(a|I) = \int_{\mathcal{S}} q(s|I)\pi_E(a|s)ds$. Later, we will discuss the performance of the surrogate delayed expert policy π_D and show how DAIL can imitate the policy and behave well in the delayed environment.

The performance of a delayed policy is measured by $\mathbb{E}_{s \sim q(\cdot|I)}[V^*(s)] - V^{\pi_I}(I)$ with $q(s|I)$. Based on the assumption that the undelayed expert π_E which generates demonstrations is close to the optimal policy π^*, proofs are done in our work. With several achievements in RL, the premise assumption holds water reasonably. Therefore, it is easy to derive Lemma 4.1 from the assumption above and the definition of value function of information state [17].

Lemma 4.1. *For all undelayed expert π_E and surrogate delayed expert π_D,*

$$\mathbb{E}_{s \sim q(\cdot|I)}[V^{\pi_E}(s)] \geq V^{\pi_D}(I).$$

After that, the total performance difference between the optimal policy and the imitation policy can be divided into three parts:

- The optimal-expert difference: $\mathbb{E}_{s \sim q(\cdot|I)}[V^*(s) - V^{\pi_E}(s)]$.
- The expert-surrogate difference: $\mathbb{E}_{s \sim q(\cdot|I)}[V^{\pi_E}(s)] - V^{\pi_D}(I)$.
- The surrogate-imitation difference: $V^{\pi_D}(I) - V^{\pi_I}(I)$.

First, the optimal-expert difference that reveals the performance of the expert policy that generates demonstrations is the performance difference between the undelayed optimal policy π^* and the undelayed expert policy π_E. Based on the premise assumption, the expert policy can make the difference quite small.

Besides, the expert-surrogate difference which is positive based on Lemma 4.1 shows the gap between the undelayed expert π_E and surrogate delayed expert π_D validating the effectiveness of rearrangement. Previous work [8] bounds the difference and derives Theorem 4.1 where L_Q, L_T, L_π are the Lipschitz constants.

Theorem 4.1. *For a $L_Q - LC$, L_T-TLC MDP with a $L_\pi - LC$ expert policy π_E and a DMDP with the delay of d timesteps with a delayed policy π_D, $\forall I \in \mathcal{I}$,*

$$\mathbb{E}_{s \sim q(\cdot|I)}[V^{\pi_E}(s)] - V^{\pi_D}(I) \leq \frac{2}{1 - \gamma} L_Q L_T L_\pi d.$$

Theorem 4.1 illustrates that the expert-surrogate difference is linear to the Lipschitz constant L_π of π_E which shows that with a smooth expert policy, the Lipschitz constant L_π would be small that results in the reduction of the difference and derives a better policy π_D. Therefore, in DAIL, SAC [19] is selected to provide a smooth expert policy. Besides, Theorem 4.1 expresses theoretically that the performance of π_D would degrade which damages DAIL as the delay increases. Several experiments will be conducted later to verify this conclusion.

Finally, the surrogate-imitation difference which indicates the advantage of DAIL over other methods is the performance difference between the surrogate delayed policy π_D and imitation policy π_I trained by DAIL. Detailed discussion about it will be presented later by analysing the upper bound theoretically.

4.2   The Surrogate-Imitation Difference

In this section, we analyze the gap between π_D and π_I. Firstly, we compare AIL with BC to show how AIL outperforms the latter. By further derivation, it is shown that DAIL can minimize the gap and achieve good performance.

AIL comes to play by minimizing the occupancy measure ρ_π gap between the expert and the agent while BC takes effect by minimizing the policy π difference between them. Kullback-Leibler (KL) divergence $D_{KL}(\cdot, \cdot)$ is chosen as the measure in our work. So, AIL and BC can be formulated as:

$$\min_{\pi \in \Pi} D_{\mathrm{KL}}\left(\rho_\pi, \rho_{\pi_{\mathrm{E}}}\right). \tag{1}$$

$$\min_{\pi \in \Pi} \mathbb{E}_{s \sim d_{\pi_{\mathrm{E}}}}\left[D_{\mathrm{KL}}\left(\pi(\cdot \mid s), \pi_{\mathrm{E}}(\cdot \mid s)\right)\right]. \tag{2}$$

In order to compare AIL with BC, we introduce Lemma 4.2, where D_{TV} means the total variation distance, that bounds the performance difference between the expert and imitation policy by IL.

Lemma 4.2. *For all imitation policy π and expert policy π_{E},*

$$|V_\pi - V_{\pi_{\mathrm{E}}}| \leq \frac{2R_{\max}}{1-\gamma} D_{\mathrm{TV}}\left(\rho_\pi, \rho_{\pi_{\mathrm{E}}}\right).$$

Further, by extending Lemma 4.2 to AIL and BC, Theorem 4.2 and Theorem 4.3 are derived respectively.

Theorem 4.2. *For all delayed AIL policy π_I and surrogate delayed expert policy π_D, if $D_{KL}\left(\rho_{\pi_I}, \rho_{\pi_D}\right) \leq \epsilon$ is achieved by AIL, then,*

$$|V_{\pi_I} - V_{\pi_D}| \leq \frac{\sqrt{2}R_{\max}}{1-\gamma}\sqrt{\epsilon}.$$

Theorem 4.3. *For all delayed BC policy π_I and surrogate delayed expert policy π_D, if $\mathbb{E}_{I \sim d_{\pi_D}}\left[D_{\mathrm{KL}}\left(\pi_I(\cdot \mid I), \pi_D(\cdot \mid I)\right)\right] \leq \epsilon$ is achieved by BC, then,*

$$|V_{\pi_I} - V_{\pi_D}| \leq \frac{2\sqrt{2}R_{\max}}{(1-\gamma)^2}\sqrt{\epsilon}.$$

Theorem 4.2 and Theorem 4.3 show that with the same upper bound of optimization objective, the gap of AIL has a linear dependency on $\frac{1}{1-\gamma}$ while that of BC has a quadratic dependency on it. With a γ, for example 0.995 or 0.999, $\frac{1}{1-\gamma}$ is huge resulting that BC suffers from more performance degradation than AIL. Therefore, AIL outperforms BC by a large margin in many tasks.

Moreover, we focus on AIL gap obtained by DAIL. Given the Gaussian surrogate delayed expert and imitation policy $\pi_D(\cdot \mid I) = \mathscr{N}\left(\mu_D(I), \sigma_D^2(I)\right)$, $\pi_I(\cdot \mid I) = \mathscr{N}\left(\mu_I(I), \sigma_I^2(I)\right)$, the upper bound of performance gap can be written as:

$$\frac{2R_{\max}}{(1-\gamma)^2}\mathbb{E}_{I \sim d_{\pi_D}}\left[D_{\mathrm{TV}}\left(\mathscr{N}\left(\mu_D(I), \sigma_D^2(I)\right), \mathscr{N}\left(\mu_I(I), \sigma_I^2(I)\right)\right)\right]. \tag{3}$$

There exists a lower bound of the total variation distance [20], so the upper bound of the performance difference between the surrogate delayed expert π_D and the delayed imitation policy π_I trained by DAIL is greater than:

$$\frac{R_{\max}\mathbb{E}_{I \sim d_{\pi_D}} \min\left\{1, \max\left\{\frac{\left|\sigma_D^2(I) - \sigma_I^2(I)\right|}{\min\{\sigma_D(I), \sigma_I(I)\}^2}, \frac{40|\mu_D(I) - \mu_I(I)|}{\min\{\sigma_D(I), \sigma_I(I)\}}\right\}\right\}}{100(1-\gamma)^2}. \tag{4}$$

As the formula (4) reveals, even the means and variances of π_D and π_I are similar, the difference can not come to zero. The minimum of the two variances in the denominator $\frac{1}{\min\{\sigma_D(I), \sigma_I(I)\}}$, illustrates that with high variance of the policy the lower bound can be reduced which helps π_I imitate π_D better and perform well in delayed environments. In DAIL, several works have been executed to minimize the lower bound. The maximum causal policy entropy is introduced to increase the policy variance. Besides, there is a noisy Gaussian network in DAIL that can also provide a high-variance policy. In the next section, experiments will be conducted to show the performance of DAIL in addressing delays.

5   Experiments

In order to evaluate the performance of DAIL, experiments are designed on a suite of high dimensional continuous control tasks in MuJoCo [21]. Comparison experiments are conducted to show the advantage of DAIL over previous methods. By ablation experiments, the impacts of key modules in DAIL are analysed. In confirmation experiments, it is verified that the increasement of delay does harm to DAIL while DAIL can overcome substantial delays. In this section, 4 undelayed expert trajectories are provided to IL methods and the returns are normalized using $\frac{return-random}{expert-random}$, where 1 means the expert level while 0 represents the random level. Additionally, all methods are performed 5 runs with different seeds for each task in one million timesteps.

5.1   Comparison Experiments

In this subsection, DAIL is tested against three baselines in addressing delays:

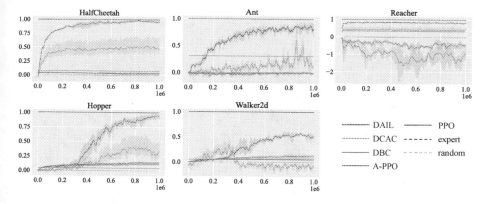

Fig. 2. Comparison experiments of DAIL using 4 undelayed demonstrations against DCAC, DBC, A-PPO and PPO in the environment with the delay of 4 timesteps. x-axis corresponds timestep and y-axis corresponds to normalized return (0 corresponds to a random policy, while 1 corresponds to an expert policy).

(1) DCAC [7]: an RL algorithm, known as a kind of augmented RL methods, with a good performance in high dimensional tasks.
(2) DBC [8]: an imitation learning based approach for delays.
(3) PPO [22]: a standard policy-gradient RL method that ignores delay and takes the current observed state as input for decision.

To make the comparison fair, we introduce an augmented version of PPO called Augmented PPO (A-PPO) whose input is information state.

Figure 2 shows the results of comparison experiments where all methods above are trained to solve 5 MuJoCo tasks in the environment with delay of 4 timesteps which is the middle-level one.

Figure 2 shows that DCAC converges to medium performance with high variance in most tasks, which reveals that DCAC can not solve problems with middle-level delay. With a few undelayed demonstrations, DBC fails in most tasks which means that DBC suffers from compounding errors and can not achieve tasks with a small amount of expert information. PPO and A-PPO work poorly in all tasks demonstrating that standard RL methods are unable to deal with delays directly. However, A-PPO with state-augmentation performs better than PPO showing that augmented RL methods can help overcome delays. Further, DAIL outperforms all baselines in all tasks by a huge margin. With a well-designed AIL framework, DAIL utilizes a few undelayed expert demonstrations and learns a delayed policy which converges to a high performance. We will analyse the reasons of the high performance of DAIL with more experiments.

5.2 Ablation Experiments

In this section, we would like to conduct some experiments to validate the impacts of the absorbing states module and off-policy networks. Specifically, we

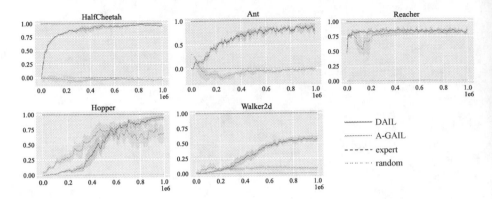

Fig. 3. Ablation experiments of DAIL using 4 undelayed demonstrations in the environment with the delay of 4 timestep. x-axis corresponds timesteps and y-axis corresponds to normalized return (0 corresponds to a random policy, while 1 corresponds to an expert policy).

remove absorbing states from DAIL, equip it with the on-policy discriminator and on-policy PPO method. Then a naive version of DAIL named Augmented GAIL (A-GAIL) is derived. We then test DAIL and A-GAIL in the same experiment settings as before: running with 5 different seeds to deal with 5 tasks in the environments with the delay of 4 timesteps.

The results presented in Fig. 3 show that DAIL and A-GAIL perform well at the same level in the easy Reacher. In Hopper, A-GAIL achieves good performance early but DAIL wins finally. In other tasks, DAIL converges to high performance fast but A-GAIL fail. Besides, we fine-tune A-GAIL parameters for each task which we do not do for DAIL. We can empirically conclude that:

- With absorbing states, DAIL relieves the biased reward and works well in kinds of tasks with diverse MDPs.
- The off-policy updating of the discriminator and policy make DAIL converge to high performance with an excellent sample efficiency therefore the delayed policy can be trained rapidly with only a few undelayed demonstrations.
- DAIL is insensitive to the parameters owing to the key modules thus the policy is easy to train.

5.3 Confirmation Experiments

In the Theory section, it is proved that DAIL policy performs worse with the increasement of delays. We would like to verify the conclusion and show the real influence. In the confirmation experiments, we run DAIL with 5 seeds to deal with 5 tasks in 5 different environments that respectively have delays of 0, 2, 4, 6, 8 timesteps.

The results depicted in Fig. 4 indicate that except for the simple-dynamics Reacher, the performance of DAIL degrades gradually with the increasement of

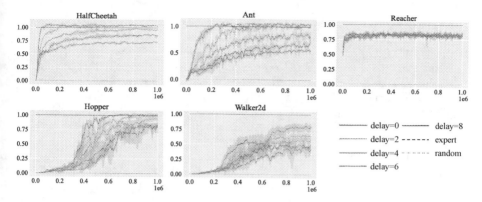

Fig. 4. Confirmation experiments of DAIL using 4 undelayed demonstrations in the environments with delays of 0, 2, 4, 6, 8 timesteps. x-axis corresponds timestep and y-axis corresponds to normalized return (0 corresponds to a random policy, while 1 corresponds to an expert policy).

the delay which demonstrates the correctness of the conclusion in the Theory section. Surprisingly, even in an environment with the substantial delay, e.g. the delay of 8 timesteps, DAIL can achieve high performance. This prove that with the powerful AIL framework, well-designed networks and modules DAIL can make accurate decisions on substantial-delay information and solve difficult delay problems.

6   Conclusion

In this paper, we propose a novel algorithm, named Delayed Adversarial Imitation Learning (DAIL), to deal with delays. A theoretical analysis is provided to validate the rationality of DAIL and guide the design. Equipped with absorbing states and off-policy updating networks, DAIL can achieve excellent performance in environments with delays by learning a few undelayed expert trajectories. As the experiments demonstrates, DAIL outperforms other baselines by a huge margin in kinds of tasks. At the same time, DAIL can converge to high performance with an excellent sampling efficiency and deal with substantial delays.

References

1. Imaida, T., Yokokohji, Y., Doi, T., Oda, M., Yoshikawa, T.: Ground-space bilateral teleoperation of ETS-VII robot arm by direct bilateral coupling under 7-s time delay condition. IEEE Trans. Robot. Autom. **20**(3), 499–511 (2004)
2. Lampe, T., Fiederer, L.D.J., Voelker, M., Knorr, A., Riedmiller, M., Ball, T.: A brain-computer interface for high-level remote control of an autonomous, reinforcement-learning-based robotic system for reaching and grasping. In: Proceedings of the 19th international conference on Intelligent User Interfaces, pp. 83–88 (2014)

3. Altman, E., Nain, P.: Closed-loop control with delayed information. ACM Sigmetrics Perform. Eval. Rev. **20**(1), 193–204 (1992)
4. Chen, B., Mengdi, X., Li, L., Zhao, D.: Delay-aware model-based reinforcement learning for continuous control. Neurocomputing **450**, 119–128 (2021)
5. Firoiu, V., Ju, T., Tenenbaum, J.: At human speed: deep reinforcement learning with action delay. arXiv preprint arXiv:1810.07286 (2018)
6. Schuitema, E., Buşoniu, L., Babuška, R., Jonker, P.: Control delay in reinforcement learning for real-time dynamic systems: a memoryless approach. In: 2010 IEEE/RSJ International Conference on Intelligent Robots and Systems, pp. 3226–3231. IEEE (2010)
7. Ramstedt, S., Bouteiller, Y., Beltrame, G., Pal, C., Binas, J.: Reinforcement learning with random delays. arXiv preprint arXiv:2010.02966 (2020)
8. Maran, D.: Delayed reinforcement learning, an imitation game (2021)
9. Bain, M., Sammut, C.: A framework for behavioural cloning. In: Machine Intelligence 15, pp. 103–129 (2000)
10. Pomerleau, D.A.: ALVINN: an autonomous land vehicle in a neural network. In: Advances in Neural Information Processing Systems, vol. 1 (1988)
11. Finn, C., Christiano, P., Abbeel, P., Levine, S.: A connection between generative adversarial networks, inverse reinforcement learning, and energy-based models. arXiv preprint arXiv:1611.03852 (2016)
12. Abbeel, P., Ng, A.Y.: Apprenticeship learning via inverse reinforcement learning. In: Proceedings of the Twenty-First International Conference on Machine Learning, p. 1 (2004)
13. Goodfellow, I., et al.: Generative adversarial networks. Commun. ACM **63**(11), 139–144 (2020)
14. Ho, J., Ermon, S.: Generative adversarial imitation learning. In: Advances in Neural Information Processing Systems, vol. 29 (2016)
15. Fu, J., Luo, K., Levine, S.: Learning robust rewards with adversarial inverse reinforcement learning. arXiv preprint arXiv:1710.11248 (2017)
16. Ramstedt, S., Pal, C.: Real-time reinforcement learning. In: Advances in Neural Information Processing Systems, vol. 32 (2019)
17. Katsikopoulos, K.V., Engelbrecht, S.E.: Markov decision processes with delays and asynchronous cost collection. IEEE Trans. Autom. Control **48**(4), 568–574 (2003)
18. Kostrikov, I., Agrawal, K.K., Dwibedi, D., Levine, S., Tompson, J.: Discriminator-actor-critic: addressing sample inefficiency and reward bias in adversarial imitation learning. arXiv preprint arXiv:1809.02925 (2018)
19. Haarnoja, T., Zhou, A., Abbeel, A., Levine, S.: Soft actor-critic: off-policy maximum entropy deep reinforcement learning with a stochastic actor. In: International conference on machine learning, pp. 1861–1870. PMLR (2018)
20. Devroye, L., Mehrabian, A., Reddad, T.: The total variation distance between high-dimensional gaussians. arXiv preprint arXiv:1810.08693 (2018)
21. Todorov, E., Erez, T., Tassa, Y.: MuJoCo: a physics engine for model-based control. In: 2012 IEEE/RSJ International Conference on Intelligent Robots and Systems, pp. 5026–5033. IEEE (2012)
22. Schulman, J., Wolski, F., Dhariwal, P., Radford, A., Klimov, O.: Proximal policy optimization algorithms. arXiv preprint arXiv:1707.06347 (2017)

An Evaluation of Self-supervised Learning for Portfolio Diversification

Yongxin Yang[1]([⊠])[iD] and Timothy M. Hospedales[2][iD]

[1] Queen Mary University of London, London, UK
yongxin.yang@qmul.ac.uk
[2] University of Edinburgh, Edinburgh, UK
t.hospedales@ed.ac.uk

Abstract. Recently self-supervised learning (SSL) has achieved impressive performance in computer vision (CV) and natural language processing (NLP) tasks, and some early attempts are made in the area of finance. In this paper, we apply SSL to extract features from financial time series data, and use those features to measure the similarities between assets in the market. As similarity measurement is the key to portfolio diversification, we consider two portfolio optimisation problems: index tracking (IT) and minimum variance portfolio (MVP), with the additional diversification terms linked to different similarity measurements, which are sourced from different SSL algorithms. Both IT and MVP are both convex optimisation problems with deterministic solutions, therefore the performance difference is traced back to SSL algorithms, rather than other factors. Extensive experiments are conducted with eight SSL algorithms, and the analysis of the results of the experiments demonstrates the advantages of SSL over non-SSL alternatives.

1 Introduction

Deep learning has undoubtedly achieved superior performance across numerous domains, but it usually requires costly annotations of big data [25]. Recently, self-supervised learning (SSL) has been introduced as a means to reduce the annotation cost. SSL is a type of machine learning strategy that involves supervised feature learning where the supervision tasks are generated from data itself [5]. Over the last few years, several methods of SSL have been proposed in many different areas, such as image representation [4,24,25] and natural language processing [14,27], alleviating the need for large labelled data by utilising unlabelled data. There have also been some early attempts to apply SSL to time series data [31,41].

Time series analysis has received considerable interests over the last two decades [38]. One of the main challenges in time series stems from the fact that there are no explicit features in sequence [39]. With data labels being unavailable or unreliable, many unsupervised learning algorithms have been proposed to carry out representation learning for time series, such as Random Wraping Series [38], TimeNet [30], and k-Shape [34]. Those methods have gained much popularity due to their highly competitive performances, which motivates us applying SSL to extract features for financial time series data. The remaining question is then how to evaluate those features.

In this work, we propose to calculate the similarity between two assets using the feature extracted from their time series data by a certain SSL algorithm. The similarity contributes to portfolio optimisation with *diversification*, and the backtesting of portfolio optimisation provides a common standard to compare SSL algorithms. More specifically, we choose two tasks: index tracking [1] and minimum variance portfolio [23], which are classic portfolio optimisation problems. These are convex optimisation problems with the added diversification term, which means once the parameters are given, the solution is unique. Thus, the performance difference can only be credited to the diversification term, which is further traced back to the SSL algorithm.

While a number of SSL algorithms designed for CV/NLP tasks can be applied to finance data in principle, there is no comprehensive evaluation under the same setting. In this work, we run eight SSL algorithms for two finance tasks across six markets, and demonstrate the effectiveness of applying SSL to financial time series data.

2   Related Work

2.1   Self-supervised Learning

SSL is a machine learning paradigm and it learns representations without human annotated labels. The most popular ones are based on contrastive, and they have achieved remarkable performance in vision tasks. SimSiam [8] introduced a stop-gradient mechanism to prevent collapse without using negative sample pairs, large batches, and momentum encoders. BYOL [20] directly predicted the output from one perturbed image from another. It was a Siamese network in which one branch was a momentum encoder. SimCLR [7] used negative samples coexisting in the current batch. It learned representations by maximising agreement between differently augmented views of the same input. MoCo [21] trained the visual representation encoder by matching an encoder query to dictionary keys using the contrastive loss. There are also some attempts to apply SSL to NLP [14, 27]. [27] presented continuous distributed vector representations for pieces of texts. The vector representations were trained to be useful in predicting words in a paragraph. [14] proposed a model to pretrain deep bidirectional representations from the unlabelled texts by jointly conditioning on both the left and right contexts in all layers. In contrast to these SSL methods designed for NLP, the algorithms developed for vision tasks can be applied to financial time series data more easily, as we only need to change the data augmentation (Sect. 3.6) and encoder accordingly.

2.2   Portfolio Diversification

Diversification has been at the centre of finance for over fifty years [3]. There are extensive studies on portfolio diversification. For example, [9] defined a diversification ratio for any portfolio and then maximised it, instead of minimising the portfolio's total variance. [3] proposed the use of cross-entropy measure as the objective function to diversified portfolios. [10] proposed most diversified portfolio (MDP) by imposing a non-negative constraint on the maximum diversification problem. [35] also found the link between entropy and diversification in the notion of uncertainty, and then built a framework for assembling a fully diversified risk parity-like portfolio, through a constrained entropy-maximisation process. [6] proposed a semi-variance method for diversified portfolio selection, in which the security returns were given and were depicted as uncertain variables, subject to experts' estimations. [26] investigated three regularisation techniques, including the spectral cut-off, the Tikhonov, and the Landweber-Fridman, to achieve diversification. In addition, $1/N$ [13] and market capitalisation-weighted [29] strategies were also used to get diversified portfolios.

The key ingredient for diversification is to measure the similarity of assets accurately, and we find that the similarity measured in the feature space usually outperforms the similarity measured in the raw data space. Thus, it is important to train a good feature extractor, and our study suggests that SSL methods provide a competitive choice.

2.3   IT and MVP with Diversification

Index tracking (IT), as a popular passive management strategy, aims to minimise tracking error that measures how closely the tracking portfolio mimics the performance of a specific index such as S&P 500 [1]. Minimum variance portfolio (MVP) is derived from the traditional mean-variance framework [32] as the latter is quite limited in practice due to the difficulty in estimating means of returns. [12,35] suggest that the errors in estimates of the means have a larger impact than errors in estimates of the covariances, thus MVP is a more robust choice. Although diversification has been studied extensively for general portfolio construction problems [37], it is underused in IT or MVP. Several researches attempted to introduce norm constraints on the weights to obtain diversified portfolios for IT [15,16,42] and MVP [2,11]. These methods often made a trade-off between optimality on the tracking error (or variance) of the portfolio and diversification. In this paper, we attempt to introduce diversification by measuring similarity of assets using the features extracted by SSL methods.

3   Methodology

3.1   Diversification

To obtain a diversified portfolio, we adopt the following regularisation term for the weight vector w from [42],

$$w^T A w \qquad (1)$$

where w is the weight vector of different assets and A_{ij} is a similarity measure between assets i and j, where 0 means most dissimilar and 1 means most similar.

We have $A_{ii} = 1$ since they are exactly the same asset, and we also assume $A_{ij} = A_{ji}$. We will discuss the construction of similarity matrix A in the following section.

To better understand the role of this term, we can extend $w^T A w$ as,

$$w^T A w = \|w\|_2^2 + 2 \sum_{i=1}^{N-1} \sum_{j=i+1}^{N} w_i A_{ij} w_j \tag{2}$$

The first term is referred to as the Herfindahl index [22], which is a common concentration indicator in portfolio optimisation [19]. The second term complements diversity, as it discourages buying two assets if they are similar to each other.

3.2   Similarity Matrix Construction

To calculate the regularisation term, we need to construct the similarity matrix A first. In this work, we use the radial basis function (BRF) kernel as the similarity measure:

$$K(z_i, z_j) = \exp\left(-\gamma \|z_i - z_j\|^2\right) \tag{3}$$

where z_i and z_j are the features extracted from the original time series data of two assets x_i and x_j, through a certain SSL method: $z_i = \text{SSL}(x_i)$ and $z_j = \text{SSL}(x_j)$. We set the similarity A_{ij} between two assets x_i and x_j as:

$$A_{ij} = K(z_i, z_j) \tag{4}$$

3.3   Portfolio Optimisation

IT with Diversification. IT can be formulated as a regression problem,

$$\min_{w} \ \|Xw - y\|_2^2 \tag{5}$$

where $X \in \mathbb{R}^{D \times N}$ is the daily return of assets and $y \in \mathbb{R}^D$ is the daily return of target index (benchmark). D is the number of timesteps (e.g., $D = 720$ trading days in three consecutive years), and N is the number of assets (e.g., $N = 500$ stocks). $w \in \mathbb{R}^N$ is the weight of each asset to hold in order to approximate the index y.

In practice, there are two constraints on w: (i) long only, which means $w_i \geq 0$, $\forall i$, and (ii) utilise all of the capital, which means $\sum_{i=1}^{N} w_i = 1$. Therefore, the objective function becomes,

$$\min_{w \geq 0, \sum_i w_i = 1} \ \|Xw - y\|_2^2 \tag{6}$$

IT with the regularisation term, long only, and sum-to-one constraints can be expressed as:

$$\min_{w \geq 0, \sum_i w_i = 1} \ \|Xw - y\|_2^2 + \lambda w^T A w \tag{7}$$

which can be solved by quadratic programming (QP) easily. λ is a hyper-parameter and we can make a trade-off between the tracking error and diversification by adjusting λ.

The quadratic form of Eq. 7 is,

$$\min_{w} \frac{1}{2} w^T P w + q^T w \tag{8}$$
$$\text{subject to: } Gw \leq h \text{ and } Aw = b$$

where $P = 2(X^T X + \lambda A)$, $q = -2X^T y$, $G = -I$, $h = 0$, $A = 1^T$, and $b = 1$. This is a convex optimisation problem that can be handled by most of the off-the-shelf solvers.

MVP with Diversification. According to [23], MVP with long only and sum-to-one constraints can be expressed as:

$$\min_{w \geq 0, \sum_i w_i = 1} w^T \Sigma w \tag{9}$$

where $w \in \mathbb{R}^N$ is the vector of portfolio weights, $\Sigma \in \mathbb{R}^{N \times N}$ is the covariance matrix. We can add a regularisation term to the objective function to obtain a diversified portfolio. MVP with the regularisation term, long only, and sum-to-one constraints can be expressed as:

$$\min_{w \geq 0, \sum_i w_i = 1} w^T \Sigma w + \lambda w^T A w \tag{10}$$

which also can be solved by QP easily. Similar to IT with the regularisation term, λ is a hyper-parameter and we can make a trade-off between the risk (variance) and diversification by adjusting λ. According to Eq. 8, we have $P = 2(\Sigma + \lambda A)$, $q = 0$, $G = -I$, $h = 0$, $A = 1^T$, and $b = 1$ in this case.

3.4 Self-supervised Learning

We evaluate the following eight SSL algorithms for feature extraction from financial time series data:

SimSiam [8] takes as input two randomly augmented views of data. The two views are processed sequentially by an encoder network f, consisting of a backbone and a projection MLP head, and a prediction MLP head that transforms the output of one view and matches it to the other view. A stop-gradient operation plays an essential role in preventing collapse in SimSiam.

BYOL [20] uses two neural networks: the online and target networks. The online network is defined by a set of weights and is comprised of three stages: an encoder f, a projector g, and a predictor h. Predictor h is only applied to the online branch, making the architecture asymmetric between the online and target pipelines. BYOL updates the target network with a slow-moving average of the online network and does not use an explicit term to prevent collapse.

SimCLR [7] learns representations by maximising agreement between different augmented views of the same data via a contrastive loss. A base encoder network f and a projection head g are trained. SimCLR relies on negative samples (dissimilarity) to prevent collapse. A learnable nonlinear transformation between the representation and the contrastive loss has been introduced to SimCLR.

MoCo [21] trains a representation encoder f by matching an encoded query to a dictionary of encoded keys via a contrastive loss. A momentum update is used to solve the intractability of updating the key encoder by back-propagation. Neither projector nor predictor is used in MoCo. InfoNCE [33] loss is used, with similarity measured by dot product.

SimCSE [17] is a simple contrastive learning framework for sentence embeddings. It predicts the input sentence itself from in-sample negatives, with different hidden dropouts mask applied. Positive instances are generated by using standard dropout on intermediate representation.

CPC [33] is a SSL approach for extracting representations from high-dimensional data (e.g., audio, text). CPC compresses high-dimensional data into a much more compact latent embedding space by using a non-linear encoder f. Autoregressive model g is used in the latent space to make predictions and a context latent representation is produced. Both the encoder f and g are trained to jointly optimise a loss based on InfoNCE loss.

Wav2Vec [36] is a convolutional neural network designed for representation learning on raw audio input. An encoder network f embeds the raw audio signal in a latent space and a context network g combines multiple time-steps of the encoder f to obtain contextualised representations. Both f and g are then used to compute the contrastive objective.

TS2Vec [40] is a framework for learning representations of time series in an arbitrary semantic level. It hierarchically discriminates positive and negative samples at instance-wise and temporal dimensions. Inputs are fed into the encoder network f, which is jointly optimised with temporal and instance-wise contrastive loss functions.

3.5   Non-SSL Methods

In addition to SSL, we consider the following non-SSL methods to complement our evaluation:

TimeNet [30] is a multilayered recurrent neural network (RNN) trained in an unsupervised manner to extract features from time series. We use the RBF kernel to construct similarity matrix A after feature extraction by TimeNet.

k-Shape [34] is an algorithm for time series clustering. k-Shape relies on a scalable iterative refinement procedure, which creates homogeneous and separated clusters. We build the similarity matrix A based on these separated clusters: the similarity A_{ij} between asset i and asset j equals to 1 if the two assets are in the same cluster else 0.

Spearman (SP) is a nonparametric measure of rank correlation between the ranking of two variables. Here we use SP to calculate distance of raw time series data and construct the similarity matrix as follows: first the distance of asset

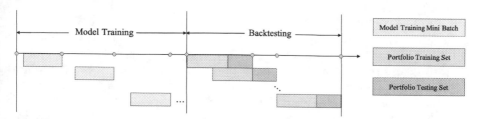

Fig. 1. Illustration of the rolling windows. The dataset (2010-01-01 to 2019-12-31) is split into two parts: (1) the first five years are used for SSL model training, (2) the second five years are used for backtesting including portfolio training and testing.

i and asset j is calculated by $d_{ij} = \mathrm{SP}(x_i, x_j)$, then we transform the distance into similarity by $A_{ij} = \exp(-d_{ij})$.

Industry Sector (IS). The thought behind IS is very simple: to obtain diversified portfolios, we want the stocks to be spread across multiple departments as much as possible. The similarity matrix A construction is similar to k-Shape method: the similarity A_{ij} between asset i and asset j equals to 1 if the two assets are in the same industry sector else 0.

To demonstrate the effectiveness of the diversification itself, two additional baselines are added: IT without a regularisation term as the Eq. 6, and MVP without a regularisation term as the Eq. 9.

3.6   Data Augmentation

As these SSL methods start from data augmentation for images, we implement a family of data augmentation methods for time series, including translation, flipping, adding noise, etc. Three data augmentation techniques are used in this paper: adding noise, drifting, and quantization.

4   Experiment

4.1   Data Preparation

To rigorously evaluate the performances of self-supervised learning methods, we conduct the experiments on six indices and their components in this paper: S&P 500, Nikkei 225, CSI 300, FTSE 100, HSI, and CAC 40. These are part of the most important indices in the world and represent barometers of the capital markets for different countries. We use the adjusted daily closing prices over the period from 2010-01-04 to 2019-12-31 for both stocks and indices.

4.2   Training Testing Split

As the Fig. 1 shows, the dataset is divided into two parts: the first half, from 2010-01-04 to 2015-01-01, is used for SSL model training; the second half, from

2015-01-01 to 2019-12-31, is used for backtesting including portfolio optimisation and testing. For the training of SSL methods, one random mini-batch contains 720-day data. More specifically, we randomly select 720 days from 2010-01-04 to 2015-01-01 and run one-step of gradient based optimisation for SSL algorithm. This process is repeated n times. Once the model training is complete, we use its encoder only, and do not change it afterwards. For each period of backtesting from 2015-01-01 to 2019-12-31, we apply the encoder to produce the feature for each training set (in terms of portfolio optimisation, i.e., Eq. 7 and Eq. 10). Note that portfolio optimisation training set has 720 days as well, which is consistent with the size of mini-batch for SSL training. This consistence reduces the risk of having a bias from training to deployment. Portfolio optimisation produces the weighting vector w, and we buy the stocks suggested by w then hold them until the next rebalance date. In all experiments, we use monthly balance. As shown in Fig. 1, this process is a sliding window and is rebalanced monthly until the last trade day. In total, we rebalance our portfolio for 24 times and obtain a daily return series. For some non-SSL baseline methods that do not have the model training step, we omit the data from 2010-01-04 to 2015-01-01.

4.3   Backtesting

Backtesting is performed with the help of the python module Backtrader from www.backtrader.com, which accounts for all necessary trading details including transaction costs, strategies, indicators, etc. We adopt a target percent strategy to rebalance our portfolio: the current percent of the asset in the portfolio and the target percent are both taken into account to decide what the final underlying operation will be. For example, the share of stock A is 2% in the current portfolio, if the target share is 3%, then we should only buy 1% for stock A; if the target share is 1%, then we should sell 1% for stock A. So the transaction fee for stock A is from the additional 1%. These measures ensure Backtrader simulates real trading process as close as possible.

4.4   Performance Measure

We have three measures of interest are presented in this paper: (i) The volatility of portfolio return (VO), as a basic quantitative risk measure in finance, is offered to gauge risk for each portfolio, (ii) Sharpe ratio (SR), as the most broadly adopted risk-adjusted return measure, aims to measure the desirability of a risky investment strategy, and (iii) Maximum drawdown (MDD), is one of the topmost risk measures for money management professionals, as large drawdowns often lead to fund redemptions [28]. From the point of view of measuring a portfolio's performance, we prefer lower, higher, and higher numbers respectively for VO, SR, and MDD.

4.5   Hyper-parameter Setting

Apart from the SSL training part, we have three hyper-parameters: (i) γ for the similarity matrix construction in RBF kernel in Eq. 3, (ii) λ for the objection

Table 1. Performance of diversified IT. TE and TEV are multiplied by 10^4. The smaller the TE and TEV, the better.

Category	Regulariser	Method	CAC 40		NIKKEI 225		S&P 500		SENSEX 30		BOVESPA		CSI 300		Avg. Rank	
			TE	TEV	TE	TEV	TE	TEV	TE	TEV	TE	TEV	TE	TEV	TE	TEV
SSL	$w^T Aw$	SimSiam	1.44	0.16	2.13	0.35	2.77	0.58	2.63	0.54	**2.27**	**0.40**	6.36	2.94	5.00	4.83
		BYOL	1.66	0.21	2.27	0.40	3.30	0.82	2.74	0.59	3.81	1.14	8.45	5.18	11.83	11.83
		SimCLR	1.41	0.15	2.04	0.33	2.82	0.60	2.20	0.38	3.00	0.70	6.56	3.13	6.33	6.17
		MoCo	1.52	0.18	2.17	0.37	3.27	0.81	2.72	0.58	2.88	0.65	6.48	3.06	8.50	8.50
		SimCSE	1.38	0.15	2.21	0.38	2.66	0.53	2.96	0.68	2.28	0.41	5.27	2.01	5.83	5.50
		CPC	1.45	0.16	**1.92**	**0.29**	**2.49**	**0.48**	**2.02**	**0.32**	2.41	0.45	6.62	3.19	**4.00**	**3.67**
		Wav2Vec	1.49	0.17	2.65	0.55	2.84	0.62	2.93	0.67	3.11	0.76	7.06	3.82	11.33	11.33
		TS2Vec	**1.24**	**0.12**	2.42	0.46	2.79	0.57	2.62	0.54	2.67	0.56	**5.09**	**1.88**	6.00	5.67
Non-SSL	$w^T Aw$	TimeNet	1.73	0.23	2.19	0.38	2.71	0.55	2.77	0.60	2.91	0.66	8.22	4.92	9.50	9.50
		k-Shape	1.53	0.18	2.30	0.41	2.76	0.57	2.65	0.55	3.40	0.91	9.94	7.20	10.50	10.33
Non-Learning	None	CO	1.34	0.14	2.21	0.38	2.66	0.53	3.01	0.71	2.28	0.41	5.18	1.95	5.67	5.33
	$w^T w$	ℓ_2-only	1.27	0.13	2.10	0.35	2.55	0.49	2.72	0.58	2.84	0.63	8.39	5.12	5.50	5.50
	$w^T Aw$	SP	1.44	0.16	2.27	0.40	2.62	0.52	2.77	0.60	2.36	0.43	6.09	2.70	6.17	6.17
	$w^T Aw$	IS	1.74	0.24	2.16	0.36	2.65	0.53	2.61	0.53	2.59	0.52	11.19	9.10	7.67	7.67

function in Eq. 7, and (iii) λ for the objective function in Eq. 10. We have different choices for setting different hyper-parameters.

We set hyper-parameter γ for RBF kernel according to [18], avoiding the use of a grid search. Specifically, we set $\gamma = \sqrt{H_n/2}$, and $H_n > 0$ is defines as:

$$H_n = \mathrm{Med}\left\{ ||X_{n,i} - X_{n,j}||^2 \mid 1 \leq i < j \leq n \right\} \tag{11}$$

where Med is the empirical median. More precisely, H_n is obtained by first ordering the $||X_{n,i} - X_{n,j}||^2$ in increasing order. We set H_n to be the first central element if $n(n-1)/2$ is odd, or the mean of the two most central elements if $n(n-1)/2$ is even. λ in Eq. 7 and Eq. 10 are set by a grid search: $\lambda \in [1, 10]$ and we sample ten evenly spaced numbers. Note that we cannot do the conventional k-fold cross-validation here: as the data are real-time series, k-fold cross-validation may result in invalid situations in which the validation set is earlier than a part of training set (information leak in terms of backtesting). Thus, the training validation split has to strictly follow time.

4.6 Result Analysis

Table 1 and Table 2 present the performance of each individual method for IT and MVP problems respectively across six indices. SR, VO, and MDD are all measured in percentage (%). Black and bold number represents the best result out of nine methods for each column (the optimal result does not include the index). From the two tables we can see: (i) SSL and non-SSL methods apparently outperform the baseline method in most cases, which means that the regularisation term helps obtain a competitive result. Among all the 36 best performances for IT and MVP, the baseline method only accounts 1 and 2, respectively. Note that, the difference for objective functions between the baseline and the remaining methods is the regularisation term, with the latter having a regularisation

Table 2. Performance of diversified MVP. SR and VO are percentages (%). The bigger the SR/the lower the VO, the better.

Category	Regulariser	Method	CAC 40		NIKKEI 225		S&P 500		SENSEX 30		BOVESPA		CSI 300		Avg. Rank	
			SR	VO	SR	VO	SR	VO	SR	VO	SR	VO	SR	VO	SR	VO
SSL	$w^T A w$	SimSiam	24.93	20.46	11.07	17.90	56.31	15.26	85.51	17.85	75.31	11.39	41.80	19.68	9.83	6.67
		BYOL	25.59	20.33	22.13	17.41	56.65	16.66	**139.60**	17.50	**85.06**	10.66	20.11	20.68	7.33	7.67
		SimCLR	36.70	20.29	16.22	17.02	88.10	16.64	96.23	18.03	49.45	16.33	72.98	20.41	6.17	8.50
		MoCo	20.63	20.33	23.74	16.12	98.97	16.15	94.82	17.00	33.78	17.65	77.80	19.62	6.50	6.67
		SimCSE	31.81	16.17	13.44	15.22	76.29	16.28	79.30	20.88	61.85	7.76	70.68	24.89	8.50	6.50
		CPC	38.31	19.53	24.10	17.03	**101.37**	15.36	87.55	17.95	57.75	10.64	**82.44**	**17.38**	**5.00**	**5.17**
		Wav2Vec	24.24	20.90	**56.60**	18.76	85.44	15.95	76.34	**16.24**	29.60	15.38	13.67	17.49	9.83	7.33
		TS2Vec	46.48	19.44	-16.04	16.41	43.89	17.10	92.97	18.96	30.19	15.88	19.38	20.53	10.17	9.00
Non-SSL	$w^T A w$	TimeNet	41.73	17.61	21.60	**14.79**	70.44	17.11	76.73	17.98	19.92	**4.09**	66.60	25.75	9.33	6.17
		k-Shape	**60.68**	20.93	31.95	16.33	72.35	**14.33**	105.73	18.23	28.54	9.23	57.03	22.30	5.83	7.00
Non-Learning	None	CO	29.13	**13.23**	33.62	15.60	81.85	17.38	74.31	35.42	72.44	14.20	28.14	27.71	7.83	9.17
	$w^T w$	ℓ_2-only	45.62	18.68	25.23	18.15	77.30	15.72	99.93	19.67	71.41	13.24	52.94	22.69	5.17	8.67
	$w^T A w$	SP	43.35	13.52	15.57	22.42	98.64	23.53	86.33	18.11	66.88	15.54	23.81	26.64	7.33	10.33
	$w^T A w$	IS	56.07	17.19	5.02	15.52	88.03	16.25	89.38	18.35	84.23	8.68	48.62	22.32	6.17	6.00

term to promote its diversification. Thus, this validates the effectiveness of diversification. (ii) Compared with non-SSL methods, SSL achieves a slightly better performance, especially for SimSiam and BYOL. The two algorithms exhibit best performances in various performance measures across six indices for both IT and MVP problems. This confirms the effectiveness of applying SSL to financial time series. It is also noteworthy that unsupervised learning methods do not achieve superior performances to the non-learning-based methods. (iii) From the average point of view, we would like to emphasise that regardless of SR, VO, or MDD, SSL outperforms the non-SSL methods and the baseline. (iv) In terms of VO and MDD, the worst performance for SSL even outperforms the HSI and S&P 500 indices respectively.

Overall, the above results lay out two facts to us: (i) Adding a regularisation term into objective functions for IT and MVP helps get a competitive result. (ii) It is effective and promising to apply SSL to financial time series, especially for SimSiam and BYOL. Turning our attention to some interesting results from Table 1 and Table 2: (i) In terms of VO and MDD, CSI 300 index exhibits worst performance, S&P 500 and FTSE 100 indices achieve superior performance compared with other indices. This results from the high volatility discrepancies and different levels of development over different markets: the CSI 300 market is the most immature capital market among the six markets, especially compared with the S&P 500 market in US. (ii) Sometimes the best result from SSL, non-SSL, and the baseline cannot outperform the index. Best results for Sharpe ratio from nine methods over HSI and S&P 500 indices are 0.06 and 0.81 respectively, compared with the 0.12 and 0.82 for the two indices themselves. Outperforming the index is not easy for either SSL or the alternatives.

5   Conclusion

In this paper, we have evaluated the self-supervised learning (SSL) algorithms to portfolio diversification. We consider two portfolio optimisation problem: index tracking (IT) and minimum variance portfolio (MVP). SSL algorithms provided competitive performances compared with several non-SSL methods on the extensive experiments of six markets. This result suggests that SSL can be a valuable tool to support investment decisions, and we hope this work attracts more interest on this direction.

Disclaimer. All authors are faculty. Neither graduate students nor small animals were hurt while producing this paper.

References

1. Beasley, J.E., Meade, N., Chang, T.J.: An evolutionary heuristic for the index tracking problem. Eur. J. Oper. Res. **148**(3), 621–643 (2003)
2. Behr, P., Guettler, A., Miebs, F.: On portfolio optimization: imposing the right constraints. J. Bank. Financ. **37**(4), 1232–1242 (2013)
3. Bera, A.K., Park, S.Y.: Optimal portfolio diversification using the maximum entropy principle. Economet. Rev. **27**(4–6), 484–512 (2008)
4. Caron, M., Bojanowski, P., Joulin, A., Douze, M.: Deep clustering for unsupervised learning of visual features. In: Ferrari, V., Hebert, M., Sminchisescu, C., Weiss, Y. (eds.) Computer Vision – ECCV 2018. LNCS, vol. 11218, pp. 139–156. Springer, Cham (2018). https://doi.org/10.1007/978-3-030-01264-9_9
5. Chen, L., Bentley, P., Mori, K., Misawa, K., Fujiwara, M., Rueckert, D.: Self-supervised learning for medical image analysis using image context restoration. Med. Image Anal. **58**, 101539 (2019)
6. Chen, L., Peng, J., Zhang, B., Rosyida, I.: Diversified models for portfolio selection based on uncertain semivariance. Int. J. Syst. Sci. **48**(3), 637–648 (2017)
7. Chen, T., Kornblith, S., Norouzi, M., Hinton, G.: A simple framework for contrastive learning of visual representations. In: ICML (2020)
8. Chen, X., He, K.: Exploring simple Siamese representation learning. In: CVPR (2021)
9. Choueifaty, Y., Coignard, Y.: Toward maximum diversification. J. Portfolio Manag. **35**(1), 40–51 (2008)
10. Choueifaty, Y., Froidure, T., Reynier, J.: Properties of the most diversified portfolio. J. Investment Strat. **2**(2), 49–70 (2013)
11. Coqueret, G.: Diversified minimum-variance portfolios. Ann. Finance **11**(2), 221–241 (2015)
12. DeMiguel, V., Garlappi, L., Nogales, F.J., Uppal, R.: A generalized approach to portfolio optimization: improving performance by constraining portfolio norms. Manage. Sci. **55**(5), 798–812 (2009)
13. DeMiguel, V., Garlappi, L., Uppal, R.: Optimal versus Naive diversification: how inefficient is the 1/N portfolio strategy? Rev. Financ. Stud. **22**(5), 1915–1953 (2009)
14. Devlin, J., Chang, M.W., Lee, K., Toutanova, K.: BERT: pre-training of deep bidirectional transformers for language understanding. arXiv preprint arXiv:1810.04805 (2018)
15. Fastrich, B., Paterlini, S., Winker, P.: Cardinality versus q-Norm constraints for index tracking. Quant. Financ. **14**(11), 2019–2032 (2014)
16. Fernholz, R., Garvy, R., Hannon, J.: Diversity-weighted indexing. J. Portf. Manag. **24**(2), 74 (1998)

17. Gao, T., Yao, X., Chen, D.: SimCSE: simple contrastive learning of sentence embeddings. arXiv preprint arXiv:2104.08821 (2021)
18. Garreau, D., Jitkrittum, W., Kanagawa, M.: Large sample analysis of the median heuristic. arXiv preprint arXiv:1707.07269 (2017)
19. Goetzmann, W.N., Kumar, A.: Equity portfolio diversification. Rev. Financ. **12**(3), 433–463 (2008)
20. Grill, J.B., et al.: Bootstrap your own latent: a new approach to self-supervised learning. arXiv preprint arXiv:2006.07733 (2020)
21. He, K., Fan, H., Wu, Y., Xie, S., Girshick, R.: Momentum contrast for unsupervised visual representation learning. In: CVPR (2020)
22. Herfindahl, O.: Concentration in the steel industry. Columbia University (1950)
23. Jagannathan, R., Ma, T.: Risk reduction in large portfolios: why imposing the wrong constraints helps. J. Financ. **58**(4), 1651–1683 (2003)
24. Kim, D., Cho, D., Yoo, D., Kweon, I.S.: Learning image representations by completing damaged Jigsaw puzzles. In: WACV (2018)
25. Kolesnikov, A., Zhai, X., Beyer, L.: Revisiting self-supervised visual representation learning. In: CVPR (2019)
26. Koné, N., et al.: Regularized maximum diversification investment strategy. Econometrics **9**(1), 1 (2021)
27. Le, Q., Mikolov, T.: Distributed representations of sentences and documents. In: ICML (2014)
28. Magdon-Ismail, M., Atiya, A.F.: Maximum drawdown. Risk Mag. **17**(10), 99–102 (2004)
29. Maillard, S., Roncalli, T., Teïletche, J.: The properties of equally weighted risk contribution portfolios. J. Portfolio Manag. **36**(4), 60–70 (2010)
30. Malhotra, P., TV, V., Vig, L., Agarwal, P., Shroff, G.: TimeNet: pre-trained deep recurrent neural network for time series classification. arXiv preprint arXiv:1706.08838 (2017)
31. Marin Zapata, P.A., Roth, S., Schmutzler, D., Wolf, T., Manesso, E., Clevert, D.A.: Self-supervised feature extraction from image time series in plant phenotyping using triplet networks. Bioinformatics **37**(6), 861–867 (2021)
32. Markowitz, H.: Portfolio selection. J. Financ. **7** (1952)
33. Oord, A.V.D., Li, Y., Vinyals, O.: Representation learning with contrastive predictive coding. arXiv preprint arXiv:1807.03748 (2018)
34. Paparrizos, J., Gravano, L.: K-shape: efficient and accurate clustering of time series. In: SIGMOD (2015)
35. Pola, G.: On entropy and portfolio diversification. J. Asset Manag. **17**(4), 218–228 (2016)
36. Schneider, S., Baevski, A., Collobert, R., Auli, M.: wav2vec: unsupervised pre-training for speech recognition. arXiv preprint arXiv:1904.05862 (2019)
37. Woerheide, W., Persson, D.: An index of portfolio diversification. Financ. Serv. Rev. **2**(2), 73–85 (1992)
38. Wu, L., Yen, I.E.H., Yi, J., Xu, F., Lei, Q., Witbrock, M.: Random warping series: a random features method for time-series embedding. In: AIStats (2018)
39. Xing, Z., Pei, J., Keogh, E.: A brief survey on sequence classification. ACM SIGKDD Explor. Newsl. **12**(1), 40–48 (2010)
40. Yue, Z., et al.: TS2Vec: towards universal representation of time series. arXiv preprint arXiv:2106.10466 (2021)
41. Zhang, P., et al.: Self-supervised learning for fast and scalable time series hyperparameter tuning. arXiv preprint arXiv:2102.05740 (2021)
42. Zheng, Y., Hospedales, T.M., Yang, Y.: Diversity and sparsity: a new perspective on index tracking. In: ICASSP (2020)

An Exploitation-Enhanced Bayesian Optimization Algorithm for High-Dimensional Expensive Problems

Yuqian Gui[ID], Dawei Zhan[(✉)][ID], and Tianrui Li[ID]

School of Computing and Artificial Intelligence, Southwest Jiaotong University, Chengdu 611756, China
qiyiguo497@my.swjtu.edu.cn, {zhandawei,trli}@swjtu.edu.cn

Abstract. The Bayesian optimization (BO) algorithm is widely used to solve expensive optimization problems. However, when dealing with high-dimensional problems, the accuracy of the global Gaussian process (GP) model is often inadequate due to the limited number of training points. As a result, the search based on the expected improvement criterion can lead to misguided exploration. To address this issue, we propose an exploitation-enhanced Bayesian optimization (EE-BO) algorithm. Our approach incorporates a local GP model built around the evaluated solution from the previous iteration, which is used to find the next infill solution if the current selection from the global GP model is not an improvement. The inclusion of the local model mitigates the impact of inaccurate models and enhances the algorithm's ability to perform local searches when the global model struggles to find better solutions. Our numerical experiments show that the proposed EE-BO algorithm outperforms the vanilla BO algorithm and achieves competitive performance compared to five state-of-the-art algorithms.

Keywords: Expensive optimization · Bayesian optimization · Expected improvement · Local model

1 Introduction

Expensive optimization problems, which refer to a kind of problem whose objectives or constraints are computationally or financially expensive to obtain, are very common in real-world applications. These problems arise in scenarios such as hyperparameter tuning for machine learning algorithms [8], meta-heuristics [3], and finite element simulation [2]. For example, training a deep learning model can take several days and require substantial computing power. Since different parameter configurations yield different experimental results, it is crucial to minimize the number of trials and errors required to make design and configuration decisions. Due to the high computational cost of each evaluation, the total number of evaluations of these problems is often restricted to a few hundred. Therefore, modern meta-heuristics are not suitable for solving

© The Author(s), under exclusive license to Springer Nature Switzerland AG 2023
L. Iliadis et al. (Eds.): ICANN 2023, LNCS 14256, pp. 295–306, 2023.
https://doi.org/10.1007/978-3-031-44213-1_25

these expensive optimization problems because they often cannot obtain reliable results with so few function evaluations. Currently, surrogate-based optimization algorithms are the primary techniques used to tackle expensive optimization problems. In a surrogate-based optimization algorithm, surrogate models are utilized to approximate the expensive functions using a small set of evaluated points. The new design points can be approximated using the fast surrogate models during the optimization process. Based on whether or not the algorithm allows the evaluation of new points during the optimization process, surrogate-based optimization algorithms can be classified as offline and online optimization algorithms. In offline optimization, no new points can be obtained, and the search is executed on surrogate models built based on historical data. This approach is similar to training a neural network on past data and directly using the trained model. On the contrary, online optimization algorithms can select one or multiple candidate points in each iteration to perform expensive evaluations and use the results to update the surrogate models during the optimization process. Due to their flexibility in computational framework and their ability to learn new information in expensive optimization problems, online surrogate-based optimization algorithms are more widely studied and used than offline algorithms.

One of the most representative surrogate-based optimization algorithms is the Bayesian optimization (BO) algorithm [7] in statistics and machine learning. In each iteration of the BO algorithm, a Gaussian process (GP) model is built to approximate expensive function, and an infill criterion is utilized to find a candidate point for expensive evaluation. The newly evaluated point is then added to the design set, and the GP model is re-trained by incorporating the new point [4]. The BO algorithm proceeds in this manner until a stopping condition is met. After being popularized by Jones et al. [4], the BO algorithm soon became the standard benchmark algorithm for later-developed surrogate-based optimization algorithms.

However, most successful BO algorithm applications are limited to low-dimensional or medium-dimensional problems. Directly applying the BO algorithm to high-dimensional problems encounters several challenges. One major issue is that the local search ability of BO gradually decreases as the dimension of the problem increases [10]. When dealing with high-dimensional problems, it becomes difficult to fit an accurate global GP model that covers the entire design space with a limited number of training points. The infill criterion, based on the inaccurate GP model, tends to select points with large prediction errors, leading to misguided exploration. The loss of local search ability poses a significant challenge in extending the BO algorithm to high-dimensional problems. In this work, we propose a new approach to address this issue. The proposed algorithm, referred to as exploitation-enhanced Bayesian optimization (EE-BO), aims to improve the performance of the BO algorithm in high-dimensional problems. The main difference between EE-BO and the vanilla BO algorithm lies in the construction of a local area based on the evaluated solution from the previous iteration. We build a local GP model within this area to search for better solutions when the infill solution from the global GP model does not provide improvement.

As the dimensionality of the optimization problem increases, the search space expands rapidly. In high-dimensional problems, constructing an accurate global GP model that captures the details of the entire search space becomes challenging. The vanilla BO algorithm focuses on capturing the contour of the search space, often leading to quick convergence to a local optimum and under-utilization of the remaining budget. By incorporating a local area around the last evaluated solution, our approach helps compensate for inaccuracies in the global GP model and enhances the algorithm's ability to conduct more effective local search. Through numerical experiments, we demonstrate that our proposed EE-BO algorithm outperforms the vanilla BO algorithm on eighteen test problems. Furthermore, the EE-BO algorithm shows competitive performance when compared with five state-of-the-art algorithms.

The rest of this paper is organized as follows. Section 2 introduces the vanilla BO algorithm. The related work is introduced in Sect. 3. Section 4 describes the proposed EE-BO algorithm and Sect. 5 presents the numerical experiments. Conclusions of this work are given in Sect. 6.

2   The Bayesian Optimization Algorithm

The vanilla BO algorithm was designed to solve an expensive single-objective bound-constrained optimization problem.

$$\mathbf{x}^{\star} = \underset{\mathbf{x} \in \mathbb{X}}{\operatorname{argmin}} \quad y(\mathbf{x}), \tag{1}$$

where $\mathbf{x} = [x_1, x_2, \cdots, x_d]^{\mathrm{T}}$ is design variables and d is the number of the design variables, $y(\mathbf{x})$ is the objective function and is assumed to be computationally expensive, $\mathbb{X}$ is the design space and is a d-dimensional hyper-rectangle $\mathbb{X} = \{\mathbf{x} \in \mathbb{R}^d : a_i \leq x_i \leq b_i\}$. In each cycle of the iteration stage, a global GP model is built based on the current design set. Then, a candidate point is selected by maximizing the infill criterion function of the GP model and is evaluated using the expensive objective function. After that, the new point is added to the design set, and the best solution is updated.

2.1   The Gaussian Process

A Gaussian process (GP) is a statistical model of the black-box function. It represents the function value, $f(\mathbf{x})$, at each point, $\mathbf{x} \in \chi$ as infinitely many correlated Gaussian random variables. As such it is completely characterized by its mean function values, and covariance functions, $m(\mathbf{x})$ and $k(\mathbf{x}^i, \mathbf{x}^j)$. More formally, we assume that $f(\mathbf{x}) \sim GP(\mu(\mathbf{x}), \sigma^2(\mathbf{x}))$, and the $\hat{\mu}$ and kernel function $\hat{\sigma}^2$ given by:

$$\hat{\mu}(\mathbf{x}) = k(\mathbf{x})\Sigma^{-1}y \tag{2}$$

$$\hat{\sigma}^2(\mathbf{x}) = k(\mathbf{x}, \mathbf{x}) - k(\mathbf{x})\Sigma^{-1}k(\mathbf{x})^{\mathrm{T}} \tag{3}$$

where the Σ is $K(\mathbf{x}^{(1:n)}, \mathbf{x}^{(1:n)})$ and $k(\mathbf{x})$ is $K(\mathbf{x}, \mathbf{x}^{(1:n)})$. By this way, we could build a response surface and describe the rough rule of f.

2.2   The Expected Improvement Criterion

After building the GP model, the next question would be how to select new samples to do expensive evaluations. The EI criterion is an elegant trade-off between exploration and exploitation. Based on the GP model, the objective value of an unknown point $Y(\mathbf{x})$ can be seen as a random variable with posterior distribution $N(\hat{\mu}(\mathbf{x}), \hat{\sigma}^2(\mathbf{x}))$. If the current best objective value of the n sampled points is $y_{\min}$, the improvement of the unknown point beyond the current minimum is

$$I(\mathbf{x}) = \begin{cases} y_{\min} - Y(\mathbf{x}), & \text{if } Y(\mathbf{x}) \leq y_{\min} \\ 0, & \text{if } Y(\mathbf{x}) > y_{\min}. \end{cases} \quad (4)$$

Then the EI function is the mathematical expectation of the improvement function, and can be calculated in closed-form [4]

$$\text{EI}(\mathbf{x}) = (y_{\min} - \hat{y}(\mathbf{x})) \, \Phi\left(\frac{y_{\min} - \hat{y}(\mathbf{x})}{\hat{\sigma}(\mathbf{x})}\right) + \hat{\sigma}(\mathbf{x})\phi\left(\frac{y_{\min} - \hat{y}(\mathbf{x})}{\hat{\sigma}(\mathbf{x})}\right), \quad (5)$$

where $\phi(x)$ and $\Phi(x)$ are the density and cumulative distribution function of standard normal distribution respectively. As can be seen, the EI function is in fact a nonlinear combination of the GP prediction $\hat{\mu}(\mathbf{x})$ and the GP standard deviation $\hat{\sigma}(\mathbf{x})$.

3   The Related Work

Expensive optimization problems have gained increased attention in recent years, particularly with the rapid development of artificial intelligence. These problems arise in various fields, such as hyperparameter tuning and simulation experiments. Surrogate-based optimization algorithms have emerged as the primary technique to address these expensive optimization problems, and among them, Bayesian optimization (BO) is the most representative and widely used. However, the success of BO has been mostly limited to low-dimensional or medium-dimensional problems. To overcome this limitation, several variants of BO have been proposed to extend its applicability to high-dimensional problems. For instance, Kandasamy [5] proposed the additive hypothesis, which utilizes multiple Gaussian process (GP) models in low dimensions and integrates their information through an additive approach. Wang [12], on the other hand, employed a low inherent dimension hypothesis to transform high-dimensional problems into low-dimensional ones using random linear embedding. However, the partition size and the number of inherent dimensions pose limitations on the application of these methods. Another approach is the incremental method proposed by Zhan [14], which reduces the time complexity of updating the GP model to $O(n2)$ instead of building the model from scratch when new samples arrive. Eriksson [1] introduced the TuRBO algorithm, which fits a collection of local models and performs a principled global allocation of samples across these models using an implicit bandit approach. However, it updates the local area in a batch approach within each iteration, which can lead to excessive evaluations and is not suitable for expensive optimization problems. In addition to BO variants, surrogate-assisted evolutionary algorithms (SAEAs) have also been developed to tackle expensive optimization problems. Liu [6] proposed an surrogate-assisted evolutionary algorithm that utilizes GP as a surrogate to predict the most promising candidate solutions. Sun [9] proposed a cooperative algorithm that aims to find high-quality solutions. Wang [11] proposed an evolutionary sampling-assisted optimization algorithm. Furthermore, Wei [13] introduced a classifier-assisted level-based learning swarm optimizer to improve the robustness and scalability of SAEAs.

4   The EE-BO Algorithm

Because of the "curse of dimensionality", the volume of the design space exponentially increases as the dimension increases. However, the number of expensive samples that we can afford to build the GP model increases at a much slower rate than the expansion of the design space. For expensive optimization problems, the number of affordable expensive samples is often restricted to several hundred. Therefore, the accuracy of the GP model inevitably decreases as the dimension of the problem increases. This decrease in accuracy adversely affects the search efficiency of the EI criterion and, consequently, the overall optimization efficiency of the BO algorithm.

4.1   The Basic Idea

An intuitive way to increase the EI efficiency for high-dimensional problems is increasing the global GP model accuracy by using more training points. However, this is often impractical in real-world engineering since the computational budget is often restricted. In this work, we propose to add a local GP model in the BO framework to ease the loss of inaccurate models and improve the local search ability for the EI criterion. For the sake of visually direct presentation, we choose a 2D problem as the basis for visualization to show the advantage of using the local area. Figure 1 (a) and Fig. 1 (b) show the real surfaces of the 2-D Ackley function in the whole design space $[-32.728, 32.728]^2$ and in a subspace $[-0.5, 0.5]^2$, respectively. Figure 1 (c) and Fig. 1 (d) show the global GP model with 50 training points and the local GP model with 10 training points, respectively. It can be seen that the global GP model has difficulty in approximating the Ackley function in small local areas but can find the overall trend of the real function. In comparison, the local GP model is able to approximate the real function in the local area accurately with only 10 sample points. As a result, we can use the global GP model to identify interesting areas and then use the local GP model to find the local optima quickly. This is the basic idea of our proposed algorithm.

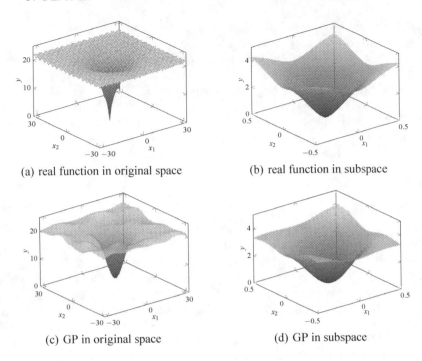

(a) real function in original space   (b) real function in subspace

(c) GP in original space   (d) GP in subspace

Fig. 1. The real surfaces and GP approximations of the 2-D Ackley function.

4.2 The Computational Framework

In this work, we propose an exploitation-enhanced Bayesian optimization (EE-BO) to ease the loss of inaccurate models and improve the local search ability of the BO for solving high-dimensional expensive problems. At the beginning of the algorithm, a global GP model is built in the whole design space and is used to capture the overall trend of the original function. The EI criterion based on the global GP model is used to find promising areas. If the infill solution offered by the global EI criterion is a better solution, the global EI criterion is then used for finding the next infill solution, as the vanilla BO algorithm does. However, when the infill solution selected by the global EI criterion brings no improvement, we build a local GP model around the infill solution to ease the loss of inaccurate model and employ a local EI to find the next infill solution. After that, the proposed EE-BO algorithm shifts to the global GP model again to find other promising areas. The framework of the proposed EE-BO is given in Algorithm 1. It can be seen that the framework of the EE-BO is identical to the vanilla when only the global GP model is used, and the modification that the EE-BO makes is utilizing an additional local GP model. In the EE-BO algorithm, all the infill sampling points are identified either by the global EI criterion or by the local EI criterion. Since the local GP model is built using all the sampled points in the local area, the local EI function can be proved to be zero at sampled points and be positive at un-sampled points [4]. This indicates that the sampling based on the local EI criterion can also converge anywhere in the local area as the number of samples goes to infinite. Therefore, the proposed EE-BO algorithm also keeps the convergence property of the vanilla BO algorithm.

Algorithm 1. Computational framework of the proposed EE-BO algorithm

---

1: generate the initial design $\mathbf{X}$, evaluate them with the original function to get $y(\mathbf{X})$.
2: set the current best solution $\mathbf{x}_{min} = \text{argmin}_{\mathbf{x} \in \mathbf{X}} y(\mathbf{x})$, $y_{min} = \min_{\mathbf{x} \in \mathbf{X}} y(\mathbf{x})$.
3: **while** the stop condition is not met **do**
4:     build a global GP model using the current design set $(\mathbf{X}, y(\mathbf{X}))$ in the whole design space.
5:     select the candidate point using the global EI criterion $\mathbf{x}_{new} = \text{argmax}_{\mathbf{x} \in \mathbb{X}} \text{EI}(\mathbf{x})$.
6:     evaluate $\mathbf{x}_{new}$ with the original expensive function.
7:     add the new infill solution $(\mathbf{x}_{new}, y(\mathbf{x}_{new}))$ to the design set.
8:     **if** $y(\mathbf{x}_{new}) > y_{min}$ **then**
9:         build a local GP model around the infill solution $(\mathbf{x}_{new}, y(\mathbf{x}_{new}))$.
10:        select the candidate point using the local EI criterion $\mathbf{x}_{local} = \text{argmax}_{\mathbf{x} \in \mathbb{X}_{local}} \text{EI}_{local}(\mathbf{x})$.
11:        evaluate $\mathbf{x}_{local}$ with the original expensive function.
12:        add the new point $(\mathbf{x}_{local}, y(\mathbf{x}_{local}))$ to the design set.
13:    **end if**
14:    update the current best solution $\mathbf{x}_{min} = \text{argmin}_{\mathbf{x} \in \mathbf{X}} y(\mathbf{x})$, $y_{min} = \min_{\mathbf{x} \in \mathbf{X}} y(\mathbf{x})$.
15: **end while**
16: output the best solution $(\mathbf{x}_{min}, y_{min})$.

---

5 Numerical Experiments

In this section, we conduct two sets of numerical experiments to verify the effectiveness of the proposed exploitation-enhanced Bayesian optimization (EE-BO) algorithm. In the first set of experiments, we compare the proposed EE-BO with the vanilla BO algorithm to study whether the proposed approach has improvements compared with the basic approach. In the second set of experiments, we compare the proposed EE-BO with five algorithms to study how the proposed algorithm performs when compared with state-of-the-art approaches.

5.1 Experiment Settings

In this section, we evaluate EE-BO on a wide range of problems: the Ellipsoid, Rosenbrock, Ackley, Griewank, Shifted Rotated Rastrigin (SRR), and Rotated Hybrid Composition with a narrow basin (RHC). To test the efficiency of the proposed EE-BO algorithm for high-dimensional problems, the dimensions of these test problems are set to 50, 100, and 200. We use the Latin hypercubic design method to generate 200 initial design points for all test problems, and as an expensive optimiazation, we set the budget as 1000. For calculation time considerations, the incremental learning approach [14] is used to build the global GP models in this work to save computational time, while for the local GP model, we use a primitive GP model. All experiments are run 30 times using 30 different initial design sets to deliver reliable results. The initial samples are the same for the compared algorithms.

5.2   Comparison with Vanilla BO

First, we compare the proposed EE-BO algorithm with the vanilla BO algorithm. The convergence histories of the compared algorithms on the test problems are shown in Fig. 2, where the vertical axis is the average optimization result of 30 runs and is plotted in logarithm scale, and the horizontal axis is the number of expensive evaluations. We can see from the convergence histories that the proposed EE-BO algorithm converges faster and finds better solutions at the end of 1000 evaluations than the vanilla BO algorithm on all the test problems, except for the 50-D RHC function on which the compared algorithms get similar results. By employing local GP models to ease the loss of inaccurate models and further exploit the infill solutions, the proposed approach is able to improve the searchability of the BO algorithm, therefore can improve the optimization performances.

The final optimization results of the compared algorithms on the test problems are given in Table 1, where the average and standard derivation values of the 30 runs are shown. To find out whether the results of the two algorithms have a significant difference, we run the paired Wilcoxon signed rank test using significance level $\alpha = 0.05$, and highlight the significantly better (smaller) results using boldface. The significant tests show that the proposed EE-BO obtains significantly better results on sixteen test problems and similar results on the rest two problems compared with the vanilla BO algorithm. The average optimization results found by the vanilla BO and the proposed EE-BO are 230.62 and 9.2590 on the 50-D Ellipsoid problem, 2512.0 and 215.09 on the 100-D Ellipsoid problem, and 52812 and 5722.8 on the 200-D Ellipsoid problem. The values are 11.420 and 3.3002 on the 50-D Rosenbrock problem, 36.120 and 13.462 on the 100-D Rosenbrock problem, and 439.17 and 89.414 on the 200-D Rosenbrock problem. This indicates that the proposed EE-BO is able to find better solutions than the vanilla BO algorithm, and the improvements of the proposed EE-BO beyond the vanilla BO get larger as the dimension of the problem increases. In addition, we can find from Table 1 that, the standard deviation values of the optimization results obtained by the proposed EE-BO are lower than the results obtained by the vanilla BO algorithm. On the 50-D Ellipsoid problem, the standard deviation values of the optimization results are 33.291 and 2.6260 for the vanilla BO and the EE-BO respectively. The values are 202.63 and 41.517 on the 100-D Ellipsoid problem, and 2578.7 and 440.87 on the 200-D Ellipsoid problem. This means the proposed EE-BO is not only able to find better results but also able to find more robust results than the vanilla BO algorithm on the test problems. In summary, the proposed EE-BO algorithm converges faster than the vanilla BO algorithm on the test problems. At the end of 1000 evaluations, the EE-BO algorithm gets better and more robust optimization results than the vanilla BO algorithm. The experiment results can empirically verify the effectiveness of the proposed EE-BO algorithm.

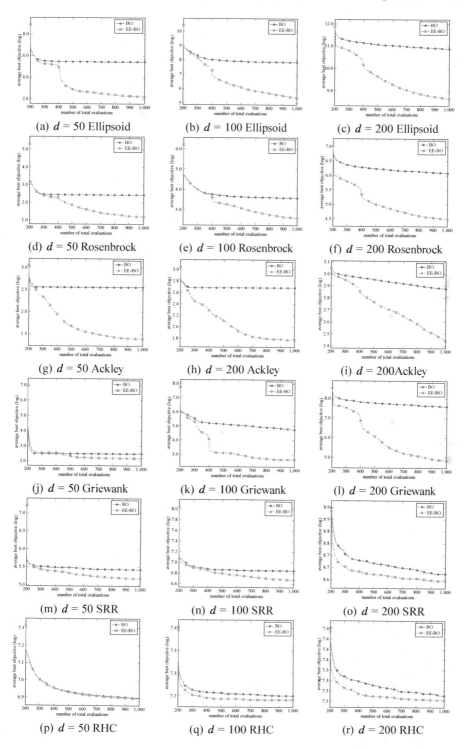

Fig. 2. Convergence histories of the vanilla BO and EE-BO on the test problems.

Table 1. Optimization results obtained by the vanilla BO and EE-BO on the test problems.

problem	d	BO		EE-BO	
		mean	SD	mean	SD
Ellipsoid	50	230.62	33.291	**9.2590**	2.6260
	100	2512.0	202.63	**215.09**	41.517
	200	52812	2578.7	**5722.8**	440.87
Rosenbrock	50	11.420	1.3057	**3.3002**	0.85933
	100	36.120	3.5060	**13.462**	2.0408
	200	439.17	19.600	**89.414**	6.8662
Ackley	50	12.852	0.56228	**4.0307**	0.19628
	100	14.630	0.50945	**5.9078**	0.34427
	200	17.779	0.20787	**11.498**	0.50051
Griewank	50	11.980	2.0577	**8.8613**	2.0713
	100	115.12	22.744	**13.937**	2.5842
	200	1978.6	76.033	**125.72**	13.694
SRR	50	226.69	20.421	**175.60**	25.197
	100	941.93	68.913	**789.32**	42.289
	200	5563.8	179.07	**5399.6**	213.11
RHC	50	989.00	13.485	**987.49**	34.339
	100	1409.2	29.589	**1396.6**	25.086
	200	1467.1	21.007	**1453.4**	23.819

Table 2. Optimization results obtained by the five comparison algorithms and the EE-BO on the test problems.

problem	d	GPEME		SA-COSO		ESAO		CA-LLSO		IKAEA		EE-BO	
		mean	SD	mean	SD	mean	SD	mean	SD	mean	SD	mean	SD
Ellipsoid	50	221.08	81.612	51.475	16.246	**0.7395**	0.5549	57.015	24.248	9.3411	4.4212	9.2590	2.6260
	100	20047	2417.3	1033.2	317.18	1282.9	134.39	1003.3	162.35	668.59	193.99	**215.09**	41.517
	200	82305	8097.2	16382	2981.1	17616	1174.8	9144.2	800.37	22051	4762.9	**5722.8**	440.87
Rosenbrock	50	258.28	80.188	252.58	40.744	47.391	1.7118	95.367	11.518	**1.8902**	0.83101	3.3002	0.85933
	100	1.47e+05	2067.3	2714.2	117.02	578.84	44.767	458.35	46.814	28.644	4.4528	**13.462**	2.0408
	200	3.10e+05	2505.8	16411	4096.5	4138.5	284.4	1806.6	140.77	238.01	24.443	**89.414**	6.8662
Ackley	50	13.233	1.5846	8.9318	1.0668	**1.4311**	0.2491	6.4079	0.5624	8.1978	0.74563	4.0307	0.196328
	100	20.616	0.0719	15.756	0.5025	10.364	0.2113	10.632	0.4275	12.622	0.60255	**5.9078**	0.34427
	200	20.708	0.0605	20.698	0.2329	14.696	0.2193	13.704	0.2987	16.588	0.81425	**11.498**	0.50051
Griewank	50	36.646	13.176	6.0062	1.1043	**0.9404**	0.0421	8.2489	1.8111	1.1884	0.11397	8.8613	2.0713
	100	1456.5	101.44	63.353	19.021	57.342	5.8387	78.803	10.636	38.252	15.734	**13.937**	2.5842
	200	4999.1	181.01	577.76	101.4	572.9	36.043	348.60	26.514	869.44	131.15	**125.72**	13.694
SRR	50	667.01	53.392	207.78	60.182	198.61	45.825	197.33	60.026	285.25	52.796	**175.60**	25.197
	100	2393.9	95.797	1273.1	117.19	**713.47**	26.454	1079.1	69.238	1189.2	80.87	789.32	42.289
	200	6576.4	436.54	3927.5	272.54	5389.1	156.85	**3467.3**	122.12	5075.5	137.74	5399.6	213.11
RHC	50	1228.2	42.454	1080.9	32.589	**975.32**	37.11	1120.7	30.027	1015.1	27.419	987.49	34.339
	100	1524.2	48.521	1365.7	30.867	1275.4	27.539	**1244.6**	16.689	1389.2	31.641	1396.6	25.086
	200	1608	41.034	1347.3	24.665	1456.4	20.432	**1275.4**	13.442	1419.4	18.105	1453.4	23.819

5.3 Comparisons with State-of-the-Art Alogorithms

In order to further demonstrate the effectiveness of the proposed EE-BO algorithm, we compare it with five state-of-the-art algorithms, which are the Gaussian process surrogate model assisted evolutionary algorithm for medium-scale computationally expensive optimization problems (GPEME) [6], surrogate-assisted cooperative swarm optimization algorithm (SA-COSO) [9], evolutionary sampling assisted optimization (ESAO) [11], classifier-assisted level-based learning swarm optimizer (CA-LLSO) [13] and incremental Kriging-assisted evolutionary algorithm (IKAEA) [14] algorithms. Overall, we can find in Table 2 that the proposed EE-BO is able to achieve competitive optimization results compared with the five state-of-the-art algorithms. Among eighteen test problems, the proposed EE-BO algorithm finds the best optimization results on nine test problems. On the other nine problems, the results found by the proposed EE-BO are also very competitive. Specifically, the proposed EE-BO algorithm finds better results than the compared algorithms on most of the Ellipsoid, Rosenbrock, Ackley, and Griewank problems, and finds competitive results on the SRR and RHC test problems. On the 100-D and 200-D Ellipsoid, Rosenbrock, Ackley, and Griewank problems, the optimization results found by the proposed EE-BO are the lowest among the six compared algorithms, which shows the advantages of the proposed EE-BO on higher-dimensional optimization problems. On the 200-D Ellipsoid problem, the average results found by GPEME, SA-COSO, ESAO, CA-LLSO, and IKAEA are 82305, 16382, 17616, 9144.2, and 22051, respectively. In comparison, the results found by the proposed EE-BO is 5722.8, which is significantly smaller than the compared algorithms. On the 200-D Rosenbrock problem, the average results found by the five SAEAs are 3.10e+05, 16411, 4138.5, 1806.6, and 238.01 respectively. In comparison, the average result found by the proposed EE-BO is 89.414. In addition, we can also find that the standard derivation of the results found by the proposed EE-BO is lower than the results found by the five compared algorithms. In summary, the proposed EE-BO is able to find very competitive optimization results compared with the five state-of-the-art algorithms.

6 Conclusions

The efficiency of the expected improvement criterion in searching decreases as the dimension of the problem increases due to the inaccuracies in the model. To address this issue, we propose the exploitation-enhanced Bayesian optimization (EE-BO) algorithm in this work. By utilizing a local GP model to mitigate the impact of inaccurate models and enhance the exploitation of infill solutions, our approach significantly improves the local search capability of the vanilla BO algorithm. We compare the performance of the proposed EE-BO algorithm with the vanilla BO algorithm and five state-of-the-art hyperparameter tuning algorithms. The results demonstrate that EE-BO outperforms the vanilla BO algorithm on the test problems and achieves competitive or superior performance compared to the five state-of-the-art hyperparameter tuning algorithms.

This work provides an effective solution to improve the performance of the BO algorithm in high-dimensional expensive optimization problems.

References

1. Eriksson, D., Pearce, M., Gardner, J., Turner, R.D., Poloczek, M.: Scalable global optimization via local Bayesian optimization. In: Advances in Neural Information Processing Systems, vol. 32 (2019)
2. Hamza, K., Shalaby, M.: A framework for parallelized efficient global optimization with application to vehicle crashworthiness optimization. Eng. Optim. **46**(9), 1200–1221 (2014)
3. Hutter, F., Hoos, H.H., Leyton-Brown, K.: Sequential model-based optimization for general algorithm configuration. In: Coello, C.A.C. (ed.) LION 2011. LNCS, vol. 6683, pp. 507–523. Springer, Heidelberg (2011). https://doi.org/10.1007/978-3-642-25566-3_40
4. Jones, D.R., Schonlau, M., Welch, W.J.: Efficient global optimization of expensive black-box functions. J. Global Optim. **13**(4), 455–492 (1998)
5. Kandasamy, K., Schneider, J., Póczos, B.: High dimensional Bayesian optimisation and bandits via additive models. In: International Conference on Machine Learning, pp. 295–304. PMLR (2015)
6. Liu, B., Zhang, Q., Gielen, G.G.: A gaussian process surrogate model assisted evolutionary algorithm for medium scale expensive optimization problems. IEEE Trans. Evol. Comput. **18**(2), 180–192 (2014)
7. Shahriari, B., Swersky, K., Wang, Z., Adams, R.P., De Freitas, N.: Taking the human out of the loop: a review of Bayesian optimization. Proc. IEEE **104**(1), 148–175 (2015)
8. Snoek, J., et al.: Scalable Bayesian optimization using deep neural networks. In: International Conference on Machine Learning, pp. 2171–2180 (2015)
9. Sun, C., Jin, Y., Cheng, R., Ding, J., Zeng, J.: Surrogate-assisted cooperative swarm optimization of high-dimensional expensive problems. IEEE Trans. Evol. Comput. **21**(4), 644–660 (2017)
10. Tian, J., Tan, Y., Zeng, J., Sun, C., Jin, Y.: Multiobjective infill criterion driven gaussian process-assisted particle swarm optimization of high-dimensional expensive problems. IEEE Trans. Evol. Comput. **23**(3), 459–472 (2018)
11. Wang, X., Wang, G.G., Song, B., Wang, P., Wang, Y.: A novel evolutionary sampling assisted optimization method for high-dimensional expensive problems. IEEE Trans. Evol. Comput. **23**(5), 815–827 (2019)
12. Wang, Z., Hutter, F., Zoghi, M., Matheson, D., De Feitas, N.: Bayesian optimization in a billion dimensions via random embeddings. J. Artif. Intell. Res. **55**, 361–387 (2016)
13. Wei, F.F., et al.: A classifier-assisted level-based learning swarm optimizer for expensive optimization. IEEE Trans. Evol. Comput. **25**(2), 219–233 (2021)
14. Zhan, D., Xing, H.: A fast kriging-assisted evolutionary algorithm based on incremental learning. IEEE Trans. Evol. Comput. **25**(5), 941–955 (2021)

Balancing Selection and Diversity in Ensemble Learning with Exponential Mixture Model

Kosuke Sugiyama[(✉)] and Masato Uchida[iD]

Waseda University, 3-4-1 Okubo, Shinjuku, Tokyo 169-8555, Japan
kohsuke0322@asagi.waseda.jp, m.uchida@waseda.jp

Abstract. In practical machine learning scenarios, there may be multiple predictors available for the same task. Ensemble learning combines these predictors to obtain a predictor with higher generalization performance. Weighted averaging is one of the most basic methods, which can be generalized by a formulation of an exponential mixture model. In this formulation, the weight optimization in ensemble learning is represented as selecting the predictors to be used by concentrating the weights and maintaining the diversity of the predictors to be used by distributing the weights. It has been theoretically shown that if the balance between these two factors is adjusted to be equal, the generalization performance improves. However, having an equal balance may not always be optimal, as there could be better alternatives. In this paper, we propose a method to obtain a predictor with higher generalization performance by adjusting the balance between selecting predictors and maintaining their diversity. Numerical experiments showed that when there is a large amount of training data and an unbiased label distribution, adjusting the balance can result in improved generalization performance.

Keywords: Ensemble Learning · Weight Parameter Estimation · Exponential Mixture Model · Predictor Selection · Predictor Diversity

1 Introduction

Ensemble learning is a method that builds a predictor with higher generalization performance by combining multiple predictors. In this method, high generalization performance is achieved by selecting the predictors that are given more weight when combined and considering their diversity. Various methods based on different combining methods have been proposed and applied to practical problems, including weighted averaging, majority voting, boosting [12], bagging [2], and stacking [6]. These methods can be categorized into two classes depending on whether multiple predictors are already available. The first class includes methods such as weighted averaging, majority voting, and stacking, which are applied when multiple predictors are already available. The main difference between these methods is how they combine multiple predictors.

This work was supported in part by the Japan Society for the Promotion of Science through Grants-in-Aid for Scientific Research (C) (23K11111).

The second class includes methods such as boosting and bagging, which are applied when multiple predictors are not yet available. These methods involve creating multiple predictors for combining and then combining them.

In this study, we considered the former class, where multiple predictors are already available for the same task. Weighted averaging is one of the simplest examples in this class. To enhance generalization performance using weighted averaging, it is essential to optimize the weight parameters. The optimization of weight parameters can be formulated as a minimization problem with mean squared error as the objective function on supervised data [15]. This formulation can be generalized by representing the predictors as probability density functions, the objective function as KL divergence, and the ensemble predictor as an exponential mixture model [13,14]. Here, the weight parameters of the exponential mixture model correspond to those of weighted averaging.

The objective function in this generalized ensemble learning can be decomposed into to two terms: one for selecting component predictors to be combined and the other for maintaining their diversity [13]. This decomposition mathematically represents the idea of ensemble learning: predictor selection and predictor diversity. Optimizing only the term for selection contributes to concentrating larger weights on higher-performing predictors. Meanwhile, optimizing only the term for diversity contributes to distributing the weights among a larger number of predictors without biasing them towards a small subset. In ensemble learning with an exponential mixture model, the weight parameters are optimized by equally considering the contributions of these two terms. It has been theoretically shown that using weight parameters optimized in this way improves generalization performance compared to individual predictors [13].

However, achieving optimal performance with the exponential mixture model does not always require an equal balance between selecting component predictors and maintaining their diversity. Our experimental results show that the influence of selection or diversity can be excessive depending on the combination of predictors. To adjust this balance, we propose introducing a variable λ into the objective function of ensemble learning using the exponential mixture model. Conventional ensemble learning ($\lambda = 0.5$) is a special case of our method. Our numerical experiments show that selecting λ through cross-validation leads to higher predictive accuracy, particularly when there is a large amount of data and less bias in the labels. Additionally, we found that selection becomes more important when combining with component predictors including those with extremely low performance, while maintaining diversity becomes more important when combining with component predictors of comparable performance.

2 Related Works

2.1 Classification of Ensemble Learning Methods

Ensemble learning is a method that enhances generalization performance by combining multiple predictors, and can be categorized into two classes based on whether multiple predictors are already available.

The first class combines multiple predictors when they are available in advance. This includes weighted averaging, majority voting, and stacking [6]. Weighted averaging calculates the output of the ensemble predictor by taking a weighted average of the individual predictor outputs. Majority voting outputs the most commonly predicted outcome among multiple predictors. Stacking builds a predictor that takes the outputs of multiple predictors as inputs.

The second class creates multiple predictors for combining when multiple predictors are not available in advance. This includes boosting [12] and bagging [2]. Boosting improves prediction accuracy by training weak predictors sequentially and weighting them based on their prediction errors. There are various boosting methods, such as AdaBoost [8] and gradient boosting decision tree (GBDT) [9], which uses decision trees as weak predictors. GBDT is enhanced by XGBoost [5] and LightGBM [11] to handle larger datasets. Bagging creates multiple predictors from multiple training datasets sampled using the bootstrap method and aggregates their predictions. An example of this approach is random forest [3].

2.2   Estimating Ensemble Weights in Exponential Mixture

This paper focuses on combining multiple predictors that are available in advance, which is one of the classes of ensemble methods described earlier. One simple method in this class is the weighted average of multiple predictors. In [13,14], a method was proposed for representing ensemble learning through weighted averaging with probability distributions, as briefly outlined below.

Let us denote the set of all probability density functions (pdfs) on $\boldsymbol{\mathcal{X}}$ ($\in \mathbb{R}^m$) by $\mathcal{P}(\boldsymbol{\mathcal{X}})$ and the set of all conditional pdfs on $\boldsymbol{\mathcal{Y}}$ ($\in \mathbb{R}^l$) given $\boldsymbol{\mathcal{X}}$ ($\in \mathbb{R}^m$) by $\mathcal{P}(\boldsymbol{\mathcal{Y}}|\boldsymbol{\mathcal{X}})$. Let us consider a subset $\mathcal{P}_i(\boldsymbol{\mathcal{Y}}|\boldsymbol{\mathcal{X}})$ of $\mathcal{P}(\boldsymbol{\mathcal{Y}}|\boldsymbol{\mathcal{X}})$, $i = 1, \ldots, M$. Suppose that we have M pdfs $p_i(\boldsymbol{y}|\boldsymbol{x})$ ($\in \mathcal{P}_i(\boldsymbol{\mathcal{Y}}|\boldsymbol{\mathcal{X}}) \subset \mathcal{P}(\boldsymbol{\mathcal{Y}}|\boldsymbol{\mathcal{X}})$, $i = 1, \ldots, M$). Now, we can define a new conditional pdf using these pdfs as follows:

$$\bar{p}_{\boldsymbol{\beta}}(\boldsymbol{y}|\boldsymbol{x}) \stackrel{\text{def}}{=} \frac{\prod_{i=1}^{M} p_i(\boldsymbol{y}|\boldsymbol{x})^{\beta_i}}{\int_{\boldsymbol{\mathcal{Y}}} \prod_{i=1}^{M} p_i(\boldsymbol{y}|\boldsymbol{x})^{\beta_i} \, \mathrm{d}\boldsymbol{y}}, \tag{1}$$

where we assume

$$\boldsymbol{\beta} = (\beta_1, \ldots, \beta_{M-1})^T \in \mathbb{R}^{M-1},$$

$$\sum_{i=1}^{M} \beta_i = 1, \quad \int_{\boldsymbol{\mathcal{Y}}} \prod_{i=1}^{M} p_i(\boldsymbol{y}|\boldsymbol{x})^{\beta_i} \, \mathrm{d}\boldsymbol{y} < \infty \ (\forall \boldsymbol{x} \in \boldsymbol{\mathcal{X}}).$$

We refer to $\bar{p}_{\boldsymbol{\beta}}(\boldsymbol{y}|\boldsymbol{x})$ as an *exponential mixture model*. Then, ensemble learning with supervised weight parameter estimation results in a three-step operation:

$$\widehat{p}_i(\boldsymbol{y}|\boldsymbol{x}) \stackrel{\text{def}}{=} \underset{p(\boldsymbol{y}|\boldsymbol{x}) \in \mathcal{P}_i(\boldsymbol{\mathcal{Y}}|\boldsymbol{\mathcal{X}})}{\arg \min} D_{\mathrm{KL}}(p_*(\boldsymbol{y}|\boldsymbol{x}) || p(\boldsymbol{y}|\boldsymbol{x})), \tag{2}$$

$$\widehat{\bar{p}}_{\boldsymbol{\beta}}(\boldsymbol{y}|\boldsymbol{x}) \stackrel{\text{def}}{=} \underset{p(\boldsymbol{y}|\boldsymbol{x}) \in \mathcal{P}(\boldsymbol{\mathcal{Y}}|\boldsymbol{\mathcal{X}})}{\arg \min} \sum_{i=1}^{M} \beta_i D_{\mathrm{KL}}(p(\boldsymbol{y}|\boldsymbol{x}) || \widehat{p}_i(\boldsymbol{y}|\boldsymbol{x})), \tag{3}$$

$$\widehat{\boldsymbol{\beta}} \stackrel{\text{def}}{=} \underset{\boldsymbol{\beta}}{\arg \min} D_{\mathrm{KL}}(p_*(\boldsymbol{y}|\boldsymbol{x}) || \widehat{\bar{p}}_{\boldsymbol{\beta}}(\boldsymbol{y}|\boldsymbol{x})), \tag{4}$$

where $p_*(\boldsymbol{y}|\boldsymbol{x})$ denotes the pdf of a true probability distribution, $\widehat{p}_i(\boldsymbol{y}|\boldsymbol{x})$ is a pre-estimated pdf for $p_*(\boldsymbol{y}|\boldsymbol{x})$, and $\overline{\overline{p}}_{\widehat{\beta}}(\boldsymbol{y}|\boldsymbol{x})$ is the final ensemble-based pdf using the results of the three-step operation. It is known that $\overline{\overline{p}}_\beta(\boldsymbol{y}|\boldsymbol{x})$ obtained by the second step of the three-step operation in Eq. (3) is equivalent to $\bar{p}_\beta(\boldsymbol{y}|\boldsymbol{x})$ defined in Eq. (1). This formulation is equivalent to weighted averaging with mean square error as the objective function, where the target variable $\boldsymbol{y}$ is assumed to follow a normal distribution with the predictor output as the mean.

2.3   Decomposition of Objective Function in Ensemble Learning

In [13], it was shown that the objective function for optimizing the weight parameters of the exponential mixture model can be decomposed as follows:

$$
\begin{aligned}
D_{\mathrm{KL}}&(p_*(\boldsymbol{y}|\boldsymbol{x})\|\overline{\overline{p}}_\beta(\boldsymbol{y}|\boldsymbol{x})) \\
&= \sum_{i=1}^{M} \beta_i D_{\mathrm{KL}}(p_*(\boldsymbol{y}|\boldsymbol{x})\|\widehat{p}_i(\boldsymbol{y}|\boldsymbol{x})) - \sum_{i=1}^{M} \beta_i D_{\mathrm{KL}}(\overline{\overline{p}}_\beta(\boldsymbol{y}|\boldsymbol{x})\|\widehat{p}_i(\boldsymbol{y}|\boldsymbol{x})).
\end{aligned}
\tag{5}
$$

The interpretation of this decomposition is explained below.

The first term on the right-hand side of Eq. (5) aims to increase the weight parameters of the pdfs that are closer to the true distribution among the set of M pdfs when optimizing the left-hand side of Eq. (5). Thus, minimizing only the first term is expected to concentrate the weight on the pdf that is closest to the true distribution, which is equivalent to selecting component predictors. We refer to this term as the *predictor selection term*.

The second term on the right-hand side of Eq. (5) indicates that the weight parameters of the ensemble predictor $\overline{\overline{p}}_\beta$ should be adjusted to deviate from the M pdfs $\widehat{p}_i$ ($i = 1, \ldots, M$) when optimizing the left-hand side of Eq. (5). Thus, minimizing only the second term is expected to distribute the weights among all pdfs to be combined, which is equivalent to maintaining the diversity of component predictors. We refer to this term as the *predictor diversity term*. Note that the predictor diversity term is independent of the true distribution p_* and can be evaluated using unsupervised data. This key feature motivated the development of an unsupervised ensemble learning method that uses an exponential mixture model with the predictor diversity term as the sole objective function [13].

3   Proposed Method

According to the interpretation presented in Sect. 2.3, the formulation of supervised ensemble learning with an exponential mixture model can be seen as equally considering both predictor selection and predictor diversity and optimizing them together. In [13], it has been shown that optimizing weight parameters by considering an equal balance between the predictor selection term and predictor diversity term can improve the generalization performance. However, it is not always optimal to treat this balance equally; there may be a better balance. This leads to the following hypothesis.

Hypothesis 1. *The balance between the predictor selection and predictor diversity terms in Eq. (5) may not be optimal.*

If Hypothesis 1 is true, the optimal balance is expected to vary depending on the combination of component predictors, as illustrated by the following examples. Example 1) Including a predictor with poor generalization performance and focusing on predictor diversity may result in a higher weight on that predictor, reducing the generalization performance of the exponential mixture model. Example 2) When the component predictors have comparable generalization performance but are diverse, focusing on predictor selection may bias the weights towards a particular predictor, leading to loss of diversity and reduced generalization performance of the exponential mixture model. Therefore, if Hypothesis 1 holds true, the following hypothesis is possible.

Hypothesis 2. *The optimal balance between the predictor selection and predictor diversity terms depends on the combination of component predictors.*

Through the experiments in Sect. 4.2, we confirm the validity of Hypotheses 1 and 2. The truth of Hypothesis 1 suggests that the balance between predictor selection and predictor diversity in existing formulations of supervised ensemble learning with exponential mixture models is not always optimal. Moreover, the truth of Hypothesis 2 suggests the need to search for the optimal balance between predictor selection and predictor diversity. Thus, we propose a supervised ensemble learning method to obtain a predictor with superior generalization performance. This method uses an objective function that optimizes the balance between the predictor selection and predictor diversity terms in Eq. (5).

In our proposed method, we introduce a hyperparameter $\lambda \in [0, 1]$ and define the objective function as follows:

$$\lambda \sum_{i=1}^{M} \beta_i D_{\mathrm{KL}}(p_*(\boldsymbol{y}|\boldsymbol{x})\|\widehat{p}_i(\boldsymbol{y}|\boldsymbol{x})) - (1-\lambda) \sum_{i=1}^{M} \beta_i D_{\mathrm{KL}}(\overline{\overline{p}}_\beta(\boldsymbol{y}|\boldsymbol{x})\|\widehat{p}_i(\boldsymbol{y}|\boldsymbol{x})). \quad (6)$$

When $\lambda > 0.5$, predictor selection is more important than predictor diversity. When $\lambda < 0.5$, predictor diversity is more important than predictor selection. When $\lambda = 0.5$, the objective function is equivalent to that of conventional supervised ensemble learning. When $\lambda = 0$, the objective function is equivalent to that of unsupervised ensemble learning proposed in [13]. Therefore, our proposed method is a generalization that includes the existing supervised and unsupervised ensemble learning as special cases.

Table 1. Outline of Datasets.

Dataset	Abbreviation	Size	Classes	Imbalance
MNIST	MNIST	70000	10	No
Fashion-MNIST	F-MNIST	70000	10	No
Kuzushiji-MNIST	K-MNIST	70000	10	No
Sensorless Drive Diagnosis	Sensorless	58509	11	No
volkert	volkert	58310	10	Yes
Bank Marketing	Bank	45211	2	Yes

4   Experiments

In this section, we verify the hypotheses presented in Sect. 3 and evaluate our proposed method using different datasets and component predictors. We describe the experimental setup in Sect. 4.1 and present our experiment to confirm the hypotheses in Sect. 4.2. In Sect. 4.3, we compare the performance of our proposed method with that of the existing method on practical classification tasks.

4.1   Datasets and Experimental Settings

We conducted classification experiments using datasets from the UCI repository [7] and OpenML [16]. The details of the datasets, including names, abbreviations, total data size, number of classes, and whether they are unbalanced, are summarized in Table 1. We normalized or standardized the features in each dataset as needed. For each dataset, we sampled training data to train component predictors, test data to evaluate component predictors and the ensemble predictor, and training data to optimize weight parameters of the ensemble predictor using simple random sampling without replacement. In all experiments, we used five component predictors, each trained on a different set of 200 samples. We used 40,000 test samples to evaluate component predictors and an ensemble predictor obtained by combining them. The number of training data for optimizing weight parameters was set for each experiment.

We used several algorithms to train component predictors to provide diversity in subsequent experiments: logistic regression (LR) [1], support vector machine (SVM) [1], K nearest neighbors (KNN) [1], naive Bayes with Gaussian model (GNB) [10], and random forest (RF) [3]. The number of neighborhoods in KNN was set to the number of classes of the target variable. The number of RF decision trees was set to 100. More details of the configuration and implementation are available at https://github.com/KOHsEMP/balancing_ensemble.

Table 2 summarizes the average results of five experiments, where each predictor was trained on 200 randomly selected training samples and evaluated on the same 40,000 test samples. From this table, it can be seen that the accuracy of LR on MNIST is high, while that of GNB is low. Similarly, for other datasets,

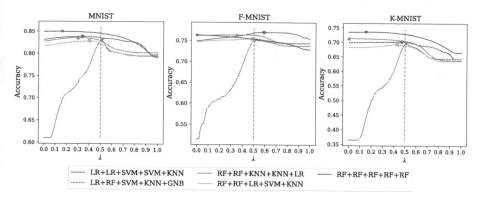

Fig. 1. Transition of λ and accuracy on test data.

Table 2. Performance of component models.

Dataset	LR	SVM	KNN	GNB	RF
MNIST	0.7948	0.7043	0.7002	0.5710	0.7865
F-MNIST	0.7380	0.6328	0.6553	0.4752	0.7316
K-MNIST	0.6438	0.5691	0.5908	0.3545	0.6410
Sensorless	0.4212	0.3424	0.4627	0.7231	0.8444
volkert	0.4378	0.4929	0.4366	0.3263	0.4807
Bank	0.8866	0.8813	0.8796	0.3268	0.8902

we found that there are different predictors with high and low accuracy. Combining predictors with varying performance allows us to investigate the behavior of ensemble learning for different combinations, including those with predictors of low or comparable performance. Note that the component predictors used in the experiments differed from those shown in Table 2, as they were trained using randomly selected training samples for each experiment.

4.2   Verification of Hypotheses and Properties of Proposed Method

This section contains two experiments. The first experiment verified the hypotheses described in Sect. 3. The second experiment confirmed that changes in the balance between selecting predictors and maintaining their diversity correspond to changes in the optimized weight parameters, as discussed in Sect. 2.3.

Verification of Hypotheses. Figure 1 shows the relationship between λ and test accuracy for different datasets and component predictor combinations. Accuracy was averaged over five experiments. The dotted line representing $\lambda = 0.5$ in the figure shows accuracy for the existing supervised ensemble learning. The plotted points represent the optimal values for each combination. To examine

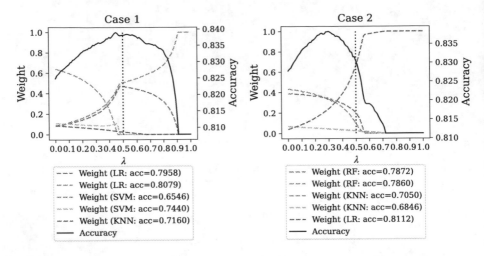

Fig. 2. Correspondence between λ, accuracy on test data, and optimized weight parameters.

the influence of λ in various situations, the combinations shown in the figure include those with large performance differences (green), nearly identical performances (purple), and slight performance differences (others). The number of training data for optimizing weight parameters was 500.

First, we verify Hypothesis 1 that the equal balance between selecting predictors and maintaining their diversity in the existing supervised ensemble learning may not be optimal. Figure 1 shows that the accuracy at $\lambda = 0.5$ is not necessarily the highest on all datasets. Therefore, it is confirmed that Hypothesis 1 is true. Next, we verify Hypothesis 2 that the optimal balance differs depending on the combination of component predictors. Figure 1 shows that in three datasets (MNIST, F-MNIST, and K-MNIST), the inclusion of GNB in the combination (green) results in a decrease in accuracy as λ decreases when $\lambda \leq 0.5$. Table 2 shows that GNB has the lowest accuracy on the three datasets shown in Fig. 1. Thus, it is possible that the observed trend is due to excessive influence from maintaining diversity among component predictors, which in turn led to an unnecessary emphasis on a predictor with low accuracy. In addition, Fig. 1 indicates that when using RF for all component predictors on the three datasets (purple), larger λ values lead to lower accuracy. This may be because the loss of diversity resulted in an excessive emphasis on a slightly more accurate predictor, despite the small performance difference between the component predictors. From the above, it is confirmed that Hypotheses 2 is true.

Weight Transition and Predictor Selection-Diversity Balance. The results of this experiment demonstrate that changes in the balance between predictor selection and predictor diversity correspond to changes in optimized weight parameters, as discussed in Sect. 2.3. Figure 2 shows one of five experiments using the MNIST dataset in Fig. 1. The left vertical axis shows the weight parameter value for each component predictor, while the right vertical axis shows the accuracy of the ensemble predictor for the test data. Cases 1 and 2 correspond to the solid blue and red lines in Fig. 1, respectively. The component predictor accuracies shown in the legend are values evaluated for the same 40,000 test data. The weight parameters were optimized using 500 training data.

In both cases in Fig. 2, an increase in λ from 0 leads to a faster approach of weight parameters of predictors with lower accuracy to 0. In particular, when $\lambda = 1$, the weight is concentrated on the predictor with the highest accuracy, reflecting a focus on selecting predictors, as discussed in Sect. 2.3. In addition, the number of positive weight parameters increases as λ decreases from 1. When $\lambda = 0$, all weight parameters of the predictors become positive, indicating that the weights are distributed. This corresponds to the case where model diversity is emphasized, and is consistent with the discussion in Sect. 2.3. Thus, changes in the balance between predictor selection and predictor diversity and the transition of the obtained weight parameters follow the trend discussed in Sect. 2.3.

4.3   Performance of Proposed Method

The discussion in Sect. 4.2 regarding Fig. 1 suggests that our proposed method can outperform the existing method by choosing an appropriate value of λ. However, obtaining the optimal λ is not always possible in real-world problems. In this section, we investigate whether the proposed method performs better than the existing method in actual classification tasks. To apply the proposed method, we only need to use known training data to determine the value of λ. In this experiment, we used stratified 5-fold cross-validation with the training data to determine the value of λ. We tested 101 different values of λ in increments of 0.01 from 0.0 to 1.0, and the value of λ that produced the best performance in cross-validation was selected.

Figure 3 compares the performances of the proposed and existing methods using multiple datasets and combinations of component predictors. In all figures, the number of component predictors is five, but the number of learning algorithms used to learn them ranges from three to five. When MNIST, F-MNIST, and K-MNIST are used as datasets, these combinations of component predictors correspond to the red, light blue, and green cases in Fig. 1, respectively. The displayed points represent the average accuracy obtained from five trials on the test data, with error bars indicating the standard deviation.

Figure 3 shows that the proposed method outperforms the existing method in many cases on the MNIST, K-MNIST, and Sensorless datasets. We observed that when the proposed method performs better on these datasets, its average value is often above the upper limit of the error bar for the existing method, or the average value of the existing method is often below the lower limit of the error bar for the proposed method. Therefore, the proposed method is significantly superior to the existing method in actual classification problems.

However, Fig. 3 shows that the proposed method performs worse than the existing method on the F-MNIST, volkert, and Bank datasets due to suboptimal λ selection. In particular, it can be difficult to determine λ through cross-

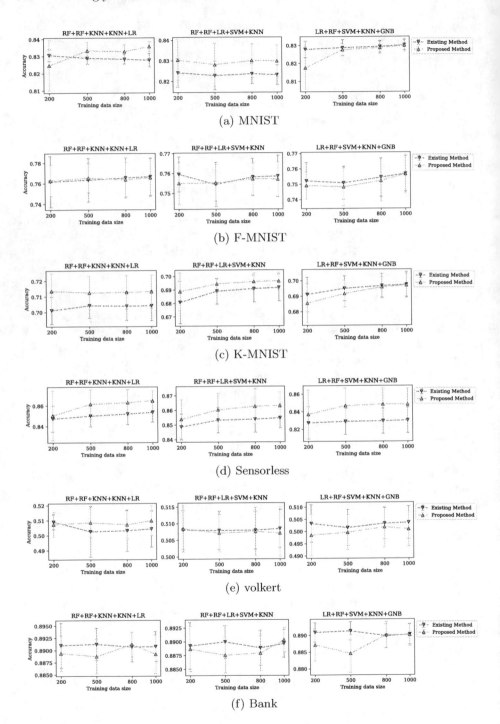

Fig. 3. Performance comparison of the proposed and existing methods.

validation for imbalanced datasets like volkert and Bank (see Table 1), which can result in inferior performance of the proposed method. However, oversampling can help reduce the impact of imbalance. Figure 4 compares the performance of the proposed method with and without oversampling during cross-validation to determine λ, taking the unbalanced data set volkert as an example. We used SMOTE [4] for oversampling. To avoid excessive oversampling, classes with sample sizes less than 0.3 times that of the class with the largest sample size were designated as minority classes, and samples generated by SMOTE were added until the threshold was reached for a minority class. From Fig. 4, we observe that applying oversampling to the proposed method improves its performance when it performs worse than the existing method without oversampling. Therefore, it is probable that label imbalance mitigation through oversampling has led to better cross-validation accuracy.

However, as shown in Fig. 3, the proposed method can perform worse than the existing method, even when the data are not imbalanced, such as in the case of F-MNIST. This can be explained by the trends of the red and light blue lines in Fig. 1. On F-MNIST, unlike MNIST and K-MNIST, the accuracy at the optimal value of λ is close to the accuracy achieved with $\lambda = 0.5$, which is the value used in the existing method. Therefore, even for balanced data, adjusting λ appropriately is crucial to outperform the existing method. Moreover, the proposed method tends to outperform the existing method on MNIST and K-MNIST, but when combined with GNB, the proposed method performs worse. This may be due to the narrow range of λ with high accuracy, as seen from the green line in Fig. 1. On the other hand, Fig. 3 shows that as the number of training data increases, the accuracy of the proposed method tends to be higher than that of the existing method. Although the accuracy of the existing method also tends to increase with more training data, the proposed method shows a stronger tendency towards higher accuracy. These findings suggest that by mitigating class imbalance and using sufficient training data, we can properly adjust λ and enable the proposed method to work effectively.

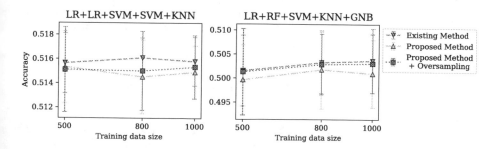

Fig. 4. Oversampling applied during optimization of λ.

5 Conclusion

In this paper, we introduced a novel approach to ensemble learning. Our proposed method optimizes predictor selection and predictor diversity simultaneously by utilizing a supervised ensemble learning method that can adjust the balance between the two factors. Our proposed method is a generalization of existing supervised ensemble learning using an exponential mixture model. Through numerical experiments, we showed that choosing an appropriate balance between predictor selection and predictor diversity can lead to better generalization performance than the existing method. We also emphasized the importance of cross-validation in accurately approximating generalization performance when optimizing this balance. Our results indicate that the proposed method performs better than the existing method, especially for large and balanced datasets.

References

1. Bishop, C.M., Nasrabadi, N.M.: Pattern Recognition and Machine Learning, vol. 4. Springer, New York (2006)
2. Breiman, L.: Bagging predictors. Mach. Learn. **24**(2), 123–140 (1996)
3. Breiman, L.: Random forests. Mach. Learn. **45**(1), 5–32 (2001)
4. Chawla, N.V., Bowyer, K.W., Hall, L.O., Kegelmeyer, W.P.: SMOTE: synthetic minority over-sampling technique. J. Artif. Intell. Res. **16**, 321–357 (2002)
5. Chen, T., Guestrin, C.: XGBoost: a scalable tree boosting system. In: Proceedings of the 22nd ACM SIGKDD International Conference on Knowledge Discovery and Data Mining, pp. 785–794 (2016)
6. David, H.W.: Stacked generalization. Neural Netw. **5**(2), 241–259 (1992)
7. Dua, D., Graff, C.: UCI machine learning repository (2017). http://archive.ics.uci.edu/ml
8. Freund, Y., Schapire, R.E.: A decision-theoretic generalization of on-line learning and an application to boosting. J. Comput. Syst. Sci. **55**(1), 119–139 (1997)
9. Friedman, J.H.: Greedy function approximation: a gradient boosting machine. Ann. Stat., 1189–1232 (2001)
10. Hastie, T., Tibshirani, R., Friedman, J.H., Friedman, J.H.: The Elements of Statistical Learning: Data Mining, Inference, and Prediction, vol. 2. Springer, New York (2009). https://doi.org/10.1007/978-0-387-84858-7
11. Ke, G., et al.: LightGBM: a highly efficient gradient boosting decision tree. In: Advances in Neural Information Processing Systems, vol. 30 (2017)
12. Schapire, R.E.: The strength of weak learnability. Mach. Learn. **5**(2), 197–227 (1990)
13. Uchida, M., Maehara, Y., Shioya, H.: Unsupervised weight parameter estimation method for ensemble learning. J. Mathe. Model. Algorithms **10**(4), 307–322 (2011)
14. Uchida, M.: Tight lower bound of generalization error in ensemble learning. In: 2014 Joint 7th International Conference on Soft Computing and Intelligent Systems (SCIS) and 15th International Symposium on Advanced Intelligent Systems (ISIS), pp. 1130–1133 (2014). https://doi.org/10.1109/SCIS-ISIS.2014.7044723

15. Ueda, N., Nakano, R.: Generalization error of ensemble estimators. In: Proceedings of International Conference on Neural Networks 1996 (ICNN 1996), vol. 3, pp. 90–95 (1996)
16. Vanschoren, J., van Rijn, J.N., Bischl, B., Torgo, L.: OpenML: networked science in machine learning. SIGKDD Explor. **15**(2), 49–60 (2013). https://doi.org/10.1145/2641190.2641198

CIPER: Combining Invariant and Equivariant Representations Using Contrastive and Predictive Learning

Xia Xu[1,2] and Jochen Triesch[1(✉)]

[1] Frankfurt Institute for Advanced Studies, Ruth-Moufang-Straße 1,
Frankfurt am Main, Germany
{xiaxu,triesch}@fias.uni-frankfurt.de
[2] Xidian-FIAS International Joint Research Center, Technology Road 9, Xi'an, China

Abstract. Self-supervised representation learning (SSRL) methods have shown great success in computer vision. In recent studies, augmentation-based contrastive learning methods have been proposed for learning representations that are invariant or equivariant to predefined data augmentation operations. However, invariant or equivariant features favor only specific downstream tasks depending on the augmentations chosen. They may result in poor performance when the learned representation does not match task requirements. Here, we consider an active observer that can manipulate views of an object and has knowledge of the action(s) that generated each view. We introduce Contrastive Invariant and Predictive Equivariant Representation learning (CIPER). CIPER comprises both invariant and equivariant learning objectives using one shared encoder and two different output heads on top of the encoder. One output head is a projection head with a state-of-the-art contrastive objective to encourage invariance to augmentations. The other is a prediction head estimating the augmentation parameters, capturing equivariant features. Both heads are discarded after training and only the encoder is used for downstream tasks. We evaluate our method on static image tasks and time-augmented image datasets. Our results show that CIPER outperforms a baseline contrastive method on various tasks. Interestingly, CIPER encourages the formation of hierarchically structured representations where different views of an object become systematically organized in the latent representation space.

Keywords: self-supervised representation learning · contrastive learning · invariance learning · equivariance learning · active observer

1 Introduction

Recent advances in self-supervised representation learning (SSRL) have achieved performance comparable to supervised methods [17]. SSRL utilizes internal structures of the data as supervisory information. Among SSRL methods, contrastive learning with deep neural networks has shown promising performance [2,15,24].

© The Author(s), under exclusive license to Springer Nature Switzerland AG 2023
L. Iliadis et al. (Eds.): ICANN 2023, LNCS 14256, pp. 320–331, 2023.
https://doi.org/10.1007/978-3-031-44213-1_27

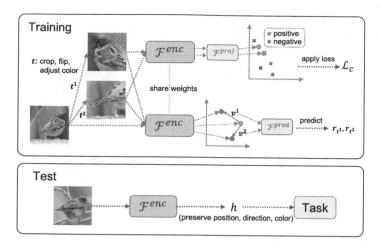

Fig. 1. Overview of CIPER. **Top:** During training, t^1 and t^2 are two randomly sampled augmentations. $\mathcal{F}^{\mathrm{proj}}$ and $\mathcal{F}^{\mathrm{pred}}$ are the contrastive and predictive projectors applied on the same encoder $\mathcal{F}^{\mathrm{enc}}$. The InfoNCE contrastive loss $\mathcal{L}_c$ is applied to the output of the projector $\mathcal{F}^{\mathrm{proj}}$. The prediction head $\mathcal{F}^{\mathrm{pred}}$ predicts the parameters of augmentations r_{t^1} and r_{t^2} given the difference between the representations of the anchor image and the augmented images in the latent space (v^1 and v^2). **Bottom:** During the test phase, the projectors are discarded and the output of the encoder h is used for downstream tasks. Images are retrieved from [11,30] under CC BY-SA 4.0 licence.

Recent progress in contrastive learning has been achieved through strong image augmentations such as random cropping, color jittering, and random horizontal flipping, assuming these operations do not alter the semantic meaning of an image [2]. Augmentations encourage invariance, and representations of differently augmented versions of the same image are made similar, while representations of different images are made dissimilar to avoid representation collapse. However, strong augmentations impose a bias that downstream tasks require little augmentation-related information in the representation. Otherwise, contrastive learning would lose valuable information [14]. For example, when the task is to recognize hand-written digits, while the model learns to be invariant to in-plane image rotations, it will be incapable of distinguishing "9" from "6".

On the other hand, equivariant representation learning aims to learn features that change according to augmentations. This learning paradigm has been facilitated using contrastive and predictive learning paradigms for static images and time series [4–7,12,36]. Equivariant representations, like their counterpart, may focus on certain features and ignore other useful information. In the context of self-driving cars, for instance, representations trained to be equivariant to image rotations may focus on the road's direction and ignore cars in images. These representations may be useful for road direction detection, but they may be of little use for, e.g., identifying cars on roads in the context of some other task.

To balance the trade-off between invariant and equivariant features, some recent studies have proposed to combine them [4,25,32,34,35]. Here, we propose a new approach, CIPER (Contrastive Invariant and Predictive Equivariant Representation learning), which trains an encoder with two output heads: one for contrastive learning and the other for predictive learning on augmentation parameters (Fig. 1). This method enables the extraction of both invariant semantic meanings and the factors manipulated by the augmentations. By doing so, CIPER maximizes the use of augmentations without biasing the learning process exclusively towards either invariant or equivariant features. The resultant representations become hierarchically organized: views of the same object become organized into clusters as for contrastive learning methods. Moreover, in CIPER these clusters develop a systematic substructure reflecting augmentation-related information.

2   Related Work

2.1   Invariant Representation Learning

Contrastive learning is a simple and effective method to promote invariance to augmentations. InfoNCE [31] uses a unified categorical cross-entropy loss to identify positive pairs against negative ones. SimCLR [2] improves generalization by using heavy data augmentations and large batch sizes. Several other methods also bring the representations of two augmented versions of an image together [8]. ReLIC [20] introduces a regularizer to isolate style information. A simulated dataset is used in [14] to control the separation of content and style. Our method extends the conventional contrastive learning by preserving augmentation-related information.

2.2   Equivariant Representation Learning

Inspired by the equivariant map in mathematics, representation learning with deep neural networks seeks to create equivariant representations that reflect the applied transformations [3]. Equivariant representation paradigms aim to create representation spaces that are mathematically equivariant to group actions (image transformations) [3]. Other methods aim to create representations that are equivariant to augmentation parameters such as image transformation matrices [5,36], pre-defined tasks like four-fold rotation prediction [7], and temporal auxiliary tasks for time series [12]. Prelax [32] uses residual relaxation and additional augmentations to encourage equivariance beyond invariance. CIPER predicts all augmentation parameters given the difference vector between the original image representation and the augmented one, unlike Prelax, which requires a target network, extra augmentations, and residual relaxation. CIPER adopts the SimCLR network structure and augmentations without any additional modifications.

2.3   Combining Invariant and Equivariant Learning

Several methods have been proposed to combine invariant and equivariant representations. Closest to our work are [4,25,32,34,35]. Specifically, LooC [34] learns subspaces invariant to all but one augmentation, which may limit extension to many augmentations. E-SSL [4] uses an extra prediction head to predict an augmentation parameter, arguing that representations should be either invariant or equivariant to a specific augmentation. However, we show that both can be encoded at the same time as clusters with organized substructures. In addition, we do not pick specific augmentations other than those already used in SimCLR while E-SSL chooses a four-fold rotation augmentation for the equivariant objective which requires training on 4 extra augmented versions of an image, resulting in a huge training burden. A residual relaxation-based method [32] has also been proposed. It uses extra augmentations to encourage equivariance beyond invariance for few-shot learning problems. Our method combines contrastive and predictive objectives to naturally encode both invariant and equivariant information without explicit relaxation. Furthermore, although these methods manage to encode both, it is still unclear how equivariant information is encoded in the representations, while CIPER manages to incorporate this as substructures within a clustered representation.

3 Methods

Given unlabelled high-dimensional data $x \in \mathbb{R}^m$, self-supervised representation learning trains an encoder network $\mathcal{F}^{\text{enc}}$ to extract low-dimensional representations $h = \mathcal{F}^{\text{enc}}(x) \in \mathbb{R}^n, n \ll m$, that are informative for a downstream task target variable g. The goal is to maximize $\mathcal{I}(h; g)$. Augmentations are general transformations $t \in \mathcal{T}$ that create augmented views x^t from raw data x as proxies for downstream tasks. Typically, a single augmentation t is a sequence of random image operations parameterized by r_t. For example, if t is random cropping at (i, j) and random horizontal flipping with an indicator p, then $r_t = [i, j, p]$. For some datasets we also consider time-based augmentations, where an active observer can change the viewpoint of an object and/or view it against a different background [1]. In the following, we refer to these as *dataset-provided augmentations* (see below). Throughout the paper, augmentations are performed in a fixed order (see Sect. 3.4).

3.1 Invariant Contrastive Learning

Contrastive learning generates representations that are invariant to data augmentations. For an anchor data point x_i, its two differently augmented versions $x_i^{t_i^1}$ and $x_i^{t_i^2}$ are positive samples, and different data points with different augmentations $x_j^{t_j^1}$ and $x_j^{t_j^2}$ are negative samples. The goal is to maximize the similarities between positive pairs and minimize the similarities between positive and negative samples. CIPER adopts SimCLR, in which a batch of N data points are augmented twice and encoded by $\mathcal{F}^{\text{enc}}$ to obtain representations h_i. The representations are projected by $\mathcal{F}^{\text{proj}}$ to z where the InfoNCE loss $\mathcal{L}_c$ is applied. If the training fully converges, which is rare in practice, then $z_i^{t_i^1}$, $z_i^{t_i^2}$ and z_i

Table 1. Augmentations and their parameters. p indicates the probability of applying a particular augmentation. Binary parameters are indicators for whether an image is augmented. Viewpoint and Session are dataset-specific augmentations (See Sect. 3.4). Parameters are randomly drawn and returned using the TorchVision package [19].

Augmentation	Type	# Dims	Meaning	Setting
Cropping	continuous	4	[location x, location y, height, width]	$p = 1$; scale: (0.2, 1.0)
Horizontal Flip	binary	1	0 for not flipped, 1 otherwise	$p = 0.8$
Color Jittering	continuous	4	[brightness, contrast, saturation, hue]	$p = 0.8$
Grayscale	binary	1	0 for grayscale, 1 otherwise	$p = 0.2$
Viewpoint(TDW only)	continuous	3	change in azimuth, elevation, distance	$p = 1$; normalized
Session(CORe50 only)	categorical	1	target session	$p = 1$

should be indistinguishable. Similarly, h should also reflect little information about the augmentations. We show in Sect. 4 that some augmentation-related information remains in the latent representation despite the contrastive learning objective. Furthermore, reducing $\mathcal{I}\left(\mathcal{F}^{\mathrm{enc}}\left(x^t\right); t\right)$ is not guaranteed to increase $\mathcal{I}\left(\mathcal{F}^{\mathrm{enc}}\left(x^t\right); g\right)$.

3.2 Equivariant Predictive Learning

We consider equivariant representations that change with input data according to an equivariant map from mathematics. The representation reflects how image augmentations alter data rather than preserving input information. Equivariant representation learning maximizes $\mathcal{I}\left(\mathcal{F}^{\mathrm{enc}}\left(x^t\right); t\right)$ where $\mathcal{F}^{\mathrm{enc}}$ is an encoder with a prediction head and loss as in Sect. 3.1. This may increase $\mathcal{I}\left(\mathcal{F}^{\mathrm{enc}}\left(x^t\right); g\right)$ if t affects task g. We use static image augmentations from SimCLR (Table 1) with 10 dimensions and dataset-specific special augmentations (Sect. 3.4). In CIPER, we add a predictor $\mathcal{F}^{\mathrm{pred}}$ to $\mathcal{F}^{\mathrm{enc}}$ to predict augmentation parameters, thereby maximizing $\mathcal{I}\left(\mathcal{F}^{\mathrm{enc}}\left(x^t\right); r_t\right)$. This is straightforward and easy to implement. Following Sect. 3.1, we augment each image twice as a pair. For an anchor image x_i and its augmentation $x_i^{t_i^1}$, the prediction head $\mathcal{F}^{\mathrm{pred}}$ takes their representation difference $h_i - h_i^{t_i^1}$ as input and feeds it into the prediction objective. For static augmentations, we normalize the target (the parameters) across batches and use the mean squared error (MSE) loss:

$$
\mathcal{L}_p = -\frac{\sum_i^N \left(\sum_k^M \left(r_k^{t_i^1} - \hat{r}_k^{t_i^1}\right)^2 + \sum_k^M \left(r_k^{t_i^2} - \hat{r}_k^{t_i^2}\right)^2\right)}{2 \cdot N \cdot M}, \tag{1}
$$

where $\hat{r}$ is the output of the prediction head, M is the total number of dimensions of the augmentations and N is the batch size. For dataset-provided augmentations, we use cross-entropy for categorical and MSE for continuous parameters.

3.3 Combining Invariant and Equivariant Representations

To allow the combination of invariant and equivariant learning, we simply apply at the same time the InfoNCE loss on the output z of the prediction head and the prediction loss (Eq. 1) on the output $\hat{r}$ of the prediction head. The total loss is then:

$$\mathcal{L} = \mathcal{L}_c + \alpha \cdot \mathcal{L}_p, \qquad (2)$$

where α is the weighting hyper-parameter of the predictive loss. We use $\alpha = 1.0$ for CIPER except for the ablation study described below. After training, we discard both heads and use only the encoder for h. Combining two counteracting objectives may seem counter-intuitive, but Sect. 4 shows that h benefits from both.

3.4   Datasets, Augmentations, Experimental Setup

We evaluate our method on CIFAR10 [13] and two image datasets with time-based augmentations: CORe50 [18] and TDW [27]. CORe50 contains videos of objects (e.g., cups, balls) in different environments (e.g., kitchen, garden), called sessions. We use 2 sessions for training and 9 for testing to avoid trivial session encoding. TDW consists of sequences of rendered objects from different perspectives. We follow the split in [27]. A common augmentation [27] is sampling the next image in the sequence as the positive pair for contrastive learning. However, this type of augmentation lacks the ability to be parameterized. We propose new augmentations using the view and session parameters of TDW and CORe50, respectively. In TDW, we manipulate the 3D view (azimuth, elevation, distance) of an object. In CORe50, we use 11 session categories (2 for training). An object is augmented by randomly changing the session and the target session label becomes the augmentation parameter. We call these "Dataset Aug." in Table 2. We also apply standard image transformations ("Image Aug.") from SimCLR (see Table 1). We compare these augmentations on CIFAR10, CORe50 and TDW.

We use ResNet18 [9] as our encoder backbone with a 3×3 convolutional kernel and no max pooling in the first layer, as in SimCLR [2]. The projection head is a two-layered MLP [26] with 2048 hidden units in each layer and batch normalization [10] and ReLU [22] after each layer, following E-SSL [4]. The predictor is another two-layered MLP with 512 hidden units and Layer-Norm [16] and ReLU after the first layer. The output dimension depends on the augmentation parameters to be predicted. See Table 1 for more details on the augmentations. For standard image augmentations, we use TorchVision [19] with a wrapper to apply random augmentations and access their parameters. To facilitate easier encoding of relative position information for the encoder, we concatenate Cartesian coordinates with RGB-channels for positional encoding as in [21]. We use stochastic gradient descent (SGD) with 0.03 initial learning rate (cosine decay), 5×10^{-4} weight decay and 0.9 momentum. We train both networks for 800/100 epochs with 256/64 batch size on CIFAR10/TDW and CoRE50 using Sect. 3 losses. We freeze the encoder and train a linear layer on top of it for linear evaluation as in SimCLR. For CIFAR10, we use training data and test accuracy. For TDW and CORe50, we also train a regressor/classifier for view/session identification. For CORe50, we sample from 9 unseen sessions for both training and test sets. The linear layer is trained for 100 epochs with SGD

Table 2. CORe50 and TDW Results. The object and session classification accuracy (%) are referred to as Obj Acc. and Sess Acc., respectively. For the TDW dataset, we mark the regression coefficient of determination of the view as View R^2. Regular image-based augmentations and dataset-specific augmentations are marked as Image Aug. and Data Aug. Each reported value is shown as mean ± std across 5 runs.

Method	CORe50 (Obj Acc.)	TDW (Obj Acc.)	CORe50 (Sess Acc.)	TDW (View R^2)
Random encoder	18.44 ± 10.01	60.73 ± 8.39	81.29 ± 5.51	0.11 ± 0.06
Contrastive w/Image Aug.	66.95 ± 0.84	95.91 ± 0.17	99.08 ± 0.09	0.21 ± 0.01
Contrastive w/Dataset Aug.	60.55 ± 0.87	98.32 ± 0.15	96.81 ± 0.61	0.13 ± 0.07
E-SSL w/Image Aug.	59.59 ± 0.68	96.24 ± 0.29	98.86 ± 0.23	0.29 ± 0.03
CIPER w/Image Aug.	**75.43 ± 0.61**	97.36 ± 0.16	**99.97 ± 0.02**	0.52 ± 0.01
CIPER w/Dataset Aug.	67.46 ± 0.41	**98.92 ± 0.41**	99.72 ± 0.07	**0.87 ± 0.02**

(10^{-6} weight decay, 0.9 Nesterov momentum [23,29]) and initial learning rate 1 (decayed by 3.33 every 10 epochs). We report mean accuracy and standard deviations over five runs with different random seeds.

4   Results

We evaluate CIPER on the CORe50 and TDW datasets, which offer additional augmentation choices. We also report the results of classifying the session in CORe50 and regression on the view parameters of TDW datasets. From the results shown in Table 2 we observe that dataset-specific augmentations can achieve better performance than general image-based augmentations. We further find that the contrastive representations would fail to achieve high view identification R^2 score, while CIPER can solve this problem and improve the contrastive method on other tasks. These findings show that the combined CIPER objective retains rich information about the augmentations compared to the invariant objective alone. Another interesting finding is that compared with the untrained randomly-initialized encoder, the contrastive representations achieve higher session classification accuracy on CORe50. Furthermore, we evaluate our encoder on CIFAR10 with the contrastive objective and with CIPER, which uses both contrastive and predictive objectives (Table 3). The encoder trained with the predictive network alone can not match the performance of the state-of-the-art contrastive learning methods. This shows that CIPER is robust to situations where one of the two objectives alone would fail. The results support our hypothesis that the invariant representations generally discard the information about the augmentation and the equivariant representations do the opposite, while neither of them achieves the goal of discarding or preserving augmentation information completely. However, by combining both contrastive and predictive objectives CIPER can robustly preserve rich information and achieves better performance in both situations.

In Fig. 2 we visualize the learned representations for the TDW dataset. We use PacMap [33] to reduce the dimension of the representations to 2, revealing a clustering of learned representations with the contrastive and the full CIPER

Table 3. Linear classification accuracy (%) on CIFAR10. The "(n×)" means that n augmented/original images are used for one image sample during training. For a fair comparison, only the methods with the SimCLR backbone are shown. The results of SimCLR and E-SSL are retrieved from [4].

Method	Acc.
SimCLR (2×)	91.1
SimCLR (re-production) (2×)	91.7 ± 0.1
E-SSL (6×)	94.1 ± 0.0
Predictive (3×)	53.4 ± 2.3
CIPER (3×)	92.2 ± 0.3

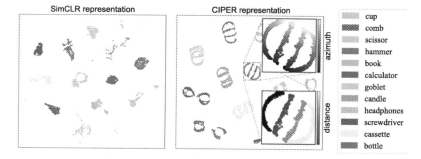

Fig. 2. PacMap [33] representation visualizations of the TDW dataset after 100 epochs of training with dataset-specifc augmentations. **Left:** representations with SimCLR objective. **Right:** representations with CIPER objective. Note how CIPER encodes and systematically organizes view point information without losing the ability to cluster representations of the same object.

objective. We can see that the contrastive objective drives representations to form compact clusters of objects, while the CIPER objective also encodes structure related to the augmentations.

To further illustrate the representations learned by CIPER, we adopt the FullGrad method [28] on CORe50 using the dataset-specific augmentation and the linear object classifier obtained at test phase to generate saliency maps as shown in Fig. 3. Since CIPER retains information about the object as well as the augmentation (in this case: against which background the object is seen) the saliency maps cover both object and background. This finding suggests that CIPER could be utilized to learn disentangled representations of objects against backgrounds.

To study what augmentations contribute most to the downstream classification task when training with CIPER, we remove each augmentation and test the performance. Similar to the findings in [2], our results in Fig. 4 (left) show that every augmentation benefits the downstream task while random cropping and color jittering contribute most to the performance.

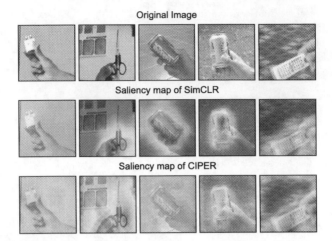

Fig. 3. Example FullGrad [28] saliency maps of images from the CORe50 dataset for the encoders trained with SimCLR and CIPER (ours). The augmentations used are the data-specific augmentation defined in Sect. 3.4. As the prediction head seeks to identify the recording session in CORe50, CIPER also pays attention to the background.

Next, to study the impact of the prediction head, we vary the weighting hyper-parameter α and conduct experiments on TDW and CORe50. Results are shown in Fig. 4 (right). Intermediate values of α lead to highest object classification accuracy on both TDW and CORe50, as well as higher session classification accuracy and lower view regression R^2 score on CORe50 and TDW, respectively. Based on this, we set $\alpha = 1$ as default for other experiments.

5   Discussion

We have proposed a new method (CIPER) for combining invariant and equivariant objectives in self-supervised representation learning. Invariance is promoted via the popular SimCLR method. For equivariance we adopted a prediction approach that learns to estimate the parameters of the augmentations applied to the input data. In the test phase, the output heads are simply discarded and the encoder is used for downstream tasks.

Experiments show the benefits of our method compared to similar state-of-the-art works. In particular, we show that the incorporation of the equivariant objective of CIPER improves the representation.

The use of the TDW and CORe50 datasets allowed us to consider an *active observer* that can manipulate the view of an object, since the used augmentations were essentially view point (TDW) and background (CORe50) changes. The incorporation of the predictive objective is therefore related to the difference between a passive observer that only sees different views of an object and an active observer that has access to the information *how* the view changed between two positive samples. CIPER exploits this additional information to learn an

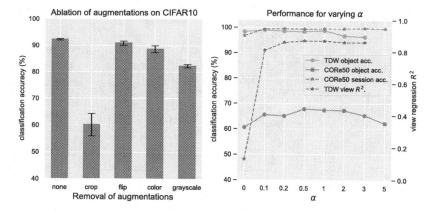

Fig. 4. Ablation studies. **Left:** CIFAR10 object classification accuracy for ablation of single augmentations. **Right:** Effect of varying α. Object/Session classification accuracy on TDW and CORe50 (solid) and view regression R^2 score on TDW (dotted). Training with $\alpha > 3$ is unstable on TDW.

improved representation. This suggests that learning in biological vision systems may also benefit from active control over the viewpoint by an active observer. In fact, the combination of invariant and equivariant representation learning objectives used in CIPER is reminiscent of the separation of the primate visual system into a so-called ventral or "what" stream for invariant object recognition and a so-called dorsal or "where/how" stream for physical interaction with objects. This may reflect a general design principle for versatile vision systems capable of supporting qualitatively different tasks.

Acknowledgements. This research was supported by the research group ARENA (Abstract Representations in Neural Architectures) of the Deutsche Forschungsgemeinschaft (DFG) under grant agreement TR 881/10-1. We also acknowledge support by "The Adaptive Mind" and "The Third Wave of Artificial Intelligence," funded by the Excellence Program of the Hessian Ministry of Higher Education, Science, Research and Art. JT is supported by the Johanna Quandt foundation.

References

1. Aubret, A., Ernst, M., Teulière, C., Triesch, J.: Time to augment contrastive learning. arXiv preprint arXiv:2207.13492 (2022)
2. Chen, T., Kornblith, S., Norouzi, M., Hinton, G.: A simple framework for contrastive learning of visual representations. In: International Conference on Machine Learning, pp. 1597–1607. PMLR (2020)
3. Cohen, T., Welling, M.: Group equivariant convolutional networks. In: Balcan, M.F., Weinberger, K.Q. (eds.) Proceedings of The 33rd International Conference on Machine Learning. Proceedings of Machine Learning Research, vol. 48, pp. 2990–2999. PMLR, New York, New York, USA, 20–22 June 2016

4. Dangovski, R., et al.: Equivariant contrastive learning. arXiv e-prints arXiv:2111.00899, October 2021

5. Feng, Z., Xu, C., Tao, D.: Self-supervised representation learning by rotation feature decoupling. In: Proceedings of the IEEE/CVF Conference on Computer Vision and Pattern Recognition, pp. 10364–10374 (2019)

6. Gidaris, S., Bursuc, A., Komodakis, N., Pérez, P., Cord, M.: Boosting few-shot visual learning with self-supervision. In: Proceedings of the IEEE/CVF International Conference on Computer Vision, pp. 8059–8068 (2019)

7. Gidaris, S., Singh, P., Komodakis, N.: Unsupervised representation learning by predicting image rotations. arXiv e-prints arXiv:1803.07728, March 2018

8. He, K., Fan, H., Wu, Y., Xie, S., Girshick, R.: Momentum contrast for unsupervised visual representation learning. In: Proceedings of the IEEE/CVF Conference on Computer Vision and Pattern Recognition, pp. 9729–9738 (2020)

9. He, K., Zhang, X., Ren, S., Sun, J.: Deep residual learning for image recognition. In: Proceedings of the IEEE Conference on Computer Vision and Pattern Recognition, pp. 770–778 (2016)

10. Ioffe, S., Szegedy, C.: Batch normalization: accelerating deep network training by reducing internal covariate shift. In: International Conference on Machine Learning, pp. 448–456. PMLR (2015)

11. Italian: English: Italian Sparrow pair, January 2009

12. Jenni, S., Jin, H.: Time-equivariant contrastive video representation learning. In: Proceedings of the IEEE/CVF International Conference on Computer Vision, pp. 9970–9980 (2021)

13. Krizhevsky, A.: Learning multiple layers of features from tiny images. Technical report, Computer Science, University of Toronto (2009)

14. von Kügelgen, J., et al.: Self-supervised learning with data augmentations provably isolates content from style. In: Advances in Neural Information Processing Systems, vol. **34**, pp. 16451–16467 (2021)

15. Laskin, M., Srinivas, A., Abbeel, P.: CURL: contrastive unsupervised representations for reinforcement learning. In: International Conference on Machine Learning, pp. 5639–5650. PMLR (2020)

16. Lei Ba, J., Kiros, J.R., Hinton, G.E.: Layer normalization. arXiv e-prints arXiv:1607.06450, July 2016

17. Liu, X., et al.: Self-supervised learning: Generative or contrastive. IEEE Trans. Knowl. Data Eng. (2021)

18. Lomanco, V., Maltoni, D.: CORe50: a new dataset and benchmark for continual object recognition. In: Proceedings of the 1st Annual Conference on Robot Learning, pp. 17–26 (2017)

19. Marcel, S., Rodriguez, Y.: Torchvision the machine-vision package of torch. In: Proceedings of the 18th ACM International Conference on Multimedia, pp. 1485–1488 (2010)

20. Mitrovic, J., McWilliams, B., Walker, J., Buesing, L., Blundell, C.: Representation learning via invariant causal mechanisms. arXiv e-prints arXiv:2010.07922 (Oct 2020)

21. Murase, R., Suganuma, M., Okatani, T.: How can CNNs use image position for segmentation? arXiv e-prints arXiv:2005.03463, May 2020

22. Nair, V., Hinton, G.E.: Rectified linear units improve restricted Boltzmann machines. In: Fürnkranz, J., Joachims, T. (eds.) Proceedings of the 27th International Conference on Machine Learning (ICML-10), 21–24 June 2010, Haifa, Israel, pp. 807–814. Omnipress (2010)

23. Nesterov, Y.: A method for solving the convex programming problem with convergence rate $o(1/k^2)$. Proc. USSR Acad. Sci. **269**, 543–547 (1983)
24. Radford, A., et al.: Learning transferable visual models from natural language supervision. In: International Conference on Machine Learning, pp. 8748–8763. PMLR (2021)
25. Rizve, M.N., Khan, S., Khan, F.S., Shah, M.: Exploring complementary strengths of invariant and equivariant representations for few-shot learning. In: Proceedings of the IEEE/CVF Conference on Computer Vision and Pattern Recognition, pp. 10836–10846 (2021)
26. Rumelhart, D.E., Hinton, G.E., Williams, R.J.: Learning internal representations by error propagation. Technical report, California University San Diego La Jolla Institute for Cognitive Science (1985)
27. Schneider, F., Xu, X., Ernst, M.R., Yu, Z., Triesch, J.: Contrastive learning through time. In: SVRHM 2021 Workshop @ NeurIPS, pp. 1–14 (2021)
28. Srinivas, S., Fleuret, F.: Full-gradient representation for neural network visualization. In: Advances in Neural Information Processing Systems, vol. 32 (2019)
29. Sutskever, I., Martens, J., Dahl, G., Hinton, G.: On the importance of initialization and momentum in deep learning. In: International Conference on Machine Learning, pp. 1139–1147. PMLR (2013)
30. Tadepalli, P.: English: a Western Bluebird sitting on a branch at in Los Gatos, California, March 2021
31. van den Oord, A., Li, Y., Vinyals, O.: Representation learning with contrastive predictive coding. arXiv e-prints arXiv:1807.03748, July 2018
32. Wang, Y., et al.: Residual relaxation for multi-view representation learning. In: Advances in Neural Information Processing Systems, vol. 34, pp. 12104–12115 (2021)
33. Wang, Y., Huang, H., Rudin, C., Shaposhnik, Y.: Understanding how dimension reduction tools work: an empirical approach to deciphering t-SNE, UMAP, TriMap, and PaCMAP for data visualization. J. Mach. Learn. Res. **22**(201), 1–73 (2021)
34. Xiao, T., Wang, X., Efros, A.A., Darrell, T.: What should not be contrastive in contrastive learning. arXiv e-prints arXiv:2008.05659, August 2020
35. Zhang, L.: Equivariance and invariance for robust unsupervised and semi-supervised learning. Ph.D. thesis, University of Central Florida (2020)
36. Zhang, L., Qi, G.J., Wang, L., Luo, J.: AET vs. AED: unsupervised representation learning by auto-encoding transformations rather than data. In: Proceedings of the IEEE/CVF Conference on Computer Vision and Pattern Recognition, pp. 2547–2555 (2019)

Contrastive Learning and the Emergence of Attributes Associations

Daniel N. Nissani (Nissensohn)[✉]

Tel Aviv, Israel
dnissani@post.bgu.ac.il

Abstract. In response to an object presentation, supervised learning schemes generally respond with a parsimonious label. Upon a similar presentation we humans respond again with a label, but are flooded, in addition, by a myriad of associations. A significant portion of these consist of the presented object attributes (e.g. "comprises one long quasi vertical segment"). Contrastive learning is a self supervised learning scheme based on the application of identity preserving transformations on the object input representations. It is intuitively assumed in this work that the same applied transformations preserve, in addition to the identity of the presented object, also the identity of its semantically meaningful attributes. The natural outcome of this intuition is that the output representations of such a contrastive learning scheme contain valuable information not only for the classification of the presented object, but also for the decision regarding the presence or absence of any attribute of interest. Simulation results which demonstrate this idea and the feasibility of this hypothesis are presented.

Keywords: Contrastive Learning · Self-supervised Learning · Learning Representations · Relations · Attributes

1 Introduction

It is our goal in this paper to point out to a computational scheme by which attribute relations naturally and seamlessly emerge as result of sensory perception.

In response to an image presentation a supervised trained neural network such as ResNet (He et al., 2015) outputs a parsimonious label (e.g. "horse"). Unless explicitly supervised trained for another purpose (e.g. Rumelhart, 1990), no additional information is usually extracted from the presented stimulus.

In contrast, and as we know by introspection, when presented with a familiar image, we humans respond again with a label, but are flooded, in addition, by a myriad of associations. These can be divided into extrinsic and intrinsic relations. The extrinsic relations can be expressed as triplets relating the subject image to external objects or, more generally, to the environment ("horse eats grass"). The intrinsic or attribute relations, on the other hand, relate the subject image to its intrinsic properties or attributes ("horse has elongated face").

D. N. Nissani—Independent Research.

It is these fore mentioned intrinsic attribute relations which are the subject of this paper.

Within the field of artificial neural networks it is useful and common practice to divide the task of classification into two stages, namely 1. the non-linear mapping from raw input (say pixel level) representations to linearly separable output representations (by 'linearly separable output representations' we more precisely mean that the set of representations created by samples of a given class can be separated, fully or mostly, from all other samples by an hyperplane); and 2. the manipulation of this fore mentioned hyperplane into its optimal position, by means of training a supervised or unsupervised linear classifier (Zhang et al., 2016; Nissani (Nissensohn), 2018, respectively).

Contrastive learning is a self-supervised learning scheme which has attracted significant attention in recent years. It has achieved classification results which compete well with those of state of the art supervised learning schemes. In a typical implementation (e.g. Chen et al., 2020) it applies 2 'benign' transformations to the raw (input) representation of each sample in a training mini-batch. This is followed by minimizing the distance between both neural network output representations of this transformed sample while simultaneously maximizing the sum of the distances between the output representations of one of these transformed samples and all the other transformed samples in a mini-batch. By benign transformations we mean such that preserve the identity of the perceived object, that is the resulting transformed raw representation can still be visually recognized as belonging to the same class. Permutating the pixels of an image is *not* a benign transformation, while translating, resizing, or mildly deforming or rotating the image is: its associated class can be still clearly recognized. Amongst all benign transformations, the most efficient for contrastive learning purpose are those which when applied to any sample of a given class distribution result in another sample belonging to the same class distribution. The implementation outlined above tacitly assumes that all samples for which distances are maximized belong to classes different than that for which distance is minimized: this seems to be a valid approximation, especially in the large number of classes' scenario.

After contrastive training completion the resultant output representations (as typically captured from a near to last layer of the network) have been shown to exhibit good linear separability and the application of a (supervised) linear classifier to these representations has resulted in competitive classification accuracy (Chen et al., 2020).

At a bird's eye view the core idea behind contrastive learning may be interpreted as the exploitation of symmetry transformations under which the identity or class of a studied object is maintained invariant. Numerous important laws of physics have resulted during the last few centuries from application of symmetry transformations under which some entity (such as the Lagrangian) is maintained invariant and it is thus not surprising that similar principles may successfully apply to pattern recognition as well.

In Sect. 2 we present our main hypothesis regarding the natural emergence of attribute relations. Section 3 demonstrates by simulation the possible validity of our hypothesis and contrasts our contrastive learning results with those of supervised learning. Section 4 points out to related works and Sect. 5 provides concluding remarks and outlines potential future lines of research.

2 Main Hypothesis

We will now present our main hypothesis and the intuition behind it. We pick hand-written digits, such as in the popular MNIST dataset (LeCun, 1998) to concretize and illustrate our discussion, but our assertions are general. Applying translation, resizing, mild rotation or mild distortion to a digit sample input (raw pixels) representation does not evidently change the perceived identity of the object, say a '4' as an example, and thus these may be considered benign transformations. In addition, it would be reasonable to assume that the distribution of the transformed samples closely resembles the distribution of the original (pre-transformed) samples. As result, the output representations of a contrastive learning model trained under such transformations will exhibit good linear separability (separability in the sequel for short). Hence, if presented with a '4', the softmax layer of a trained linear classifier (followed by hard decision) to which this contrastive learning scheme output representations are applied will generally output '0 0 0 1 0 0 0 0 0 0 ', as expected (here the classifier output vector elements represent digits in their natural order i.e. '1', '2', ...'9','0'). Summarizing, transformation satisfies class invariance and distributions similarity, these in turn lead to separability, and, finally, separability results in good classification accuracy.

After some reflection we may be intuitively led to suspect that not only the nature of the observed object (i.e. its class) remains invariant under these transformations. Its semantically meaningful attributes do so as well. For example, for our '4' digit above each of the following attributes: "has one long quasi vertical segment", "has one short horizontal segment", "has one diagonal segment from mid-lower left to upper right" (and many more) will all remain invariant under our transformations.

This is then our main hypothesis: that transformations satisfy attributes invariance and attributes distributions similarity, that these lead to attributes separability and that attributes separability leads to accurate decisions on whether each and every attribute is present or not in the given object sample. Thus in accordance with our hypothesis, from the point of view of contrastive learning classes and their attributes will be treated alike.

We use the term 'semantically meaningful attribute' (and 'attribute' in the sequel for short) to distinguish between this term and the terms 'feature', or 'abstract feature' which are commonly used in relevant literature to describe a feature vector element, and which do not necessarily carry along with them any concrete semantically meaningful property.

To probe into the feasibility of our hypothesis we could in principle multi-label each sample in a dataset with a long list of its attributes; this would be impractically tedious. At the cost of some loss in attribute resolution we will take instead a very simple alternative approach. We notice in the above examples that each of the fore mentioned attributes may be shared by more than one class. For example "has one long quasi vertical segment" is an attribute which, in addition to '4', is shared also by '1', '6', '7' and '9'. With some abuse of language we may thus say that this attribute implies the *super-class* expression '1 0 0 1 0 1 1 0 1 0' which should be equivalently read as "our sample belongs to either class '1' or '4' or '6' or '7' or '9'", but not to '2', '3', '5', '8' nor '0'. Super-class expressions which contain a large number of 1's are implied by highly common attributes, i.e. those which are shared by many classes, and vice-versa. For example, "has curved arcs, closed curves or straight segments" is an attribute shared by all digits and thus implies an all '1's super-class expression. Composite attributes, that is such that are defined by the intersection of several 'simple' attributes (and thus contain in their semantic description several "and"s) will imply, in the limit, a single (or even no) class. An example would be the logical conjunction of the 3 fore-mentioned attributes of the digit '4'. We note that there might be some cases where 2 or more distinct attributes imply the same super-class; this would lead to the fore mentioned resolution loss.

We have 2^{10} super-classes (including 10 'pure' classes) in the MNIST case, each implied by one or more attributes. Following contrastive training completion and provided that our hypothesis is not false, then a trained linear classifier to which the contrastive learning output representations are fed will be able to decide with high accuracy whether a sample belongs to any selected super-class out of the 2^{10} super-classes, or not.

We will call this conjectured surprisingly strong capability of the output representations of contrastive learning by the term 'hyper-separability'.

We would also expect, in striking contrast, that the ubiquitous supervised trained neural network classifiers, such as (He et al., 2015), will not exhibit such hyper-separability of representations, and thus will be able to classify digit samples and infer their labels in a multi-class classification task, but not any more than that.

3 Probing Our Hypothesis

To probe the possible validity of our hypothesis we carry on an experiment utilizing the MNIST (LeCun, 1998; 60000 training and 10000 test samples, 10 classes, handwritten digits) and the balanced EMNIST (Cohen et al., 2017; 112800 training and 18800 test samples, 47 classes, handwritten digits and letters) datasets. MNIST allows us to check the separability of all the 2^{10} super-classes, while EMNIST allows only (random) super-class sampling (due to their huge quantity, 2^{47} in total), but provides a significantly more challenging and realistic task. Both datasets were augmented during training by means of elastic distortion (applied prior to the application of the benign transformations pair), following the suggested scheme and steps of (Simard et al., 2003).

Contrastive learning is generally agnostic to the details of the underlying neural network architecture. We implement here 2 simple fully connected feed-forward neural networks with similar architectures and 2 hidden layers each. One neural network is used for contrastive learning (784, 400, 400, 100 units per layer) and one for a standard supervised learning classifier (784, 400, 400, and 10 or 47 units per layer for MNIST and balanced EMNIST respectively). Several loss functions have been in use within the contrastive learning paradigm. We picked for this work the mini-batch based loss function which was found best for their purpose by (Chen et al., 2020). This loss, denoted $l(i, j)$, is function of (z_i, z_j), the neural network last layer representations (of dimension 100 each) of the transformed pair (x_i, x_j) of a given sample, and of z_k, the last layer representations of all other mini-batch samples x_k. This loss is namely expressed as (see Chen et al., 2020 for details):

$$l(i,j) = -\frac{sim(z_i, z_j)}{\tau} + \log\left(\sum_{k=1}^{2N} 1_{k \neq i} \exp\left(\frac{sim(z_i, z_k)}{\tau}\right)\right) \qquad (1)$$

where $sim(.,.)$ is the normalized inner product (i.e. the cosine similarity), τ is the system temperature, N is the mini-batch size, and $1_{k\neq i}$ is a binary indicator function which vanishes when k = i and equals 1 otherwise. The overall mini-batch loss will then be

$$L = \frac{1}{2N} \sum_{k=1}^{N} [l(2k-1, 2k) + l(2k, 2k-1)] \tag{2}$$

which can be minimized by stochastic gradient descent. We have used $\tau = 1$, N = 1000 and ADAM (Kingma and Ba, 2015) optimization scheme. Again, following (Chen et al., 2020) we use the penultimate layer (and not the last layer) for output representations capture (of dimension 400) for both the contrastive learning and the supervised learning schemes (for which a standard MSE loss was used).

The benign (symmetry) transformations adopted by (Chen et al., 2020) are suitable for the Imagenet dataset (Deng et al., 2009), but not for handwritten characters. We checked the contrastive learning multi-class classification error performance (empiric error probability, P_{err}) of mild elastic distortion (Simard et al., 2003), mild rotation, re-sizing and translation transformations, both separately for each transformation type (standalone) and in selected sequential transformation pairs. We found that elastic distortion alone provides the best performance. This is probably due to the fact that in both MNIST and balanced EMNIST datasets most of the characters are centered (and thus translation does not play a major role), of similar size (same for re-sizing), and of quasi-vertical position (same for rotation). We thus applied elastic distortion alone in all our experiments. Table 1 shows the multi-class test set error probability results for contrastive and supervised learning. The number of training epochs (e.g. 200 for MNIST contrastive learning) was set so that no further loss descent was observed. For both schemes, the output representations (of dimension 400), captured after training completion, were supplied as input to a multi-class supervised linear classifier with 10 (MNIST) and 47 (balanced EMNIST) units at softmax layer, which was trained for 10 epochs.

Table 1. Contrastive and Supervised Learning training epochs and multi-class classification error probability (P_{err}) for MNIST and balanced EMNIST datasets

	Method	Training Epochs	Test Set P_{err}
MNIST	Contrastive	200	0.014
	Supervised	50	0.009
Balanced EMNIST	Contrastive	300	0.186
	Supervised	50	0.132

It should not surprise us that, for similar contrastive and supervised learning network architectures (as those which we applied in our tests), the performance of supervised learning was significantly better than that of contrastive learning e.g. 0.186 for contrastive vs. 0.132 for supervised, in the EMNIST case. This was also reported by (Chen et al., 2020) where in order to achieve similar error performance a wider and deeper architecture was used for contrastive learning as compared to that of supervised learning. But we are studying hyper-separability here (and not classification accuracy) so we may proceed with this.

The error performance results provided in Table 1 will serve as reference points, for checking the possible validity of our hyper-separability conjecture, as follows: multi-class classification has expected random choice error probability of 0.90 (MNIST) and 0.98 (balanced EMNIST) and thus are a much more challenging task than the 2-class super-class decision task ("does this sample belong to a specified super-class, or not?") which has, in average, 0.50 random choice error probability for both MNIST and balanced EMNIST. In order that our hyper-separability conjecture regarding contrastive learning be possibly valid we would thus expect that for contrastive learning, super-class decision error probability will be in general better than multi-class classification error probability. The opposite would be true of supervised learning: since no hyper-separability is expected in this case (there is no force driving towards super-class separability during the training period) then the 2-class super-class decision would have in general worse error performance than the more difficult multi-class classification.

Please refer to Fig. 1 where histograms of super-class decision error probability are plotted for MNIST (for all its 1024 super-classes) and for balanced EMNIST (for 1000 super-classes uniformly randomly chosen from the integer interval $[0, (2^{47} - 1)]$). The multi-class classification error probabilities cited in Table 1 which serve us as references are also shown for convenience in each respective plot.

In the MNIST case, when applying contrastive learning, 93% of the super-classes exhibit *better* (lower) decision error probability than that of the multi-class classification task. This is in striking contrast with supervised learning where 77% of the super-classes yield *worse* error performance.

Balanced EMNIST shows similar results. In this case, in contrastive learning 98% of the super-classes exhibit *better* performance than that of the multi-class classification task, while in supervised learning 68% of the super-classes yield *worse* performance.

Our results above clearly support our contrastive learning related hyper-separability conjecture. Contrastive learning representations carry upon their shoulders not only class but also semantically meaningful attributes information. Supervised learning representations, in contrast, carry with them merely class information.

As mentioned above learning hyper-separable representations is a necessary but not sufficient condition to implement attribute detection. We still need a firing neuron (i.e. a separating hyperplane), which detects or decides upon each of the semantically meaningful attributes of interest (recall – we have at least 2^{47} attributes in the EMNIST case, only a miniscule bunch of these would be typically of interest to us). We can train such hyperplanes either supervised or unsupervised. In the supervised case we should utilize selected attributes labeled samples to train a linear classifier, as we have done for example in our experiments above. In (Nissani (Nissensohn), 2018) an unsupervised learning classifier model has been proposed. Guided by local density estimates, the model gradually shifts and rotates individual hyperplanes until they settle near the density 'valleys' which separate between (separable) classes. See (Nissani (Nissensohn), 2018) for details. Such a model, with slight modifications, can be used for our purpose here as well.

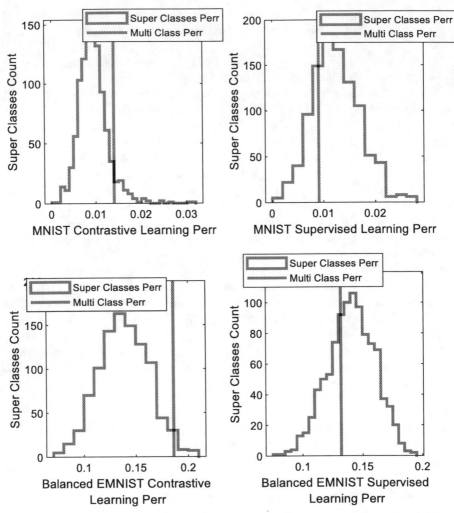

Fig. 1. Super-class decision vs. Multi-class classification error probability. Top: MNIST, Bottom: Balanced EMNIST. Left: Contrastive, Right: Supervised

4 Related Work

We are not aware of any prior neuro-computational research or study related to the spontaneous emergence of attributes associations in an unsupervised or self-supervised learning framework.

The idea that human perception results not only in an identification label but is also accompanied by a large set of associations is old and goes at least as far back as (Locke, 1689).

Connectionist models which supervised learn both extrinsic as well as intrinsic relations go back to the early days of neural networks (e.g. Rumelhart and Todd, 1993; McClelland et al., 1995) and extend up to date (Santoro et al., 2017). One of the main tracks that this approach has taken in later works is that of graph neural net models (Scarselli et al., 2009). A second similar significant track has been that of relational embeddings (Bordes et al., 2013, Wang et al., 2014) in which multi-relational knowledge bases (such as Freebase or Wordnet) are embedded in a metric space wherein the distance between the embeddings of two concepts reflects its semantic similarity. An extensive research corpus exists for both these tracks, see (Zhang et al., 2021) for a survey. Again, the proposed models of these works above are explicitly trained for their respective purposes, and this is done within the supervised learning paradigm.

The intuition lying behind contrastive learning is that identity preserving transformations are naturally available to living organisms (through variation of object pose and lighting, through object manipulation, and so on) and that these, complemented by a (possibly innate) invariance principle prior, can become an important instrument to arrive to useful internal representations. This intuition has guided many researchers, including (Hadsell et al., 2006; Bouvrie et al., 2009; diCarlo et al., 2012; Anselmi et al., 2013).

We have followed in general (Chen et al., 2020) contrastive learning scheme due to its methodical and slim approach. We have replaced their ResNet (He et al., 2015) neural network of choice by a much simpler one (we are not competing on accuracy performance in this work and our datasets are less demanding) and replaced their set of benign transformations (suitable for the Imagenet dataset) with our own. One possible disadvantage of this scheme is its computational and memory complexity for mini-batch processing and storage as reflected in Eqs. (1) and (2) above. There exists a significant line of work on contrastive learning and we could possibly have similarly picked any of e.g. (Grill et al., 2020; Chen and He, 2020; Mikolov et al., 2013; Dosovitskiy et al., 2014; Oord et al., 2018; Bachman et al., 2019).

5 Concluding Remarks

We have provided demonstrative evidence that the output representations of a contrastive learning scheme carry along with them information not only about class identity but also regarding attribute relations of the perceived object. This property which we have denoted 'hyper-separability' is characteristic of contrastive learning and does not seem to show up in supervised learning schemes.

Interestingly, this identity and relational information appears in a single representation package, as a single "bundle", as opposed for example to some neural graph models where object identity and attribute relations are represented as separate entities (nodes and edges). In order to express this bundle contents as a semantically meaningful sentence it would be required to sequentially fetch the information of interest, piece by piece (Bickerton, 1990). To do this one should first extract (decode) this embedded information. A simple way to carry out such information extraction consists, as was described above, in placing linear multi-class classifiers (for identity) and 2-class classifiers (for attributes of interest) as a last 'decoding' neural layer.

Significant efforts (Zeiler and Fergus, 2014; Yosinski, 2015; Nguyen et al., 2016) have been invested in attempts to decipher the attributes or interpretable features which individual neurons of neural nets hidden layers maximally respond to. These studies have been carried solely upon supervised learning networks. After reading the present work, it should not be a major surprise to us that they all resulted in no major findings. It seems that attributes related information not only is available in contrastive learning but not in supervised learning, but also that, perhaps counter-intuitively, it is available in the output representation layer and not embedded within hidden layers; the attribute responsive neurons are output neurons, just like classification neurons, and they are fed by the same output representation layer that feeds the final linear classification layer. This is a more 'democratic' view than the traditional one where attributes have been traditionally viewed as lower level components of a hierarchical structure. In this respect this paper apparent observation and discovery may also result in the Gordian knot cutting of the infamous 'Binding Problem' (Riesenhuber and Poggio, 1999; von der Malsburg, 1981).

It has been suspected for decades that animal learning is mainly based upon some unsupervised (or self-supervised) strategy. The works of (Chen et al., 2020) and others which demonstrate contrastive learning competitive accuracy performance along with this present work (spontaneous attributes association) may provide additional support for the idea that benign transformations combined with a tacit innate principle of permanence or continuity (which are the main components of contrastive learning) constitute one of the basic strategies for animal learning.

We have dealt in this work with the emergence of attributes related associations, namely intrinsic relations. The seamless emergence of environment related associations, i.e. extrinsic relations, remains an open problem, and is left for future work. Perhaps answers to this could be found within the Reinforcement Learning (Sutton and Barto, 2018) paradigm, which purposely deals with the interaction between organisms and their surrounding environment.

To facilitate replication of our results a simulation package will be provided by the author upon request.

References

Anselmi, F., Leibo, J.Z., Rosasco, L., Mutch, J., Tacchetti, A., Poggio, T.: Unsupervised learning of invariant representations in hierarchical architectures. arXiv 1311.4158 (2013)

Bachman, P., Hjelm, R.D., Buchwalter, W.: Learning representations by maximizing mutual information across views. In: NIPS 2019 (2019)

Bickerton, D.: Language and Species. University of Chicago Press, Chicago (1990)

Bordes, A., Usunier, N., Garcia-Duran, A., Weston, J., Yakhnenko, O.: Translating embeddings for modeling multi-relational data. In: NIPS 2013 (2013)

Bouvrie, J., Rosasco, L., Poggio, T.: On invariance in hierarchical models. In: NIPS 2009 (2009)

Chen, T., Kornblith, S., Norouzi, M., Hinton, G.: A simple framework for contrastive learning of visual representations. In: PMLR 2020 (2020)

Cohen, G., Afshar, S., Tapson, J., vanSchaik, A.: EMNIST: an extension of MNIST to handwritten letters arXiv 1702.05373 (2017)

Chen, X., He, K.: Exploring simple Siamese representation learning. arXiv 2011.10566 (2020)

Deng, J., Dong, W., Socher, R., Li, L., Li, K., Fei-Fei, L.: 'ImageNet: a large-scale hierarchical image database. In: CVPR 2009 (2009)

diCarlo, J.J., Zoccolan, D., Rust, N.C.: How does the brain solve visual object recognition. Neuron **73**, 415–434 (2012)

Dosovitskiy, A., Springenberg, J.T., Riedmiller, M., Brox, T.: Discriminative unsupervised feature learning with convolutional neural networks. In: NIPS 2014 (2014)

Grill, J., et al.: Bootstrap your own latent. a new approach to self-supervised learning. arXiv 2006.07733 (2020)

Hadsell, R., Chopra, S., LeCun, Y.: Dimensionality reduction by learning an invariant mapping. In: CVPR 2006 (2006)

He, K., Zhang, X., Ren, S., Sun, J.: Deep residual learning for image recognition. arXiv 1512.03385 (2015)

Kingma, D.P., Ba, J.L.: ADAM: a method for stochastic optimization. In: ICLR 2015 (2015)

LeCun, Y.: The MNIST database of handwritten digits (1998). http://yann.lecun.com/exdb/mnist

Locke, J.: Of the association of ideas. In: Chapter 33 of 'An Essay Concerning Human Understanding' (1689)

McClelland, J.L., McNaughton, B.L., O'Reilly, R.C.: Why there are complementary learning systems in the hippocampus and neocortex: insights from successes and failures of connectionist models of learning and memory. Psychol. Rev. **102**, 419–457 (1995)

Mikolov, T., Chen, K., Corrado, G., Dean, J.: Efficient estimation of word representations in vector space. arXiv 1301.3781 (2013)

Nguyen, A., Yosinski, J., Clune, J.: Multifaceted feature visualization: uncovering the different types of features learned by each neuron in deep neural networks. In: ICML 2016 (2016)

Nissani (Nissensohn), D.N.: An unsupervised learning classifier with competitive error performance. In: Nicosia, G., Pardalos, P., Giuffrida, G., Umeton, R., Sciacca, V. (eds.) Machine Learning, Optimization, and Data Science. LOD 2018. LNCS, vol. 11331, pp. 341–356. Springer, Cham (2019). https://doi.org/10.1007/978-3-030-13709-0_29

Riesenhuber, M., Poggio, T.: Are cortical models really bound by the "Binding Problem". Neuron **24**, 87–93 (1999)

Rumelhart, D.E.: Brain style computation: learning and generalization. In: Zornetzer, et al. (eds.) An Introduction to Neural and Electronic Networks. Academic Press, San Diego, CA (1990)

Rumelhart, D.E., Todd, P.M.: Learning and connectionist representations. In: Meyer, D.E., Kornblum, S. (eds.) Attention and Performance XIV: Synergies in Experimental Psychology, Artificial Intelligence and Cognitive Neuroscience. MIT Press, Cambridge (1993)

Santoro, A., et al.: A simple neural network module for relational reasoning. arXiv 1706.01427 (2017)

Scarselli, F., Gori, M., Tsoi, A., Hagenbuchner, M., Monfardini, G.: The graph neural network model. IEEE Trans. Neural Netw. **20**, 61–80 (2009)

Simard, P.Y., Steinkraus, D., Platt, J.C.: Best practices for convolutional neural networks applied to visual document analysis. In: ICDAR 2003 (2003)

Sutton, R.S., Barto, A.G.: Reinforcement Learning: An Introduction. MIT Press, Cambridge (2018)

vanDerOord, A., Li, Y., Vinyals, O.: Representations learning with contrastive predictive coding. arXiv 1807.03748 (2018)

von der Malsburg, C.: The Correlation Theory of Brain Function, MPI Biophysical Chemistry, Internal Report, pp. 81–2 (1981)

Wang, Z., Zhang, J., Feng, J., Chen, Z.: Knowledge graph embedding by translating on hyperplanes. In: AAAI 2014 (2014)

Yosinski, J., Clune, J., Nguyen, A., Fuchs, T., Lipson, H.: Understanding neural networks through deep visualization. In: ICML 2015 (2015)

Zeiler, M.D., Fergus, R.: Visualizing and understanding convolutional networks. In: Fleet, D., Pajdla, T., Schiele, B., Tuytelaars, T. (eds.) ECCV 2014. LNCS, vol. 8689, pp. 818–833. Springer, Cham (2014). https://doi.org/10.1007/978-3-319-10590-1_53

Zhang, R., Isola, P., Efros, A.A.: Colorful image colorization. In: Leibe, B., Matas, J., Sebe, N., Welling, M. (eds.) ECCV 2016. LNCS, vol. 9907, pp. 649–666. Springer, Cham (2016). https://doi.org/10.1007/978-3-319-46487-9_40

Zhang, J., Chen, B., Zhang, L., Ke, X., Haipeng, D.: Neural, symbolic, and neural-symbolic reasoning on knowledge graphs. arXiv 2010.05446 (2021)

Contrastive Learning for Sleep Staging Based on Inter Subject Correlation

Tongxu Zhang and Bei Wang[✉]

School of Information Science and Engineering, East China University of Science and Technology, Shanghai 200237, China
juk@mail.ecust.edu.cn, beiwang@ecust.edu.cn

Abstract. In recent years, multitudes of researches have applied deep learning to automatic sleep stage classification. Whereas actually, these works have paid less attention to the issue of cross-subject in sleep staging. At the same time, emerging neuroscience theories on inter-subject correlations can provide new insights for cross-subject analysis. This paper presents the MViTime model that has been used in sleep staging study. And we implement the inter-subject correlation theory through contrastive learning, providing a feasible solution to address the cross-subject problem in sleep stage classification. Finally, experimental results and conclusions are presented, demonstrating that the developed method has achieved state-of-the-art performance on sleep staging. The results of the ablation experiment also demonstrate the effectiveness of the cross-subject approach based on contrastive learning. The code can be accessed through: https://github.com/jukieCheung/MViTime.

Keywords: Deep learning · Contrastive learning · Sleep stage · Cross subject

1 Introduction

Sleep is an essential part of everyone's life. Good sleep is crucial in maintaining one's mental and physical health [9,16]. With the rapid development of modern society, high-intensity work and study, irregular lifestyles affect the sleep of most people. Currently, sleep problems have gradually become one of the important public health issues.

Sleep stage discrimination takes an important role to monitor sleep quality and diagnose sleep disorders. Sleep stages are manually classified by physicians with professional qualifications and clinical experience for each sleep data segment. Obviously, the manual classification of sleep stages is time-consuming. Compared with manual classification, the algorithm/model-based automatic classification method is more efficient as an important tool in clinical applications. In recent years, deep learning models have been applied to many fields. With the increasing popularity of deep learning, many automatic sleep stage classification methods based on convolutional neural networks (CNNs), recurrent neural networks (RNNs), and transformers have been developed [12,13,17].

L. Iliadis et al. (Eds.): ICANN 2023, LNCS 14256, pp. 343–355, 2023.
https://doi.org/10.1007/978-3-031-44213-1_29

Those deep learning models are all end-to-end networks, but have been only implemented using supervised learning.

Apart from this, there are still many problems that need to be investigated and explored in the practical clinical application of deep learning models for sleep stage classification. The electrophysiological signals of different subjects inevitably have individual differences, which will affect the actual discrimination performance of the well-trained model. Studies in the literature [8] and [1] have demonstrated that EEG signals are unstable in cases of cross-subject due to user fatigue, different electrode placements, different impedances, etc. Therefore, how to design and implement a sleep stage automatic classification model to deal with the problem of cross-subject is essential.

To solve the cross-subject problem, researchers have applied domain adaptation (DA) methods to EEG signals [5]. However, domain adaptation methods require to access the test data, which cannot guarantee any information leakage problems. At the same time, based on the emerging neuroscience theory of inter-subject correlation (ISC) and combined with contrastive learning methods, a new approach can be provided to explore subject invariance and develop cross-subject analysis. CLISA [15] is such a work that starts from the perspective of inter-subject correlation and uses contrastive learning methods to perform emotional recognition based on EEG. Contrastive learning has been widely used in many fields. For example, in computer vision (CV), the representation of the network can be improved by learning from large amounts of unlabeled data based on the contrast between images [2]. In the existing literature, only one study was found that used contrastive learning for automatic sleep staging [6]. However, the literature [6] did not consider the inter-subject correlation but only compared the signals.

In summary, our study considers using comparative learning methods to distinguish sleep stages from the perspective of inter subject correlation, in order to overcome the impact of individual differences. The ultimate purpose is to provide feasible and implementable solutions for cross-subject sleep staging. The main contributions of this paper are summarized as follows:

1. MobileViT is improved for time series tasks and combined with comparative learning methods to achieve optimal sleep stage classification.
2. Based on the method of comparative learning and the correlation between subjects, a cross-subject solution is designed for sleep staging.

2   Method

2.1   Contrasting Learning Methods

The contrastive learning approach used in this study is mainly based on the work of SimClr [2]. However, the contrastive learning strategy is different including the self-contrast and cross-subject contrast which are designed to solve the cross-subject problem as well as to take into account the characteristics of the sleep EEG signal and the sleep staging task.

In practice, contrastive learning is a way of pre-training, where the input training set is used to initialise the parameters of the network by contrastive learning. The training set is re-input to fine-tune the network and train the classifier at the same time.

Applying contrastive learning to EEG signals requires learning the representation of EEG signals by calculating the similarity between different features in the cosine metric space. Here, note x and y as vector representations of the two EEG signals, and note $sim(x, y)$ as the similarity measure of the two vectors x and y,

$$sim(x, y) = \cos(\theta_{x,y}) = \frac{x^T y}{\|x\|\|y\|}, sim(x, y) \in [0, 1] \tag{1}$$

If the cosine value is close to 1, it indicates that the angle between the two vectors is smaller and the signals are more similar. When the cosine value comes to 0, it indicates that the angle between the two vectors is larger and the signals are more different.

The self-contrast of the model is based on the work of SimClr, where two different transformations of the signal are referred to the work of SSL [6]. The original signal sequence of n epochs is firstly transformed twice respectively, by Cropping and Permutation, to produce $2n$ transformed signals. It is then fed into the network to extract features. During the training process, for each epoch, the similarity of the features is measured by the network. In the remaining $2n - 1$ samples, the corresponding identical signals but with different transformations are found, i.e. the network with the same epoch is taken as the positive pair and the rest as the negative pair. The loss of the cross-entropy function is calculated using the ground truth as in Fig. 1.

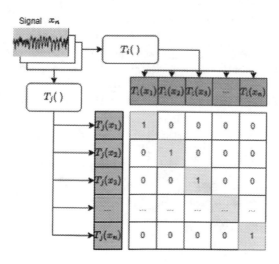

Fig. 1. Ground truth for contrastive learning of EEG signals.

There are totally five sleep stages that need to be identified, i.e. Wake, REM in the rapid eye movement phase, and S1, S2 and S3 in the non-rapid eye movement phase. In order to implement the cross-subject contrast learning model, five epochs (each 30 s) corresponding to the above sleep stages are selected. By using PCA (principle component analysis) for dimensionality reduction, a segment of 30 s is used as a feature for one subject. Assuming that there are n subjects, there are n subject features. Again, two different transformations are performed to generate $2n$ transformed signals that are fed into the network for feature extraction. Different transformations of the same subjects are positive pairs and transformed signals between different subjects are negative pairs. The same cross-entropy function is used to calculate the loss.

In addition, the above two different transformations are specified as,

Cropping: the raw EEG signal $T(t)$ ($t = 1, 2, \ldots, L$) is randomly separated into a number of segments $\{T_1(t), T_2(t), \ldots, T_n(t)\}$; a $T_r(t)$ is then selected randomly and is adjusted to the original length L.

Permutation: the raw EEG signal $T(t)$ ($t = 1, 2, \ldots, L$) is randomly separated into a number of segments $\{T_1(t), T_2(t), \ldots, T_n(t)\}$; those segments are disorganized into $\{T_{k_1}(t), T_{k_2}(t), \ldots, T_{k_n}(t)\}$ where $\{k_1, k_2, \ldots, k_n\}$ is of $\{1, 2, \ldots, n\}$; those segments are then reorganized together.

The above contrastive learning strategy can maximize the difference of a sample from other samples. Meanwhile, it considered the inter-subject correlation to maximize the relevant data. Thus, for cross-subject sleep staging, the trained model can be applied to new subjects. It can improve the utility of automatic sleep stage classification based on deep learning models.

2.2 Sleep Staging Contrastive Learning Model

The sleep stage classification model used in this study was mainly referred to in the literature [4] and [14]. The MobileViT from the literature [10] was adopted due to the ability of the transformer to extract long local features and the ability of CNN to extract global features. The main difference is that MobileViT is an image model. Therefore, we adjusted MobileViT to make it suitable for deep learning models dealing with one-dimensional time series. The developed model is named MViTime. The architecture of MViTime is shown in Fig. 2.

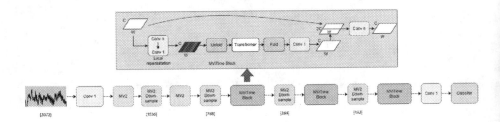

Fig. 2. Network structure of MViTime.

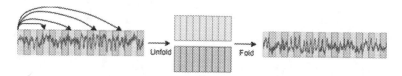

Fig. 3. Unfold and Fold for MViTime.

In Fig. 3, the signal input to the MViTime module is divided into many segments of Tokens by Patch size. A position encoding is performed to represent the characteristic of the signal. Therefore, each Hertzian signal is related to the other signals in the MViTime module. In Table 1, taking the signal input to the MViTime module for the first time as an example, ignoring the channels in the network, the signal length is 768. Among them, a patch size of 2 can divide the signal into 384 tokens. During the process of Unfold and Fold, tokens of the same color will be rearranged and self attention will be done through the Transformer. Among them, tokens with the same color will implement a self attention mechanism after Unfold. By doing so, we can reduce the computational complexity of the self attention mechanism.

Table 1. The structure of MViTime.

Layer	Input
Convolutional Layer	[1,3072]
MV2 Block	[16,3072]
MV2 Block (Downsize)	[16,3072]
MV2 Block	[24,1536]
MV2 Block (Downsize)	[24,1536]
MViTime Block	[48,768]
MV2 Block (Downsize)	[48,768]
MViTime Block	[64,384]
MV2 Block (Downsize)	[64,384]
MViTime Block	[80,192]
Convolutional Layer	

SiLU is used as the activation function and the optimizer is SGD, where the SiLU function is smoother and less monotonic than the ReLU function, which improves the generalisation performance of the model. The batchsize of contrastive learning module is set to 128, mainly to allow the model to be loaded onto the GPU (Nvidia RTX 3090). For the training of the classifier, the batchsize is set to 512, using a cosine warm-up strategy.

2.3   Sleep Staging Classification Model

Figure 4 shows the contrastive learning strategy for the developed MViTime model. The input datasets are entered into the MViTime backbone network for pre-training to initialize the parameters by the contrastive learning method. These datasets are re-entered to perform fine-tuning and train the classifier. The reason for choosing fine-tuning instead of linear probe is that linear probe freezes the backbone to train the classifier, i.e. it is equivalent to fine-tuning the last classification layer. The neural network is supposed to be optimised as a whole to achieve the final classification. It is unlikely that only the last layer is operated. Therefore, it is argued that overall fine-tuning is consistent with the mode of operation of neural networks.

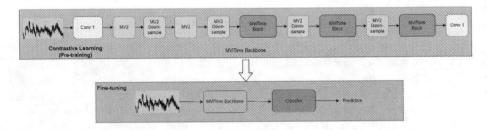

Fig. 4. MViTime initializes the network parameters by pre-training with a contrastive learning method and subsequently fine-tunes these parameters.

2.4   Cross-Subject Strategy for Sleep Staging Based on Contrastive Learning

Figure 5 shows the cross-subject contrastive learning strategy for the MViTime model. In the experiments of the cross-subject strategy, the output of the backbone based on the self-contrast and the cross-subject contrast was weighted and combined. It is then loaded into the network to train the classifier. The main objective was to maximise the difference between the different sleep stages and to maximise the difference between subjects. There are two methods of combination: one is that the contrastive learning modules of the two contrasts are combined but not the classifiers after the two contrasts; another is that the whole network of the two contrasts is combined containing the contrastive learning modules and the classifiers. Both methods are also trained using fine-tuning.

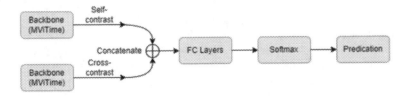

Fig. 5. Cross-subject contrastive learning strategy for MViTime.

3   Experiments

3.1   Dataset

The polysomnographic data in this study were from the Sleep-EDF dataset [7], which contains 197 full-night polysomnographic recordings. The sleep staging markers in the Sleep-EDF dataset are based on the definitions and characteristics of sleep staging corresponding to the R&K sleep staging guidelines. The Sleep-EDF data is divided into two parts, Sleep Cassette and Sleep Telemetry. There are a total of 153 SC recordings (SC = Sleep Cassette) and 44 ST recordings (ST = Sleep Telemetry).

The Sleep-EDF dataset is the publicly available dataset, of which the SC data is also the more commonly used dataset in research work on automatic sleep staging methods. The amount of data used in the literature work varies depending on the processing method: 222,479 record data segments were used in the literature [11], 177,411 record data segments in the literature [5] and 195,479 record data segments in the literature [3]. In addition, the EEG signal in Sleep-EDF contained both Fpz-Cz and Pz-Oz channels. In the literature [5] it is argued that the Fpz-Cz channel is closer to the eye than the Pz-Oz channel and that this channel would be better to capture the characteristics of the sleep state corresponding to the electrical activity of eye movements.

In this study, the same 195,479 recording segments as in the literature [3] were considered and the Fpz-Cz single channel was chosen for automatic sleep stage classification.

Data from 78 healthy subjects from the Sleep-EDF dataset were used for the experiments. The 78 healthy subjects constitute a dataset that is often divided into two datasets, EDF-20 (also known as Sleep-EDF-2013) and EDF-78 (also known as Sleep-EDF-2018), where EDF-20 is the first 20 subjects out of 78 subjects. The distribution of epochs corresponding to the five stages in the two datasets is shown in Table 2.

Table 2. The number and percentage of 30-Second epochs of each sleep stage in the two datasets.

Dataset	Total number	Wake	Stage1	Stage2	Stage3	REM
Sleep-EDF-20	42308	8285	2804	17799	5703	7717
		(19.6%)	(6.6%)	(42.1%)	(13.5%)	(18.2%)
Sleep-EDF-78	195479	65951	21522	69132	13039	25835
		(33.7%)	(11.0%)	(35.4%)	(6.7%)	(13.2%)

3.2   Performance Metrics

To evaluate the classification performance of the presented model, their indicators including Accuracy, Recall and F1-score are calculated based on the confusion matrix. The description of the indicators is described in Table 3.

Table 3. Meaning of Accuracy, Recall and F1-score.

Indicators	Description
Accuracy	This measures the proportion of correctly classified instances among all instances.
Recall	This measures the proportion of positive instances that are correctly identified by the model.
F1-score	This is the harmonic mean of precision and recall. It provides a balance between precision and recall, taking into account both false positives and false negatives.

3.3   Results of Sleep Staging Experiment

Figure 6 shows the confusion matrix and performance metrics obtained by using our proposed method on the two datasets of Sleep-EDF-20 and Sleep-EDF-78, respectively. The row of confusion matrix represents the sleep staging inspected by the physician, while the column represents the automatic classification results of sleep stages. The classification performance compared with the visual inspection is evaluated by three indicators.

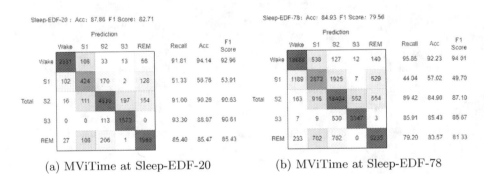

(a) MViTime at Sleep-EDF-20   (b) MViTime at Sleep-EDF-78

Fig. 6. Confusion matrix and performance metrics for MViTime

In addition, the obtained results by our method are compared with other deep learning methods in recent literatures. The results of sleep staging are summarized in Table 4, where the overall accuracy and F1-score, and the F1-score of each stage are given.

The obtained results in Fig. 6 and Table 4 showed that our proposed method of MViTime achieved optimal overall performance metrics (State-of-the-art) on both the Sleep-EDF-20 and Sleep-EDF-78 datasets. According to the comprehensive indicator of F1-score of each sleep stage, the classification performance on sleep stages is rather satisfactory, especially of W, S2, S3 and REM. S1 is a kind of transmission state from wake to sleep, the characteristic is difficult to precisely identify. Although the F1-score of S1 is lower than the other sleep stages, it still reached a fairly well level compared with other deep learning models.

Table 4. Performance comparison of the Sleep-EDF with state-of-the-art methods.

Dataset	Method	Acc	F1	Per Class F1				
				W	S1	S2	S3	REM
EDF-20	DeepSleepNet [17]	81.9	76.6	86.7	45.5	85.1	83.3	82.6
	SleepEEGNet [11]	81.5	76.6	89.4	44.4	84.7	84.6	79.6
	He's work [5]	85.2	78.9	–	–	–	–	–
	AttnSleep [3]	84.4	78.1	89.7	42.6	88.8	90.2	79.0
	XSleepNet [18]	86.3	80.6	–	–	–	–	–
	SSL [6]	87.5	82.1	92.4	51.5	**90.9**	90.6	85.1
	MViTime(Our)	**87.8**	**82.7**	**93.0**	**53.9**	90.6	**90.6**	**85.4**
EDF-78	SleepEEGNet [11]	74.2	69.9	89.8	42.1	75.2	70.4	70.6
	U-Time [12]	81.3	76.3	92.0	**51.0**	83.5	74.6	80.2
	He's work [5]	83.9	77.6	–	–	–	–	–
	AttnSleep [3]	81.3	75.1	92.0	42.0	85.0	82.1	74.2
	XSleepNet [18]	84.0	77.8	–	–	–	–	–
	SleepTransformer [13]	**84.9**	78.9	93.5	48.5	86.5	80.9	**84.6**
	SSL [6]	84.2	79.0	94.0	50.4	86.1	84.5	80.1
	MViTime(Our)	**84.9**	**79.6**	**94.0**	49.7	**87.1**	**85.7**	81.3

3.4 Results of Cross-Subject Experiments

Further experiments are conducted to validate the cross-subject strategy based on MViTime. Here, one subject is randomly selected from the Sleep-EDF-20 dataset. The selected sleep recording is used as the test data and the other subjects are as the training data. The performance of MViTime and the effectiveness of the cross-subject strategy based on MViTime are evaluated and compared. Table 5 showed the comparison results by using MViTime, MViTime+ and MViTime++ of three subjects. MViTime represents the developed deep learning model, MViTime+ and MViTime++ correspond to the two types of cross-subject strategy which is described in Sect. 2.4 and Fig. 5.

Table 5. Effect of cross-subject protocol on five-stage F1 scores for three subjects.

Subject	Method	W	S1	S2	S3	REM
SC4131	MViTime	91.7	60.2	**91.4**	**91.3**	**90.8**
	MViTime+	**92.3**	**71.2**	90.7	90.3	88.5
	MViTime++	91.6	47.6	90.9	90.7	87.5
SC4052	MViTime	83.1	37.3	92.0	85.9	76.4
	MViTime+	85.1	36.5	88.7	83.1	68.1
	MViTime++	**89.4**	**41.4**	**92.6**	**86.5**	**78.6**
SC4032	MViTime	93.0	35.8	86.4	82.3	79.5
	MViTime+	92.6	34.2	86.8	86.7	78.2
	MViTime++	**93.7**	**37.7**	**89.6**	**89.4**	**82.5**

In Table 5, it can be observed that the cross-subject strategy of MViTime++ significantly improved the F1-score of S1 of subject SC4032 and SC4052E0, i.e. from 35.8% to 37.7% and from 37.3% to 41.4% respectively. For subject SC4131, MViTime and MViTime+ are slightly better than MViTime++. It seems that MViTime itself is already performing well enough which may prevent the cross-subject solution MViTime++ from optimising the network parameters further. Overall, however, the presented cross-subject strategy based on inter subject correlation has effectiveness on sleep staging when the deep learning model is facing a new sleep recording with individual differences.

3.5   Ablation

Ablation experiments are conducted to verify the importance of contrastive learning pre-training and the potential for large-scale pre-training by removing the contrastive learning module. The following models are defined: (1) Baseline: MViTime network but without contrastive learning pre-training, (2) Baseline + CL: MViTime network and with contrastive learning pre-training, which is the result in Sect. 3.3, (3) Baseline + CL-Large: MViTime network and with contrastive learning pre-training where the pre-training using the remaining 58 individuals in Sleep-EDF-78 by excluding the 20 subjects of Sleep-EDF-20. The results of the ablation experiments are presented in Table 6.

Table 6. Ablation experiments on the Sleep-EDF.

Dataset	Method	Acc	F1	Per Class F1				
				W	S1	S2	S3	REM
EDF-20	Baseline	86.1	80.0	92.5	46.0	89.6	89.1	82.9
	Baseline + CL	87.8	82.7	93.0	53.9	90.6	90.6	85.4
	Baseline + CL-Large	88.2	82.1	93.2	48.7	90.9	91.0	86.5
EDF-78	Baseline	83.6	76.8	93.9	41.8	86.1	83.8	78.7
	Baseline + CL	84.9	79.6	94.0	49.7	87.1	85.7	81.3

It can be seen from Table 6 that the pre-training module of contrastive learning improves the classification performance of the model. Moreover, in EDF-20, the accuracy of the model is improved from 87.8% to 88.2% when the data of 58 people unrelated to EDF-20 are used for the contrastive learning pre-training. The increment in the amount of pre-training data leads to an improvement in the model effect. The results show that the proposed contrastive learning module is effective in further improving the model performance and demonstrates the potential to bring improvements in model performance when the amount of data pre-trained for contrastive learning is increased.

In addition, the potential of large-scale contrastive learning pre-training on the cross-subject problem is explored. The results are compared in Table 7.

Here, MViTime-58 is using MViTime without cross-subject strategy where contrastive learning pre-training using the remaining 58 individuals in Sleep-EDF-78. MViTime++ is the same as in Table 5.

Table 7. Effect of increased pre-training data on five stage F1 scores for three subjects.

Subject	Method	W	S1	S2	S3	REM
SC4131	MViTime-58	93.5	64.2	91.1	90.2	88.0
	MViTime++	91.6	47.6	90.9	90.7	87.5
SC4052	MViTime-58	89.9	47.3	94.5	93.4	76.9
	MViTime++	89.4	41.4	92.6	86.5	78.6
SC4032	MViTime-58	96.7	53.9	91.3	90.9	88.5
	MViTime++	93.7	37.7	89.6	89.4	82.5

From Table 7, it can be seen that contrastive learning with an increased amount of pre-training data leads to an improvement in the model's performance across the subjects. MViTime-58 achieves significant performance of more than 5% across the three subjects in both Wake and the more difficult S1 which is comparable to or better than MViTime++ in S2, S3 and REM. It is worth noting that MViTime-58 does not require additional inter-subject correlation contrasts compared to MViTime++, but only an increase in the amount of pre-training data for self-contrast. Such a result is due to the internal structure of MViTime, as it has the self-attention mechanism of the transformer.

4 Conclusion

In this study, a contrastive learning method is developed for sleep staging which is combined with the theory of inter-subject correlation. A deep learning sleep stage classification model of MViTime is proposed dealing with single-channel EEG signals. The sleep recording of two datasets from Sleep-EDF is utilized for evaluation. The main improvements of our method are validated and analyzed by several comparison experiments. The ablation experiments show that the contrastive learning module was effective and the importance of contrastive learning pre-training. Besides, the lightweight cross-subject strategy is more meaningful than large-scale pre-training in clinical applications. Whereas, using contrastive learning for pre-training has significant potential to improve classification performance and cross-subject performance when fine-tuning.

Acknowledgements. This research was supported by the National Natural Science Foundation of China under Grant 61773164.

References

1. Buttfield, A., Ferrez, P.W., Millan, J.R.: Towards a robust BCI: error potentials and online learning. IEEE Trans. Neural Syst. Rehabil. Eng. **14**(2), 164–168 (2006)
2. Chen, T., Kornblith, S., Norouzi, M., Hinton, G.: A simple framework for contrastive learning of visual representations. In: International Conference on Machine Learning, pp. 1597–1607. PMLR (2020)
3. Eldele, E., et al.: An attention-based deep learning approach for sleep stage classification with single-channel EEG. IEEE Trans. Neural Syst. Rehabil. Eng. **29**, 809–818 (2021)
4. Hannun, A.Y., et al.: Cardiologist-level arrhythmia detection and classification in ambulatory electrocardiograms using a deep neural network. Nat. Med. **25**(1), 65–69 (2019)
5. He, Z., et al.: Single-channel EEG sleep staging based on data augmentation and cross-subject discrepancy alleviation. Comput. Biol. Med. **149**, 106044 (2022)
6. Jiang, X., Zhao, J., Du, B., Yuan, Z.: Self-supervised contrastive learning for EEG-based sleep staging. In: 2021 International Joint Conference on Neural Networks (IJCNN), pp. 1–8. IEEE (2021)
7. Kemp, B., Zwinderman, A.H., Tuk, B., Kamphuisen, H.A., Oberye, J.J.: Analysis of a sleep-dependent neuronal feedback loop: the slow-wave microcontinuity of the EEG. IEEE Trans. Biomed. Eng. **47**(9), 1185–1194 (2000)
8. Li, Y., Kambara, H., Koike, Y., Sugiyama, M.: Application of covariate shift adaptation techniques in brain-computer interfaces. IEEE Trans. Biomed. Eng. **57**(6), 1318–1324 (2010)
9. Maquet, P.: The role of sleep in learning and memory. Science **294**(5544), 1048–1052 (2001)
10. Mehta, S., Rastegari, M.: Mobilevit: light-weight, general-purpose, and mobile-friendly vision transformer. arXiv preprint arXiv:2110.02178 (2021)
11. Mousavi, S., Afghah, F., Acharya, U.R.: SleepEEGnet: automated sleep stage scoring with sequence to sequence deep learning approach. PLoS ONE **14**(5), e0216456 (2019)
12. Perslev, M., Jensen, M., Darkner, S., Jennum, P.J., Igel, C.: U-time: a fully convolutional network for time series segmentation applied to sleep staging. In: Advances in Neural Information Processing Systems, vol. 32 (2019)
13. Phan, H., Mikkelsen, K., Chén, O.Y., Koch, P., Mertins, A., De Vos, M.: Sleep-transformer: automatic sleep staging with interpretability and uncertainty quantification. IEEE Trans. Biomed. Eng. **69**(8), 2456–2467 (2022)
14. Ronneberger, O., Fischer, P., Brox, T.: U-net: convolutional networks for biomedical image segmentation. In: Navab, N., Hornegger, J., Wells, W.M., Frangi, A.F. (eds.) MICCAI 2015. LNCS, vol. 9351, pp. 234–241. Springer, Cham (2015). https://doi.org/10.1007/978-3-319-24574-4_28
15. Shen, X., Liu, X., Hu, X., Zhang, D., Song, S.: Contrastive learning of subject-invariant EEG representations for cross-subject emotion recognition. IEEE Trans. Affect. Comput. (2022)
16. Siegel, J.M.: Clues to the functions of mammalian sleep. Nature **437**(7063), 1264–1271 (2005)

17. Supratak, A., Dong, H., Wu, C., Guo, Y.: Deepsleepnet: a model for automatic sleep stage scoring based on raw single-channel EEG. IEEE Trans. Neural Syst. Rehabil. Eng. **25**(11), 1998–2008 (2017)
18. Phan, H., Chén, O.Y., Tran, M.C., Koch, P., Mertins, A., De Vos, M.: Xsleep-net: multi-view sequential model for automatic sleep staging. IEEE Trans. Pattern Anal. Mach. Intell. **44**(9), 5903–5915 (2021)

Diffusion Policies as Multi-Agent Reinforcement Learning Strategies

Jinkun Geng, Xiubo Liang$^{(\boxtimes)}$, Hongzhi Wang, and Yu Zhao

School of Software Technology, Zhejiang University, Ningbo, China
xiubo@zju.edu.cn

Abstract. In the realm of multi-agent systems, the application of reinforcement learning algorithms frequently confronts distinct challenges rooted in the non-stationarity and intricate nature of the environment. This paper presents an innovative methodology, denoted as Multi-Agent Diffuser (MA-Diffuser), which leverages diffusion models to encapsulate policies within a multi-agent context, thereby fostering efficient and expressive inter-agent coordination. Our methodology embeds the action-value maximization within the sampling process of the conditional diffusion model, thereby facilitating the detection of optimal actions closely aligned with the behavior policy. This strategy capitalizes on the expressive power of diffusion models, while simultaneously mitigating the prevalent function approximation errors often found in offline reinforcement learning environments. We have validated the efficacy of our approach within the Multi-Agent Particle Environment, and envisage its future extension to a broader range of tasks.

Keywords: Multi-agent reinforcement learning · Diffusion model · Offline reinforcement learning

1 Introduction

Multi-Agent Reinforcement Learning has garnered significant interest in recent years due to its extensive applicability across diverse domains, including multi-robot control [6], multiplayer games [2,30], communication [5], and social analysis [18]. Traditional reinforcement learning approaches, such as Q-Learning [22] and policy gradient [27], often struggle to address the non-stationary and complex nature of multi-agent environments. Consequently, several MARL algorithms, such as MADDPG [20], COMA [7], and MAAC [13], have been proposed to tackle these challenges. However, these temporal difference(TD) based reinforcement learning algorithms encounter issues such as function approximation, bootstrapping, and off-policy training [29], which limit their practical applicability.

In recent years, denoising diffusion models [10] have achieved remarkable success, making significant strides in image [24], audio [12], and video [11] generation. The denoising diffusion model is a generative model that produces high-quality results by allowing neural networks to fit the noise added to data in

L. Iliadis et al. (Eds.): ICANN 2023, LNCS 14256, pp. 356–364, 2023.
https://doi.org/10.1007/978-3-031-44213-1_30

advance. Inspired by diffusion models, some researchers have sought to treat single-agent behavior planning problems as generative problems [1,14]. By considering trajectories as generative objects and utilizing the reward function as guidance, the model can directly plan an agent's behavior trajectory. This approach mitigates estimation errors and long-term credit assignment issues prevalent in traditional reinforcement learning methods, yielding relatively favorable results across various environments. We aim to extend these methods to the multi-agent domain by employing diffusion models as policy representations in multi-agent reinforcement learning. Consequently, we propose a novel diffusion-based multi-agent reinforcement learning method, the Multi-Agent Diffuser (MA-Diffuser) method. Our approach simultaneously predicts the plans for all agents at all time steps, avoiding autoregressive forward prediction to circumvent rollout errors. Additionally, we guide multi-agent behavior planning by controlling the reward function.

In summary, the primary contributions of this paper are as follows:

- We pioneer the integration of diffusion models into multi-agent reinforcement learning and propose the MA-Diffuser model.
- In our model, we found that sharing action information during agent trajectory generation can effectively enhances the model's overall performance.
- Experiments in the multiagent-particle-envs (MPE) environment showed that MA-diffuser has competitive performance compared to traditional multi-agent reinforcement learning methods.

2 Related Works

In this section, we will discuss the related works in multi-agent reinforcement learning, diffusion models, and diffusion reinforcement learning. Various approaches have been proposed in these fields over the past few years, and we will summarize these methods.

2.1 Multi-Agent Reinforcement Learning

Multi-Agent Reinforcement Learning (MARL) involves learning optimized policies for multiple agents operating in a shared environment using reinforcement learning techniques. With the growing popularity of deep learning methods, deep learning-based MARL approaches have attracted increasing attention. The simplest approach to learning in multi-agent settings involves using independently learning agents. Tampuu et al. applied the Deep Q-learning method to the Pong game [28]. However, in most cases, independently learning policies for intelligent agents perform poorly in MARL, as each agent's policy changes, resulting in an unstable environment and difficulty in utilizing historical experiences. Several algorithms have been proposed to address these challenges, such as optimistic and hysteretic Q function updates [17] and sharing of policy parameters [9]. However, the applicability of these methods is limited. In the past few years, methods based on the Actor-Critic architecture have gained popularity. Multi-Agent Deep Deterministic Policy Gradient (MADDPG) is an extension of the DDPG algorithm [19] algorithm, employing a centralized critic for each agent to guide the learning of decentralized actors. Counterfactual Multi-Agent (COMA) utilizes a centralized critic to train decentralized actors, estimating a counterfactual advantage function for each agent to address the multi-agent credit assignment problem. Attention models have also been integrated into MARL. Iqbal et al. proposed the Multi-Actor-Attention-Critic (MAAC), which employs an attention mechanism to enable each agent to focus on relevant interactions with the environment and other agents, while ignoring irrelevant ones. Value-Decomposition Networks (VDN) [26], developed by Sunehag et al., is another approach that addresses team rewards in cooperative settings. VDN autonomously learns the value-decomposition from experience, optimizing for total reward.

In addition to these online strategies, offline MARL has been receiving increasing attention recently. Offline MARL aims to learn multi-agent policies from previously collected non-expert datasets without requiring further interaction with the environment. Because interacting with the real-world environment can sometimes be costly, offline MARL carries particular value in many situations. Studies by Fujimoto et al. [8] shows that offline Multi-Agent Reinforcement Learning is more likely to be influenced by extrapolation error. Some methods have been proposed to address this issue, such as the CQL method presented by Kumar et al. [16] in 2020 and ICQ approach presented by Yang et al. [32] in 2021. Each of these methods has subsequent multi-agent versions.

2.2   Diffusion Models

Denoising Diffusion Probabilistic Models (DDPM) [10] is a powerful generative model and has demonstrated very advanced performance in the field of image generation. The foundation for DDPMs was laid in this seminal work by Sohl-Dickstein et al. [25], which introduced the concept of using diffusion processes for unsupervised learning. They developed a scalable algorithm by simulating the diffusion process in reverse. Compared with other unsupervised learning algorithms, this method produces competitive results.DDPM can generate high quality picture data. Compared to GANs [21], DDPM does not require adversarial training, which can often result in unstable training dynamics and mode collapse. DDPM offers a more stable and robust training process. Unlike VAEs [15], which can suffer from the problem of posterior collapse, DDPM can capture a rich and diverse set of modes in the data distribution. In addition to images, DDPM can also be extended to audio or video generation, and it is easier to control the generated content [33].

2.3   Diffusion Reinforcement Learning

The use of diffusion models in reinforcement learning was first proposed by Janner et al. They proposed the Diffuser model [14] that applies the diffusion model as a trajectory generator. The complete trajectories of state-action pairs are combined to form a single sample of the diffusion model. This model is similar to the Decision Transformer [4] proposed by Chen et al. It applies the self-attention mechanism to extract and learn long-term decision-making information from historical trajectories. Since the proposal of Diffuser, many reinforcement learning algorithms based on diffusion have been proposed. Wang et al. proposed Diffusion-QL [31], which leverages diffusion models for precise policy regularization and successfully incorporates Q-learning guidance into the reverse diffusion chain to seek optimal actions. Chen et al. using diffusion probabilistic models to decouples policy learning into behavior learning and action evaluation, and proposed SfBC [3] method.

3   Method

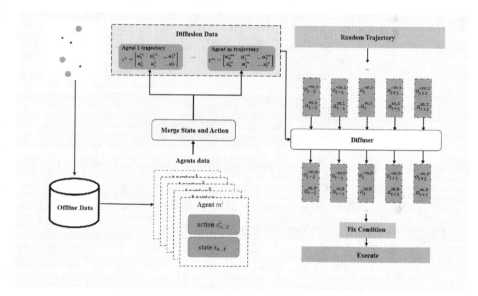

Fig. 1. Overall framework of MA-Diffuser

Our Multi-Agent Diffuser (MA-Diffuser) model is specifically illustrated in Fig. 1. Consider a standard MARL environment $\langle \mathcal{M}, \mathcal{O}, \mathcal{A}, R \rangle$, $\mathcal{M} = \{1, \ldots, m\}$ is the set of agents, $\mathcal{O} = \prod_{i=1}^{m} \mathcal{O}^i$ is the product of local observation spaces of the agents, $\mathcal{A} = \prod_{i=1}^{m} \mathcal{A}^i$ is the agents action space, and $R : \mathcal{O} \times \mathcal{A}$ is the environment reward function. Considering a specific time step t, we denote s_t as global state of the environment, a_t^i as the agent i's action, o_t^i as the agent i's observation.

We hope we can apply the experience of diffusion models to multi-agent behavior control. From the perspective of the diffusion model, trajectories are similar to images. By fitting manually added noise in the data using neural networks, we can gradually generate sequence that are consistent with the distribution of the original data from completely random noise. Consider a trajectory τ, assuming that τ_0 has undergone standard diffusion process to become τ_N, we can gradually reconstruct τ_0 using the following formula:

$$p_\theta(\tau_0) = p_\theta(\tau_N) \prod_{n=1}^{N} p_\theta(r_{n-1} \mid r_n) \tag{1}$$

In our method, we represent trajectory of the agent as a sequence of action-observation pairs, which forms a 2D array. For each agent, it will have its own representation of trajectory. Considering the information exchange among agents, for diffusion time step t, we concatenate the actions a_{t-1} of all agents taken at time step $t-1$ with the observation o_t^i of agent i to form a new observation vector o_t^{*i} (for o_0^{*i}, we set the action to 0). Finally, we represent the trajectory of the agents i as:

$$\tau^i = \begin{bmatrix} \mathbf{o}_0^{*i} & \mathbf{o}_1^{*i} & \dots & \mathbf{o}_T^{*i} \\ \mathbf{a}_0^i & \mathbf{a}_1^i & \dots & \mathbf{a}_T^i \end{bmatrix} \tag{2}$$

In the process of trajectory diffusion, we will alternate training the diffusion strategy of the i-th agent in the n-th time step. We execute gradient descent by minimizing the following loss:

$$\mathcal{L}^i(\theta) = \mathbb{E}_{n,\epsilon,\tau_n^i} \left[\left\| \epsilon - \epsilon_\theta(\tau_n^i, n) \right\|^2 \right] \tag{3}$$

Algorithm 1. Trajectory Generation Algorithm

Require: Diffuser p_θ, reward guid function $\mathcal{J}$, scale α
  while not done **do**
    Obtain state s from the environment;
    Generate a trajectory for each agent $\tau_N^i \sim \mathcal{N}(\mathbf{0}, I)$
    while n in N **do**
      get a_{n-1} and update o_n^* by p_n
      while i in M **do**
        $\tau_{n-1}^i \sim \mathcal{N}(p_n + \alpha\Sigma\nabla\mathcal{J}(s, p_n), \Sigma^n)$
        $\tau_{n-1,o_0}^i \leftarrow s$
      end while
    end while
  end while

The procedure for the sampling phase is delineated in Algorithm 1. Each agent initiates a trajectory drawn from a standard Gaussian distribution, progressively formulating strategies via an N-step denoising process. Within this denoising operation, we incorporate a reward function as a guidance mechanism and facilitate information exchange among distinct agents. The diffusion model is then trained on the data originating from these diverse agents under uniform conditions. Consequently, upon the conclusion of the training, the parameters of our model exhibit efficacy across all agents.

4   Experiment

In this section, we will present comprehensive descriptions of the dataset and experimental details utilized in our research. We will compare MA-Diffusion to other conventional multi-agent reinforcement learning baseline methods. Finally, we will focus on the effectiveness of action information exchange in the MA-Diffusion method.

4.1   Experimental Setting

We evaluate of our MA-Diffuser method in the Multi-Agent Particle Environment (MPE) [23]. MPE is a simple yet powerful multi-agent world that incorporates continuous observation and discrete action spaces along with basic simulated physics. We conduct our experiments in it's simple spread environment, which consists of 3 agents and 3 landmarks. In this environment, agents receive more rewards when they are closer to the nearest landmark, and are penalized for collisions with other agents. Agents must learn to avoid collisions while covering all landmarks. We used multiple pre-trained external models to generate four sets of trajectory samples, each with a size of 5M, and mixed them together as our offline data. We select MA-ICQ and MA-CQL as our baseline experiments. For all experiments, we control batch-size $= 4$, learning-rate$=1e-4$, and the max train iterations is 180,000.

4.2   Results and Analysis

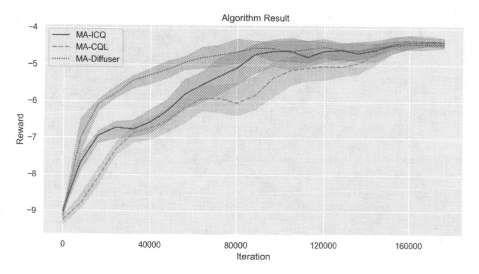

Fig. 2. The average reward in the MPE's Simple Spread environment.

Figure 2 shows our experience result. We can see that our MA-Diffuser model has a faster convergence rate and better performance compared to multi-agent reinforcement learning algorithms based on temporal difference. After a sufficient number of iterations, all four algorithms tend to stabilize and converge to a similar value. MA-Diffuser outperforms other algorithms in both early performance and convergence rate. This suggests that applying the diffusion model to multi-agent reinforcement learning is feasible.

4.3   Mean Reward of the MA-Diffuser Under Different Information Exchange Method

Table 1. Mean reward of the MA-Diffuser under different information exchange method.

Method	Mean Reward
No Exchange	−7.396
Action Exchange(with 0% random error)	−5.248
Action Exchange(with 25% random error)	−5.419
Action Exchange(with 50% random error)	−6.171
Action Exchange(with 75% random error)	−6.584
Action Exchange(with 100% random error)	−7.321

In this section, we studied the method of information exchange between multiple agents. We attempted to introduce noise interference into the process of action information exchange between multiple intelligent agents during the running of MA-Diffuser. We iterated the model 10000 times, and then tested it 100 times in evaluate environment to validate the performance of the model using average reward. The experimental results are shown in Table 1. This indicates that exchanging action information in multi-agent trajectory diffusion can effectively improve the performance of the model.

When multiple agents acquire the actions of other intelligent agents, the environment can be considered an approximately deterministic environment. Since we do not use real-time action information but rather historical actions, the intelligent agents must try to learn the strategies of other intelligent agents. In this process, the model can effectively enhance the planning ability of the intelligent agents to improve the performance of the model.

5   Conclusions

In this study, we introduced a novel approach to multi-agent reinforcement learning called Multi-Agent Diffuser (MA-Diffuser), which employs diffusion models to represent policies in a multi-agent setting. The primary contributions of this paper include the integration of diffusion models into multi-agent reinforcement learning, and the introduction of the MA-Diffuser model. We found that sharing action information during agent trajectory generation can effectively enhance the model's overall performance. This finding has implications for the design of future multi-agent reinforcement learning algorithms and applications. The MA-Diffuser method can be expanded to other tasks in the future, and this research provides a promising foundation for further developments in the field of multi-agent reinforcement learning.

Acknowledgements. This work is supported by "Pioneer" and "Leading Goose" R&D Program of Zhejiang (2023C01045).

References

1. Ajay, A., Du, Y., Gupta, A., Tenenbaum, J., Jaakkola, T., Agrawal, P.: Is conditional generative modeling all you need for decision-making? arXiv preprint arXiv:2211.15657 (2022)
2. Berner, C., et al.: Dota 2 with large scale deep reinforcement learning. arXiv preprint arXiv:1912.06680 (2019)
3. Chen, H., Lu, C., Ying, C., Su, H., Zhu, J.: Offline reinforcement learning via high-fidelity generative behavior modeling. arXiv preprint arXiv:2209.14548 (2022)
4. Chen, L., et al.: Decision transformer: reinforcement learning via sequence modeling. Adv. Neural. Inf. Process. Syst. **34**, 15084–15097 (2021)
5. Cui, J., Liu, Y., Nallanathan, A.: Multi-agent reinforcement learning-based resource allocation for UAV networks. IEEE Trans. Wirel. Commun. **19**(2), 729–743 (2019)
6. Fan, T., Long, P., Liu, W., Pan, J.: Distributed multi-robot collision avoidance via deep reinforcement learning for navigation in complex scenarios. Int. J. Robot. Res. **39**(7), 856–892 (2020)
7. Foerster, J., Farquhar, G., Afouras, T., Nardelli, N., Whiteson, S.: Counterfactual multi-agent policy gradients. In: Proceedings of the AAAI Conference on Artificial Intelligence, vol. 32 (2018)
8. Fujimoto, S., Meger, D., Precup, D.: Off-policy deep reinforcement learning without exploration. In: International Conference on Machine Learning, pp. 2052–2062. PMLR (2019)
9. Gupta, J.K., Egorov, M., Kochenderfer, M.: Cooperative multi-agent control using deep reinforcement learning. In: Sukthankar, G., Rodriguez-Aguilar, J.A. (eds.) AAMAS 2017. LNCS (LNAI), vol. 10642, pp. 66–83. Springer, Cham (2017). https://doi.org/10.1007/978-3-319-71682-4_5
10. Ho, J., Jain, A., Abbeel, P.: Denoising diffusion probabilistic models. Adv. Neural. Inf. Process. Syst. **33**, 6840–6851 (2020)
11. Ho, J., Salimans, T., Gritsenko, A., Chan, W., Norouzi, M., Fleet, D.J.: Video diffusion models. arXiv preprint arXiv:2204.03458 (2022)
12. Huang, R., et al.: Fastdiff: a fast conditional diffusion model for high-quality speech synthesis. arXiv preprint arXiv:2204.09934 (2022)
13. Iqbal, S., Sha, F.: Actor-attention-critic for multi-agent reinforcement learning. In: International Conference on Machine Learning, pp. 2961–2970. PMLR (2019)
14. Janner, M., Du, Y., Tenenbaum, J.B., Levine, S.: Planning with diffusion for flexible behavior synthesis. arXiv preprint arXiv:2205.09991 (2022)

15. Kingma, D.P., Welling, M.: Auto-encoding variational Bayes. arXiv preprint arXiv:1312.6114 (2013)
16. Kumar, A., Zhou, A., Tucker, G., Levine, S.: Conservative q-learning for offline reinforcement learning. Adv. Neural. Inf. Process. Syst. **33**, 1179–1191 (2020)
17. Lauer, M.: An algorithm for distributed reinforcement learning in cooperative multiagent systems. In: Proceedings of 17th International Conference on Machine Learning (2000)
18. Leibo, J.Z., Zambaldi, V., Lanctot, M., Marecki, J., Graepel, T.: Multi-agent reinforcement learning in sequential social dilemmas. arXiv preprint arXiv:1702.03037 (2017)
19. Lillicrap, T.P., et al.: Continuous control with deep reinforcement learning. arXiv preprint arXiv:1509.02971 (2015)
20. Lowe, R., Wu, Y.I., Tamar, A., Harb, J., Abbeel, O.P., Mordatch, I.: Multi-agent actor-critic for mixed cooperative-competitive environments. In: Advances in Neural Information Processing Systems, vol. 30 (2017)
21. Mirza, M., Osindero, S.: Conditional generative adversarial nets. arXiv preprint arXiv:1411.1784 (2014)
22. Mnih, V., et al.: Playing Atari with deep reinforcement learning. arXiv preprint arXiv:1312.5602 (2013)
23. Mordatch, I., Abbeel, P.: Emergence of grounded compositional language in multi-agent populations. arXiv preprint arXiv:1703.04908 (2017)
24. Rombach, R., Blattmann, A., Lorenz, D., Esser, P., Ommer, B.: High-resolution image synthesis with latent diffusion models. In: Proceedings of the IEEE/CVF Conference on Computer Vision and Pattern Recognition, pp. 10684–10695 (2022)
25. Sohl-Dickstein, J., Weiss, E., Maheswaranathan, N., Ganguli, S.: Deep unsupervised learning using nonequilibrium thermodynamics. In: International Conference on Machine Learning, pp. 2256–2265. PMLR (2015)
26. Sunehag, P., et al.: Value-decomposition networks for cooperative multi-agent learning. arXiv preprint arXiv:1706.05296 (2017)
27. Sutton, R.S., McAllester, D., Singh, S., Mansour, Y.: Policy gradient methods for reinforcement learning with function approximation. In: Advances in Neural Information Processing Systems, vol. 12 (1999)
28. Tampuu, A., et al.: Multiagent cooperation and competition with deep reinforcement learning. PLoS ONE **12**(4), e0172395 (2017)
29. Van Hasselt, H., Doron, Y., Strub, F., Hessel, M., Sonnerat, N., Modayil, J.: Deep reinforcement learning and the deadly triad. arXiv preprint arXiv:1812.02648 (2018)
30. Vinyals, O., et al.: Grandmaster level in starcraft ii using multi-agent reinforcement learning. Nature **575**(7782), 350–354 (2019)
31. Wang, Z., Hunt, J.J., Zhou, M.: Diffusion policies as an expressive policy class for offline reinforcement learning. arXiv preprint arXiv:2208.06193 (2022)
32. Yang, Y., et al.: Believe what you see: implicit constraint approach for offline multi-agent reinforcement learning. Adv. Neural. Inf. Process. Syst. **34**, 10299–10312 (2021)
33. Zhang, L., Agrawala, M.: Adding conditional control to text-to-image diffusion models. arXiv preprint arXiv:2302.05543 (2023)

Dynamic Memory-Based Continual Learning with Generating and Screening

Siying Tao[1], Jinyang Huang[1], Xiang Zhang[2], Xiao Sun[1,3], and Yu Gu[4(✉)]

[1] School of Computer Science and Information Engineering,
Hefei University of Technology, Hefei, China
siyingtao@mail.hfut.edu.cn, {hjy,sunx}@hfut.edu.cn
[2] School of Cybers Science and Technology,
University of Science and Technology of China, Hefei, China
zhangxiang@ieee.org
[3] Institute of Artificial Intelligence, Hefei Comprehensive National Science Center,
Hefei, China
[4] I+ Lab, School of Computer Science and Engineering,
University of Electronic Science and Technology of China, Chengdu, China
yugu.bruce@ieee.org

Abstract. Deep neural networks suffer from catastrophic forgetting when continually learning new tasks. Although simply replaying all previous data alleviates the problem, it requires large memory and even worse, often infeasible in real-world applications where access to past data is limited. Therefore, We propose a two-stage framework that dynamically reproduces data features of previous tasks to reduce catastrophic forgetting. Specifically, at each task step, we use a new memory module to learn the data distribution of the new task and reproduce pseudo-data from previous memory modules to learn together. This enables us to integrate new visual concepts with retaining learned knowledge to achieve a better stability-malleability balance. We introduce an N-step model fusion strategy to accelerate the memorization process of the memory module and a screening strategy to control the quantity and quality of generated data, reducing distribution differences. We experimented on CIFAR-100, MNIST, and SVHN datasets to demonstrate the effectiveness of our method.

Keywords: Continual Learning · Generative replay · Deep learning

1 Introduction

While the majority of deep learning literature mainly focuses on learning models using fixed datasets, real-world data is constantly evolving and generating new classes or domains. This often results in the catastrophic forgetting problem when models are fine-tuned directly with new data, and previous data is not accessible due to concerns such as privacy or device storage limitations. Catastrophic forgetting can result in a loss of previous data distributions and seriously degrade the performance of models to process previous data classes. Continual

© The Author(s), under exclusive license to Springer Nature Switzerland AG 2023
L. Iliadis et al. (Eds.): ICANN 2023, LNCS 14256, pp. 365–376, 2023.
https://doi.org/10.1007/978-3-031-44213-1_31

learning aims to keep the model learning new tasks without forgetting the knowledge of the old ones, solving the stability-plasticity dilemma [1], which refers to the challenge of achieving a balance between model stability and plasticity in continual learning. In detail, excessive plasticity can lead to a dramatic decline in the model's performance for old tasks, while excessive stability can increase the difficulty for the model to learn new tasks.

There has been a significant effort to tackle catastrophic forgetting in the field of machine learning. Typical methods [7,8], such as knowledge distillation or fixing important parameters in the model, aim to retain previous knowledge by reusing well-trained network components. However, when a large number of new tasks are added to the model, these methods can have limitations. Other approaches [7,9] attempt to store samples from old tasks to inform new ones, but the imbalance between the number of samples and new tasks can lead to a classifier that is biased towards old tasks due to storage capacity limitations. To address this, some methods [2,3] dynamically expand the classification network to accommodate new tasks. However, as the number of tasks increases, the classification network can become increasingly large in parameters and complex in structure, which requires careful pruning as post-processing.

To address the above weaknesses, we propose a two-stage learning framework that decouples the process of remembering old classes and the learning process of new classes to achieve a better stability-malleability trade-off in continuous learning. We nicknamed our framework, DMCL, for Dynamic Memory-based Continual Learning with generating and screening. Within this framework, we design the memory module consisting of a diffusion model [4] and a screening network in pairs that can learn old classes of data distributions and generate pseudo-data with the same distribution. Our main idea is to dynamically generate old class samples by memory module and to learn them together with the new samples, thus allowing both adequate retention of existing knowledge and sufficient flexibility to learn new knowledge. In addition, our framework can be broken down into multiple discrete modules stored on the hard disk and loaded into different memory modules in turn during use. Therefore, the machine memory consumed is very limited, even when there are many tasks.

To achieve this, we propose the N-step model fusion strategy and the screening strategy for the memory module. Specifically, when memorizing the old class data, our N-step model fusion strategy fuses Gaussian transfer kernels from different time steps of the diffusion model in the memory module to speed up convergence. When generating the old class data samples, our screening strategy controls the quantity and quality of generated samples, avoiding class imbalances and reducing distribution differences with actual data.

We validated DMCL on image classification tasks with three commonly used benchmark tests, including the CIFAR-100 [16], MNIST [17], and SVHN [18] datasets. The empirical results and ablation studies show that our method outperforms the existing state-of-the-art methods. In fact, DMCL can be applied to many tasks, not only image classification tasks, as long as the memory module can reliably reproduce the old data distribution.

2   Related Work

2.1   Continual Learning

Continual learning is to address the catastrophic forgetting of machine learning on old classes, and common settings include Task-IL, Domain-IL, and Class-IL. In computer vision, most of strategies applied on large-scale datasets use rehearsal learning: a limited amount of the data of old task is kept during training [1]. These data can be either raw pixels or compressed vectors. Others [7,9,11] acquire knowledge of old classes by knowledge distillation and apply some constraints in training new data. These constraints [8] can be directly applied to the model weights, sample intermediate features, and prediction probabilities of the classifier. In addition, there are approaches [5,14] that generate instead of storing old samples through generative models (e.g.,GAN) to alleviate the difficulties of limited storage space for old samples.

2.2   Diffusion Model

The diffusion model is a generative model surpassing GAN as the current state-of-the-art proposal in the field of image generation [12]. The model consists of two processes. The first process gradually adds noise to perturb or destroy the data distribution by the forward process, and then the reverse process learns to remove the noise and restore the structure of the original data distribution, resulting in a highly flexible and easily handled generative model. Recently diffusion models have been applied to many works [4] (e.g., image super-resolution, image translation, image segmentation, text-to-image generation, etc.) and showed great potential.

3   Our Approach

In this section, we demonstrate the processing flow of our framework for image classification tasks and the details of the n-step model fusion strategy and the screening strategy.

3.1   Method Overview

We expect DMCL to be capable of classifying an increasing number of classes. We define the image classification tasks to be solved as a sequence of N tasks, represented as $Task = (task_1, task_2, ..., task_n)$. Each task includes different categories of pictures (x_i, y_i) with completely different distributions D. The classification labels y may be the same (for domain incremental learning) or completely different (for class incremental learning). DMCL will learn the $task_n$ data sequentially while retaining the knowledge of previously learned $task_{1,2,...,n-1}$. The main challenge is that DMCL can only temporarily access the data from the current $task_i$, but it must be able to efficiently classify test data from all previous classes $C(task_1, ..., task_i)$.

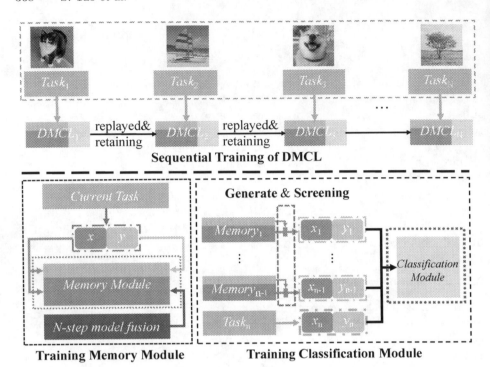

Fig. 1. The process of sequential training of DMCL. In the top subplot, when a new $task_n$ arrives, DMCL first learns the data distribution features of $task_n$ with a memory model, and then replays the old sample data$(x_{1...n-1}, y_{1...n-1})$ from the previous memory modules to retrain the classification module together with the $task_n$ data(x_n, y_n). The left subplot is the current $task_n$ data for the training process of diffusion model and screening network in the memory module, and the N-step model fusion strategy is applied to training diffusion model. The right subplot is a retraining process of the classification module. All memory modules generate samples, select and label pseudo data $(x_{1...n-1}, y_{1...n-1})$ by screening strategy. Then, the pseudo data$(x_{1...n-1}, y_{1...n-1})$ and $task_n$ data (x_n, y_n) work together to retrain the classification module.

To address the forgetfulness of previous tasks, our DMCL learns the sample data for each task by the memory module and re-trains the pseudo-sample data jointly in the new task. The sequence training process of DMCL is at the top of Fig. 1. When the $task_n$ arrives, the DMCL first trains the memory module with the current task sample data, and then trains the classification module with the current task sample data and replayed sample data from all the previous memory modules. Formally, the loss function of the i-th classification model is given as

$$L_{train}(\theta_i) = r_i E_{(x,y)\sim C_i}[L(C(x_i, \theta_i), y] + \sum_{t=0}^{i-1} r_t E_{x'\sim M_t}[L(C(x', \theta_i), SN_t(x')] \quad (1)$$

where θ_i are network parameters of the i-th classification module, M_t is the t-th memory module, SN_t is the t-th screening network in the t-th memory module, and r_t is a ratio of mixing data.

3.2 Classification Module

The classification module used in our study is compatible with any classification network, and we chose the Resnet [15] network for our experiments in this paper. When a new task is presented, we first update the number of classification heads in the last layer of the classification network to match the total number of classes, given by $C(task_1, ..., task_{n-1})$. Next, we combine the pictures and labels generated by the memory module, i.e.,$x(Memory_1, ..., Memory_{n-1})$ and $y(Memory_1, ..., Memory_{n-1})$, with the samples of the current $task_n$, in a certain ration depending on the task's importance. As shown in the training classification module of Fig. 1, the diffusion models in the memory module generate samples, and then the screening network then selects and labels the categories through the screening strategy with output pseudo-data $(x_{1...n-1}, y_{1...n-1})$. Finally, the pseudo-data and current task data work together to retain the classification module.

3.3 Memory Module

The memory module is the core part of DMCL and consists of two parts: the diffusion model and the screening network. The diffusion model in our work uses the denoising diffusion probabilistic model [12] (DDPM), which can generate samples with the same distribution as the original data in a limited time by variational inference. The forward chain of DDPM perturbs the data distribution by gradually adding Gaussian noise with a pre-designed schedule until the data distribution converges to a Gaussian distribution. The reverse chain of DDPM starts with the given prior and uses a parameterized Gaussian transition kernel, learning to gradually restore the undisturbed data structure. The noise-adding process q for the forward chain and the noise-removal process p for the reverse chain are defined formally as:

$$q(x_t|x_{t-1}) = N(x_t; \sqrt{1 - \beta_t}x_{t-1}, \beta_t I) \tag{2}$$

$$p_\theta(x_t - 1|x_t) = N(x_{t-1}; \mu_\theta(x_t, t), \textstyle\sum_\theta(x_t, t) \tag{3}$$

where the x_t is the sampling noise to image at times step t, and the β_t is a fixed-variance strategy. The $q(x_t|x_0)$ is the process of forward chain, deriving the noise distribution of x_t from x_{t-1}, and I is the constant value. The $p_\theta(x_t - 1|x_t)$ is the process of reverse chain, removing the noise distribution from x_t to $xt - 1$, and the $\mu_\theta(x_t, t)$ is a noise reduction network for predicting the noise at t step.

The screening network in the memory module is a small classification network. Compared with the classification module, the screening network is trained with only one task data, so it has better performance than the classification module in a single task. Like the classification module, the screening network is compatible with any classification network. The role of the screening network is to remove samples with poor generation quality and match the corresponding pseudo-labels.

On the left of Fig. 1, the training process of the memory module is shown. The diffusion model and the screening network in the memory module are trained simultaneously and independently. The image x and category label y from the current task are used to train the screening network. And for the training of the diffusion model only use the image x of the current task. When training the diffusion model, use the N-step model fusion strategy to speed up its convergence.

The generation and screening processes of the memory module are shown on the right side of Fig. 1. The diffusion model in different memory modules generates various classes of pseudo-sample data. And the corresponding screening network in the memory module selects and marks the generated samples by the screening strategy. In this way, The resulting image $x_{1,...,n-1}$ is closer to the data distribution of the original task and reduces the ambiguity between the different categories $y_{1,...,n-1}$.

3.4   Screening Strategy

The screening strategy is acting when generating samples. Firstly, set a reasonable confidence threshold. After that, the Screening network is used to classify the generated samples and give the confidence level. Samples below the confidence threshold are directly dropped, and the remainders go to the joint training of the next task. Each memory module selects the same number of samples by screening strategy as the number of the new task to decrease the category imbalance problem.

The confidence threshold is finalized by repeated pre-experiments. Using different confidence threshold values, samples are generated by the same memory module and selected using the same screening strategy for training of the classification module. The appropriate confidence threshold value is selected according to the variation in the accuracy of the classification module. The confidence threshold in this paper is 0.98.

Algorithm 1 describes the entire flow of the screening strategy. In the follow-up ablation experiments, we found that the strategy was helpful to improve the classification accuracy, especially when the diffusion model was not fully converged.

3.5   N-step Model Fusion Strategy

The N-step model fusion strategy is applied to the diffusion model training. The core of the diffusion model is the training of a noise-reducing U-Net [12], using a Monte Carlo algorithm. At each training, a time step t is randomly selected from the total time step T. Then the loss is calculated by forward propagation and gradient descent for the U-Net in time step t, with updated parameters of the diffusion model (DM_t). Based on the **Law of Large Numbers** theorem, the U-Net will eventually converge after many iterations.

Algorithm 1 The screening strategy, Pytorch-like

```
#Input:DM(diffusion model),SN( screening network),
#N(number of generation samples),threshold
#Output:X(image generated),Y(label of image)
X = list()        #store images
Y = list()        #store labels
while len(X)<N:
    sample = DM()         #generate sample
    #calculate the label and degree of confidence
    Label, CF = SN(sample)
    if CF >=threshold:
        X.append(sample)        #screening
        Y.append(Label)
return   X,Y
```

Assuming that each gradient descent decreases the loss, the KL scatter between the samples generated by DM_t and the samples from the original task is $KL(D|DM_t)$. By **Jensen's inequality**, it is known that:

$$E(KL(D||DM_t)) \geq KL(D||E(DM_t)) \tag{4}$$

where E is the expectation. If $E(DM_t)$ is used instead of DM_t for the next iteration, a lower KL scatter is obtained. However, the performance of the overhead of computing $E(DM_t)$ is high in practice. As indicated by Algorithm 2, we calculate the mean value of the n-step model fusion in terms to approximate $E(DM_t)$ as follows

$$E(DM_t) \approx \frac{1}{n} \sum_{i=1}^{n} DM_t^i \tag{5}$$

Algorithm 2 N-step model fusion strategy, Pytorch-like

```
#Input:CM(the updated model),now(number of iterations)
#Output:model(model for the next training)
old_models        #temporary strorage models
previous_model        #the model before gradient descent
old_models.append(copy(CM))        #save updated model
#check whether the number of steps has reached N
if check_step(now):
    previous_model=mean(old_models)
return previous_model
```

4   Experiments

4.1   Experiment Setup and Implementation Details

Datasets. We experimented with class incremental experiments on the CIFAR-100 [16] dataset, and domain incremental experiments on the MNIST [17] and SVHN [18] datasets. Due to the fact that the MNIST dataset is a 28 * 28 grayscale image, we transform it into a 32 * 32 pixel and 3-channel image (keeping with SVHN).

Benchmarks. In CIFAR-100, we compare performances on 10 steps (10 new classes per step), 20 steps (5 new classes per step), and 50 steps (2 new classes per step) and report the top-1 accuracy (%) for each step. In both MNIST and SVHN, we conducted domain increment experiments from MNIST to SVHN and from SVHN to MNIST, and report the change in top-1 accuracy (%).

The performance of the classification module directly affects the accuracy of class incremental experiments and domain incremental experiments. Our experimental framework is based on the open-source PYCIL [6] secondary development. We experimented the classification experiments with various specifications of Resnet [15] at CIFAR-100 dataset, and the performance is shown (accuracy of the Resnet18 is 70.55%, Resnet32 is 72.34%, Resnet34 is 74.12%, Resnet50 is 74.56% and Resnet101 is 74.28%). To facilitate comparison with DyTox [2] (Transf. Joint accuracy 76.12%), we chose Resnet34 (Joint accuracy 74.12%) as the benchmark network for the classification module.

We perform repeated pre-experiments on task data of CIFAR-100 to determine the confidence threshold of the screening strategy. As the results are shown in Table 1, We find with a rising threshold, the accuracy rate will start to rise, but will remain the same after reaching a certain value. The experiment was chosen with a threshold value of 0.98.

Table 1. The accuracy of different confidence thresholds on test data.

threshold	0.9	0.91	0.92	0.93	0.94	0.95	0.96	0.97	0.98	0.99
accuracy	0.801	0.826	0.833	0.847	0.852	0.861	0.872	0.878	0.883	0.882

4.2   Class Incremental Learning

Table 2 shows the results for all approaches on CIFAR-100. The more steps there are, the larger the forgetting is and thus the lower the performances are. These settings are shown in Fig. 2. In the setting, DMCL is close to DER [3] for much fewer parameters(up to 25x less). Critically, DMCL is significantly above other baselines and has better-forgetting resistance for the case of a consistently huge number of tasks: e.g. DMCL is up to +30% in "Last" accuracy in the 20 steps setup.

Table 2. Results on CIFAR-100 averaged over three different class orders. Baseline results come from [2]. The * symbol means that [3] needed setting-sensitive hyperparameters and its reported parameters count was an average over all steps.

Methods	10 steps			20 steps			50 steps		
	#P	Avg	Last	#P	Avg	Last	#P	Avg	Last
Res. Joint	22.45	–	74.12	22.45	–	74.12	22.45	–	74.12
iCaRL [7]	11.22	65.27	50.74	11.22	61.2	43.75	11.22	56.08	35.62
UCIR [8]	11.22	58.66	43.39	11.22	58.17	40.63	11.22	56.86	37.09
BiC [9]	11.22	68.8	53.54	11.22	66.48	47.02	11.22	62.09	41.04
WA [10]	11.22	69.46	53.78	11.22	67.33	47.31	11.22	64.32	42.14
PODNet [11]	11.22	58.03	41.05	11.22	53.97	35.02	11.22	51.19	35.99
RPSNet [13]	56.5	68.6	57.05	–	–	–	–	–	–
DER* [3]	112.27	74.64	64.35	224.55	73.98	62.55	561.39	72.05	59.76
DyTox [2]	10.73	73.66	60.67	10.74	72.27	56.32	10.77	70.2	52.34
DMCL	22.45	71.97	**64.94**	22.45	72.69	**65.08**	22.45	71.03	**60.01**

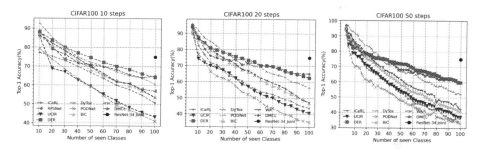

Fig. 2. Performance evolution on CIFAR100. The top-1 accuracy (%) is reported after learning each task. Left is evaluated with 10 steps, middle with 20 steps, and right with 50 steps.

4.3 Domain Incremental Learning

Table 3 shows the results for DMCL and Joint training on MNIST and SVHN. Whether the domain is changed from MNIST to SVHN or vice versa, DMCL achieves the same level of performance as joint training, with 97% average accuracy.

Table 3. The top-1 accuracy results of domain increment experiments on MNIST and SVHN.

	MNIST	SVHN	MNIST to SVHN	SVHN to MNIST
DMCL	99.6	96.56	97.24	96.65
Joint	–	–	96.97	

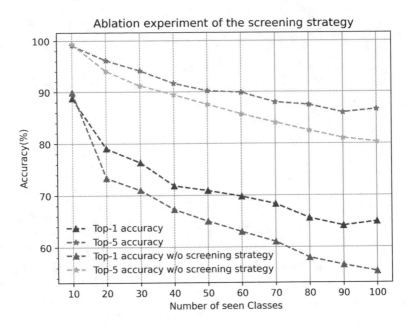

Fig. 3. Performance evaluation of the ablation experiment of screening strategy at CIFAR-100 with 10 steps.

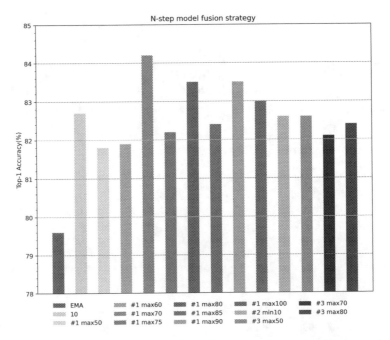

Fig. 4. Performance evaluation of the ablation experiment of the N-step model fusion strategy at CIFAR-100 with the same task. where max or min denotes the maximum or minimum number of fusion steps, and EMA denotes the original exponential moving average of the diffusion model.

4.4   Ablation Experiments

Screening Strategy. We experimented on CIFAR-100 with a setting of 10 steps. Using the same diffusion model and screening network, the threshold value of the screening strategy is set to 0.98. In Fig. 3, the screening strategy can effectively reduce the difference in the distribution between the generated samples and the original task. In each task, the screening strategy contributed to the quality of sample replication, with a maximum improvement of 9.6% on top1 accuracy and 6.3% on top5 accuracy.

N-step Model Fusion Strategy. We conducted experiments on CIFAR100, with the same network structure of diffusion model, the same screening strategy, and the same task data, to compare the memory effect with different fusion steps. Fig. 4 displays the performance comparison of different fusion step strategies, and the baseline strategy is the exponential moving average (EMA) of the diffusion model. We compared the 10 steps fusion and linear adjustment step fusion methods. The linear function is as follows:

$$\#1 : N = \left\lfloor 10 + \frac{steps}{1000} \right\rfloor \quad \#2 : N = \left\lfloor 100 - \frac{steps}{1000} \right\rfloor \quad \#3 : N = \left\lfloor 10 + \frac{steps}{2000} \right\rfloor$$

From Fig. 4, it can be seen that the N-step model fusion strategy has a noticeable performance improvement over the EMA strategy(up to +4.6% in top 1 accuracy).

5   Conclusion

In this paper, we proposed a two-stage framework for reducing catastrophic forgetting in deep neural networks when learning new tasks. At each step, we use a new memory module to memorize the data features of the new task and dynamically generate the pseudo-data of the previous tasks from the previous memory modules. We introduced the N-step model fusion strategy to accelerate the memorization process of the memory module and the screening strategy to select the generated samples and control the quantity and quality of the generated data. Experimental results on CIFAR-100, MNIST, and SVHN datasets show that our method outperforms the state-of-the-art methods in terms of accuracy, which achieves a better stability-malleability balance. Our proposed method provides a practical solution to address catastrophic forgetting in continual Learning, and our approach is easily modularly extended and optimized to suit different demands.

References

1. Grossberg, S.: Adaptive resonance theory: how a brain learns to consciously attend, learn, and recognize a changing world. Neural Netw. **37**, 1–47 (2013). https://doi.org/10.1016/j.neunet.2012.09.017

2. Douillard, A., Ramé, A., Couairon, G., Cord, M.: Dytox: transformers for continual learning with dynamic token expansion. In: Proceedings of the IEEE/CVF Conference on Computer Vision and Pattern Recognition, pp. 9285–9295 (2022)

3. Yan, S., Xie, J., He, X.: Der: dynamically expandable representation for class incremental learning. In: Proceedings of the IEEE/CVF Conference on Computer Vision and Pattern Recognition, pp. 3014–3023 (2021)

4. Yang, L., et al.: Diffusion models: a comprehensive survey of methods and applications. arXiv preprint arXiv:2209.00796. https://doi.org/10.48550/arXiv.2209.00796 (2022)

5. Shin, H., Lee, J.K., Kim, J., Kim, J.:Continual learning with deep generative replay. In: Advances in Neural Information Processing Systems, vol. 30 (2017)

6. Zhou, D.W., Wang, F.Y., Ye, H.J., Zhan, D.C.: Pycil: a Python toolbox for class-incremental learning. arXiv preprint arXiv:2112.12533. https://doi.org/10.1007/s11432-022-3600-y (2021)

7. Rebuffi, S.A., Kolesnikov, A., Sperl, G., Lampert, C.H.: ICARL: incremental classifier and representation learning. In: Proceedings of the IEEE Conference on Computer Vision and Pattern Recognition, pp. 2001–2010 (2017)

8. Hou, S., Pan, X., Loy, C.C., Wang, Z., Lin, D.: Learning a unified classifier incrementally via rebalancing. In: Proceedings of the IEEE/CVF Conference on Computer Vision and Pattern Recognition, pp. 831–839 (2019)

9. Wu, Y., et al.: Large scale incremental learning. In: Proceedings of the IEEE/CVF Conference on Computer Vision and Pattern Recognition, pp. 374–382 (2019)

10. Zhao, B., Xiao, X., Gan, G., Zhang, B., Xia, S.T.:Maintaining discrimination and fairness in class incremental learning. In: Proceedings of the IEEE/CVF Conference on Computer Vision and Pattern Recognition, pp. 13208–13217 (2020)

11. Douillard, A., Cord, M., Ollion, C., Robert, T., Valle, E.: PODNet: pooled outputs distillation for small-tasks incremental learning. In: Vedaldi, A., Bischof, H., Brox, T., Frahm, J.-M. (eds.) ECCV 2020. LNCS, vol. 12365, pp. 86–102. Springer, Cham (2020). https://doi.org/10.1007/978-3-030-58565-5_6

12. Ho, J., Jain, A., Abbeel, P.: Denoising diffusion probabilistic models. Adv. Neural. Inf. Process. Syst. **33**, 6840–6851 (2020)

13. Rajasegaran, J., Hayat, M., Khan, S., Khan, F.S., Shao, L., Yang, M.H.: An adaptive random path selection approach for incremental learning. arXiv preprint arXiv:1906.01120 (2019)

14. Lesort, T., Caselles-Dupré, H., Garcia-Ortiz, M., Stoian, A., Filliat, D.: Generative Models from the perspective of continual learning. In: 2019 International Joint Conference on Neural Networks (IJCNN), Budapest, Hungary, pp. 1–8 (2019). https://doi.org/10.1109/IJCNN.2019.8851986

15. He, K., Zhang, X., Ren, S., Sun, J.: Deep residual learning for image recognition. In: Proceedings of the IEEE Conference on Computer Vision and Pattern Recognition, pp. 770–778 (2016)

16. Krizhevsky, A., Hinton, G.: Learning multiple layers of features from tiny images (2009)

17. Lecun, Y., Bottou, L., Bengio, Y., Haffner, P.: Gradient-based learning applied to document recognition. Proc. IEEE **86**(11), 2278–2324 (1998). https://doi.org/10.1109/5.726791

18. Netzer, Y., Wang, T., Coates, A., Bissacco, A., Wu, B., Ng, A.Y.: Reading digits in natural images with unsupervised feature learning (2011)

Enhancing Text2SQL Generation with Syntactic Information and Multi-task Learning

Haochen Li[1] and Minghua Nuo[1,2,3]([✉])

[1] College of Computer Science, Inner Mongolia University, Hohhot 010021, Inner Mongolia, China
nuominghua@163.com
[2] National and Local Joint Engineering Research Center of Intelligent Information Processing Technology for Mongolian, Hohhot 010021, Inner Mongolia, China
[3] Inner Mongolia Key Laboratory of Mongolian Information Processing Technology, Hohhot 010021, Inner Mongolia, China

Abstract. The Text2SQL task aims to convert natural language (NL) questions into SQL queries. Most rule-based traditional syntactic parsers are often ignoring the syntactic information in the question and unseen database schemas, which lead to lower generalization ability. To breakthrough these limitations, we propose a novel model Syn-RGAT that leverages syntactic information of questions. Specifically, our model jointly encodes database schemas and questions by mapping them into a graph, which is then passed through a relation-aware graph attention network (RGAT). For the questions, map it as a syntax information graph and use syntactic augmentation module to learn all the nodes representations of the graph. Then the outputs of RGAT and syntactic augmentation module are integrated. Additionally, to assist the model distinguish between different database schemas, we introduce a graph pruning task and form a multi-task framework which shares the encoder of Text2SQL task. We use a heuristic learning method to combine graph pruning tasks with Text2SQL. In experimental part, Syn-RGAT outperforms all baseline models on the Spider dataset, and we further improve the performance more than 8% with BERT.

Keywords: Text2SQL · Graph neural network · syntactic parsing · multi-task Learning

1 Introduction

In recent years, the NLP researchers have shown significant interest in Text2SQL [1–4], which enables users unfamiliar with SQL to query databases using natural language. Numerous neural network approaches have been proposed to translate questions into executable SQL queries, achieving high exact match accuracies exceeding 80% on public Text2SQL benchmarks WikiSQL [5]. However, the cross-domain problem is still a critical challenge, which has been ignored by earlier parser.

L. Iliadis et al. (Eds.): ICANN 2023, LNCS 14256, pp. 377–388, 2023.
https://doi.org/10.1007/978-3-031-44213-1_32

The recent dataset Spider [6] poses a challenge of generalization ability of models for unseen database schemas. In this dataset, each SQL query is conditioned on a multi-table, and database schemas of the validation and test set do not overlap during the model training step. This presents a challenge for domain adaptation for two main reasons. Firstly, as far as schema concerned, the intersection of test set, validation set, and the training set is small. Specifically, 35% of words in the database schemas of the validation set do not appear in the training set, making it difficult to match the domain information in the user query and schema. Secondly, the database schemas differ significantly in structure, with syntactic information present in all of them, leading to difficulty in obtaining a unified schema representation. The main challenge under the cross-domain setup is to strengthen the ability of understanding questions and learn different database schemas quickly and adequately. The method proposed by us aims to address these challenges.

To effectively translate questions into SQL queries, it is important to identify the role of the syntactic information of the database schema. One of the primary tasks of Text2SQL parsers is to locate all the mentioned columns and tables in the syntactic schema. Once the relevant schema components are identified, the words in the questions and the database schema can be aligned by schema linking. In addition to the schema information, the syntactic information is also taken into the model account to ensure that the question is understand correctly. To address this, we propose a two-module encoder for the Text2SQL model that learn the mapping between the questions and the database schemas by used RGAT [7]. Furthermore, we introduce a new multi-task called graph pruning to enhance the schema linking capability of the model.

Our approach, named Syn-RGAT, is evaluated on the challenging cross-domain Text2SQL dataset, Spider. Contributions are summarized as:

- We propose the Syn-RGAT to jointly encode the database schema graph and the questions. For the questions, we analysis the syntax of it and use the syntactic enhancement module to learn the syntactic information of the questions. Then fuse the database schema graph and the syntactic component graph.
- We proposed a graph pruning task to assist model select the database schemas which should appear in the SQL query and combined it with the Text2SQL task by using multi-task framework with heuristic learning to improve the generalization of the model.
- The Experimental results show that our approach outperforms baseline models on the Spider dataset.

2   Related Work

The recent state-of-the-art models evaluated on Spider dataset use encoder-decoder architectures for encoding and AST-based structural architectures for query decoding. IRNet [17] encodes the question and schema separately with LSTM and self-attention respectively, augmenting them with custom type vectors for schema linking. They further use the AST-based decoder to decode a query in an intermediate representation that exhibits higher-level abstractions than SQL. But intermediate representations take more time to write and maintain. Meanwhile, Bogin [8] published Global-GNN, a different approach to schema linking on Spider, which applies global reasoning between question words and database schema. Global reasoning is implemented by gating the GNN that encodes the schema using the question token representations. But this work focuses on extracting the features of the database schema graph, ignoring the understanding of the questions by the model. Concurrently, ShadowGNN [20] presents a graph project neural network to abstract the representation of the question and schema. ShadowGNN uses Graph Attention Neural networks (GAT) which are widely used in other fields [21]. Scholak [22] proposes a method PICARD for constraining autoregressive decoders of pre-trained language models through incremental parsing. Most of this work focuses on the optimization of the model without analyzing the question, and only considers the Text2SQL task itself independently. In contrast, the Syn-RGAT provides a unified way to encode arbitrary relational information among inputs, our relation-aware transformer mechanism allows encoding relations between question words and schema elements explicitly, and these representations are computed jointly over all inputs using self-attention. Syn-RGAT is special in two important ways: (1) to make the model pay more attention to the real meaning of the question, we analyze the syntax of the question and integrate it with the representation; (2) additional graph pruning tasks are used to co-train the ability of our model to generate SQL queries.

3 Methods

In this section, we propose Syn-RGAT model. It utilizes the classic encoder-decoder [9] architecture as the backbone of our model. Firstly, a relation-aware graph neural network is employed to iteratively encode the database schema graph. Secondly, a syntactic enhancement module is applied to extract features from the natural language question and combine them with the encoding results of the database schema graph. The RGAT enables model to effectively capture the complex relationships between the database schemas, while the syntactic enhancement module enhances the ability to understand the questions of model and then we fuse the extracted features with the encoded database schema graph, resulting in improved performance.

3.1 Problem Definition

Syn-RGAT model takes the questions Q and the database schema S as input. Given a question $Q = \{q_i\}_{i=1}^{N}$ with length N and the corresponding database schema $S = T \cup C, S = \{s_j\}_{j=1}^{m}$, the goal of this paper is to generate a SQL query Y. The database schema S include multiple tables $T = \{t_1, t_2, \ldots, t_M\}$ and columns $C = \{C_1, C_2, \ldots, C_u\}$. The entire input database schema graph $G_N = (V_N, E_N)$ consists of question nodes, table nodes and column nodes.

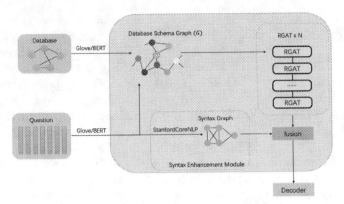

Fig. 1. The architecture of Syn-RGAT model. The database schema graph is composed of the natural language questions and the database schema. For the questions, we further build a syntax graph, and use Graph Convolutional Neural Networks (GCN) [11] to learn its nodes embeddings, and finally fuse the two graphs.

3.2 Schema Linking

Database schema linking [10], also known as database schema alignment, is a critical task that aligns entities in user questions with entities in database schemas. In our work, we present two methods to determine the database schema entities which mentioned in questions: text linking and value linking. Although text linking is the main way to determine the schema link, it leads to some errors. On the other hand, value linking has high accuracy, but it involves sensitive issues such as user privacy and has limited usage scenarios. To achieve more accurate linking, we integrate both and construct three types of relations for the token in the question and the database schema token: full match, partial match, and no match. Specifically, we use an N-gram based string-matching algorithm to calculate the similarity between the question and database schema, then assign the result to corresponding edge which related the database schema graph. We also introduce edge value links to construct the database schema graph when a specific value is mentioned in the question, and the corresponding field name in the database is mentioned in the user questions. For example, in question "For an artist with four exhibits, which one has the highest price", we can use "four" locate the table "artist" not the others.

3.3 The Construction of Database Schema Graph

In the proposed approach, heterogeneous graph G is constructed to achieve a joint representation of the database schema and questions. The nodes in G contain not only the tokens of the database schema and questions, but also edges connecting them. In addition to the text linking and value linking defined in Sect. 3.2, various edges are introduced to represent relationships between question tokens and database schemas. Specifically, the edge relations can be grouped into three main categories: question-question edge, table-column edge, and table-table edge. In our work, we expand the possible relationships between the database schema and user question and enhances the graph representation of the data.

Thus, the words in the questions and the database schema together determine the nodes in the database schema graph. The edges in the graph can be clearly categorized into two kinds: one is from the schema link between the questions and the database schema, while the other comes from the defined edge relationship.

3.4 Relation-Aware Graph Attention Network

RGAT has gained considerable attention in NLP tasks due to their capacity to model graph-structured data. These networks are capable of propagating and aggregating information from each node to generate a new representation for the node. As the depth of the network increases, it could aggregate information from higher-order neighbors.

In the framework we proposed (see Fig. 1. The architecture of Syn-RGAT model.), each node in the graph G is initialized as feature x_i by Glove or BERT, which is the initial hidden state of the database schema graph. The attention weights of the nodes in the graph are computed as follows:

$$
e_{ij}^{(h)} = \frac{x_i W_Q^{(h)} \left(x_j W_K^{(h)} + r_{ij,K} \right)^T}{\sqrt{\frac{d_z}{H}}} \tag{1}
$$

$$
\alpha_{ij}^{(h)} = softmax \left\{ e_{ij}^{(h)} \right\} \tag{2}
$$

where x_i and x_j are the representations of node i and node j respectively, $r_{ij,K}$ represents the representation of the relationship between two nodes, $W_K^{(h)}$ and $W_Q^{(h)}$ are two learnable parameter matrixes, d_z is the dimension of the nodes embedding, and H is the number of heads of multi-head attention. The final representation of node i in each attention head will be aggregated as follows:

$$
z_i^{(h)} = \sum_{j=1}^{n} \alpha_{ij}^{(h)} \left(x_j W_V^{(h)} + r_{ij,V} \right) \tag{3}
$$

where $W_V^{(h)}$ is a learnable matrix, and $r_{ij,V}$ is the embedding of the relationship between nodes i and j. Finally, we concatenate the results of each attention head to obtain the node representation of layer l:

$$
z_i^{(l)} = \sigma \left(\frac{1}{H} \sum_{h=1}^{H} z_i^{(h)} \right) \tag{4}
$$

where H is the number of heads of multi-head attention.

3.5 Syntactic Enhancement Module

We believe that database entities mentioned by natural language questions are usually noun components, so we introduce syntactic parsers to capture database schema in questions. From the previous work [12, 13], we have observed that the currently used syntactic parsers are insufficient for complicated questions. Thus, we propose a syntactic enhancement module that integrates syntactic information into the embeddings of nodes of database schema graph. Firstly, we will parse the questions to build a syntax tree, specifically, the relationship between words is extracted, and syntactic rules are applied to analyze grammatical structure of the sentence. Then, we convert the tree into a graph where each node is words of question. Finally, to make our model learn the topology of the syntactic graph of each question, we use GCN to extract features of the syntactic graph.

In Syn-RGAT, we train a syntactic enhancing module to improve the feature extraction ability from syntactic graph. Formally, in each GCN layer, the feature of each node is updated by aggregating the features of its neighboring nodes. The updated feature is then passed through a nonlinear activation function to generate the output feature of the current layer. We use multiple GCN layers to capture higher-order relationships between nodes in the syntactic graph, which allows the module to extract complex features and capture the syntax of the questions even better. The hidden state of node i in the current GCN layer is calculated as follows:

$$h_i^{(l+1)} = \sigma\left(D^{-\frac{1}{2}}AD^{-\frac{1}{2}}h_i^{(l)}W_g^{(l)}\right) \tag{5}$$

where $W_g^{(l)}$ is a learnable parameter matrix and σ is the activation function. A is the adjacency matrix of the graph and D is the degree matrix of A, which is shared between GCNS with different levels.

3.6 Graph Pruning

It is difficult for existing approaches to accurately predict column names using slot filling method to predict tables and columns in the SQL query. To solve this problem, we introduce graph pruning task that aims to eliminate irrelevant database schemas, and experiments show that graph pruning can improve the performance of our model (Fig. 2).

To improve the discernment of whether a database schema should be included in an SQL query, we propose an attention-based graph pruning task for Text2SQL, aimed at predicting the relationship between the database schema and the SQL query. Initially, the node representations of questions and database schemas are trained by RGAT. Then, we calculate the correlation between the two, as follows:

$$\beta_{ij}^h = softmax\left(\frac{(x_{si}W_{sq}^h)(x_{qj}W_{sk}^h)^T}{\sqrt{\frac{d}{H}}}\right) \tag{6}$$

where x_{si} and x_{qj} represent the embedding of the database schemas and the question words respectively, W_{sq}^h and W_{sk}^h are two learnable matrixes, d is the word embedding dimension, and H is the number of heads of multi-head attention. The database schema entities for each header are represented as follows:

$$\widetilde{x_{si}^h} = \left(\sum_j \beta_{ij}^h x_{qj}W_{sv}^h\right)W_o \tag{7}$$

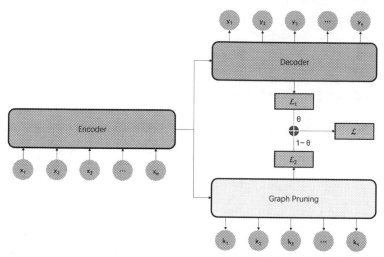

Fig. 2. The details of the decoder of Syn-RGAT model. Not all table and column names in the database will appear in SQL queries. Thus, we propose a graph pruning task to improve the ability of the model to select database schemas.

where x_{qj} is the representation of the questions words, W_{sv}^h, W_o are two learnable parameter matrixes. Finally, the results of each attention head are concatenated to obtain the transformed database schema representation:

$$\widetilde{x_{si}} = concat\left(\widetilde{x_{si}^1}, \widetilde{x_{si}^2}, \ldots, \widetilde{x_{si}^H}\right) \tag{8}$$

where, H is the number of attention heads. To calculate the relevance of database schemas and the questions, we evaluate the similarity between them. This similarity calculation aims at determining whether the database schema should appear in the generated SQL query or not.

$$sim\left(\widetilde{x_{si}}, x_q\right) = \left[\widetilde{x_{si}}; x_q\right]W_{bs} + b_{bs} \tag{9}$$

where, [;] is the concatenation operation, W_{bs} is the learnable matrix, and b_{bs} is the bias value.

To integrate the SQL query prediction task and the graph pruning task, we use a heuristic learning approach that utilizes shared encoding layer but different output layers in the decoder. Specifically, we define cross-entropy loss functions for both the SQL query prediction and graph pruning tasks. The loss functions from the output layers of the two tasks which guide the backpropagation of the model gradient together.

$$\mathcal{L} = \theta\mathcal{L}_{SQL} + (1 - \theta)\mathcal{L}_{gp} \tag{10}$$

where $\mathcal{L}_{SQL}$ and $\mathcal{L}_{gp}$ denote the loss functions for the Text2SQL task and the graph pruning task, respectively, and θ is a learnable parameter.

4 Experiment

4.1 Dataset

Spider is a comprehensive and extensive benchmark for the zero-shot cross-domain Text2SQL task, comprising of 8659 training examples across 146 databases. The benchmark encompasses multiple domains, Table 1 presents the detailed statistics. As the test set of this benchmark is not publicly available, the verification set is utilized as the test set in this study. The performance of each model on the verification set is reported as the experimental results in this paper.

Table 1. Statistics for dataset Spider.

	Train	Dev
# of samples	8659	1034
# of databases	146	20
Avg # of question nodes	13.4	13.8
Avg # of table nodes	6.6	4.5
Avg # of column nodes	33.1	25.8
Avg # of nodes	53.1	44.1
Avg # of actions	16.3	15.4

4.2 Setup

In the encoder, the RGAT hidden size d is set to 256 for GLOVE and 512 for BERT. The number of RGAT layers L is 8. In the decoder, the dimension of hidden state, action embedding, and node type embedding are set to 512, 128 and 128 respectively, the dropout is 0.2 for ON-LSTM. The number of heads in multi-head attention is 8 and the dropout rate of features is set to 0.2 in both the encoder and decoder. Throughout the experiments, we use Adam optimizer with linear warmup scheduler. For GLOVE, the learning rate is 5e−4 and the weight decay coefficient is 1e−4; for BERT, we use smaller leaning rate 2e−5, and larger weight decay rate 0.1. The optimization of the PLM encoder is carried out more carefully with layer-wise learning rate decay coefficient 0.8. The number of training epochs is 100 for GLOVE, and 200 for BERT respectively.

4.3 Results

Table 2 presents the exact match accuracy of the main results of the baseline model and the Syn-RGAT model. Syn-RGAT model outperforms all previous methods, achieving state-of-the-art results in all configurations at the time of writing. Using GLOVE word vectors, our model achieves an accuracy of 67.7%. Furthermore, when utilizing the pre-trained language model BERT-wwm, Syn-RGAT surpasses all previous models, including the ensemble model, and achieves an impressive 76.5% accuracy.

As shown in the Table 2, the performance of our raw Syn-RGAT and Syn-RGAT with BERT models are better than baseline models on the dev set. The addition of BERT further improves the performance of Syn-RGAT, and we believe that it has the potential to outperform newer models in the future. On the dev set, our proposed method with BERT-Large outperforms others method with BERT-Large. It should be noted that our focus is on dev set rather than a specific solution for the Spider dataset.

Table 2. Execution accuracy results on the Spider train set and dev set

Dataset	Model	EM
Spider	TypeSQL [14]	8.03
	SyntaxSQLNet [15]	18.97
	GNN/Global-GNN [8]	40.75
	EditSQL [16]	40.62
	IRNetv2 [17]	55.40
	RATSQL [10]	62.72
	LGESQL [18]	66.14
	SADGA [19]	64.73
	Syn-RGAT(ours)	67.68
	EditSQL (with BERT)	57.63
	IRNetv2 (with BERT)	63.98
	RATSQL (with BERT)	69.76
	LGESQL (with BERT)	74.12
	SADGA (with BERT)	71.66
	Syn-RGAT (ours) (with BERT)	76.58

As the Table 2 show, our proposed syntactic enhancement RGAT(Syn-RGAT) and Syn-RGAT with BERT achieve 67.68% and 76.58% respectively. The SyntaxSQLNet model, utilizing a template-based data augmentation method and slot filling, outperforms TypeSQL by 10.94%, reaching an accuracy of 18.97%. The GNN-based Global-GNN model is the first to apply graph neural networks to the Text2SQL task. The Syn-RGAT model outperforms Global-GNN and EditSQL, which introduces BERT for encoding, by utilizing syntactic information, achieving an improvement of 27 percentage points over EditSQL. The IRNet model treats Text2SQL as a machine translation task and introduces a custom intermediate representation, while the Syn-RGAT model uses an abstract syntax tree to generate SQL queries, resulting in a 12.28% improvement over IRNet. The RATSQL model implements Transformer on graph neural networks, but Syn-RGAT improves performance by introducing syntactic information and global nodes to guide schema selection. The LGESQL model, which utilizes the dual graph method, achieves

66.1% accuracy; however, Syn-RGAT further improves accuracy by introducing global information and syntactic representation, mining the graph structure at a deeper level. Finally, the SADGA model utilizes the dual graph aggregation mechanism to encode the question graph and database schema graph into a single graph. In comparison, Syn-RGAT introduces a pruning task to determine the most relevant tables and columns and trains the model using the loss of this task and the model loss, achieving 2.75% higher accuracy than SADGA.

In this experiment, the initial word vector representation of the model is obtained by fine-tuning the pre-trained BERT model, which is then used in place of the trained Glove word vector. The effectiveness of this approach is demonstrated by the improved performance of all models, including the substantial 8.9% improvement achieved by the model in this paper. Notably, the use of initial word vector replacement with the BERT model is also employed in comparison experiments with other baseline models. The performance of the model is positively correlated with schema link accuracy, and while the addition of the BERT model has significantly enhanced the prediction accuracy of the model, there remains room for improvement. Specifically, the model's prediction error is largely attributed to SQL queries involving cross-table queries and multiple clause nesting, as well as inconsistent statements between the questions and column names of the data table. Thus, the model's ability to handle such inconsistencies requires further improvement.

4.4 Ablation

We explore the impact of syntactic enhancement modules on model performance under different GCN layers and aggregation methods. We report the results on the Spider with 6 random seeds.

Table 3. Fusion methods with different number of GCN layers

Different feature fusion methods	# of GCN Layers	EM
Pooling	1	64.81
	2	65.38
	3	65.52
Cross-Attention	1	66.02
	2	67.68
	3	67.33

The RGAT model is a baseline system that does not utilize syntactic information. The results of the experiments on the effectiveness of different fusion methods are presented in Table 3. We find that the cross-attention method generally outperforms the pooling method, and as the number of GCN layers increases, the performance of the cross-attention method tends to decline. The reason for this trend is attributed to the syntactic analysis errors in some short questions, which leads to a descend in the performance of the more layers. However, the performance of the pooling method has been improving, as it corrects some samples and reduce the noise. Overall, increasing the number of GCN layers is better than adjusting the fusion method, with the two layers GCN being the optimal choice.

Table 4. Comparison of combination methods of graph pruning

Dataset	Feature fusion	Text2SQL task weights	Graph pruning task weights	EM
Spider	No	1	0	64.20
	Add	–	–	66.09
	Fix	0.3	0.7	67.13
		0.5	0.5	66.47
		0.7	0.3	66.28
	Heuristic learning	–	–	67.68

Based on the experimental results presented in Table 4, the heuristic learning method is utilized for joint training during model training. The result indicates that multi-task training significantly improves the performance of model. Significantly, the graph pruning task help model more accurately inferring related database schema. As the number of shared layers increases, the model becomes more like multi-task, and this increase has the potential to further boost the performance of our model.

5 Conclusion

The present study puts forth Syn-RGAT, a novel Text2SQL parser, to augment the transformation of NL into SQL query. The proposed Syn-RGAT parser incorporates a syntactic information graph, which can learn its topology, and a graph pruning task that boosts the schema selection ability of model. The experimental findings demonstrate the superiority of this approach over other existing parsers on the cross-domain dataset Spider, and its ability to significantly enhance the performance of cross-domain SQL generation.

Acknowledgments. This work was supported by the National Natural Science Foundation of China (No. 61966025), and Natural Science Foundation of Inner Mongolia (No. 2019MS06010, No. 2023MS06010).

References

1. Cao, R., et al.: Unsupervised dual paraphrasing for two-stage semantic parsing (2020)

2. Deng, X, et al.: Structure-grounded pretraining for Text-to-SQL (2020)
3. Gan, Y, et al.: Towards robustness of Text-to-SQL models against synonym substitution, https://doi.org/10.48550/arXiv.2106.01065 (2021)
4. Elgohary, A., Hosseini, S., Awadallah, A.H.: Speak to your parser: interactive Text-to-SQL with natural language feedback (2020)
5. Zhong, V., Xiong, C., Socher, R.: Seq2SQL: generating structured queries from natural language using reinforcement learning (2017)
6. Yu, T., et al.: Spider: a large-scale human-labeled dataset for complex and cross-domain semantic parsing and Text-to-SQL task (2018)
7. Wang, K., et al.: Relational graph attention network for aspect-based sentiment analysis (2020)
8. Bogin, B., Gardner, M., Berant, J.: Global reasoning over database structures for Text-to-SQL parsing (2019)
9. Sutskever, I., Vinyals, O., Le, Q.V.: Sequence to sequence learning with neural networks. In: Advances in Neural Information Processing Systems (2014)
10. Wang, B., et al.: RAT-SQL: relation-aware schema encoding and linking for Text-to-SQL parsers (2019)
11. Kipf, T.N., Welling, M.: Semi-supervised classification with graph convolutional networks (2016)
12. Huang, B., Carley, K.M.: Syntax-aware aspect level sentiment classification with graph attention networks (2019)
13. Wei, L., Mccallum, A.: Semi-supervised sequence modeling with syntactic topic models. In: National Conference on Artificial Intelligence AAAI Press (2005)
14. Tao, Y., Li, Z., Zhang, Z., et al.: TypeSQL: knowledge-based type-aware neural Text-to-SQL generation (2018)
15. Yu, T., Yasunaga, M., Yang, K., et al.: SyntaxSQLNet: syntax tree networks for complex and cross-domain Text-to-SQL task (2018)
16. Zhang, R., Yu, T., Er, H., et al.: Editing-based SQL query generation for cross-domain context-dependent questions (2019)
17. Guo, J., Zhan, Z., Gao, Y., et al.: Towards complex Text-to-SQL in cross-domain database with intermediate representation (2019)
18. Cao, R., Chen, L., Chen, Z., et al.: LGESQL: line graph enhanced Text-to-SQL model with mixed local and non-local relations (2021)
19. Cai, R., Yuan, J., Xu, B., et al.: SADGA: structure-aware dual graph aggregation network for Text-to-SQL (2021)
20. Chen, Z., Chen, L., Zhao, Y., et al.: ShadowGNN: Graph projection neural network for text-to-SQL parser (2021)
21. Veličković, P., Casanova, A., et al.: Graph attention networks (2017)
22. Scholak, T., Schucher, N., Bahdanau, D.: PICARD: parsing incrementally for constrained auto-regressive decoding from language models (2021)

Fast Generalizable Novel View Synthesis with Uncertainty-Aware Sampling

Zhixiong Mo[1], Weijun Wu[1], Weihao Yu[2], Tinghua Zhang[3], Zhilin Ke[4], and Jin Huang[1(✉)]

[1] South China Normal University, Guangzhou, China
{mozx,huangjin}@m.scnu.edu.cn
[2] Research Institute of China Telecom Corporate, Guangzhou, China
[3] China Electronic Product Reliability and Environmental Testing, Guangzhou, China
[4] Guangzhou Pixtalks Information Technology, Guangzhou, China

Abstract. Recent generalizable NeRF methods synthesize novel view images without optimizing per-scene via constructing radiation fields from 2D features. However, most of the existing methods are slow in the rendering process due to querying millions of 3D points to the NeRF model. In this paper, we propose a photorealistic novel view synthesis method with generalizable and efficient rendering. Specifically, given a set of multi-view images, we utilize a multi-scale scene geometry predictor consisting of MVS and NeRF to infer key points from coarse to fine. In addition, to obtain more accurate key point positions and features, we design an uncertainty-guided sampling strategy based on depth prediction and uncertainty perception. With the key points and scene geometry features, we propose a rendering network to synthesize full-resolution images. This process is fully differentiable, allowing us to train the network with only RGB images. Compared with state-of-the-art baselines, the experimental results show that our model is more efficient and has higher rendering quality on various synthetic and real datasets. With the multi-scale scene geometry predictor and uncertainty-aware sampling strategy, our approach infers geometry information efficiently and improves the rendering speed significantly.

Keywords: Novel view synthesis · Neural radiance field · Uncertainty-aware

1 Introduction

Novel View Synthesis (NVS) is an important research field in computer graphics and computer vision. In recent, NVS is widely used in a variety of applications including virtual tourism, television, and sports broadcasting. Given a set of input images and camera poses, the task of NVS is synthesizing the photorealistic image for the target view.

With the advent of deep learning, learning-based NVS methods made a significant impact on synthesizing image quality. Recently, Neural Radiance Field

L. Iliadis et al. (Eds.): ICANN 2023, LNCS 14256, pp. 389–401, 2023.
https://doi.org/10.1007/978-3-031-44213-1_33

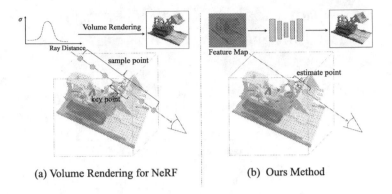

(a) Volume Rendering for NeRF   (b) Ours Method

Fig. 1. Comparison of our method (b) with the traditional NeRF method (a).

(NeRF) [16], a new implicit 3D representation, has shown great success in rendering high-quality novel view images. Despite the impressive results, NeRF exists two main drawbacks. First, NeRF trains the network for every scene separately with a very long optimization process. Second, NeRF synthesizes a novel view image with low rendering speed due to querying multiple sampling points during the rendering process.

Several works [2,12,13,22,24,28] address the former issue via generalizing NeRF rendering technique to unseen scenes. These works construct a radiance field dynamically by extracting the spatial features from a set of input images and training the NeRF renderer. They can produce photorealistic rendering results without per-scene optimization. Another line of works [8,18,21,27] are devoted to improving the slow rendering issue of NeRF. These methods often rely on explicit voxel representation, octree representation, or cache to store feature information. Although both of them achieve excellent results in their respective fields, efficient and generalizable NeRF variants are still under-explored.

In this work, we propose a photorealistic novel view synthesis method for generalizable and efficient rendering with sparse inputs. Previous methods query millions of 3D points in the entire space, but only a few key points play an important role in rendering images, which causes a slow rendering time. Our method leverages a multi-scale scene geometry predictor that accelerates the rendering process via reducing the number of rendering points. In particular, inspired by recent work (MVSNeRF) [2], we first construct the cost volume on the target view to compute the depth probability distribution and uncertainty by utilizing the MVS method [26]. Via the uncertainty-aware sampling strategy, we sample a few confident points near the scene surface. Then we propose a nerf-like network to estimate the refinement depth map and ray feature map of the target view. Aggregating entire scene ray features and 2D image features, we introduce a full-resolution render network based on a 2DCNN structure to synthesize images (Fig. 1).

We evaluate our method on the DTU [1], Real Forward-facing [15], and NeRF Synthetic [16] datasets. Experiments show that our method has the ability to synthesize high-quality novel view images across different scenes without per-scene training. Most importantly, compared with generalized novel view synthesis models, our method can significantly improve the rendering speed while maintaining the image quality. In summary, our main contributions are as follows: **1.** We propose an NVS approach that leverages a multi-scale geometric predictor consisting of the MVS and NeRF, which achieves fast and generalizable view synthesis. **2.** We design an uncertainty-guided sampling strategy that leads our method to learn to sample key points, which accelerates the rendering process without losing synthesis quality. **3.** We employ a rendering network to synthesize full-resolution images via entire space ray features and geometry, which also improve the rendering speed.

2   Related Works

Multi-View Stereo. Multi-View Stereo (MVS) is a classic computer vision problem that aims to estimate dense reconstruction via images from multiple viewpoints, which is widely researched by MVS traditional methods [6,7,20]. Recently, deep learning-based methods [11,26] have been extensively studied and have shown better performance than traditional methods. To improve the quality of geometric reconstruction, the following works extend this approach by utilizing point-based densification [3], multi-scale cost volume [9,25], confidence aggregation [4] and other techniques. In recent, via combining MVS methods with differentiable volume rendering, some works [2,5] have inferred the 3D geometry features of the scene to train generalizable neural radiance fields. In this work, we adopt the MVSNet method to obtain coarse geometric features and estimate the depth probability of the entire scene.

Uncertainty Estimation. Uncertainty estimation in deep learning is a rapidly growing field and is considered to have significant value in computer vision. Recently, with the development of novel view synthesis, several works have explored the possibility of applying uncertainty estimation in this field. NeRF-W [14] introduces uncertainty estimation to avoid the effect of transient objects in training process. ActiveNeRF [17] estimates uncertainty to select the training sample that brings the most information gain, which promotes the quality of novel view synthesis with minimal additional resources. [19] generates sparse depth maps by using SfM, converts it into dense depth maps and estimates uncertainty to guide the NeRF optimization while in sparse inputs. In our work, to improve the rendering performance, we propose an uncertainty-aware sampling strategy to infer the key points.

Novel View Synthesis. Early learning-based works demonstrate powerful capabilities in the NVS. Recently, NeRF [16] shows impressive results in high-quality novel view synthesis by combining MLP with differentiable volume rendering. However, NeRF synthesizes images with low speed and cannot generalize to unseen scenes without retraining the network. The following works [2,12,13,22,24,28] aim to improve the generalization ability of NeRF by constructing a radiance field dynamically. Although these methods synthesize novel view high-quality images without per-scene optimization, they are required to query a large number of 3D sample points to the MLP network, which costs a long time in rendering. In addition, several works attempt to accelerate the rendering process of NeRF. KiloNeRF [18] uses teacher-student distillation to train a smaller and faster MLP. [8,21] propose a graphics-inspired factorization to estimate the pixel values efficiently. Nevertheless, they require training the network for each new scene. To achieve a novel view synthesis model with high speed and generalizability, we propose a NeRF method to infer the feature and depth of each camera ray through key points, which are critical in the full-resolution rendering.

3   Method

In this section, our goal is to synthesize novel view images that are efficient and generalizable. Our architecture is presented in Fig. 2. The following sections provide our method in detail.

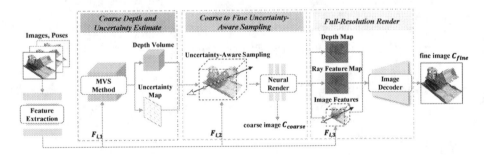

Fig. 2. Pipeline of our method. Our method is divided into 3 parts: Coarse Depth and Uncertainty Prediction, Coarse to Fine Uncertainty-Aware Sampling and Full-Resolution Rendering.

3.1   Coarse Depth and Uncertainty Prediction

Given a set of input images $\{I_i\}_{i=1}^{N_v}$ and their camera parameters, the method is designed to compute the coarse depth probability and uncertainty of the scene via MVS method [26].

Cost Volume Construction. For each input image $I_i \in \mathbb{R}^{H \times W \times 3}$, we feed it into a feature pyramid network (FPN) to extract three-stage feature maps $F_{i,1} \in \mathbb{R}^{H/4 \times W/4 \times C_1}$, $F_{i,2} \in \mathbb{R}^{H/2 \times W/2 \times C_2}$ and $F_{i,3} \in \mathbb{R}^{H \times W \times C_3}$. Subsequently, to predict coarse 3D scene geometry, we construct the cost volume by image feature maps $F_{i,1}$. Given the camera parameters, we warp 2D image features to a plane sweep volume via homography warping, which is defined as: $F_i^w \in \mathbb{R}^{H/8 \times W/8 \times C_1}$. Then, we leverage the variance-based metric to construct the cost volume based on the warped feature maps F_i^w of each input view.

Depth and Uncertainty Prediction. Previous MVS method predicts the depth probabilities from the cost volume. Similarly, in our approach, we regularize the target-view cost volume by a 3D UNet to predict depth probability volume $\mathbf{P}^{mvs} \in \mathbb{R}^{H/8 \times W/8 \times N_d}$ and geometry feature volume F_{voxel}. Then, inspired by [29], we design the uncertainty based on Shannon Entropy, which represents the confidence of depth estimation. With depth probability volume $\mathbf{P}^{mvs}$, the uncertainty map $\mathbf{U}^{mvs}$ is inferred by a shallow 2DCNN network S_c:

$$\mathbf{U}^{mvs} = S_c(-\sum_{j=1}^{N_d} \mathbf{P}_j^{mvs} \log \mathbf{P}_j^{mvs}) \qquad (1)$$

where N_d is the number of initial depth planes. Then depth probability volume and uncertainty map are used to estimate the coarse sampling points.

3.2 Coarse to Fine Uncertainty-Aware Sampling

The generalizable NeRF methods [2,12,13] rendering process is slow, as they sample many points in empty space when inferring radiance fields. Therefore, we propose an uncertainty-aware sampling strategy that leverages depth probabilities and uncertainty to estimate accurate key points from coarse to fine.

Uncertainty-Aware Sampling Strategy. Previous methods [9,26] estimate the depth by unimodal distribution, but they tend to ignore small objects and boundary regions with abrupt depth changes. To address this issue, according to the inverse transform sampling strategy, we use the depth probability volume $\mathbf{P}$ and its corresponding depth plane L to compute the initial depth sampling point $X \in \mathbb{R}^{H \times W \times N}$. For each sample point, we utilize uncertainty to calculate two additional points near the original ones, which are defined as follows:

$$X_{un} = X \pm clamp(\mathbf{U}, 0, 1) \times d_{inter} \qquad (2)$$

where d_{inter} is the depth interval, and $X_{un} \in \mathbb{R}^{H \times W \times N \times 2}$ is the uncertainty-based sampling points set.

Feature Fusion. After obtaining the uncertainty-based sampling points, we proceed to fuse the image features from each input view in order to render the target view image. Following the approach described in IBRNet [28], we project each sampling point to image feature maps $\{F_{i,n}\}_{i=1}^{N_v}$ and extract corresponding pixel-aligned features $\{f_{i,n}\}_{i=1}^{N_v}$. These features are then aggregated with a pooling network $\varphi_{fusion}(f_{1,n}, ..., f_{N_v,n})$ to output the image point features f_{img}^u. Finally, based on the pairs of uncertainty points and their point features, we employ a mean and variance-based network to fuse them:

$$f_{mean}, f_{var} = mean(\{f_{img}^u\}_{u=1,2}), var(\{f_{img}^u\}_{u=1,2})$$
$$f_{img} = \varphi_{m,v}(f_{mean}, f_{var}) \tag{3}$$

where $\varphi_{m,v}$ is a two-layer perceptron. The output feature f_{img} is used in the rendering process.

Coarse to Fine Sampling. For capturing the high-resolution scene geometry efficiently, we propose a multi-scale sampling method. We adopt the uncertainty-aware sampling strategy, utilizing $\mathbf{P}^{mvs}$ and $\mathbf{U}^{mvs}$ to compute coarse sampling points $X_{un,c} \in \mathbb{R}^{H/8 \times W/8 \times N_c \times 2}$. These points $X_{un,c}$ are then upsampled two times, and image features $f_{img,c}$ for each sampling point are aggregated from feature maps $F_{i,2}$ using the feature fusion approach. Additionally, for each sampling point, our method uses trilinear interpolation to obtain voxel features f_{voxel} from F_{voxel}. Leveraging both geometry and image information, we use an MLP network φ_{nerf} to generate the color features f_r and density σ for each point:

$$\sigma, f_r = \varphi_{nerf}(f_{voxel}, f_{img,c}) \tag{4}$$

In order to predict fine scene geometry, we utilize density estimation to establish the fine sampling prior. Similar to [16], we trace a ray through each pixel and calculate the depth probability:

$$\tau_k = \sum_{k=1}^{N_c} T_k \left(1 - \exp\left(-\sigma_k \delta_k\right)\right), \ where \ T_k = \exp(-\sum_{k'=1}^{k} \sigma_{k'} \delta_{k'}) \tag{5}$$

where k denotes the point number of each ray. δ_k represents the distance between two adjacent points, and T_k indicates the accumulated transmittance when reaching k. As described in Sect. 3.1, we use τ_k to construct the depth probability volume $\mathbf{P}^{nerf}$ and evaluate the uncertainty map $\mathbf{U}^{nerf}$ by a 2DCNN network S_f. Subsequently, $\mathbf{P}^{nerf}$ and $\mathbf{U}^{nerf}$ are used to compute fine sampling points $X_{un,f} \in \mathbb{R}^{H/4 \times W/4 \times N_f \times 2}$, where N_f is set to one. We also obtain the ray feature map F_r and depth map D for each ray, which are defined as follows:

$$F_r(r) = \sum_{k=1}^{N_c} T_k \left(1 - \exp\left(-\sigma_k \delta_k\right)\right) f_{r,k}$$
$$D(r) = \sum_{k=1}^{N_c} T_k \left(1 - \exp\left(-\sigma_k \delta_k\right)\right) \delta_k' \tag{6}$$

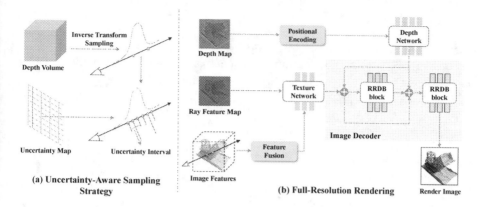

Fig. 3. The details of the (a) uncertainty-aware sampling strategy and (b) full-resolution rendering.

where δ'_k represents the distance from the sampling point k to the camera center. Furthermore, for training our network to learn low-resolution information accurately, we utilize a rendering network $\varphi_{color}(f_r, f_{i,2})$ to generate a low-resolution image $\widehat{C}_{coarse}$ by volume rendering (Fig. 3).

3.3 Full-Resolution Rendering

After computing the rough scene geometry and information, we utilize an image decoder to render the final full-resolution target view image. Rendering high-quality images from low-resolution features can be a challenging task. Fortunately, integrating local information of nearby pixels has proven to be effective for recovering high frequency details in rendering. Therefore, we upsample the ray feature map F_r, depth map D and fine uncertainty-based sampling point $X_{un,f}$ four times. According to the feature fusion approach, we also compute the image feature $f_{img,f}$ for each fine sampling point from the feature map $F_{i,3}$.

To provide guidance of the 3D structure, we feed depth map D into the 2DCNN network and infer the depth feature map D', which is designed as follows:

$$D' = \phi_{depth}(\gamma(D)) \tag{7}$$

where $\gamma()$ denotes the positional embedding. ϕ_{depth} is a four-layer ResNet [10]. Then, the depth, ray and image features are used to generate the target view image $\widehat{C}_{fine}$ by an image decoder:

$$\widehat{C}_{fine} = \phi_{decoder}(D', f_{img,f}, F_r) \tag{8}$$

where $\phi_{decoder}$ is RRDB-Net with two residual in residual dense blocks [23]. Instead of concatenating depth features with ray and image features, our method injects depth features into each block.

3.4   Loss Function

During training, our model is trained only from RGB images. Following NeRF [16], the model is trained by minimizing the mean squared errors (MSE) between the predicted image $\widehat{\mathbf{C}}(\mathbf{r})$ and the ground-truth image $\mathbf{C}(\mathbf{r})$:

$$\mathcal{L}_{\text{MSE}} = \frac{1}{|\mathcal{R}|} \sum_{\mathbf{r} \in \mathcal{R}} \|\widehat{\mathbf{C}}(\mathbf{r}) - \mathbf{C}(\mathbf{r})\|_2^2 \tag{9}$$

where $\mathcal{R}$ denotes the ray number of the image. To jointly learn the rendered color and its uncertainty, we minimize the negative log likelihood described above:

$$\mathcal{L}_{un} = \frac{1}{|\mathcal{R}|} \sum_{\mathbf{r} \in \mathcal{R}} \frac{1}{\mathbf{U}(\mathbf{r})} \|\widehat{\mathbf{C}}(\mathbf{r}) - \mathbf{C}(\mathbf{r})\|_2^2 + \log \mathbf{U}(\mathbf{r}) \tag{10}$$

where $\mathbf{U}(\mathbf{r})$ denotes the ray uncertainty after the upsampling operation. We found that the model tends to produce blurry or oversmoothed images during training. Therefore, we utilize the perceptual loss to regularize fine detail in the rendering process:

$$\mathcal{L}_{perc} = \frac{1}{|\mathcal{R}|} \sum_{\mathbf{r} \in \mathcal{R}} \left\| \Phi\left(\hat{\mathbf{C}}(\mathbf{r})\right) - \Phi\left(\mathbf{C}(\mathbf{r})\right) \right\| \tag{11}$$

where $\Phi()$ is a pre-trained 19-layer VGG network to estimate the similarity between the predicted image $\hat{\mathbf{C}}$ and ground-truth image $\mathbf{C}$ in the feature space. We integrate multiple loss functions $\mathcal{L}_{mul} = \lambda_{\text{MES}} \mathcal{L}_{\text{MES}} + \lambda_{perc} \mathcal{L}_{perc} + \lambda_{un} \mathcal{L}_{un}$ by a weighted approach. For each scale rendered image $\hat{\mathbf{C}}_{coarse}$ and $\hat{\mathbf{C}}_{fine}$, our model calculates their multiple losses individually and computes the total loss function as $\mathcal{L}_{total} = \lambda_{coarse} \mathcal{L}_{coarse} + \lambda_{fine} \mathcal{L}_{fine}$.

4   Experiments

4.1   Experiments Setup

Model Detail. During training process, our model is trained using the Adam optimizer with an initial learning rate of 0.0005. In the 2D image feature extraction, the number of feature channels is $C_1 = 32$, $C_2 = 16$, $C_3 = 8$. During the sampling process, the number of sampling points is $N_d = 64$, $N_c = 8$. The multiple loss parameters λ_{MES}, λ_{un}, λ_{perc} and the total loss parameters λ_{coarse}, λ_{fine} are respectively set to 1, 0.1, 0.01 and 0.1, 1. In pretraining, our method is trained on a GTX 3090 GPU and tends to converge after approximately 170k iterations, which takes about 14 h. In per-scene optimization, we train our model with 15 min based on the pretrained model.

Dataset. We only use the DTU dataset [1] to train our pretrained model, which consists of 124 different scenes. We use the same dataset processing approach as MVSNeRF [2] and PixelNeRF [28], dividing the dataset into 88 training scenes, 15 validation scenes and 16 testing scenes. To demonstrate the generalization capability of our model, we also test on the NeRF Synthetic datasets [15] and the Real Forward Face dataset [16]. According to the same rules of MVSNeRF, we choose three images of the nearby source views as inputs to train the model and generate the target view images.

Baselines. In our work, we compare our method with PixelNeRF, IBRNet, and MVSNeRF without per-scene optimization, which are the SOTA generalizable NeRF variants with sparse inputs. During the fine-tuning process, we conducted a comparative analysis of our method with other techniques.

Metric. We compare our model with others to show the performance of generalization and rendering speed. PSNR, SSIM and LPIPS are often used to indicate image quality in the NVS. We also use FPS to measure the rendering speed.

4.2 Comparison with Baselines

We compare our model with pixelNeRF, MVSNeRF and IBRNet in terms of generalizable ability and rendering speed. During the pretraining, all generalizable methods are pretrained on the DTU dataset and tested on other unseen datasets with the same principle as MVSNeRF.

As shown by the quantitative results in Table 1, our approach consistently outperforms baselines in generalizable ability. In addition, to demonstrate the rendering efficiency of our method, we utilize these models to render a DTU image with 512×640 resolution on a single RTX 3090 GPU. Table 1 exhibits that our model runs at least 50 times faster than previous generalizable radiance field methods. The slow rendering speed of previous methods can be attributed to their need to infer many sampling points for each pixel. In contrast, our model leverages an uncertainty-aware sampling strategy and a multi-scale geometry predictor to estimate the range of depths incrementally and filter accurate key points. These strategies help reduce the rendering time. Specifically, our model first costs 14 ms to evaluate the scene geometry at low resolution using the mvs method. Then, it takes 17 ms to obtain the geometry information from coarse to fine and finally takes 25 ms to render a full-resolution image by the image decoder. We also compare our fine-tuning results with other methods. After 15 minutes of fine-tuning, our model obtains high quality results on several datasets, especially on the metric of LPIPS.

We provide qualitative comparisons of generalizable results in Fig. 4. Obviously, other models tend to produce obvious blurring and artifacts when generating novel view images in sparse inputs. This is because reflective regions and

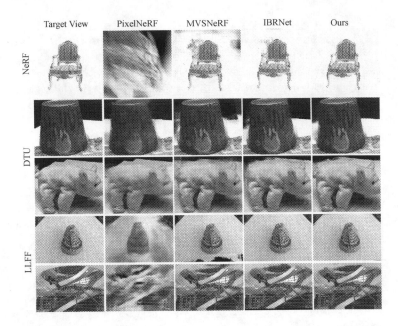

Fig. 4. Qualitative comparisons of view synthesis on the NeRF Synthetic, DTU and Real Forward Face datasets.

low-texture surfaces often lead to predict wrong density for empty points during volume rendering. In contrast, our method uses a multi-scale geometric predictor to estimate the depth probabilities of the scene and samples key points near the scene surface, which avoids the interference of empty points. This approach benefits from reasonable sampling for uncertain regions, enabling our model to generate higher-quality images even with sparse views. Moreover, our rendering 2D network incorporates depth information during full-resolution rendering, leading to images with better restored scene details and fewer artifacts.

Table 1. Quantitative comparison of image synthesis results on datasets of NeRF Synthetic, DTU and Real Forward-facing.

Methods	Rendering Time (FPS)	NeRF Synthetic			DTU			Real Forward-facing		
		PSNR↑	SSIM↑	LPIPS↓	PSNR↑	SSIM↑	LPIPS↓	PSNR↑	SSIM↑	LPIPS↓
PixelNeRF	0.018	7.39	0.658	0.411	19.31	0.789	0.382	11.24	0.486	0.671
IBRNet	0.203	22.44	0.874	0.195	26.04	0.917	0.191	21.79	0.786	0.279
MVSNeRF	0.397	23.62	0.897	0.176	26.63	0.931	0.168	21.93	0.795	0.252
Ours	**17.81**	**24.80**	**0.929**	**0.118**	**27.32**	**0.936**	**0.133**	**22.31**	**0.830**	**0.236**
NeRF$_{10.2h}$	0.160	**30.63**	**0.962**	0.093	27.01	0.902	0.263	**25.97**	0.870	0.236
IBRNet$_{1.0h}$	0.203	25.62	0.939	0.111	**31.35**	**0.956**	0.131	24.88	0.861	0.189
MVSNeRF$_{15min}$	0.397	27.07	0.931	0.168	28.51	0.933	0.179	25.45	**0.877**	0.192
Ours$_{15min}$	**17.81**	26.76	0.938	**0.086**	27.83	0.946	**0.118**	24.93	0.855	**0.186**

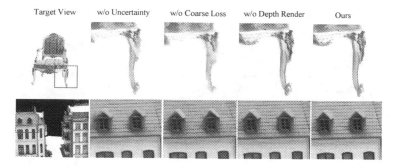

Fig. 5. Qualitative ablation analysis of the influence of each component.

4.3   Ablation Studies and Analysis

Ablation of Main Proposed Components. We perform ablation experiments on the DTU test dataset to examine the impact of various modules. The quantitative and qualitative results are individually recorded in Table 2 and Fig. 5.   We first analyze the impact of uncertainty estimation in our model. The uncertainty predicts the confidence of depth estimates, which leads the model to infer more accurate depth information. Through uncertainty estimation and sampling, we demonstrate that our model improves the rendering performance. Next, we remove the depth injection in the image decoder. Our approach utilized low-resolution ray features to produce full-resolution images, where the detailed position information is critical for image rendering. Therefore, the missing of depth information produces a blurry image. With depth injection in the image decoder, we obviously improved the clarity of complex and subtle object details. Finally, we show the vital role of coarse loss. In the coarse depth estimation process, predicting the depth probability of the scene at low-resolution is challenging without depth supervision. Therefore, it leads to errors in coarse geometry estimation and low image quality without the use of coarse loss.

Ablation of Sample Number and View Number. We also investigate the impact of different sampling points and input views on speed and rendering quality. As shown in Table 3, we try to vary the number of sampling points of each ray in the coarse sampling process. The results indicate that increasing the number of sample points improves image quality but also increases rendering time. Then, we also show the impact of varying the number of nearest input views in the rendering process, and find that the increase of input views results in better image quality but lower rendering speed. In summary, our approach achieves the optimal balance between rendering quality and speed.

Table 2. Quantitative ablation analysis of the influence of each component, test on the DTU dataset

Algorithm	PSNR↑	SSIM↑	LPIPS↓
w/o Uncertainty	26.84	0.912	0.158
w/o Depth Render	26.97	0.915	0.161
w/o Coarse Loss	26.57	0.891	0.175
ours	27.32	0.936	0.133

Table 3. Quantitative ablation analysis of the number of samples and input source views on the DTU dataset.

Samples	PSNR↑	FPS	Views	PSNR↑	FPS
2	26.93	19.80	2	25.24	19.56
4	27.19	19.13	3	27.32	17.81
8	27.32	17.81	4	27.43	14.53
16	27.35	13.84	5	27.47	13.12

5 Conclusion

In this paper, we propose a photorealistic novel view synthesis method that can rapidly generate high-quality images for complex scenes without per-scene optimization. Our approach employs a multi-scale depth predictor to improve rendering speed, which obtains key points using an uncertainty-guided sampling strategy and synthesizes images with a 2D structured network. Although our method can synthesize high-quality novel view images generally and efficiently, there are failure cases when regions are unseen in the input view. How to achieve high-quality rendering in invisible regions is a significant concern.

Acknowledgements. This work was supported by the Natural Science Foundation of Guangdong Province, China No. 2022A1515010148.

References

1. Aanæs, H., Jensen, R.R., Vogiatzis, G., Tola, E., Dahl, A.B.: Large-scale data for multiple-view stereopsis. Int. J. Comput. Vision **120**(2), 153–168 (2016)
2. Chen, A., et al.: MVSNeRF: fast generalizable radiance field reconstruction from multi-view stereo. In: CVPR, pp. 14124–14133 (2021)
3. Chen, R., Han, S., Xu, J., Su, H.: Point-based multi-view stereo network. In: CVPR, pp. 1538–1547 (2019)
4. Cheng, S., et al.: Deep stereo using adaptive thin volume representation with uncertainty awareness. In: CVPR, pp. 2524–2534 (2020)
5. Chibane, J., Bansal, A., Lazova, V., Pons-Moll, G.: Stereo Radiance Fields (SRF): learning view synthesis for sparse views of novel scenes. In: CVPR, pp. 7911–7920 (2021)
6. De Bonet, J.S., Viola, P.: Poxels: probabilistic voxelized volume reconstruction. In: ICCV, vol. 2 (1999)
7. Furukawa, Y., Ponce, J.: Accurate, dense, and robust multiview stereopsis. IEEE Trans. Pattern Anal. Mach. Intell. **32**(8), 1362–1376 (2009)
8. Garbin, S.J., Kowalski, M., Johnson, M., Shotton, J., Valentin, J.: FastNeRF: high-fidelity neural rendering at 200 FPS. In: CVPR, pp. 14346–14355 (2021)
9. Gu, X., Fan, Z., Zhu, S., Dai, Z., Tan, F., Tan, P.: Cascade cost volume for high-resolution multi-view stereo and stereo matching. In: CVPR, pp. 2495–2504 (2020)
10. He, K., Zhang, X., Ren, S., Sun, J.: Deep residual learning for image recognition. In: CVPR, pp. 770–778 (2016)

11. Im, S., Jeon, H.G., Lin, S., Kweon, I.S., et al.: DPSNet: end-to-end deep plane sweep stereo. In: ICLR (2019)
12. Johari, M.M., Lepoittevin, Y., Fleuret, F.: GeoNeRF: generalizing NeRF with geometry priors. In: CVPR, pp. 18365–18375 (2022)
13. Liu, Y., et al.: Neural rays for occlusion-aware image-based rendering. In: CVPR, pp. 7824–7833 (2022)
14. Martin-Brualla, R., Radwan, N., Sajjadi, M.S., Barron, J.T., Dosovitskiy, A., Duckworth, D.: NeRF in the wild: neural radiance fields for unconstrained photo collections. In: CVPR, pp. 7210–7219 (2021)
15. Mildenhall, B., et al.: Local light field fusion: practical view synthesis with prescriptive sampling guidelines. ACM Trans. Graph. (TOG) 38(4), 1–14 (2019)
16. Mildenhall, B., Srinivasan, P.P., Tancik, M., Barron, J.T., Ramamoorthi, R., Ng, R.: NeRF: representing scenes as neural radiance fields for view synthesis. In: Vedaldi, A., Bischof, H., Brox, T., Frahm, J.-M. (eds.) ECCV 2020. LNCS, vol. 12346, pp. 405–421. Springer, Cham (2020). https://doi.org/10.1007/978-3-030-58452-8_24
17. Pan, X., Lai, Z., Song, S., Huang, G.: ActiveNeRF: learning where to see with uncertainty estimation. In: Avidan, S., Brostow, G., Cissé, M., Farinella, G.M., Hassner, T. (eds.) Computer Vision – ECCV 2022. ECCV 2022. LNCS, vol. 13693, pp. 230–246. Springer, Cham (2022). https://doi.org/10.1007/978-3-031-19827-4_14
18. Reiser, C., Peng, S., Liao, Y., Geiger, A.: KiloNeRF: speeding up neural radiance fields with thousands of tiny MLPs. In: CVPR, pp. 14335–14345 (2021)
19. Roessle, B., Barron, J.T., Mildenhall, B., Srinivasan, P.P., Nießner, M.: Dense depth priors for neural radiance fields from sparse input views. In: CVPR, pp. 12892–12901 (2022)
20. Schönberger, J.L., Zheng, E., Frahm, J.-M., Pollefeys, M.: Pixelwise view selection for unstructured multi-view stereo. In: Leibe, B., Matas, J., Sebe, N., Welling, M. (eds.) ECCV 2016. LNCS, vol. 9907, pp. 501–518. Springer, Cham (2016). https://doi.org/10.1007/978-3-319-46487-9_31
21. Wadhwani, K., Kojima, T.: SqueezeNeRF: further factorized FastNeRF for memory-efficient inference. In: CVPR, pp. 2717–2725 (2022)
22. Wang, Q., et al.: IBRNet: learning multi-view image-based rendering. In: CVPR, pp. 4690–4699 (2021)
23. Wang, X., et al.: ESRGAN: enhanced super-resolution generative adversarial networks. In: Leal-Taixé, L., Roth, S. (eds.) ECCV 2018. LNCS, vol. 11133, pp. 63–79. Springer, Cham (2019). https://doi.org/10.1007/978-3-030-11021-5_5
24. Xu, Q., et al.: Point-NeRF: point-based neural radiance fields. In: CVPR, pp. 5438–5448 (2022)
25. Yang, J., Mao, W., Alvarez, J.M., Liu, M.: Cost volume pyramid based depth inference for multi-view stereo. In: CVPR, pp. 4877–4886 (2020)
26. Yao, Y., Luo, Z., Li, S., Fang, T., Quan, L.: MVSNet: depth inference for unstructured multi-view stereo. In: Ferrari, V., Hebert, M., Sminchisescu, C., Weiss, Y. (eds.) ECCV 2018. LNCS, vol. 11212, pp. 785–801. Springer, Cham (2018). https://doi.org/10.1007/978-3-030-01237-3_47
27. Yu, A., Li, R., Tancik, M., Li, H., Ng, R., Kanazawa, A.: PlenOctrees for real-time rendering of neural radiance fields. In: CVPR, pp. 5752–5761 (2021)
28. Yu, A., Ye, V., Tancik, M., Kanazawa, A.: pixelNeRF: neural radiance fields from one or few images. In: CVPR, pp. 4578–4587 (2021)
29. Zhang, J., Yao, Y., Li, S., Luo, Z., Fang, T.: Visibility-aware multi-view stereo network. BMVC (2020)

Find Important Training Dataset by Observing the Training Sequence Similarity

Zhengchang Liu[1], Hang Diao[2], Fan Zhang[2(✉)], and Samee U. Khan[3]

[1] College of Computer and Information Engineering, Nanjing Tech University,
Nanjing, China
[2] Ocean College, Zhejiang University, Zhoushan, China
f.zhang@zju.edu.cn
[3] Mississippi State University, Starkville, MS, USA

Abstract. It is imperative to eliminate training data that has minimal impact on model accuracy. In addition to eliminating training data that share similar features, we propose a novel concept called *training sequence*, which signifies the trajectory of each training data in terms of correct or incorrect prediction during each training epoch. We eliminate training data that exhibit similar training trajectories. We complement this approach with the identification of hard-to-forget training data that consistently demonstrate accurate prediction. We conducted extensive experiments on various classical classification tasks and compared our approach with forgetting-score method. Our experimental findings demonstrate that our approach outperforms the forgetting-score approach by up to 13.2% and is particularly effective at low training data retention ratios, implying that our method can choose important training datasets with satisfactory performance. Our open-source code is available at the following link: https://github.com/sheldonlll/angle_method.

Keywords: Training sequence · Data pruning · Similarity matrix

1 Introduction

With the increasing size of deep learning models and datasets, there is a proportional increase in the computing resources required for training. The Transformer-based model currently has $3.3 * 10^{18}$ floating-point computing capabilities (Vaswani et al. 2017 [12]), while the ImageNet dataset comprises 14.1 million images (Russakovsky et al. 2015 [10]), requiring a storage space of approximately over 100 GB. Training large models and datasets can take several days or weeks to obtain the desired results. In their empirical study, Toneva et al. 2018 [11] present a novel approach that leverages forgetting dynamics to identify training samples that are hard or easy to forget by a machine learning model which we called forgetting-score method. Specifically, the hard-to-forget training samples as those that are consistently and correctly predicted throughout all training epochs, while easy-to-forget training samples are mostly predicted incorrectly during the training process.

L. Iliadis et al. (Eds.): ICANN 2023, LNCS 14256, pp. 402–413, 2023.
https://doi.org/10.1007/978-3-031-44213-1_34

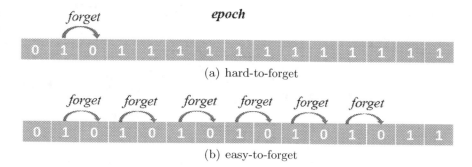

(a) hard-to-forget

(b) easy-to-forget

Fig. 1. In Fig. 1(a), we present a training sample that exhibits a low rate of forgetting events, making it difficult to forget during the training process. Conversely, in Fig. 1(b), we illustrate a training sample that experiences multiple forget events, categorizing it as an easy-to-forget sample.

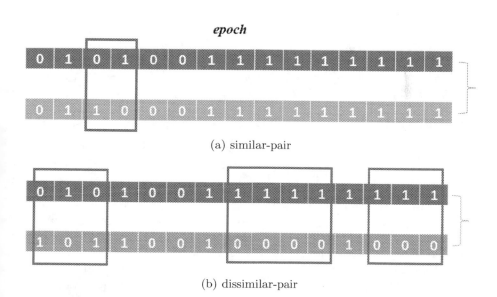

(a) similar-pair

(b) dissimilar-pair

Fig. 2. In Fig. 2(a), we demonstrate two training samples that display similar training sequences, while in Fig. 2(b), we depict a pair of training samples that exhibit dissimilar training sequences.

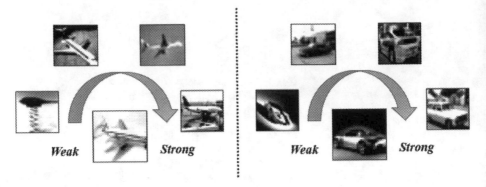

Fig. 3. The four selected images visually exemplify the continuum of similarity, ranging from weak to strong, in comparison with the central image within the same class.

We show the difference between these two sorts of training samples using the training sequence in Fig. 1. To select the training dataset, the authors employ a differentiated sampling approach, wherein a higher percentage of easy-to-forget training samples are included compared to the hard-to-forget ones. This methodology aims to improve the overall performance and robustness of the trained model by prioritizing samples that are more challenging for the model to learn. Upon observation, it has been noted that training samples can be categorized as easy-to-forget ones or hard-to-forget ones. However, it is also evident that training samples exhibit other distinct features that could be utilized to enhance the training process. Specifically, we define the training sequence acc_x of a training sample x as a list of binary values, where each value acc_x^k represents whether it was correctly or wrongly predicted in the kth epoch. It is observed that certain training samples, such as x and y, may exhibit similar acc_x and acc_y patterns, indicating similar behaviors during the training process. We hypothesize that this information could be effectively leveraged to improve the performance of the model further.

When the training sequence of the x and y are not similar, it indicates that the model has the capability to distinguish the two training samples, or the two training samples are *far* in the distance and visa versa. We detail the concepts in Fig. 2. Figure 3 shows the continuum of distances between training samples within the same class. Using the methodology described above, the findings are presented in Fig. 4, which illustrates a comparison between easy-to-forget samples and hard-to-forget training samples. The results reveal that hard-to-forget training samples exhibit common characteristics, including simple-color backgrounds and sharp contours, making them easily identifiable at a glance. As a result, we refer to these hard-to-forget training samples as baseline training samples. Our intention is to extract training samples that deviate significantly from this baseline, as we believe they would be beneficial in enhancing the model's generalization capabilities.

Fig. 4. The top portion of the dataset contains one exemplary hard-to-forget training sample from each class. Meanwhile, the bottom portion of the dataset showcases the image within each class that bears the least similarity to the aforementioned hard-to-forget training sample. This meticulous selection process ensures that the dataset encompasses a diverse range of representative examples, promoting robust model training and performance.

2   Related Work

Curriculum Learning. Curriculum Learning is an optimization method in machine learning, which makes learning more efficient by gradually increasing the difficulty of training. Bengio et al. 2009 [1] proposed a language model-based approach to curriculum learning that trains the model by gradually increasing the sentence length. Katharopoulos et al. 2018 [6] argue that the importance of samples is related to the gradient norm of their loss function to network parameters. Jiang et al. 2018 [5] improves the generalization performance of the student model in the context of corrupted labels based on the teacher model's judgment of how easy it is to train on data. Wang et al. 2019 [13] propose a dynamic curriculum learning method to solve the data imbalance problem. Chang et al. 2017 [2] use a "sample variance" indicator to measure the difficulty of each sample. Training from high-variance samples allows the model to obtain better generalization capabilities. Li et al. 2019 [8] use a noise filter to allow the model to learn in high-noise tough training samples. Toneva et al. 2018 [11] proposed a screening method based on forgetting dynamics, which can delete most hard-to-forget samples without affecting the model's generalization performance.

Deep Generalization. Masters et al. 2018 [9], Wu et al. 2017 [14], and Zhang et al. [15] mentioned that the generalization ability of the model is not only affected by the complexity of the model. Krizhevsky et al. 2017 [7] use data enhancement methods such as rotation, scaling, and cropping on training data and uses dropout and L2 regularization techniques to improve the model. Ilyas et al. 2019 [4] increase the accuracy by adding adversarial samples (such as noise, etc.) to the training data set. In this paper, we present empirical results from several benchmark datasets to demonstrate that our method can achieve good generalization performance with only a small fraction of the training data retained without compromising the complexity of the dataset.

3   Methodology

3.1   Definition

Our study is built on top of a deep neural network, e.g., CNN or Transformer, that deals with a standard classification task. For a given dataset $D = \{x_i, y_i\}_i$ of observation/label pairs, a deep neural network with parameters Θ is utilized to learn the conditional probability distribution $P(y|x; \Theta)$. We denote by $\hat{y}_i^k = argmax_k P(y_{ik}|x_i; \Theta^k)$ the predicted label for example x_i obtained after $k + 1$ epochs of optimizer.

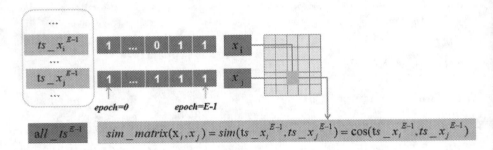

Fig. 5. The similarity matrix represents the comparison of training sequences between two training samples denoted as x_i and x_j.

Training Sequence. Let $acc_{x_i}{}^k = \mathbb{1}_{\hat{y}_i^k = y_i}$ be a binary variable indicating whether the example x_i is correctly classified at epoch k. We record the $acc_{x_i}{}^k (0 <= k <= E - 1)$ corresponding to the training sample x_i in the list

$$training\_sequence\_x_i{}^k = [acc_{x_i}{}^0, acc_{x_i}{}^1, ..., acc_{x_i}{}^k] \tag{1}$$

We denote $trainig\_sequence\_x_i{}^k$ as $ts\_x_i{}^k$ and save the $ts\_x_i{}^k$ of all training samples in $training\_sequences^k$. We abbreviate $training\_sequences^k$ to ts^k.

$$ts^k = [ts\_x_0{}^k, ts\_x_1{}^k, ..., ts\_x_{|D|-1}{}^k] \tag{2}$$

We define a continuous subsequence of length len in the ts^k as $sub\_ts_{len}^k (0 <= len <= |D|)$.

Similarity Matrix of Training Sequence. We define the similarity between the training sequences $ts\_x_i^k$, $ts\_x_j^k$ corresponding to the training samples x_i and x_j as the cosine distance

$$sim(x_i, x_j) = cos(ts\_x_i^k, ts\_x_j^k) \tag{3}$$

Next, we calculate the pairwise similarity on all training samples and save the calculated results in a matrix called sim_matrix, where $sim\_matrix[i][j] = sim(x_i, x_j)$. We define a subregion of shape $n\_num * m\_num$ in the sim_matrix as sub_sim_matrix, where $0 <= n\_num, m\_num <= |D|$. In Fig. 5, we give the specific details of obtaining sim_matrix.

3.2 Determine the Training Convergence Epoch

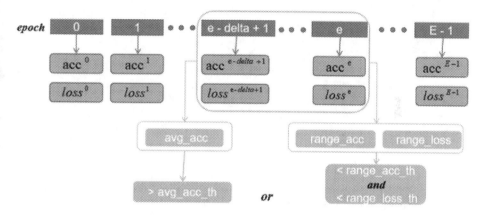

Fig. 6. A sliding window with *delta* steps in the training process to determine the convergence epoch. *avg_acc*, *range_acc* and *range_loss* are jointly evaluated. And the epoch = e is denoted by *th_epoch* when the logical condition requirement is satisfied.

Consider a training process that encompasses a maximum of E epochs, ranging from epoch 0 to $E - 1$, as depicted in Fig. 6. To determine if the training process has converged, we initiate the evaluation process from a predefined training epoch e. We retrospectively analyze *delta* epochs, calculating accuracy and loss metrics from epoch e to $e - delta + 1$, as denoted by the orange rectangular box in the figure, and we define e as *th_epoch*. Typically, we assess the following three metrics:

$$avg\_acc = \frac{\sum(acc^{e-delta+1}, acc^{e-delta+2}, ..., acc^e)}{delta} \tag{4}$$

$$range\_acc = \max(acc^{e-delta+1}, acc^{e-delta+2}, ..., acc^e) - \\ \min(acc^{e-delta+1}, acc^{e-delta+2}, ..., acc^e) \tag{5}$$

$$range\_loss = \max(loss^{e-delta+1}, loss^{e-delta+2}, ..., loss^e) - \\ \min(loss^{e-delta+1}, loss^{e-delta+2}, ..., loss^e) \tag{6}$$

In our evaluation process, we collectively assess the three metrics and conduct a comparison against three predetermined threshold values, namely avg_acc_th,

$range\_acc\_th$, and $range\_loss\_th$. Convergence of the model is determined when either the avg_acc metric surpasses the avg_acc_th threshold, or both the $range\_acc$ and $range\_loss$ metrics fall below their respective threshold values, $range\_acc\_th$, and $range\_loss\_th$. The detail is revealed in Algorithm 1.

Algorithm 1: Finding the th_epoch and Recording ts^{th_epoch}

Require: D^{train} # the training dataset
Require: E # the total number of training epochs
Require: $delta$ # the size of a sliding window
Require: $range\_acc\_th$, $range\_loss\_th$, avg_acc_th
Ensure: th_epoch # the qualified epoch
Ensure: ts^{th_epoch} # the qualified training sequences
1: Initialize $acc\_list, loss\_list$ as empty lists
2: **for** epoch $e = 0$ to $E - 1$ **do**
3:     $ts^{th\_epoch} \cup$ Compute $acc^e_{D^{train}}$;
4:     $acc\_list \cup$ Compute Acc of D^{train} ;
5:     $loss\_list \cup$ Compute Loss of D^{train} ;
6:     **if** $length(acc\_list) \geq delta + 1$ **then**
7:         $acc\_list, loss\_list \leftarrow acc\_list[-delta :], loss\_list[-delta :]$
         #Select the last delta elements in the sequence;
8:         Compute $avg\_acc, range\_acc, range\_delta$ from $acc\_list, loss\_list$
9:         **if** $avg\_acc \geq avg\_acc\_th$ or ($range\_acc \leq range\_acc\_th$ and $range\_delta \leq range\_loss\_th$) **then**
10:            Set $th\_epoch = epoch$
11:            Break the loop
12:        **end if**
13:    **end if**
14: **end for**
15: **return** th_epoch, ts^{th_epoch}

3.3   Prune the Training Dataset

In our experimental design, we first used the forgetting statistics algorithm by using forgetting-score method to identify training samples with very few occurrences of forgetting events and defined them as hard-to-forget training samples. Training samples not belonging to the hard-to-forget category were defined as easy-to-forget training samples. Next, we implemented Algorithm 1 to determine if the model has converged, which gave us the value of th_epoch and ts^{th_epoch}. We calculate the pairwise similarity among ts^{th_epoch} and store it in the sim_matrix.

Subsequently, it is imperative to discern the training samples that exhibit the greatest dissimilarity with the training sequences of the hard-to-forget samples, which are referred to as D^{train_subset}. Ultimately, the identified D^{train_subset} is used as the new training dataset, and the model is retrained accordingly.

Algorithm 2: Prune Training Dataset

Input: D^{train} # training dataset; E # total training epochs;
     r # retention ratio of the training dataset;
     $D^{hard-to-forget}$ # the hard-to-forget samples;
     ts^{th_epoch} # training sequences from 0 to th_epoch epoch;
Output: D^{train_subset} # remaining training dataset after pruning;

1 **Function** $prune\_training\_dataset(D^{train}, E, r, D^{hard-to-forget},$
   $ts^{th\_epoch})$:

2      $D^{train\_subset} = \{\}$

3      $S \leftarrow r * |D^{train}|$;# size of the remaining training dataset after pruning

4   **while** $|D^{train\_subset}| < S$ **do**

5         $sub\_ts^{th\_epoch}_{n\_num} \leftarrow ts^{th\_epoch}[s1 : s1 + n\_num]$# s1 is a random integer

6         $sub\_ts^{th\_epoch}_{m\_num} \leftarrow ts^{th\_epoch}[s2 : s2 + m\_num]$# s2 is a random integer

7   Initialize $sub\_sim\_matrix[n\_nums][m\_nums]$

8   **for** $i \leftarrow 0$ **to** $n\_nums - 1$ **do**

9   **for** $j \leftarrow 0$ **to** $m\_nums - 1$ **do**

10              $sub\_sim\_matrix[i][j] =$
              $sim(sub\_ts^{th\_epoch}_{n\_num}[i], sub\_ts^{th\_epoch}_{m\_num}[j])$

11   **end**

12   **end**

13         $subregion \leftarrow sub\_sim\_matrix[:, m\_nums * r :]$# choose a subregion with dissimilar training samples

14   **for** $training\ sample\ x, y \in subregion$ **do**

15   **if** $x \in D^{hard-to-forget}$ and $y \notin D^{hard-to-forget}$ **then**

16              $D^{train\_subset} \cup y$

17   **end**

18   **if** $x \notin D^{hard-to-forget}$ and $y \in D^{hard-to-forget}$ **then**

19              $D^{train\_subset} \cup x$

20   **end**

21   **end**

22   **end**

23   **return** D^{train_subset}

It should be noted that storing the entire sim_matrix would entail substantial memory usage. To optimize this process, we select two subsequences, namely $sub\_ts^{th\_epoch}_{n\_num}$ and $sub\_ts^{th\_epoch}_{m\_num}$, generated from the ts^{th_epoch}, and store their pairwise similarity values in a considerably smaller matrix, which we refer to as sub_sim_matrix. The sub_sim_matrix is sorted based on similarity on each row, which is significantly smaller than the original sim_matrix.

We partition the sub_sim_matrix based on the desired proportion of the training dataset to be retained and identify the most dissimilar subset. We add the easy-to-forget training samples from this subset to our new training subset only if their corresponding sequences exhibit high dissimilarity with the hard-to-forget samples. Additional details regarding the pruning process can be found in Fig. 7 and Algorithm 2.

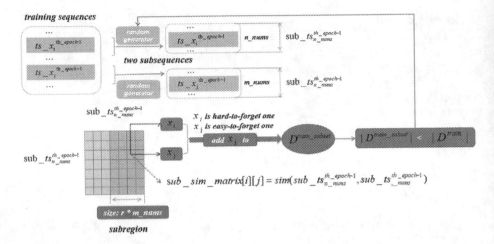

Fig. 7. The process of pruning a training dataset involves utilizing a binary-value training sequence as input, where each row represents a training sample index and each column represents an epoch number. The binary value indicates whether the training sample was correctly predicted or not. Instead of generating an exhaustive all-pair similarity matrix, an expedited approach was adopted, whereby a smaller similarity matrix, termed the sub_sim_matrix, was randomly generated. This iteration is repeated for several loops until a subset of training samples, denoted as D^{train_subset}, is identified that meets the specified retention ratio criteria.

4 Experiments

4.1 Experimental Setup

Data. The evaluation of the performance of our proposed approach is conducted using four benchmark datasets, namely $MNIST$, $FashionMNIST$, $CIFAR-10$, and $CIFAR-100$. Although the training datasets we have used for our evaluation are relatively small in size, they are still considered appropriate and representative since they are well-established datasets that have been thoroughly tested and verified by the community. Other than that, these datasets are carefully curated and designed to cover a wide range of real-world scenarios.

Model and Optimizer. Various models and optimizers were assessed across four datasets in our evaluation. For the experiment on the $MNIST$ dataset, a fundamental convolutional neural network model was employed, featuring two convolutional layers, two maximum pooling layers, a fully connected layer, and an output layer. The training was conducted using the SGD optimizer with momentum. In the experiments involving the $FashionMNIST$ dataset, a convolutional neural network model was utilized, comprising two convolutional layers, two batch normalization layers, one pooling layer, two dropout layers, and two fully connected layers. The training was performed using the SGD optimizer with momentum. As for the $CIFAR-10$ and $CIFAR-100$ datasets, the ResNet18 model was employed, accompanied by the SGD optimizer with momentum and a learning rate scheduler with a specific step size for training.

Hardware. All experiments are performed on a machine with NVIDIA GeForce RTX 3090 39.9 GB graphics card and 12th Gen Intel(R) Core(TM) i7-12700KF@ 2.38 GHz CPU.

Training Hyper-parameters. Data augmentation techniques such as rotation and shearing are applied to these datasets. Notably, during the retraining process after selecting data based on the forgetting-score method, a simple cutout method for regularization of convolutional neural networks (DeVries et al., 2017 [3]) is added, and the cutout method is not used for the selected training dataset when using our method.

For the threshold evaluation, specific threshold values are set for various parameters, including a range loss threshold ($range\_loss\_th$) and range accuracy threshold ($range\_acc\_th$) both set to 1e−3, average accuracy threshold (avg_acc_th) set to 0.85, delta (δ) set to 3, number of samples (n_nums) and margin samples (m_nums) set to 128.

4.2   Experimental Results

In Fig. 8, we report the results of our experiment. The x-axis in each figure represents the retention percentage on each dataset using the corresponding methods, and the y-axis represents the test accuracy by only using the retention dataset for training from scratch.

In the majority of percentage settings, our method outperforms the forgetting-score method. Notably, our approach demonstrates significant competitive advantage in experiments where a majority of the training data is pruned, such as 99% on $MNIST$, 95% on the $FashionMNIST$, 90% on the $CIFAR-10$, and 80% on $CIFAR-100$, which means our approach shows a competing advantage when the retention percentage is small. This clearly indicates that our method could pick up the most important dataset that is instrumental in improving the model performance. In most cases, the forgetting-score method shows marginal or no noticeable advantage in high retention percentage.

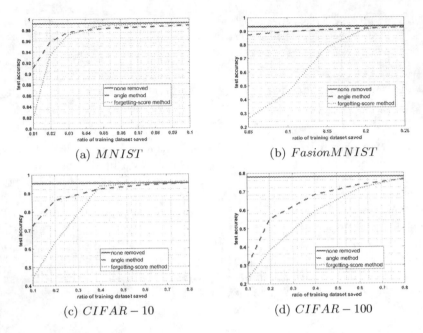

Fig. 8. The evaluation results are presented for varying percentages of training dataset retention in $MNIST$, $FasionMNIST$, $CIFAR-10$, and $CIFAR-100$ datasets. The solid line in each figure indicates the results obtained without data pruning. A dashed line represents our method, while the forgetting-score method is depicted by a dotted line.

5   Conclusion and Future Work

This study explores the concept of pairwise training sample similarity, referred to as *training_sequences*, and proposes a novel method for efficiently pruning training datasets based on similarity evaluation. Our experiments demonstrate that training samples that exhibit feature dissimilarity to hard-to-forget samples can significantly benefit model training. Consequently, our proposed approach enables the reduction of the training set proportion without compromising generalization performance.

Further research is needed to better comprehend the relationship between training data similarity and redundancy, as well as to assess the method's applicability to complex training sets. In addition, potential applications in other areas of supervised learning by means of training sample pruning using our proposed approach should be investigated.

References

1. Bengio, Y., Louradour, J., Collobert, R., Weston, J.: Curriculum learning. In: Proceedings of the 26th Annual International Conference on Machine Learning, pp. 41–48 (2009)
2. Chang, H.S., Learned-Miller, E., McCallum, A.: Active bias: training more accurate neural networks by emphasizing high variance samples. In: Advances in Neural Information Processing Systems, vol. 30 (2017)
3. DeVries, T., Taylor, G.W.: Improved regularization of convolutional neural networks with cutout. arXiv preprint arXiv:1708.04552 (2017)
4. Ilyas, A., Santurkar, S., Tsipras, D., Engstrom, L., Tran, B., Madry, A.: Adversarial examples are not bugs, they are features. In: Advances in Neural Information Processing Systems, vol. 32 (2019)
5. Jiang, L., Zhou, Z., Leung, T., Li, L.J., Fei-Fei, L.: MentorNet: learning data-driven curriculum for very deep neural networks on corrupted labels. In: International Conference on Machine Learning, pp. 2304–2313. PMLR (2018)
6. Katharopoulos, A., Fleuret, F.: Not all samples are created equal: deep learning with importance sampling. In: International Conference on Machine Learning, pp. 2525–2534. PMLR (2018)
7. Krizhevsky, A., Sutskever, I., Hinton, G.E.: ImageNet classification with deep convolutional neural networks. Commun. ACM **60**(6), 84–90 (2017)
8. Li, J., Wong, Y., Zhao, Q., Kankanhalli, M.S.: Learning to learn from noisy labeled data. In: Proceedings of the IEEE/CVF Conference on Computer Vision and Pattern Recognition, pp. 5051–5059 (2019)
9. Masters, D., Luschi, C.: Revisiting small batch training for deep neural networks. arXiv preprint arXiv:1804.07612 (2018)
10. Russakovsky, O., et al.: ImageNet large scale visual recognition challenge. Int. J. Comput. Vision **115**, 211–252 (2015)
11. Toneva, M., Sordoni, A., Combes, R.T.D., Trischler, A., Bengio, Y., Gordon, G.J.: An empirical study of example forgetting during deep neural network learning. arXiv preprint arXiv:1812.05159 (2018)
12. Vaswani, A., et al.: Attention is all you need. In: Advances in Neural Information Processing Systems, vol. 30 (2017)
13. Wang, Y., Gan, W., Yang, J., Wu, W., Yan, J.: Dynamic curriculum learning for imbalanced data classification. In: Proceedings of the IEEE/CVF International Conference on Computer Vision, pp. 5017–5026 (2019)
14. Wu, L., Zhu, Z., et al.: Towards understanding generalization of deep learning: perspective of loss landscapes. arXiv preprint arXiv:1706.10239 (2017)
15. Zhang, C., Bengio, S., Hardt, M., Recht, B., Vinyals, O.: Understanding deep learning (still) requires rethinking generalization. Commun. ACM **64**(3), 107–115 (2021)

Generating Question-Answer Pairs
for Few-Shot Learning

YuChen Wang and Li Li[✉]

School of Computer and Information, Southwest University, Chongqing, China
ainloy9@email.swu.edu.cn, lily@swu.edu.cn

Abstract. In the real world, obtaining question-answer pairs for a target domain text is often an expensive process, an approach to tackle the problem is to use automatically generated question-answer pairs from the problem context and large amount of unstructured texts (e.g. Wikipedia). However, current approaches to generate question-answer pairs typically require fine-tuning tens of thousands of examples to achieve good results. Obtaining these instances involves high labor costs, and once the model lacks sufficient training data, the performance of the model with few-shot (< 100 examples) drops dramatically. To address this problem, we propose a method for generating question-answer pairs with few examples, generating answers and questions using the input context, and then filtering the results through a model. By tuning the fine-tuned structure of the model to improve the few-shot performance, we also input different levels of features into the model through granularity decomposition, solving an important issue when data is limited: the inability to perform answer-span detection (or answer generation). We evaluate our method in three aspects: the diversity of generated answers, the quality of generated questions, and the training of a new model entirely using the generated QA pairs. Our experimental results demonstrate that our proposed method can effectively generate question-answer pairs with low resources.

Keywords: Few-shot learning · Question generation · Question answer generation

1 Introduction

Question answering (QA) and question generation (QG) are two fundamental tasks in natural language processing (NLP) that have seen substantial progress in recent years, QA involves generating answers to questions, while QG involves generating questions from input text. These tasks have a wide range of applications. While state-of-the-art models have been developed for QA and QG, the task of question-answer generation (QAG), in which generating QA pairs involves taking a given passage as input and generating the corresponding QA pairs, has not been fully explored and studied, this task is essential for data augmentation and generating diverse QA pairs to fulfill domain-specific task requirements, for example, creating educational materials for reading exercises and assessments [8,14], or generating QA pairs to improve children's narrative comprehension through storybooks [21].

Some recent synthetic QA data generation methods based on large pretrained language models (LM) have been proposed [2,13]. These methods are divided into two modules: a span/answer detector (or answer generation module), and a question generation module. However, these methods typically require a large number of data samples, and their performance decreases dramatically in data-scarce contexts, such as minority languages or specialized domains, especially in the answer generation module, which has been studied by a few researchers in the few-shot scenario.

To address this problem, we propose a few-shot learning method for generating QA pairs. Specifically, in the answer generation module, the Named Entity Recognition (NER) technique was previously commonly used as a span/answer detector. Given an input passage, the span detector is responsible for extracting the spans that will be used as answers to the generated questions. This approach requires a large amount of data to fine-tune the NER model and extracts answers that are mostly solid words, we transform the span detection task into a generation task through granularity decomposition to generate answers with limited training data. In the question generation module, We adjust the fine-tuned input-output design to be consistent with the pre-training framework by constructing the model inputs as a combination of question, mask token and context, and generating the question using the same way the mask token were recovered in the pre-training task. Our proposed fine-tuning framework is similar to the pre-training framework, allowing the model to make maximum use of the pre-training knowledge for the fine-tuning task of question generation. To ensure consistency between the generated questions and their corresponding answers, we adopt a round-trip filtering approach to filter the question-answer pairs.

Our contribution is threefold:

1. We propose a new framework for generating diverse QA pairs from a single context, which is, to our knowledge, the first few-shot learning generative model for question-answer pair generation (QAG).
2. Our approach tackles a significant challenge of previous QA data generation methods when data is limited: span/answer detector (or answer generation). We show that answers can be efficiently generated after different levels of features are fed into the model through granularity decomposition.
3. We evaluate our framework on several benchmark datasets by three aspects, i.e., diversity of generated answers, quality of generated questions, and training a new model entirely using generated QA pairs (QA-based evaluation). We demonstrate that our method can generate high-quality and diverse question-answer pairs in data-scarce settings (Table 1).

Table 1. In the few-shot setting (32 examples), our method generates two examples of question-answer pair compared to the NER approach.

NER answer	Generated answer	Generated question
Nordic	Closer ties to the Nordic Countries.	What has been a major factor in the restoration of Estonia after winning their independence?
QWIPs	Advanced forms of thermographic cameras such as those that incorporate QWIPs.	What can see stealth aircraft even with RCS?

2   Related Work

2.1   Question-Answer Pair Generation

In previous studies, most researchers used rule-based methods for question generation (QG) [9]. Recently, attention-based seq-to-seq models have been developed for QG [6], and the QG task achieved better generation by fine-tuning the pre-training models. While stand-alone question generation tasks have been thoroughly researched, in-context question and answer pair generation tasks are still being explored.

In the past, rule-based approaches were used to select answer spans or generate answers. These approaches used lexical features like POS and NER tags to select answer phrases or words [18]. Some recent work involves using cloze fill-in-the-blank passages to select an answer in a context by NER or linguistic parsers [2], but these methods can only generate answers for a single entity. Alberti et al. [1] uses model-based methods to match the answer distribution of the QA dataset and extract more complex answers.

Over the years, researchers have used QA and QG as dual tasks for joint learning [19], such as controls the latent space (e.g. VAE) and controls the generative space (e.g. random sampling) to improve the diversity of generative problems [10], or using synthetic QA pairs to provide more training data for models, developed to reduce the cost of manual annotation and improve model performance. Unsup.QA [12] generate pairs of synthetic context, question and answer triples by sampling contextual passages from a large corpus of documents, but additionally require named entity recognizers and lexical taggers.

However, the above work and methods require a large amount of data, and these manually labeled data are costly and not suitable for applications where data are scarce. Our work deviates from these because we do not rely on additional synthetic data, and do not use external NLP tools. Instead, we only use a few training examples for fine-tuning.

2.2   Few-Shot Learning

With the swift advancement of pre-training models in the field of natural language processing, there has been a growing interest in utilizing the acquired knowledge of such models to address the few-shot problem. While the GPT3 model [3] has shown exceptional performance in few-shot and zero-shot cases owing to its vast number of parameters and pre-training data, its high cost restricts its access to a limited group of researchers. In contrast, the PET model [17] has adopted prompt-learning to transform text classification into an ideal fill-in-the-blank task, thereby enabling it to achieve favorable performance with few-shot. By aligning the downstream task with the pre-training task, it can better utilize the knowledge gained in the pre-training phase. Similarly, the FewshotQA framework [4] improves the performance of QA scenarios by aligning only the inputs, targets, and outputs of the pre-training and fine-tuning phases without any model modification. This approach has yielded a significant boost in few-shot performance.

3   Methods

In this work, we aim to generate good-quality QA pairs for few-shot. Previous generative models such as GPT-2 [15], BART [11] have great performance in generating text using an auto-regressive form. However, the disadvantage is that when faced with the challenge of data scarcity, the model cannot control the generated text well based on the given answer because the model does not have enough data to learn the direction to be controlled, and the input to the model is just a sequence of text containing the control text. Our approach uses a bidirectional masking model (MLM) instead of the commonly used auto-regressive language models (e.g. GPT-2 [15]), and we achieve control output by aligning the few shot fine-tuning framework with the pre-training framework using mask token.

3.1   Few-Shot Fine-Tuning

Empirically [4] showed that aligning the fine-tuning with the pre-training framework allows the model to take advantage of the knowledge gained in the

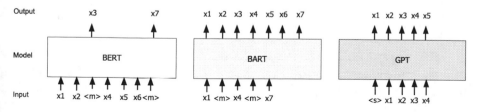

Fig. 1. Comparison of pre-training frameworks. xi represents a single token at the ith position. m represents a special mask token.

pre-training phase during the fine-tuning stage. When we need to generate question-answer pairs based on the context, the limited data does not allow the model to learn the relationship between the context and the question-answer pairs, so we make adjustments in the fine-tuning phase for few-shot learning.

The task of generating question-answer pairs requires predicting the span of text containing multiple tokens during fine-tuning. However, models such as BERT [5] predict only a single word (or subword) of the mask token during pre-training. Considering that the pre-training objective for such tasks involves multi-token span generation, we use the BART model to accomplish this by appending a mask token as part of the input that corresponds to the answer or question in the target. Figure 1 illustrates the comparison of the three pre-trained models for the pre-training. Our method involves adapting the fine-tuning structure differently for each aspect of generating question-answer pairs and constructing a robust, few-shot question-answer pair generation system by varying the input-output design with the placement of the mask token. Our different improvements when fine-tuning each model in the framework are described in detail in the subsequent sections.

3.2   Question-Answer Generation

The generation of question-answer pairs involves a series of steps, the first step is to decompose the context granularity, followed by fine-tuning of the different models, and then sequentially completing the answer generation, question generation and round-trip filtering. The primary objective is to model the joint conditional distribution $p(a, q|c)$, where c denotes the input context, q represents a question, and a is a span of text in the paragraph as an answer. The overall framework of our approach is shown in Fig. 2.

Granularity Decomposition and AnGen Model: The answers in datasets have varying distributions, in the SQuAD dataset [7], 55.1% of the answers are numeric and solid objects, and another 44.9% of the answers are composed of various types of phrases and clauses. Previous research [18] has demonstrated that the performance of models trained with named entities and noun phrases as answers are limited to datasets with similar answer distributions. When applied to datasets with different answer distributions, performance degrades.

To address this issue, we propose a new approach. First, we decompose the paragraph-level context into sentence-level, enabling the AnGen $p(a|s)$ model to learn the feature-attention relationship between sentence-level features and answers. We subsentence the contextual text passages in all examples, group the sentences containing true answers and the true answers themselves into the training set S^t, and use mask tokens to replace the true answers in the training examples after inputting them into the AnGen model. We then train the model to reconstruct the output to generate the true answers, thereby enabling the model to learn the answers in sentence-level text with varying utterance distributions. When predicting answers, we group the sentences that do not contain the true

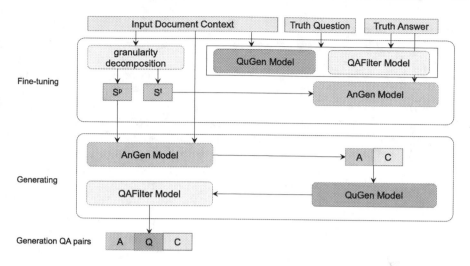

Fig. 2. Question-Answer pair generation framework.

answer after dividing the contextual document into sentences as the prediction set S^p. We add the mask token to the test example in the position of the answer, put it into the AnGen model for prediction as input, and the AnGen model generates the answer in this sentence by replacing the mask token in the output. Be aware that if you put in fine-tuning directly without gradient decomposition, the model will overfit due to data scarcity.

We also adjust the input and output during model fine-tuning. The input of the model is a text sequence $[m_1, s_1]$, consisting of two texts in series. The first text, m_1, is a mask token that replaces the answer word or phrase and generates the answer word or phrase at this position after the model output. The second text, s_1, is a sentence containing the word or phrase replaced by m_1 and is taken from one of the d_1 documents in the e_1 sample. The document d_1 comprises n sentences, $d_1 = [s_1, s_2 ...... s_n]$. When generating answers, the target output is $[a_1, s_1]$, where a_1 is the word or phrase corresponding to replaced by the m_1 mask token in the input to be generated. The AnGen model is shown in Fig. 3.

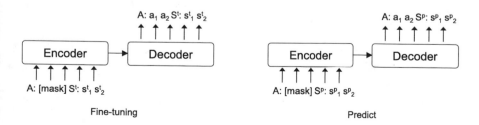

Fig. 3. AnGen Model.

QuGen Model and Round-Trip Filtering: For question generation, we also developed a conditional question generation model QuGen $p(q|a, c)$ using the pretrained BART model. Once the answer a is generated by the AnGen model, the question q is generated by inputting the context c. We improved the fine-tuning phase of question generation by designing the input for fine-tuning as a sequence of three texts in series $[m_1, a_1, c_1]$. The first text m_1 of the input is the mask token that replaces the question, the second a_1 is the corresponding answer to the question, and the third c_1 is the input context where the question and answer are located. When generating questions, the target output is $[q_1, a_1, c_1]$, where q_1 is the question replaced by the mask token that is recovered and generated by the QuGen model. The QuGen model is shown in Fig. 4.

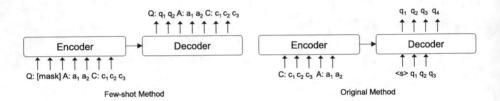

Fig. 4. QuGen Model.

To ensure the quality of the generated QA pairs, we employ a round-trip filtering approach [2]. First, we use a QA filtering model $p(a|q, c)$ to provide answers to the generated questions, and second, we discard QA pairs whose answers from the QA filter model do not match the generated answers. We also incorporate fuzzy matching to remove low-quality QA pairs, because the filtering model has noise when data is sparse. The QA filter model is shown in Fig. 5.

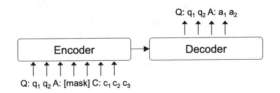

Fig. 5. QA filter Model.

4 Experiments

We evaluate three different aspects of our question-answer pair generation framework: (i) the diversity of generated answers, (ii) the quality of the generated questions, and (iii) the quality of the generated QA pairs.

During validation and testing, we generated text in an autoregressive manner and limited the generation length to 50, using training batches of size 2. We trained a total of 25 epochs.

4.1 Dataset

We chose the SQuAD dataset and the NewsQA dataset, and fine-tune and evaluate our model using the same training and testing segments provided by Ram et al. [16], who sliced the above dataset into segments with different numbers of examples. To avoid experimental errors, we ran each experiment three times using different random seeds. We set the number of training examples to 32 in the few-shot setting. Because, at 32 examples, the original BART model was able to generate simple questions. Furthermore, in the answer generation phase, for comparison, we utilized the BERT model to extract answers by employing the NER approach. To achieve this, we fine-tuned the BERT model on the NER task in the additional CoNLL-2003 English dataset [20], which consists of 946 articles. We then applied the NER approach to the target dataset to extract answers. All of our experiments were conducted on an RTX 3090 GPU.

SQuAD: SQuAD is a benchmark dataset for question-answering systems. The train set consists of 86,821 QA pairs and the dev set consists of 10,507 QA pairs.

NewsQA: NewsQA consists of question-answer pairs from CNN news articles. The train set consists of 74,160 QA pairs and the dev set consists of 4,212 QA pairs.

4.2 Results and Analysis

Answer Generation. In our experiments on generating question-answer pairs, we found that it is crucial to choose which texts in the context are used as answers, and we have compared our answer generation method with the NER method and found that the latter has a low F1 score. This can be attributed to the fact that entities account for only a fraction of the answer distribution in the dataset, and the NER approach tends to extract only entities consisting of a single or a few words and cannot interrogate specific phrases or sentences. Hence, it becomes necessary to adopt a learning model that can effectively model the different answer sets that exist in a targeted manner. Figure 6 presents the word count distribution of the answers generated by the two methods under the SQuAD dataset. Our approach generates answer words or phrases with a richer word count. The NER approach uses a BERT model trained with an additional dataset (12,000 data examples), while our approach (32 data examples) by considering a wider range of contextual textual information without needing additional data and additional models.

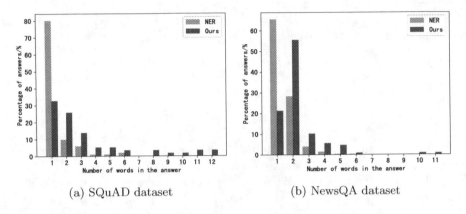

(a) SQuAD dataset   (b) NewsQA dataset

Fig. 6. Answer distribution of word count for different methods.

Question Generation. To better examine the quality of the generated questions when data is limited, we tested the question generation model separately, where we used real answers from the dataset to generate questions and then examined the generated questions. Table 2 presents the specific performance of our method on different datasets. With only 32 data examples in the training set, our QuGen model showed improvements in performance across all test sets. For instance, on the SQuAD dataset, the ROUGE-L value increased by 1.37 to reach 33, while the range of improvement in the BLEU tests was from 1.03 to 2.51. The performance improvement was even more significant on the NewsQA dataset, where the ROUGE-L value improved by 6.21 and the BLEU-4 value improved by 2.48. We think that the performance improvement is due to the fact that the model can make better use of the knowledge learned from pre-training by adjusting the input-output design. However, generating diverse questions based on different types of questions in the dataset can be challenging. In contrast, the question types in the NewsQA dataset are more focused, therefore the performance of the model improves even more. Our experiments show that our question generation model, QuGen, can generate high-quality questions even with limited data.

Question-Answer Generation. One of the significant challenges encountered in the assessment of QA pair generation models is the absence of reliable quantitative assessment metrics. To address this issue, we use the quality assurance based assessment (QAE) metric proposed by Zhang and Bansal [22] to measure

Table 2. BLEU and ROUGE scores across all datasets.

Model	SQuAD				
	BLEU-1	BLEU-2	BLEU-3	BLEU-4	ROUGE-L
BARTL	29.96 ± 2.35	19.48 ± 1.77	13.65 ± 1.38	9.94 ± 1.11	31.74 ± 1.11
QuGen	$\mathbf{32.47 \pm 1.25}$	$\mathbf{21.33 \pm 1.12}$	$\mathbf{15.01 \pm 1.03}$	$\mathbf{10.97 \pm 0.94}$	$\mathbf{33.00 \pm 0.95}$
Model	NewsQA				
	BLEU-1	BLEU-2	BLEU-3	BLEU-4	ROUGE-L
BARTL	18.19 ± 0.97	9.05 ± 0.58	5.03 ± 0.29	2.78 ± 0.16	19.15 ± 0.38
QuGen	$\mathbf{21.76 \pm 1.02}$	$\mathbf{12.39 \pm 0.64}$	$\mathbf{7.77 \pm 0.42}$	$\mathbf{5.16 \pm 0.26}$	$\mathbf{25.36 \pm 0.40}$

the quality of QA pairs. QAE is obtained by first training the QA model on synthetic data and evaluating the quality of the QA pairs generated by our models by comparing them with different approaches.

Table 3 presents the number of different question-answer pairs and the F1 scores obtained on two datasets. To gain further insight, we conducted ablation experiments to analyze the impact of each model component in our framework.

When using NER-extracted answers to generate questions, the resulting questions are more numerous than those generated by our method. However, the questions generated by our method exhibit higher F1 scores. Subsequently, by incorporating the QA filtering model, we were able to remove low-quality question-answer pairs, thereby significantly enhancing the quality of generated pairs. Notably, although our method generates more pairs than the manually curated dataset, its F1 score is approaching or even surpassing that of the dataset's human-guided question-answer pairs.

Table 3. The results of QAE experiments on SQuAD and NewsQA.

Approach	SQuAD		NewsQA	
	F1	Numbers	F1	Numbers
NER Answers + Generation Questions	45.95	101	23.81	280
Generation Answers + Generation Questions	57.71	84	28.15	178
Generation Answers + Generation Questions + QA-filter	69.11	58	46.95	108
True Answers + Generation Questions	64.48	32	52.35	32
True Answers + True Questions	71.12	32	51.72	32

5   Conclusion

In this paper, we propose a novel approach for generating high-quality question-answer pairs with limited training data. The proposed framework consists of three stages: answer generation, question generation, and round-trip filtering. We adjust the fine-tuning method in the pre-trained model to align it with the input-output of the pre-training phase, which improves the few-shot performance approach. Through experiments with different settings, it is found that the quality of QA pairs generated by our proposed method with a few shot configurations is close to that of QA pairs that can be manually annotated. While the improvement in ROUGE-L value is up to 6.21 and BLEU4 value is up to 2.48 when generating questions alone, and solves the problem of not being able to generate answer span when data is scarce.

However, our approach is currently limited by the number and quality of sentences in the articles. Therefore, future research could focus on how to better break the limitations.

Acknowledgments. This work was supported by NSFC (grant No. 61877051).

References

1. Alberti, C., Andor, D., Pitler, E., Devlin, J., Collins, M.: Synthetic QA corpora generation with roundtrip consistency (2019)
2. Alberti, C., Andor, D., Pitler, E., Devlin, J., Collins, M.: Synthetic QA corpora generation with roundtrip consistency. In: Proceedings of the 57th Annual Meeting of the Association for Computational Linguistics, pp. 6168–6173 (2019)
3. Brown, T., et al.: Language models are few-shot learners. Adv. Neural. Inf. Process. Syst. **33**, 1877–1901 (2020)
4. Chada, R., Natarajan, P.: FewshotQA: a simple framework for few-shot learning of question answering tasks using pre-trained text-to-text models. In: Proceedings of the 2021 Conference on Empirical Methods in Natural Language Processing, pp. 6081–6090 (2021)
5. Devlin, J., Chang, M.W., Lee, K., Toutanova, K.: BERT: pre-training of deep bidirectional transformers for language understanding. arXiv preprint arXiv:1810.04805 (2018)
6. Du, X., Shao, J., Cardie, C.: Learning to ask: neural question generation for reading comprehension. arXiv preprint arXiv:1705.00106 (2017)
7. Fisch, A., Talmor, A., Jia, R., Seo, M., Choi, E., Chen, D.: MRQA 2019 shared task: evaluating generalization in reading comprehension. In: Proceedings of the 2nd Workshop on Machine Reading for Question Answering, pp. 1–13 (2019)
8. Jia, X., Zhou, W., Sun, X., Wu, Y.: EQG-Race: examination-type question generation. In: Proceedings of the AAAI Conference on Artificial Intelligence, vol. 35, pp. 13143–13151 (2021)
9. Labutov, I., Basu, S., Vanderwende, L.: Deep questions without deep understanding. In: Proceedings of the 53rd Annual Meeting of the Association for Computational Linguistics and the 7th International Joint Conference on Natural Language Processing (Volume 1: Long Papers), pp. 889–898 (2015)

10. Lee, D.B., Lee, S., Jeong, W.T., Kim, D., Hwang, S.J.: Generating diverse and consistent QA pairs from contexts with information-maximizing hierarchical conditional VAEs. arXiv preprint arXiv:2005.13837 (2020)

11. Lewis, M., et al.: BART: denoising sequence-to-sequence pre-training for natural language generation, translation, and comprehension. arXiv preprint arXiv:1910.13461 (2019)

12. Lewis, P., Denoyer, L., Riedel, S.: Unsupervised question answering by cloze translation. In: Proceedings of the 57th Annual Meeting of the Association for Computational Linguistics, pp. 4896–4910 (2019)

13. Puri, R., Spring, R., Shoeybi, M., Patwary, M., Catanzaro, B.: Training question answering models from synthetic data. In: Proceedings of the 2020 Conference on Empirical Methods in Natural Language Processing (EMNLP), pp. 5811–5826 (2020)

14. Qu, F., Jia, X., Wu, Y.: Asking questions like educational experts: automatically generating question-answer pairs on real-world examination data. arXiv preprint arXiv:2109.05179 (2021)

15. Radford, A., et al.: Language models are unsupervised multitask learners. OpenAI Blog **1**(8), 9 (2019)

16. Ram, O., Kirstain, Y., Berant, J., Globerson, A., Levy, O.: Few-shot question answering by pretraining span selection. In: Proceedings of the 59th Annual Meeting of the Association for Computational Linguistics and the 11th International Joint Conference on Natural Language Processing (Volume 1: Long Papers), pp. 3066–3079 (2021)

17. Schick, T., Schütze, H.: Exploiting cloze-questions for few-shot text classification and natural language inference. In: Proceedings of the 16th Conference of the European Chapter of the Association for Computational Linguistics: Main Volume, pp. 255–269 (2021)

18. Subramanian, S., Wang, T., Yuan, X., Zhang, S., Trischler, A., Bengio, Y.: Neural models for key phrase extraction and question generation. In: Proceedings of the Workshop on Machine Reading for Question Answering, pp. 78–88 (2018)

19. Tang, D., Duan, N., Qin, T., Yan, Z., Zhou, M.: Question answering and question generation as dual tasks. arXiv preprint arXiv:1706.02027 (2017)

20. Tjong Kim Sang, E.F., De Meulder, F.: Introduction to the CoNLL-2003 shared task: language-independent named entity recognition. In: Proceedings of the Seventh Conference on Natural Language Learning at HLT-NAACL 2003, pp. 142–147 (2003). https://www.aclweb.org/anthology/W03-0419

21. Yao, B., et al.: It is AI's turn to ask humans a question: question-answer pair generation for children's story books. In: Proceedings of the 60th Annual Meeting of the Association for Computational Linguistics (Volume 1: Long Papers), pp. 731–744 (2022)

22. Zhang, S., Bansal, M.: Addressing semantic drift in question generation for semi-supervised question answering. In: Proceedings of the 2019 Conference on Empirical Methods in Natural Language Processing and the 9th International Joint Conference on Natural Language Processing (EMNLP-IJCNLP) (2019)

GFedKRL: Graph Federated Knowledge Re-Learning for Effective Molecular Property Prediction via Privacy Protection

Yangyou Ning[1,2,3], Jinyan Wang[1,2,3(✉)], De Li[3], Dongqi Yan[1,2,3], and Xianxian Li[1,2,3]

[1] Key Lab of Education Blockchain and Intelligent Technology, Ministry of Education, Guangxi Normal University, Guilin 541004, China
wangjy612@gxnu.edu.cn
[2] Guangxi Key Lab of Multi-Source Information Mining and Security, Guangxi Normal University, Guilin 541004, China
[3] School of Computer Science and Engineering, Guangxi Normal University, Guilin 541004, China

Abstract. Graph Neural Networks (GNNs) are one of the primary methods for molecular property prediction due to their ability to learn state-of-the-art level representations from graph-structured molecular data. In addition, the Federated Learning (FL) paradigm, which allows multiple ends to collaborate on machine learning training without sharing local data, is being considered for introduction to improve the performance of multiple ends. However, in FL, the molecular graph data among clients are not only Non-Independent Identically Distribution (Non-IID) but also skewed in quantity distribution. In this paper, we propose the GFedKRL framework to perform knowledge distillation and re-learning during the interaction between clients and servers in each cluster after clustering the graph embeddings uploaded. We also analyze the risk of privacy leakage in the GFedKRL and propose personalized local differential privacy to protect privacy while better controlling the amount of noise input and improving model performance. In addition, to resist the impact of noise data on the clients' model, graph representation learning is enhanced by knowledge contrast learning at the local clients. Finally, our approach achieves better results in three experimental datasets compared with four public benchmark methods.

Keywords: Graph Neural Networks · Federated Learning · Personalized Local Differential Privacy

1 Introduction

Molecular property prediction in graph classification is a hot topic, such as determining whether a molecular compound has properties that hinder cancer cell

L. Iliadis et al. (Eds.): ICANN 2023, LNCS 14256, pp. 426–438, 2023.
https://doi.org/10.1007/978-3-031-44213-1_36

growth, mutagenicity, or toxicity. However, deep learning methods have difficulty in achieving satisfactory results when dealing with graph data in these non-Euclidean spaces. To extract more effective latent features on graph-structured data, graph neural networks have thus been introduced [1].

Drug data are usually stored on multiple local ends in the drug discovery scenario. The research and development companies try to enhance the mining capabilities of drug graph data by federated learning. However, the drug data are heterogeneous [2], and the inconsistent progress of each company's drug development, resulting in different quantities of data uploaded to the central server. These problems can lead to the fact that predicting the properties of molecules is challenging to achieve better results under the FL. In addition, molecule drugs are carefully collected by R&D companies from high-consumption experiments and considered their proprietary assets. The leakage and misuse of these privacy data may damage the company's interests. Therefore, to obtain a robust local model, the following two challenges need to be addressed.

Challenge 1. Heterogeneity and quantity skew of the graph data distribution can seriously impair the model performance in FL. **Challenge 2.** Since the server is honest-but-curious, participating users' privacy information is easily leaked. Specifically, GNNs are more vulnerable to membership inference attacks [3] due to the encoding of the graph structure.

Existing work on federated learning has addressed the problems of missing labels, heterogeneous graph structure features, or reliable learning in mobile networks, as shown in [2,4,5]. However, in reality, graph data is not only heterogeneous, but the quantity skew problem will cause a significant challenge to the FL model. And existing methods do not achieve the expected results in our scenario. In addition, most of the current work focuses on improving the model performance of FL and ignoring the security issue of client-sensitive information leakage [6]. Differential privacy [7,8] gives mathematically rigorous proof that can effectively prevent the leakage of private information. Currently, there are differential privacy methods for GNN models [9,10], which investigate the assumption that the central server preserves and does not preserve the global graph topology in the case of local differential privacy, respectively, and allow the server to collect nodes that satisfy local differential privacy. Qiu et al. [11] investigated differential privacy protection under subgraph settings in the recommendation system scenario of federal graph neural networks, which addresses both the Non-IID problem and adequately protects the privacy of clients. A two-stage pipeline framework is designed to resist privacy attacks in heterogeneous graph neural networks based on differential privacy [12]. However, these privacy protection methods address node-level and subgraph-level privacy issues, which are different from the graph-level data privacy in our study of molecular property prediction problem setting and cannot be used to solve our challenge 2.

To solve the above problems, we propose a novel Graph Neural Network Federated Knowledge Re-Learning method based on Local Differential Privacy named GFedKRL. Specifically, the uploaded embeddings are clustered according to the K-means algorithm and relearned to get more accurate logits (probabilistic

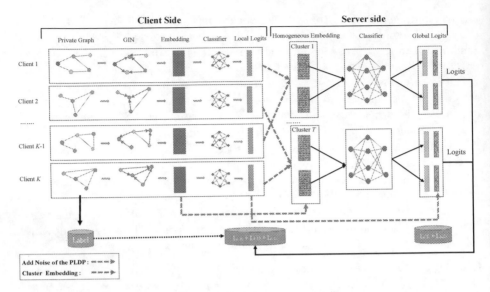

Fig. 1. The privacy data of each client is learned to embedding and logits, and uploaded to the server after adding personalized local differential privacy. The server calculates the similarity of embeddings to divide homogeneous embeddings into the same cluster, to train to get more accurate logits. Then the logits are returned to guide the client's learning.

predictions). And then, these logits are used to guide the training of client models in a knowledge distillation paradigm. In addition, we analyze the risk of local clients' privacy information leakage in GFedKRL, and propose personalized local differential privacy to protect local private graph data. Since adding noise to local private data reduces the utility of the model, we construct contrast learning [13] to further enhance the graph representation learning ability. The client regards the local knowledge as the anchor, the knowledge returned from the current cluster of the corresponding server as a positive sample, and the knowledge in other clusters as a negative sample. We summarize the main contributions as follows:

- We propose a GFedKRL method that allows the client to learn a more robust models from Non-IID and quantity-skewed data.
- We analyze the risk of privacy leakage of the GFedKRL and protect users' private data by personalized local differential privacy.
- We introduce a graph contrast learning approach in GFedKRL to mitigate the impact of global knowledge with noise on local models.
- Experimental results show that our method can achieve better than baseline results for clients. The properties of molecules can still be effectively predicted while protecting privacy.

2 Proposed Framework

2.1 Overview

This section introduces an overall learning framework of GFedKRL, i.e., a graph neural network knowledge relearn in federated learning with differential privacy, as shown in Fig. 1.

Server Side: The server side first calculates the similarity of graph embeddings based on K-means to divide homogeneous graph embeddings into the same cluster. It uses these graph embeddings as the input of the server classification model, which can accelerate the model convergence and get more accurate global logits. Then the global logits are returned to the local client, i.e., the paradigm of **knowledge distillation** is used to guide the client relearning.

Client Side: The privacy data of each client is learned to graph embedding by Graph Isomorphism Network (GIN), trained by a linear classifier to obtain local probabilistic predictions, i.e., local logits. Then the labels, embeddings, and local logits of the clients are uploaded to the server by adding **personalized local differential privacy**. Also, the **contrast learning** is used to reduce the adverse effect of noise on the model.

2.2 Knowledge Distillation

Similar Graph Embedding Cluster. When the model converges, the server calculates the similarity of graph embeddings based on the K-means algorithm to prevent drift. Then it divides homogeneous graph embeddings into the same clusters, which facilitates that these homogeneous graph embeddings can be relearned for better logits, i.e., K graph embeddings $\{\mathbb{H}_1, \mathbb{H}_2, ..., \mathbb{H}_K\}$ are divided into T clusters $\{\mathbb{C}_1, \mathbb{C}_2, ..., \mathbb{C}_T\}$, as shown in Fig. 1, where embedding is learning in local, i.e., $H^{(k)} = f_e^{(k)}\left(W_e^{(k)}; X^{(k)}\right)$.

Graph Knowledge Re-Learning. After the server clustering, we relearn homogeneous embeddings to obtain better probabilistic prediction Z_s, i.e., $Z_s = f_s\left(W_s; H^{(k)}\right)$. For better training of the server model, we construct server knowledge distillation loss l_{KD}^s by the Kullback Leibler (KL) Divergence:

$$l_{KD}^s = l_{KD}(Z_s, Z_c^{(k)}) = l_{KD}(f_s(W_s; H^{(k)}), f_c^{(k)}(W_c; H^{(k)})). \tag{1}$$

The logit $Z_c^{(k)}$ are the probabilistic prediction of the client model, i.e., $Z_c^{(k)} = f_c^{(k)}\left(W_c; H^{(k)}\right)$. The local client knowledge distillation loss l_{KD}^c of the server is constructed by probabilistic predictions $Z_c^{(k)}$ and Z_s of the client model and the server model, respectively:

$$l_{KD}^c = l_{KD}(Z_c^{(k)}, Z_s) = l_{KD}(f_c^{(k)}(W_c; H^{(k)}), f_s(W_s; H^{(k)})), \tag{2}$$

where f_s is the server model, $f_c^{(k)}$ is the client classifier model, and $f_e^{(k)}$ is the client feature extractor model. W_s, $W_c^{(k)}$, $W_e^{(k)}$ are the network weight of f_s, $f_c^{(k)}$, $f_e^{(k)}$, respectively. $H^{(k)}$ is the graph embedding output by $f_e^{(k)}$.

2.3   Personalized Local Differential Privacy

Privacy Leakage Scenario. In drug discovery scenarios, drugs that impede the growth of cancer cells tend to be more valuable than drugs that have no effect. Since the central server is honest-but-curious in the federated learning paradigm, these malicious users are more comfortable stealing all the information about these valuable drugs.

Private Preserve of Labels. Since the presence of labels during model training can increase the success rate of member inference attacks [14], the random response (RR) mechanism [15] is used to protect the labels' privacy before uploading them to the server in each communication. We flip them according to the following distribution, which are later exploit in our learning algorithm:

$$p(y^{'}|y) = \begin{cases} \frac{e^{\epsilon y}}{e^{\epsilon y}+c-1}, if \quad y^{'} = y \; ; \\[2mm] \frac{1}{e^{\epsilon y}+c-1}, \text{otherwise} \; , \end{cases} \tag{3}$$

where y and $y^{'}$ are clean and perturbed labels, respectively. c is the number of classes, and ϵ_y is the privacy budget of label.

Private Preserve of Embedding or Logits. For the privacy of continuous data, such as embedding or logits, we further utilize a multi-bit mechanism to protect the privacy of every vector, which is roughly the same as the one used in specific. The multi-bit mechanism consists of two components which include the encoder and rectifier [9,10]. To randomize vector of logits or embedding, the encoder uniformly samples m vector out of the D dimensions, where each element $x_{i,j}$ falls into the range $[x_{min}, x_{max}]$ in the vector. Each of the selected vectors is encoded into -1 or 1, and the rest of the $d - m$ dimensional vectors are mapped to 0, with a probability formulated as

$$\tilde{x}_{i,j} = \frac{1}{e^{\epsilon_x/m} + 1} + \frac{x_{i,j} - x_{min}}{x_{max} - x_{min}} \cdot \frac{e^{\epsilon_x/m} - 1}{e^{\epsilon_x/m} + 1}. \tag{4}$$

The rectifier is to calibrate the encoded vector $\tilde{x}$ to ensure the outcome of the randomized mechanism $x^{'}$ is statistically unbiased. Formally, the rectifier is instantiated as

$$x^{'}_{i,j} = \frac{|D| \cdot (x_{max} - x_{min})}{2m} \cdot \frac{e^{\epsilon_x/m} + 1}{e^{\epsilon_x/m} - 1} \cdot \tilde{x}_{i,j} + \frac{x_{max} + x_{min}}{2}, \tag{5}$$

where x is the vector of logits or embedding, m is the parameter for the dimension of the sampling vector, ϵ_x is the privacy budget of the vector logits and embedding, and D is the total number of dimensions of the vector.

Our Method of Personalized Local Differential Privacy. As mentioned earlier, malicious users are more inclined to steal valuable sample graph data. Specifically, we firstly determine which data are valuable by labeling, and then

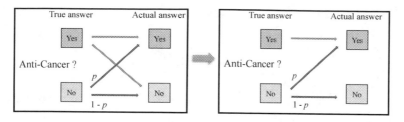

Fig. 2. The personalized random response (right side) based on improved traditional random response mechanism (left side) to protect the privacy label.

use other known intermediate information (e.g., logits and embedding) to invert the specific structural features and other information of these valuable graph data. Therefore, to prevent this risk of privacy leakage, we focus more on noise addition for more sensitive information by improving the original two noise addition methods, random response and multi-bit mechanism, to achieve the purpose of precise noise addition. We can provide better protection to sensitive information and reduce the utility impact of noise on the model.

As shown in Fig. 2, to protect the privacy of labels in a binary graph classification task for molecular drug property prediction, the traditional random response algorithm is shown on the left side, which achieves the privacy protection goal by reversing the two real answers with a certain probability. It makes it impossible for malicious users to obtain information about sensitive labels through the actual answers. However, this method can add too much noise to the data. We propose an improved random response method inspired by [16], as shown on the right side of Fig. 2, because molecules without anticancer effect (i.e., the "No" label) are not of excessive value. Therefore, only the "No" label is perturbed, and it is impossible to determine the answer from which the "Yes" label comes. We focus only on the security of sensitive label, reducing noisy input to the data while achieving the privacy protection.

To prevent malicious users from inversion of sensitive information such as features and structure. In the multi-bit mechanism algorithm, instead of the traditional approach of applying the same noise to the logits and embeddings of the samples, more noise is applied to the logits and embeddings of sensitive samples than to non-sensitive samples by personalization. In this way, not only are sensitive samples are protected, but also less noise is imposed on the data in general, thus improving the utility of the data.

Corollary 1. *The random response mechanism for sensitive labels $\mathcal{M}_y$ satisfies ϵ_y-local differential privacy.*

Proof. Consider the sensitive labels that Y and Y' only differ in one sample. Concretely, we assume that $y_{i,j} \neq y'_{i,j}$, and given any output $d = (d_1, ..., d_n)$ from $\mathcal{M}_y$, where $1 - p$ is the probability of retaining original label, p is the probability of reversing label, then we have

$$\frac{\Pr\left[\mathcal{M}_y\left(Y\right)=d\right]}{\Pr\left[\mathcal{M}_y\left(Y'\right)=d\right]} = \frac{\mathrm{pr}\left[y_{i,1}\to d_1\right]\cdots\mathrm{pr}\left[y_{i,n}\to d_n\right]}{\mathrm{pr}\left[y'_{i,1}\to d_1\right]\cdots\mathrm{pr}\left[y'_{i,n}\to d_n\right]}$$

$$= \frac{\mathrm{pr}\left[y_{i,j}\to d_j\right]}{\mathrm{pr}\left[y'_{i,j}\to d_j\right]} = \frac{1-p}{p} \le e^{\epsilon_y}.$$

Corollary 2. *The muti-bit mechanism for the vector of embedding or logits $\mathcal{M}_x$ satisfies ϵ_x-local differential privacy of every graph.*

Proof. Since different vectors in the graph data have different sensitivities, for any two input vectors X_1 and X_2, let $X^* = \mathcal{M}_x\left(X\right)$, then we have

$$\frac{\Pr\left[\mathcal{M}_x\left(X_1\right)=X^*\right]}{\Pr\left[\mathcal{M}_x\left(X_2\right)=X^*\right]} = \prod_{x_k^*\in\{-1,1\}} \frac{\Pr\left[\mathcal{M}_x\left(x_1\right)_k\in\{-1,1\}\right]}{\Pr\left[\mathcal{M}_x\left(x_2\right)_k\in\{-1,1\}\right]}$$

$$\le \prod_{x_k^*\in\{-1,1\}} \frac{\frac{m}{d}\cdot\frac{e^{\epsilon_x/m}}{e^{\epsilon_x/m}+1}}{\frac{m}{d}\cdot\frac{1}{e^{\epsilon_x/m}+1}} \le \prod_{x_k^*\in\{-1,1\}} e^{\epsilon_x/m} \le e^{\epsilon_x}.$$

Corollary 3. *The protection for labels, logits and embedding satisfies $(\epsilon_y + \epsilon_x)$-local differential privacy of every graph.*

Proof. Before the local client graph data is uploaded, labels use a random response mechanism, and logits and embedding use multi-bit encoders, i.e., ϵ_y-LDP and ϵ_x-LDP, for each graph, respectively. The multi-bit encoder and random response mechanism are called only once for each graph. By a theorem of composition [7], the protection for labels, logits and embedding satisfies $(\epsilon_y + \epsilon_x)$-LDP of every graph.

2.4   Contrast Learning to Reduce Negative Effects of Noise

In the previous subsection, the model utility may be reduced after imposing some noise on the local data due to the need to protect the privacy of the local data. Contrast learning can enhance the learning of graph representations in noisy data and we verify in the experimental section that contrast learning can resist the adverse effects of noise. The idea of contrast learning is to make the target samples closer to the semantically similar samples (positive samples) and further away from the semantically dissimilar samples (negative samples) in the representation space [13].

For example, we consider the embedding can learn more similar global logits Z_s in the cluster $\mathbb{C}_k$. Therefore, we take client logits Z_c and global logits Z_s in the cluster $\mathbb{C}_k$ as positive pair, and client logits Z_c and global logits Z_s^* in the other clusters $\mathbb{C}_i$ as negative pair, as shown in Fig. 3. We decrease the distance between Z_c and Z_s and increase the distance between Z_c and Z_s^*.

Figure 3 describes how our method enhances the graph representation learning of client k through contrast learning. We define the client's knowledge contrast learning loss as

$$l_{CL} = -\log\frac{exp(sim(Z_c,Z_s)/\tau)}{exp(sim(Z_c,Z_s)/\tau)+exp(sim(Z_c,Z_s^*)/\tau)}, \tag{6}$$

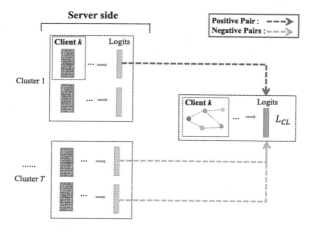

Fig. 3. The local contrast learning in GFedKRL. For an example of client k, the server obtains the global logarithm by relearning the embedding of client k and uses this global logits with the logits of local client k as the positive pair and the logits learned in other clusters as the negative pairs, and then constructs the contrast learning loss to enhance the graph representation learning ability of client k.

where $sim\left(\cdot,\cdot\right)$ is a cosine similarity function and τ denotes a temperature parameter, Z_c is the client logits, Z_s is the global logits of cluster $\mathbb{C}_k$ and Z_s^* is the global logits of other clusters.

2.5   Optimization the GFedKRL

Our global loss consists of two terms, and local loss consists of three terms. The first part is a cross-entropy loss between the logits and the ground truth label, i.e., $l_{CE}^c\left(Z_c^{(k)}, Y^{(k)}\right)$ or $l_{CE}^s\left(Z_s, Y\right)$. The second part is a knowledge distillation term, i.e., l_{KD} is the Kullback Leibler (KL) Divergence between clients and servers to transfer knowledge from one network to another. The third part is a contrast learning loss term l_{CL}.

In summary, the global server loss l_s and the local clients loss l_c that we want to optimize are defined as

$$l_s = l_{CE}^s + \alpha l_{KD}^s, \tag{7}$$

$$l_c = l_{CE}^c + \alpha l_{KD}^c + \beta l_{CL}, \tag{8}$$

where α and β are hyper-parameter to control the weight of knowledge distillation and contrast learning loss, respectively.

3   Experiments

3.1   Experimental Settings

Datasets. We use eight molecule datasets, MUTAG, BZR, COX2, PTC_MR, DHFR, AIDS, NCI1, and Mutagenicity. We set up two scenarios for experiments:

the first scenario is where all clients are from the first seven datasets in the molecular domain, with each client having a molecular graph dataset; the second scenario is where all clients hold from the same type of molecular dataset. We use 90% of each client's data for training and the rest for testing.

Baselines. We use self-train, FedAvg [17], FedProx [18] and GCFL [2] as a baseline for FL. The self-train is used as the first baseline to test whether FL can bring improvements to each client through collaborative training. It only trains locally after each client downloads the initialized model without any communications. The FedAvg algorithm can overcome non-convex problems when the client graph data is IID. FedProx can deal with data and system heterogeneity in non-graph FL. GCFL mainly handles Non-IID graph data, and it can dynamically find clusters of local systems based on the gradients of GNNs to reduce the structure and feature heterogeneity among graphs owned. For the graph classification model, we use the GIN architecture, which is the state-of-the-art GNN for graph-level tasks.

Parameter Settings. We use the three-layer GINs with a hidden size of 64. We use a batch size of 128 and an Adam optimizer with a learning rate of 0.001 and weight decay $5e^{-4}$. The μ for FedProx is set to 0.01. All clients' local epoch E is set to 1. And the skew of client data quantity is controlled by the hyperparameter α. We run all of the experiences conducted on a single NVIDIA GeForce RTX 3090 GPU.

3.2 Experimental Results

Two scenarios for Molecular Property Prediction. For the graph classification task in our federated learning method, two scenarios are set up, i.e., all clients predict the property of different or identical type molecules, respectively. In addition, the quantity of data is skewed among clients, i.e. the quantity is not equal. As shown in Table 1, in the first scenario, there is a large heterogeneity among the client's data distribution in the prediction of different molecular properties since seven different molecular datasets are used in MOLECULES. The results show a 2.98% improvement compared to self-train, a 2.24% improvement compared to FedAvg, a 2.53% improvement compared to FedProx, and comparable performance to GCFL. In the second scenario, when predicting identical molecules, all clients experiment with the NCI1 or Mutagenicity datasets. Our method can significantly improve the performance of graph classification by 4.35% and 4.86% relative to FedAvg method and 2.98% and 6.51% relative to FedProx method, respectively, and compared to the current state-of-the-art model GCFL is still improved. Knowledge distillation and contrast learning ablation experiments were also performed, experiments show that knowledge distillation and contrast learning give a significant performance boost to the GFedKRL framework. These experimental results show that our framework is effective in predicting homogeneous and different molecular datasets in a multi-client FL setup.

Table 1. Results on the molecular property prediction task

Dataset	MOLECULES (7)	NCI1(7)	Mutagenicity (7)
Self-train	0.7418	0.6496	0.6807
FedAvg [17]	0.7492	0.6321	0.7207
FedProx [18]	0.7463	0.6478	0.7042
GCFL [2]	0.7644	0.6742	0.7502
GFedKRL (Our)	**0.7716**	**0.6765**	**0.7693**
GFedKRL (KD)	0.7594	0.6627	0.7585
GFedKRL (CL)	0.7572	0.6483	0.7557

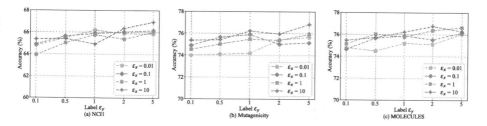

Fig. 4. Performance under varying privacy budgets on three datasets.

The Utility-Privacy Trade-Off. We experimented on three datasets to analyze the trade-off between the utility and privacy of our privacy-preserving PLDP method. We evaluate our method's performance under varying privacy budgets. We changed the label privacy budget in $\{0.1, 0.5, 1, 2, 5\}$, the logits and embedding privacy budget within $\{0.01, 0.1, 1, 10\}$. As shown in Fig. 4, although with a lower privacy budget, our method maintains an efficient result in a privacy-preserving training mode. And the model's accuracy gradually improves as the privacy budget increases in our experiment.

Contrast Learning to Resist Negative Effects of Noise. Personalized local differential privacy can reduce some of the noise addition. However, noise addition still damages the model's utility. Graph contrast learning can enhance graph representation learning ability in sparse or noisy data, so we consider using it to mitigate the impact of noise on the model. When the privacy budget of embedding and logits is set to 1, and the privacy budget of labels is varied in the range $\{0.1, 0.5, 1, 2, 5\}$. Compare the model's accuracy with or without the use of contrast learning. As shown in Fig. 5, the results show that using contrast learning in our framework can improve the model's accuracy under different privacy budgets. Thus, the experiments demonstrate that contrast learning can mitigate the negative effect of noise on the model.

Parameter Sensitivity Analysis. We split these molecular datasets NCI1 and Mutagenicity by Dirichlet distribution with parameter α. We control the degree of skewing of these dataset quantities by the parameter α and research how the

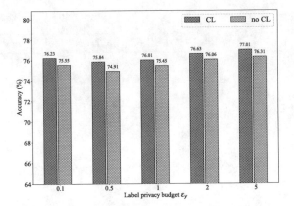

Fig. 5. The experiment with or without contrast learning on Mutagenicity dataset.

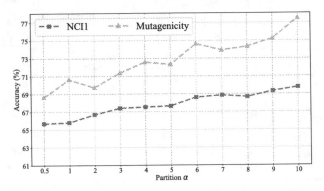

Fig. 6. Sensitivity experiments on NCI1 and Mutagenicity.

parameter α affects the model's accuracy. When the value of parameter *alpha* is small, the data quantity distribution among clients is more skewed, but our model can still maintain high accuracy. As the value of *alpha* increases, the distribution of data quantity of clients becomes more and more balanced. The classification accuracy of our model also tends to increase, as shown in Fig. 6.

4   Conclusion

This paper identifies Non-IID graph data and skew data quantity as significant obstacles preventing Molecular property prediction tasks in federated learning. To address this issue, we propose a GFedKRL framework. First, knowledge distillation is used to guide model training. Then, we analyze the risk of privacy leakage in the framework and propose personalized local differential privacy to protect private data. Also, contrast learning is introduced to mitigate the negative impact of noise on the model. Finally, rigorous theoretical analysis and experiments demonstrate that personalized local differential privacy preserves private information while maintaining the model's utility.

Acknowledgment. This paper was supported by the National Natural Science Foundation of China (Nos. 62162005 and U21A20474), Guangxi Science and Technology Project (GuikeAA22067070), Innovation Project of Guangxi Graduate Education (YCBZ2023058), Guangxi "Bagui Scholar" Teams for Innovation and Research Project, and Guangxi Collaborative Innovation Center of Multisource Information Integration and Intelligent Processing.

References

1. Ma, Y., Wang, S., Aggarwal, C.C., Tang, J.: Graph convolutional networks with EigenPooling. In: Proceedings of the 25th ACM SIGKDD International Conference on Knowledge Discovery & Data Mining (2019)
2. Xie, H., Ma, J., Xiong, L., Yang, C.: Federated graph classification over non-IID graphs. ArXiv, abs/2106.13423 (2021)
3. Wu, B., Yang, X., Pan, S., Yuan, X.: Adapting membership inference attacks to GNN for graph classification: approaches and implications. In: 2021 IEEE International Conference on Data Mining (ICDM), pp. 1421–1426 (2021)
4. Kang, J., Xiong, Z., Niyato, D.T., Zou, Y., Zhang, Y., Guizani, M.: Reliable federated learning for mobile networks. IEEE Wirel. Commun. **27**, 72–80 (2019)
5. Lim, W.Y.B., et al.: Hierarchical incentive mechanism design for federated machine learning in mobile networks. IEEE Internet Things J. **7**, 9575–9588 (2020)
6. Geiping, J., Bauermeister, H., Dröge, H., Moeller, M.: Inverting gradients - how easy is it to break privacy in federated learning? ArXiv, abs/2003.14053 (2020)
7. Dwork, C., Roth, A.: The algorithmic foundations of differential privacy. Found. Trends Theor. Comput. Sci. **9**, 211–407 (2014)
8. Li, D., Wang, J., Li, Q., Yuhang, H., Li, X.: A privacy preservation framework for feedforward-designed convolutional neural networks. Neural Netw. Off. J. Int. Neural Netw. Soc. **155**, 14–27 (2022)
9. Sajadmanesh, S., Gática-Pérez, D.: Locally private graph neural networks. In: Proceedings of the 2021 ACM SIGSAC Conference on Computer and Communications Security (2020)
10. Lin, W., Li, B., Wang, C.: Towards private learning on decentralized graphs with local differential privacy. IEEE Trans. Inf. Forensics Secur. **17**, 2936–2946 (2022)
11. Qiu, Y., Huang, C., Wang, J., Huang, Z., Xiao, J.: A privacy-preserving subgraph-level federated graph neural network via differential privacy. In: Knowledge Science, Engineering and Management (2022)
12. Wei, Y., et al.: Heterogeneous graph neural network for privacy-preserving recommendation. In: 2022 IEEE International Conference on Data Mining (ICDM), pp. 528–537 (2022)
13. He, K., Fan, H., Wu, Y., Xie, S., Girshick, R.B.: Momentum contrast for unsupervised visual representation learning. In: 2020 IEEE/CVF Conference on Computer Vision and Pattern Recognition (CVPR), pp. 9726–9735 (2019)
14. Shokri, R., Stronati, M., Song, C., Shmatikov, V.: Membership inference attacks against machine learning models. In: 2017 IEEE Symposium on Security and Privacy (SP), pp. 3–18 (2016)
15. Wang, T., Blocki, J., Li, N., Jha, S.: Locally differentially private protocols for frequency estimation. In: USENIX Security Symposium (2017)
16. Mangat, N.S.: An improved randomized response strategy. J. Royal Stat. Soc. Ser. B Methodol. **56**(1), 93–95 (1994)

17. McMahan, H.B., Moore, E., Ramage, D., Hampson, S., y Arcas, B.A.: Communication-efficient learning of deep networks from decentralized data. In: International Conference on Artificial Intelligence and Statistics (2016)
18. Sahu, A.K., Li, T., Sanjabi, M., Zaheer, M., Talwalkar, A.S., Smith, V.: Federated optimization in heterogeneous networks. arXiv: Learning (2018)

Gradient-Boosted Based Structured and Unstructured Learning

Andrea Treviño Gavito[1](✉) ⓘ, Diego Klabjan[1]ⓘ, and Jean Utke[2]ⓘ

[1] Northwestern University, Evanston, IL, USA
andrea.tg@u.northwestern.edu d-klabjan@northwestern.edu
[2] Allstate Insurance Company, Northbrook, IL, USA
jutke@allstate.com

Abstract. We propose two frameworks to deal with problem settings in which both structured and unstructured data are available. Structured data problems are best solved by traditional machine learning models such as boosting and tree-based algorithms, whereas deep learning has been widely applied to problems dealing with images, text, audio, and other unstructured data sources. However, for the setting in which both structured and unstructured data are accessible, it is not obvious what the best modeling approach is to enhance performance on both data sources simultaneously. Our proposed frameworks allow joint learning on both kinds of data by integrating the paradigms of boosting models and deep neural networks. The first framework, the boosted-feature-vector deep learning network, learns features from the structured data using gradient boosting and combines them with embeddings from unstructured data via a two-branch deep neural network. Secondly, the two-weak-learner boosting framework extends the boosting paradigm to the setting with two input data sources. We present and compare first- and second-order methods of this framework. Our experimental results on both public and real-world datasets show performance gains achieved by the frameworks over selected baselines by magnitudes of 0.1%–4.7%.

Keywords: Deep learning · Multimodal learning · Gradient boosting

1 Introduction

Data in modern machine learning problems can be represented by a variety of modalities or data sources. We consider the setting in which structured data and unstructured data are available simultaneously[1]. A common application area of this setting is medical diagnosis, in which the decision making process

---

[1] In the context of this paper, structured data refers to data that is organized and easily searchable in a specific format. It is typically stored in a database or spreadsheet,

Supplementary Information The online version contains supplementary material available at https://doi.org/10.1007/978-3-031-44213-1_37.

is supported by unstructured data such as medical imaging and doctors' notes, in combination with patient historical data, lab analyses and blood tests, in the form of structured data.

The settings where structured or unstructured data are available individually have been extensively researched. Deep neural networks (DNNs) have consistently proven successful at solving problems with unstructured data [1]. On the other hand, traditional boosting methods have shown significant advantages over DNNs in modeling structured data inputs [3,5,13]. Examples of such benefits are observed in terms of training time, interpretability, amount of required training data, tuning efforts, and computational expense. This is commonly observed in Kaggle competitions, where better performance is achieved by boosted methods when the available data is structured [21,22], and by deep learning models when the available data is unstructured [15,35]. In particular, LightGBM [17] and XGBoost [7], have become de-facto modeling standards for structured data. Conversely, in the setting in which both structured and unstructured data are accessible (*US*), it is not obvious what the best modeling approach is to enhance performance on both data sources simultaneously. In general, the simplest method consists of training independent models for each data modality and then combining the results by averaging or voting over the individual predictions. A big caveat is the missed opportunity of capturing any cross-data source interactions or underlying complementary information that might exist in the data. Training concurrently on both modalities of data is deemed crucial if we attempt to learn such relationships. A common approach to joint training consists of using DNNs for representation learning on each data source, concatenating the learned embeddings, and having it as input to a third DNN. This approach serves as a baseline for our experiments, and performs sub-optimally given that boosting algorithms excel on structured data settings.

We propose two frameworks for the *US* setting that address the above-mentioned considerations. Our frameworks aim at better capturing the best and most informative features of each data source, while simultaneously enhancing performance though a joint training scheme. To achieve this, our novel approaches combine the proven paradigms for structured and unstructured data respectively: gradient boosting machines and DNNs. The first framework is the boosted-feature-vector deep learning network (BFV+DNN). BFV+DNN learns features from the structured data using gradient boosting and combines them with embeddings from unstructured data via a two-branch deep neural network. It requires to train a boosted model on the structured data as an initial step. Then, each neural network branch learns embeddings specific to each data input, which are further fused into a shared trainable model. The post-fusion shared architecture allows the model to learn the complementary cross-data source interactions. The key novelty is the feature extraction process from boosting. Following standard terminology, we refer to model inputs as "features" and to DNN-

---

can be numerical or categorical, and is also referred to as tabular data. On the other hand, unstructured data refers to data that does not have a predefined structure or format. This can include text, images, audio, and video data, among others.

learned representations as "embeddings." In our proposed framework, BFVs are used as inputs to BFV+DNN and hence, are named features accordingly.

In addition, we propose a two-weak-learner boosting framework (2WL) that extends the boosting paradigm to the $\mathcal{US}$setting. The framework is derived as a first-order approximation to the gradient boosting risk function and further expanded to a second-order approximation method (2WL2O). It should be noted that this framework can be used in the general multimodal setting and is not restricted to the $\mathcal{US}$use case. Our experimental results show significant performance gains over the aforementioned baseline. Relative improvements on F1 metrics are observed by magnitudes of 4.7%, 0.1%, and 0.34% on modified Census, Imagenet, and Covertype datasets, respectively. We also consider a real-world dataset from an industry partner where the improvement in accuracy is 0.41%.

2   Related Work

Boosting methods combine base models (referred to as weak learners) as a means to improve the performance achieved by individual learners [28]. AdaBoost [10] is one of the first concrete adaptive boosting algorithms, whereas Gradient Boosting Machines (GBM) [12] derive the boosting algorithm from the perspective of optimizing a loss function using gradient descent, see [23]. A formulation of gradient boosting for the multi-class setting and two algorithmic approaches are proposed in [30]. LightGBM [17] incorporates techniques to improve GBM's efficiency and scalability. Traditionally, trees have been the base learners of choice for boosting methods, but the performance of neural networks as weak learners for AdaBoost has also been investigated in [32]. More recently, CNNs were explored as weak learners for GBM in [24], integrating the benefits of boosting algorithms with the impressive results that CNNs have obtained at learning representations on visual data [27]. Second-order information is employed in boosting algorithms such as Logitboost [11], Taylorboost [29], and XGBoost [7]. However, unlike our proposed second-order model, all these algorithms consider a single family of weak learners and individual data inputs, whereas we handle two families of weak learners and both structured and unstructured data simultaneously.

Boosting approaches have also been applied to the setting in which more than one data source is available as input. For instance, [14,18,26] employ traditional decision stumps as weak learners regardless of the data input sources and do not make use of DNN approaches. In contrast, [19] uses DNNs as weak learners, but overlooks the benefits of tree-based approaches for structured data. These methods do not take into account the underlying properties of these different data sources, nor do they consider specific algorithmic approaches that better suit each one of them.

Approaches that directly target the $\mathcal{US}$setting are scarce, more so those that address the structured data characteristics. In [6], the authors deal with demographics, living habits, and examination results from patients in the form of structured data, and with doctor's records and patient's medical history presented as unstructured text data. Similarly, in [31] speech and text data are transformed into structured and unstructured features to use as inputs to a boosting ensemble. In both cases, intuitive DNN approaches are used for feature embedding, with the drawbacks that have already been discussed as no special treatment is given to structured data.

An application to credit modeling is presented in [25], where structured data from financial statements and market data are integrated with text data from the Securities and Exchange Commission filings. Models such as K-nearest neighbors, random forests, DNNs, and boosted decision trees are compared. However, yet again in each model both modalities are given the same treatment. Conversely, in [20] the $\mathcal{US}$ setting is tackled by combining the benefits of tree-based models and DNNs. To do so, they use stacking and boosted stacking of independently trained models. Their approaches differ from our BFV+DNN in two main aspects. First, their models are heavily tailored for the learning-to-rank use case and second, they use direct outputs from the first model as input to the second model, whereas we propose a novel way to extract boosted-feature vectors from the first model, rather than using its direct output.

3   Proposed Models

3.1   Boosted-Feature-Vector Deep Learning Network (BFV+DNN)

The boosted-feature-vector deep learning network aims at using DNNs as the primary learning method, while incorporating boosted-feature vectors (BFV) from the structured data source. As a means of comparison, the baseline DNN approach to the $\mathcal{US}$ setting is shown in Fig. 1a and the BFV+DNN architecture in Fig. 1b. Both contain two branches, a fusion stage and a joint learning architecture. Each branch learns representations from one data source (see DNN1 and DNN2 in Fig. 1). Then, a fusion yields a joint embedding that combines the data-source-specific representations. Finally, the combined vector is used as input to a trainable DNN to model cross-data source interactions (DNN3 in Fig. 1). The common baseline ignores the structured or unstructured nature of the data source and directly learns representations via DNNs, whereas BFV+DNN uses BFVs as input to DNN2. To do so, we assume that a GBM model is first trained on the structured data. For the multiclass setting with M classes and N iterative GBM stages, M CARTs [4] are fitted per iteration. Let $R_{i,j,k}$ be the region defined by class i, tree j, and leaf k, and $w_{i,j,k}$ the value representing the raw prediction of a sample falling in the corresponding region ($1 \leq i \leq M, 1 \leq j \leq N$). Moreover, let each fitted tree j of class i have a number of leaves $l_{i,j}$. We define the boosted-feature vector of the structured portion of a sample x as $BFV(x) \in \mathbb{R}^{M \times N}$,

$$
BFV(x) = \begin{bmatrix} \sum_{k=1}^{l_{1,1}} w_{1,1,k} \mathbb{1}\{x \in R_{1,1,k}\} \ , \ \dots \ , \ \sum_{k=1}^{l_{M,1}} w_{M,1,k} \mathbb{1}\{x \in R_{M,1,k}\} \\ \sum_{k=1}^{l_{1,2}} w_{1,2,k} \mathbb{1}\{x \in R_{1,2,k}\} \ , \ \dots \ , \ \sum_{k=1}^{l_{M,2}} w_{M,2,k} \mathbb{1}\{x \in R_{M,2,k}\} \\ \vdots \qquad\qquad\qquad\qquad \vdots \\ \sum_{k=1}^{l_{1,N}} w_{1,N,k} \mathbb{1}\{x \in R_{1,N,k}\} \ , \dots , \ \sum_{k=1}^{l_{M,N}} w_{M,N,k} \mathbb{1}\{x \in R_{M,N,k}\} \end{bmatrix}.
$$

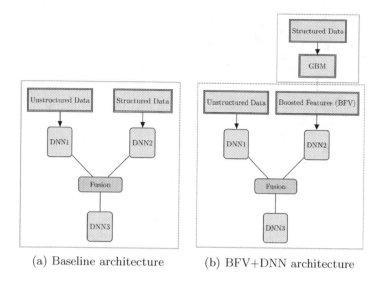

(a) Baseline architecture   (b) BFV+DNN architecture

Fig. 1. $\mathcal{U}S$deep neural networks

The outputs of DNN1 and DNN2 are combined into a joint representation using a fusion method. In our experiments in Sect. 4, fusing steps are performed by concatenatation or element-wise multiplication of the DNNs' embeddings.

3.2 Two-Weak-Learner-Gradient-Boosting Framework

Multi-class boosting aims at finding a classifier $F(x) = \arg\max_k \langle y^k, f(x) \rangle$ where f is some predictor, y^k is the kth class unit vector identifier, and $\langle \cdot, \cdot \rangle$ is the standard dot product. Following the GD-MCBoost [30] multi-class boosting approach, f is a boosted predictor trained to minimize classification risk $R(f) = \mathbb{E}_{X,Y}[L(y, f(x))] \approx \frac{1}{n} \sum_{i=1}^{n} L(y_i, f(x_i))$ where n is the number of training samples and $L(y, f(x)) = \sum_{k=1}^{M} e^{-\frac{1}{2}[<f(x),y-y^k>]}$ is the M-class loss function. At each iteration t, the update of the predictor is given by $f^{t+1}(x) = f^t(x) + g(x)$ with $g(x)$ a weak learner. Although the most common choices for weak learners are decision trees, we posit that weak learners must be chosen according to the available data source, such that they best capture their specific properties. In the $\mathcal{U}S$setting, each training sample is of the form $((x^U, x^S), y)$, and we have two families of weak learners denoted by $g = g(x^U)$ and $h = h(x^S)$.

Two-Weak-Learner-First-Order-Gradient-Boosting Framework (2WL). The two-weak-learner-gradient-boosting framework integrates the boosting paradigm to the $\mathcal{U}S$setting by including two families of weak learners that target each specific data input. In the two-weak-learner case, given f^t we have weak learners g and h. We update the predictor at iteration $t + 1$ to $f^{t+1}((x^U, x^S)) = f^t((x^U, x^S)) + \epsilon g^*(x^U) + \delta h^*(x^S)$. The optimization step is taken via gradient descent along directions g and h of largest decrease of $R(f)$. We have that[2]: $R(f^t + \epsilon g + \delta h) \approx R(f^t) - \epsilon \sum_{i=1}^{n} <g(x_i^U), w_i> -\delta \sum_{i=1}^{n} <h(x_i^S), w_i>$,

$$w_i = \frac{1}{2} e^{-\frac{1}{2}<f^t(x_i^U, x_i^S), y_i>} \sum_{k=1}^{M}(y_i - y^k) e^{\frac{1}{2}<f^t(x_i^U, x_i^S), y^k>}, \tag{1}$$

which yields optimization problems:

$$g^* \in \arg\min_{g} \quad ||g - w||^2 = \sum_{i=1}^{n} ||g(x_i) - w_i||, \tag{2}$$

$$h^* \in \arg\min_{h} \quad ||h - w||^2 = \sum_{i=1}^{n} ||h(x_i) - w_i||, \tag{3}$$

$$(\epsilon^*, \delta^*) \in \arg\min_{\epsilon, \delta} \quad R(f + \epsilon g^* + \delta h^*). \tag{4}$$

These problems are solved iteratively using Algorithm 1. For 2 and 3 we use standard mean squared error algorithms. Optimization 4 can be approximated in different ways such as heuristics, grid search, randomized search, or Bayesian optimization. Our experimental study, detailed in Sect. 4, uses heuristic values or Bayes optimization.

Algorithm 1 Two-Weak-Learner-Gradient-Boosting

Input: Number of classes M, number of boosting iterations N and training dataset $\mathcal{D} = \{(x_1, y_1), ..., (x_n, y_n)\}$, where x_i are training samples of the form $x_i = (x_i^1, x_i^2)$, with x_i^1 corresponding to one modality, x_i^2 corresponding to the second modality, and y_i are the class labels. In our use case, $x_i = (x_i^U, x_i^S)$.

   Initialization: Set $f^0 = 0 \in \mathbb{R}^M$

   for $t = 0$ to N **do**

      Compute w_i as in (1).

      Fit learners g^* and h^* as in (2) and (3).

      Find ϵ^* and δ^* as in (4).

      Update $f^{t+1}(x) = f^t(x) + \epsilon^* g^*(x_{i_1}) + \delta^* h^*(x_{i_2})$.

   end for

Output: $F(x) = \arg\max_k \langle y^k, f^N(x) \rangle$

---

[2] Further details can be found in Section A of the Supplementary Material.

Two-Weak-Learner-Second-Order Gradient Boosting Framework (2WL2O). The two-weak-learner-gradient-boosting framework is derived from the first-order approximation to the multi-class risk function R. In order to improve the estimation, we use second-order Taylor approximation. We now have that[3]:

$$(\epsilon^*, \delta^*) \in \arg\min_{\epsilon, \delta} \quad R(f + \epsilon g^*(\epsilon, \delta) + \delta h^*(\epsilon, \delta)) \tag{5}$$

$$\text{s.t.} \quad g^* \in \arg\min_{g} \quad \left\| g - (\epsilon w - \frac{\epsilon^2}{4}\tilde{w} - \frac{\epsilon\delta}{2}w) \right\|^2 \tag{6}$$

$$h^* \in \arg\min_{h} \quad \left\| h - (\delta w - \frac{\delta^2}{4}\tilde{w} - \frac{\epsilon\delta}{2}w) \right\|^2, \tag{7}$$

where

$$\tilde{w}_i = \sum_{k=1}^{M} \left[(y_i - y^k)(e^{-\frac{1}{2}<f^t(x_i^U, x_i^S), y_i - y^k>})^{\frac{1}{2}} \right], \tag{8}$$

and w_i as in (1). We solve these using Algorithm 2. In the experimental study in Sect. 4, the initialization values for ϵ_0^* and δ_0^* are set to 0.1, mimicking the default learning rate used in standard GBM implementations.

Algorithm 2 Two-Weak-Learner-Gradient-Boosting-Second-Order

Input: Number of classes M, number of boosting iterations N_1, number of inner iterations N_2 and training dataset $\mathcal{D} = \{(x_1, y_1), ..., (x_n, y_n)\}$, where x_i are training samples of the form $x_i = (x_i^1, x_i^2)$, with x_i^1 corresponding to one modality, x_i^2 corresponding to the second modality, and y_i are the class labels.

  Initialization: Set $f^0 = 0 \in \mathbb{R}^M$
  for $t = 0$ to N_1 **do**
    Compute w_i and $\tilde{w}_i$ as in (1), and (5).
    Initialize ϵ_0^*, δ_0^*.
    for $j = 0$ to N_2 **do**
      Fit learners g_j^* and h_j^* as in (6) and (7) by using ϵ_j^*, δ_j^* .
      Find ϵ_{j+1}^* and δ_{j+1}^* as in (5).
      Compute risk function value R_j at point $(g_j^*, h_j^*, \epsilon_{j+1}^*, \delta_{j+1}^*)$.
    end for
    $j^* = \arg\min_j R_j$
    $g^* = g_{j*}, h^* = h_{j*}, \epsilon^* = \epsilon_{j*}, \delta^* = \delta_{j*}$
    Update $f^{t+1}(x) = f^t(x) + \epsilon^* g^*(x) + \delta^* h^*(x)$.
  end for
Output: $F(x) = \arg\max_k \langle y^k, f^{N_1}(x) \rangle$

---

[3] Further details can be found in Section B of the Supplementary Material.

4   Computational Study

4.1   Datasets

Census-Income Dataset (CI). The census-income dataset [9] consists of 40 features presented in the form of structured data. We adjust it to the $\mathcal{US}$ setting in two ways: CI-A) by randomly splitting the set of features and assigning them to two sets $\mathcal{S}$ and $\mathcal{U}$, representing the structured and unstructured modalities, respectively; CI-B) by using backward elimination to identify the most informative features and assigning them to one of the sets ($\mathcal{S}$), while the rest of the features were assigned to the other ($\mathcal{U}$). The latter setting CI-B represents the case of one modality being much stronger correlated to the labels than the other.

Modified Imagenet Dataset (MI). We sample from Imagenet ($\mathcal{I}$) [8] and construct $\mathcal{U}$ with two classes: $\mathcal{C}_0 = \{x_U | x_U \in \mathcal{I}$ and x_U is a dog$\}$ and $\mathcal{C}_1 = \{x_U | x_U \in \mathcal{I}$ and x_U is a feline, primate, reptile or bird$\}$. These classes were selected so that the dataset has a reasonable size and is balanced. We adjust it to the $\mathcal{US}$ setting as follows: we generate $\mathcal{S}$ by creating a structured sample $x_S \in \mathbb{R}^{500}$ for each image x_U in $\mathcal{U}$ such that, for a fixed $w \in \mathbb{R}^{500}$ we have that $w^T x_S > 0$ if $x_U \in \mathcal{C}_0$ and $w^T x_S < 0$ otherwise. Since there are many such x_S, we select one at random. Finally, we randomly switch 9% of the labels in $\mathcal{S} \cup \mathcal{U}$ which provides a balance between further introducing noise to the data, while keeping more than 90% of the dataset's deterministic label assignment unchanged.

Forest Covertype Dataset (CT). We construct $\mathcal{S}$ with the 3 most represented classes in the original dataset [2]. We adjust it to the $\mathcal{US}$ setting by generating an image $x_U \in \mathbb{R}^{128 \times 128}$ for each structured sample x_S in $\mathcal{S}$ as follows. Each x_U consists of a white background and a random number in $\{1, ..., 10\}$ of randomly positioned: a) mixed type shapes if $x_s \in \mathcal{C}_0$; b) triangles if $x_s \in \mathcal{C}_1$; and c) rectangles if $x_s \in \mathcal{C}_2$. Again, we randomly switch 9% of the labels in $\mathcal{S} \cup \mathcal{U}$ to introduce noise[4].

Real-World Multimodal Dataset (RW). We use a proprietary dataset with both structured and unstructured data inputs, which allows us to test our models in a real-world $\mathcal{US}$ setting. The dataset constitutes a binary classification problem with two data sources: one is presented in the form of images $\mathcal{U}$ and the other as structured data $\mathcal{S}$ where GBM works very well. Tens of thousands of samples were curated for training and validation, with each structured data sample containing approximately 100 features.

---

[4] Examples of generated images can be found in Section C of the Supplementary Material.

4.2 Experimental Results

For our experiments, we employ Bayesian Optimization (BO) [34] to find ϵ^* and δ^*. The tracked metric is F1 for all datasets, except for RW, where accuracy is used[5]. In Table 1a, we summarize our results. For each dataset, we compare the performance of the boosted-feature vector DNN (BFV$_S$ +DNN$_U$), the two-weak-learner-gradient-boosted model with BO (2WL), and the two-weak-learner-second-order-gradient-boosted model with BO (2WL2O). Additionally, we analyze the impact of finding optimal steps ϵ^* and δ^* for the two-weak-learner models and conduct the same experiments with fixed $\epsilon^* = \delta^* = 0.1$ (2WL_Fix and 2WL2O_Fix). The value of 0.1 is again selected to mimick the default learning rate used in standard GBM implementations. All results are given as percentage of relative improvement over the chosen baseline (see Fig. 1 for reference), which was chosen to account for both data modalities. As additional comparison, the single-modality one-weak-learner results for the datasets with both structured (1WL$_S$) and unstructured (1WL$_U$) data are also shown in Table 1b, for which relative improvements are consistently negative for all datasets. This is expected due to the absence of a modality.

Table 1. Percentage of metric relative improvement w.r.t. baseline per dataset

a) Multimodal methods

Model	CI-A	CI-B	CT	MI	RW
BFV$_S$ +DNN$_U$	1.87	**4.70**	0.08	**0.34**	0.11
2WL	3.50	0.14	−0.37	−0.09	−0.60
2WL_Fix	0.68	−2.10	−0.36	−3.45	−2.37
2WL2O	**3.97**	0.25	**0.10**	0.13	**0.41**
2WL2O_Fix	−7.87	−19.85	−0.23	−0.14	−5.37

b) Single-modality methods

Model	CT	MI	RW
1WL$_S$	−7.04	−8.17	−9.21
1WL$_U$	−0.48	−0.16	−1.93

In general, BFV$_S$ +DNN$_U$ and 2WL2O models exhibit the best performance. The results in the different considered datasets help to differentiate the individual strengths of each of our proposed models. For datasets CI-A and CI-B, we observe that given the underlying structured nature of the data, the BFVs used for BFV$_S$ +DNN$_U$ are responsible for a large portion of the predictive power, making this model perform significantly better than the baseline. This behavior is notably exhibited in CI-B, were the most informative features have been grouped in S and used to generate the BFVs. On the other hand, due to the random variable split in CI-A, not all of the most informative features are used for generating the BFV, which is reflected in the performance gap between both datasets for this model and in the two-weak-learner models outperforming BFV+DNNs for CI-A. In datasets with both modalities, CT, MI and RW, we observe closer gaps between

---

[5] Further details of the implementation and dataset-specific hyperparameters used for the models can be found in Section D of the Supplementary Material.

the performances of BFV$_\mathcal{S}$ +DNN$_\mathcal{U}$ and 2WL2O, but quite large improvements of these over 2WL in all cases. BFV$_\mathcal{S}$ +DNN$_\mathcal{U}$ achieves the best performance for CI-B and MI. On the other hand, 2WL2O outperforms all models for CI-A, CT, and RW. The predictive power and complexity of each data input versus the other appears to play an important role both in the best model's performance and in the usefulness of the second order approximation. We further observe this in Figs. 2 and 3. Interestingly, the deterioration is shown only in one of the two-weak-learner models per dataset, possibly as a result of conducting independent optimizations to find ϵ^* and δ^* in step (4) of Algorithm 1 and (5) of Algorithm 2.

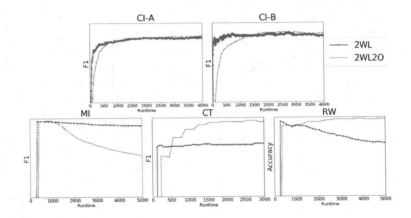

Fig. 2. First- (2WL) and second-order (2WL2O) two-weak-learners performance vs runtime in minutes

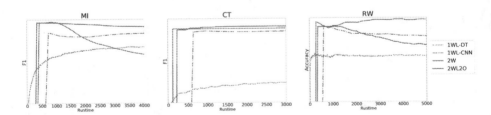

Fig. 3. One- (1WL-DT, 1WL-CNN) and two-weak-learners (2WL, 2WL2O) perfor-mance vs runtime in minutes

In Fig. 4, we compare 2WL and 2WL2O with their corresponding 2WL_Fix and 2WL2_Fix runs. In all experiments, fixing the values of ϵ^* and δ^* results in a significant drop in performance, further emphasizing the key role played by the Bayes optimization steps and careful choice of learning rates ϵ and δ. As a final remark, an important factor to consider when evaluating and comparing

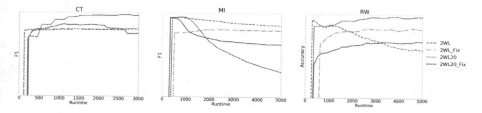

Fig. 4. Performance of first- and second-order two-weak-learners with fixed (2WL_Fix, 2WL2O_Fix) and optimized (2WL, 2WL2O) learning rates vs runtime in minutes

the proposed models is computational time. In Algorithms 1 and 2 for the two-weak-learner frameworks, we have that one DNN is trained per iteration for the first order approximation, yielding a total of N trained DNNs per run. For the second order approximation, N_2 DNNs are trained per iteration, for a total of $N_1 N_2$ DNNs per run. On the other hand, we have that the BFV+DNN model trains a single DNN (plus a previously trained GBM). Hence, BFV+DNN has a clear advantage in terms of runtime, whereas the two-weak-learner-boosted frameworks can be leveraged to improve performance when time does not pose a hard constraint.

5 Conclusion

Traditionally, boosted models have shown stellar performance when dealing with structured data, whereas DNNs excel in unstructured data problems. However, in many real-world applications both structured and unstructured data are available. In this paper, we presented two frameworks that address these scenario. The proposed models are compared to a standard baseline model and demonstrate strong results, outperforming the baseline approach when data is presented as a combination of these two data sources.

References

1. Balas, V.E., Roy, S.S., Sharma, D., Samui, P.: Handbook of Deep Learning Applications. Springer, Cham (2019). https://doi.org/10.1007/978-3-030-11479-4
2. Blackard, J.A.: UCI machine learning repository (1999). https://archive.ics.uci.edu/ml/machine-learning-databases/covtype/covtype.info
3. Borisov, V., Leemann, T., Seßler, K., Haug, J., Pawelczyk, M., Kasneci, G.: Deep neural networks and tabular data: a survey. arXiv preprint arXiv:2110.01889 (2021)
4. Breiman, L., Friedman, J.H., Olshen, R.A., Stone, C.J.: Classification and Regression Trees (1984)
5. Caruana, R., Karampatziakis, N., Yessenalina, A.: An empirical evaluation of supervised learning in high dimensions. In: International Conference on Machine Learning (2008)
6. Chen, M., Hao, Y., Hwang, K., Wang, L., Wang, L.: Disease prediction by machine learning over big data from healthcare communities. IEEE Access **5**, 8869–8879 (2017)

7. Chen, T., Guestrin, C.: XGBoost: a scalable tree boosting system. In: International Conference on Knowledge Discovery and Data Mining (2016)
8. Deng, J., Dong, W., Socher, R., Li, L.J., Li, K., Fei-Fei, L.: ImageNet: a large-scale hierarchical image database. In: IEEE Conference on Computer Vision and Pattern Recognition (2009)
9. Dua, D., Graff, C.: UCI machine learning repository (2017). https://archive.ics.uci.edu/ml/datasets/Census-Income+%28KDD%29
10. Freund, Y., Schapire, R.E.: A decision-theoretic generalization of on-line learning and an application to boosting. J. Comput. Syst. Sci. **55**, 119–139 (1997)
11. Friedman, J., Hastie, T., Tibshirani, R.: Additive logistic regression: a statistical view of boosting. Ann. Stat., 337–374 (2000)
12. Friedman, J.H.: Greedy function approximation: a gradient boosting machine. Ann. Stat., 1189–1232 (2000)
13. Gorishniy, Y., Rubachev, I., Khrulkov, V., Babenko, A.: Revisiting deep learning models for tabular data. In: International Conference on Advances in Neural Information Processing Systems (2021)
14. Goyal, A., Morvant, E., Germain, P., Amini, M.: Multiview boosting by controlling the diversity and the accuracy of view-specific voters. arXiv preprint arXiv:1808.05784 (2018)
15. Graham, B.: Kaggle diabetic retinopathy detection competition report. Technical report, University of Warwick (2015)
16. He, K., Zhang, X., Ren, S., Sun, J.: Deep residual learning for image recognition. In: IEEE Conference on Computer Vision and Pattern Recognition (2016)
17. Ke, G., et al.: LightGBM: a highly efficient gradient boosting decision tree. In: Advances in Neural Information Processing Systems, vol. 30 (2017)
18. Koço, S., Capponi, C., Béchet, F.: Applying multiview learning algorithms to human-human conversation classification. In: Conference of the International Speech Communication Association (2012)
19. Lahiri, A., Paria, B., Biswas, P.K.: Forward stagewise additive model for collaborative multiview boosting. IEEE Trans. Neural Netw. Learn. Syst. **29**, 470–485 (2018)
20. Li, P., Qin, Z., Wang, X., Metzler, D.: Combining decision trees and neural networks for learning-to-rank in personal search. In: International Conference on Knowledge Discovery and Data Mining (2019)
21. Lloyd, J.R.: GEFCom2012 hierarchical load forecasting: gradient boosting machines and Gaussian processes. Int. J. Forecast. **30**, 369–374 (2014)
22. Mangal, A., Kumar, N.: Using big data to enhance the Bosch production line performance: a Kaggle challenge. arXiv preprint arXiv:1701.00705 (2017)
23. Mayr, A., Binder, H., Gefeller, O., Schmid, M.: The evolution of boosting algorithms - from machine learning to statistical modelling. Methods Inf. Med. **53**, 419–27 (2014)
24. Moghimi, M., Belongie, S., Saberian, M., Yang, J., Vasconcelos, N., Li, L.J.: Boosted convolutional neural networks. In: British Machine Vision Conference (2016)
25. Nguyen, C.V., et al.: Multimodal machine learning for credit modeling. In: IEEE Computer Society Signature Conference on Computers, Software and Applications (2021)
26. Peng, J., Aved, A.J., Seetharaman, G., Palaniappan, K.: Multiview boosting with information propagation for classification. IEEE Trans. Neural Netw. Learn. Syst. **29**, 657–669 (2018)

27. Redmon, J., Divvala, S.K., Girshick, R.B., Farhadi, A.: You only look once: unified, real-time object detection. In: IEEE Conference on Computer Vision and Pattern Recognition (2016)
28. Ridgeway, G.: The state of boosting. In: Computing Science and Statistics (1999)
29. Saberian, M.J., Masnadi-Shirazi, H., Vasconcelos, N.: TaylorBoost: first and second-order boosting algorithms with explicit margin control. In: IEEE Conference on Computer Vision and Pattern Recognition (2011)
30. Saberian, M.J., Vasconcelos, N.: Multiclass boosting: theory and algorithms. In: Advances in Neural Information Processing Systems, vol. 24 (2011)
31. Sarawgi, U., Khincha, R., Zulfikar, W., Ghosh, S., Maes, P.: Uncertainty-aware boosted ensembling in multi-modal settings. arXiv preprint arXiv:2104.10715 (2021)
32. Schwenk, H., Bengio, Y.: Boosting neural networks. Neural Computation (2000)
33. Simonyan, K., Zisserman, A.: Very deep convolutional networks for large-scale image recognition. In: International Conference on Learning Representations (2015)
34. Snoek, J., Larochelle, H., Adams, R.P.: Practical Bayesian optimization of machine learning algorithms. In: Advances in Neural Information Processing Systems, vol. 25 (2012)
35. Zou, H., Xu, K., Li, J.: The YouTube-8M Kaggle Competition: challenges and methods. arXiv preprint arXiv:1706.09274 (2017)

Graph Federated Learning Based on the Decentralized Framework

Peilin Liu[1], Yanni Tang[2,3], Mingyue Zhang[3], and Wu Chen[3(✉)]

[1] College of Computer and Information Science and College of Software,
Southwest University, Chongqing 400715, China
[2] School of Computer Science, University of Auckland, Auckland 1142, New Zealand
[3] College of Software, Southwest University, Chongqing 400715, China
chenwu@swu.edu.cn

Abstract. Graph learning has a wide range of applications in many scenarios, which require more need for data privacy. Federated learning is an emerging distributed machine learning approach that leverages data from individual devices or data centers to improve the accuracy and generalization of the model, while also protecting the privacy of user data. Graph-federated learning is mainly based on the classical federated learning framework i.e., the Client-Server framework. However, the Client-Server framework faces problems such as a single point of failure of the central server and poor scalability of network topology. First, we introduce the decentralized framework to graph-federated learning. Second, determine the confidence among nodes based on the similarity of data among nodes, subsequently, the gradient information is then aggregated by linear weighting based on confidence. Finally, the proposed method is compared with FedAvg, Fedprox, GCFL, and GCFL+ to verify the effectiveness of the proposed method. Experiments demonstrate that the proposed method outperforms other methods.

Keywords: Federated Learning · Graph Neural Network · Decentralized Framework

1 Introduction

Graph learning refers to a class of methods that use the graph structure for machine learning. Specifically, graph learning uses information such as topology and neighbor relationships of graph structures to perform tasks such as feature learning, classification, and clustering of nodes or edges. Graph learning has a wide range of applications in healthcare [4,8,19], social network analysis [7,23], and intelligent transportation [5,11,16], where the need for data privacy increases as well as the problem of data silos arises. Federated learning(FL) has received attention as a major hot topic in recent years. FL is an emerging distributed machine learning approach that ensures that multiple devices or data centers can collaboratively train a machine model without the data leaving the device or data center. FL leverages data from individual devices or data centers to

L. Iliadis et al. (Eds.): ICANN 2023, LNCS 14256, pp. 452–463, 2023.
https://doi.org/10.1007/978-3-031-44213-1_38

improve the accuracy and generalization of the model, while also protecting the privacy of user data.

Like the classical FL framework, graph-federated learning(GFL) is also based on the FL framework. Currently, FL usually adopts the Client-Server(CS) framework, in which clients compute model parameters locally and upload them to the server, and the server aggregates the model parameters uploaded by each client and distributes them to the clients. One of the most important parts is the model aggregation method, such as FedAvg [13](which is based on a weighted average) and Fedprox [10](which adds regularization terms to the loss function).

However, the CS framework faces problems such as a single point of failure of the central server and poor scalability of network topology [3,12]. Inspired by the blockchain domain, the decentralized framework has better robustness and scalability [15,17]. Therefore, in this paper, we consider introducing the decentralized framework into GFL. Nevertheless, FL under this framework without centralized control of the server has challenges in designing reasonable interaction mechanisms and effective client-side model aggregation methods.

In this paper, to address these challenges, we propose the Decentralized Graph-Federated Learning(DGFL) approach. First, we introduce the decentralized framework to GFL, which consists of fully peer-to-peer learning nodes without a central server. Each node has its own local data, aiming to train GNNs [18] models that are more suitable for local data. Second, determine the confidence among nodes based on the similarity of data among nodes, subsequently, the gradient information is then aggregated by linear weighting based on confidence. Finally, the proposed method is compared with FedAvg [13], Fedprox [10], GCFL, and GCFL+ [22] to verify the effectiveness(accuracy, convergence speed, and computational time) of the proposed method. In summary, the main contributions of this paper are as follows: (1) a gradient interaction mechanism is proposed in the framework of decentralized architecture, which greatly reduces the communication overhead while ensuring no inefficiency. (2) introduces the confidence between nodes which is based on a local model gradient sequence and a new model gradient aggregation method based on the confidence for linear weighted aggregation is proposed. (3) experiments conducted on standard graph datasets, and the result of experiments demonstrate the proposed method outperforms other methods.

The rest of this paper is organized as follows. Section 2 presents related works. Section 3 describes the preliminaries of GNNs and the classic federated aggregation method. Section 4 provides details and the implementation of the proposed approach. Section 5 lists the experiments to demonstrate the effectiveness of the proposed method. At last, Sect. 6 summarizes the entire article.

2   Related Works

2.1   Federated Learning

Federated Learning(FL) [13] is a distributed machine learning framework that effectively helps multiple nodes or data centers to train models by performing machine learning. The participants of FL mainly consist of a central server and nodes. The server aims to train an optimal model based on the aggregated data of all parties, and the model trained by each node or data center serves local data goals. Importantly, FL allows participants (e.g., smartphones, sensors, mobile devices, servers, etc.) to not share data during the information exchange process so that the user's raw data remains local to the node or data center throughout the model training process, so FL simultaneously solves the problem of data silos while meeting the requirements of user privacy, data security, and government regulations. FL also reduces the pressure on network bandwidth because the local models are trained on local computers and only the model parameters need to be transmitted. The advantage of the CS framework is that it is easy to manage and easy to implement, and the centralized architecture makes it easier to control, coordinate and monitor. However, its centralized architecture will lead to a single point of failure, and once the server crashes, the whole system will not work properly and has poor scalability.

FL [13] has three major elements: data source, federated learning system, and users. Under the federated learning system, each data source performs data preprocessing, jointly establishes its learning model, and feeds back the output results to the user. There are two main frameworks in FL:

- *client-server(CS) framework.* The client-server framework is the most commonly used framework for federated learning and was the first to be proposed. In this framework, there is a central server, which is responsible for coordinating the computation and communication among the various clients. Specifically, clients download models from the server, then train them using local data and upload the updated models to the server. The server aggregates all the models uploaded by the clients and calculates the average model, which is then sent back to the clients for the next round of training.
- *decentralized framework.* The decentralized framework eliminates the reliance on a central server, and individual clients can communicate and collaborate directly with each other. In this framework, each client has its own model and uses local data for training, and then sends the updated model to other clients for model aggregation(such as gradient averaging). During model aggregation, clients can verify and monitor each other to ensure security and correctness. The decentralized framework has no single point of failure, each client is independent, and the system is more stable and robust. Data privacy is better because data does not need to be uploaded to the central server. However, the decentralized framework is relatively complex and requires more management and coordination efforts because there is no central server for management and control.

2.2   Graph Learning

A graph is a mathematical structure used to represent entities and their relationships, consisting of vertices and edges. Nodes represent entities (such as people, places, or objects), and edges represent relationships between entities (such as friendship, distance, or similarity). Machine learning on graphs is referred to as "graph learning", and methods used in this field convert graph features to feature vectors of the same dimensionality in the embedding space. Without projecting the graph into a lower dimensional space, a graph learning model or algorithm directly converts graph data into the output of a graph learning architecture. Most graph learning approaches are based on or generalized from deep learning techniques since these techniques can encode and represent graph data as vectors. The objective of graph learning is to extract the desirable features of the graph, and the output vectors are in a continuous space. As a result, downstream activities like node classification and link prediction can employ graph representations with ease without using an explicit embedding procedure. Many graph analysis problems, including link prediction, recommendation, and classification, may be solved quickly and effectively in the representation space thanks to graph learning approaches [1,6]. Different facets of social life, including communication patterns, community structures, and information diffusion, are shown by graph network representations [21,24]. The three kinds of graph learning tasks-vertex-based, edge-based, and subgraph-based-can be separated depending on the characteristics of vertices, edges, and subgraphs. For categorization, risk identification, clustering, and community finding, a graph's vertex relationships can be leveraged [20]. We can do recommendation and knowledge inference by determining whether an edge exists between any two vertices in a network.

3 Preliminaries

3.1 Graph Neural Networks (GNNs)

The core idea behind GNN [18] is to use the information interplay between neighbor nodes to replace the function illustration of every node and to procedure the total graph. Usually, a GNN model consists of a multi-layer neural network, and every layer of the community is accountable for updating the node function representation, and weighting and summing the characteristic vectors of the nodes to acquire a new characteristic illustration of the node. The shape and function data in the graph are normally expressed as $G = (V, E, X)$, where V, E, X denotes nodes, links, and node features. Next, an illustration of an L-layer GNN is given as

$$h_v^{(l+1)} = \sigma(h_v^l, agg(\{h_u^l; u \in N_v\})), \forall l \in [L] \tag{1}$$

the place N_v is the set of neighbours of node v, $\sigma(\cdot)$ is the activation function, and the h_v^l is the illustration of the node v at the lth-layer. $agg(\cdot)$ is the combination characteristic with special GNNs models. The Eq. 1 is the node-level representation, and the graph-level illustration can be pooled from the illustration of all nodes, as

$$h_G = readout(\{h_v; v \in V\}) \tag{2}$$

where the $readout(\cdot)$ represents the different pooling methods, such as mean pooling, sum pooling, etc., which is to aggregate and embed the vectors of each node in the graph into a single vector and then perform classification tasks.

3.2   FedAvg

FedAvg [13] is a model parameter aggregation algorithm widely used in FL, which can be used to aggregate local model parameters from multiple clients into global model parameters. The main idea is to combine the parameters of the local model through the weighted average and use the weighted average parameters as the parameters of the global model. For example, there are n clients in total, and k is a specific communication round. The server will sample the client to select a set of participants $\{P\}_k$. For every participant P_i in $\{P\}_k$, they use local data D_i to train the model locally, and then pass its updated parameters $w_i^{(k)}$ to the server. The server then aggregates these incoming parameters by

$$w^{(k+1)} = \sum_{i=1}^{n} \frac{|D_i|}{|D_{all}|} w_i^{(k)} \tag{3}$$

where $|D_i|$ is the local data size of P_i, and $|D_{all}|$ represents the total data size of all $P_i \in \{P\}_k$. After the server aggregation update is completed, the new parameters of the global model will be passed to all clients.

4   Decentralized Graph Federated Learning

4.1   The Design of DGFL

Suppose there is a set of local clients based on a decentralized network framework under the set $C = \{c_1, c_2, ..., c_n\}$, and the graph formed by the connections between the default clients is a fully connected graph. Unlike the classical CS framework, without the control of a central server, each local client needs to execute the federated algorithm once in each round of communication as a receiver. In contrast to Cluster Federated Learning (CFL) [2], which also does not rely on the central server to perform clustering, each local client decides its confidence weight based on the local data information and the messages received. Then, clients aggregate the sender's gradient information received in this round with the local gradient information in this round according to the confidence weight and then update the local gradient information.

Figure 1, which is a random situation in the interaction process, describes the main steps of the proposed algorithm. The left part of the figure shows the process of randomly sampling and sending messages to the selected client. Take client B as an example, the right part of the figure demonstrates the gradient updating process.

The definition of the local client set has been given: $C = \{c_1, c_2, ..., c_n\}$, assuming that each client maintains a local neighbor set $N_i = \{n_1, n_2, n_3, ..., n_k\}$,

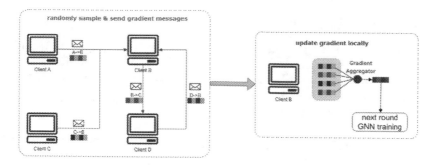

Fig. 1. The design of the proposed method

where N_i represents the neighbor list of c_i. From the above process, we can know that in each round of communication, when a client acts as the sender, it will use random single sampling which randomly selects a neighbor as the message receiver of the current round. Of course, each client also needs to maintain a set of senders $S_i = \{s_1, s_2, s_3, ..., s_k\}$, where S_i represents the sender list of C_i, which is used to record who send a message to yourself in this round. Then the client C_i selects the senders greater than the average confidence value from the sender list to aggregate their messages. Next, define confidence($Conf$) as

$$Conf_{i,j}^t = 1 - DTW_{std}(g_i^t, g_j^t) \tag{4}$$

The average confidence value($\overline{Conf^t}$) in the t-th round is denoted as

$$\overline{Conf_i^t} = \frac{1}{|S_i|} \sum_{k \in S_i} Conf_{i,k}^t \tag{5}$$

$Conf_{i,j}^t$ represents the confidence of client c_i on c_j during the t-th round of communication, and $Conf \in [0,1]$, where DTW_{std} represents the standardized $DTW()$ function which is used to calculate the dynamic time wrapping (DTW) [14] distance between two gradient sequences. Obviously, we can get $Conf_{i,i} = 1$.

It should be emphasized that $DGFL$ is different from the classic federated algorithm. What the client updates after each round of communication is no longer the model parameters, but the gradient. The specific equation of the strategy is as follows:

$$g_i^{(t+1)} = \frac{Conf_{i,i}^t * g_i^t + \sum_{j \in Sample} Conf_{i,j}^t * g_j^t}{Conf_{i,i}^t + \sum_{j \in Sample} Conf_{i,j}^t} \tag{6}$$

The Eq. 6 is the gradient update strategy of the client c_i, where t represents the communication round, g is the gradient, and $Sample$ is the selected senders after a de-mean confidence filtering. At the same time, the local and received gradient information is normalized.

4.2   Algorithm Implementation

The implementation of DGFL is illustrated in algorithm 1. Lines 1 to 5 show the preparations before starting which initialize all clients. From line 6 to the end is the FL process. In the process of FL, sending process is from lines 7 to 12, and the receiving process is from lines 13 to 20. The random single-sampling process is shown in line 9. The computation of confidence between clients on line 15 is based on Eq. 4. The gradient updating is shown on line 20.

Algorithm 1: Decentralized Graph Federated Learning

Initialization: Set clients $C = \{c_1, c_2, ..., c_n\}$, divide the dataset unevenly among clients, E is the number of local epochs, n is the total number of clients

1 **for** *each client $k \in C$* **do**
2 $\quad$ $S_k \leftarrow \{\}$;
3 $\quad$ $N_k \leftarrow C \backslash c_k$;
4 $\quad$ $Sample \leftarrow \{\}$
5 **end**
6 **for** *each round $t = 1, 2, 3, ...$* **do**
7 $\quad$ **for** *each client $i \in C$* **do**
8 $\quad\quad$ $g_i^t \leftarrow \texttt{ClientLocalTrain}(E)$;
9 $\quad\quad$ $r \leftarrow$ randomly select a client from N_i;
10 $\quad\quad$ $S_r \leftarrow i$(append client i to client r's sender list);
11 $\quad\quad$ send g_k^t to r
12 $\quad$ **end**
13 $\quad$ **for** *each client $i \in C$* **do**
14 $\quad\quad$ **for** $j \in S_i$ **do**
15 $\quad\quad\quad$ compute $Conf_{i,j}^t$
16 $\quad\quad$ **end**
17 $\quad\quad$ $Sample \leftarrow j \in S_i$, for $Conf_{i,j}^t \geq \overline{Conf_i^t}$(append client j to sample list);
18 $\quad\quad$ $g_i^{(t+1)} \leftarrow \dfrac{Conf_{i,i}^t * g_i^t + \sum_{j \in Sample} Conf_{i,j}^t * g_j^t}{Conf_{i,i}^t + \sum_{j \in Sample} Conf_{i,j}^t}$(update gradient);
19 $\quad\quad$ $Sample \leftarrow \{\}$
20 $\quad$ **end**
21 **end**

---

5   Experiments

5.1   Experimental Settings

Datasets. The datasets we use is TuDataset from the official datasets set of PyG (PyTorch Geometric), which mainly selects different data sets from three fields, namely Small molecules (AIDS, DHFR, P388), Bioinformatics (DD), Social networks(COLLAB, IMDB-BINARY, IMDB-MULTI), where each dataset has a set of graphs. The graph labels are binary or multi-class and our task is a graph classification task. We randomly distribute the graphs of a single dataset to multiple clients and keep 10% of the graphs as the test set (Table 1).

Table 1. Data Set Stat.

Name	Graphs	Classes	Avg.nodes	Avg.edges
COLLAB	5000	3	74.49	2457.78
AIDS	2000	2	15.69	16.20
DD	1178	2	284.32	715.66
PTC_FR	351	2	14.56	15.00
IMDB-BINARY	1000	2	19.77	96.53

Parameters. The local epoch E is set to 5 for each different FL algorithm. In the neural network layer, we choose the 3-layer Graph Isomorphism Networks(GINs) with a hidden size of 64. The batch size is set to 128 and the optimizer is Adam [9] with weight decay of $5e^{-4}$ and a learning rate of 0.001. The parameter μ of Fedprox [10] is set to 0.01. All experiments are run on the server with 16GB NVIDIA Tesla T4 GPUs.

Topology. Like the decentralized framework introduced by DGFL in Chap. 4, each node in the experiment is composed of a fully connected graph, meaning that each node has communication channels with all other nodes. In the experiment, we set the number of clients to 10 by default.

5.2 Research Questions

In this section. We will mainly conduct experiments to address the following research questions:

- How do the convergence speed, loss, and accuracy of the proposed method compare with other methods (Effectiveness)
- How does the time cost of the proposed method compare with other methods? (Time Overhead)

Effectiveness. To illustrate the superiority of the proposed method in terms of effectiveness, we mainly compare the proposed method with the existing baseline methods from three aspects which are accuracy, loss, and convergence speed.

Accuracy. Figure 2 shows the accuracy variation of the proposed method compared to the baseline method over 500 rounds for the same dataset IMDB-BINARY. Table 2 shows the final accuracy comparison of all methods with different data sets for a fixed number of rounds. The horizontal axis is the exchange rounds, and the vertical axis represents the average accuracy of all clients.

Table 2. Accuracy comparison of all methods for a fixed number of rounds with different datasets.

	COLLAB$_{500}$	AIDS$_{500}$	DD$_{1000}$	PTC_FR$_{1000}$	IMDB-B$_{1000}$
FedAvg [13]	0.7253	0.9859	0.7277	0.7250	0.6329
Fedprox [10]	0.7141	0.9858	0.7039	0.7250	0.6540
GCFL [22]	0.6879	0.9808	0.7369	0.7250	0.6613
GCFL+ [22]	0.6962	0.9808	0.7181	0.7250	0.6511
DGFL	**0.7374**	**0.9906**	**0.7628**	**0.7500**	**0.6732**

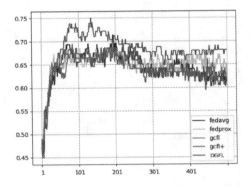

Fig. 2. 500 rounds accuracy comparison on IMDB-BINARY

Loss. Here are the results of three comparative experiments of different methods based on the loss to demonstrate the advantages of the proposed method. The vertical axis of each graph is the loss, and the horizontal axis is the communication round. From the first result Fig. 3(a) of the experiment on dataset AIDS of 200 rounds, we can find that the loss performance of all methods is very similar, however, compared with the baseline methods, the proposed method has better stability, which means that the baseline method has a larger "shake range". After that, the number of AC rounds is increased to 1000, and it can be seen from Fig. 3(c) that the proposed method has the highest curvature of the convergence curve in the case where the final convergence of the losses of each method is almost the same.

Table 3. Convergence comparison of methods on AIDS.

Method Name	FedAvg [13]	Fedprox [10]	GCFL [22]	GCFL+ [22]	DGFL
Convergence round	65	62	"63"	"61"	**47**

Convergence speed. When the fluctuation range of the accuracy within a certain number of rounds remains within a certain threshold, we consider that the

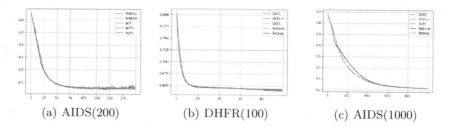

| (a) AIDS(200) | (b) DHFR(100) | (c) AIDS(1000) |

Fig. 3. Loss comparison of methods.

method has reached convergence. Since most datasets cannot achieve convergence within a short communication round, we give the dataset AIDS where all methods can converge within a short communication round for comparative experiments, and the results are shown in Fig. 4.

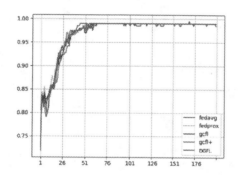

Fig. 4. 200 rounds convergence speed comparison on AIDS.

Obviously, in Table 3, we can see that the number of convergence rounds of other baseline methods is around 60, while the proposed method is reduced below 50 which is a big boost. The reason why we put quotation marks on the convergence round of $GCFL$ and $GCFL+$ for these two methods is that they have not reached absolute convergence. It can be seen that there is still a slight shake in the follow-up.

Time overhead. Under the premise of ensuring that the proposed method has an advantage in accuracy, compare the time consumption with the existing baseline method under the same dataset and the same number of rounds.

It can be seen from Table 4 that except for the time consumption of the proposed method under COLLAB(500 rounds) is slightly higher than that of GCFL, the time consumption of the proposed method under other datasets is optimal. Moreover, with the number of communication rounds increasing, the proposed method has no disadvantage in accuracy, and the speed of training highlights a greater advantage.

Table 4. Time consumption comparison of methods for a fixed number of rounds with different datasets.

	COLLAB$_{500}$	AIDS$_{500}$	DD$_{1000}$	IMDB-B$_{1000}$
FedAvg [13]	6467 ss	842 s	2552 ss	1475 ss
Fedprox [10]	6153 ss	998 s	2584 ss	1591 ss
GCFL [22]	**5843 ss**	887 s	2751 ss	1373 ss
GCFL+ [22]	6374 ss	867 s	2568 ss	1279 ss
DGFL	6012 ss	**838 s**	**2270 ss**	**1128 ss**

6 Conclusion

Taking the interaction of graph-federated learning based on a decentralized structure into consideration, this paper adopted GIN and a new federated aggregator algorithm, by introducing the proposed algorithm. Following, we considered four algorithms (i.e., FedAvg, Fedprox, GCFL, and GCFL+), and conducted a set of experiments to validate the effectiveness of the proposed algorithms. The experimental results illustrated that the proposed algorithms could achieve graph-federated learning [13] based on a decentralized structure. The success of graph learning and federated learning in this area demonstrates its great potential for other applications.

However, heterogeneity of each client's local data structure (e.g. distributing each client's different local data from different datasets) and Byzantine problems in communication (e.g. a certain client intentionally sends false information to other clients) will affect the training results. Therefore, there is still a need to address the problem of working under more dynamic topological conditions. Furthermore, the success of the proposed algorithm in graph-federated learning based on a decentralized framework shows the potential to be applied to more real-world scenarios, such as medical institutions sharing patient data for model training. In the future, we aim to improve the deficiencies in the proposed algorithm and apply it to more realistic scenarios.

References

1. Bengio, Y., Courville, A., Vincent, P.: Representation learning: a review and new perspectives. IEEE Trans. Pattern Anal. Mach. Intell. **35**(8), 1798–1828 (2013)
2. Caldarola, D., Mancini, M., Galasso, F., Ciccone, M., Rodolà, E., Caputo, B.: Cluster-driven graph federated learning over multiple domains. In: Proceedings of the IEEE/CVF Conference on Computer Vision and Pattern Recognition, pp. 2749–2758 (2021)
3. Coulouris, G.F., Dollimore, J., Kindberg, T.: Distributed systems: concepts and design. Pearson Education (2005)
4. Covert, I.C., et al.: Temporal graph convolutional networks for automatic seizure detection. In: Machine Learning for Healthcare Conference, pp. 160–180. PMLR (2019)

5. Diao, C., Zhang, D., Liang, W., Li, K.C., Hong, Y., Gaudiot, J.L.: A novel spatial-temporal multi-scale alignment graph neural network security model for vehicles prediction. IEEE Trans. Intell. Transp. Syst. **24**(1), 904–914 (2023). https://doi.org/10.1109/TITS.2022.3140229
6. Guo, T., et al.: Graduate employment prediction with bias. In: Proceedings of the AAAI Conference on Artificial Intelligence, vol. 34, pp. 670–677 (2020)
7. Hamilton, W., Ying, Z., Leskovec, J.: Inductive representation learning on large graphs. Advances in Neural Information Processing Systems, vol. 30 (2017)
8. Jiang, H., Cao, P., Xu, M., Yang, J., Zaiane, O.: Hi-GCN: a hierarchical graph convolution network for graph embedding learning of brain network and brain disorders prediction. Comput. Biol. Med. **127**, 104096 (2020)
9. Kingma, D.P., Ba, J.: Adam: a method for stochastic optimization. arXiv preprint arXiv:1412.6980 (2014)
10. Li, T., Sahu, A.K., Zaheer, M., Sanjabi, M., Talwalkar, A., Smith, V.: Federated optimization in heterogeneous networks. Proc. Mach. Learn. Syst. **2**, 429–450 (2020)
11. Lv, M., Hong, Z., Chen, L., Chen, T., Zhu, T., Ji, S.: Temporal multi-graph convolutional network for traffic flow prediction. IEEE Trans. Intell. Transp. Syst. **22**(6), 3337–3348 (2020)
12. Maly, R.J., Mischke, J., Kurtansky, P., Stiller, B.: Comparison of centralized (client-server) and decentralized (peer-to-peer) networking. Semester thesis, ETH Zurich, Zurich, Switzerland, pp. 1–12 (2003)
13. McMahan, B., Moore, E., Ramage, D., Hampson, S., y Arcas, B.A.: Communication-efficient learning of deep networks from decentralized data. In: Artificial Intelligence and Statistics, pp. 1273–1282. PMLR (2017)
14. Müller, M.: Dynamic time warping. Information retrieval for music and motion, pp. 69–84 (2007). https://doi.org/10.1007/978-3-540-74048-3_4
15. Pilkington, M.: Blockchain technology: principles and applications. In: Research handbook on digital transformations, pp. 225–253. Edward Elgar Publishing (2016)
16. Qiu, H., Zheng, Q., Msahli, M., Memmi, G., Qiu, M., Lu, J.: Topological graph convolutional network-based urban traffic flow and density prediction. IEEE Trans. Intell. Transp. Syst. **22**(7), 4560–4569 (2020)
17. Raval, S.: Decentralized applications: harnessing Bitcoin's blockchain technology. O'Reilly Media, Inc. (2016)
18. Scarselli, F., Gori, M., Tsoi, A.C., Hagenbuchner, M., Monfardini, G.: The graph neural network model. IEEE Trans. Neural Netw. **20**(1), 61–80 (2008)
19. Wang, T., et al.: MORONET: multi-omics integration via graph convolutional networks for biomedical data classification. bioRxiv, pp. 2020–07 (2020)
20. Xia, F., Ahmed, A.M., Yang, L.T., Luo, Z.: Community-based event dissemination with optimal load balancing. IEEE Trans. Comput. **64**(7), 1857–1869 (2014)
21. Xia, F., Ahmed, A.M., Yang, L.T., Ma, J., Rodrigues, J.J.: Exploiting social relationship to enable efficient replica allocation in ad-hoc social networks. IEEE Trans. Parall. Distrib. Syst. **25**(12), 3167–3176 (2014)
22. Xie, H., Ma, J., Xiong, L., Yang, C.: Federated graph classification over non-IID graphs. Adv. Neural. Inf. Process. Syst. **34**, 18839–18852 (2021)
23. Xu, K., Hu, W., Leskovec, J., Jegelka, S.: How powerful are graph neural networks? arXiv preprint arXiv:1810.00826 (2018)
24. Zhang, J., Wang, W., Xia, F., Lin, Y.R., Tong, H.: Data-driven computational social science: a survey. Big Data Res. **21**, 100145 (2020)

Heterogeneous Federated Learning Based on Graph Hypernetwork

Zhengyi Xu, Liu Yang[✉], and Shiqiao Gu

College of Intelligence and Computing, Tianjin University, Tianjin 300350, China
{2022244243,yangliuyl,2020244163}@tju.edu.cn

Abstract. Federated learning is a distributed machine learning framework over a large number of possible clients without data leakage. However, most federated learning methods are limited to clients with isomorphic network architectures. This restricts heterogeneous clients equipped with different computation and communication resources. To address this issue, this paper introduces a new heterogeneous federated learning method called heterogeneous federated graph hyperNetwork (hFedGHN), which takes the clients as a graph to integrate both structure and content information for deep latent representation learning and generates heterogeneous model for each client. HFedGHN can share effective parameters across clients, and maintain the capacity to generate unique and diverse personal models. Moreover, hFedGHN can be regarded as a process to learn a meta-model for federated learning, therefore it has better generalization ability to novel clients. As a group of novel clients are added dynamically, they can get acceptable performance after just one round of communication. With extensive experiments on MNIST, CIFAR-10, and CIFAR-100, the results demonstrate the superiority of hFedGHN.

Keywords: Federated learning · Heterogeneous clients · Graph hypernetwork

1 Introduction

Federated learning (FL) is a distributed machine learning framework that enables multiple clients to train a strong model without data leakage. The most well known FL technique is FedAvg [12], utilizing gradient descent iterations and suggesting more local training steps before aggregating models to reduce communication cost. The FL framework exists many challenges, such as data heterogeneity and model heterogeneity. Data heterogeneity makes it hard to learn a single shared global model acceptable for all clients, which triggers poor convergence on highly heterogeneous data and a lack of personalized solutions. To handle such heterogeneity across clients and provide personalized solutions, personalized federated learning (PFL) [1–3, 8–10, 13, 15, 16, 18, 20] allows each client to use a personalized model instead of a shared global model. Many papers

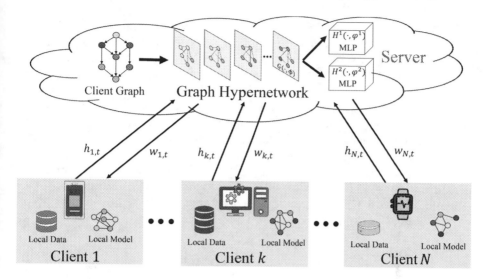

Fig. 1. The framework of hFedGHN. The graph hypernetwork is located on the server, generating heterogeneous models $w_{k,t}$ for each client. In turn, the clients upload local update $h_{k,t}$ to optimize the graph hypernetwork.

proposed a decentralized version of the model agnostic meta-learning problem [3,8,9], these methods focus on client-server relation to get stronger generalization ability to novel clients. Another approach to PFL is model mixing where the clients learn a mixture of the global and local models [1,10,16]. However, most PFL approaches do not allow client models to be heterogeneous.

Existing heterogeneous FL methods [5,7,11,14,17] focus on improving components of model personalization while processing knowledge sharing by simply aggregating all local models like FedAvg [12]. The simple aggregation overlooks the topological relationship across clients with heterogeneous data distribution. In other words, they do not allow pairwise collaboration among clients with similar data distribution, and thus may meet dramatic difficulty on non-IID data. Furthermore, previous models are not easily generalized to new clients.

In this paper, we propose a novel heterogeneous FL framework called Heterogeneous Federated Graph Hypernetwork as shown in Fig. 1, which trains heterogeneous local models with different computational graphs based on graph hypernetwork (GHN) [19]. The GHN takes as input a description of the client graph integrating both structure and content information for deep latent representation learning and emits weights to populate their model architecture. GHN is composed of two sub-networks: a graph convolutional neural network (GCN) and a set of multi-layer perceptrons (MLPs). GCN generates better client embedding vectors by sampling from the neighborhood and aggregating features according to the adjacency relation, which could be viewed as federated learning between clients with similar data distribution. These embedded representation vectors, output by GCN, are then fed into MLPs to produce heterogeneous personalized model weights. Therefore, MLPs could be view as some maps between the embedding space and the personal networks' parameter space.

Furthermore, the trained GHN can be shared by all clients. The training process of GHN could be regarded as learning a meta-model for federated learning. Thus, a well trained GHN can be easily generalized to novel clients. As shown in the experiments results, hFedGHN can achieve better results than other compared methods. Our contributions of this work can be summarized as follows:

(1) A new heterogeneous federated learning framework called hFedGHN is introduced. It allows clients to have different model sizes, that is, the client models are heterogeneous. (2) HFedGHN constructs a graph for the clients, uses GHN to learn an aggregation from similar local data distribution, and generates heterogeneous model for each client. (3) HFedGHN provides effective parameter sharing across clients like meta-learning, which can be easily generalized to novel clients. Extensive experiment results demonstrate that the proposed method can achieve better performance than other compared methods.

2   Method

In this work, we introduce a new approach called hFedGHN, which uses GHN to provide effective parameter sharing across heterogeneous clients. The framework of hFedGHN is shown in Fig. 1. The server firstly constructs clients as a graph to perform initialization. Then the GHN located on the server generates heterogeneous models for clients. After local training, the clients upload their local updates to server for optimizing GHN.

2.1   Problem Formulation

PFL aims to collaboratively train personalized models for a set of N clients, each client with its own personal private data. Unlike conventional FL, the objective of PFL can be written as:

$$\min_{w} \frac{1}{N} \sum_{k=1}^{N} f_k(\boldsymbol{w_k}; \boldsymbol{x_k}) \tag{1}$$

where $\boldsymbol{x_k}$ and $\boldsymbol{w_k}$ are the k-th client's data and model respectively, $f_k(\boldsymbol{w_k}; \boldsymbol{x_k})$ represents the loss function of k-th client.

In order to take advantage of the relationship between heterogeneous clients and share parameters, GHN is utilized for client personalization. Let $GH(\mathcal{G}; \theta)$ denote the GHN parameterized by θ. The GHN is located at the server and acts on a client graph $\mathcal{G}$. Given $\mathcal{G}$ the GHN outputs the weights for the clients, i.e., $\{\boldsymbol{w_k}\}_{k=1}^{N} = GH(\mathcal{G}; \theta)$. Moreover, hFedGHN allows the local models $\{\boldsymbol{w_k}\}_{k=1}^{N}$ to be heterogeneous. Hence, we adjust the PFL objective (Eq. (1)) as:

$$\min_{\theta} \frac{1}{N} \sum_{k=1}^{N} f_k(GH(\mathcal{G}; \theta); \boldsymbol{x_k}) \tag{2}$$

HFedGHN provides a natural way for sharing information across clients while maintaining the flexibility of heterogeneous personalized models, by sharing the GHN's parameters θ. In the following sections, this paper describes how to construct the client graph and how to train the GHN model.

2.2 Construction of Client Graph

With federated learning, clients in a system necessarily have a variety of complex relationships. For example, some clients have similar data distribution, while some clients have very different data distribution. Traditional federated learning incorporates all client models that participate in federated learning without considering the relationship between clients. In other words, traditional federated learning considers clients to form a complete graph.

In this paper, we use deep latent representation learning to dig the topological information between data distributions among clients and construct a special client graph. Constructing a client graph allows each client to benefit from the updates of others by data distribution similarity. Specifically, this paper uses the local model updates to calculate the relationship between clients. First, the clients perform multi-step SGD on their local data with learning rate η to obtain the updates after initializing local models $\{\bar{\boldsymbol{u}}_k\}_{k=1}^N$:

$$\tilde{\boldsymbol{u}}_k \leftarrow \bar{\boldsymbol{u}}_k - \eta \nabla f_k(\bar{\boldsymbol{u}}_k), \quad k = 1, \ldots, N \tag{3}$$

where $\tilde{\boldsymbol{u}}_k$ represents the updated model for k-th client. To better capture the relationship between clients, the generated gradient vector $\boldsymbol{u}_k := \bar{\boldsymbol{u}}_k - \tilde{\boldsymbol{u}}_k$ during local training is sent to the server to obtain a correlation matrix $\boldsymbol{A}$:

$$\boldsymbol{A} = (a_{ij})_{N \times N}, \quad a_{ij} = 1 - \cos\langle \boldsymbol{u}_i, \boldsymbol{u}_j \rangle \tag{4}$$

where $\cos\langle \cdot, \cdot \rangle$ is the cosine function, and a_{ij} is the cosine similarity between i-th client and j-th client. By specifying a threshold τ, the correlation matrix $\boldsymbol{A}$ can be transferred to an adjacency matrix by sign function $Sign(\cdot)$:

$$\tilde{\boldsymbol{A}} = Sign(\boldsymbol{A} - \tau) \tag{5}$$

The adjacency matrix $\tilde{\boldsymbol{A}}$ is approximate to the relationship between data distributions among clients. Then, for each client, we need to get its initial embedding representation. Because the original dimension of $\boldsymbol{u}_k$ is too high, we concatenate all $\boldsymbol{U} = \{\boldsymbol{u}_k\}_{k=1}^N$ to form matrix $\boldsymbol{U}$ and adopt Principal Component Analysis (PCA) to dimension reduction. The initial client embedding representation $\boldsymbol{V}^0$ of all N clients is obtained by

$$\boldsymbol{V}^0 = PCA(\boldsymbol{U}) \tag{6}$$

where $\boldsymbol{V}^0$ consists of N client embedding representations $\{\boldsymbol{v}_k^0\}_{k=1}^N$.

Finally, the client graph $\mathcal{G} = (\boldsymbol{V}^0, \tilde{\boldsymbol{A}})$ is obtained as an input to the GHN.

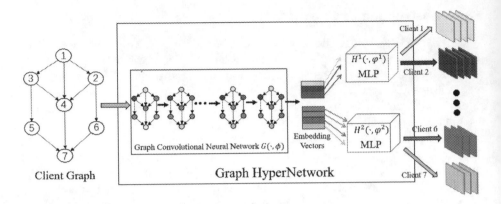

Fig. 2. Generation of heterogeneous models by hFedGHN on server. A shared graph representation is obtained by graph convolutional neural network G, and heterogeneous models are generated by multiple MLP function H^m.

2.3   Generation of Heterogeneous Models

$GH(\cdot; \theta)$ is a generalization of standard hypernetwork that allows generating models for heterogeneous local network architectures, which can be divided into two stages: (1) processing a graph representation using a GCN $G(\cdot; \phi)$. (2) generating models for clients by MLPs $\{H^m(\cdot; \varphi^m)\}_{m=1}^M$. Then the parameters are $\theta = \{\phi, \{\varphi^m\}_{m=1}^M\}$. The overall process for generating heterogeneous models of hFedGHN is shown in Fig. 2.

At the first stage, in the round t, GCN takes as input the client graph $\mathcal{G} = \left(\boldsymbol{V}^0, \tilde{\boldsymbol{A}}\right)$ with learnable parameters ϕ_t:

$$\forall k \in \mathcal{S}_t, \quad \boldsymbol{v}_{k,t}^L = G\left(\boldsymbol{v}_k^0, \tilde{\boldsymbol{A}}; \phi_t \mid \forall k \in \mathcal{S}_t\right) \tag{7}$$

where $\mathcal{S}_t$ clients are selected to perform local training at the t-th epoch. $\boldsymbol{v}_{k,t}^L$ is the result of $\boldsymbol{v}_{k,t}^0$ passing through GCN with L layers. GCN learns a function that generates $\boldsymbol{v}_{k,t}^L$ by sampling and aggregating features from the neighborhood according to the similarity between client data distributions, which can be regarded as performing FL aggregation between clients with similar data distribution contributing to superior performance. In this paper, the GraphSAGE [4] method is used as the messaging mechanism in GCN.

At the second stage, a set of MLPs with different output dimensions act as a hypernetwork for generating heterogeneous models. Supposed that clients participating in federated learning can be divided into M groups according to their model structure, the client set of the m-th group is $\mathcal{S}_t^m$.

Specifically, for each client embedding representation vector $\boldsymbol{v}_{k,t}^L$, input it into the corresponding MLP to get the model weights for that client:

$$\forall k \in \mathcal{S}_t^m, \quad \boldsymbol{w}_{k,t} = H^m\left(\boldsymbol{v}_{k,t}^L; \varphi_t^m\right) \tag{8}$$

where φ_t^m is the parameter of m-th MLP. In other words, the clients with the same model structure share the same MLP. Local models with different model structures use different MLPs to output personalized models that can be adapted to different computational graphs.

We simply use two different MLPs as examples shown in Fig. 2. According to the graph representation G and model generation H, heterogeneous model can be output for all clients. In summary, hFedGHN not only makes use of the topological relationship of data distribution between clients to achieve more efficient federated aggregation but also produces heterogeneous local models for clients. In addition, hFedGHN abandons the linear average aggregation method in the traditional federated learning method but uses GHN to learn the aggregation method instead.

2.4   Training Procedure

Based on Eq.(2) and utilizing the chain rule, we have the optimization form of the MLP $H^m(\cdot; \varphi_t^m)$:

$$\nabla_{\varphi_t^m} f_k(\boldsymbol{w}_{k,t}) = \nabla_{\boldsymbol{w}_{k,t}} f_k(\boldsymbol{w}_{k,t}) \cdot \nabla_{\varphi_t^m} H^m(\boldsymbol{v}_{k,t}^L; \varphi_t^m) \tag{9}$$

where $\nabla_{\varphi_t^m} f_k(\boldsymbol{w}_{k,t})$ represents the gradient of the loss function to the weights of the MLP, and $\nabla_{\boldsymbol{w}_{k,t}} f_k(\boldsymbol{w}_{k,t})$ can be approximated by $\boldsymbol{h}_{k,t} := \boldsymbol{w}_{k,t} - \boldsymbol{w}_{k,t+1}$. Similarly, the gradient of GCN can be calculated by:

$$\nabla_{\phi_t} f_k(\boldsymbol{w}_{k,t}) \approx \boldsymbol{h}_{k,t} \cdot \nabla_{\boldsymbol{v}_{k,t}^L} H^m(\boldsymbol{v}_{k,t}^L; \varphi_t^m) \cdot \nabla_{\phi_t} \boldsymbol{v}_{k,t}^L \tag{10}$$

where $\nabla_{\phi_t} f_k(\boldsymbol{w}_{k,t})$ represents the gradient of the loss function to the weights of GCN $G(\cdot; \phi_t)$. Therefore, the communication efficiency is only determined by $\boldsymbol{h}_{k,t}$. An optimal GHN can be learned that generates heterogeneous models for each client by solving Eq. (2).

The overall training process of hFedGHN is shown in Algorithm 1, which can be described as follow: The server takes clients' updates to obtain the client graph as initialization. The client graph will not change if novel clients don't join. Then, the GHN outputs local models $\{\boldsymbol{w}_{k,t} \mid \forall k \in \mathcal{S}_t\}$ to selected clients via inputting the client graph. The clients perform local training and send their model updates $\{\boldsymbol{h}_{k,t} \mid \forall k \in \mathcal{S}_t\}$ back to optimize GHN based on Eq. (9-10). One superior property of hFedGHN is that it decouples communication cost. The amount of data transferred in FL only depends on the complexity of local model updates $\boldsymbol{h}_{k,t}$ during the forward and backward communications. Consequently, the size of GHN can be arbitrarily large without weakening communication efficiency.

3   Experiments

3.1   Datasets and Implementation Details

Datasets and Compared Methods. Three benchmark datasets MNIST, CIFAR-10, and CIFAR-100 are used in the experiments to evaluate the per-

---

Algorithm 1: The Algorithm of HFedGHN

   Input: Local data $\{x_k\}_{k=1}^N$, learning rate η, number of rounds T.

1   Initialize $\{v_k^0\}_{k=1}^N$ and construct $\tilde{A}$ via Eqs. (3-6)

2   **Server Execution**:

3   **for** $t = 1, \ldots, T$ **do**

4   Randomly select clients $\mathcal{S}_t$;

5   Obtaining $w_{k,t}$ via Eqs. (7-8);

6   **for** $k \in \mathcal{S}_t$ *in parallel* **do**

7          $h_{k,t+1} \leftarrow$ **ClientUpdate** $(k, w_{k,t})$;

8          $\varphi_{t+1}^m \leftarrow \varphi_t^m - \eta \nabla_{\varphi_t^m} f_k(w_{k,t})$ based on Eq. (9);

9   **end**

10      $\phi_{t+1} \leftarrow \phi_t - \eta \frac{1}{|\mathcal{S}_t|} \sum_{k \in \mathcal{S}_t} \nabla_{\phi_t} f_k(w_{k,t})$ based on Eq. (10);

11   **end**

12   Return the final parameters ϕ_T, φ_T.

13   **Client Execution**:

14   **ClientUpdate** $(k, w_{k,t})$:

15   **for** $e = 1, \ldots, E$ **do**

16      $w_{k,t+1} \leftarrow w_{k,t} - \eta \nabla f_k(w_{k,t})$;

17   **end**

18   $h_{k,t+1} = w_{k,t} - w_{k,t+1}$;

19   Return $h_{k,t+1}$

---

formance of hFedGHN. Six methods, FedAvg [12], Per-Fed [3], pFedMe [16], LG-Fed [10], HeteroFL [17] and pFedHN [14], are used to compare with the proposed hFedGHN.

Hyperparameters. GHN adopts 2 convolutional layers and 3 fully connected neural network layers by default. The learning rate of GHN and local training is 0.01. We train the local classifier with 50 local update epoch and 64 batch size. For most methods, the experiments limit the training process to a maximum of 5000 communication steps. Since LG-FedAvg [10] needs to use the pre-trained FedAvg [12] model, it requires an additional 1000 communication steps. The experiments distribute 2/2/10 categories for each client on MNIST/CIFAR-10/CIFAR-100 datasets respectively to generate heterogeneous data distributions for clients, which is the same as the work of pFedHN [14].

Heterogeneous Setting. It is assumed that all clients participating in FL can be divided into three groups according to local resources. Clients in the same group share the same model structure. In this section, the width-based model heterogeneity denotes that the local model's computational graph is same between clients, but the output channels of some layers are different. According to their local resources, the width with large, medium and small sizes are marked as W_L, W_M and W_S, respectively. The client models under such settings are composed of two convolutional layers and three fully connected layers. The

Table 1. Experimental results of width-based heterogeneous model on CIFAR-10 and CIFAR-100. #Par is the parameters transmitted in FL.

Method	CIFAR-10				
	W_S	W_M	W_L	Acc	#Par
FedAvg [12]	39.17%	44.46%	49.48%	44.37%	3,635M
Per-Fed [3]	73.29%	74.90%	75.74%	74.64%	3,635M
pFedMe [16]	82.44%	85.71%	85.60%	84.58%	3,635M
LG-Fed [10]	77.58%	56.62%	57.22%	63.81%	5,089M
pFedHN [14]	83.45%	84.01%	85.28%	84.24%	758M
hFedGHN	**84.09%**	**85.21%**	**86.10%**	**85.13%**	**758M**
Method	CIFAR-100				
	W_S	W_M	W_L	Acc	#Par
FedAvg [12]	9.98%	12.90%	20.28%	14.39%	3,635M
Per-Fed [3]	42.40%	43.38%	45.80%	43.86%	3,635M
pFedMe [16]	40.72%	42.54%	46.56%	43.27%	3,635M
LG-Fed [10]	38.71%	30.66%	24.42%	31.26%	5,089M
pFedHN [14]	47.73%	51.50%	51.34%	50.19%	758M
hFedGHN	**49.94%**	**52.23%**	**52.05%**	**51.41%**	**758M**

output channels of the first convolutional layer is 16. However, for the second convolutional layer, the output channels of W_L, W_M and W_S are respectively 32, 16, 8.

For the depth-based model heterogeneity, the experiments also set three different model structures, which are marked with D_L, D_M and D_S, whose number of convolutional layers is 5, 4, and 3 respectively while other settings are same. Additionally, 80 clients are used and divided into three groups. Among them, clients 0–26 belong to W_S/D_S, clients 27–53 belong to W_M/D_M, and clients 54–79 belong to W_L/D_L. Additionally, because some methods, such as FedAvg [12], do not allow heterogeneous model settings, we choose to train each group separately for such methods.

3.2 Experiment Results

Width-Based Heterogeneous Model. The heterogeneity of models may differ in output channels. We evaluate different model widths shown in Table 1, which shows the average test accuracy of each group. The communication cost is included as well. HFedGHN achieves the best performance in accuracy under all the large, medium, and small scale model structures. HFedGHN saves about 79.15% communication cost compared with FedAvg [12], Per-FedAvg [3], and pFedMe [16]. What's more, the test accuracy of pFedAvg also achieves the best superiority. Compared with pFedHN [14], the average test accuracy increases

Table 2. Experiment results of depth-based heterogeneous model on CIFAR-10 and CIFAR-100.

Method	CIFAR-10				
	D_S	D_M	D_L	Acc	#Par
Local	54.45%	68.34%	80.10%	67.63%	–
FedAvg [12]	54.10%	77.54%	82.44%	71.36%	36,694M
pFedHN [14]	83.43%	86.05%	83.82%	84.43%	12,231M
hFedGHN	**84.42%**	**87.42%**	**85.97%**	**85.94%**	**12,231M**

Method	CIFAR-100				
	D_S	D_M	D_L	Acc	#Par
Local	12.38%	21.41%	36.05%	23.27%	–
FedAvg [12]	10.37%	41.41%	44.84%	32.21%	36,694M
pFedHN [14]	43.61%	47.25%	49.48%	46.78%	12,231M
hFedGHN	**45.78%**	**47.70%**	**49.94%**	**47.81%**	**12,231M**

0.89% at the same communication overhead. Similarly, the average test accuracy of hFedGHN is about 1.22% higher than pFedHN [14] on CIFAR-100.

Depth-Based Heterogeneous Model. In the framework of hFedGHN, a set of MLPs can take embedding vectors as input to adapt to different computational graphs. We perform experiments on different model depths. Table 2 shows the results under depth-based heterogeneous settings. Compared with pFedHN [14], hFedGHN proposed in this paper has achieved the best performance on CIFAR-10 and CIFAR-100. This is mainly because all clients share the same hypernetwork (which is essentially a MLP) in pFedHN [14], ignoring the relationship of client data distribution, therefore its ability to utilize relationships between clients with a high degree of heterogeneity is weaker than hFedGHN.

Generalization of New Clients. Another advantage of hFedGHN is the ability to generalization. In the general methods of sharing models across clients, they should perform more retraining or fine-tuning iterations to share the model. While hFedGHN is communication efficient to generalize to novel clients. The experiments are conducted with 100 clients on MNIST, and divide all clients into training clients or novel clients according to the ratio of 5:5, 6:4, 7:3, and 8:2. The results are shown in Table 3. HFedGHN only requires a round of communication to obtain the embedding vectors of novel clients as Eq. (3) without additional communication cost. The success of this process mainly depends on the training process of GHN which can be regarded as a process to learn a meta-model according to the clients' different data distributions. Once the shared GHN has been trained on a set of clients, it hardly requires extra effort to expand to a novel group of clients. The final results prove the superiority of hFedGHN.

3.3   Ablation Experiments

Personalization Ability. HFedGHN can be applied to isomorphic models as well. The experiments are carried out with 10, 50, and 100 client participants. The model structure selected in the experiments is W_M, which is the same as the model structure used in pFedHN [14]. The results shown in Table 4 show that hFedGHN has significantly improved the performance compared with other methods, which fully demonstrate the advantages of hFedGHN on non-IID data under both isomorphic and heterogeneous settings.

Different GHN's Hidden Layers. The depth of hidden layers indicates different complexity of GHN. The experiments are respectively conducted in which $L=1$–5, using 10, 50, and 100 clients respectively. With the increment of GCN layers, the performance becomes progressively worse, which is shown in Fig. 3. The reason is the inherent problem of over-smoothing in graph neural networks [6]. As the network becomes deeper, the representation of clients within the same connected component tends to converge to the same value, which makes the representation of different clients indistinguishable.

Table 3. The hypernetwork's generalization ability to novel clients on MNIST. Acc_t is the average accuracy of trained clients, and Acc_n is the average accuracy of novel clients.

Method	5:5			6:4		
	Acc_t	Acc_n	#Par	Acc_t	Acc_n	#Par
pFedHN [14]	99.07%	98.53%	172M	99.11%	98.57%	172M
hFedGHN	**99.35%**	**99.26%**	**4.3M**	**99.52%**	**99.46%**	**3.4M**
Method	7:3			8:2		
	Acc_t	Acc_n	#Par	Acc_t	Acc_n	#Par
pFedHN [14]	98.63%	98.36%	172M	98.59%	98.64%	172M
hFedGHN	**99.58%**	**99.48%**	**2.6M**	**99.65%**	**99.54%**	**1.7M**

Different Local Update Steps. Local training rounds can affect the performance. The experiments are conducted on CIFAR-10 and CIFAR-100 using 50 clients with different values of the local training round. As shown in Fig. 4, the final performance is similar for most settings of local update steps, which fully illustrates the robustness of hFedGHN.

Table 4. Results of model isomorphism on CIFAR-10 and CIFAR-100. 10, 50 and 100 denote the number of clients.

Method	CIFAR-10			CIFAR-100		
	10	50	100	10	50	100
Local	90.48%	75.50%	64.91%	60.36%	21.39%	15.62%
FedAvg [12]	53.83%	52.27%	47.22%	16.51%	16.06%	14.99%
Per-FedAvg [3]	81.49%	83.28%	82.18%	51.20%	46.65%	48.98%
FedPer [1]	88.66%	83.86%	81.70%	56.11%	49.78%	42.26%
pFedMe [16]	89.62%	87.22%	85.81%	53.26%	50.19%	46.59%
LG-FedAvg [10]	89.11%	85.77%	82.05%	55.11%	55.34%	53.12%
pFedHN [14]	90.83%	88.38%	**87.97%**	64.55%	58.51%	**53.24%**
hFedGHN	**91.70%**	**88.60%**	87.62%	**65.52%**	**59.28%**	53.12%

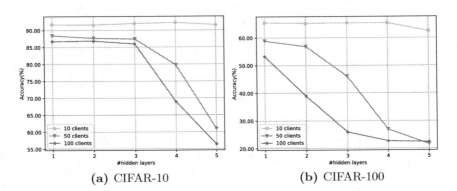

(a) CIFAR-10   (b) CIFAR-100

Fig. 3. Experiment results on different number of hidden layers of graph hypernetwork.

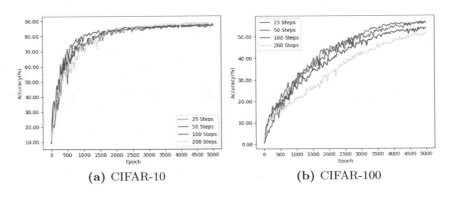

(a) CIFAR-10   (b) CIFAR-100

Fig. 4. Experiment results of different local training rounds.

4   Conclusion

In this paper, we introduce a new heterogeneous federated learning method hFedGHN, which trains a GHN on the server and outputs heterogeneous models for all clients. All clients are constructed as a graph in the server for deep latent representation learning by shared GCN, and heterogeneous model can be generated by MLPs for each client. HFedGHN can share effective parameters across clients, and maintain the capacity to generate unique and diverse personal models. Moreover, hFedGHN can be regarded as a process to learn a meta-model for federated learning, which has better generalization ability to new clients. Experimental results show it outperforms the state-of-the-art methods.

Acknowledgement. This work was supported in part by the National Natural Science Foundation of China under Grant 62076179.

References

1. Arivazhagan, M.G., et al.: Federated learning with personalization layers. arXiv preprint arXiv:1912.00818, pp. 1–13 (2019)
2. Chen, F., et al.: Personalized federated learning with graph. arXiv preprint arXiv:2203.00829 (2022)
3. Fallah, A., Mokhtari, A., Ozdaglar, A.: Personalized federated learning: a meta-learning approach. arXiv preprint arXiv:2002.07948, pp. 1–29 (2020)
4. Hamilton, W., Ying, Z., Leskovec, J.: Inductive representation learning on large graphs. Neural Information Processing Systems, pp. 1–11 (2017)
5. Huang, Y., et al.: Personalized cross-silo federated learning on non-IID data. In: AAAI, pp. 7865–7873. PMLR (2021)
6. Jin, W., et al.: Feature overcorrelation in deep graph neural networks: a new perspective. arXiv preprint arXiv:2206.07743, pp. 1–11 (2022)
7. Li, D., Wang, J.: FedMD: heterogenous federated learning via model distillation. arXiv preprint arXiv:1910.03581 (2019)
8. Li, J., Khodak, M., Caldas, S., et al.: Differentially private meta-learning. arXiv preprint arXiv:1909.05830 (2019)
9. Li, X., Li, Y., Wang, J., et al.: Decentralized federated meta-learning framework for few-shot multitask learning. Int. J. Intell. Syst. **37**(11), 8490–8522 (2022)
10. Liang, P.P., Liu, T., Ziyin, L., et al.: Think locally, act globally: federated learning with local and global representations. arXiv preprint arXiv:2001.01523, pp. 1–34 (2020)
11. Lin, T., et al.: Ensemble distillation for robust model fusion in federated learning. Advances in Neural Information Processing Systems, pp. 2351–2363 (2020)
12. McMahan, B., Moore, E., Ramage, D., et al.: Communication-efficient learning of deep networks from decentralized data. In: Artificial Intelligence and Statistics. pp. 1273–1282. PMLR (2017)
13. Mills, J., Hu, J., Min, G.: Multi-task federated learning for personalised deep neural networks in edge computing. IEEE Trans. Parallel Distrib. Syst. **33**(3), 630–641 (2022)
14. Shamsian, A., et al.: Personalized federated learning using hypernetworks. In: International Conference on Machine Learning, pp. 9489–9502. PMLR (2021)

15. Smith, V., Chiang, C.K., Sanjabi, M., et al.: Federated multi-task learning. In: Neural Information Processing Systems, pp. 1–11 (2017)
16. Dinh, T., Tran, C., Nguyen, N.: Personalized federated learning with Moreau envelopes. J. Neural Inf. Process. Syst. **33**, 21394–21405 (2020)
17. Wang, K., et al.: Federated evaluation of on-device personalization. arXiv preprint arXiv:1910.10252 (2019)
18. Yu, F., Rawat, A.S., Menon, A., Kumar, S.: Federated learning with only positive labels. In: International Conference on Machine Learning, pp. 10946–10956. PMLR (2020)
19. Zhang, C., Ren, M., Urtasun, R.: Graph hypernetworks for neural architecture search. arXiv preprint arXiv:1810.05749, pp. 1–17 (2018)
20. Zhang, X., et al.: Personalized federated learning via variational Bayesian inference. In: International Conference on Machine Learning, pp. 26293–26310. PMLR (2022)

Learning to Resolve Conflicts in Multi-Task Learning

Min Tang[1], Zhe Jin[3], Lixin Zou[2], and Liang Shiuan-Ni[1(✉)]

[1] Monash University, 47500 Kuala Lumpur, Malaysia
{min.tang,liang.shiuan-ni}@monash.edu
[2] Wuhan University, Wuhan 430072, China
[3] Anhui University, Hefei 230039, China

Abstract. Multi-task learning, a promising direction for sharing structure and knowledge between different tasks, has been widely studied for improving the data efficiency of deep learning. Unfortunately, training the MTL model is non-trivial since multi-tasks might negatively influence each other due to gradient conflicts.

Toward this end, many algorithms have been proposed to handle the gradient conflicts by designing sophisticated neural architectures or gradient modification methods in task granularity. However, in this work, we argue that it is necessary to resolve the conflicts from the sample granularity. Specifically, we propose a framework named learning to resolve conflicts (LTRC), which adaptively reweights the sample gradient for diminishing the gradient conflicts over multi-tasks. Finally, we conduct extensive experiments on two benchmark datasets. The superior experimental results of the proposed method demonstrate its effectiveness.

Keywords: Multi-task Learning · Meta-Learning · Gradient Conflicts

1 Introduction

With the emerging success of deep learning in natural language processing, computer vision, and information retrieval, a variety of applications have been developed in web search engines [30,33], machine translation [26], and recommendation systems [31,32]. However, deploying deep learning-based models is not always feasible in practice due to the heavy cost of collecting corresponding training examples [29]. For instance, gathering a large-scale training dataset in biometrics features regarding privacy protection [24] or medical diagnosis [1] might be perceived as intrusive by the users. Therefore, a common practice is to develop a shared model for multiple tasks [9,23,28], i.e., multi-task learning [2] (MTL). Specifically, MTL aims to attain higher performance and better generalization than individual tasks by learning the same model to perform multiple tasks. Furthermore, the shared parameters of the MTL intrinsically reduce the size of the multi-task model compared to single-task models, thereby speeding up the training and inferences. However, obtaining the ideal MTL is a non-trivial

© The Author(s), under exclusive license to Springer Nature Switzerland AG 2023
L. Iliadis et al. (Eds.): ICANN 2023, LNCS 14256, pp. 477–489, 2023.
https://doi.org/10.1007/978-3-031-44213-1_40

task as negative-sharing is observed due to the *gradient conflicts* [27], i.e., the gradients of different tasks might be in opposite directions. Consequently, training multiple tasks simultaneously can lead to degradation in certain tasks and worsen overall performance.

As a result, various algorithms have been proposed to handle this challenge, which can be categorized into two groups: (a) neural architecture design and (b) gradient conflict optimization. The first group aims to discover suitable neural architectures that can eliminate the gradient conflicts, such as the MMOE [16], and Multitask-CenterNet [5]. They have been extensively studied and can significantly boost performance. The second group, on the other hand, tries to resolve the gradient conflicts through loss-reweighting [8,12,15] and gradient modification [3,13,19,25,27]. For example, Nash-MTL [19] utilizes Nash bargaining to find the optimal updating weights for different tasks. CAGrad [13] tries to find a gradient that is consistent with the averaging neighborhood gradients. However, all these methods are considering the gradient conflicts from the task granularity. Few works have been considered to resolve the conflicts from sample granularity.

In this work, we argue that it is beneficial to study the gradient conflicts from sample granularity and reweight the multi-samples gradient to reach a conflict-free gradient. Specifically, we design a bi-level optimization procedure named LTRC (learning to resolve conflicts) to find the best sample weighting function. It follows a simple assumption that the best gradient should resolve the conflicts and minimize the losses on all tasks. Therefore, we adaptively select the sample weights by maximizing the performance on a randomly reselected batch sample, which is used to verify the sample weights' effectiveness on the overall tasks. Furthermore, we theoretically analyze the learned weighting function and give an intuitive explanation for it.

Finally, we conducted extensive experiments on two benchmark datasets, Census-Income and CIFAR-100. Compared with the state-of-the-art methods for resolving conflicts, our proposed method suppress them by a large margin, which indicates the superiority of the proposed methods. The main contribution of this work can be summarized as follows:

- We proposed a framework named LTRC, which adaptively reweights the sample gradient for diminishing the gradient conflicts over multi-tasks.
- We provide explanations for LTRC by theoretically analyzing the weighting function.
- Extensive experimental results demonstrate the superiority of the proposed methods.

2   Proposed Method

In the following, we describe the technical details of our proposed approach. We first discuss some prerequisites that are necessary to formulate the multi-task learning. Then, solving gradient conflict is formulated as a bi-level meta-learning problem. Further, we provide a practical implementation of the bi-level optimization task in a typical training procedure of deep neural networks.

Finally, we analyze the gradient of weights and give an intuitive understanding of the proposed method.

2.1 Prerequisite

In this section, we present multi-task learning formulation and then introduce how the conflicting phenomenon arises in the training process.

Multi-task Learning. Given a set of K ($K \geq 2$) tasks, each of them is associated with a set of shared parameters θ across different tasks, a set of task-specific parameters ϕ_i and a corresponding empirical loss $\mathcal{L}_i(\theta, \phi_i)$ as $\mathcal{L}_i(\theta, \phi_i) = \sum_{j \in \mathcal{D}_i} \ell_{i,j}(\theta, \phi_i)$, where $\mathcal{D}_i$ consists of samples from task i and $\ell_{i,j}(\theta, \phi_i)$ is the loss on a specific sample j. We are required to find the optimal θ and $\{\phi_i\}_{i=1}^K$ that minimize the loss across all tasks as:

$$\theta^*, \{\phi_i^*\}_{i=1}^K = \arg\min_{\theta, \{\phi_i\}_{i=1}^K} \frac{1}{K} \sum_{i=1}^K \mathcal{L}_i(\theta, \phi_i). \tag{1}$$

However, directly optimizing the objective with vanilla gradient descent needs to consider the optimization of individual losses, leading to a well-known problem known as gradient conflicts.

Gradient Conflict. Let $g_i = \partial_\theta \mathcal{L}_i(\theta, \phi_i) = \sum_{j \in \mathcal{D}_i} g_{i,j}$ be the gradient of task i on shared parameters, where $g_{i,j}$ is the gradient of a specific sample j. Furthermore, assume that $\bar{g} = \partial_\theta \frac{1}{K} \sum_{i=1}^K \mathcal{L}_i(\theta, \phi_i)$ be the overall gradient across tasks. With the learning rate $\alpha \in \mathbb{R}^+$, $\theta \leftarrow \theta - \alpha \bar{g}$ would be the steepest descent update that appears to be the most natural update for minimizing Eq. (1). However, the overall gradient $\bar{g}$ might be conflicting with the individual gradient g_i. There might be a task i satisfying $\langle g_i, \bar{g} \rangle < 0$. When the frequency of observing the discrepancy between g_i and $\bar{g}$ is high, using overall gradient $\bar{g}$ might result in the performance degradation of individual tasks.

2.2 Resolving Conflicts by Gradient Recombination

Existing works mitigate the conflicts by optimizing the gradient [8,14,15] or searching better neural architectures [5,17]. However, few works notice that the gradient g_i is the sum of multi-gradients of samples. Therefore, we argue that it is beneficial to recombine the gradient as $g_i' = \sum_{j \in \mathcal{D}_i} \omega_{i,j} \cdot g_{i,j}$ for resolving conflicts, i.e., reweighting the training samples for negotiation between different tasks. As a result, the objective of this work is to find optimal hyper-parameters set $\Omega_i = \{\omega_{i,j}\}_{j \in \mathcal{D}_i}$ that minimizes the gradient conflicts as

$$\Omega_i^* = \arg\max_{\Omega_i} \langle g_i', g \rangle, \text{ where } g_i' = \sum_{j \in \mathcal{D}_i} \omega_{i,j} \cdot g_{i,j} \text{ and } \omega_{i,j} \geq 0. \tag{2}$$

Notice that the $\omega_{i,j} > 0$ is necessary since minimizing the negative training loss may result in unstable behavior. Furthermore, $\omega_{i,j} > 0$ ensures that g_i' minimizes the loss $\mathcal{L}_i(\theta, \phi_i)$ to some extent. Otherwise, the performance of task i will be sacrificed in MTL.

2.3   Meta-Learning for Gradient Recombination

Reformulation as a Bi-level Optimization Task. Unfortunately, directly optimizing the target in Eq. (2) is difficult. We, therefore, approximate the gradient recombination as reweighting the individual loss of the samples since weighting the gradient is equivalent to weighting the loss. Consequently, the problem can be viewed as finding the optimal Ω_i^* through a bi-level optimization task as

$$\overbrace{\Omega_i^* = \arg\min_{\Omega_i^*} \frac{1}{K} \sum_{i=1}^{K} \sum_{j \in \mathcal{D}_i^{\mathrm{val}}} \ell_{i,j}(\theta^*, \phi_i^*)}^{\text{Outer Level}}, \text{where } \overbrace{\theta^*, \phi_i^* = \arg\min_{\theta, \phi} \frac{1}{K} \sum_{i=1}^{K} \sum_{j \in \mathcal{D}_i} \omega_{i,j} \ell_{i,j}(\theta^*, \phi_i^*)}^{\text{Inner Level}}. \quad (3)$$

Here, $\mathcal{D}_i^{\mathrm{val}}$ is the validation dataset. The inner level optimizes the reweighted empirical loss that generates the weighted gradient g_i'. The outer level aims to optimize the reweighting hyper-parameters Ω_i^*. The optimal modified gradient g_i' is designed to achieve the best performance on a validation dataset $\mathcal{D}_i^{\mathrm{val}}$.

Online Approximation. The optimization of the inner and outer objectives in Eq. (3) is a non-trivial task due to two facts: **(1)** the time cost of iterating between these two tasks is intolerable; **(2)** a small validation dataset typically leads the performance deterioration during training. Therefore, during the training iteration for a specific task i, we inspect the descent direction of a batch training examples $\mathcal{B}_i$ locally on the training loss surface and reweight them according to their similarity to the descent direction of another different batch training samples $\mathcal{B}'_{k=1}^{K}$, i.e., approximately using the whole training dataset as the validation set for learning the reweighting function.

Specifically, during the t-th iteration of training, we approximate the optimal θ^*, ϕ_i^* using the $\mathcal{B}_i$ with one step vanilla SGD updating of θ', ϕ_i' as

$$\theta' = \theta - \alpha \sum_{j \in \mathcal{B}_i} \frac{\partial \omega_{i,j} \ell_{i,j}(\theta, \phi_i)}{\partial \theta}, \phi' = \phi - \alpha \sum_{j \in \mathcal{B}_i} \frac{\partial \omega_{i,j} \ell_{i,j}(\theta, \phi_i)}{\partial \phi_i}, \quad (4)$$

where α is the learning rate. We expect that the updated θ' would be beneficial or at least not bad for all tasks' performance. Therefore, following [20], we optimize the weight by minimizing the overall loss on a randomly sampled different batch samples $\{\mathcal{B}_i'\}_{i=1}^{K}$ as

$$\omega_{i,j} \leftarrow \max\{\omega_{i,j} - \beta \sum_{i=1}^{K} \sum_{j \in \mathcal{B}_i'} \frac{\partial \ell_{i,j}(\theta', \phi')}{\partial \omega_{i,j}}, 0\}, \quad (5)$$

where β is the learning rate. The max operation is to avoid the negative weight. In practice, we found that $\omega_{i,j} = 1$ is a good initializer for resolving the conflicts. After updating the Ω_i, on the same batch samples $\mathcal{B}_i$, the model parameters are updated as original multi-task learning as $\theta \leftarrow \theta - \alpha \sum_{j \in \mathcal{B}_i} \frac{\partial \omega_{i,j} \ell_{i,j}(\theta, \phi_i)}{\partial \theta}, \phi \leftarrow \alpha \sum_{j \in \mathcal{B}_i} \frac{\partial \omega_{i,j} \ell_{i,j}(\theta, \phi_i)}{\partial \phi_i}$. A detailed training procedure of LTRC is illustrated in Fig. 1.

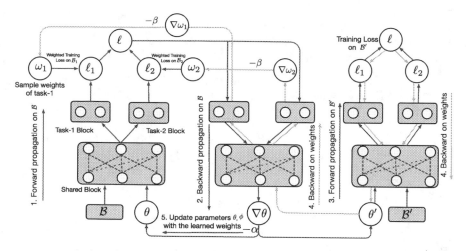

Fig. 1. The proposed workflow of learning to resolve conflicts. Due to the space limitation and without losing generalization, we only plot two tasks for a demo illustration. Its optimization consists of the following five steps: **(1)** Compute weighted loss $\sum_{j \in \mathcal{B}_i} \omega_{i,j} \ell_i(\theta, \phi_i)$ for all the task $i \in [1, K]$. **(2)** Calculate the updated parameters with the weighted loss, including shared parameters θ' and task-independent parameters ϕ'_i for $i \in [1, K]$. **(3)** Compute the overall tasks' loss $\sum_{i=1}^{K} \sum_{j \in \mathcal{B}'_i} \ell_{i,j}(\theta', \phi'_i)$ with the updated parameters θ', ϕ'_i, and another batch datasets $\{\mathcal{B}'_i\}_{i=1}^{K}$. **(4)** Update the loss weights $\omega_{i,j} \leftarrow \max\{\omega_{i,j} - \beta \sum_{i=1}^{K} \sum_{j \in \mathcal{B}'_i} \frac{\partial \ell_{i,j}(\theta', \phi')}{\partial \omega_{i,j}}, 0\}$. **(5)** Update the model parameters $\theta \leftarrow \theta - \alpha \sum_{j \in \mathcal{B}_i} \frac{\partial \omega_{i,j} \ell_{i,j}(\theta, \phi_i)}{\partial \theta}$, $\phi \leftarrow \alpha \sum_{j \in \mathcal{B}_i} \frac{\partial \omega_{i,j} \ell_{i,j}(\theta, \phi_i)}{\partial \phi_i}$ using the same batch samples $\mathcal{B}_i$ for $i \in [1, K]$.

Analysis on the Weighting Scheme. The computation of Eq. (5) by backward propagation can be rewritten as

$$\omega_{i,j} \leftarrow \max \left\{ \omega_{i,j} - \beta\alpha \left. \frac{\partial \sum_{i=1}^{K} \sum_{j \in \mathcal{B}'_i} \ell_{i,j}(\Theta')}{\partial \Theta'} \right|_{\Theta'}^{\top} \frac{\partial \ell_{i,j}(\Theta)}{\partial \Theta}, 0 \right\}, \quad (6)$$

where $\Theta' = \{\theta', \phi'_i\}_{i=1}^{K}$, $\Theta = \{\theta, \phi_i\}_{i=1}^{K}$. From Eq. (6), the weight $\omega_{i,j}$ depends on the similarity between its gradient and the average gradient of the randomly sampled batch's samples. That means if the learning gradient of a training sample $g_{i,j}$ is similar to that of overall samples $\bar{g}$, then it will be considered beneficial for boosting overall performance and its weight tends to be more possibly increased. Conversely, the weight of the sample inclines to be suppressed.

3   Experiments

To assure the effectiveness of the proposed solutions, we conducted extensive experiments on the multi-task benchmark datasets. This section details the experimental setup and presents several insights demonstrating that the proposed approach is an effective way of solving the gradient conflict for multi-task learning.

3.1   Experimental Settings

Dataset. We train and evaluate the proposed method with two benchmark datasets Census-Income[1] and CIFAR-100[2], which have been used to demonstrate the task conflicts [16]. The **Census-Income** was extracted from the 1994 Census Bureau database. It contains 299,285 samples with 40 features. Following the setting in [16], we construct two tasks: **(1) Income** determines whether a person earns over $50K$ dollars a year; **(2) Marital** guesses whether the person is ever married. The **CIFAR-100** [11] is a labeled subset of the 80 million tiny images dataset that contains 100 classes with 6,000 images per class. We follow the setting in [21] and construct twenty tasks of five-class classification problems by consolidating the 100 classes into 20 superclasses [11] according to their similarity of species, such as fish, people, and flower. The statistics of the datasets are available at Table 1.

Table 1. Summary Statistics of Datasets.

Dataset	train	test	tasks	class
Census-Income	199,523	99,762	2	2
CIFAR-100	372,392	76,141	20	5

Parameter Settings. For the Census-Income dataset, we randomly select 33% instances as the test set and leave the remaining 67% samples as the training set. For the neural network, an MLP with the size of $\{490, 80, 50\}$ is selected as the backbone model. The task-specific parameter is a two-layer $\{10, 2\}$ MLP. Its whole parameters are initialized with a uniform distribution ranging from -0.01 to 0.01.

The maximum iteration of LTRC is set as 300 in the experiments. The CIFAR-100 dataset is divided into the 17% test set (76,141 images) and the 83% training set (372,392 images). Following Merity et al. work [18], we employ the VGG-16 as the backbone model and the linear classifier as the task-specific head. Therefore, a total of 20 heads are attached to the backbone. For both datasets, all the models are trained with the Adam optimizer [10].

The models are defined and trained with Pytorch on an Nvidia Tesla P40 GPU. Due to the limitation of GPU memory, the training batch size is set to 32.

---

[1] https://www.kaggle.com/datasets/uciml/adult-census-income.
[2] https://www.cs.toronto.edu/~kriz/cifar.html.

Evaluation Protocol

- **Single Task Evaluaion.** For Census-Income, since the task of predicting the salary is a highly imbalanced classification problem, we utilize AUC (Area Under Curve) metric to evaluate models' performance, where AUC is insensitive to the imbalance labels in test data and suitable for evaluation [16]. Besides, for CIFAR-100 tasks, the accuracy score is employed to indicate the models' performance.
- **Multi-Task Evaluaion.** Furthermore, following the common practice in [12,13,19], we choose Mean Rank (MR) and Δ_{MTL} as the metrics to evaluate the model's overall effectiveness on the multi-tasks. Specifically, the MR represents the average rank of each method across the different tasks. Therefore, the smallest value of MR indicates the best performance, i.e., MR $=1$, if it ranks first in all tasks. Δ_{MTL}^m is the tuning performance score of method m with respect to a specific single-task baseline, which is defined as

$$\Delta_{MTL}^m = \frac{1}{K} \sum_{i \in [1,K]} 100 \cdot (-1)^{l_i} (M_{m,i} - b_i)/b_i, \qquad (7)$$

where b_i denotes the score of the single task learning method for task i. $M_{m,i}$ is the score of the multi-task learning method m on task i. l_i is an indicator function. $l_i = 0$ if a higher value is better for $M_{m,i}$ and b_i in the i-th task, and $l_i = 1$ otherwise. As a result, the higher score of Δ_{MTL}^m indicates better performance.

Baseline. We compared LTRC with the following methods, which include both basic and state-of-the-art methods. (1) **SingleTask** trains independent models for every single task. (2) **EquWeight** uses the fixed and equal weights for all tasks' loss in the training process. (3) **UncWeight** [8] scales the training loss of each task differently based on task uncertainty. (4) **DWA** [15] adapts the task weight based on the changing of loss for each task. (5) **Nash-MTL** [19] prompts that overall tasks negotiate to get an agreement on a joint direction for parameters updating, which is inspired by the Nash Bargaining Solution.

Table 2. Multi-task learning performance of different methods on Census-Income.

Method	Income (AUC)↑	Marital (AUC)↑	RM↓	Δ_{MTL} ↑
SingleTask	0.9399	0.9761	–	–
EquWeight	0.9411	0.9769	2.0	+0.1048
UncWeight	0.9393	0.9766	3.0	−0.0063
DWA	0.9388	0.9763	4.5	−0.0482
Nash-MTL	0.9378	0.9765	4.5	−0.0912
LTRC	**0.9422***	**0.9771***	**1.0***	**+0.1735***

Bold: the best performance among all models. *: the statistically significant improvements (i.e., two-sided t-test with $p < 0.05$) over the best baseline.

Table 3. Multi-task learning performance of different methods on CIFAR-100. To save space, we only report the accuracy of 5 representative tasks from the whole twenty tasks in the table. But the average accuracy is calculated on the twenty tasks' scores.

Method	Fish↑	Aquatic↑	Scenes↑	Trees↑	Vegetables↑	Average↑	RM↓	Δ_{MTL} ↑
SingleTask	79.20%	66.00%	88.40%	73.80%	86.80%	80.36%	-	-
EquWeight	77.50%	70.10%	**89.90%**	72.00%	85.50%	80.40%	2.4	+0.3651
UncWeight	79.20%	68.90%	88.40%	71.80%	**88.40%**	80.67%	2.6	+0.7054
DWA	79.20%	69.40%	87.40%	70.80%	85.40%	80.31%	3.8	−0.3315
Nash-MTL	77.80%	67.80%	87.50%	71.60%	81.80%	78.14%	4.2	−1.7599
LTRC	**80.20%***	**72.80%***	89.40%	**73.80%***	86.20%	**81.08%***	**1.2***	**+2.4010***

Bold: the best performance among all models. ∗: the statistically significant improvements (i.e., two-sided t-test with $p < 0.05$) over the best baseline.

3.2 Evaluation Results

All the experiments have run at least 3 times with different random seeds and only the average best results are reported in this section. The results of all methods over the benchmark datasets are shown in Table 2 and Table 3. From the results shown in these two tables, we have the following observations:

- The results indicate that our method LTRC can indeed improve multi-task learning performance by solving conflicts in the shared models. The reason is that LTRC outperformed all baseline methods on RM and Δ_{MTL} by a large margin on both datasets.
- The gradient conflicts reduce the models' effectiveness. As shown in Table 2 and Table 3, the DWA and Nash-MTL are worse than the SingleTask method on both datasets, which verifies the performance deterioration effect of gradient conflict in multi-task learning.
- Inappropriate loss reweighting may further deteriorate models' performance. From Table 2 and Table 3, the Δ_{MTL} of UncWeight and Nash-MTL are smaller than EquWeight, which directly sum the multi-task losses for naive multi-task learning.

3.3 Ablation Study

The Influence of the Initializer for Weights. We analyze the influence of the initializer for weights by following the experiment setting on CIFAR-100 in Section 3.2 and only change the initializer to zero, i.e., setting $\omega_{i,j} = 0$. In Fig. 2, we plot the LTRC with different initializing weights. From the Figure, initializing the weights with zero will significantly decrease the average accuracy, i.e., the overall performance. This is because initializing weight with zero leads to the ignorance of many samples and partial usage of training data.

Effectiveness of Randomly Selected Batch Samples. In this section, we study the influence of using different validation datasets. Therefore, in Fig. 3, we

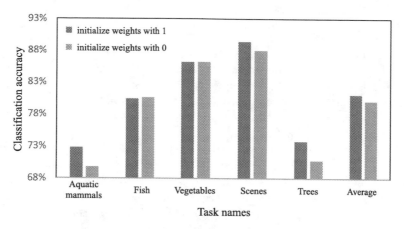

Fig. 2. The performance of LTRC with different initialized weights on CIFAR-100.

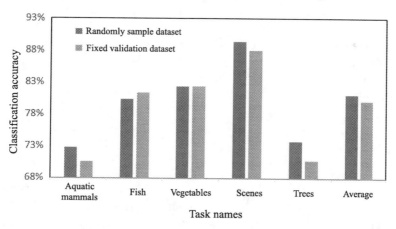

Fig. 3. Performance of LTRC with randomly sample dataset and fixed validation set on CIFAR-100.

plot the comparison between using randomly sampled batch samples and a fixed validation dataset. As shown in the figure, the former, i.e., using a randomly sampled dataset, surpasses the latter, which is consistent with our intuition and verified the effectiveness of the proposed technique.

4   Related Work

Generally, the research for sharing knowledge on multi-task learning can be roughly grouped into neural architecture design and gradient-conflicts optimization. In this section, we briefly review the relevant work.

4.1   Neural Architecture Design

During the past years, many successful neural architectures have been developed for boosting multi-task learning performance. The existing methods mainly approach this problem from two different directions. **Hard Parameter Sharing** [2] employed a shared neural network to learn multiple tasks simultaneously. In [5], the Multitask-CenterNet architecture was designed for diverse tasks including object detection, semantic segmentation, and human pose estimation, in order to save computation time and resources. Based on Transformer-based encoder-decoder architecture, UniT model [6] encoded each input modality with an encoder and made predictions on each task with a shared decoder over the encoded input representations, followed by task-specific output heads. Ma et al. [17] used ESMM with a shared lookup table to estimate the conversion rate, addressing the sample selection bias and data sparsity problems. Differing from the previous setting, **Soft Parameter Sharing** model [4] uses separate parameters and hidden layers, thereby simplifying the calculations to find the appropriate weights for different task loss functions. As mentioned in [22], a sluice meta-network was capable to learn what layers and subspaces should be shared and at what layers the meta-network has learned the best representations of the input sequences. Nevertheless, designing a more powerful neural architecture isn't the main focus of this work.

4.2   Gradient-Conflicts Optimization

Since the gradient directions of different tasks may conflict, training a joint model for MTL typically yields lower performance than its corresponding single-task model. Accordingly, a series of works have been proposed to resolve the conflicts and improve the performance of the MTL model. Specifically, Uncertainty Weights (UW) [8], Dynamic Weight Average (DWA) [15], and IMTL-L [14] studied how to acquire appropriate loss weights to balance the performance of multiple objectives. However, Random Loss Weighting (RLW) [12] demonstrated that the MTL model trained with random loss weights sampled from a distribution may obtain better generalization ability. In particular, a dynamic reweighing loss has been proposed and achieved superior performance than using fixed loss weights. Another set of methods seeks to mitigate optimization challenges in multi-task learning by finding a better strategy to update gradients. Such representative works include Gradient Normalization (GradNorm) [3], Projecting Conflicting Gradient (PCGrad) [27], Impartial Multi-Task Learning (IMTL-G) [14], and Gradient Vaccine [25]. Recently, Conflict-Averse Gradient descent (CAGrad) [13] intended to search for a gradient direction that maximizes the worst local improvement of any objective in a neighborhood of the average gradient. RotoGrad [7] and Nash-MTL [19] attempted to reach an agreement on a joint direction of parameter update by playing a bargaining game.

Though these methods are technically sound for solving gradient conflicts, rare work has been done from the perspective of sample granularity. Consequently, in this work, we aim to automatically find particular sample weights for every task, which relieves the gradient conflicts. Therefore, the LTRC procedure is built to find the optimal sample weights using another randomly reselected batch sample. Compared to other solutions, LTRC is capable of saving the cost of heuristically designing the complicated neural architecture or the intricate reweighting function.

5   Conclusions

This work has introduced LTRC, a practical optimization method for multi-task learning, which decreases the gradient conflicts from the perspective of sample granularity. Furthermore, LTRC is model-agnostic and can be combined with other state-of-the-art approaches based on neural architecture design for more significant benefit. Remarkably, exploring asynchronously updating shared modules and task-independent modules with particular step speeds and directions might be a promising future direction. Additionally, we theoretically analyze the method of the proposed methods and conduct extensive experiments on two benchmark datasets for proving the effectiveness of the proposed method.

References

1. Bakator, M., Radosav, D.: Deep learning and medical diagnosis: a review of literature. Multimodal Technol. Interact. **2**(3), 47 (2018)
2. Caruana, R.: Multitask learning: a knowledge-based source of inductive bias1. In: Proceedings of ICML, pp. 41–48. Citeseer (1993)
3. Chen, Z., Badrinarayanan, V., Lee, C.Y., Rabinovich, A.: Gradnorm: gradient normalization for adaptive loss balancing in deep multitask networks. In: Proceedings of ICML, pp. 794–803. PMLR (2018)
4. Duong, L., Cohn, T., Bird, S., Cook, P.: Low resource dependency parsing: cross-lingual parameter sharing in a neural network parser. In: Proceedings of the 53rd annual meeting of the Association for Computational Linguistics and the 7th international joint conference on natural language processing (volume 2: short papers), pp. 845–850 (2015)
5. Heuer, F., Mantowsky, S., Bukhari, S., Schneider, G.: Multitask-centernet (MCN): efficient and diverse multitask learning using an anchor free approach. In: Proceedings of ICCV, pp. 997–1005 (2021)
6. Hu, R., Singh, A.: Unit: multimodal multitask learning with a unified transformer. In: Proceedings of ICCV, pp. 1439–1449 (2021)
7. Javaloy, A., Valera, I.: RotoGrad: gradient homogenization in multitask learning. arXiv preprint arXiv:2103.02631 (2021)
8. Kendall, A., Gal, Y., Cipolla, R.: Multi-task learning using uncertainty to weigh losses for scene geometry and semantics. In: Proceedings of CVPR, pp. 7482–7491 (2018)
9. Kiela, D., Conneau, A., Jabri, A., Nickel, M.: Learning visually grounded sentence representations. arXiv preprint arXiv:1707.06320 (2017)

10. Kingma Diederik, P., Adam, J.B.: A method for stochastic optimization. arXiv preprint arXiv:1412.6980 (2014)
11. Krizhevsky, A., et al.: Learning multiple layers of features from tiny images (2009)
12. Lin, B., Ye, F., Zhang, Y., Tsang, I.W.: Reasonable effectiveness of random weighting: a litmus test for multi-task learning (2021)
13. Liu, B., Liu, X., Jin, X., Stone, P., Liu, Q.: Conflict-averse gradient descent for multi-task learning. Adv. Neural. Inf. Process. Syst. **34**, 18878–18890 (2021)
14. Liu, L., et al.: Towards impartial multi-task learning. In: ICLR (2021)
15. Liu, S., Johns, E., Davison, A.J.: End-to-end multi-task learning with attention. In: Proceedings of CVPR, pp. 1871–1880 (2019)
16. Ma, J., Zhao, Z., Yi, X., Chen, J., Hong, L., Chi, E.H.: Modeling task relationships in multi-task learning with multi-gate mixture-of-experts. In: Proceedings of SIGKDD, pp. 1930–1939 (2018)
17. Ma, X., et al.: Entire space multi-task model: an effective approach for estimating post-click conversion rate. In: Proceedings of SIGIR, pp. 1137–1140 (2018)
18. Merity, S., Xiong, C., Bradbury, J., Socher, R.: Proceedings of the International Conference on Learning Representations (2017)
19. Navon, A., et al.: Multi-task learning as a bargaining game. arXiv preprint arXiv:2202.01017 (2022)
20. Ren, M., Zeng, W., Yang, B., Urtasun, R.: Learning to reweight examples for robust deep learning. In: Proceedings of ICML, pp. 4334–4343. PMLR (2018)
21. Rosenbaum, C., Klinger, T., Riemer, M.: Routing networks: adaptive selection of non-linear functions for multi-task learning. arXiv preprint arXiv:1711.01239 (2017)
22. Ruder, S., Bingel, J., Augenstein, I., Søgaard, A.: Latent multi-task architecture learning. In: Proceedings of the AAAI, vol. 33, pp. 4822–4829 (2019)
23. Søgaard, A., Goldberg, Y.: Deep multi-task learning with low level tasks supervised at lower layers. In: Proceedings of the 54th Annual Meeting of the Association for Computational Linguistics (Volume 2: Short Papers), pp. 231–235 (2016)
24. Talreja, V., Valenti, M.C., Nasrabadi, N.M.: Deep hashing for secure multimodal biometrics. IEEE Trans. Inf. Forensics Secur. **16**, 1306–1321 (2020)
25. Wang, Z., Tsvetkov, Y., Firat, O., Cao, Y.: Gradient vaccine: investigating and improving multi-task optimization in massively multilingual models. arXiv preprint arXiv:2010.05874 (2020)
26. Wu, Y., et al.: Google's neural machine translation system: bridging the gap between human and machine translation. arXiv preprint arXiv:1609.08144 (2016)
27. Yu, T., Kumar, S., Gupta, A., Levine, S., Hausman, K., Finn, C.: Gradient surgery for multi-task learning. Adv. Neural. Inf. Process. Syst. **33**, 5824–5836 (2020)
28. Zamir, A.R., Sax, A., Shen, W., Guibas, L.J., Malik, J., Savarese, S.: Taskonomy: disentangling task transfer learning. In: Proceedings of CVPR, pp. 3712–3722 (2018)
29. Zou, L., et al.: Approximated doubly robust search relevance estimation. In: Proceedings of the 31st ACM International Conference on Information & Knowledge Management, pp. 3756–3765 (2022)
30. Zou, L., et al.: Pre-trained language model-based retrieval and ranking for web search. ACM Trans. Web **17**(1), 1–36 (2022)
31. Zou, L., Xia, L., Ding, Z., Song, J., Liu, W., Yin, D.: Reinforcement learning to optimize long-term user engagement in recommender systems. In: Proceedings of the 25th ACM SIGKDD International Conference on Knowledge Discovery & Data Mining, pp. 2810–2818 (2019)

32. Zou, L., et al.: Neural interactive collaborative filtering. In: Proceedings of the 43rd International ACM SIGIR Conference on Research and Development in Information Retrieval, pp. 749–758 (2020)
33. Zou, L., et al.: Pre-trained language model based ranking in Baidu search. In: Proceedings of the 27th ACM SIGKDD Conference on Knowledge Discovery & Data Mining, pp. 4014–4022 (2021)

Neighborhood-Oriented Decentralized Learning Communication in Multi-Agent System

Hao Dai[1,2], Jiashu Wu[1,2], André Brinkmann[3], and Yang Wang[1,2(✉)]

[1] Shenzhen Institute of Advanced Technology,
Chinese Academy of Science, Shenzhen, China
yang.wang1@siat.ac.cn
[2] University of Chinese Academy of Science, Beijing, China
[3] Zentrum für Datenverarbeitung, Johannes Gutenberg-Universität Mainz,
Mainz, Germany

Abstract. Partial observations are one of the critical obstacles in multi-agent systems (MAS). The Centralized Training Decentralized Execution (CTDE) paradigm has been widely studied to integrate global observations into the training process. However, the traditional CTDE paradigm suffers from local observations during the execution phase, and numerous efforts have been made to study the communication efficiency among agents to promote cognitive consistency and better cooperation. Furthermore, training still operates in a centralized manner, requiring agents to communicate with each other in a broadcast fashion. As a consequence, this centralized broadcast-based training process is not feasible when being applied to more complex scenarios. To address this issue, in this paper we propose a neighborhood-based learning approach to enable agents to perform training and execution in a decentralized manner based on information received from their neighboring nodes. In particular, we design a novel encoder network and propose a two-stage decision model to improve the performance of this decentralized training. To evaluate the method, we further implement a prototype and perform a series of simulation-based experiments to demonstrate the effectiveness of our method in multi-agent cooperation compared to selected existing multi-agent methods to achieve the best rewards and drastically reduce data transmission during training.

Supported by the Key-Area Research and Development Program of Guangdong Province (2021B010140005), Shenzhen Science and Technology Plan Project (Shenzhen-Hong Kong-Macau Category C, No. SGDX20220530111001003), and the Joint Research Project of Suntang-SIAT Research Lab for Big Data and AI, the National Key R&D Program of China (No. 2021YFB3300200), National Natural Science Foundation of China (No. 62072451, 92267105), Industrial application research project of Shenzhen for undertaking the national key project of China (No.CJGJZD20210408091600002), Chinese Academy of Sciences President's International Fellowship Initiative (No. 2023DT0003), Guangdong Special Support Plan (No. 2021TQ06X990), Shenzhen Basic Research Program (No. JCYJ20200109115418592, JCYJ20220818101610023).

L. Iliadis et al. (Eds.): ICANN 2023, LNCS 14256, pp. 490–502, 2023.
https://doi.org/10.1007/978-3-031-44213-1_41

Keywords: Multi-Agent System · Deep Reinforcement Learning · Learning Communication

1 Introduction

Multi-agent reinforcement learning (MARL) has emerged as a cutting-edge artificial intelligence technology that has achieved significant success in massive challenging tasks [10,13,17]. However, although MARL shows excellent prospects in solving optimization problems, it encounters many additional obstacles when adapted to real-world tasks [8,19,20]. One of them is the well-known non-stationary problem. The simultaneous action of multiple agents brings not only the dimensional explosion of the observation space, but also the difficulty of reaching consistency between actions and environment. Another is the partial observation problem. A single agent has a limited perspective and can only observe the situation in its own neighborhood, which leads to a lack of overall consideration in its decision-making. To overcome these technical hurdles, an approach is to aggregate all observations for centralized model training. Meanwhile, in the execution phase, the trained model relies on local observations to make decisions independently. Through optimization algorithms, such as value decomposition and credit assignment, this paradigm, called Centralized Training and Decentralized Execution (CTDE) [13,15,17], alleviates some of the difficulties in model training convergence. However, CTDE still suffers from chaotic decisions caused by partial observation at the execution stage.

Another intuitive idea comes from bionics, where animals use communication to negotiate and cooperate. Introducing communication into multi-agents means that agents can share their perceptions of the environment and their intentions to act, thus achieving unanimity. Agents typically encode their own observations and send them to other agents for decision-making. Open problems in learning communication include how to encode and decode messages, how to select communication objects, and how to design communication mechanisms [2,7,14,19,21]. Recent research including CommNet [16], IC3Net [14], TarMAC [1], and I2C [2] has significantly advanced the state of the art in these aspects and demonstrated the benefits of communication in MARL. Although promising, these methods all imply some form of centralization, such as broadcast communication [1,6,16], or concentrating all observations to train the encoder [2,7].

To address these issues, we draw inspiration from social psychology, which finds that cognitive consistency within a neighborhood is important, and people tend to cooperate with their neighbors [11]. We design a novel neighbor-oriented learning communication approach, in which agents make decisions and train models using their neighbors' messages. In this paper, we make the following contributions: (1) We design an encoder network according to the idea of neighborhood cognitive consistency. By calculating the Kullback-Leibler (KL) divergence of messages from different neighbors, the encoder network can represent the consensus information of the neighborhood. (2) We propose a *pseudo-pre-acting* mechanism. This mechanism can send decision information along with messages to support the neighbors' decision-making and reduce the non-stationarity of MAS. (3) We develop a new learning communication method based on the actor-critic (AC) algorithm, *Neighborhood-Oriented Actor-Critic (NOAC)*, and construct experiments to validate our findings.

The organization of the paper is as follows: we discuss related works regarding MARL in Sect. 2 and introduce some background knowledge in Sect. 3. We illustrate the formulation and methodology in Sect. 4. Afterward, we present the simulation studies to validate our findings in Sect. 5, followed by the conclusion of the paper in the last section.

2   Related Work

An important challenge in MARL is how to characterize the interaction between agents, so numerous works propose that we can learn a joint value to guide agents' actions [5,10,13,15,17]. Based on this idea, researchers developed a widely used paradigm, Centralized Training Decentralized Execution (CTDE). In this paradigm, all agents share the information of joint value to mitigate non-stationarity. Although this paradigm has significantly improved the applicability of MARL, the lack of additional information in the execution phase still plagues the robustness of the action policy. To address the problem of agents' limited perspective, exchanging observations among agents to gain an understanding of the entire environment is an intuitive and advantageous idea. Many works have shown that learning communication is a promising approach [1–3,6,7,14,16]. These methods mainly focus on how to combine communication and deep reinforcement learning networks.

DIAL [3], a pioneer of learning communication, uses DQN to implement a learnable communication, introducing backpropagation to communication networks for the first time. The shortcoming of DIAL is that it can only handle discrete messages. Therefore, CommNet [16] employs a hidden layer to encode observations as continuous messages. DIAL and CommNet exchange messages between agents in a fully connected network, i.e. they communicate in a broadcast fashion. This mode of message delivery introduces redundant communication and massive inter-message interference. Lowe *et al.* [9] analyzed the urgency of messages and proposed two indicators, positive signaling and positive listening, to measure the utility of messages. Based on the concern that messages are not always useful for decision making, some works have tried to investigate how to communicate efficiently. One type of method, represented by ATOC [6] and IC3Net [14], introduced a gate mechanism to determine whether a message needs to be sent. In contrast, other alternative approaches, such as SchedNet [7], TarMAC [1], and I2C [2], adopted some weighting mechanisms to reduce communication between agents.

However, all these methods inevitably share a common problem: global information (including all observations and actions) is needed to compute TD-error during training. This leads to scalability problems when dealing with large-scale multi-agent systems. The dilemma stems from the fact that non-stationarity requires global information to counteract it. To this end, we designed a learning communication method that trains and executes depending on neighborhood information. One of the main differences between previous work and ours is that we no longer use global information to compute the TD-error. This setting is more practical and allows for flexible parallelization of training.

3 Background

3.1 Dec-POMDP

Decentralized Partially Observable Markov Decision Process (*Dec-POMDP*), is commonly used to characterize multi-agent systems where each agent can only partially observe the environment and follows a hidden Markov decision process for state transitions. A *Dec-POMDP* can be defined as a tuple:

$$\mathcal{D} = \langle \mathcal{N}, \mathcal{A}, \mathcal{R}, \mathcal{O} \rangle \tag{1}$$

here, $\mathcal{N}$ denotes the number of agents in total, $\mathcal{A} = a_1 \times ... \times a_\mathcal{N}$ is the set of joint action, $\mathcal{R} = \{r_1, ..., r_\mathcal{N}\}$ is the reward set, $\mathcal{O} = \{o_1, ..., o_\mathcal{N}\}$ is the set of observations, which satisfies $o_i \cup o_j \not\subseteq o_i$ or o_j.

Our goal is to guide the agent to achieve the maximum cumulative reward $\mathbb{E}[\sum_{t=0}^{+\infty} \gamma \vec{r}_t]$, here γ is the discount factor. To this end, we define a set of policies $\vec{\pi} = \{\pi_1(a_1|o_1), ..., \pi_\mathcal{N}(a_\mathcal{N}|o_\mathcal{N})\}$, and the final objective is to learn the optimal policy to maximize the cumulative reward.

$$\mathcal{J}(\theta) = \mathbb{E}_{a \sim \pi(\theta)}[\sum_{t=0}^{+\infty} \gamma \vec{r}_t] \tag{2}$$

Remarkably, considering that we are mainly focusing on the cooperative agents, there is typically only one global reward r, which is one of the main reasons why the convergence of MARLs is challenging.

3.2 Actor-Critic

Actor-Critic is a typical reinforcement learning algorithm that combines the advantages of value-based and policy gradient methods. It consists of two networks: the actor network and critic network. The critic network is used to estimate the current status value $V(o; \theta^c)$, which is updated by calculating the current TD-error:

$$\mathcal{L}(\theta^c) = \gamma * V(o'; \theta^c) + r - V(o; \theta^c) \tag{3}$$

Meanwhile, the actor network adopts the policy gradient method to perform actions for agents. The idea of policy gradient is to give the larger action value higher sampling probability. Therefore, combined with the advantage function of the critic network, its updating method is as follows:

$$\nabla_{\theta^a} \mathcal{J}(\theta^a) = \nabla_{\theta^a}[\log_{\theta^a} \pi_{\theta^a}(a|o)\mathcal{L}(\theta^c)] \tag{4}$$

It is worth noting that to avoid non-stationary problems in multi-agent training, it is typically assumed that the critic network is centralized, or that each critic can obtain global information through communication or other means.

That is, o and a in the above formula are the set of observations and actions of all agents, respectively. Although this type of method has shown good convergence guarantees, the cost of aggregating all information is prohibitive in large-scale multi-agent systems.

4   Methodology

To overcome the centralized dilemma of multi-agent training, we take inspiration from [11]. In most cases, agents interact only with their neighbors, which is also consistent with interaction in human society. Therefore, we design a neighborhood-oriented method for multi-agent training in the subsequence section.

4.1   Neighborhood Cognitive

We denote the set of neighbors of agent i as $N(i)$, *i.e.*, agent $j \in N(i)$ is a neighbor of agent i. According to [11], there is a so-called **true hidden cognitive variable** C in each neighborhood, and all partial observations are the interplay of these variables. This assumption is intuitive, we can imagine that multiple neighbors observe a global state S and attain multiple hidden variables C_k, and agent i observes C_k and get observation o_i, as shown in Fig. 1. We can assume that $\{C_k\}$ has a strong representation of global state S, and the observation of agent i can be derived as follows:

$$p(o_i|S) = \sum_k p(o_i|C_k) \tag{5}$$

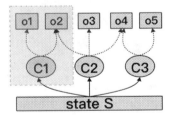

Fig. 1. The partial observations are generated from the hidden cognitive variables.

Therefore, we can consider the aggregation of C_k as an intermediate representation of S. Although this hidden state does not change the situation that the global reward cannot be decomposed to a single agent (or neighborhood), it does mitigate some of the uncertainties through this transformation. As a consequence, we design an encoder network, $m_i = \mathcal{M}(o_i)$, to encode the observation of agent i and send it to its neighbors. We can rewrite the AC algorithm with neighborhood communication as follows:

$$\mathcal{L}(\theta_i^c) = \gamma * V_{j \in N(i)}(m_i', m_j'; \theta_i^c) + r - V_{j \in N(i)}(m_i, m_j; \theta_i^c)$$
$$\nabla_{\theta_i^a} \mathcal{J} = \nabla_{\theta_i^a}[\log_{\theta_i^a} \pi_{\theta_i^a; j \in N(i)}(a_i|m_i, m_j)\mathcal{L}(\theta_i^c)] \tag{6}$$

Note that the input to the AC algorithm becomes an encoded set of messages. Neighborhood consistency assumes that all observations are based on the same hidden variable C_k, which means that o_i and o_j are inherently correlated, so we can achieve consistency in cognition by minimizing the differences between messages. Although the exact value of C_k is unknown, we can leverage KL-divergence to measure the difference between messages. Therefore, we derive the loss function of the encoder network as follows:

$$\mathcal{L}^e(\theta_i^m) = \sum_{j \in N(i)} D_{\mathrm{KL}}(P(m_i; \theta_i^m) \| P(m_j)) \tag{7}$$

This encoder network improves cognitive consistency in neighborhoods and significantly reduces the amount of data transferred.

4.2   Pseudo Pre-Acting

Passing messages brings additional information to the actor network and affects its decision-making by integrating neighborhood information. The neighborhood messages change the receiver's decision, and we use this differential to indicate the impact of these messages. Using the causal inference method, we can define indicators to show how an agent's decision making is influenced by its neighbors.

$$\mathbb{I}_i = D_{\mathrm{KL}, j \in N(i) \cup i}(\pi(a|o_i, m_j) \| \pi(a|o_i)) \tag{8}$$

Unfortunately, this influence shows the effect of neighborhood information on decision-making and does not indicate whether the changes increase or decrease the reward. Therefore, we consider the role of messages from a game theory perspective.

Multi-agent systems can usually be formalized as a game in which each agent takes its own action and receives a payoff. An important concept in game theory is the Nash equilibrium (NE), which means that the system is in a sort of steady state. Although the NE does not always maximize the social welfare (reward), it is robust enough and usually better than non-stationary solutions. Moreover, the maximum reward must also be an element of the NE set. Therefore, if we let multiple agents cooperatively reach a NE, we can change the problem of maximizing rewards to finding the optimal point among multiple NE states.

There are many ways to solve Nash equilibrium, and the most effective is to compute the best response. Let A_i and u be the action space and the utility function of agent i, respectively, then the best response can be computed as follows:

$$a^* = \arg\max_{a_i \in A_i} u(a_i, \vec{a}_{-i}) \tag{9}$$

here, $\vec{a}_{-i}$ represents the action set of all agents except i. One of the definitions of Nash equilibrium is that all agents are in the best response state, which means that no agent can unilaterally change its action to get better rewards. That is, if agents know the actions of other agents, they can adopt strategies to get better rewards. We can share agents' actions through communication and calculate actions through $\pi_i(a_i|o_i, a_j; j \in N(i))$.

However, it is not practical to send all neighborhood actions to agent i for decision-making, because agents act simultaneously rather than sequentially.

When an agent receives messages from other agents and changes its action, this change will lead to new changed actions of other agents. To avoid this chain reaction, we propose a two-step decision-making method:

1) obtain $\hat{a}_i$ by $\hat{\pi}_i(\hat{a}_i|o_i)$, and send it to neighbors;
2) execute action $\pi_i(a_i|o_i, a_j; j \in N(i))$ after the actions of neighbors are received.

We refer to this approach as **pseudo-pre-acting (PPA)** mechanism, in which $\hat{a}$ and $\hat{\pi}$ are called pseudo action and pseudo policy, respectively. Note that π_i is the policy we actually learned by interacting with the environment, so we update the pseudo-policy network $\hat{\pi}_i$ with the causal inference indicator mentioned above:

$$\mathcal{L}^{\hat{\pi}}(\theta_i^m) = D_{\text{KL}, j \in N(i)}(\hat{\pi}_i(\hat{a}_i|o_i; \theta_i^m) \| \pi_i(a_i|o_i, a_j, m_j)) \tag{10}$$

There are two perspectives to explain why we make the pseudo action approximate the actual action: On the one hand, the consistency of the pseudo action and the actual action makes the best response calculated by other agents effective; on the other hand, under the premise of receiving other actions, the consistency of the two types of actions indicates that the current state is in some kind of equilibrium.

4.3   Neighborhood-Oriented Actor-Critic

Combined with the above methods, we propose a neighborhood-oriented MARL approach based on actor-critic: **Neighborhood-Oriented Actor-Critic (NOAC)**. The overall architecture of NOAC is illustrated in Fig. 2, which consists of three parts: encoder network, actor network, and critic network.

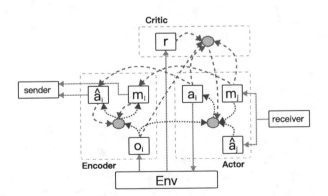

Fig. 2. The overall architecture of NOAC. The blue lines are the execution dataflow, while the red lines are training dataflow. Gray circles are neural networks. (Color figure online)

In the execution phase, the encoder network encodes the local observations, outputs the message m_i and pseudo action $\hat{a}_i$, and then sends them to its neighbors. After receiving messages and pseudo actions from its neighbors, the actor network selects appropriate actions to interact with the environment and then moves to the next epoch.

In the training stage, the encoder network calculates $\mathcal{L}^e$ and $\mathcal{L}^{\hat{\pi}}$ according to the received messages and the actions performed by the actor network, respectively, and updates parameters with the following loss function:

$$\mathcal{L}(\theta_i^m) = \mathcal{L}^e(\theta_i^m) + \mathcal{L}^{\hat{\pi}}(\theta_i^m) \tag{11}$$

Concerning the actor network, we adopt the policy gradient to update parameters as follows:

$$\nabla_{\theta_i^a}\mathcal{J} = \nabla_{\theta_i^a}[\log_{\theta_i^a}\pi_{\theta_i^a;j\in N(i)}(a_i|o_i, m_i, a_j, m_j)\mathcal{L}(\theta_i^c)] \tag{12}$$

The main concern for training of the critic network is the calculation of TD-loss. As mentioned above, the critic network is usually centralized because it needs to estimate Q_{total}, which directly influences the global reward. Since the global reward cannot be directly assigned to individuals in multi-agent cooperation, the centralized network is needed to evaluate the value function. Likewise, although we propose that C_k can characterize part of the global state, we still cannot assign the global reward to a concrete C_k. However, considering that in some environments where agents move, each agent transforms the C value as it moves, we have relaxed this constraint. Since the size of the neighborhood directly affects the approximation of Q_C and Q_{total}, we define the TD-loss of the critic network as follows:

$$\mathcal{L}(\theta_i^c) = \gamma * V_{j\in N(i)\cup i}(m_i', m_j'; \theta_i^c) + \frac{|N(i)|}{\mathcal{N}} * r - V_{j\in N(i)\cup i}(m_i, m_j; \theta_i^c) \tag{13}$$

Due to the decentralized network design, all agents run in parallel during execution and training, which only need to be synchronized during communication and environment steps. Therefore, the networks of agents can be deployed in different servers and communicate over protocols such as GLOO, NCCL, or TCP. This feature is particularly efficient in large-scale multi-agent environments.

5   Experiments

To validate our findings, we conducted empirical studies to evaluate the performance of the proposed NOAC. We implemented a test platform based on multi-agent particle environment [12] and took a cooperative game as the environment simulator.

5.1   Setup

Environment. We took the cooperative navigation game [10] as the simulation environment. As shown in Fig. 3, there are $\mathcal{N}$ agents and $\mathcal{N}$ landmarks in the environment, and the agents need to cooperate with each other to occupy all the landmarks. The environment takes the sum of the minimum distance between all agents and landmarks as the global reward value, that is, there is no individual reward for each agent.

Each agent has its own observation o_i and takes the closer agents as its neighbors. Each agent can only stand on one landmark, and there is a penalty (negative reward) for collisions. In the experiment, we set $\mathcal{N} = 7$, $N(i) = 3$, and each agent starts at a random position. All other settings, such as the agent's speed, are default values from the open source library *PettingZoo* [18]. Note that the agent's environment is open and not restricted to a specific area, which may differ from some other cooperative navigation settings.

Baselines. We compared the proposed method NOAC with the following state-of-the-art MARL baselines:

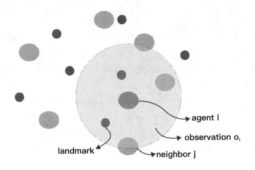

Fig. 3. Cooperative navigation environment.

- *TarMAC* [1]: An attention-based learning communication method that weighs the importance of incoming messages.
- *IC3Net* [14]: A gate-based method for deciding whether to communicate with others, in which messages are sent in broadcast mode.
- *MADDPG* [10]: A classical CTDE algorithm without communication.
- *DDQN* [4]: A typical single agent algorithm. In our setting, it can sense the global state and output all agents' actions simultaneously.

Hyperparameters. To reduce the off-site factors in the comparison, we adopted the same network structure in most baselines. In addition, we set the learning rate $lr = 1 \times 10^{-3}$ and $batch\_size = 64$ for all methods. We implemented the testbed based on *PyTorch* and *PettingZoo* and ran it on a $3 \times$ Tesla V-100 server.

5.2   Numerical Results

Global Reward. First, we examined the rewards of multiple baselines, which is the primary concern in MARL problems. Previous cooperative navigation experiments often focused only on the average reward during the entire training (referred to as "total reward" in the subsequent section), while we are more concerned with the final state of the agent at the end of the round, the final

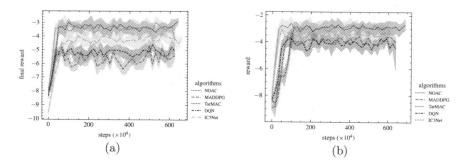

Fig. 4. Comparison of final reward (a) and total reward (b).

reward. Therefore, we compared the two types of rewards of baselines: final reward and total reward.

The comparison of the final rewards is illustrated in Fig. 4*(a)*, where the final rewards of *NOAC* are approximately equal to *TarMAC*, and more significant than other baselines. This result shows the effectiveness of our approach. It is worth noting that the baselines, including *TarMAC*, require centralized information exchange, while *NOAC* only collects neighborhood information. Similarly, *NOAC* also performs well on total rewards, as shown in Fig. 4*(b)*. It should be noted that the gap between baselines on total rewards differs less than that on final rewards, so we treat the final reward as the metric for the following experiments.

We executed 500 episodes with these trained models, and Table 1 shows the means and standard deviations of the total and final rewards. *NOAC* outperforms all baselines with the highest average final rewards. These results suggest that our partial information and message training approach is comparable to methods that require centralized training.

Table 1. Summary of final reward and total reward of MARL baselines

Algorithms	NOAC	MADDPG	TarMAC	IC3Net	DQN
Final Reward Mean	**−3.292036**	−5.627667	−3.335745	−4.164599	−5.120261
Final Reward Std	0.595101	0.646373	0.766422	0.457646	0.626979
Total Reward Mean	−3.358014	−4.168850	−3.201513	−3.512844	−4.132432
Total Reward Std	1.430986	1.219422	1.408928	0.964834	0.860662

Neighborhood Impact. Although *NOAC* is designed for neighborhoods, it can also handle broadcast messages. To investigate whether *NOAC* does indeed includes neighbors' messages into decision making, we compare it with two cases: one where there is no communication at all, which is a decentralized AC algorithm with independent control, which we call "*NOAC-No-Comm*"; the other is a fully connected communication network with *NOAC*, which we call "*NOAC-FC*".

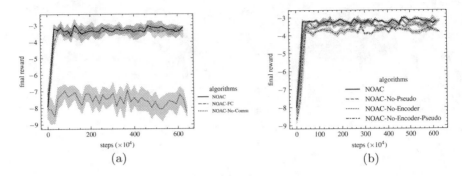

Fig. 5. Reward comparison of different neighborhood impacts (a) and ablation experiments (b).

After training with the same settings, the comparison of the experimental results is illustrated in Fig. 5*(a)*. Not surprisingly, the decentralized algorithm *NOAC-No-Comm* without communication performs the worst. In fact, it performs worse than all other baselines because it uses only local observations to train the agents. This result confirms that communication significantly improves MARL.

Nevertheless, it is worth noting that *NOAC-FC* with fully connected communication does not provide a significant improvement in performance. At the beginning of training, the convergence of *NOAC-FC* is even slower than that of the partially connected case. This result illustrates that more messages are not always better, and actually is consistent with the selective communication proposition in related work. It also shows that neighborhood cognitive consistency exists, and the agent can achieve an approximate effect of global observation through the messages of neighbors.

Ablation. Finally, to further investigate the contribution of the encoder network and pseudo-pre-acting to *NOAC*, we performed ablation experiments. We conducted three different sets of experiments: 1) *NOAC* without pseudo-pre-acting mechanism, "*NOAC-No-Pseudo*"; 2) NOAC without encoding the neighbor observations, "*NOAC-No-Encoder*". Note that the raw neighbor observations are still transmitted; 3) the "*NOAC-No-Encoder-Pseudo*" algorithm without encoder or pseudo-pre-acting mechanism, where each agent aggregates the neighbor observations for training.

Figure 5*(b)* shows a comparison of the ablation experiments, and it can be seen that the removal of either mechanism leads to a slight decrease in performance. In particular, the *NOAC-No-Encoder-Pseudo* with the encoder and **PPA** removed shows a significant drop in reward. To illustrate the difference more clearly, Table 2 shows the difference in reward for each setting. Note that all methods use information from neighbors.

Despite the lack of an encoder, the actor and critic networks can still extract information from raw observations. Thus, the gap is not that significant. However, the encoded messages are about 3/4 times smaller than the original obser-

Table 2. Summary of the final reward of ablation experiments

	NOAC	No-Encoder	No-PPA	No-Encoder-PPA
Final Reward Mean	−3.292036	−3.458257	−3.514603	−3.828242
Final Reward Std	0.595101	0.411429	0.955895	0.592898

vations $(42 \to 12)$, which shows a significant advantage in terms of latency in both network transmission and tensor operations.

6   Conclusions

In this paper, we proposed a neighborhood-oriented MARL training method that uses only messages from neighbors instead of global information to learn policies. Experiments show that this decentralized training method is comparable to mainstream CTDE methods. This approach shows the potential of decentralized learning methods for solving MARL problems. This decentralized MARL learning is not only closer to real-world scenarios, but also has excellent advantages in terms of computational efficiency. We expect that this paradigm could be further developed and applied to more practical problems.

References

1. Das, A., et al.: TarMAC: targeted multi-agent communication. In: ICML (2019)
2. Ding, Z., Huang, T., Lu, Z.: Learning individually inferred communication for multi-agent cooperation. In: NeurIPS (2020)
3. Foerster, J., Assael, I.A., de Freitas, N., Whiteson, S.: Learning to communicate with deep multi-agent reinforcement learning. In: NeurIPS (2016)
4. Hasselt, H.V., Guez, A., Silver, D.: Deep reinforcement learning with double Q-learning. In: AAAI (2016)
5. Iqbal, S., Sha, F.: Actor-attention-critic for multi-agent reinforcement learning. In: International Conference on Machine Learning (ICML) (2019)
6. Jiang, J., Lu, Z.: Learning attentional communication for multi-agent cooperation. Advances in Neural Information Processing Systems (NeurIPS) (2018)
7. Kim, D., et al.: Learning to schedule communication in multi-agent reinforcement learning. In: International Conference on Learning Representations (ICLR) (2019)
8. Leonardos, S., Overman, W., Panageas, I., Piliouras, G.: Global convergence of multi-agent policy gradient in Markov potential games. In: ICLR (2022)
9. Lowe, R., Foerster, J., Boureau, Y.L., Pineau, J., Dauphin, Y.: On the pitfalls of measuring emergent communication. In: AAMAS (2019)
10. Lowe, R., Wu, Y., Tamar, A., Harb, J., Abbeel, O.P., Mordatch, I.: Multi-agent actor-critic for mixed cooperative-competitive environments. In: NeurIPS (2017)
11. Mao, H., et al.: Neighborhood cognition consistent multi-agent reinforcement learning. In: AAAI (2020)
12. Mordatch, I., Abbeel, P.: Emergence of grounded compositional language in multi-agent populations. arXiv preprint arXiv:1703.04908 (2017)

13. Rashid, T., Samvelyan, M., de Witt, C.S., Farquhar, G., Foerster, J., Whiteson, S.: QMIX: monotonic value function factorisation for deep multi-agent reinforcement learning. In: International Conference on Machine Learning (ICML) (2018)
14. Singh, A., Jain, T., Sukhbaatar, S.: Individualized controlled continuous communication model for multiagent cooperative and competitive tasks. In: International Conference on Learning Representations (ICLR) (2019)
15. Son, K., Kim, D., Kang, W.J., Hostallero, D.E., Yi, Y.: QTRAN: learning to factorize with transformation for cooperative multi-agent reinforcement learning. In: International Conference on Machine Learning (ICML) (2019)
16. Sukhbaatar, S., Fergus, R., et al.: Learning multiagent communication with backpropagation. In: NeurIPS (2016)
17. Sunehag, P., et al.: Value-decomposition networks for cooperative multi-agent learning based on team reward. In: AAMAS (2018)
18. Terry, J.K., et al.: PettingZoo: gym for multi-agent reinforcement learning. arXiv preprint arXiv:2009.14471 (2020)
19. Wang, T., Wang, J., Zheng, C., Zhang, C.: Learning nearly decomposable value functions via communication minimization. In: ICLR (2020)
20. Wen, Y., Yang, Y., Wang, J.: Modelling bounded rationality in multi-agent interactions by generalized recursive reasoning. In: Proceedings of the Twenty-Ninth International Joint Conference on Artificial Intelligence, IJCAI'20 (2021)
21. Zhang, S.Q., Zhang, Q., Lin, J.: Efficient communication in multi-agent reinforcement learning via variance based control. In: Advances in Neural Information Processing Systems (NeurIPS) (2019)

NN-Denoising: A Low-Noise Distantly Supervised Document-Level Relation Extraction Scheme Using Natural Language Inference and Negative Sampling

Mengting Pan, Ye Wang, and Zhiyun Chen[✉]

East China Normal University, Shanghai 200000, China
{pmt,yewang}@stu.ecnu.edu.cn, chenzhy@cc.ecnu.edu.cn

Abstract. The task of document-level relation extraction (DocRE) is crucial in the field of natural language processing, as it aims to extract semantic relations between entities in a given document to facilitate deeper comprehension. Previous methods have primarily focused on fully supervised learning for DocRE, which requires a large amount of human-annotated training data, making it a tedious and laborious task. Recently, more and more attention has been paid to the incomplete labeling problem in human-annotated data, and it is believed to be the bottleneck of model performance. To address this limitation and mitigate annotation costs, we propose a low-noise distant supervision scheme for DocRE, called NN-Denoising, that combines natural language inference (NLI) models and negative sampling to filter out noise in the training data. The NLI model serves as a pre-filter for denoising the distant supervision (DS) labels, while negative sampling is employed to overcome the false negative problem in the filtered data. Our experimental results on a large-scale DocRE benchmark demonstrate the superiority of the proposed approach over existing baselines in distant supervision learning. Specifically, NN-Denoising achieves an improvement of 15.83 F1 points and 10.34 F1 points compared to the ATLOP and SSR-PU models, respectively.

Keywords: Document-level Relation Extraction · Distantly Supervised Learning · Low-Noise

1 Introduction

Relation extraction (RE) extracts semantic relationships among entities in text and has various applications such as sentiment analysis, information extraction,

Supported by Development of University Computer Fundamental Curriculum and Training Platform for Kunpeng Ecosystem, a Ministry of Education Industry-Academia-Research Project (No.201902146018).

and knowledge graph construction. Most previous work has focused on sentence-level RE [12,34], which is limited as it cannot extract relationships between multiple sentences. To overcome this limitation, document-level relation extraction (DocRE) has been proposed [1,28,30,36], which extracts relationships within and between sentences.

Previous methods for DocRE have primarily focused on fully supervised learning, which can be time-consuming and labor-intensive in real-world scenarios due to the need for a large amount of human-annotated training data. Distantly supervised (DS) learning is a more efficient alternative, but it can introduce false positive (FP) problems [11]. In addition, the incomplete labeling problem, also known as the false negative (FN) problem, has received increasing attention in recent years [7,23]. To address the FN problem, previous work [25] proposed a unified positive-unlabeled learning framework - shift and squared ranking loss positive-unlabeled (SSR-PU) learning, to adapt DocRE with different levels of incomplete labeling. However, the SSR-PU method still faces challenges such as expensive labeling costs. To address these challenges, we propose a novel method for improving the FN and FP problems in distantly supervised learning for DocRE. Our approach, called NN-Denoising, aims to combine natural language inference (NLI) models and negative sampling to denoise the training data generated by DS. The NLI model serves as a pre-filter for denoising the DS labels, while negative sampling is employed to overcome the FN problem in the filtered data. This approach effectively improves the performance of the RE model by filtering out noisy training data and reducing the impact of incomplete labeling.

We conducted extensive experiments on the DS dataset provided in DocRED [30]. Recent work [23] has revealed the presence of severe incomplete labeling in the human-annotated data of DocRED. Through our rigorous experiments and analysis, we further identified prevalent FP and FN problems in the DS data. Subsequently, We compared the performance of our model with the state-of-the-art DocRE models under distantly supervised learning and observed a significant improvement in performance.

The contribution of this paper can be summarized as follows:

- We propose a novel approach to mitigate the FN problem in DocRE by introducing negative sampling, which, to the best of our knowledge, has not been applied before in this task.
- We present a low-noise distant supervision scheme, NN-Denoising, which utilizes NLI models and negative sampling to filter out noise in the training data, resulting in significantly improved performance of the DocRE model.
- Our proposed approach outperforms current state-of-the-art DocRE models under distant supervision, achieving substantial improvements of 15.83 F1 points and 10.34 F1 points over ATLOP [35] and SSR-PU [25], respectively.

2   Related Work

2.1   Document-Level Relation Extraction

Document-level relation extraction (DocRE) methods can be categorized into graph-based and transformers-based models. Graph-based models [8, 15, 29, 32] use knowledge graphs to model and reason about entities and relations, while transformers-based models [22, 27, 33, 35] leverage pre-trained language models and deep learning to achieve high-precision relation extraction. Recently, attention has been given to the incomplete labeling problem in DocRE datasets, with [7, 23] pointing out that this is a bottleneck for model performance. Previous work, such as SSR-PU [25], was proposed to address this issue. However, [25] only addressed the FN problem in DocRE tasks under supervised learning and did not provide solutions for the FP problem that arises in distantly supervised learning.

2.2   Natural Language Inference

Natural language inference (NLI) is a crucial task in natural language processing that aims to determine the logical relationship between two statements. NLI models can be rule-based, logic-based [6, 13, 19], or deep learning-based [2, 5]. Recently, there has been interest in using NLI models as independent RE models by formulating RE as an entailment task [21]. This approach has shown promising results in sentence-level RE tasks. Inspired by this, [24] conducted a study on the use of NLI as a pre-filter to improve distantly supervised DocRE and found that it can effectively enhance the task's performance.

2.3   Negative Sampling

Recently, a negative sampling method was proposed by [9] to address the FN problem in named entity recognition (NER) tasks. The method randomly samples a small subset of unlabeled spans as negative instances to induce the training loss, effectively eliminating the misleading effect of FN samples and improving the performance of NER models. Building upon this work, [23] also applied the negative sampling method to investigate the FN problem in RE tasks.

3   Methodology

3.1   NLI as Pre-filter

Here, we focus on the scenario where NLI is used as a pre-filter to filter the DS dataset, as presented in [24].

We start by taking a premise (p), which is an input text containing entity mentions of *head* and *tail*, and then construct a set of templates for each relation (r). Each template (t) in the set is specific to a particular relation and provides a structured representation of the relationship between *head* and *tail*. By combining a template and the premise, we can construct a hypothesis (h), which is a sentence that expresses the relationship between *head* and *tail* in a structured way. For instance, if the relation is "location", we might have templates like "The *head* is located in *tail*" and "The *tail* is near the *head*". Given a premise that mentions "Hawaii" as the *head* entity and "America" as the *tail* entity, we could construct the hypotheses "The Hawaii is located in America" and "The America is near the Hawaii" using these templates. To filter the DS dataset, we use an NLI model as a binary entailment task classifier. Given a premise p and a hypothesis h, the NLI model outputs a prediction score indicating whether the hypothesis is entailed by the premise or not.

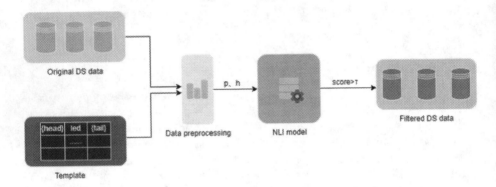

Fig. 1. The processing flow of NLI as a pre-filter.

As shown in Fig. 1, to apply this pre-filter, we integrate the original DS dataset with the template set and construct premise and hypothesis pairs for each labeled relation in the dataset. These pairs are then fed into the NLI model, which returns a prediction score. If the score is greater than a predefined threshold (τ), we retain the relation label for that hypothesis in the filtered DS dataset; otherwise, we discard it. We repeat this process for all hypotheses, resulting in a filtered DS dataset that is hopefully of higher quality.

Table 1. Percentages of triples left in the DS data after per-filtering with NLI.

Threshold τ	zero-shot
low (0.5)	73.4
med (0.95)	68.6
high (0.99)	59.0

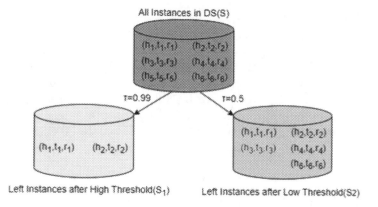

Fig. 2. Incomplete labeling problem in filtered data. FP samples are marked in red. (Color figure online)

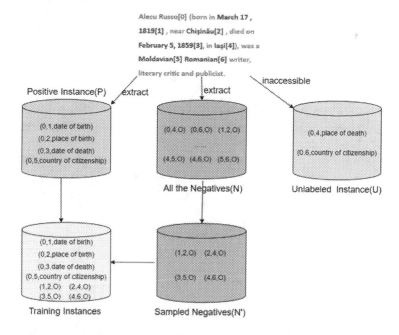

Fig. 3. An example to depict how "whole-sample negative sampling" works.

Same as in [24], we set three threshold values (τ) of 0.5, 0.95, and 0.99 to evaluate the effectiveness of filtering. A higher threshold value leads to stricter filtering conditions and the removal of more FP samples. Table 1 displays the percentage of remaining triples in the filtered DS dataset under each threshold. However, our analysis shows that a threshold value of 0.99 may lead to filtering out some positive samples, exacerbating the incomplete labeling problem of the

DS dataset. This is why the RE model's performance was worse under high threshold conditions in previous work [24].

We provide a hypothetical example in Fig. 2, illustrating the impact of filtering with different threshold values. When the threshold is set to 0.99, only two positive samples remain, and two previously positive samples become false negatives. In contrast, a threshold of 0.5 retains more samples, including one false positive, but does not introduce any new false negatives. To overcome the FN problem during training with the low-noise dataset obtained through high threshold filtering, we introduce a negative sampling method explained in Sect. 3.2.

3.2   Training via Negative Sampling

To mitigate the issue of FN problem in the filtered DS dataset after high-threshold filtering, we introduce the negative sampling method proposed in [9]. This method has been successfully applied to NER tasks and is now applied to the DocRE task for the first time.

As illustrated in Fig. 3, given a document with labeled relation triples, let $\mathbf{P} = \{(0, 1, $ "date of birth"$), (0, 2, $ "place of birth"$), (0, 3, $ "date of death"$), (0, 5, $ "country of citizenship"$)\}$ be the set of labeled relation triples, and $\mathbf{U} = \{(0, 4, $ "place of death"$), (0, 6, $ "country of citizenship"$)\}$ be the set of unlabeled relation triples. $\mathbf{P} \cup \mathbf{U}$ represents the ground-truth set of relation triples. Let $\mathbf{N}$ be the set of all negative samples, which includes all entity pairs in the document that are not part of the labeled relations, labeled as "O" to indicate that they are negative samples. The core idea of negative sampling is to randomly and uniformly select a small fraction of all negative samples for training to mitigate the misleading impact of false negatives. Let $\mathbf{N}'$ be a subset of $\mathbf{N}$, the final training data used in the model is $\mathbf{P} \cup \mathbf{N}'$.

Ultimately, a cross entropy loss used for training is incurred as:

$$\left(\sum_{(i,j,l) \in \mathbf{P}} - \log(o_{i,j}[l]) \right) + \left(\sum_{(i',j',l') \in \mathbf{N}'} - \log(o_{i',j'}[l']) \right) \tag{1}$$

where the term $o_{i,j}[l]$ is the predicted score of a relation(i, j, l).

The negative sampling method based on [9] mentioned above is referred to as "whole-sample negative sampling" in this study. In addition, we propose a "label-specific negative sampling" method to better adapt to multi-label classification tasks. Instead of randomly and uniformly sampling negative samples from the entire dataset, we dynamically generate negative samples during training by considering each label individually. Specifically, we treat all samples other than those labeled with a particular label as negative examples for that label, and then perform uniform random sampling on these negative examples. This approach allows us to better capture the specific characteristics of each label and improve the model's ability to learn the nuances of the dataset. For example, in Fig. 3, when calculating the loss for the label "date of birth", we treat samples predicted as "date of birth" as positive samples and all other samples (including those predicted as "date of death", "place of birth", "place of death", "country of citizenship", and "O") as negative samples. Then, we randomly sample a subset of these negative samples for final loss calculation.

4   Experiments

Datasets and Evaluation Metric. This study uses the distantly supervised dataset from DocRED [30] as training data. For evaluation, the test set provided by Re-DocRED [23], a revised version of DocRED with more comprehensive annotations, is used. Evaluation metrics include micro F1(F1), micro ignore F1(Ign F1), precision(P), and recall(R), with Ign F1 measuring the F1 score excluding the relations shared by the training and test sets.

NLI Model. We used DeBERTaV3 [4], a pre-trained language model, as our NLI pre-filter. This model replaces masked language modeling (MLM) with replacement token detection (RTD) and achieves state-of-the-art performance. It was trained on 1.3 million hypothesis-premise pairs from 8 NLI datasets: MNLI [26], FEVER-NLI [16], NLI dataset from [18], and DocNLI [31](which is curated from ANLI [17], SQuAD [20], DUC20016[1], CNN/DailyMail [14], and Curation[2].

DocRE Model. For the DocRE model, we utilized ALTOP (Adaptive Thresholding and Localized Context Pooling) proposed in [35], which incorporates adaptive thresholding loss and localized context pooling techniques. This model addresses the issue of decision errors caused by using a global threshold in the original multi-label classification task and leverages pre-trained models to obtain better entity representations.

Implementation Details. We used pre-trained models from Huggingface[3] for the NLI pre-filter and considered only zero-shot scenarios. It is worth noting that the NLI pre-filter only filters the training data (DocRED) [30] and does not need to filter the test data (Re-DocRED) [23], as the test dataset is already a revised version. For the DocRE model, we implemented ATLOP model based on $BERT_{Base}$ [3] and $RoBERTa_{Large}$ [10], respectively. The learning rate was adjusted to 3e$-$5, and the training epochs were set to 10 when using BERT as the encoder. For RoBERTa, the hyperparameters remained unchanged. Negative sampling rates were adjusted from 0.01 to 0.1. We report the final model's performance rather than the best checkpoint, and all experiments were conducted on an NVIDIA A100-40GB GPU.

---

[1] https://www-nlpir.nist.gov/projects/duc/guidelines/2001.html.
[2] Curation. 2020. Curation corpus base.
[3] https://huggingface.co/MoritzLaurer/DeBERTa-v3-base-mnli-fever-docnli-ling-2c.

Baseline. We re-implemented distantly supervised learning on ATLOP [35] and SSR-PU [25] and used their results as the baseline for our task. We used similar settings as our own method, with a learning rate of 3e−5 and 10 training epochs when using BERT as the encoder, while keeping other parameters unchanged. We reported the performance of the final model instead of the best checkpoint.

5   Results and Analysis

Table 2. Main result on DocRED. The number in the subscript represents the filtering threshold for NLI.

Model	F1	Ign F1	P	R
ATLOP+$BERT_{Base}$	42.35	39.36	75.55	29.42
SSR-PU+ATLOP+$BERT_{Base}$	47.84	41.61	50.29	45.62
NLI-filtering$_{0.99}$+ATLOP+$BERT_{Base}$	36.18	35.65	**92.40**	22.50
Negative-Sampling+$BERT_{Base}$	46.60	44.53	62.61	40.59
NN-Denoising$_{0.5}$+ATLOP+$BERT_{Base}$	56.02	51.84	63.40	50.17
NN-Denoising$_{0.95}$+ATLOP+$BERT_{Base}$	56.86	52.22	57.98	**55.78**
NN-Denoising$_{0.99}$+ATLOP+$BERT_{Base}$	**58.18**	**54.44**	64.32	53.10
ATLOP+$RoBERTa_{Large}$	43.47	40.47	76.06	30.43
SSR-PU+ATLOP+$RoBERTa_{Large}$	49.11	42.88	50.74	47.58
NLI-filtering$_{0.99}$+ATLOP+$RoBERTa_{Large}$	36.95	36.53	**93.81**	23.01
Negative-Sampling+$RoBERTa_{Large}$	46.50	39.57	37.88	**60.19**
NN-Denoising$_{0.5}$+ATLOP+$RoBERTa_{Large}$	55.49	50.16	51.82	59.72
NN-Denoising$_{0.95}$+ATLOP+$RoBERTa_{Large}$	57.54	52.66	55.92	59.25
NN-Denoising$_{0.99}$+ATLOP+$RoBERTa_{Large}$	**59.03**	**54.95**	60.72	57.43

Our experimental results, as shown in Table 2, emphasize the effectiveness of our proposed negative sampling method in addressing the FN problem in distant supervision DocRE models. Specifically, we set the filtering threshold for NLI and varied the negative sampling rate to achieve the best results. We implemented our models using both $BERT_{Base}$ and $RoBERTa_{Large}$ encoders.

From the results, we observe that: (1) our method outperforms the baseline models ATLOP and SSR-PU, achieving the best F1 score in both settings. With the BERT encoder, our model achieves 58.18 F1 points, surpassing the baseline models ATLOP (15.83 F1 points) and SSR-PU (10.34 F1 points), and with the RoBERTa encoder, our model achieves 59.03 F1 points, surpassing the baseline models ATLOP (15.56 F1 points) and SSR-PU (9.92 F1 points). This improvement in performance emphasizes the effectiveness of our method in mitigating the negative impact of FN and FP problem on DocRE models. (2) our results show that our model performs better with a high threshold for NLI filtering compared to a low threshold, which differs from the findings of previous studies [24]. This demonstrates the effectiveness of our negative sampling method in addressing the FN problem, which is the main bottleneck for RE model performance. Moreover, it confirms our hypothesis that the high threshold filtered DS dataset suffers from a more severe incomplete labeling problem than the low threshold filtered DS dataset. (3) when using only the NLI filtering method (NLI-filtering$_{0.99}$+ATLOP+$BERT_{Base}$), the performance of the DocRE model was the worst, even lower than that of directly training on the original DS dataset. This is because the incomplete labeling phenomenon in the high threshold filtered DS dataset is more severe, reducing the performance of the DocRE model. This finding further confirms that the FN problem, rather than the FP problem, is the performance bottleneck of distant supervision DocRE models. (4) our model's performance was improved compared to the baseline model ATLOP (+4.25 F1 points) when trained only with negative sampling (Negative-Sampling+ATLOP+$BERT_{Base}$). The performance was also comparable to the SSR-PU model that effectively addressed the FN problem. This further confirms the effectiveness of our negative sampling method in mitigating the FN problem in distant supervision DocRE models. (5) Our proposed method exhibits superior stability in terms of precision and recall compared to other methods, indicating that it does not suffer from overfitting and possesses excellent predictive capability.

Table 3. Effect of different sampling methods on model performance. "w" means "whole-document negative sampling" and "l" means "label-specific negative sampling".

Model	F1	Ign F1	P	R
NN-Denoising$_{0.99}$+ATLOP+$BERT_{Base}$(w)	55.98	52.58	**66.22**	48.48
NN-Denoising$_{0.99}$+ATLOP+$BERT_{Base}$(l)	**58.18**	**54.44**	64.32	**53.10**

To comprehensively evaluate the effectiveness of our proposed sampling methods, we conducted a comparative analysis using the high threshold NLI filtering and the optimal negative sampling rate (0.01). As shown in Table 3, our proposed "label-specific negative sampling" method outperforms the "whole-document negative sampling" method by 2.2 F1 points. This improvement is mainly due to our method's ability to sample negative examples specific to each label, effectively addressing the label imbalance problem in DocRE datasets.

To investigate the impact of negative sampling rate on addressing the FN problem in the distant supervision DocRE task, we conducted experiments under both low and high threshold conditions in NLI filtering, with negative sampling rates ranging from 0.01 to 0.1. The results, as shown in Fig. 4, revealed that lower negative sampling rates led to better performance in both scenarios, indicating the effectiveness of negative sampling in reducing the risk of training the model with FN samples.

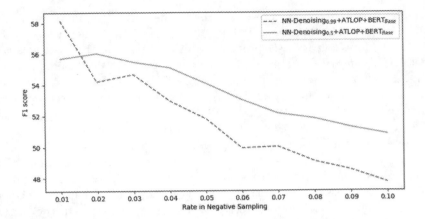

Fig. 4. Effect of different negative sampling rates on model performance.

We observed that the performance of the model was more sensitive to the negative sampling rate in the high threshold scenario compared to the low threshold scenario. This finding indicates that negative sampling is particularly effective in scenarios where the incomplete labeling problem is more severe, thus highlighting the potential of our proposed sampling method in addressing the FN problem in distant supervision DocRE models. This insight can guide future research in this area.

6   Conclusion and Future Work

The aim of this work was to address the issue of expensive human annotation in DocRE tasks by introducing DS learning. During the training of DocRE models, we noticed the potential bottleneck in performance caused by false negatives, as well as the severe FP problem introduced by DS. To address these issues, we proposed a method that improves the performance of DocRE models by combining NLI as a pre-filter to remove most false positive samples and negative sampling to solve the severe FN problem in the filtered DS dataset. Our experiments demonstrated that our model significantly outperforms baseline models under complete DS learning, with a performance improvement of 15.83 F1 points over the ATLOP and 10.34 F1 points over the SSR-PU.

In addition, we observed that different sampling methods have a significant impact on addressing incomplete labeling problem. In this work, we used two simple sampling methods based on random uniform sampling, there is still much room for improvement in this area. Future work can explore more effective sampling methods that can further enhance the training performance of our model. Furthermore, developing more robust and accurate NLI models is also a potential research avenue.

References

1. Christopoulou, F., Miwa, M., Ananiadou, S.: Connecting the dots: document-level neural relation extraction with edge-oriented graphs (2019). https://doi.org/10.48550/ARXIV.1909.00228. https://arxiv.org/abs/1909.00228
2. Das, R., Munkhdalai, T., Yuan, X., Trischler, A., McCallum, A.: Building dynamic knowledge graphs from text using machine reading comprehension (2018). https://doi.org/10.48550/ARXIV.1810.05682. https://arxiv.org/abs/1810.05682
3. Devlin, J., Chang, M.W., Lee, K., Toutanova, K.: BERT: pre-training of deep bidirectional transformers for language understanding. North American Chapter of the Association for Computational Linguistics (2018)
4. He, P., Gao, J., Chen, W.: DeBERTaV 3: improving deBERTa using ELECTRA-style pre-training with gradient-disentangled embedding sharing (2021). https://doi.org/10.48550/ARXIV.2111.09543. https://arxiv.org/abs/2111.09543
5. Henaff, M., Weston, J., Szlam, A., Bordes, A., LeCun, Y.: Tracking the world state with recurrent entity networks (2016). https://doi.org/10.48550/ARXIV.1612.03969. https://arxiv.org/abs/1612.03969
6. Hobbs, J.R., Stickel, M.E., Appelt, D.E., Martin, P.: Interpretation as abduction. Artif. Intell. **63**(1), 69–142 (1993). https://doi.org/10.1016/0004-3702(93)90015-4. https://www.sciencedirect.com/science/article/pii/0004370293900154
7. Huang, Q., Hao, S., Ye, Y., Zhu, S., Feng, Y., Zhao, D.: Does recommend-revise produce reliable annotations? An analysis on missing instances in docRED (2022). https://doi.org/10.48550/ARXIV.2204.07980. https://arxiv.org/abs/2204.07980
8. Li, B., Ye, W., Sheng, Z., Xie, R., Xi, X., Zhang, S.: Graph enhanced dual attention network for document-level relation extraction. In: Proceedings of the 28th International Conference on Computational Linguistics, Barcelona, Spain, pp. 1551–1560. International Committee on Computational Linguistics (Online), December 2020. https://doi.org/10.18653/v1/2020.coling-main.136. https://aclanthology.org/2020.coling-main.136
9. Li, Y., Liu, L., Shi, S.: Empirical analysis of unlabeled entity problem in named entity recognition (2020). https://doi.org/10.48550/ARXIV.2012.05426. https://arxiv.org/abs/2012.05426
10. Liu, Y., et al.: RoBERTa: a robustly optimized BERT pretraining approach (2019). https://doi.org/10.48550/ARXIV.1907.11692. https://arxiv.org/abs/1907.11692
11. Mintz, M., Bills, S., Snow, R., Jurafsky, D.: Distant supervision for relation extraction without labeled data. In: Proceedings of the Joint Conference of the 47th Annual Meeting of the ACL and the 4th International Joint Conference on Natural Language Processing of the AFNLP, Suntec, Singapore, pp. 1003–1011. Association for Computational Linguistics, August 2009. https://aclanthology.org/P09-1113
12. Miwa, M., Bansal, M.: End-to-end relation extraction using LSTMs on sequences and tree structures (2016). https://doi.org/10.48550/ARXIV.1601.00770. https://arxiv.org/abs/1601.00770
13. Moldovan, D.I., Clark, C., Harabagiu, S.M., Maiorano, S.J.: COGEX: a logic prover for question answering. In: North American Chapter of the Association for Computational Linguistics (2003)
14. Nallapati, R., Zhou, B., dos Santos, C.N., Gulcehre, C., Xiang, B.: Abstractive text summarization using sequence-to-sequence RNNs and beyond. arXiv: Computation and Language (2016)

15. Nan, G., Guo, Z., Sekulić, I., Lu, W.: Reasoning with latent structure refinement for document-level relation extraction (2020). https://doi.org/10.48550/ARXIV.2005.06312. https://arxiv.org/abs/2005.06312
16. Nie, Y., Chen, H., Bansal, M.: Combining fact extraction and verification with neural semantic matching networks. arXiv: Computation and Language (2018)
17. Nie, Y., Williams, A., Dinan, E., Bansal, M., Weston, J., Kiela, D.: Adversarial NLI: a new benchmark for natural language understanding. arXiv: Computation and Language (2019)
18. Parrish, A., et al.: Does putting a linguist in the loop improve NLU data collection. Empirical Methods in Natural Language Processing (2021)
19. Raina, R., Ng, A.Y., Manning, C.D.: Robust textual inference via learning and abductive reasoning. In: Proceedings of the 20th National Conference on Artificial Intelligence, AAAI 2005, vol. 3, pp. 1099–1105. AAAI Press (2005)
20. Rajpurkar, P., Zhang, J., Lopyrev, K., Liang, P.: SQuaD: 100,000+ questions for machine comprehension of text (2016)
21. Sainz, O., de Lacalle, O.L., Labaka, G., Barrena, A., Agirre, E.: Label verbalization and entailment for effective zero and few-shot relation extraction. Empirical Methods in Natural Language Processing (2021)
22. Tan, Q., He, R., Bing, L., Ng, H., Academy, D., Group, A.: Document-level relation extraction with adaptive focal loss and knowledge distillation (2023)
23. Tan, Q., Xu, L., Bing, L., Ng, H.T., Aljunied, S.M.: Revisiting docRED - addressing the false negative problem in relation extraction (2022). https://doi.org/10.48550/ARXIV.2205.12696. https://arxiv.org/abs/2205.12696
24. Vania, C., Lee, G., Pierleoni, A.: Improving distantly supervised document-level relation extraction through natural language inference. In: Proceedings of the Third Workshop on Deep Learning for Low-Resource Natural Language Processing, pp. 14–20. Association for Computational Linguistics, Hybrid, July 2022. https://doi.org/10.18653/v1/2022.deeplo-1.2. https://aclanthology.org/2022.deeplo-1.2
25. Wang, Y., Liu, X., Hu, W., Zhang, T.: A unified positive-unlabeled learning framework for document-level relation extraction with different levels of labeling (2022). https://doi.org/10.48550/ARXIV.2210.08709. https://arxiv.org/abs/2210.08709
26. Williams, A., Nangia, N., Bowman, S.R.: A broad-coverage challenge corpus for sentence understanding through inference. arXiv: Computation and Language (2017)
27. Xu, B., Wang, Q., Lyu, Y., Yong, Z., Mao, Z.: Entity structure within and throughout: modeling mention dependencies for document-level relation extraction. In: Proceedings of the ... AAAI Conference on Artificial Intelligence (2021)
28. Xu, W., Chen, K., Mou, L., Zhao, T.: Document-level relation extraction with sentences importance estimation and focusing (2022). https://doi.org/10.48550/ARXIV.2204.12679. https://arxiv.org/abs/2204.12679
29. Xu, W., Chen, K., Zhao, T.: Document-level relation extraction with reconstruction. Cornell University - arXiv (2021)
30. Yao, Y., et al.: DocRED: a large-scale document-level relation extraction dataset (2019). https://doi.org/10.48550/ARXIV.1906.06127. https://arxiv.org/abs/1906.06127
31. Yin, W., Radev, D.R., Xiong, C.: DocNLI: a large-scale dataset for document-level natural language inference. Cornell University - arXiv (2021)
32. Zeng, S., Xu, R., Chang, B., Li, L.: Double graph based reasoning for document-level relation extraction. Cornell University - arXiv (2020)
33. Zhang, N., et al.: Document-level relation extraction as semantic segmentation. Cornell University - arXiv (2021)

34. Zhang, Y., Qi, P., Manning, C.D.: Graph convolution over pruned dependency trees improves relation extraction (2018). https://doi.org/10.48550/ARXIV.1809.10185. https://arxiv.org/abs/1809.10185
35. Zhou, W., Huang, K., Ma, T., Huang, J.: Document-level relation extraction with adaptive thresholding and localized context pooling (2020). https://doi.org/10.48550/ARXIV.2010.11304. https://arxiv.org/abs/2010.11304
36. Zhou, Y., Lee, W.S.: None class ranking loss for document-level relation extraction (2022). https://doi.org/10.48550/ARXIV.2205.00476. https://arxiv.org/abs/2205.00476

pFedLHNs: Personalized Federated Learning via Local Hypernetworks

Liping Yi, Xiaorong Shi, Nan Wang, Ziyue Xu, Gang Wang[✉],
and Xiaoguang Liu

College of Computer Science, TMCC, SysNet, DISSec, GTIISC,
Nankai University, Tianjin, China
{yiliping,shixiaorong,wangn,xuzy,wgzwp,liuxg}@nbjl.nankai.edu.cn

Abstract. As an emerging paradigm, federated learning (FL) trains a shared global model by multi-party collaboration without leaking privacy since no private data transmission between the server and clients. However, it still faces two challenges: statistical heterogeneity and communication efficiency. To tackle them simultaneously, we propose pFedLHNs, which assigns each client with both a small hypernetwork (HN) and a large target network (NN) whose parameters are generated by the hypernetwork. Each client pulls other clients' hypernetworks from the server for local aggregation to personalize its local target model and only interacts the small hypernetwork with other clients via the central server to reduce communication costs. Besides, the server also aggregates received local hypernetworks to construct a global hypernetwork and uses it to initialize new joining out-of-distribution (OOD) clients for cold start. Extensive experiments on three datasets with Non-IID distributions demonstrate the superiority of pFedLHNs in the trade-off between model accuracy and communication efficiency. The case studies justify its tolerance to statistical heterogeneity and new OOD clients.

Keywords: Personalized federated learning · Communication efficiency · Statistical heterogeneity · Hypernetwork

1 Introduction

Federated learning (FL) [24] aims to train a shared global model on multi-party decentralized data with privacy protection. FedAvg [24] is a typical FL algorithm where the central server broadcasts the global model to clients; clients train the received global model on local data and then upload local model updates to the server; the server aggregates received local model updates to construct a new global model. The above steps repeat until the global model converges. In

This research is supported in part by the National Science Foundation of China under Grant 62141412, 62272253, 62272252, and the Fundamental Research Funds for the Central Universities.

general, *data* is always stored in clients, and only *models* are transmitted between the server and clients.

However, FL still faces two major challenges: **a) Statistical heterogeneity**, the distributions of decentralized data from different clients are usually non-independently and identically distributed (Non-IID), which leads to large *model bias* among different clients and highly skewed Non-IID data can degrade the accuracy of the aggregated global model [18,39,40]. Some local models trained individually on local data may perform better than the shared global model. **b) Communication efficiency** is affected by three factors: the number of clients, model footprint, and communication rounds for convergence. When any of the three is large, high communication costs lead to the communication time being FL's primary bottleneck [29,35–37].

To tackle *statistical heterogeneity*, personalized federated learning (PFL) [16,30] is proposed to learn a personalized local model for each client in FL. The final personalized local models often perform better than the global model trained in traditional FL. To improve *communication efficiency*, prior arts (such as client sampling [6,32,36], model compression [36], and delay increasing [24,26]) sample partial clients to join in FL, compress the transmitted models or speed up convergence. Most PFL methods do not improve communication efficiency and most communication-efficient approaches also can not alleviate statistical heterogeneity. Although a few methods [8,13,22,34] try to solve the two issues simultaneously, the trade-off between them still requires to be improved.

To alleviate statistical heterogeneity and improve communication efficiency simultaneously, we propose a PFL framework named *pFedLHNs*, where each client locally trains a small hypernetwork and a large target network with parameters generated by the hypernetwork. It allows clients to conduct *local aggregation* to fulfil personalized local target networks, and only *small local hypernetworks* interact with others via the server, which alleviates statistical heterogeneity and saves communication costs. Besides, the server also aggregates the received local hypernetworks to construct a new global hypernetwork, which is used to initialize the local hypernetworks of new-joining OOD clients. Extensive experiments demonstrated that pFedLHNs achieves a superior trade-off between personalized model accuracy and communication costs, and case studies justify the tolerance of pFedLHNs to statistical heterogeneity and OOD clients.

Contributions. Our main contributions are summarized as follows:

- We propose a communication-efficient PFL framework dubbed as *pFedLHNs* to tackle statistical heterogeneity while improving communication efficiency.
- We evaluate *pFedLHNs* and baselines on three datasets with Non-IID distributions and demonstrate that it performs the state-of-the-art trade-off between model accuracy and communication efficiency.
- Extensive case studies verify that *pFedLHNs* is robust to statistical heterogeneity (Non-IID degrees and imbalance rates) and it also performs tolerance to new joining clients with OOD data distributions.

2   Related Work

2.1   Personalized Federated Learning

Prior PFL arts include: fine-tuning [23,33], federated meta-learning [11], federated multi-task learning [10,30], model mixup [2,4,7,21,31], regularization [1,9,19,20,27], and federated clustering [3,14,25]. Recent PFL methods involve: **Local aggregation**, FedFomo [38] makes each client pull other clients' *complete* models and select more benefited models for local aggregation to update their local models. It directly optimizes local learning objectives, but the communication cost increases exponentially since each client has to pull other clients' *complete* models from the server. **Hypernetwork-based**, pFedHN [28] deploys a hypernetwork with a *larger* size than local target models on the *server*. The hypernetwork learns the parameter distributions of local models and generates personalized local models for each client, but the communication overhead is still the *same* as FedAvg. In the latest Fed-RoD [5], each client involves one feature extractor and two headers: one is a global header that combines with the feature extractor for aggregation to update the global model, and the other is a personalized header with parameters generated by a local hypernetwork. Although it improves personalized local models, *extra communication cost* is consumed due to transmitting hypernetworks between clients and the server.

2.2   Hypernetwork

As shown in Fig. 1, a hypernetwork [12] is a model that generates parameters for target models. It belongs to the category of *generative networks*. The output of hypernetworks is the parameters of target models, which varies with the input (an embedding vector representing the target model). The hypernetwork (HN) and target model (NN) are trained in an end-to-end manner. During training, the input embedding vector of HN is a trainable variable. The detailed training pipeline involves: 1) HN generates parameters for NN, which transfers knowledge (parameter distribution) from HN to NN; 2) NN is directly trained on data; 3) The parameter variances of NN before/after training are used to update HN's parameters, which transfers the latest NN's knowledge to HN. The above steps repeat until the target model converges. In short, a hypernetwork as information media continuously learns the parameter distributions of target models during end-to-end training.

3   Preliminary

In this section, we first introduce the background of FL, and then we verify the feasibility of using small hypernetworks to generate parameters for large target models.

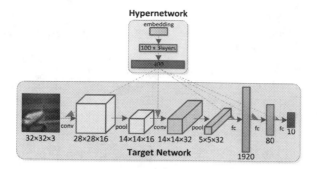

Fig. 1. The structures of a hypernetwork and its generated target model. The output dimension of the hypernetwork is 400, which is smaller than the target model's parameter capacity, so we call the hypernetwork multiple times to generate parameters in a stacked way. The input of the hypernetwork is an embedding of (client id + chunk id). Every 400 parameters constitute a chunk with id started from 0 and increased by 1.

3.1 Background of FL

With a typical FL algorithm *FedAvg* as the background, we introduce the definition of FL. Assuming that there are total N clients, the server randomly samples a fraction C of clients (set of sampled clients: $S^t, |S^t| = C \cdot N = K$) to participate in each round of FL. The server first sends the global model to sampled clients as their initial local models. Then the k-th client trains its local model ω_k on local datasets D_k with the training objective: $min\ F_k(\omega_k) = \frac{1}{n_k}\sum_{i \in D_k} f_i(\omega_k)$, where $n_k = |D_k|$; $f_i(\omega_k) = \ell(\boldsymbol{x}_i, y_i; \omega_k)$, i.e., the loss of i-th instance $(\boldsymbol{x}_i, y_i)$ on the local model ω_k. The local epoch is E, batch size is B, so local training executes $E\frac{n_k}{B}$ iterations. Next, clients upload trained local models to the server, and the server aggregates the received local models to update the global model with the whole goal of FL:

$$\min f(\omega) = \sum_{k=0}^{K-1} \frac{n_k}{n} F_k(\omega_k), \tag{1}$$

where n is the total number of samples held by all clients. Finally, the server broadcasts the updated global model ω to clients. All the above steps repeat until the global model converges.

3.2 Feasibility of Hypernetworks

To verify whether a small HN can generate parameters for NN with acceptable model performance, we carry out an experiment on CIFAR-10, where the structures of HN and NN are the same as the settings in Sect. 5. We train a large NN *independently* on one client while training a large NN through the *end-to-end training*: HN generates NN $\rightarrow$ training NN on data $\rightarrow$ updating HN with NN's parameter variance before/after training. Figure 2 displays that training NN w/ HN obtains lower training loss and higher test accuracy than training NN solely,

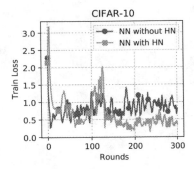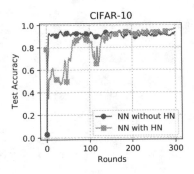

Fig. 2. Train loss and test accuracy of NN w/o or w/ HN on CIFAR-10 dataset.

which may be attributed to that training NN with HN in an end-to-end format inherently trains more parameters to learn knowledge from data than training NN without HN. *Hence, we can safely regard an HN as a "meta model" to extract an NN's knowledge.*

4   Methodology

In this section, we first formulate pFedLHNs's training object, then detail its workflow, and finally analyze its generalization to new out-of-distribution (OOD) clients and budgets about computation and communication.

4.1   Problem Formulation and Notations

We deploy one small local hypernetwork and one large local target model for each client. The local target model is actually the local model in traditional FL. The hypernetwork is responsible for learning the target model's parameter distributions and generating parameters for the target model.

Hypernetwork Generating (Forward). Assuming that the local hypernetwork of the k-th client in the $(t-1)$-th round is φ_k^{t-1} and the generated target model of the k-th client in the t-th round is $\hat{\omega}_k^t$. Referred to [28], we can use a hypernetwork φ_k^{t-1} to generate parameters for a target model $\hat{\omega}_k^t$ with

$$\hat{\omega}_k^t = h(v_k; \varphi_k^{t-1}), \tag{2}$$

where v_k is a *unique* embedding vector representing the target model $\hat{\omega}_k^t$, as shown in Fig. 1. Since each client's local hypernetwork has diverse parameters φ_k and different input embeddings v_k, the generated target models are *personalized*.

Local Training. After generating a target model, we train it on the local dataset to get the latest *trained* target model ω_k^t, which will be used to update the hypernetwork.

Hypernetwork Updating (Backward). Also referred to [28], we can use the target model after local training to further carry out a one-shot updating of the hypernetwork's parameters in the following way:

$$\varphi_k^t \leftarrow \varphi_k^{t-1} - \eta_{HN} \nabla_{\varphi_k^{t-1}}(\omega_k^t)^T \Delta\omega_k^t, \tag{3}$$

where $\nabla_{\varphi_k^{t-1}}(\omega_k^t)^T$ is the derivative of the latest trained target model ω_k^t in the t-th round with respect to the hypernetwork φ_k^{t-1} in the $(t-1)$-th round; $\Delta\omega_k^t = \omega_k^t - \hat{\omega}_k^t$, the variation of the generated target model before and after local training. That is, updating HN requires HN's parameters φ_k^{t-1}, NN's parameters ω_k^t, and the parameter variations of NN $\Delta\omega_k^t$, but no private data of clients.

Training Object. Next, each client only communicates the small local hypernetwork φ_k with the server to learn other clients' knowledge. Based on Eq. (1), the training object of pFedLHNs is formulated as:

$$\min f(\omega) = \sum_{k=0}^{K-1} \frac{n_k}{n} F_k(h(v_k; \varphi_k)). \tag{4}$$

4.2   Overview of pFedLHNs

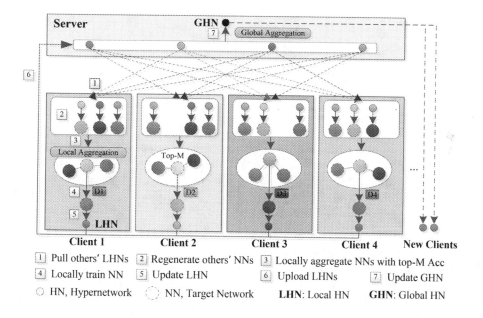

Fig. 3. The workflow of pFedLHNs.

To achieve the training objective in Eq. (4), as shown in Fig. 3, pFedLHNs execute the following steps: 1) $client_k$ participating in the current t-th round pulls other clients' hypernetworks $[\varphi_{k_1}^{t-1}, \varphi_{k_2}^{t-1}, ...]$ received by the server in the last round. 2) $client_k$ uses pulled hypernetworks $[\varphi_{k_1}^{t-1}, \varphi_{k_2}^{t-1}, ...]$ to regenerate corresponding target models $[\omega_{k_1}^{t-1}, \omega_{k_2}^{t-1}, ...]$. 3) $client_k$ tests the regenerated target models' accuracies $[Acc_{k_1}^{t-1}, Acc_{k_2}^{t-1}, ...]$ on its local dataset D_k.

Then $client_k$ puts the regenerated target models with top-M accuracies and itself into its collaboration group G_k^t, and executes *local aggregation* within G_k^t. The aggregation weights of target models are defined by normalized accuracy $Acc_i^{t-1} / \sum_{i \in G_k^t} Acc_i^{t-1}$, and the locally aggregated rule is formulated as:

$$\textbf{NN's Local Aggregation:} \quad \hat{\omega}_k^t = \sum_{i \in G_k^t} \frac{Acc_i^{t-1}}{\sum_{i \in G_k^t} Acc_i^{t-1}} \omega_i^{t-1}. \qquad (5)$$

4) The locally aggregated target model $\hat{\omega}_k^t$ continues being trained on the local dataset D_k and finally updates to ω_k^t. 5) The local hypernetwork's parameters can be updated using ω_k^t and $\hat{\omega}_k^t$ according to Eq. (3), and the updated local hypernetwork is φ_k^t. 6) $client_k$ uploads φ_k^t to the server. 7) The server stores and aggregates the received local hypernetworks to update the global hypernetwork φ^t with the following rule:

$$\textbf{HN's Global Aggregation:} \quad \varphi^t = \sum_{k \in S^t} \frac{n_k}{n} \varphi_k^t. \qquad (6)$$

The above steps repeat until all local target models converge.

4.3   Discussion

Next, we analyze pFedLHNs's personalization, the generalization to new out-of-distribution (OOD) clients, and budgets of communication and computation.

Personalization. Since each client performs *local aggregation*, the aggregated target models and updated hypernetworks are both *personalized*. Besides, each client only chooses other clients' target models with top-M accuracy and itself for local aggregation, which enhances the *preference* of aggregated target models to local data, hence boosting the accuracy of personalized local target models and alleviating statistical heterogeneity.

Generalization to Out-of-distribution (OOD) Clients. New-appeared clients holding data with diverse distributions from old joined clients are regarded as OOD clients [2,38]. pFedLHNs stores a *global hypernetwork* φ^t on the server. When a new OOD client joins in the t-th round, its local hypernetwork will be initialized with the latest global hypernetwork in the $(t-1)$-th round, i.e., $\varphi_{new}^t = \varphi^{t-1}$, as shown in Fig. 3. The initialized new client can acquire old clients' knowledge indirectly to converge quickly within a few rounds.

Budgets. We discuss the budgets for communication and computation:

Communication Efficiency. In *uplink* communication, each client uploads a *small local hypernetwork* to the server, so the uplink communication cost is much lower than uploading *complete target models* in FedAvg. In *downlink* communication, although each client has to pull other clients' hypernetworks from the server, when the hypernetwork size is much smaller than the target model size, the communication cost consumed by pulling others' hypernetworks may be lower than transmitting one *complete* global target model in FedAvg.

Computational Cost. pFedLHNs's main computations are in clients, i.e., steps 2–5 in Fig. 3. Except for step-5 (locally training NN), pFedLHNs incurs extra computation compared with FedAvg. In *cross-silo* FL scenarios, since multiple participating enterprises often take sufficient computation power such as server clusters, sacrificing computation for improved accuracy benefits economic gains.

5 Experiments

We implement pFedLHNs and baselines with PyTorch and simulate the FL environment on NVIDIA GeForce RTX 3090 GPUs with 24G memory. We evaluate pFedLHNs and baselines on MNIST[1] [17] and CIFAR-10/100[2] [15] datasets.

5.1 Settings

Datasets and Models. Referred to the Non-IID division in [28], we manually divide three datasets into *Non-IID* distributions. For MNIST, we set 50 clients, and each client only has 2 classes of data. For CIFAR-10/100 datasets, we set 50 clients, and each client has only 2/10 classes of data. Besides, in the above three divisions, to construct imbalance, one class in different clients involves *different* numbers of samples, and the different sample ratios are generated randomly by a *random.uniform (low, high)* function with $(low, high \leq 1)$, the larger distances of *low* and *high*, the more imbalance one class takes. We train one LeNet and two CNN models compromised of two convolution layers and three fully-connected layers on MNIST and CIFAR-10/100 datasets, respectively. The hypernetwork used in three tasks is an MLP model with two hidden layers.

Baselines. We compare pFedLHNs with: 1) **Local Training**, where each client trains its model individually. 2) **FedAvg** [24], the typical FL algorithm. PFL methods related to our work: 3) **FedFomo** [38] with local aggregation, 4) **pFedHN** [28] and 5) **Fed-RoD** [5] with hypernetworks.

Metrics. a) Accuracy (%), we evaluate the performance of algorithms with the mean test accuracy of local target models. **b) Communication traffic (GB)** is measured by parameters volume bi-communicated between the server and clients until algorithms reach the designated target accuracy.

Training Strategy. We set consistent grid-searched optimal FL hyperparameters for all algorithms: the client sampling rate C is 0.1; the learning rate of local target models (η_{NN}) is $5e-3$, using an SGD optimizer with the momentum of 0.9, weight decay of $5e-5$, and batch size of 64. In pFedLHNs, M is set to be 20%, and the learning rate of hypernetworks (η_{HN}) is 0.01. All algorithms perform 1000 training rounds and $\{1, 10, 50, 100\}$ local epochs per round to guarantee convergence.

---

[1] http://yann.lecun.com/exdb/mnist/.

[2] https://www.cs.toronto.edu/%7Ekriz/cifar.html.

Table 1. The experimental results of pFedLHNs and baselines on three Non-IID datasets. 'Traffic (xx%)' represents the consumed communication traffic (GB) until algorithms reach xx% target accuracy. '-' denotes not reaching the target accuracy xx%. All the results are the average of five trials.

Dataset Method	MNIST		CIFAR-10		CIFAR-100	
	Accuracy	Traffic (90%)	Accuracy	Traffic (40%)	Accuracy	Traffic (10%)
Local Training	98.12	-	40.62	-	6.56	-
FedAvg	97.81	11.90	34.06	-	7.19	-
FedFomo	48.44	-	70.31	**1.82**	15.62	**0.52**
pFedHN	98.19	11.90	86.12	2.08	53.56	10.86
Fed-RoD	95.62	7.43	58.44	9.58	23.75	6.17
pFedLHNs (ours)	**98.99**	**6.63**	**86.88**	7.97	**54.97**	10.62

5.2 Comparisons with State-of-the-Art

We evaluate pFedLHNs and baselines on the three datasets with Non-IID distributions. It can be observed from Table 1 that *pFedLHNs achieves the highest accuracy with acceptable communication cost*, indicating it takes the best trade-off between model accuracy and communication cost. FedFomo takes the lowest communication overhead on CIFAR-10/100 datasets, but its accuracy is far lower than our pFedLHNs.

5.3 Generalization to New OOD Clients

To evaluate the generalization of pFedLHNs and baselines to new OOD clients, we construct the following scenario: there are 55 clients, the first 50 clients from the old client group, and the last 5 clients from the new client group; the old client group is first trained for $R/2$ rounds, and the new group joins in training from the $((R/2)+1)$-th round, while the local hypernetworks of new clients are initialized by the global hypernetwork updated in the $(R/2)$-th round. To construct clients with OOD data, we fix the old clients with 2 classes of data (Non-IID (2/10)) and set the new clients with Non-IID ({2, 4, 6, 8, 10}/10) data. We evaluate the generalization ability to new clients through *generalization distance*, the gap between the mean accuracy of old clients' local models and the mean accuracy of new clients' local models, which is a common metric used in [2,28], and the smaller gap indicates the stronger generalization ability.

From Fig. 4, we see that *our pFedLHNs has the lowest generalization gaps at all Non-IID degrees, i.e., the most powerful generalization capability*. This is because the shared global hypernetwork has sufficiently learned the knowledge of the old clients' local models, and new OOD clients with local hypernetworks initialized by the global hypernetwork can converge fast due to absorbing old knowledge indirectly.

5.4 Case Study

We explore the robustness of pFedLHNs and baselines to statistical heterogeneity (*Non-IID degrees* and *imbalance rates*) on the CIFAR-10 dataset.

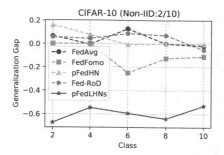

Fig. 4. When old clients hold CIFAR-10 (Non-IID: 2/10) data, the generalization gaps vary as the Non-IID degrees ({2, 4, 6, 8, 10}/10) of new clients' data.

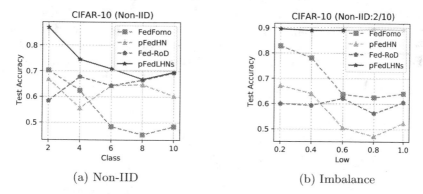

(a) Non-IID   (b) Imbalance

Fig. 5. The accuracy of pFedLHNs and baselines vary as (a): Non-IID degrees ('Class' in the x-axis denotes the number of classes owned by one client) and (b): imbalance rates ('Low' in the x-axis denotes that the value of low rate in $random.uniform(low, high)$ function for generating imbalance rates when $high = 1.0$) on CIFAR-10 datasets.

Robustness to Non-IID Degree. We assign $\{2, 4, 6, 8, 10\}$ classes of data for each client and Fig. 5 (a) displays that *our pFedLHNs exhibits the highest model accuracy for all degrees of Non-IID, which verifies its strong robustness to Non-IID data*.

Robustness to Imbalance Rate. To produce different imbalance rates, we fix $high = 1.0$ and set $low = \{0.2, 0.4, 0.6, 0.8, 1.0\}$, the larger distance between *low* and *high* means the higher imbalance rate. From the results depicted in Fig. 5 (b), we find that *our pFedLHNs shows the highest accuracy among different imbalance rates, demonstrating the tolerance of pFedLHNs to imbalance rates*.

6 Conclusions and Future Work

This paper proposed a personalized and communication-efficient FL framework named pFedLHNs. It allows each client to locally aggregate its target model and others' target models preferred to its local data, enhancing the personalization of the aggregated target model and alleviating statistical heterogeneity. Only small local hypernetworks are transmitted between the server and clients, so the communication cost is saved. Extensive experiments verify that pFedLHNs performs state-of-the-art model accuracy and acceptable communication cost on Non-IID datasets while providing strong generalization capability to new OOD clients and robustness to Non-IID degrees and imbalance rates. To sum up, our pFedLHNs can be effectively applied in cross-silo FL scenarios due to its benefits of accuracy and communication.

Since one hypernetwork can generate parameters for target models with different structures and only hypernetworks are communicated in pFedLHNs, it can support collaborative training across clients with heterogeneous models. In future, we will explore whether pFedLHNs can perform satisfied model accuracy in model-heterogeneous FL.

References

1. Acar, D.A.E., et al.: Federated learning based on dynamic regularization. In: Proceedings of ICLR, Virtual, Austria. OpenReview.net (2021)
2. Achituve, I., et al.: Personalized federated learning with gaussian processes. CoRR abs/2106.15482 (2021)
3. Agrawal, S., et al.: Genetic CFL: optimization of hyper-parameters in clustered federated learning. CoRR abs/2107.07233 (2021)
4. Arivazhagan, M.G., et al.: Federated learning with personalization layers. CoRR abs/1912.00818 (2019)
5. Chen, H., et al.: On bridging generic and personalized federated learning. CoRR abs/2107.00778 (2021)
6. Chen, T., et al.: LAG: lazily aggregated gradient for communication-efficient distributed learning. In: Proceedings of NeurIPS 2018, pp. 5055–5065 (2018)
7. Collins, L., et al.: Exploiting shared representations for personalized federated learning. In: Proceedings of ICML, Virtual Event. vol. 139, pp. 2089–2099. PMLR (2021)
8. Diao, E.: Heterofl: Computation and communication efficient federated learning for heterogeneous clients. In: Proceedings of ICLR (2021)
9. Dinh, C.T., et al.: Personalized federated learning with moreau envelopes. In: Proceedings of NeurIPS virtual (2020)
10. Dinh, C.T., et al.: Fedu: A unified framework for federated multi-task learning with laplacian regularization. CoRR abs/2102.07148 (2021)
11. Fallah, A., et al.: Personalized federated learning with theoretical guarantees: a model-agnostic meta-learning approach. In: Proceedings of NIPS, virtual (2020)
12. Ha, D., et al.: Hypernetworks. In: Proc. ICLR 2017, Toulon, France. OpenReview.net (2017)
13. Horváth, S.: FjORD: Fair and accurate federated learning under heterogeneous targets with ordered dropout. In: Proceedings of NIPS (2021)

14. Huang, Y., et al.: Personalized cross-silo federated learning on non-iid data. In: Proceedings of AAAI. pp. 7865–7873. AAAI Press (2021)
15. Krizhevsky, A., et al.: Learning multiple layers of features from tiny images (2009)
16. Kulkarni, V., et al.: Survey of personalization techniques for federated learning. CoRR abs/2003.08673 (2020)
17. LeCun, Y., et al.: Gradient-based learning applied to document recognition. Proc. IEEE **86**(11), 2278–2324 (1998)
18. Li, Q., et al.: Federated learning on non-iid data silos: An experimental study. CoRR abs/2102.02079 (2021)
19. Li, T., et al.: Federated optimization in heterogeneous networks. In: Proceedings MLSys, Austin, TX, USA. mlsys.org (2020)
20. Li, T., et al.: Ditto: Fair and robust federated learning through personalization. In: Proceedings of ICML, Virtual Event. vol. 139, pp. 6357–6368. PMLR (2021)
21. Liang, P.P., et al.: Think locally, act globally: Federated learning with local and global representations. CoRR abs/2001.01523 (2020)
22. Liu, S., et al.: Adaptive network pruning for wireless federated learning. IEEE Wirel. Commun. Lett. **10**(7), 1572–1576 (2021)
23. Mansour, Y., et al.: Three approaches for personalization with applications to federated learning. CoRR abs/2002.10619 (2020)
24. McMahan, B., et al.: Communication-efficient learning of deep networks from decentralized data. In: Proceeidngs of AISTATS, Fort Lauderdale, FL, USA. vol. 54, pp. 1273–1282. PMLR (2017)
25. Ouyang, X., et al.: Clusterfl: a similarity-aware federated learning system for human activity recognition. In: Proceedings of MobiSys, USA, pp. 54–66. ACM (2021)
26. Reisizadeh, A., et al.: Fedpaq: A communication-efficient federated learning method with periodic averaging and quantization. In: Proceedings of AISTATS. vol. 108, pp. 2021–2031. PMLR, Online (2020)
27. Sai, et al.: SCAFFOLD: stochastic controlled averaging for federated learning. In: Proceedings ICML, Virtual Event. vol. 119, pp. 5132–5143. PMLR (2020)
28. Shamsian, A., et al.: Personalized federated learning using hypernetworks. In: Proceedings of ICML, Virtual Event. vol. 139, pp. 9489–9502. PMLR (2021)
29. Shi, X., et al.: FFedCL: Fair Federated Learning with Contrastive Learning. In: Proceedings of ICASSP (2023)
30. Smith, V., et al.: Federated multi-task learning. In: Proceedings of NIPS, Long Beach, CA, USA, pp. 4424–4434 (2017)
31. Sun, B., et al.: Partialfed: Cross-domain personalized federated learning via partial initialization. In: Proceedings of NIPS, Virtual Event (2021)
32. Sun, J., et al.: Communication-efficient distributed learning via lazily aggregated quantized gradients. In: Proceedings of NeurIPS, Canada, pp. 3365–3375 (2019)
33. Wang, K., et al.: Federated evaluation of on-device personalization. CoRR abs/1910.10252 (2019)
34. Yang, T., et al.: Designing energy-efficient convolutional neural networks using encrgy-aware pruning. In: Proceedings of CVPR, USA, pp. 6071–6079. IEEE Computer Society (2017)
35. Yi, L., et al.: SU-Net: an efficient encoder-decoder model of federated learning for brain tumor segmentation. In: Proceedings of ICANN (2020)
36. Yi, L., et al.: QSFL: A two-level uplink communication optimization framework for federated learning. In: Proceedings of ICML. vol. 162, pp. 25501–25513. PMLR (2022)

37. Yi, L., et al.: FedRRA: reputation-aware robust federated learning against poisoning attacks. In: Proceedings of IJCNN (2023)
38. Zhang, M., et al.: Personalized federated learning with first order model optimization. In: Proceedings of ICLR Virtual Event, Austria. OpenReview.net (2021)
39. Zhao, Y., et al.: Federated learning with non-iid data. CoRR abs/1806.00582 (2018)
40. Zhu, H., et al.: Federated learning on non-iid data: a survey. Neurocomputing **465**, 371–390 (2021)

Prototype Contrastive Learning
for Personalized Federated Learning

Siqi Deng and Liu Yang[✉]

College of Intelligence and Computing, Tianjin University, Tianjin 300350, China
{2021244166,yangliuyl}@tju.edu.cn

Abstract. Federated learning (FL) is a decentralized learning paradigm in which multiple clients collaborate to train the global model. However, the generalization of a global model is often affected by data heterogeneity. The goal of Personalized Federated Learning (PFL) is to develop models tailored to local tasks that overcomes data heterogeneity from the clients' perspective. In this paper, we introduce Prototype Contrastive Learning into FL (FedPCL) to learn a global base encoder, which aggregates knowledge learned by local models not only in the parameter space but also in the embedding space. Furthermore, given that some client resources are limited, we employ two prototype settings: multiple prototypes and a single prototype. The federated process combines with the Expectation Maximization (EM) algorithm. During the iterative process, clients perform the E-step to compute prototypes and the M-step to update model parameters by minimizing the ProtoNCE-M (ProtoNCE-S) loss. This process leads to achieving convergence of the global model. Subsequently, the global base encoder that extracts more compact representations is customized according to the local task to ensure personalization. Experimental results demonstrate the consistent increase in performance as well as its effective personalization ability.

Keywords: Contrastive Learning · Prototype · Embedding Space

1 Introduction

Federated Learning (FL) is a machine learning framework that trains a model on data from multiple clients in a decentralized manner. The clients collaborate to train a global model without sharing individual data. Federated Averaging algorithm (FedAvg) [15] is a popular approach that trains a global model by averaging local model updates. In practice, the data across different clients is frequently non-independent and identically distributed (Non-IID) [10,14]. When this occurs, the convergence of the learned model can be impaired, resulting in reduced generalization performance. To address this issue, several effective FL algorithms have been developed based on FedAvg, such as FedProx [14], MOON [13], and FedProc [16]. FedProx [14] directly limits the magnitude of local updates by considering the dissimilarity between the global model and

© The Author(s), under exclusive license to Springer Nature Switzerland AG 2023
L. Iliadis et al. (Eds.): ICANN 2023, LNCS 14256, pp. 529–540, 2023.
https://doi.org/10.1007/978-3-031-44213-1_44

local models. MOON [13] corrects the local updates by a model-contrastive loss, while FedProc [16] using a global prototypical contrastive loss.

However, a shared global model may not necessarily generalize better than models trained on the local clients' data alone. Hence the development of Personalized Federated Learning (PFL) emerges as the times require [1,5,6,8,9,17,18]. L2GD [8] seeks an explicit trade-off between the two by a mixture of global and local models. These studies [1,5,17,18] decouple the global model into two distinct parameter sets: global shared parameters and local private parameters. Additionally, the study [9] demonstrates that FedAvg is a Meta Learning algorithm and careful fine-tuning has a significant contribution to adapting the global model to the local. Per-FedAvg [6] learns an initial shared model that can be generalized quickly to clients and FedBABU [17] also can be personalized rapidly with fine-tuning.

Our observation aligns with the findings in previous works [13,16,19], indicating that the use of FedAvg results in a disorganized feature distribution, but it can learn more compact representations using a unified prototype. Accordingly, we integrate the principle of Prototype Contrastive Learning [12] into the federated learning process and train a global model comprising of a base encoder and a MLP projector. After this step, we fine-tune the base encoder on clients to improve personalization. During each round of FL, clients compute prototypes to utilize their local models' knowledge in the embedding space by performing the Expectation step. Next, the Maximization step is used to minimize the ProtoNCE loss [12], which encourages representations to be closer to their prototypes. When aggregating prototypes, the client only use the base encoder's extracted representations and disregards the task-specific representations of the MLP. Based on the convergent global model, the client trains a classifier to learn a definite decision boundary.

The main contributions of this work can be summarized as follows:

- We propose FedPCL to learn a global base encoder, which can learn more compact representations and it can be fine-tuned to local tasks for both clients participating and not participating in FL for personalization.
- We encode the semantic structure learned by the clients into the embedding space through the prototypes and minimize the ProtoNCE loss to alleviate the influence of the Non-IID.
- To address the limitation in client computing power, we extend the Multiple Prototypes Contrastive Learning for FL (FedPCL-M) to A Single Prototype (FedPCL-S), where the server aggregates a single prototype for each class.

2 Related Work

2.1 Personal Federated Learning

There have been many studies exploring PFL from various different perspectives [1,5,6,17–19]. The most common personalization method is parameter decoupling where the model parameters are decoupled into two parts: the global shared parameters and the local private parameters [1,5,17,18]. FedRep [5] learns a shared data representation across clients and unique local heads for each client. FedBABU [17] demonstrates that the body of the model is related to representation learning, while the head is related to linear decision boundary learning. The study [18] proposes two FL optimization algorithms: FedSim updates shared and personal parameters simultaneously and FedAlt updates them alternately.

However, when the knowledge aggregation of the clients occurs in the parameter space, it usually has a worse impact on the convergence speed and generalization performance. FedProto [19] and Fedproc [16] abstract class prototypes in the embedding space and use prototypes' distance as the regularization term to solve heterogeneous problems. In this work, FedPCL takes full advantage of the knowledge learned by the local models not only in the parameter space but also in the embedding space. Moreover, we directly minimize the ProtoNCE loss to update the model rather than as a regularization term, mitigating the influence of Non-IID on the model.

The study in [9] empirically demonstrates that FedAvg is a meta learning algorithm and fine-tuning can achieve more stable personalization performance. Per-FedAvg [6] aims to learn an initial shared model that can be generalized quickly, but it needs to calculate the Hessian term, resulting in high resource consumption. Considering the clients with limited resources, we extend the Multiple Prototype Contrastive Learning for FL (FedPCL-M) to the Single Prototype (FedPCL-S), where a single prototype of each class is computed on the server.

2.2 Representative Learning and Contrastive Learning

The study [2] shows that representation learning maps raw data domain to a feature space that makes it easier to extract better representations. Contrastive learning [3,7,11,12] is a self-supervised representation learning algorithm minimizing the InfoNCE loss, the key idea of which is that semantically similar (positive) pairs of data point are pulled closer while dissimilar (negative) pairs are pushed apart. SimCLR [3] proposes a simple framework and systematically examines the primary components of contrastive learning. In subsequent studies [7,11], MLP projection head and stronger data augmentation are employed as fundamental components. SupCon [11] extends the self-supervised contrastive learning to the fully-supervised setting, leveraging label information effectively. PCL [12] proposes the ProtoNCE loss, which uses representation centroids as prototypes.

3 Prototype Contrastive Learning for Federated Learning

This section introduces FedPCL, an innovative federated learning framework, and its overview is shown in Fig. 1. FedPCL uses an Expectation Maximization (EM) algorithm, where the E-step occurs in the previous round of federated communication, and the M-step occurs in the current round. In the following,

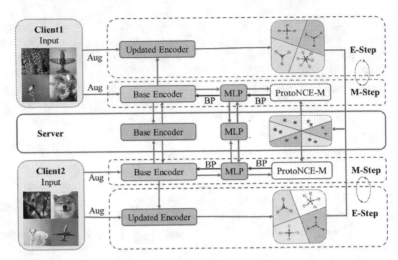

Fig. 1. The framework overview of FedPCL-M. The server broadcasts the global model and prototypes to the clients, each of which executes an EM iteration. In M-step, the clients update the received model by minimizing the ProtoNCE-M loss. In E-step, the clients update their prototypes. Finally, the clients upload their models and prototypes.

we first give relevant notations and problem statement, then show the theoretical frameworks of FedPCL-M and FedPCL-S, and give the algorithm procedure.

3.1 Notations and Problem Statement

Suppose there are K clients and the client k has a local dataset $\mathcal{D}_k$. Let $X_k \in \mathbb{R}^{N_k \times d}$, where it represents a dataset consisting of multiple vector data points x on client k, and the corresponding label $Y_k \in \mathbb{R}^{N_k \times c}$. X is the observed global data, $X = \sum_{k=1}^{K} X_k$ and Y is the label associated with X, $Y = \sum_{k=1}^{K} Y_k$. N_k denotes the number of data points on client k, N is the total number of data points, $N = \sum_{k=1}^{K} N_k$, d represents the input dimension and c is the number of classes. Let Z_k denotes the local prototypes on client k and $Z_k \in \mathbb{R}^{c_k \times r}$, where c_k is the number of the classes on client k and r represents the dimension of the prototype. Z denotes the global prototypes and $\bar{Z}$ denotes the average prototypes computed on sever.

A model parameterized by $\boldsymbol{\theta}$ consists of two components: a base encoder and a MLP projection head, which are parameterized by $\boldsymbol{\theta}_e$ and $\boldsymbol{\theta}_h$ respectively. Let $v = f(x; \boldsymbol{\theta})$ and it denotes the output of the whole model.

To obtain a global base encoder, the objective of the sever is to find the model parameters $\boldsymbol{\theta}$ that maximizes the log-likelihood function:

$$\boldsymbol{\theta}^* = \arg\max_{\boldsymbol{\theta}} \log p(X, Y; \boldsymbol{\theta}) \tag{1}$$

3.2 Multiple Prototypes Contrastive Learning for Federated Learning

As previously mentioned, the server maintains multiple prototypes Z in the embedding space, serving as the latent variables associated with the observed global data X. As a result, the log-likelihood function can be rephrased as follows:

$$\boldsymbol{\theta}^* = \arg\max_{\boldsymbol{\theta}} \sum_{i=1}^{N} \log \sum_{z \in Z} p(x_i, y_i, z; \boldsymbol{\theta}) \qquad (2)$$

where $x_i \in X$ and its label is y_i. However, the server cannot access the data on the clients and the prototypes cannot be calculated directly, so the prototypes can only be updated and uploaded by the clients:

$$Z = \{Z_k\}_{k=1}^{K} \qquad (3)$$

where $Z_k = \{z_i\}_{i=1}^{c_k}$ and z_i is the prototype of class i and c_k is the number of classes on client k, so (2) can be rewritten as:

$$\boldsymbol{\theta}^* = \arg\max_{\boldsymbol{\theta}} \sum_{k=1}^{K} \sum_{i=1}^{N_k} \log \sum_{k'=1}^{K} \sum_{z \in Z_{k'}} p(x_i, y_i, z; \boldsymbol{\theta}) \qquad (4)$$

(4) represents the maximum likelihood value of the data across all clients, where z is a latent variable associated with each client. It is hard to optimize (4) directly. Following the previous work [12], we use ProtoNCE loss to tackle this difficulty within an Expectation-Maximization framework. The ultimate objective is presented as follows:

$$\boldsymbol{\theta}^* = \arg\min_{\boldsymbol{\theta}} \sum_{k=1}^{K} \sum_{i=1}^{N_k} \sum_{k'=1}^{K} - \log \frac{\exp\left(\cos(v_i, z_{s_{k'}}) / \phi_{s_{k'}} \right)}{\sum_{j_{k'}=1}^{c_{k'}} \exp\left(\cos(v_i, z_{j_{k'}}) / \phi_{j_{k'}} \right)} \qquad (5)$$

where $v_i = f(x_i; \boldsymbol{\theta}^k)$, $z_{s_{k'}}$ denotes the prototype of class s on the client k', and the label of x_i is s. The class prototype is used as the anchor point to make v_i closer to the class prototype $z_{s_{k'}}$ and farther away from other prototype $z_{j_{k'}}$. Besides, $\phi_{s_{k'}}$ denotes the concentration level of the representation distribution around the prototype $z_{s_{k'}}$ and it is defined as:

$$\phi_{s_{k'}} = \frac{\sum_{m'=1}^{M'} ||v_{m'} - z_{s_{k'}}||_2}{M' \log(M' + \alpha)} \qquad (6)$$

where $v_{m'}$ belongs to the prototype $z_{s_{k'}}$ and α is a smoothing parameter used to prevent excessively large ϕ values for prototypes with few data representations. Additionally, we normalize ϕ for each set of prototypes $Z_{k'}$ on client k'.

E-step: To solve (5), each client k' calculates $Z_{k'}$. Specifically, $z_{s_{k'}}$ is the mean vector of the embedded training data associated with class s on client k' and it is a hard clustering.

$$z_{s_{k'}} = \frac{1}{|\{X_{k'}|y_i = s\}|} \sum_{(x_i,y_i)\in\{X_{k'}|y_i=s\}} f(x_i;\boldsymbol{\theta}_e^{k'}) \qquad (7)$$

where $\boldsymbol{\theta}_e^{k'}$ represents the local base encoder updated by the client k'.

M-step: The client k initializes its model with the received global model θ and optimizes the local model $\boldsymbol{\theta}^k$ by minimizing ProtoNCE-M loss with the prototypes Z.

$$L_M(x_i, y_i; \boldsymbol{\theta}^k) = -\sum_{i=1}^{N_k}\sum_{k'=1}^{K} \log \frac{\exp\left(\cos(v_i, z_{s_{k'}})/\phi_{s_{k'}}\right)}{\sum_{j_{k'}=1}^{c_{k'}} \exp\left(\cos(v_i, z_{j_{k'}})/\phi_{j_{k'}}\right)} \qquad (8)$$

During each round of FL, clients update their local model and calculate the prototypes using their individual data, and then upload them to the server.

3.3   The Extension to a Single Prototype Contrastive Learning for Federated Learning

When computing resources are limited, it becomes challenging to optimize (8) because of the need to calculate the similarity of v_i to all other client prototypes. It is the increasing linear complexity with respect to the number of clients. As a solution, we propose an extension of the Multiple Prototypes Contrastive Learning for FL (FedPCL-M) to A Single Prototype Contrastive Learning (FedPCL-S). FedPCL-S works by aggregating multiple client prototypes $\{z_{i_k}\}_{k=1}^K$ into a single prototype $\bar{z}_i$. $\bar{z}_i$ is computed on the server and it is the mean of the prototypes with the same label across all clients.

$$\bar{z}_i = \frac{1}{K}\sum_{k=1}^{K} z_{i_k} \qquad (9)$$

We replace the normalized concentration parameter ϕ with the temperature parameter τ and the ProtoNCE-S loss is as follows:

$$L_S(x_i, y_i; \boldsymbol{\theta}^k) = -\sum_{i=1}^{N_k} \log \frac{\exp\left(\cos(v_i, \bar{z}_s)/\tau\right)}{\sum_{j=1}^{c} \exp\left(\cos(v_i, \bar{z}_j)/\tau\right)} \qquad (10)$$

where x_i belongs to class s and $\bar{z}_s$ is a single prototype calculated by the server.

The algorithms for FedPCL-M and FedPCL-S are described in Alg. 1. During the first round of federated training, the server only transmits the initialized global model to the clients. The clients compute prototypes using the received base encoder without performing gradient descent, and then upload the prototypes to the server. In each subsequent round, the server sends the global model and prototypes to the clients. In FedPCL-S, the server calculates $\bar{z}_i$ based on (9). In FedPCL-M and FedPCL-S, the client updates the model parameters according to (8) and (10), respectively. FedPCL iteratively applies the aforementioned process, combined with the EM algorithm, until the model converges.

Algorithm 1: FedPCL-M and FedPCL-S

Input: local dataset $\mathcal{D}_k$, number of clients K, communication rounds R,
         number of local epoch E, local minibatch size B, learning rate η.
Output: the base encoder $\boldsymbol{\theta}^R$

1   **Server executes :**
2   initial $\boldsymbol{\theta}^0$ and $Z = \emptyset$ ($\&\bar{Z}$ in FedPCL-S)
3   **for** $r = 0, 1, ..., R - 1$ **do**
4   **for** $k = 1, 2, ..., K$ **do**
5   send global model $\boldsymbol{\theta}^r$ and prototypes Z^r $(\bar{Z}^r)$ to client k
6         $\boldsymbol{\theta}^{k,r}, Z_k^r \longleftarrow$ **LocalTraining**$(k, \boldsymbol{\theta}^r, Z^r(\bar{Z}^r))$
7      $\boldsymbol{\theta}^{r+1} \longleftarrow \sum_{k=1}^K \frac{N_k}{N} \boldsymbol{\theta}^{k,r}$
8   **if** $FedPCL - S$ **then**
9   Update $\bar{Z}^{r+1}$

10   **return** $\boldsymbol{\theta}^{R-1}$
11   **LocalTraining** $(k, \boldsymbol{\theta}^r, Z^r(\bar{Z}^r))$:
12   $\boldsymbol{\theta}^{k,r} \longleftarrow \boldsymbol{\theta}^r$
13   **if** $Z = \emptyset$ **then**
14   Update Z_k^r

15   **else**
16   **for** $epoch = 1, 2, ..., E$ **do**
17   **for** $each\ batch\ \boldsymbol{b} = \{x_i, y_i\}_{i=1}^B$ **do**
18   **if** $FedPCL - M$ **then**
19              $l \longleftarrow \sum_{i=1}^B L_M(x_i, y_i; \boldsymbol{\theta}^{k,r})$
20   **else if** $FedPCL - S$ **then**
21              $l \longleftarrow \sum_{i=1}^B L_S(x_i, y_i; \boldsymbol{\theta}^{k,r})$
22            $\boldsymbol{\theta}^{k,r} \longleftarrow \boldsymbol{\theta}^{k,r} - \eta \nabla l$

23   Update Z_k^r
24   **return** $\boldsymbol{\theta}^{k,r}, Z_k^r$

---

4   Experiments

4.1   Experiment Setup

Baselines. FTFA [4] uses FedAvg [15] as a warm-start for local training. FedRep [5] iteratively updates the local header and global feature extractor. Fed-BABU [17] only updates the body of the model during training. Per-FedAvg [6] learns an initial shared model that can be generalized quickly.

Dataset. We conduct experiments on three image datasets: MNIST, CIFAR-10 and CIFAR-100. Like previous works [13], we model Non-IID data distributions using a Direchlet distribution $\text{Dir}(\beta)$, in which a smaller value of β indicates greater data heterogeneity. The data on each client is randomly split with 60% for training and 40% for testing.

FedAvg   FedBABU   FedRep

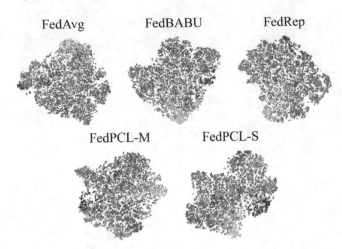

FedPCL-M   FedPCL-S

Fig. 2. t-SNE visualization of the learned representations on CIFAR-10, where different colors represent different categories

Local Model. We use a CNN network consisting of two 5×5 convolution layers, each followed by 2×2 max pooling, and a fully connected layer with 50 units and ReLU activation. It is used as the base encoder for MNIST. For CIFAR-10, we use the same CNN network with two fully connected layers following the convolutional layers as the base encoder. For CIFAR-100, a ResNet-18 without the linear classification layer is used as the base encoder. All base encoders are followed by a MLP projection head helping increase nonlinearity.

4.2   Implement Details

We implement FedPCL and the other baselines in PyTorch. Unless otherwise specified, we use 10 clients for all datasets and all clients are sampled in each communication round. We use the SGD optimizer, with a learning rate of 0.01 for all approach. The SGD weight decay is set to 0.00001, and the SGD momentum is set to 0.9. The local epoch is set to 4, and the local batch size is set to 128 for all FL approaches. The value of β is set to 0.9. For FedPCL-S, we set the temperature parameter to 0.1.

4.3   Visualization of Learning Representation

In Fig. 2, we visualize the learned representations of CIFAR-10 training images using t-SNE. Compared to the representations learned by FedAvg [15], Fed-BABU [17] and FedRep [5], the representations learned by the proposed FedPCL are more compact and have lower entropy.

Table 1. Personalized accuracy comparison under various settings

Dataset	Method	Direchlet(β)		
		0.9	0.5	0.1
MNIST	FedPCL-M(Ours)	**94.91 ± 0.81**	95.23 ± 0.79	95.28 ± 0.60
	FedPCL-S(Ours)	94.23 ± 1.06	94.59 ± 1.02	94.89 ± 0.98
	FTFA	94.43 ± 0.81	**95.36 ± 0.98**	95.47 ± 0.89
	FedBABU	94.40 ± 0.76	95.15 ± 1.02	**95.60 ± 0.84**
	FedRep	91.21 ± 1.25	95.03 ± 1.17	95.26 ± 0.93
	Per-FedAvg	93.86 ± 0.64	94.55 ± 1.31	94.36 ± 1.07
CIFAR-10	FedPCL-M(Ours)	63.73 ± 3.29	**68.02 ± 5.82**	**80.32 ± 9.53**
	FedPCL-S(Ours)	**63.84 ± 3.39**	67.28 ± 5.50	79.81 ± 9.29
	FTFA	60.32 ± 3.99	64.37 ± 6.09	78.85 ± 9.76
	FedBABU	60.32 ± 4.05	64.67 ± 6.11	79.66 ± 9.75
	FedRep	61.58 ± 4.06	65.34 ± 5.80	79.45 ± 9.77
	Per-FedAvg	61.98 ± 3.86	65.41 ± 5.78	79.02 ± 9.45
CIFAR-100	FedPCL-M(Ours)	**48.97 ± 1.82**	**53.36 ± 3.87**	**66.92 ± 4.38**
	FedPCL-S(Ours)	48.61 ± 2.64	52.87 ± 4.09	65.51 ± 4.11
	FTFA	39.75 ± 2.99	48.49 ± 3.63	59.01 ± 3.34
	FedBABU	40.05 ± 2.61	48.28 ± 3.27	58.92 ± 3.41
	FedRep	26.48 ± 2.56	29.67 ± 2.48	39.32 ± 3.54
	Per-FedAvg	33.50 ± 4.29	35.27 ± 4.46	36.48 ± 5.56

4.4   Performance Overview

In Table 1, we present the average accuracy and variance of personalized models across all clients. We find that FedAvg [15] provides a strong baseline but FedPCL outperforms in most cases.

Impacts of Different Datasets. On MNIST, the performances of FedPCL-M and FedPCL-S are comparable to that of most methods based on representation learning. However, the variance of clients' accuracy is consistently the smallest in FedPCL-M, indicating that the base encoder learned by FedPCL-M can be stably generalized. For CIFAR-10 and CIFAR-100, our methods consistently outperform other methods, especially on CIFAR-100. This is due to the use of ResNet-18 with BN layers. The parameters of the BN layers imply the statistical information of the local data. Averaging them across clients results in the aggravation of the negative impact of data heterogeneity.

Impacts of Data Heterogeneity. Our Methods are highly robust algorithms that perform excellently across varying levels of data heterogeneity. As mentioned in Sect. 4.1, a smaller value of β indicates a higher heterogeneity and fewer data categories to which clients are assigned. It makes the convergence more challenging for global model but it simplifies the local task by reducing the number of assigned categories, resulting in higher average accuracy.

Table 2. The performance on unseen clients

Method	CIFAR-10	CIFAR-100	MNIST
FedPCL-M(Ours)	62.85 ± 4.56	$\mathbf{59.02 \pm 2.07}$	$\mathbf{94.76 \pm 1.24}$
FedPCL-S(Ours)	$\mathbf{62.88 \pm 4.55}$	58.01 ± 2.94	94.23 ± 1.20
FAFT	60.23 ± 4.50	44.82 ± 2.04	94.39 ± 1.24
FedBABU	60.14 ± 4.58	44.82 ± 2.04	94.28 ± 1.31
FedRep	61.06 ± 4.51	27.24 ± 2.64	91.81 ± 1.91
Per-FedAvg	60.16 ± 4.30	25.53 ± 4.41	93.88 ± 1.53

Table 3. The performance on different numbers of clients on CIFAR-10

Method	$K = 10$	$K = 20$	$K = 50$
FedPCL-M(Ours)	63.73 ± 3.29	$\mathbf{61.78 \pm 4.10}$	$\mathbf{60.84 \pm 6.29}$
FedPCL-S(Ours)	$\mathbf{63.84 \pm 3.39}$	61.68 ± 4.58	59.12 ± 6.29
FAFT	60.32 ± 3.99	59.26 ± 4.98	59.75 ± 5.94
FedBABU	60.32 ± 4.05	59.69 ± 4.86	59.45 ± 5.81
FedRep	61.58 ± 4.06	59.49 ± 4.94	54.46 ± 6.54
Per-FedAvg	61.98 ± 3.86	61.38 ± 4.63	60.14 ± 5.67

4.5 Scalability Analysis

Table 1 provides evidence that FedPCL-M exhibits lower accuracy variance compared to other methods, suggesting that the base encoder generalizes well. We perform more experiments to conduct a more in-depth analysis.

Performance on Unseen Clients. We perform an experiment to verify its generalization capabilities by applying the base encoder learned by FedPCL to unseen clients. In particular, we set the number of clients to 10, β to 0.9, and present the results in Table 2. Interestingly, we observe a similar performance trend, indicating that the base encoder can be adapted to local tasks for both participating and non-participating clients in the federation process.

Effects of the Number of Client. To demonstrate the scalability of FedPCL, we assess its capabilities with a larger number of clients on CIFAR-10. We conduct two experiments: (1) the dataset is partitioned into 20 clients, and all clients participate in each round. (2) the dataset is partitioned into 50 clients and we randomly select 20 clients in each round. We present the results in Table 3. Remarkably, FedPCL-M consistently outperforms all other methods, with FedPCL-S coming in a close second with a high number of clients.

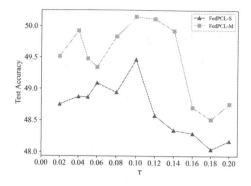

Fig. 3. Effect of τ on the test accuracy of FedPCL on CIFAR-10

Impacts of Temperature. As specified in Sect. 3.3, we utilize ϕ to evaluate the degree of dispersion of the embedding distribution surrounding each prototype in FedPCL-M. A larger value of ϕ implies more dispersion, which is normalized with a mean of τ on each client. Besides, FedPCL-S replaces ϕ with the temperature parameter τ. In this study, we examine the performance of FedPCL with different values of τ. Figure 3 highlights that the normalized ϕ in FedPCL-M provides high and consistent accuracy within a specific range of τ. However, to obtain optimum accuracy in FedPCL-S, it needs to search for an appropriate temperature value.

5   Conclusion

In this work, we propose FedPCL to learn a global base encoder, which extracts more compact representations. FedPCL aggregates knowledge learned by local models not only in the parameter space, but also in the embedding space. When the global model converges, the clients adapt the global base encoder to local tasks to achieve personalization. Considering the resource constraints of the clients, we extend FedPCL-M to FedPCL-S. Our extensive experiments show that FedPCL achieves significant improvements and can be generalized stably to unseen clients. To investigate FedPCL in greater depth in the future, we will try variational prototypes or generative models.

Acknowledgment. This work was supported in part by the National Natural Science Foundation of China under Grant 62076179.

References

1. Arivazhagan, M.G., Aggarwal, V., Singh, A.K., Choudhary, S.: Federated learning with personalization layers. arXiv preprint arXiv:1912.00818 (2019)
2. Bengio, Y., Courville, A., Vincent, P.: Representation learning: a review and new perspectives. IEEE Trans. Pattern Anal. Mach. Intell. **35**(8), 1798–1828 (2013)

3. Chen, T., Kornblith, S., Norouzi, M., Hinton, G.: A simple framework for contrastive learning of visual representations. In: International Conference on Machine Learning, pp. 1597–1607 (2020)
4. Cheng, G., Chadha, K., Duchi, J.: Fine-tuning is fine in federated learning. arXiv preprint arXiv:2108.07313 (2021)
5. Collins, L., Hassani, H., Mokhtari, A., Shakkottai, S.: Exploiting shared representations for personalized federated learning. In: International Conference on Machine Learning, pp. 2089–2099 (2021)
6. Fallah, A., Mokhtari, A., Ozdaglar, A.: Personalized federated learning: A meta-learning approach. arXiv preprint arXiv:2002.07948 (2020)
7. Grill, J.B., et al.: Bootstrap your own latent-a new approach to self-supervised learning. Adv. Neural. Inf. Process. Syst. **33**, 21271–21284 (2020)
8. Hanzely, F., Richtárik, P.: Federated learning of a mixture of global and local models. arXiv preprint arXiv:2002.05516 (2020)
9. Jiang, Y., Konečný, J., Rush, K., Kannan, S.: Improving federated learning personalization via model agnostic meta learning. arXiv preprint arXiv:1909.12488 (2019)
10. Kairouz, P., et al.: Advances and open problems in federated learning. Found. Trends® Mach. Learn. **14**(1–2), 1–210 (2021)
11. Khosla, P., et al.: Supervised contrastive learning. Adv. Neural. Inf. Process. Syst. **33**, 18661–18673 (2020)
12. Li, J., Zhou, P., Xiong, C., Hoi, S.C.: Prototypical contrastive learning of unsupervised representations. arXiv preprint arXiv:2005.04966 (2020)
13. Li, Q., He, B., Song, D.: Model-contrastive federated learning. In: Proceedings of the IEEE/CVF Conference on Computer Vision and Pattern Recognition, pp. 10713–10722 (2021)
14. Li, T., Sahu, A.K., Talwalkar, A., Smith, V.: Federated learning: challenges, methods, and future directions. IEEE Signal Process. Mag. **37**(3), 50–60 (2020)
15. McMahan, B., Moore, E., Ramage, D., Hampson, S., y Arcas, B.A.: Communication-efficient learning of deep networks from decentralized data. In: Artificial Intelligence and Statistics, pp. 1273–1282 (2017)
16. Mu, X., et al.: Fedproc: prototypical contrastive federated learning on non-iid data. Futur. Gener. Comput. Syst. **143**, 93–104 (2023)
17. OH, J.H., Kim, S., Yun, S.: Fedbabu: Toward enhanced representation for federated image classification. In: 10th International Conference on Learning Representations, ICLR 2022. International Conference on Learning Representations (ICLR) (2022)
18. Pillutla, K., Malik, K., Mohamed, A.R., Rabbat, M., Sanjabi, M., Xiao, L.: Federated learning with partial model personalization. In: International Conference on Machine Learning, pp. 17716–17758 (2022)
19. Tan, Y., et al.: Fedproto: Federated prototype learning across heterogeneous clients. In: Proceedings of the AAAI Conference on Artificial Intelligence. vol. 36, pp. 8432–8440 (2022)

PTSTEP: Prompt Tuning for Semantic Typing of Event Processes

Wenhao Zhu[1,2], Yongxiu Xu[1,2], Hongbo Xu[1,2(✉)], Minghao Tang[1,2], and Dongwei Zhu[1,2]

[1] Institute of Information Engineering, Chinese Academy of Sciences, Beijing, China

[2] School of Cyber Security, University of Chinese Academy of Sciences, Beijing, China
hbxu@iie.ac.cn

Abstract. Giving machines the ability to understand the intent of human actions is a basic goal of Natural Language Understanding. In the context of that, a task called the Multi-axis Event Processes Typing is proposed, which aims to comprehend the overall goal of an event sequence from the aspect of action and object. Existing works utilize fine-tuning to mine the semantic information of the event processes in the pre-trained language models and achieve good performance. Prompt tuning is effective in fully exploiting the capabilities of pre-trained language models. To mine more sufficient semantic information of the event process, it is crucial to utilize appropriate prompts to guide the pre-trained language models. Moreover, most existing prompt tuning methods use unified prompt encodings. Due to the complex correlations between events of event processes, it is hard to capture context-sensitive semantic information of the event processes. In this paper, we propose PTSTEP, an encoder-decoder based method with continuous prompts. Specifically, we propose a context-aware prompt encoder to obtain a more expressive continuous prompt. Parameters in the pre-trained language model are fixed. On the encoder, the continuous prompt guide the model to mine more semantic information of the event process. On the decoder, the context-aware continuous prompt guide the model to better understand the event processes. PTSTEP outperforms the state-of-the-art method by 0.82% and 3.74% respectively on action MRR and object MRR. The significant improvements prove the effectiveness of our method.

Keywords: Event processes understanding · Semantic Typing · Prompt Tuning

1 Introduction

The comprehension of events is a fundamental part of the human perceptual system. According to findings from cognitive research [7,23], humans assume the objectives of co-occurring events to understand event processes. Inspired by that, Chen et al. [4] propose the Multi-axis Event Process Typing task, which utilizes

L. Iliadis et al. (Eds.): ICANN 2023, LNCS 14256, pp. 541–553, 2023.
https://doi.org/10.1007/978-3-031-44213-1_45

ultra-fine-grained types to summarize the goal and intention of the systematically connected events. Specifically, each event process is classified along two axes: action type and object type. The action type represents the movement that the event process seeks to accomplish, while the object type represents the item that is affected by the action of the performer. For example, if a performer takes the following steps, 1. *set locations and dates*, 2. *open the flight booking app*, 3. *compare airfares*, 4. *purchase a ticket*, the overall intent is *"book flight"*, where the action is *book* and the object is *flight*. Although it is easy for humans to deduce the intent of event processes, it is a hard task for machines due to the fact that action and object types may not appear in the event processes. In addition to that, a wide range of downstream tasks can benefit from event processes understanding, such as commonsense reasoning [18], story comprehension for narrative prediction [3], and reading comprehension [1].

However, despite the event processes understanding can benefit a broad range of NLP applications, the recent task of event process typing is still understudied. P2GT [4] utilizes an extra Word Sense Disambiguation (WSD) system to assign glosses to each action and object. Then it ranks their types based on the similarity with input events under indirect supervision. Although incorporated gloss knowledge supports few-shot case prediction, P2GT includes two shortcomings: i) The performance of P2GT depends extremely on the glosses provided by the Word Sense Disambiguation (WSD) system. ii) P2GT requires a fixed sense inventory to define the possible action and object types, which is not in line with the free-form nature of the classes. STEPS [15] considers the free-label nature of classes and achieves state-of-the-art results without using glosses in a sequence-to-sequence manner. STEPS also proves that harsh filtering on dataset harms the sequential nature of event processes. Despite the large boost in performance, STEPS also processes two disadvantages: i) STEPS is sensitive to input in some cases, which means small changes to the input lead to a large change in result. ii) STEPS requires huge time and computing costs during the training stage.

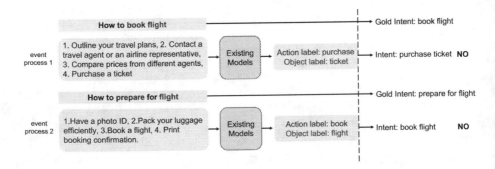

Fig. 1. Two event processes are fed in existing models. Gold action types and objects are boldfaced with green and purple colors respectively. The existing models output incorrect action types and object types. (Color figure online)

Moreover, existing works utilize fine-tuning to mine the semantic information of the event processes in the pre-trained language models and achieve good performance, but they do not fully exploit the capabilities of pre-trained language models, which leads to acquiring insufficient semantic information in event processes. For example, as shown in Fig. 1, existing models deduce that the intent of event process 1 is *purchase ticket*. Although *purchase a ticket* is a key step in the event process of *book flight*, it is not comprehensive to deem that *purchase ticket* fully expresses the overall intention of the event process. Existing models also deduce a secondary intent for event process 2. Prompt tuning is an effective method to fully exploit the capabilities of pre-trained language models. Appropriate prompts can be used to guide the pre-trained language models to mine more sufficient semantic information of the event process. Due to the complex correlations between events in event processes, it is hard to capture context-sensitive semantic information in the event processes. In summary, existing models mine and utilize insufficient semantic information in event processes, which makes it difficult to accurately infer the primary intent of event processes. In order to alleviate this problem, we propose Prompt Tuning for Multi-axis Semantic Typing of Event Processes (PTSTEP), an encoder-decoder based method with continuous prompts. Specifically, we propose a context-aware prompt encoder to obtain a more expressive continuous prompt. PTSTEP freezes the parameters of the pre-trained language model and tunes continuous prompts to gain a more comprehensive understanding of event processes. On the encoder, the continuous prompt guide the model to mine more semantic information in the event process. Due to the fact that the key objective of the task is to mine more sufficient semantic information of event processes, we call this prompt the task-aware continuous prompt. On the decoder, the context-aware continuous prompt guide the model to better understand the event processes. The main contributions of our work are as follows:

(1) We propose a novel method, which uses task-aware and context-aware prompts to guide the model to mine and utilize more sufficient semantic information in event processes.
(2) As far as we know, this is the first work to utilize prompt tuning for multi-axis semantic typing of event processes. We fix the parameters of the pre-trained language model, the trainable parameters is tuned by continuous prompts.
(3) We outperform the state-of-the-art by 0.82% and 3.74% respectively on action MRR and object MRR. The significant improvements prove that PTSTEP can mine and utilize more sufficient semantic information.

2   Related Work

2.1   Event Processes Understanding Task

Understanding event processes has attracted much attention recently. Previous works mainly focus on the completion of event processes and infer the temporal relations between events. As for the completion of event processes, Zhang et al. [24] and Wang et al. [22] predict the future event(s) of a process. Towards inferring the temporal relations, Do et al. [5] constructs a timeline from event processes, Lin et al. [11] deduces the temporal relations between events firstly, then uses a language model to generate events for completion. However, cognitive studies suggest that inferring the intentions behind event processes can better understand event processes. Event2Mind [17] relies on a sequence generation approach to produce the most likely intents and reactions of a participant, given a single-cause free-form event description. P2GT [4] focuses on processes made up of multiple event descriptions and proposes the Multi-axis Semantic Typing of Event Processes task to facilitate understanding the intentions behind event processes. STEPS [15] uses a sequence-to-sequence approach to extract the intentions from the output and achieve the state of the art without using action and object glosses. In addition to this, there are several efforts to downstream applications. A non-exhaustive list includes, Mostafazaedh et al. [14]; Chaturvedi et al. [3] for narrative prediction, Berant et al. [1] for machine comprehension, Zhang et al. [25] for diagnostic prediction.

2.2   Prompt Tuning

According to the shape of the prompt, prefix-style [2] and cloze-style [16] are proposed. Existing works on discrete prompt tuning mainly focus on the classification task, PET [19], AutoPrompt [20] use verbalizers to map from class labels to answer tokens. These methods are effective in the few-shot setting for text classification. There are also methods that explore continuous prompts directly operating in the embedding space of the model. For example, tuning on vectors: PREFIX-TUNING [10] and its simple version proposed by Lester et al. [8]; initializing with discrete prompts: OPTIPROMPT [26] and WARP [6]; use hybrid prompt tuning: P-Tuning [12]. However, most of these continuous methods use unified prompt encodings, which are not able to capture context-aware semantic information.

3   Method

This section introduces the proposed model, named PTSTEP for the Multi-axis Event Process Typing task. We first define the task and notations and depict the sequence-to-sequence formulation. Then we elaborate on our model step by step. Figure 2 gives an overview of our model.

3.1   Task Definition and Formulation

Task Definition. Given a process $\hat{p}$, composed of a sequence of n events $E_{\hat{p}} = e_1^{\hat{p}}, ..., e_n^{\hat{p}}$, the Multi-axis Event Process Typing task aims at classifying $\hat{p}$ in two axes: the type of action the event process seeks to complete ($a_{\hat{p}}$), and the type of object which is affected by the action of the performer ($o_{\hat{p}}$). Both action types ($a_{\hat{p}}$) and object types ($o_{\hat{p}}$) are free-from labels.

Sequence-to-Sequence Formulation. We follow the sequence-to-sequence formulation used in STEPS [15]. In this formulation, a fixed format is designed for output, in which we can extract the action and object types from output tokens. The input sequence of events m is defined as:

$$m= <\text{e1}>, t^1_{e^{\hat{p}}_1}, ..., t^i_{e^{\hat{p}}_1}, ... t^k_{e^{\hat{p}}_1}, </\text{e1}>,$$

$$...,$$

$$<\text{eh}>, t^1_{e^{\hat{p}}_h}, ..., t^j_{e^{\hat{p}}_h}, ... t^l_{e^{\hat{p}}_h}, </\text{eh}>,$$

$$...,$$

$$<\text{en}>, t^1_{e^{\hat{p}}_n}, ..., t^g_{e^{\hat{p}}_n}, ... t^o_{e^{\hat{p}}_n}, </\text{en}>,$$

The $t^j_{e^{\hat{p}}_h}$ represents the j-th token of the h-th event of the process $\hat{p}$ and the special tokens (<eh>, </eh>) are used to separate the h-th event. Output $\hat{s}$ is defined as "*how to* $<a>$ *action* $</a>$ $<o>$ *object* $</o>$", the action and the object types and both can be extracted by leveraging the special markers $[<a>, </a>, <o>, </o>]$. Therefore, the entire probability $p(\hat{s}|m)$ of generating the output sequence $\hat{s}$ given the input sequence m is calculated as

$$p(\hat{s}|m) = \sum_{j=2}^{|\hat{s}|} p(\hat{s}_j | \hat{s}_{1:j-1}, m) \tag{1}$$

3.2 Prompt Tuning

We propose a novel model, which uses the task-aware continuous prompt and context-aware continuous prompt to guide the model to mine and utilize more sufficient semantic information in event processes. Specifically, the task-aware continuous prompt guide the model to mine more semantic information of the event process. The context-aware continuous prompt guide the model to better understand the event processes. Our backbone model BART [9] is parameter-fixed during training and testing.

Task-Aware Continuous Prompt. Inspired by Li et al. [10], we introduce task-aware continuous prompt, which is a pair of two transformer activation sequences $\{tp_{enc}, tp_{dec}\}$, providing trainable context for encoder and decoder, each containing L continuous D-dim vectors as the history values, respectively. As shown in Fig. 2, a trainable embedding tensor $P \in \mathbb{R}^{|\varepsilon| \times L \times D}$, which we call "Prompt Embedding Table", is designed to model the task-aware continuous prompt tp_{dec}, the continuous prompt vector tp_{dec} at index i is

$$tp^i_{dec} = P[i, :] \tag{2}$$

The tp_{enc} can be obtained according to Eq. (2) using different embedding tensor P. The primary objective of the event processes typing task is to mine more semantic information of event processes, we call tp_{enc} and tp_{dec} the task-aware continuous prompt.

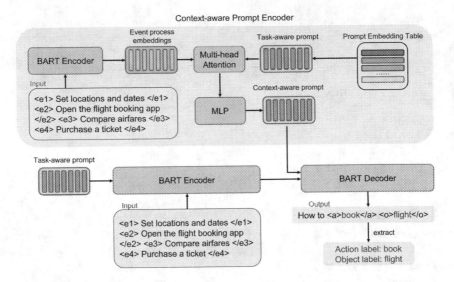

Fig. 2. An overview of our model. We first get task-aware continuous prompts $\{sp_{enc}, sp_{dec}\}$ for mining semantic information in event processes. Secondly, we obtain a context-aware continuous prompt through our prompt encoder, which aims to fully utilize semantic information of event processes from the encoder. Finally, we get outputs and extract labels with the continuous prompts steering the frozen BART model.

Context-Aware Continuous Prompt. As shown in Fig. 2, the task-aware continuous prompt tp_{dec} and event processes are fed in context-aware prompt encoder to obtain context-aware continuous prompt cp_{dec}, which is calculated by the multi-head attention module [21]. To calculate event process embedding e, we reuse the parameter-fixed BART-encoder [9]. L represents the length of continuous prompts. The tp^i_{dec} and cp^i_{dec} have the same prompt length.

$$cp^i_{dec} = \text{MultiHeadAttn}^L_{i=1}(tp^i_{dec}, e)$$
$$e = \text{BARTencoder}(m) \tag{3}$$

Following Li et al. [10], we compute the decoder transformer activation vector h_i, which is a concatenation of all layers, at time step i in the encoder-decoder language model recurrently. LM represents the BART language model.

$$h_i = \begin{cases} cp^i_{dec} & \text{if } i < L, \\ \text{LM}(\hat{s}_i, h_{<i}|m), & \text{otherwise.} \end{cases} \tag{4}$$

Overall, the continuous prompts are virtually prepended for the sequences m and $\hat{s}$ in an encoder-decoder language model.

$$m' = [sp_{enc}; m]$$
$$\hat{s}' = [dp_{dec}; \hat{s}] \tag{5}$$

Due to the interaction between the task-aware prompt tp_{dec} and event processes embeddings, the context-sensitive semantic information is captured by the context-aware continuous prompt cp_{dec}. In summary, the task-aware continuous prompt and the context-aware continuous prompt guide the model to mine and utilize more comprehensive semantic information of event processes.

3.3   Training

In our model, encoder and decoder parameters are fixed, and the trainable parameters involved embedding tensor P and parameters from a multi-head attention module in the context-aware prompt encoder. In addition to that, we reparametrize the embedding tensor P by modeling a MLP and another embedding tensor $P' \in R^{|\varepsilon| \times L \times D'}$ with small dimension $D' < D$. Then P is computed as

$$P[t,:] = MLP(P'[t,:]) \qquad (6)$$

Similar to Eq. 1, by minimizing the cross-entropy loss, We can get more reasonable outputs which leads to more correct semantic typing results.

4   Experiments

4.1   Dataset and Baseline Methods

Dataset. We use the dataset proposed by Chen et al. [4], whose data source is from how-to guides on wikiHow (https://www.wikihow.com). Chen et al. [4] collected 62,277 different event processes with 1,336 action types and 10,441 object types. However, some steps of event processes are filtered out due to harsh dataset filtering. In addition to that, Pepe et al. [15] use the raw data without filtering steps, which is used to evaluate the robustness of their models. This results in a larger dataset of 108,027 instances with longer processes and more noise. We train all the models on a split containing 80% of the whole dataset and use as validation and test sets two equally sized partitions which include the remainder of the data.

Baseline Methods. In addition to the base model, we compare our model with the following baselines: **S2L** [17]: S2L is an encoder-decoder architecture trained to directly map from sequences to unigrams of the types vocabulary. We compare with three different encoder initializations using: RoBERTa (S2L-RoBERTa), a BiGRU RNN (S2L-BiGRU), and a mean-pooling encoder (S2L mean-pool). **P2GT** [4]: Systems under the Process Typing with Gloss Knowledge (P2GT) framework, which utilizes RoBERTa [13] as their pretrained language model. We include in the evaluation both the systems trained on the glosses assigned via the Most Frequent Sense (MFS) and the glosses predicted by the external WSD model they use. We compare with a total of four different models: Single P2GT-MFS (Single training + MFS), Single P2GT-WSD (Single training + Dedicated

WSD system), Joint P2GT-MFS (Joint training of actions and objects + MFS), and Joint P2GT-WSD (Joint training of actions and objects + Dedicated WSD system). **STEPS** [15]: the state-of-the-art systems use a sequence-to-sequence approach, which performs well without glosses. We compare this method in no-gloss settings.

4.2   Main Results

The performance of baselines and our method are shown in Table 1. Firstly, S2L gets the worst performance. The possible reason is that due to the ultra-fine-grained classes, it is difficult to classify types solely based on the training data without any external knowledge. Secondly, P2GT with the Roberta-base model (125 million parameters) performs worse than generative methods with the BART-base model (139 million parameters), such as STEPS and our method. On the one hand, this indicates that generative-based methods can benefit more from pre-trained language models. On the other hand, this means our model can obtain more sufficient semantic information than P2GT. Thirdly, Our model achieves state-of-the-art results in all metrics and performs better than STEPS in the corresponding row. Compared with STEPS under the BART-base No glosses setting, our method shows little improvement on action typing metrics but gets 3.71%, 3.07%, and 4.93% on object typing MRR, recall@1, and recall@10, respectively. Under the BART-large No glosses setting, we get 0.82%, 0.46%, and 0.67% on action typing MRR, recall@1, and recall@10, respectively. As for object typing metrics, we get a 3.74% improvement on MRR, 3.07% improvement on recall@1, and 5.7% improvement on object typing recall@10. Our model has the same

Table 1. Results in the test set in terms of MRR, recall@1, and recall@10. Similar to STEPS, Ours$_{BB}$ and Ours$_{BL}$ denote our system based on BART Base and BART Large models, respectively. The best scores with a specific setting per row block are underlined, while the best across the board are shown in bold. As for our method, we conducted five experiments and calculated the average as the final result.

	Model	Action Typing			Object Typing		
		MRR	recall@1	recall@10	MRR	recall@1	recall@10
S2L	S2L-mean-pool	3.72	1.96	5.95	1.01	0.80	1.66
	S2L-BiGRU	7.94	4.40	12.71	4.20	2.72	6.19
	S2L-RoBERTa	8.36	5.31	14.69	4.88	3.24	8.10
P2GT	Single P2GT-MFS	24.10	19.67	32.40	13.71	8.86	23.09
	Single P2GT-WSD	25.83	19.93	37.50	14.19	9.32	24.84
	Joint P2GT-MFS	28.57	20.63	43.14	15.26	10.62	25.01
	Joint P2GT-WSD	29.11	21.21	42.84	15.70	11.07	25.51
STEPS$_{BB}$	No glosses	39.73	30.68	60.56	20.19	15.11	30.11
STEPS$_{BL}$		41.22	31.97	62.27	21.11	15.51	31.42
Ours$_{BB}$	No glosses	40.69	31.18	60.95	23.90	18.08	35.04
Ours$_{BL}$		**42.04**	**32.43**	**62.94**	**24.85**	**18.58**	**37.12**

model architecture as STEPS. The difference between our model and STEPS is that instead of tuning the LM parameters, our model fixes the LM parameters and tunes the parameters of continuous prompts. Therefore, it is clear that our method can mine more comprehensive semantic information with the task-aware continuous prompt and the context-aware continuous prompt.

4.3 Ablation Study

We consider the only task-aware continuous prompt setting and the hybrid of two kinds of continuous prompt setting in two different-sized models: BART-base and BART-large. As shown in Table 2, under the first setting, models with the task-aware continuous prompt perform comparative or better than existing works, especially STEPS. This proves that the task-aware continuous prompt is able to capture semantic information in event processes. Moreover, under the second setting, our model achieves the best performance in all metrics, which demonstrates that the context-aware continuous prompt is not only able to guide the model to fully utilize the semantic information of event processes but is also useful for mining more sufficient semantic information in event processes.

Table 2. Effectiveness of the task-aware continuous prompt and context-aware continuous prompt on dataset proposed by Chen et al. [4].

Model	Action Typing			Object Typing		
	MRR	recall@1	recall@10	MRR	recall@1	recall@10
Ours$_{BB}$	40.69	31.18	60.95	23.90	18.08	35.04
w/ task-aware prompt	39.37	30.39	59.41	21.69	16.27	32.63
Ours$_{BL}$	42.04	32.43	62.94	24.85	18.58	37.12
w/ task-aware prompt	41.82	32.31	62.19	22.88	17.24	33.96

4.4 Robustness Analysis

Similar to STEPS, we conduct experiments on raw data to evaluate the robustness of our models. As shown in Table 3, our model performs worse than STEPS under the BART-base model setting but performs better under the BART-large setting. This result is, potentially, due to the BART-large model having more parameters, and more semantic information can be mined by the continuous prompts. In summary, experiment results show that our model is robust to longer event processes with noise.

Table 3. Experiment results on raw data without data filtering steps. The final result is calculated by the average of five experiments

Model	Action Typing			Object Typing		
	MRR	recall@1	recall@10	MRR	recall@1	recall@10
STEPS$_{BB}$	50.49	39.43	72.87	33.01	24.41	49.93
STEPS$_{BL}$	51.55	40.38	74.34	35.84	26.28	54.14
Ours$_{BB}$	49.11	37.70	72.43	34.16	25.28	51.62
Ours$_{BL}$	**52.14**	**40.94**	**75.13**	**36.28**	**27.06**	**54.38**

4.5   Case Study

We conduct a case study using the raw data used in STEPS [15]. As shown in Table 4, after feeding three event processes to models, our model outputs more accurate action types and object types compared with STEPS. This indicates that our models can better mine and utilize the semantic information in event processes.

Table 4. The first two event processes express the same intent "*bake cheesecake*", while the intent of the last event process is "*cut cantaloupe*". The predictions are given by STEPS$_{BB}$ and Ours$_{BL}$. Each case is given top 3 predictions on both axes, ground truths are underlined, whereof reasonably correct ones are boldfaced, and relevant ones are italic.

Event Processes	Model	Predictions
1. prepare the pan. 2. blend the crust ingredients. 3. press the crust into the pan. 4. bake the crust. 5. reduce the oven temperature.	Ours	A: make, **bake**, prepare
		O: *pie, tiramisu,* **cheesecake**
	STEPS	A: make, prepare, put
		O: *pie,* apple, crescent
1. beat the cream cheese. 2. mix in the remaining ingredients. 3. heat a pot of water. 4. bake the cake. 5. let the cake cool.	Ours	A: make, **bake**, *heat*
		O: *cake,* cream, **cheesecake**
	STEPS	A: make, mix, *heat*
		O: *cake,* cream, sponge
1. wash and scrub the cantaloupe. 2. cut the melon in half. 3. scoop out the seeds. 4. cut each half into wedges. 5. serve the wedges on the rind.	Ours	A: eat,**cut**, make
		O: **cantaloupe**, wedges, salad
	STEPS	A:make, eat, prepare
		O: wedges, **cantaloupe**, wedge

5 Conclusions

We propose a novel method, which uses task-aware continuous prompt and context-aware continuous prompt to guide the model to capture and utilize more comprehensive semantic information of event processes. Experiment results prove the effectiveness of our model, and results on raw data verify the robustness of our method. However, one limitation is that the number of parameters of the model affects the performance obviously. For future work, we are interested in alleviating the problem caused by the long-tail effect of the data.

Acknowledgements. This work was supported by the Strategic Priority Research Program of Chinese Academy of Sciencecs, Grant NO.XDC02040400.

References

1. Berant, J., et al.: Modeling biological processes for reading comprehension. In: Proceedings of the 2014 Conference on Empirical Methods in Natural Language Processing (EMNLP), pp. 1499–1510 (2014)
2. Brown, T., et al.: Language models are few-shot learners. Adv. Neural. Inf. Process. Syst. **33**, 1877–1901 (2020)
3. Chaturvedi, S., Peng, H., Roth, D.: Story comprehension for predicting what happens next. In: Proceedings of the 2017 Conference on Empirical Methods in Natural Language Processing, pp. 1603–1614 (2017)
4. Chen, M., Zhang, H., Wang, H., Roth, D.: What are you trying to do? semantic typing of event processes. In: Fernández, R., Linzen, T. (eds.) Proceedings of the 24th Conference on Computational Natural Language Learning, CoNLL 2020, Online, November 19–20, 2020, pp. 531–542. Association for Computational Linguistics (2020). https://doi.org/10.18653/v1/2020.conll-1.43
5. Do, Q., Lu, W., Roth, D.: Joint inference for event timeline construction. In: Proceedings of the 2012 Joint Conference on Empirical Methods in Natural Language Processing and Computational Natural Language Learning, pp. 677–687 (2012)
6. Hambardzumyan, K., Khachatrian, H., May, J.: Warp: Word-level adversarial reprogramming. In: Proceedings of the 59th Annual Meeting of the Association for Computational Linguistics and the 11th International Joint Conference on Natural Language Processing (Volume 1: Long Papers), pp. 4921–4933 (2021)
7. Kurby, C.A., Zacks, J.M.: Segmentation in the perception and memory of events. Trends Cogn. Sci. **12**(2), 72–79 (2008)
8. Lester, B., Al-Rfou, R., Constant, N.: The power of scale for parameter-efficient prompt tuning. In: Proceedings of the 2021 Conference on Empirical Methods in Natural Language Processing, pp. 3045–3059 (2021)
9. Lewis, M., et al.: BART: Denoising sequence-to-sequence pre-training for natural language generation, translation, and comprehension. In: Proceedings of the 58th Annual Meeting of the Association for Computational Linguistics. Association for Computational Linguistics, Online (2020)
10. Li, X.L., Liang, P.: Prefix-tuning: Optimizing continuous prompts for generation. In: Proceedings of the 59th Annual Meeting of the Association for Computational Linguistics and the 11th International Joint Conference on Natural Language Processing (Volume 1: Long Papers). Association for Computational Linguistics, Online (2021)

11. Lin, S.T., Chambers, N., Durrett, G.: Conditional generation of temporally-ordered event sequences. In: Proceedings of the 59th Annual Meeting of the Association for Computational Linguistics and the 11th International Joint Conference on Natural Language Processing (Volume 1: Long Papers), pp. 7142–7157 (2021)

12. Liu, X., et al.: P-tuning: Prompt tuning can be comparable to fine-tuning across scales and tasks. In: Proceedings of the 60th Annual Meeting of the Association for Computational Linguistics (Volume 2: Short Papers), pp. 61–68 (2022)

13. Liu, Y., et al.: Roberta: A robustly optimized BERT pretraining approach. CoRR abs/1907.11692 (2019)

14. Mostafazadeh, N., Roth, M., Louis, A., Chambers, N., Allen, J.: Lsdsem 2017 shared task: The story cloze test. In: Proceedings of the 2nd Workshop on Linking Models of Lexical, Sentential and Discourse-level Semantics, pp. 46–51 (2017)

15. Pepe, S., Barba, E., Blloshmi, R., Navigli, R.: Steps: Semantic typing of event processes with a sequence-to-sequence approach. In: Proceedings of the AAAI Conference on Artificial Intelligence. vol. 36, pp. 11156–11164 (2022)

16. Petroni, F., et al.: Language models as knowledge bases? In: Proceedings of the 2019 Conference on Empirical Methods in Natural Language Processing and the 9th International Joint Conference on Natural Language Processing (EMNLP-IJCNLP), pp. 2463–2473 (2019)

17. Rashkin, H., Sap, M., Allaway, E., Smith, N.A., Choi, Y.: Event2mind: Commonsense inference on events, intents, and reactions. In: Proceedings of the 56th Annual Meeting of the Association for Computational Linguistics (Volume 1: Long Papers), pp. 463–473 (2018)

18. Sap, M., et al.: Atomic: An atlas of machine commonsense for if-then reasoning. In: Proceedings of the AAAI Conference On Artificial Intelligence, vol. 33, pp. 3027–3035 (2019)

19. Schick, T., Schmid, H., Schütze, H.: Automatically identifying words that can serve as labels for few-shot text classification. In: Proceedings of the 28th International Conference on Computational Linguistics, pp. 5569–5578 (2020)

20. Shin, T., Razeghi, Y., Logan IV, R.L., Wallace, E., Singh, S.: Autoprompt: Eliciting knowledge from language models with automatically generated prompts. In: Proceedings of the 2020 Conference on Empirical Methods in Natural Language Processing (EMNLP), pp. 4222–4235 (2020)

21. Vaswani, A., et al.: Attention is all you need. In: Advances in Neural Information Processing Systems 30: Annual Conference on Neural Information Processing Systems 2017, December 4–9, 2017, Long Beach, CA, USA, pp. 5998–6008 (2017)

22. Wang, Z., Zhang, H., Fang, T., Song, Y., Wong, G.Y., See, S.: Subeventwriter: Iterative sub-event sequence generation with coherence controller. In: Goldberg, Y., Kozareva, Z., Zhang, Y. (eds.) Proceedings of the 2022 Conference on Empirical Methods in Natural Language Processing, EMNLP 2022, Abu Dhabi, United Arab Emirates, December 7–11, 2022, pp. 1590–1604. Association for Computational Linguistics (2022). https://aclanthology.org/2022.emnlp-main.103

23. Zacks, J.M., Tversky, B.: Event structure in perception and conception. Psychol. Bull. **127**(1), 3 (2001)

24. Zhang, H., Chen, M., Wang, H., Song, Y., Roth, D.: Analogous process structure induction for sub-event sequence prediction. In: Proceedings of the 2020 Conference on Empirical Methods in Natural Language Processing (EMNLP), pp. 1541–1550 (2020)

25. Zhang, T., Chen, M., Bui, A.A.T.: Diagnostic prediction with sequence-of-sets representation learning for clinical events. In: Michalowski, M., Moskovitch, R. (eds.) AIME 2020. LNCS (LNAI), vol. 12299, pp. 348–358. Springer, Cham (2020). https://doi.org/10.1007/978-3-030-59137-3_31

26. Zhong, Z., Friedman, D., Chen, D.: Factual probing is [mask]: Learning vs. learning to recall. In: Proceedings of the 2021 Conference of the North American Chapter of the Association for Computational Linguistics: Human Language Technologies, pp. 5017–5033 (2021)

SR-IDS: A Novel Network Intrusion Detection System Based on Self-taught Learning and Representation Learning

Qinghao Wang, Geying Yang, Lina Wang[✉], Jie Fu, and Xiaowen Liu

School of Cyber Science and Engineering, Wuhan University, Wuhan, China
{anthony,yanggeying,lnwang,whuerfu,2021202210085}@whu.edu.cn

Abstract. As a proactive network security protection scheme, network intrusion detection system (NIDS) has become a powerful tool for early warning of computer and communication systems attacks. However, traditional machine learning methods struggle to pay attention to both spatial and temporal features of network traffic simultaneously, resulting in poor detection performance. In this paper, we propose SR-IDS, an Intrusion Detection System based on Self-taught learning and Representation learning, which consists of one-dimensional stacked convolutional autoencoders (1D-SCAE) and bidirectional gated recurrent units (BiGRU). SR-IDS can extract spatial features through 1D-SCAE and abstract temporal features via BiGRU. It uses self-taught learning and representation learning to simultaneously focus on the spatial and temporal characteristics of network traffic, overcoming the challenges of traditional methods in feature extraction. Experiments show that our SR-IDS model can distinguish the network traffic with 98.90% accuracy on the UNSW-NB15 dataset.

Keywords: Convolutional autoencoders · Feature extraction · Recurrent neural networks · Traffic intrusion detection

1 Introduction

Network intrusion detection system (NIDS) monitors all traffic in the network and detects each data packet passing through the web. Many researchers have begun studying intrusion detection techniques to deal with network attacks effectively. In classification problems, machine learning algorithms perform feature extraction to identify malicious behaviors in network traffic [8]. However, the statistical characteristics of traffic have changed considerably in terms of network architectures and applications today. Traditional machine learning methods have been powerless to efficiently and accurately abstract spatial and temporal features of abnormal traffic.

Self-taught learning is a typical machine learning framework for using unlabeled data in supervised classification tasks [22]. The method does not require the assumption that unlabeled data follows the same distribution as labeled data.

© The Author(s), under exclusive license to Springer Nature Switzerland AG 2023
L. Iliadis et al. (Eds.): ICANN 2023, LNCS 14256, pp. 554–565, 2023.
https://doi.org/10.1007/978-3-031-44213-1_46

Besides, representation learning analyzes the characteristic of data that makes it easier to extract helpful information when building predictors [5]. Inspired by the above ideas, we develop a noval network intrusion detection system based on self-taught learning and representation learning.

General traffic features can be divided into two categories: spatial features, such as data packet features, and temporal features, such as network flow features. NIDS often struggles to broaden the horizon and jump out of the local optimum solution when using only spatial or temporal features [27]. In this paper, we design one-dimensional stacked convolutional autoencoders (1D-SCAE), an excellent self-taught learning model which abstracts spatial features by reducing the dimensionality of complex data signals. Besides, bidirectional gated recurrent units (BiGRU) can extract temporal features of traffic sequences in representation learning. Therefore, we propose a deep neural network model based on 1D-SCAE and BiGRU, which can accurately extract spatial and temporal features and enhance the performance of malicious traffic detection. The main contributions of the proposed work include the following:

- We design 1D-SCAE—an improved network traffic spatial feature extraction model, which uses sparse regularization to reduce overfitting by invalidating a certain part of active neurons. The greedy layer-wise strategy is adopted to achieve the best detection performance.
- We propose a BiGRU-based temporal feature extraction model that utilizes TimeseriesGenerator to generate and model traffic time series. It can acquire both memories from history and information from the future.
- We develop SR-IDS, a network intrusion detection system that simultaneously focuses on network traffic's spatial and temporal characteristics. Experiments show that the accuracy of SR-IDS on the UNSW-NB15 dataset can reach 98.90%.
- We discuss different hyperparameters to determine the optimal model architecture. Furthermore, we compare the detection performance of different RNN variants.

The rest of the paper is organized as follows. The related work on NIDS is reviewed in Sect. 2. Then we present the details of the proposed SR-IDS in Sect. 3. The accuracy and the efficiency of SR-IDS are verified in Sect. 4 by comparing it with several state-of-the-art IDS algorithms. Finally, we provide our conclusions and discuss the future work in Sect. 5.

2   Related Work

NIDS is a necessary foundation and premise for dealing with complex network attacks and identifying malicious traffic behavior. The deep learning models currently applied to network anomaly detection include two categories: generative intrusion detection model and discriminative intrusion detection model.

2.1 Generative Intrusion Detection Model

Generative models often adopt an advanced hierarchical learning method to establish a multi-level model, which can flexibly analyze and restore joint probability distribution. The current famous generative model architecture mainly includes autoencoder and its variants [18].

Amir et al. [4] designed a new lightweight architecture that considers feature separation and uses surrounding information of a single value in the feature vector. The accuracy is improved while reducing the memory footprint and the need for processing power. Iliyasu et al. [12] achieved a few-shot learning intrusion detection, which uses the feature extraction model in the few-shot learning stage to fit a classifier with a small number of novel attack samples. Long et al. [17] proposed a network intrusion detection model based on an integrated autoencoder. It uses recursive feature addition to select the optimal subset of features, which can significantly reduce the training time and improve the intrusion detection performance.

2.2 Discriminative Intrusion Detection Model

Discriminative models are usually based on the excellent classification of heterogeneous data to achieve the best recognition. The common discriminative model structures mainly include recurrent neural networks and convolutional neural networks [2].

Imrana et al. [14] proposed a novel feature-driven intrusion detection system. The model first utilizes a statistical model to rank all the features, then uses best-first-search algorithm to search for the best subset, and finally classifies testing data based on the best subset. Sahu et al. [23] proposed a multi-classification intrusion detection method based on LSTM and fully connected networks. This method accurately classifies the imbalanced intrusion data. Imrana et al. [13] used an improved RNN model for network intrusion detection, which can be associated with the feature knowledge and accurately classify unknown data.

Several works sought to propose ML-based solutions with consideration of as many essential features as possible, and the approaches managed to obtain interesting results. However, there are still some challenges in extracting both spatial and temporal traffic features. Inspired by existing research progress, we propose SR-IDS—a new intrusion detection system with the advantages of generative models and discriminative models. Moreover, it can serially extract the spatial and temporal features of network traffic accurately.

3 The Proposed Model

In this section, we introduce how SR-IDS works. SR-IDS first preprocesses the UNSW-NB15 dataset, including one-hot encoding and normalization. Afterward, SR-IDS uses 1D-SCAE to extract spatial features of network traffic, and the greedy layer-wise strategy is adopted to pre-train the neural network. Finally,

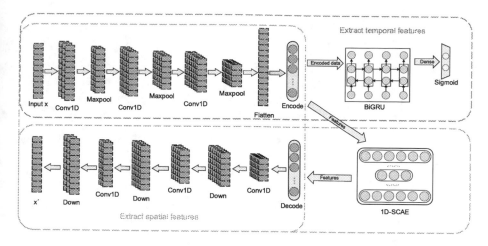

Fig. 1. The framework of our proposed SR-IDS model. 1D-SCAE (marked in blue) extracts spatial features through encoding and decoding. The output of the last encoding layer of 1D-SCAE is the input of BiGRU (marked in green). BiGRU extracts temporal features by generating time series. (Color figure online)

SR-IDS uses BiGRU to extract temporal features of network traffic. BiGRU accepts input from pre-trained 1D-SCAE and outputs to the binary classifier. Figure 1 describes the framework of our proposed SR-IDS model.

3.1 Data Preprocessing

In general, machine learning models can only process meaningful numerical data, but the actual data differs from what we expected. In order to enable machine learning models to process and analyze traffic data, assigning numerical meaning to features is necessary. One-hot encoding is a commonly used feature encoding method.

One-hot encoding expresses a specific type of different values in binary vectors. The N values used for encoding correspond to the states of N registers one by one. Only one bit in any form is activated, and the rest of the registers are inactive. The specific representation is generally $v_i = \{0, 1, 0, \ldots 0, 0\}$, and the dimension of the vector is equal to the number of possible values N of the eigenvalues to be encoded.

After encoding, we use the min-max method to standardize network traffic samples. With a fixed output range, the min-max method performs a linear operation on the sequence $\{x_1, x_2, \ldots, x_n\}$. After transformation, the new sequence $\{y_1, y_2, \ldots, y_n\} \in (0, 1)$ are dimensionless:

$$y_i = \frac{x_i - \min_{1 \leq i \leq n}\{x_j\}}{\max_{1 \leq i \leq n}\{x_j\} - \min_{1 \leq i \leq n}\{x_j\}} \tag{1}$$

It can be found that min-max forces the original input data to distribute in [0, 1], and the normalized scale transformation is only related to extreme values.

3.2   Spatial Feature Extraction

Spatial features of network traffic refer to feature sets related to packets, for example, packet size and number. We design a 1D-SCAE for spontaneously learning spatial feature representation, and Fig. 2 describes the architecture. In each layer, the autoencoder convolves the features of the lower layers to produce a high-level representation. The whole methodology is shown as follows:

$$x_j^l = f(\sum_{i \in M_j} x_i^{l-1} \times k_{ij}^l + b_j^l) \tag{2}$$

where M_j represents the input feature map, l represents the l-th layer in 1D-SCAE, and k is the convolution kernel. f represents the activation function, and b_j^l is the bias vector.

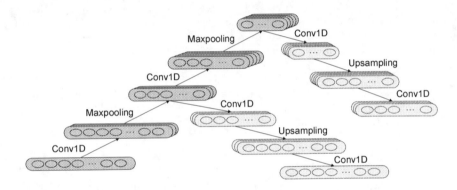

Fig. 2. The structure of proposed 1D-SCAE model

The 1D-SCAE consists of three convolutional autoencoders, and their encoder layers are stacked in the model construction process to build the complete 1D-SCAE model. After the training is completed, we discard the decoders and connect the last encoder layer to the subsequent temporal extraction model, which will be explained in the next subsection. MSE Loss is used to evaluate the effect of feature extraction and input reconstruction as follows:

$$J = \frac{1}{n} \sum_{i=1}^{n} (x_i - x_i')^2 \tag{3}$$

where i is the sample index, x_i is the original input data, and x_i' is the reconstructed data after dimensionality reduction by 1D-SCAE.

We also add a custom regularization term in 1D-SCAE to improve the generalization performance of the model. The principle is that different inputs cause different neurons to be activated, making neurons better dependent on data. In general, the constant ρ is the proportion of activated neurons, which is used to measure the average activity $\hat{\rho}$ of the activation degree of neurons:

$$\hat{\rho} = \frac{1}{N} \sum_{i=1}^{N} \Theta(x_i) \tag{4}$$

where N is the number of neurons in the hidden layer, Θ is the corresponding neuron transformation. In the field of machine learning, forward KL divergence is often used as the training cost to measure the difference between two probability distributions. Forward KL divergence makes sure $\hat{\rho}$ close to ρ, and the regularization term punishs the deviation between $\hat{\rho}$ and ρ:

$$KL(\rho\|\hat{\rho}) = \rho \log \frac{\rho}{\hat{\rho}} + (1 - \rho) \log \frac{1 - \rho}{1 - \hat{\rho}} \tag{5}$$

If $\hat{\rho}$ is equal to ρ, the KL divergence is 0; otherwise, it will gradually increase as the difference between ρ and $\hat{\rho}$ increases. Therefore, the error function J' in the sparse autoencoder is shown as follows:

$$J' = J + \mu \sum_{j=1}^{N} KL(\rho\|\hat{\rho}) \tag{6}$$

where J is the error when no sparse item is added, and μ is the impact factor used to balance the weight of KL divergence in the entire loss function.

3.3   Temporal Feature Extraction

In this work, we group traffic records by timestep and link the context with their labels. Our proposed SR-IDS can accurately reflect the time characteristics of network traffic and significantly reduce the false positive rate.

SR-IDS takes the output from the spatial feature extraction model as input and uses TimeseriesGenerator—a time series generator to convert isolated samples into a sequence. After serialization, the processed traffic is input into the BiGRU. The principle of BiGRU is to split the neurons of a regular GRU into two directions, one for positive time direction and another for negative time direction.

Assume that the current input vector is x_t, the last step activation vector is r_{t-1}, W and U are weight matrices used to represent the connection strength between neurons, and b is the bias vector. σ_g represents the sigmoid activation function, the update gate vector z_t and the reset gate vector r_t are shown as follows:

$$\begin{aligned} z_t &= \sigma_g(W_z x_t + U_z h_{t-1} + b_z) \\ r_t &= \sigma_g(W_r x_t + U_r h_{t-1} + b_r) \end{aligned} \tag{7}$$

The candidate activation vector $\hat{h}_t$ is obtained through the Hadamard product of r_t and h_{t-1}, where ϕ_h represents the hyperbolic tangent function:

$$\hat{h}_t = \phi_h(W_h x_t + U_h(r_t \odot h_{t-1}) + b_h) \tag{8}$$

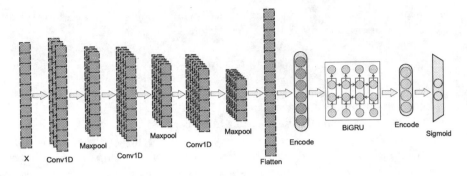

Fig. 3. Classification model based on 1D-SCAE and BiGRU

Finally, update the activation output vector of the hidden unit h_t at time t:

$$h_t = (1 - z_t) \odot h_{t-1} + z_t \odot \hat{h}_t \tag{9}$$

When the 1D-SCAE model is completely trained, we connect it with the subsequent BiGRU network, as shown in Fig. 3. We optimize the free parameters in BiGRU to achieve the global optimum. The binary cross entropy loss function in the final binary classification is adopted to evaluate the model as follows:

$$\xi = -\frac{1}{N} \sum_{i=1}^{N} y_i \log(p(y_i)) + (1 - y_i) \log(1 - p(y_i)) \tag{10}$$

where i is the sample index, N is the number of samples, y_i is the binary label of the i-th sample, and $p(y_i)$ is the probability that the output belongs to the y_i label. For the case where the label y_i is 1, if the predicted value $p(y_i)$ approaches 1, then the loss approaches 0. Conversely, if the predicted value $p(y_i)$ approaches 0, the loss should be tremendous.

4   Experiments

In this section, a series of experiments are conducted to verify the efficiency and accuracy of the proposed SR-IDS. Specifically, we first present the experimental settings and some details. Then we analyze some critical parameters to find the optimal solution. Lastly, we evaluate SR-IDS's performance and compare it with some state-of-the-art methods.

4.1   Dataset

The UNSW-NB15 dataset simulates a modern representation of network traffic [19]. Each instance in the dataset is a network flow that summarizes the activity of a sequence of unidirectional packets with contextual features. Additional features are introduced into the dataset, totaling 49 features.

Table 1. Model hierarchy and some parameters

Layers	Types	Input size	Output size
1	Conv1D	None, 200, 1	None, 200, 8
2	MaxPooling1D	None, 200, 8	None, 100, 8
3	Conv1D	None, 100, 8	None, 100, 16
4	MaxPooling1D	None, 100, 16	None, 50, 16
5	Conv1D	None, 50, 16	None, 50, 32
6	MaxPooling1D	None, 50, 32	None, 25, 32
7	Flatten	None, 25, 32	None, 800
8	Dense	None, 800	None, 32
9	TimeseriesGenerator	None, 32	None, 8, 32
10	BiGRU	None, 8, 32	None, 8, 48
11	BiGRU	None, 8, 48	None, 8, 24
12	Dense	None, 8, 24	None, 6
13	Dense	None, 6	None, 1

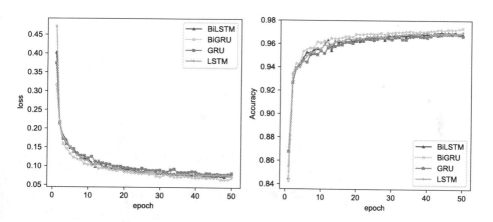

Fig. 4. Training loss and accuracy of different RNN variants

4.2 Model Hierarchy

SR-IDS inputs the preprocessed data into three independent one-dimensional convolutional autoencoders and trains them separately through a greedy layer-wise strategy. Three autoencoders' encoder layers are stacked after training by the weight-sharing method and then connects to the time series generator to produce traffic groups with contextual features. Afterwards, we use BiGRU to extract temporal feature and output the type judgment of the testing set. The complete model hierarchy and some significant parameters are shown in Table 1.

4.3   Parameters Analysis

We compare and test the influence of different learning rate and dropout ratio on convolutional layer and dense layer, as shown in Table 2. We find that the convergence speed of the entire neural network is extremely slow when the initial learning rate of the dense layer is less than 0.0001. It means the time overhead significantly increases, and the effect improvement is negligible, so we do not adopt the lower initial learning rate scheme.

Table 2. Comparison of different learning rate and dropout ratio

Layers	Learning rate	Dropout	Accuracy	FAR	F1 score
Conv1D	0.005	0.05	0.9310	0.0700	0.9184
		0.1	0.9358	0.0693	0.9300
		0.3	0.9187	0.0869	0.9226
	0.001	0.05	0.9398	0.0626	0.9301
		0.1	**0.9439**	**0.0537**	**0.9355**
		0.3	0.9106	0.0574	0.9280
	0.0005	0.05	0.9317	0.0604	0.9208
		0.1	0.9324	0.0586	0.9245
		0.3	0.9289	0.0654	0.9177
Dense	0.001	0.05	0.9401	0.0593	0.9353
		0.1	0.9439	0.0537	0.9355
		0.3	0.9422	0.0540	0.9320
	0.0005	0.05	0.9471	0.0569	0.9273
		0.1	0.9488	0.0525	0.9392
		0.3	0.9306	0.0528	0.9394
	0.0001	0.05	0.9533	0.0505	0.9314
		0.1	**0.9556**	**0.0499**	**0.9403**
		0.3	0.9485	0.0613	0.9345

We also compare the loss and accuracy of different RNN models during training iterations. Figure 4 shows the detailed performance of training loss and accuracy for attack detection. It can be seen that loss and accuracy hardly change when the epoch reaches 50, and BiGRU can achieve better performance than the other three RNN variants.

4.4   Evaluation

We compare the proposed method's performance with some state-of-the-art methods, as shown in Table 3. Additionally, we test our model on KDD CUP 99 [26] and CIC-IDS-2017 dataset [24], which also shows well performance. In summary, our proposed SR-IDS method can achieve excellent performance in network traffic anomaly detection.

Table 3. Comparison with other machine learning algorithms

Dataset	Model	Accuracy	Precision	Recall	F1 score
UNSW-NB15	DT [3]	88.30%	94.59%	77.78%	85.37%
	SVM [28]	89.63%	–	–	–
	GBT [30]	93.13%	92.38%	92.84%	92.61%
	GAN [7]	92.39%	91.46%	94.03%	94.39%
	CNN [6]	86.25%	86.92%	86.25%	86.59%
	Our SR-IDS	**98.90%**	**98.90%**	**98.90%**	**98.90%**
KDD CUP 99	DT [20]	94.46%	96.67%	–	–
	SVM [21]	96.61%	**98.04%**	95.31%	96.66%
	GBT [25]	91.82%	86.51%	–	–
	GAN [1]	–	86.76%	86.94%	85.71%
	CNN [29]	94.11%	–	93.22%	–
	Our SR-IDS	**98.15%**	97.26%	**99.01%**	**98.13%**
CIC-IDS-2017	DT [10]	94.48%	96.67%	–	–
	SVM [11]	93.75%	–	94.73%	–
	GBT [9]	**97.83%**	–	–	–
	GAN [16]	–	**98.17%**	90.57%	88.42%
	CNN [15]	97.39%	–	82.12%	–
	Our SR-IDS	96.16%	95.42%	**97.15%**	**96.28%**

5   Conclusion

In this paper, we propose SR-IDS, an intrusion detection system for network traffic based on self-taught learning and representation learning, which simultaneously focuses on traffic's spatial and temporal characteristics. Specifically, it utilizes 1D-SCAE to extract spatial features and BiGRU to extract temporal features. The greedy layer-wise strategy is adopted in the training process of 1D-SCAE, and sparse regularization is applied to reduce overfitting. BiGRU generates time series through TimeseriesGenerator to extract advanced time features. Multiple experiments have proved that BiGRU can achieve the best score among RNN variants. The accuracy rate of our proposed SR-IDS model in classifying network traffic on UNSW-NB15 dataset can reach 98.90%, which is more efficient than other current IDS methods.

In future research, we can consider online operations to improve robustness and stability. Furthermore, defense against attack techniques targeting deep learning models is also a research direction in the future.

Acknowledgements. This work is supported by the National Key Research and Development Program of China (No. 2020YFB1805403) and the National Natural Science Foundation of China (61876134).

References

1. Ahmad, R., Li, L.H., Sharma, A.K., Tanone, R.: Boundary-seeking GAN approach to improve classification of intrusion detection systems based on machine learning model. In: 2023 17th International Conference on Ubiquitous Information Management and Communication (IMCOM), pp. 1–5. IEEE (2023)
2. Alghanam, O.A., Almobaideen, W., Saadeh, M., Adwan, O.: An improved PIO feature selection algorithm for IoT network intrusion detection system based on ensemble learning. Expert Syst. Appl. **213**, 118745 (2023)
3. Anwer, H.M., Farouk, M., Abdel-Hamid, A.: A framework for efficient network anomaly intrusion detection with features selection. In: 2018 9th International Conference on Information and Communication Systems (ICICS), pp. 157–162. IEEE (2018)
4. Basati, A., Faghih, M.M.: PDAE: efficient network intrusion detection in IoT using parallel deep auto-encoders. Inf. Sci. **598**, 57–74 (2022)
5. Bengio, Y., Courville, A., Vincent, P.: Representation learning: a review and new perspectives. IEEE Trans. Pattern Anal. Mach. Intell. **35**(8), 1798–1828 (2013)
6. Cao, B., Li, C., Song, Y., Qin, Y., Chen, C.: Network intrusion detection model based on CNN and GRU. Appl. Sci. **12**(9), 4184 (2022)
7. Ding, H., Chen, L., Dong, L., Fu, Z., Cui, X.: Imbalanced data classification: a KNN and generative adversarial networks-based hybrid approach for intrusion detection. Futur. Gener. Comput. Syst. **131**, 240–254 (2022)
8. Du, R., Li, Y., Liang, X., Tian, J.: Support vector machine intrusion detection scheme based on cloud-fog collaboration. Mob. Netw. Appl. **27**(1), 431–440 (2022)
9. Faker, O., Dogdu, E.: Intrusion detection using big data and deep learning techniques. In: Proceedings of the 2019 ACM Southeast Conference, pp. 86–93 (2019)
10. Ferrag, M.A., Maglaras, L., Ahmim, A., Derdour, M., Janicke, H.: RDTIDS: rules and decision tree-based intrusion detection system for internet-of-things networks. Future Internet **12**(3), 44 (2020)
11. Gu, J., Lu, S.: An effective intrusion detection approach using SVM with naïve bayes feature embedding. Comput. Secur. **103**, 102158 (2021)
12. Iliyasu, A.S., Abdurrahman, U.A., Zheng, L.: Few-shot network intrusion detection using discriminative representation learning with supervised autoencoder. Appl. Sci. **12**(5), 2351 (2022)
13. Imrana, Y., Xiang, Y., Ali, L., Abdul-Rauf, Z.: A bidirectional LSTM deep learning approach for intrusion detection. Expert Syst. Appl. **185**, 115524 (2021)
14. Imrana, Y., et al.: χ 2-BidLSTM: a feature driven intrusion detection system based on χ 2 statistical model and bidirectional LSTM. Sensors **22**(5), 2018 (2022)
15. Le Jeune, L., Goedemé, T., Mentens, N.: Feature dimensionality in CNN acceleration for high-throughput network intrusion detection. In: 2022 32nd International Conference on Field-Programmable Logic and Applications (FPL), pp. 366–374. IEEE (2022)
16. Lee, J., Park, K.: AE-CGAN model based high performance network intrusion detection system. Appl. Sci. **9**(20), 4221 (2019)
17. Long, C., Xiao, J., Wei, J., Zhao, J., Wan, W., Du, G.: Autoencoder ensembles for network intrusion detection. In: 2022 24th International Conference on Advanced Communication Technology (ICACT), pp. 323–333. IEEE (2022)
18. Louk, M.H.L., Tama, B.A.: Dual-IDS: a bagging-based gradient boosting decision tree model for network anomaly intrusion detection system. Expert Syst. Appl. **213**, 119030 (2023)

19. Moustafa, N., Slay, J.: UNSW-NB15: a comprehensive data set for network intrusion detection systems (UNSW-NB15 network data set). In: 2015 military communications and information systems conference (MilCIS), pp. 1–6. IEEE (2015)
20. Nancy, P., Muthurajkumar, S., Ganapathy, S., Santhosh Kumar, S., Selvi, M., Arputharaj, K.: Intrusion detection using dynamic feature selection and fuzzy temporal decision tree classification for wireless sensor networks. IET Commun. **14**(5), 888–895 (2020)
21. Nerlikar, P., Pandey, S., Sharma, S., Bagade, S.: Analysis of intrusion detection using machine learning techniques. Int. J. Comput. Netw. Commun. Secur. **8**(10), 84–93 (2020)
22. Raina, R., Battle, A., Lee, H., Packer, B., Ng, A.Y.: Self-taught learning: transfer learning from unlabeled data. In: Proceedings of the 24th International Conference on Machine Learning, pp. 759–766 (2007)
23. Sahu, S.K., Mohapatra, D.P., Rout, J.K., Sahoo, K.S., Pham, Q.V., Dao, N.N.: A LSTM-FCNN based multi-class intrusion detection using scalable framework. Comput. Electr. Eng. **99**, 107720 (2022)
24. Sharafaldin, I., Lashkari, A.H., Ghorbani, A.A.: Toward generating a new intrusion detection dataset and intrusion traffic characterization. ICISSp **1**, 108–116 (2018)
25. Tama, B.A., Rhee, K.H.: An in-depth experimental study of anomaly detection using gradient boosted machine. Neural Comput. Appl. **31**, 955–965 (2019)
26. Tavallaee, M., Bagheri, E., Lu, W., Ghorbani, A.A.: A detailed analysis of the KDD CUP 99 data set. In: 2009 IEEE Symposium on Computational Intelligence for Security and Defense Applications, pp. 1–6. IEEE (2009)
27. Thakkar, A., Lohiya, R.: A survey on intrusion detection system: feature selection, model, performance measures, application perspective, challenges, and future research directions. Artif. Intell. Rev. **55**(1), 453–563 (2022)
28. Tian, Q., Li, J., Liu, H.: A method for guaranteeing wireless communication based on a combination of deep and shallow learning. IEEE Access **7**, 38688–38695 (2019)
29. Yong, L., Bo, Z.: An intrusion detection model based on multi-scale CNN. In: 2019 IEEE 3rd Information Technology, Networking, Electronic and Automation Control Conference (ITNEC), pp. 214–218. IEEE (2019)
30. Zhou, Y., Han, M., Liu, L., He, J.S., Wang, Y.: Deep learning approach for cyber-attack detection. In: IEEE INFOCOM 2018-IEEE Conference on Computer Communications Workshops (INFOCOM WKSHPS), pp. 262–267. IEEE (2018)

Task-Aware Adversarial Feature Perturbation for Cross-Domain Few-Shot Learning

Yixiao Ma[✉] and Fanzhang Li

Provincial Key Laboratory for Computer Information Processing Technology,
Soochow University, Suzhou 215006, China
yixiaoma.edu@outlook.com, lfzh@suda.edu.cn

Abstract. Currently, metric-based meta-learning methods have achieved great success in few-shot learning (FSL). However, most works assume a high similarity between base classes and novel classes, and their performance can be greatly reduced when comes to domain-shift problem. As a result, cross-domain few-shot learning (CD-FSL) methods are proposed to tackle the domain-shift problem, which places a higher demand on the robustness of the meta-knowledge. To this end, we propose a feature augmentation method called Task-Aware Adversarial Feature Perturbation (TAAFP) to improve the generalization of the existing FSL models. Compared to the traditional adversarial training, our adversarial perturbations are generated from the feature space and contain more sample relationship information, which is discovered by the Task Attention Module. Task Attention Module is designed based on a transformer to capture more discriminative features in a task. Therefore, our perturbations can easily attack the extraction process for discriminative features, forcing the model to extract more robust discriminative features. In addition, a regularization loss is introduced to ensure the predictions of the adversarial augmented task remain similar to the original task. We conduct extensive classification experiments in five datasets under the setting of cross-domain few-shot classification. The result shows that our method can significantly improve the classification accuracy in both seen and unseen domains.

Keywords: Few-shot learning · Cross-domain few-shot learning · Task-Aware Adversarial Feature Perturbation

1 Introduction

Few-shot learning (FSL) aims to classify unseen samples into novel categories with few labeled samples. Among different few-shot learning methods, metric-based methods [21, 23, 26, 29] have achieved great success in FSL by learning meta-knowledge effectively from the seen samples with the feature extractor and their specific similarity metric model. However, these existing methods usually

L. Iliadis et al. (Eds.): ICANN 2023, LNCS 14256, pp. 566–578, 2023.
https://doi.org/10.1007/978-3-031-44213-1_47

assume that the unseen samples come from the same domain as the seen samples, and perform poorly when comes to domain-shift problem [2]. Domain-shift problem places a higher demand on the model for meta-knowledge extraction. As a result, cross-domain few-shot learning (CD-FSL) methods are proposed to tackle the domain-shift problem, which aims to enhance the existing FSL methods across different domains.

In real-world application, CD-FSL methods have more practical value than the traditional FSL methods. FSL methods require a large number of labeled samples in the domain for training. However, for some domains with few available samples, we are forced to extract the knowledge from one or more seen domains and transfer the knowledge to the unseen domains. In such cases, how to extract better meta-knowledge and perform better knowledge transfer becomes the key problem of CD-FSL.

In this paper, we studies the single domain generalization problem [8], with only one seen domain for training, which is more challenging and concerned. Many CD-FSL methods have been proposed to tackle the single domain generalization problem. Tseng [28] introduces feature-wise transformation with a learned noise distribution to the intermediate layers and thus improve the robustness of the similarity metric model. However, the parameters of feature-wise transformation layers are fixed when it comes to the single domain generalization problem. Wang [32] introduces adversarial perturbations to each sample in a training task to improve the robustness of features. However, the adversarial perturbations are only applied to the raw input and generated by the standard task loss.

It follows that the robustness of the model is critical for CD-FSL. According to [19], adversarial perturbations on intermediate feature can not only provides stronger regularization compared to Dropout but also improves adversarial robustness comparable to traditional adversarial training approaches. In addition, many works on regularization [33] or knowledge transfer [14] has shown that the exploration of sample relationships can improve the robustness of feature representations. To this end, we tend to make full use of the sample relationship information in a FSL task while perturbing the intermediate blocks. Intuitively, adversarial perturbations for a FSL task with more discriminative features can be more effective. Such perturbations can easily attack the extraction process for discriminative features, forcing the model to extract more robust discriminative features. Therefore, we first propose a Task Attention Module to discover the relationship between samples and further process the feature representations for a new task. Then we generated adversarial perturbations for the intermediate feature by a hybrid loss of the standard task and the new task. Such adversarial perturbations will contain more information about sample relationship in a FSL task. Finally, we consider that the model must remain stable against the adversarial perturbations. A regularization loss is introduced to ensure the predictions of the adversarial augmented task remain similar to the original task. We will show that our method can be adopted as a plug-and-play module to the existing metric-based model and enhance the generalization on unseen domains. The main contributions of our work can be summarized as follows:

- We propose a Task Attention Module (TAM) to adjust the feature representations in a task by sample relationship information. Task Attention Module is designed based on transformer to discover the sample relationship and capture more discriminative features in a task.
- The adversarial perturbations for the intermediate feature, which is called Adversarial Feature Perturbation (AFP) are generated by a hybrid loss of the standard task and the adjusted task. Such adversarial perturbations can force the backbone to learn robust representations at each layer resulting in improved generalization.
- A regularization loss (REG) is introduced to keep the semantic meanings of samples unchanged against the adversarial perturbations in a task, which further improves the robustness of the model.
- Our method is composed of AFP, TAM and REG, which is called Task-Aware Adversarial Feature Perturbation (TAAFP). As a plug-and-play module, we combined it with the existing metric-based model GNN and evaluate the performance under the cross-domain few-shot classification setting. The result shows that our method can significantly improve the generalization in both seen and unseen domains.

2   Related Work

2.1   Few-Shot Learning

Few-shot learning methods can be roughly classified into three main categories: metric-based, optimization-based, and model-based methods. Metric-based methods [21,23,26,29] exploit a large number of base classes to learn an embedding space for the samples from novel classes and make a comparison between query set and the labeled support set. The similarity function can be parametric or nonparametric, such as Euclidean distance, cosine distance, etc. Optimization-based methods [4,18,25] aim at learning a better initialization of the model and fine-tuning the initialized model to novel classes, such as the suitable initialization of the model's parameters which can quickly converge to novel tasks, and the efficient learning-to-learn optimization algorithm for updating the model parameters with few gradient update steps. Model-based methods [17,20] focus on designing a parameterized predictor to learn meta-knowledge dynamically and generate specific parameters for novel tasks. Although these methods have achieved great performance under the assumption that the novel classes share the same domain as the base classes, the domain shift problem can make them underperform [2].

2.2   Domain Generalization

Domain generalization [1] aims at generalizing from one or more source domains to the target domains with no sample accessible from the target domain during the training stage. Domain generalization methods can be summarized from two perspectives: learning domain invariant features and augmentation for the source domain. The former [7,12,15] focuses on extracting domain invariant features which can generalize well on unseen domains by minimizing the discrepancy between source domains. Recent work [35] adds style normalization to disentangle the style and content of samples to extract generalized features. The augmentation [22] for the source domain aims at enlarging the possibility of covering the distribution of data from the target domain. Adversarial approaches [30] are widely adopted to perturb the input data to enhance the robustness of the model. These domain generalization methods assume that the source and unseen domains share the same categories. While in the setting of few-shot learning, the novel classes for testing are unseen before, which is more difficult for model generalization.

2.3 Cross-Domain Few-Shot Learning

As an emerging topic, cross-domain few-shot Learning currently has two main settings: target domain unavailable during training and target domain available during training. In recent works, FWT [28], LRP [24], ATA [32] and Wave-SAN [6] can be classified into the former setting. FWT introduces feature-wise transformation with a noise distribution to the intermediate layers and develops a learning-to-learn approach for optimizing the feature-wise transformation layer using multiple seen domains. LRP adopts explanation-guided training to re-weight the features that are more relevant to the prediction and reduce overfitting. ATA generates adversarial perturbations to the raw input for a robust representation. Wave-SAN makes good use of the wavelet transforms to augment the source styles and narrow the domain gap. STARTUP [16] and Meta-FDMixup [5] can be classified into the later setting. STARTUP conducts semi-supervised learning using a large number of unlabeled samples from the target domain with the labeled samples from the source domain. Meta-FDMixup utilizes extremely few labeled target data and mix the images of the source and the target datasets to learn domain-irrelevant features. In addition, other works like ConFT [3] and NSAE [13] propose their fine-tune algorithm to quickly adapt the model to the target domain. Our work fits the former setting without any fine-tuning. We are similar to ATA in generating adversarial perturbations, but different in perturbing the mid-level feature maps and leveraging the sample relationships in a task.

3 Method

3.1 Preliminaries

Few-Shot Learning and Cross-Domain Few-Shot Learning. We first introduce the typical setting of few-shot learning. For each training iteration i, the training samples are randomly selected as a task from a meta-training set: $\mathcal{S}^{train} = \{\mathcal{T}_i\}$, consisting of a support set and a query set. The support set contains N classes with K samples per class (N-way, K-shot), which is denoted as

$\mathcal{D}^s = \{(X^s, Y^s)\}$. The query set contains the same classes with the support set but with Q different samples per class, which is denoted as $\mathcal{D}^q = \{(X^q, Y^q)\}$. For metric-based few-shot learning methods, the samples from both support set and query set are encoded by a feature extractor $E(\cdot)$, and the followed similarity metric model $Sim(\cdot)$ will compare the embedding of support and query samples and make prediction for each query sample. After all, our goal is to minimize the classification loss of query samples in each task, the objective function is:

$$\mathcal{L}_{ce} = \mathcal{L}(Sim(Y^s, E(X^s), E(X^q)), Y^q) \qquad (1)$$

For each testing iteration j, we evaluate the model with N-way, K-shot tasks from a meta-testing set $\mathcal{S}^{test} = \{\mathcal{T}_j\}$, which shares the same domain with the meta-training set $\mathcal{S}^{train}$.

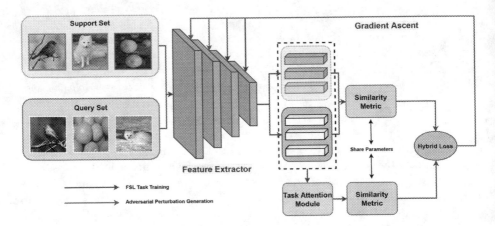

Fig. 1. Generating Adversarial Feature Perturbations with Task Attention Module.

In this paper, we develop the testing stage to the setting of cross-domain few-shot learning, which means the testing tasks are sampled from several unseen domains. Our goal is to improve the generalization of the metric-based few-shot learning model on the seen domain, so that the model can recognize the novel classes from the unseen domain.

Adversarial Training. Traditional adversarial training [27] aims at generating box-constrained adversarial perturbations on the input samples and training with the adversarial samples to improve the robustness of the base network. Given a dataset $\mathcal{D} = \{(x, y)\}$, where x is the input sample and y is the corresponding label. The loss function can be denoted as $\mathcal{J}(\theta, x, y)$, where θ is the parameters of the base network. Typical adversarial training can be formulated as the following min-max optimization problem:

$$\min_{\theta} \mathbb{E}_{(x,y) \in D} \left[\max_{\|\delta\|_p \le \epsilon} \mathcal{J}(\theta, x + \delta, y) \right] \qquad (2)$$

where δ is the adversarial perturbation bounded by the l_p norm ball with ϵ as the maximum perturbation magnitude. The adversarial perturbations are applied to the input for augmentation.

In this paper, we generate adversarial perturbations from intermediate layers rather than the raw input, and we intend to generate more task-aware attacks for different FSL tasks. The framework is shown in Fig. 1.

3.2 Adversarial Feature Perturbation

In this section, we extend the traditional adversarial training to the feature space and introduce it to FSL. We denote the collection of the support feature map for each block output as $\mathcal{X}^s = \{X_l^s\}_{l=0}^L$, and the query as $\mathcal{X}^q = \{X_l^q\}_{l=0}^L$. The collections of the corresponding adversarial perturbation for the feature map are denoted as $\Delta^s = \{\delta_l^s\}_{l=0}^L$ and $\Delta^q = \{\delta_l^q\}_{l=0}^L$. L is the number of the blocks of the feature extractor (e.g. 4 for ResNet-10). To this end, the following objective function is defined to obtain the adversarial feature perturbations for each sample in the metric-based FSL task:

$$\mathcal{L}_1 = \mathcal{L}(Sim(Y^s, E(\mathcal{X}^s + \Delta^s), E(\mathcal{X}^q + \Delta^q)), Y^q) \tag{3}$$

$$\begin{array}{c} \arg\max_{\Delta} \ \mathcal{L}_1 \\ \text{subject to} \ \ \|\delta_l^s\|_p \leq \epsilon, \ \|\delta_l^q\|_p \leq \epsilon, \ \forall l \end{array} \tag{4}$$

Specifically, we use the classical gradient ascent to compute the adversarial feature perturbation δ, and β is the perturbation strength:

$$\delta_l = \beta \nabla_{X_l} \mathcal{L}_{ce} \tag{5}$$

For each training task, after generating the task-specific adversarial feature perturbations, we re-extract the feature representations as the augmented feature, which is written as F_a, and the adversarial task loss can be denoted as:

$$\mathcal{L}_a = \mathcal{L}(Sim(Y^s, F_a^s, F_a^q), Y^q) \tag{6}$$

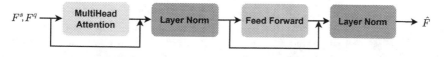

Fig. 2. An illustration of the proposed Task Attention Module.

3.3 Task Attention Module

Although the above Adversarial Feature Perturbation (AFP) is task-specific, only the category relationship information between the samples from support set and query set is exploited. In this section, we intend to take the relationship information between all samples in a FSL task into consideration while attacking the model. In order to capture more discriminative features of the sample in a FSL task, Task Attention Module (TAM) is built based on a simple transformer. The specific structure of TAM is shown in Fig. 2. Specifically, we combine the feature representations of support set F^s and query set F^q as the input, and we use the multi-head attention networks for encoding, further to process the feature representation. Let the original feature representation as $F \in \mathbb{R}^{n \times d}$, where n is the sum of the number of support and query samples, d represents the dimension of the feature representation. We compute the self-attention outputs $\widetilde{F}$ with h heads as:

$$\widetilde{F} = \text{concate}(\widetilde{F}_1, \widetilde{F}_2, ..., \widetilde{F}_h)W^O \tag{7}$$

$$\widetilde{F}_i = softmax(\frac{Q_i \times K_i^T}{\sqrt{d}})V_i \tag{8}$$

where $Q_i = FW_i^Q$, $K_i = FW_i^K$, $V_i = FW_i^V$, and $\{W_i^Q, W_i^K, W_i^V\} \in \mathbb{R}^{d \times \frac{d}{h}}$, $W^O \in \mathbb{R}^{d \times d}$ are all linearly projections. The feed-forward layer is composed of two linear transformations with a relu activation between them.

For the final output of Task Attention Module $\hat{F} = TAM(F)$, which can be viewed as an adjusted task T', the representation of each sample is related to those of other samples in the task. It is worth mentioning that due to the large number of same-labeled samples contained in the FSL task, training directly on T' leads to models that focus on the discriminative but non-robust features and converge quickly, which is not beneficial for model generalization. To this end, we adopt the above described adversarial feature perturbation to the adjusted task and force the model to extract more robust features. To preserve the information of the original task, a hybrid loss is used for generating adversarial feature perturbations:

$$\mathcal{L}_{ta} = \mathcal{L}(Sim(Y^s, TAM(E(\mathcal{X}^s), E(\mathcal{X}^q))), Y^q) \tag{9}$$

$$\delta_l = \beta \nabla_{X_l}(\mathcal{L}_{ce} + \mathcal{L}_{ta}) \tag{10}$$

Such adversarial perturbations can be called Task-Aware Adversarial Feature Perturbation (TAAFP). Compared to AFP which only contains category information, TAAFP contains more sample relationship information in a FSL task. In terms of the number of samples involved in generating the perturbation, we take a query sample x_q as an example. The former adversarial perturbation on x_q is generated by x_q and all support samples, while the later takes other query samples into consideration, which contains more information. At last, we re-extract the feature representations with the adversarial perturbations as the new augmented feature $F_{\hat{a}}$, and the hybrid loss function can be denoted as:

$$\mathcal{L}_{\hat{a}} = \mathcal{L}(Sim(Y^s, F_{\hat{a}}^s, F_{\hat{a}}^q), Y^q) + \mathcal{L}(Sim(Y^s, TAM(F_{\hat{a}}^s, F_{\hat{a}}^q)), Y^q) \tag{11}$$

3.4   Regularization Loss

Intuitively, TAAFP is not supposed to cause significant changes in the predictions of the model. Therefore, we propose a regularization loss to keep the semantic meanings of samples unchanged against the adversarial perturbations in a task. We introduce KL divergence loss as our regularization loss (REG). Firstly, we calculate the prediction of the original task P_o and the prediction of new task P_{ta} encoded by TAM. After generating adversarial feature perturbations, we re-extract the feature representations and calculate the prediction of the augmented original task P'_o and the prediction of the augmented new task P'_{ta}. The regularization loss is defined as:

$$P_o = Sim(Y^s, F^s, F^q), P'_o = Sim(Y^s, F^s_{\hat{a}}, F^q_{\hat{a}}) \tag{12}$$

$$P_{ta} = Sim(Y^s, TAM(F^s, F^q)), P'_{ta} = Sim(Y^s, TAM(F^s_{\hat{a}}, F^q_{\hat{a}})) \tag{13}$$

$$\mathcal{L}_{reg} = KL(P_o \| P'_o) + KL(P'_o \| P_o) + KL(P_{ta} \| P'_{ta}) + KL(P'_{ta} \| P_{ta}) \tag{14}$$

Our regularization loss takes a dual form of the KL loss between the original predictions and the augmented. By minimizing the regularization loss, the robustness of the model can be further improved against the adversarial feature perturbations, which is a new perspective to take full advantage of the adversarial perturbations in a FSL task.

3.5 Overall Objective

Finally, the overall objective loss function merges both the hybrid loss $\mathcal{L}_{\hat{a}}$ and the regularization loss $\mathcal{L}_{reg}$, which is denoted as follows:

$$\mathcal{L}_{total} = \mathcal{L}_{\hat{a}} + \lambda \mathcal{L}_{reg} \tag{15}$$

where λ is a positive scalar to control the impact of the regularization loss. We set $\lambda = 1$ for all experiments.

By minimizing the above loss during the training stage, the robustness of the base FSL model can be greatly improved. During the testing stage, we discard TAM and directly use the similarity metric model to make predictions on the clean output of the feature extractor, which is very convenient.

4 Experiments

4.1 Experimental Setups

Dataset. Five few-shot classification datasets are used in our experiments: mini-Imagenet [17], CUB [31], Cars [11], Places [34] and Plantae [10]. Each dataset consists of train/val/test splits. We select mini-Imagenet as the single source domain and the other four datasets as the target domains. We train and validate the model on the training set and validation set of mini-Imagenet. Then we choose the model parameters with best performance on the validation set for testing on the testing sets of four target domains.

Table 1. In-domain and Cross-domain few-shot classification accuracies(%).

5-way 1-shot	mini	CUB	Cars	Places	Plantae
MatchingNet	59.10 ± 0.64	35.89 ± 0.51	30.77 ± 0.47	49.86 ± 0.79	32.70 ± 0.60
RelationNet	57.80 ± 0.88	42.44 ± 0.77	29.11 ± 0.60	48.64 ± 0.85	33.17 ± 0.64
GNN	60.77 ± 0.75	45.69 ± 0.68	31.79 ± 0.51	53.10 ± 0.80	35.60 ± 0.56
GNN+FT	66.32 ± 0.80	47.47 ± 0.75	31.61 ± 0.53	55.77 ± 0.79	35.95 ± 0.58
GNN+LRP	65.03 ± 0.54	48.29 ± 0.51	32.78 ± 0.39	54.83 ± 0.56	37.49 ± 0.43
GNN+ATA	–	45.00 ± 0.50	33.61 ± 0.40	53.57 ± 0.50	34.42 ± 0.40
GNN+WSAN	67.21 ± 0.79	50.25 ± 0.74	33.55 ± 0.61	57.75 ± 0.82	40.71 ± 0.66
GNN+TAAFP	**69.24 ± 0.54**	**52.25 ± 0.54**	**35.17 ± 0.43**	**59.92 ± 0.59**	**41.60 ± 0.48**
5-way 5-shot	mini	CUB	Cars	Places	Plantae
MatchingNet	70.96 ± 0.65	51.37 ± 0.77	38.99 ± 0.64	63.16 ± 0.77	46.53 ± 0.68
RelationNet	71.00 ± 0.69	57.77 ± 0.69	37.33 ± 0.68	63.32 ± 0.76	44.00 ± 0.60
GNN	80.87 ± 0.56	62.25 ± 0.65	44.28 ± 0.63	70.84 ± 0.65	52.53 ± 0.59
GNN+FT	81.98 ± 0.55	66.98 ± 0.68	44.90 ± 0.64	73.94 ± 0.67	53.85 ± 0.62
GNN+LRP	82.03 ± 0.40	64.44 ± 0.48	46.20 ± 0.46	74.45 ± 0.47	54.46 ± 0.46
GNN+ATA	–	66.22 ± 0.50	49.14 ± 0.40	75.48 ± 0.40	52.69 ± 0.40
GNN+WSAN	84.27 ± 0.54	70.31 ± 0.67	46.11 ± 0.66	76.88 ± 0.63	57.72 ± 0.64
GNN+TAAFP	**85.67 ± 0.35**	**72.05 ± 0.46**	**50.19 ± 0.46**	**77.92 ± 0.45**	**58.45 ± 0.45**

Implementation Details. We use ResNet-10 [9] as the backbone network for the feature extractor and the Adam optimizer with the learning rate of 0.001, which is the same setting with Tseng [28] and Sun [24]. We use the SGD optimizer to update the parameters of TAM with a fixed learning rate of 0.005. The adversarial perturbation strength β is set to 10 for 5-way 1-shot and 20 for 5-way 5-shot. The number of heads in the multi-head attention networks is 4. We train and test our model under 5-way 1-shot and 5-way 5-shot settings. We report the average accuracy as well as 95% confidence interval over 2000 random trials with 16 query samples per class at test time. We apply the same pre-training strategy as Tseng for a fair comparison, which can make the model converge quickly and achieve better performance than training from scratch.

4.2   Main Result

We combine the proposed Task-Aware Adversarial Feature Perturbation (TAAFP) with the existing metric-based model GNN to evaluate its improvement under the settings of in-domain and cross-domain few-shot classification. We compare our method with the baseline and four existing CD-FSL methods, including FT [28], LRP [24], ATA [32], and WSAN [6], which are implemented under the same setting as our model. The results are shown in Table 1.

We can observe the in-domain and CD-FSL performance of GNN can be significantly improved by our method, which means TAAFP as a plug-and-play model can greatly improve the generalization ability of the base model. In addition, our method outperforms four CD-FSL methods in all cases, which indicates adversarial perturbations in feature space is a more effective augmentation method for CD-FSL, and the robust meta-knowledge is essential for cross-domain setting.

4.3   Ablation Study

Effect of Three Components. Here we study the effect of each component of TAAFP. We conduct an ablation study under the 5-way 1-shot setting on the adversarial feature perturbations (AFP), Task Attention Module (TAM), and the regularization loss (REG). The results are shown in Table 2.

Table 2. Ablation Study on three components of TAAFP.

AFP	TAM	REG	mini	CUB	Cars	Places	Plantae
✗	✗	✗	60.77 ± 0.75	45.69 ± 0.68	31.79 ± 0.51	53.10 ± 0.80	35.60 ± 0.56
✗	✓	✗	63.82 ± 0.55	49.43 ± 0.52	31.36 ± 0.37	51.31 ± 0.55	37.75 ± 0.43
✓	✗	✗	66.10 ± 0.54	49.28 ± 0.48	33.55 ± 0.40	56.11 ± 0.56	39.81 ± 0.46
✓	✗	✓	68.70 ± 0.52	51.52 ± 0.52	34.03 ± 0.40	58.32 ± 0.56	40.96 ± 0.46
✓	✓	✗	68.33 ± 0.54	51.56 ± 0.52	34.08 ± 0.40	58.51 ± 0.57	40.72 ± 0.46
✓	✓	✓	**69.24 ± 0.54**	**52.25 ± 0.54**	**35.17 ± 0.43**	**59.92 ± 0.59**	**41.60 ± 0.48**

From the results, we can observe that: 1) Directly training on the multi-task (the second row) composed of the original task and the task encoded by TAM can achieve improvement in the source domain, but not stable in the target domains. Due to the large number of same-labeled samples contained in the FSL task, TAM will drive the model to focus on the discriminative features within the corresponding category, which is beneficial for the in-domain classification but not robust enough for cross-domain setting. 2) Both adversarial feature perturbation and the regularization loss (the third and forth row) can bring a significant improvement to the base model by learning more robust meta-knowledge. 3) The combination of AFP and TAM (the fifth row) can achieve more significant improvement. On the one hand, TAM enables the adversarial feature perturbations to contain more sample relationship information in a FSL task, thus generating more task-aware attacks. On the other hand, TAM exploits discriminative but non-robust features. While the combination with AFP can force the model to extract more robust and discriminative features, thus further improving the accuracy of cross-domain classification. Finally, the combination of three components (the sixth row) get the best results.

Effect of Different Blocks for TAAFP. Here we study the effect of different blocks for TAAFP. We try to apply perturbations to the first block, the first and second blocks, the first, second and third blocks, and all blocks, respectively. The results are shown in Table 3.

Table 3. Ablation Study on different blocks for TAAFP.

Block	mini	CUB	Cars	Places	Plantae
1	64.20 ± 0.52	47.71 ± 0.49	33.10 ± 0.40	54.02 ± 0.53	38.96 ± 0.44
4	65.55 ± 0.52	49.72 ± 0.50	33.87 ± 0.40	57.14 ± 0.57	39.09 ± 0.44
1,2	65.48 ± 0.54	49.63 ± 0.51	33.45 ± 0.39	56.84 ± 0.57	38.58 ± 0.44
3,4	68.81 ± 0.55	50.57 ± 0.51	33.64 ± 0.40	59.52 ± 0.58	40.47 ± 0.46
1,2,3	67.05 ± 0.53	50.04 ± 0.49	34.98 ± 0.41	58.36 ± 0.56	39.17 ± 0.43
2,3,4	69.04 ± 0.54	51.62 ± 0.51	34.88 ± 0.41	59.24 ± 0.58	40.93 ± 0.47
1,2,3,4	**69.24 ± 0.54**	**52.25 ± 0.54**	**35.17 ± 0.43**	**59.92 ± 0.59**	**41.60 ± 0.48**

From the results, we can observe that: 1) Better results can be achieved by applying perturbations to more blocks. Since the feature maps output by different blocks contain corresponding high-level and low-level features, perturbing all blocks can be more comprehensive. 2) Perturbation on more backward blocks can achieve better results. We believe that perturbation on the high-level features with more semantic information can be more effective than perturbation on low-level features in a FSL task.

5   Conclusion

In this paper, we propose a simple but effective Task-Aware Adversarial Feature Perturbation (TAAFP) to further improve the generalization of the existing FSL model. Our method is composed of three main components: adversarial feature perturbation (AFP), Task Attention Module (TAM), and the regularization loss (REG). The experimental results fully confirm the validity of each component of our method, and demonstrate that TAAFP outperforms the state-of-the-art CD-FSL methods under the settings of in-domain and cross-domain few-shot classification.

References

1. Blanchard, G., Lee, G., Scott, C.: Generalizing from several related classification tasks to a new unlabeled sample. In: NIPS (2011)
2. Chen, W.Y., Liu, Y.C., Kira, Z., Wang, Y.C.F., Huang, J.B.: A closer look at few-shot classification. In: ICLR (2019)
3. Das, R., Wang, Y., Moura, J.M.F.: On the importance of distractors for few-shot classification. CoRR (2021)
4. Finn, C., Abbeel, P., Levine, S.: Model-agnostic meta-learning for fast adaptation of deep networks. In: ICML, pp. 1126–1135 (2017)
5. Fu, Y., Fu, Y., Jiang, Y.: Meta-FDMixup: cross-domain few-shot learning guided by labeled target data. In: ACM Multimedia (2021)
6. Fu, Y., Xie, Y., Fu, Y., Chen, J., Jiang, Y.: Wave-san: wavelet based style augmentation network for cross-domain few-shot learning. CoRR (2022)

7. Ghifary, M., Kleijn, W.B., Zhang, M., Balduzzi, D.: Domain generalization for object recognition with multi-task autoencoders. In: ICCV (2015)
8. Guo, Yunhui, et al.: A broader study of cross-domain few-shot learning. In: Vedaldi, Andrea, Bischof, Horst, Brox, Thomas, Frahm, Jan-Michael. (eds.) ECCV 2020. LNCS, vol. 12372, pp. 124–141. Springer, Cham (2020). https://doi.org/10.1007/978-3-030-58583-9_8
9. He, K., Zhang, X., Ren, S., Sun, J.: Deep residual learning for image recognition. In: CVPR, pp. 770–778 (2016)
10. Horn, G.V., et al.: The inaturalist species classification and detection dataset. In: CVPR (2018)
11. Krause, J., Stark, M., Deng, J., Fei-Fei, L.: 3D object representations for fine-grained categorization. In: ICCV (2013)
12. Li, H., Pan, S.J., Wang, S., Kot, A.C.: Domain generalization with adversarial feature learning. In: CVPR (2018)
13. Liang, H., Zhang, Q., Dai, P., Lu, J.: Boosting the generalization capability in cross-domain few-shot learning via noise-enhanced supervised autoencoder. CoRR (2021)
14. Long, M., Cao, Y., Wang, J., Jordan, M.: Learning transferable features with deep adaptation networks. In: ICML
15. Muandet, K., Balduzzi, D., Schölkopf, B.: Domain generalization via invariant feature representation. In: ICML (2013)
16. Phoo, C.P., Hariharan, B.: Self-training for few-shot transfer across extreme task differences. In: ICLR (2021)
17. Ravi, S., Larochelle, H.: Optimization as a model for few-shot learning. In: ICLR (2017)
18. Rusu, A.A., et al.: Meta-learning with latent embedding optimization. In: ICLR (2019)
19. Sankaranarayanan, S., Jain, A., Chellappa, R., Lim, S.: Regularizing deep networks using efficient layerwise adversarial training. In: AAAI (2018)
20. Santoro, A., Bartunov, S., Botvinick, M., Wierstra, D., Lillicrap, T.P.: Meta-learning with memory-augmented neural networks. In: ICML
21. Satorras, V.G., Estrach, J.B.: Few-shot learning with graph neural networks. In: ICLR (2018)
22. Shankar, S., Piratla, V., Chakrabarti, S., Chaudhuri, S., Jyothi, P., Sarawagi, S.: Generalizing across domains via cross-gradient training. In: ICLR (2018)
23. Snell, J., Swersky, K., Zemel, R.: Prototypical networks for few-shot learning. In: NIPS (2017)
24. Sun, J., Lapuschkin, S., Samek, W., Zhao: Explanation-guided training for cross-domain few-shot classification. In: ICPR (2020)
25. Sun, Q., Liu, Y., Chua, T.S., Schiele, B.: Meta-transfer learning for few-shot learning. In: CVPR (2019)
26. Sung, F., Yang, Y., Zhang, L., Xiang, T., Torr, P.H., Hospedales, T.M.: Learning to compare: relation network for few-shot learning. In: CVPR (2018)
27. Szegedy, C., et al.: Intriguing properties of neural networks. In: ICLR (2014)
28. Tseng, H.Y., Lee, H.Y., Huang, J.B., Yang, M.H.: Cross-domain few-shot classification via learned feature-wise transformation. In: ICLR (2020)
29. Vinyals, O., Blundell, C., Lillicrap, T., Kavukcuoglu, K., Wierstra, D.: Matching networks for one shot learning. In: NIPS (2016)
30. Volpi, R., Namkoong, H., Sener, O., Duchi, J.C., Murino, V., Savarese, S.: Generalizing to unseen domains via adversarial data augmentation. In: NIPS (2018)

31. Wah, C., Branson, S., Welinder, P., Perona, P., Belongie, S.: The Caltech-UCSD Birds-200-2011 Dataset. Technical report (2011)
32. Wang, H., Deng, Z.: Cross-domain few-shot classification via adversarial task augmentation. In: IJCAI (2021)
33. Zhang, H., Cissé, M., Dauphin, Y.N., Lopez-Paz, D.: Mixup: beyond empirical risk minimization. In: ICLR (2018)
34. Zhou, B., Lapedriza, À., Khosla, A., Oliva, A., Torralba, A.: Places: a 10 million image database for scene recognition (2018)
35. Zhou, K., Yang, Y., Qiao, Y., Xiang, T.: Domain generalization with MixStyle. In: ICLR (2021)

Ternary Data, Triangle Decoding, Three Tasks, a Multitask Learning Speech Translation Model

Linlin Zhang[1,2]([✉]), Boxing Chen[2], Shaolin Zhu[3], and Luo Si[2]

[1] Zhejiang University, Hangzhou, China
zhanglinlinlin@zju.edu.cn
[2] Alibaba DAMO Academy, Hangzhou, China
[3] Tianjin University, Tianjin, China

Abstract. Direct end-to-end approaches for speech translation (ST) are now competing with the traditional cascade solutions. However, end-to-end models still suffer from the challenge of ST data scarcity. How to effectively utilize the limited ST data or more text machine translation (MT) data is appealing but still an open problem. The end-to-end model requires the model to have both cross-modal and cross-language capabilities, which increases the mapping difficulty. In this paper, we propose a tightly tied multitask ST model. By adding a lightweight adapter, we make the ASR decoder also be the MT encoder, where they use one language model and share the source text semantic space. Thus, our model can utilize the MT data. Our end-to-end model can accomplish the ST, ASR and MT tasks simultaneously, and multitask learning can promote the overall performance of an ST model. Our method can make efficient and full use of the limited ternary ST data and even more intelligently utilize external data. When using the limited ternary data, our ST method can achieve state-of-the-art performance in end-to-end models. When adding the external data, our method shows a significant improvement on the strong baselines.

Keywords: Speech translation · speech · Machine translation · Cross-modal · Speech-to-text

1 Introduction

Speech translation (ST) is the task that automatically translates a source acoustic speech signal into a text sequence in a target language. Traditionally, the advanced ST task can be considered as a combination of automatic speech recognition (ASR) and machine translation (MT), usually called cascade or pipeline architecture [12,14,22]. In contrast, with the advance of Transformer, recent works on end-to-end (E2E) ST have reached a comparable level to the cascade method [6,17].

Although the E2E ST model has many appealing properties (e.g., less error propagation), the cascade model still dominates in the actual scene. Firstly,

L. Iliadis et al. (Eds.): ICANN 2023, LNCS 14256, pp. 579–590, 2023.
https://doi.org/10.1007/978-3-031-44213-1_48

the E2E model inputs the speech and directly outputs the final translation, requiring the model to have both cross-modal and cross-language capabilities, which increases the mapping difficulty. Secondly, the E2E model usually requires aligned ST data, and the ideal triple data (speech, transcription, translation) is scarce. And usually the external MT data is much more than ASR data [1]. Therefore, how to efficiently use limited ternary ST data and utilize external data (raw audio, ASR and especially MT data) is a hot topic.

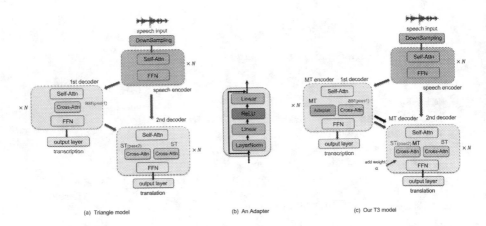

Fig. 1. The left part (a) is the original Triangle model and consists of a speech encoder and two decoders. The middle part (b) is a typical adapter. The right part (c) is our T3 method. Our method adds a lightweight adapter into the 1st decoder, so that the ASR decoder is also the MT encoder.

To combine the advantages of the above two methods and utilize the medium transcription, a tighter tied E2E model has been proposed. [13] are the first to apply the two-pass decoding on E2E ST. To alleviate error propagation, [2] add a path from the speech encoder directly to the second decoder, so-called the Triangle model. This kind of methods usually add an ASR subtask, but the tightly integrated triangle architecture has no MT subtask. As shown in Fig. 1, in the 1st decoder, we add a lightweight adapter to decouple the acoustic model and language model. Thus, the ASR decoder is also the MT encoder. The two parts use one language model and share the source text semantic space. Therefore, our ST model can naturally introduce auxiliary ASR and MT subtasks, and better use the limited ternary ST data. Moreover, under this multitask learning framework, our ST method can intelligently utilize external MT data. Our ST model can use the **T**ernary ST data, is **T**riangle decoding and has **T**hree tasks (**T3**).

Our main contributions can be summarized as follows:

First, we designed a multitask E2E ST model, including ASR and MT subtasks. By adding a lightweight Adapter into the Triangle model, we are the first to make the ASR decoder also be the MT encoder, which make full use of the ternary ST data.

Second, under this organically combined multitask learning framework, our method can break through the E2E ST limitation of scarce ternary ST data, and intelligently utilize external data.

Third, we conduct various experiments on 8 language pairs of the MuST-C corpus. When using the limited ternary data, our end-to-end ST model can achieve state-of-the-art performance. When adding the external data, our method shows a significant improvement over the strong baselines.

2   Our Proposed ST Model

In this section, we introduce our ST model, **T3**. As shown in Fig. 1, we add a lightweight Adapter into the 1st decoder to construct the MT encoder. Therefore, the ASR decoder and the MT encoder coexist in one component and share the most parameters. In this way, our method can leverage ASR and MT subtasks to use ternary ST data better.

2.1   Speech Translation Background

Speech translation (ST) automatically translate a acoustic speech sequence S into a target language text sequence Y. Usually, the ST data is a ternary corpus with the medium transcription X. We denote the ST task, where $Y, \hat{Y} \in \mathbb{Y}$ denote the oracle/best translation:

$$
\begin{aligned}
\hat{Y} &= \underset{\hat{Y} \in \mathbb{Y}}{\mathrm{argmax}} P(Y \mid S) \\
&\approx \underset{\hat{Y} \in \mathbb{Y}}{\mathrm{argmax}} \sum_{X \in \mathbb{X}} P(Y \mid X, S) P(X \mid S)
\end{aligned}
\tag{1}
$$

2.2   Ternary Data, Triangle Decoding, Three Tasks ST Model (T3)

Original Triangle Model. To alleviate the problems of cascade method such as error propagation, a strong coupling E2E method was proposed. The two-pass model [13] is conceptually similar to the cascade approach but is E2E trainable.

A Transformer encoder layer is stacked with a multihead attention block and a point-wise feed-forward network (FFN). For Transformer decoder layer, there is a multihead self attention (Self-Attn), and a mulithead cross attention (Cross-Attn).

In the Triangle model [2], the left path is two-pass decoding consisting of an acoustic encoder and two decoders. The Triangle model extends a second attention mechanism to the 2nd decoder that directly attends to the encoded output. We use H^{1-Dec}, H^{2-Dec} and H^{Enc} to represent the hidden states of 1st decoder, 2nd decoder and speech encoder:

$$
H_{out}^{2-Dec} = \mathrm{CrossAttn}\left(H_{self}^{2-Dec}, H^{1-Dec}\right) + \mathrm{CrossAttn}\left(H_{self}^{2-Dec}, H^{Enc}\right)
\tag{2}
$$

Our T3 Model. We added a learnable weight α to replace the fixed weight:

$$H_{out}^{2-Dec} = \alpha \, \mathrm{CrossAttn} \left(H_{self}^{2-Dec}, H^{1-Dec} \right) + \mathrm{CrossAttn} \left(H_{self}^{2-Dec}, H^{Enc} \right) \tag{3}$$

A triple ST data include: speech signal S, transcription X, and text translation Y. The ASR task of Triangle model can be formulated as:

$$\hat{X} = \underset{\hat{X} \in \mathbb{X}}{\mathrm{argmax}} P(X \mid S) = \underset{\hat{X} \in \mathbb{X}}{\mathrm{argmax}} \frac{P(S \mid X)P(X)}{P(S)}$$
$$\approx \underset{\hat{X} \in \mathbb{X}}{\mathrm{argmax}} P(S \mid X)P(X) \tag{4}$$

where $\hat{X} \in \mathbb{X}$ denote the best transcription. $P(S \mid X)$ is the acoustic model (AM), and $P(X)$ is the language model (LM).

If remove the Cross-Attn, the 1st decoder becomes an encoder. Thus, by adding a lightweight Adapter into the 1st decoder, we constitute the MT encoder. As shown in our T3 model of Fig. 1, if doing the ASR task, the 1st decoder chooses to go through Cross-Attn to generate transcription, if doing MT task, chooses the Adapter to encode the MT input. We use the full-visible mask for MT encoding as the common encoder, and the 2nd decoder only uses the H^{1-Dec}.

In a word, in our method, by adding a small Adapter to decouple the acoustic model and language model, the component is both the decoder of ASR and the encoder of MT. The ASR decoder and MT encoder use one language model and share the source text semantic space. We enable the transcription semantic module component to have the functions of decoding and encoding source language text.

A common **Adapter** [4] module is presented in Fig. 1(b). The first linear layer is typically a down projection to a small bottleneck dimension, and the second one projects the output back to the initial dimension.

Auxiliary External Data. Since we have different subtasks, we can use additional external MT data to train a better MT model. As the MT data increase, the performance of the MT task will be better. In the ST task, knowledge distillation (KD) is a widely introduced method.

Concretely, we assume $\mathbb{D}$ is the ternary ST dataset with a vocabulary size of $|V|$. The training criterion is to minimize negative log likelihood (NLL) for each sample $o \in \mathbb{D}$:

$$\mathcal{L}_{NLL}(\theta_{ST}) = -\sum_{o \in \mathbb{D}} \sum_{k=1}^{K} \sum_{v=1}^{|V|} \delta(y_k = v) \log p(y_k = v \mid Y_{<k}, S, \theta_{ST}) \tag{5}$$

where p is the ST distribution and $\delta(.)$ is the indicator function of the ST model. The KD loss is defined as minimizing the cross-entropy with the MT's probability distribution q:

$$\mathcal{L}_{KD}(\theta_{ST}) = -\sum_{o \in \mathbb{D}} \sum_{k=1}^{K} \sum_{v=1}^{|V|} q(y_k = v \mid Y_{<k}, X, \theta_{MT}) \log p(y_k = v \mid Y_{<k}, S, \theta_{ST})$$

(6)

The overall loss is the combination of KD loss, negative log likelihood loss of ST, ASR and MT, as follows:

$$\mathcal{L}(\theta) = \mathcal{L}_{NLL}(\theta_{ST}) + \lambda_1 \mathcal{L}_{NLL}(\theta_{ASR}) + \lambda_2 \mathcal{L}_{NLL}(\theta_{MT}) + \eta \mathcal{L}_{KD}(\theta_{ST}) \quad (7)$$

where λ_1, λ_2 and η are hyperparameters.

3 Experiments Settings

3.1 Datasets and Settings

For a fair comparison with previous works, we conduct our experiments on the widely used MuST-C corpus [9].

We introduce the LibriSpeech dataset [19] as the external ASR data. We use the WMT14 dataset as our external MT data.

Following the default preprocessing recipes of Fairseq [18], speech inputs are represented as 80D log melfilterbank with SpecAugment [20]. The shared vocabulary consists of 10,000 subword units learned by SentencePiece. We report the WER score for ASR and detokenized sacreBLEU score for ST.

3.2 Model Settings

We experiment with two architectures: a small Transformer model with 256 hidden units, 4 attention heads, 2048 feed-forward size, and a medium one with a hidden size of 512 and 8 attention heads. All ST and ASR models use the same encoder with 12 layers. The two decoders of our T3 model both have 6 layers. The corresponding MT submodel also has 6 encoder and decoder layers. For limited ST situation, we select the small settings. When using external data, we apply the medium model settings.

For limited ST, we used the Adam optimizer [15] with the learning rate $2e-3$. For auxiliary data, we set the learning rate as $2e-4$. The dropout rate and the label smoothing are both set as 0.1. We choose $\lambda_1 = 0.3$, $\lambda_2 = 0.3$ and $\eta = 0.2$ in the training loss equation through grid search ($[0.1, 1.0]$ for λ and $[0.1, 0.5]$ for η). For external situations, We select the alternative batches between ST and MT with sample ratio 1.0 and 0.25, respectively. For all models at inference, we average 10 checkpoints with beam size 5.

Table 1. BLEU scores of the speech translation results on the MuST-C tst_COMMON sets. The models are trained with the limited ST data and as small model settings. *: results reported in the ESPnet toolkit. †: the SOTA performance of all E2E methods. ‡: the best result including the cascade method.

Method	En-De	En-Fr	En-Es	En-Pt	En-It	En-Nl	En-Ro	En-Ru	Avg
ESPnet ST*	22.91	32.69	27.96	28.01	23.75	27.43	21.90	15.75	25.05
ESPnet Cascade*	23.65	33.84	28.68	29.04	24.04	27.91	22.68	16.39	25.78
AFS [28]	22.38	33.43	27.04	26.55	23.35	25.05	21.87	14.92	24.32
Dual-Decoder [16]	23.63	33.45	28.12	29.95	24.18	27.55	22.87	15.21	25.62
Cascade baseline	24.61	35.04	28.90‡	29.63	24.90‡	28.94‡	23.67‡	17.17‡	26.61
E2E ST baseline	22.69	33.02	27.18	28.17	22.86	27.27	21.82	15.26	24.78
Joint ASR	23.38	33.46	27.39	28.45	23.32	27.25	21.88	15.74	25.11
Triangle	23.87	34.32	27.41	29.02	23.69	27.69	22.53	16.14	25.58
Our T3	25.38‡	35.30‡	28.82†	30.31‡	24.72†	28.41†	23.28†	16.85†	26.63‡

4   Experiments Results

4.1   Main Results on the Ternary ST Data

As shown in Table 1, our method achieves an appealing performance on all 8 language pairs in the restricted ternary Must-c data.

Compared with the original Triangle model, our method has appealing performance improvements on the all 8 language pairs, yielding an average translation gain of 0.71–1.45 BLEU. Compared with previous multitask methods, our method can fully exploit the limited ternary ST data.

Compared with the direct E2E ST baseline, our method has enhanced 1.14 to 2.63 BLEU on the 8 language directions, with an average gain of 1.85 BLEU. In a word, our approach can achieve the SOTA translation performance among all end-to-end ST methods.

Compared with the cascade method that we have reproduced, our approach surpasses the cascade on the three language pairs En-De, En-Fr, and En-Pt, and is only slightly weaker on the remaining language pairs. In summary, our method has matched or surpassed the cascade method on the constrained triple ST data.

4.2   Auxiliary Data

As shown in Table 2, we compare with different baselines, and all models use the medium model architecture settings. Naturally, the upper limit of all ST models should be the pure text MT model.

By introducing more auxiliary data, our model further improves 3.2 and 2.4 BLEU on the two language pair En-De and En-Fr, respectively. Moreover, our method achieves better translation performance than other methods that utilize external data. Although the performance is not as good as the strong cascade method, our model can leverage the external data to improve the quality of ST.

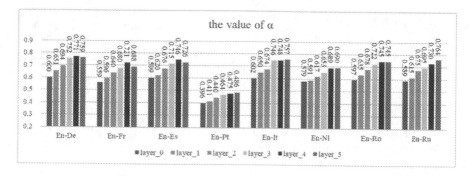

Fig. 2. The value of the weight α of our T3 models. All models use the small architecture settings.

In a word, although our method underperforms the cascade method, we can smartly utilize extra MT data to promote the ST task.

From the comparison of the parameters in Table 2, our adapter is small but smart.

4.3   Weight α and Parameters

As denoted in Eq. 3, α represents the weight of the 2nd decoder using the information from the 1st decoder. Previous works assume that the ST model prefers the information from the transcription, and adding direct speech information is just an auxiliary path to alleviate error propagation [2, 21]. However, as shown in Fig. 2, all α are less than 1. Contrary to the intuition of the previous works, our T3 model prefers the direct ST path as the main information path. In our method, the 2nd decoder uses more direct speech encoding information than the transcription information. The possible reason might be that although the two-pass decoding reduces the complexity of the ST task, it will also lead to early decisions like the cascade model.

As shown in Fig. 2, basically, as the number of layers increases, the α also tends to increase. On the En-De, En-Fr and En-Es three language pairs, the α of the sub-top layer is larger than the top level, while on all remaining language pairs the top layer has the largest value of α. In our model, the higher layer may need more information from the transcription.

4.4   Ablation Study

We conduct ablation experiments to evaluate the importance of every component of our method. We perform experiments in two situations: 1) only using the limited ternary ST data, 2) adding external data, correspond to the small model architecture settings and the medium settings, respectively. As shown in Table 4, using a learnable weight α is more effective than using a fixed value. Adding the Adapter contributes to the ST. The last row shows that KD loss can enhance the whole ST model when adding external data.

5   Related Work

For the ST task, previous work can be summarized into two classic paradigms: the cascade model and the end-to-end model.

5.1   Cascade ST

Cascade ST architecture concatenates the individual ASR and MT components [23,25], and represent an intuitive solution to achieve reasonable performance and high intelligibility. At the same time, this cascade method also faces some thorny problems: the traditional cascade method suffers from error propagation and the loss of acoustic information that might be useful to improve final translations, and it needs train two separate ASR and MT models. To alleviate the aforementioned problems, some tightly integration methods have been proposed. Instead of using the the 1-best output of ASR, more informative ASR outputs are given to MT models: ASR n-best, lattices or confusion networks [22]. Using the robust ASR data enhancement method, a strong cascade model can be constructed [3] (Table 3).

Table 2. The speech translation BLEU results when using the auxiliary extended data ($\star$) on medium model settings.

other models	En-De	En-Fr	Paras.	our implement	En-De	En-Fr	Paras.
Cascade baseline	24.7	35.6	124M	MT baseline	31.0	43.2	50M
Cascade*	28.9	38.6	124M	MT*	33.4	45.9	50M
Chimera* [10]	26.3	35.6	165M	E2E ST baseline	23.5	34.0	74M
JT-ST* [24]	26.8	37.4	–	BiKD [11]	25.3	35.3	–
XSTNet* [27]	27.8	38.0	155M	Triangle	24.4	35.0	100M
SATE* [26]	28.1	–	–	Our T3	25.6	35.9	104M
STEMM* [8]	28.7	37.4	155M	Our T3*	28.8	38.3	104M

Table 3. The BLEU ($\uparrow$) and WER ($\downarrow$) scores on limited ternary ST data.

Model	En-De	En-Fr
MT (individual)	30.97	43.21
MT in T3	30.31	42.58
ASR (individual)	12.26	12.48
ASR in T3	13.19	13.04
T3 (ground-truth MT)	30.85	43.36

5.2   End-to-End ST

To overcome the weakness of cascade models, [5] proposed the first direct neural network model of an encoder decoder architecture without the intermediate transcription. Currently, more effective solutions used in end-to-end ST models [7]. To alleviate the cross-modal difficulty in end-to-end models, two-pass [13] and triangle deooding [2] methods are proposed.

Although the former solutions are effective to some extent, end-to-end architectures have to confront a critical bottleneck, the ternary ST data paucity. Pretraining and multitask learning are widely used to improve the end-to-end ST performance [26]. However, it is still a challenge to leverage external data efficiently. Many techniques, such as adapter and knowledge distillation, have been widely used in ST. Previous work often used adapters to concatenate different encoders, or to connect encoders and decoders. No works has explored whether to decouple ST's cross-modal and cross-linguistic capabilities from the model structure.

Table 4. Ablation study on the En-De tst_COMMON set. For the constrained ternary ST data, models are conducted as small model settings, while the unrestricted case with adding the external data are medium settings. +ext data: denotes our T3 model using the external ASR and MT corpus.

BLEU	constrained	unrestricted
Triangle Baseline	23.87	24.38
+learned α	24.19	24.73
+adapter	25.29	25.45
+KD loss	25.38	–
+ext data	–	28.23
+KD loss	–	28.84

6   Conclusion and Future Work

In this paper, by adding a lightweight Adapter into the 1st decoder of the Triangle ST model, we are first to make the component can be both the ASR decoder and the MT encoder. Thus, our ST model includes three tasks: ST, ASR and MT. Our ST method can better utilize the limited ternary ST data, and achieve a SOTA end-to-end ST performance. Moreover, under this multitask learning framework, our ST method can intelligently utilize auxiliary external data to enhance the ST quality. Experiments show that our method can significantly improve the translation performance regardless of using the limited ternary data or adding the auxiliary external data.

In the future, we will explore the impact of better acoustic pretrain model.

References

1. Anastasopoulos, A., et al.: Findings of the IWSLT 2021 evaluation campaign. In: Federico, M., Waibel, A., Costa-jussà, M.R., Niehues, J., Stüker, S., Salesky, E. (eds.) Proceedings of the 18th International Conference on Spoken Language Translation, IWSLT 2021, Bangkok, Thailand (online), 5–6 August 2021, pp. 1–29. Association for Computational Linguistics (2021). https://aclanthology.org/2021.iwslt-1.1

2. Anastasopoulos, A., Chiang, D.: Tied multitask learning for neural speech translation. In: Walker, M.A., Ji, H., Stent, A. (eds.) Proceedings of the 2018 Conference of the North American Chapter of the Association for Computational Linguistics: Human Language Technologies, NAACL-HLT 2018, New Orleans, Louisiana, USA, 1–6 June 2018, vol. 1 (Long Papers), pp. 82–91. Association for Computational Linguistics (2018). https://doi.org/10.18653/v1/n18-1008

3. Bahar, P., et al.: Start-before-end and end-to-end: neural speech translation by apptek and RWTH Aachen university. In: Federico, M., Waibel, A., Knight, K., Nakamura, S., Ney, H., Niehues, J., Stüker, S., Wu, D., Mariani, J., Yvon, F. (eds.) Proceedings of the 17th International Conference on Spoken Language Translation, IWSLT 2020, Online, 9–10 July 2020, pp. 44–54. Association for Computational Linguistics (2020). https://doi.org/10.18653/v1/2020.iwslt-1.3

4. Bapna, A., Firat, O.: Simple, scalable adaptation for neural machine translation. In: Inui, K., Jiang, J., Ng, V., Wan, X. (eds.) Proceedings of the 2019 Conference on Empirical Methods in Natural Language Processing and the 9th International Joint Conference on Natural Language Processing, EMNLP-IJCNLP 2019, Hong Kong, China, 3–7 November 2019, pp. 1538–1548. Association for Computational Linguistics (2019). https://doi.org/10.18653/v1/D19-1165

5. Berard, A., Pietquin, O., Servan, C., Besacier, L.: Listen and translate: a proof of concept for end-to-end speech-to-text translation. CoRR abs/1612.01744 (2016). http://arxiv.org/abs/1612.01744

6. Dong, Q., Wang, M., Zhou, H., Xu, S., Xu, B., Li, L.: Consecutive decoding for speech-to-text translation. In: Thirty-Fifth AAAI Conference on Artificial Intelligence, AAAI 2021, Thirty-Third Conference on Innovative Applications of Artificial Intelligence, IAAI 2021, The Eleventh Symposium on Educational Advances in Artificial Intelligence, EAAI 2021, Virtual Event, 2–9 February 2021, pp. 12738–12748. AAAI Press (2021). https://ojs.aaai.org/index.php/AAAI/article/view/17508

7. Dong, Q., et al.: Listen, understand and translate: triple supervision decouples end-to-end speech-to-text translation. In: Thirty-Fifth AAAI Conference on Artificial Intelligence, AAAI 2021, Thirty-Third Conference on Innovative Applications of Artificial Intelligence, IAAI 2021, The Eleventh Symposium on Educational Advances in Artificial Intelligence, EAAI 2021, Virtual Event, 2–9 February 2021, pp. 12749–12759. AAAI Press (2021). https://ojs.aaai.org/index.php/AAAI/article/view/17509

8. Fang, Q., Ye, R., Li, L., Feng, Y., Wang, M.: STEMM: self-learning with speech-text manifold Mixup for speech translation. CoRR abs/2203.10426 (2022). https://doi.org/10.48550/arXiv.2203.10426

9. Gangi, M.A.D., Cattoni, R., Bentivogli, L., Negri, M., Turchi, M.: MuST-C: a multilingual speech translation corpus. In: Burstein, J., Doran, C., Solorio, T. (eds.) Proceedings of the 2019 Conference of the North American Chapter of the Association for Computational Linguistics: Human Language Technologies, NAACL-HLT

2019, Minneapolis, MN, USA, 2–7 June 2019, vol. 1 (Long and Short Papers), pp. 2012–2017. Association for Computational Linguistics (2019). https://doi.org/10.18653/v1/n19-1202

10. Han, C., Wang, M., Ji, H., Li, L.: Learning shared semantic space for speech-to-text translation. In: Zong, C., Xia, F., Li, W., Navigli, R. (eds.) Findings of the Association for Computational Linguistics: ACL/IJCNLP 2021, Online Event, 1–6 August 2021. Findings of ACL, vol. ACL/IJCNLP 2021, pp. 2214–2225. Association for Computational Linguistics (2021). https://doi.org/10.18653/v1/2021.findings-acl.195

11. Inaguma, H., Kawahara, T., Watanabe, S.: Source and target bidirectional knowledge distillation for end-to-end speech translation. In: Toutanova, K., et al. (eds.) Proceedings of the 2021 Conference of the North American Chapter of the Association for Computational Linguistics: Human Language Technologies, NAACL-HLT 2021, Online, 6–11 June 2021, pp. 1872–1881. Association for Computational Linguistics (2021). https://doi.org/10.18653/v1/2021.naacl-main.150

12. Iranzo-Sánchez, J., Giménez-Pastor, A., Silvestre-Cerdà, J.A., Baquero-Arnal, P., Saiz, J.C., Juan, A.: Direct segmentation models for streaming speech translation. In: Webber, B., Cohn, T., He, Y., Liu, Y. (eds.) Proceedings of the 2020 Conference on Empirical Methods in Natural Language Processing, EMNLP 2020, Online, 16–20 November 2020, pp. 2599–2611. Association for Computational Linguistics (2020). https://doi.org/10.18653/v1/2020.emnlp-main.206

13. Kano, T., Sakti, S., Nakamura, S.: Structured-based curriculum learning for end-to-end English-Japanese speech translation. In: Lacerda, F. (ed.) Interspeech 2017, 18th Annual Conference of the International Speech Communication Association, Stockholm, Sweden, 20–24 August 2017, pp. 2630–2634. ISCA (2017). http://www.isca-speech.org/archive/Interspeech_2017/abstracts/0944.html

14. Khan, A.R., Xu, J.: Diversity by phonetics and its application in neural machine translation. CoRR abs/1911.04292 (2019). http://arxiv.org/abs/1911.04292

15. Kingma, D.P., Ba, J.: Adam: a method for stochastic optimization. In: Bengio, Y., LeCun, Y. (eds.) 3rd International Conference on Learning Representations, ICLR 2015, San Diego, CA, USA, 7–9 May 2015, Conference Track Proceedings (2015). http://arxiv.org/abs/1412.6980

16. Le, H., Pino, J.M., Wang, C., Gu, J., Schwab, D., Besacier, L.: Dual-decoder transformer for joint automatic speech recognition and multilingual speech translation. In: Scott, D., Bel, N., Zong, C. (eds.) Proceedings of the 28th International Conference on Computational Linguistics, COLING 2020, Barcelona, Spain (Online), 8–13 December 2020, pp. 3520–3533. International Committee on Computational Linguistics (2020). https://doi.org/10.18653/v1/2020.coling-main.314

17. Liu, Y., Zhu, J., Zhang, J., Zong, C.: Bridging the modality gap for speech-to-text translation. CoRR abs/2010.14920 (2020). https://arxiv.org/abs/2010.14920

18. Ott, M., et al.: Fairseq: a fast, extensible toolkit for sequence modeling. In: Ammar, W., Louis, A., Mostafazadeh, N. (eds.) Proceedings of the 2019 Conference of the North American Chapter of the Association for Computational Linguistics: Human Language Technologies, NAACL-HLT 2019, Minneapolis, MN, USA, 2–7 June 2019, Demonstrations, pp. 48–53. Association for Computational Linguistics (2019). https://doi.org/10.18653/v1/n19-4009

19. Panayotov, V., Chen, G., Povey, D., Khudanpur, S.: Librispeech: an ASR corpus based on public domain audio books. In: 2015 IEEE International Conference on Acoustics, Speech and Signal Processing (ICASSP), pp. 5206–5210 (2015). https://doi.org/10.1109/ICASSP.2015.7178964

20. Park, D.S., et al.: Specaugment: a simple data augmentation method for automatic speech recognition. In: Kubin, G., Kacic, Z. (eds.) Interspeech 2019, 20th Annual Conference of the International Speech Communication Association, Graz, Austria, 15–19 September 2019, pp. 2613–2617. ISCA (2019). https://doi.org/10.21437/Interspeech. 2019-2680

21. Sperber, M., Neubig, G., Niehues, J., Waibel, A.: Attention-passing models for robust and data-efficient end-to-end speech translation. Trans. Assoc. Comput. Linguist. **7**, 313–325 (2019). https://transacl.org/ojs/index.php/tacl/article/view/1628

22. Sperber, M., Neubig, G., Pham, N., Waibel, A.: Self-attentional models for lattice inputs. In: Korhonen, A., Traum, D.R., Màrquez, L. (eds.) Proceedings of the 57th Conference of the Association for Computational Linguistics, ACL 2019, Florence, Italy, July 28–2 August 2019, Volume 1: Long Papers, pp. 1185–1197. Association for Computational Linguistics (2019). https://doi.org/10.18653/v1/p19-1115

23. Stentiford, F.W., Steer, M.G.: Machine translation of speech. Br. Telecom Technol. J. **6**(2), 116–122 (1988)

24. Tang, Y., Pino, J.M., Li, X., Wang, C., Genzel, D.: Improving speech translation by understanding and learning from the auxiliary text translation task. In: Zong, C., Xia, F., Li, W., Navigli, R. (eds.) Proceedings of the 59th Annual Meeting of the Association for Computational Linguistics and the 11th International Joint Conference on Natural Language Processing, ACL/IJCNLP 2021, (Volume 1: Long Papers), Virtual Event, 1–6 August 2021, pp. 4252–4261. Association for Computational Linguistics (2021). https://doi.org/10.18653/v1/2021.acl-long.328

25. Waibel, A., Jain, A.N., McNair, A.E., Saito, H., Hauptmann, A.G., Tebelskis, J.: JANUS: a speech-to-speech translation system using connectionist and symbolic processing strategies. In: 1991 International Conference on Acoustics, Speech, and Signal Processing, ICASSP '91, Toronto, Ontario, Canada, 14–17 May 1991, pp. 793–796. IEEE Computer Society (1991). https://doi.org/10.1109/ICASSP.1991.150456

26. Xu, C., et al.: Stacked acoustic-and-textual encoding: integrating the pre-trained models into speech translation encoders. In: Zong, C., Xia, F., Li, W., Navigli, R. (eds.) Proceedings of the 59th Annual Meeting of the Association for Computational Linguistics and the 11th International Joint Conference on Natural Language Processing, ACL/IJCNLP 2021, (Volume 1: Long Papers), Virtual Event, 1–6 August 2021, pp. 2619–2630. Association for Computational Linguistics (2021). https://doi.org/10.18653/v1/2021.acl-long.204

27. Ye, R., Wang, M., Li, L.: End-to-end speech translation via cross-modal progressive training. In: Hermansky, H., Cernocký, H., Burget, L., Lamel, L., Scharenborg, O., Motlícek, P. (eds.) Interspeech 2021, 22nd Annual Conference of the International Speech Communication Association, Brno, Czechia, 30 August–3 September 2021, pp. 2267–2271. ISCA (2021). https://doi.org/10.21437/Interspeech.2021-1065

28. Zhang, B., Titov, I., Haddow, B., Sennrich, R.: Adaptive feature selection for end-to-end speech translation. In: Cohn, T., He, Y., Liu, Y. (eds.) Findings of the Association for Computational Linguistics: EMNLP 2020, Online Event, 16–20 November 2020. Findings of ACL, vol. EMNLP 2020, pp. 2533–2544. Association for Computational Linguistics (2020). https://doi.org/10.18653/v1/2020.findings-emnlp.230

Author Index

L. Iliadis et al. (Eds.): ICANN 2023, LNCS 14256, pp. 591–593, 2023.
https://doi.org/10.1007/978-3-031-44213-1